SØREN KIERKEGAARD'S
JOURNALS AND
PAPERS

Volume 5, Autobiographical
Part One   1829–1848

EDITED AND TRANSLATED BY

Howard V. Hong and Edna H. Hong

ASSISTED BY GREGOR MALANTSCHUK

INDIANA UNIVERSITY PRESS

BLOOMINGTON AND LONDON

This book has been brought to publication with the assistance of a grant from Carlsberg Fondet.

Library of Congress Cataloging in Publication Data

Kierkegaard, Søren Aabye, 1813–1855.
Søren Kierkegaard's journals and papers.

Translation of portions of the 20 volume Danish work published 1909–48 under title: Papirer.
Includes bibliographies.
1. Philosophy—Collected works. I. Hong, Howard Vincent, 1912–   ed. II. Hong, Edna (Hatlestad) 1913–   ed. III. Malantschuk, Gregor.
B4372.E5H66 1967   198'.9   67–13025
ISBN 0-253-18244-1 (vol. 5)   1 2 3 4 5 81 80 79 78 77
      0-253-18239-5 (complete set, vols. 1-7)

Contents

Chronology

1835

Summer in north Sjælland.

1837

Between May 8 and May 12   On a visit to the Rørdams in Frederiksberg meets Regine Olsen for the first time (see II A 67,
68).
Autumn   Begins teaching Latin for a term in Borgerdydskolen.
Sept. 1   Moves from home to Løvstræde 7.

1838

"The Battle between the Old and the New Soap-Cellars" (a
philosophical comedy drafted but not completed or published; see *Pap.* II B 1–21).
May 19   About 10:30 A.M. S. K.'s entry concerning "an indescribable
joy" (see II A 228).
Aug. 8/9   Father dies, 2:00 A.M.
Aug. 14   Father buried in family plot in Assistents Cemetery.
Sept. 7   Publication of *From the Papers of One Still Living, published
against his will by S. Kierkegaard.* (About H. C. Andersen as a
novelist, with special reference to his latest work, *Only a Fiddler.*)

1840

Feb. 1   Census list gives address as Kultorvet 132 (now 11).
Apr. or Oct.   Moves to Nørregade 230A (now 38).
June 2   Presents his request for examination to theological faculty.
July 3   Completes examination for degree (*magna cum laude*).
July 19–Aug. 6   Journey to ancestral home in Jutland.
Sept. 8   Proposes to Regine Olsen.
Sept. 10   Becomes engaged to Regine.
Oct. 8   First number of *Corsaren* (*The Corsair*) published by M.
Goldschmidt.
Nov. 17   Enters the Pastoral Seminary.

1841

Jan. 12   Preaches sermon in Holmens Kirke (see II C 1).
July 16   Dissertation for the *Magister* degree, *The Concept of Irony, with
Constant Reference to Socrates,* accepted.

Aug. 11 Returns Regine Olsen's engagement ring.

Sept. 16 Dissertation printed.

Sept. 28 10 A.M.–2:00 P.M., 4:00 P.M.–7:30 P.M. Defends his dissertation. (In 1854 *Magister* degrees came to be regarded and named officially as doctoral degrees such as they are now.)

Oct. 11 Engagement with Regine Olsen broken.

Oct. 25 Leaves Copenhagen for Berlin, where he attends Schelling's lectures.

1842

March 6 Returns to Copenhagen.

Nov. 11 S.K.'s brother Peter Christian Kierkegaard ordained.
Johannes Climacus, or De omnibus dubitandum est begun but not completed or published.

1843

Feb. 20 *Either/Or,* edited by Victor Eremita, published.

May 8 Leaves for short visit to Berlin.

May 16 *Two Upbuilding [Edifying] Discourses,* by S. Kierkegaard, published.

July Learns of Regine's engagement to Johan Frederik Schlegel.

Oct. 16 *Repetition,* by Constantin Constantius; *Fear and Trembling,* by Johannes de Silentio; and *Three Upbuilding [Edifying] Discourses,* by S. Kierkegaard, published.

Dec. 6 *Four Upbuilding [Edifying] Discourses,* by S. Kierkegaard, published.

1844

Feb. 24 Preaches terminal sermon in Trinitatis Kirke.

March 5 *Two Upbuilding [Edifying] Discourses,* by S. Kierkegaard, published.

June 8 *Three Upbuilding [Edifying] Discourses,* by S. Kierkegaard, published.

June 13 *Philosophical Fragments,* by Johannes Climacus, published.

June 17 *The Concept of Anxiety [Dread],* by Vigilius Haufniensis; and *Prefaces,* by Nicolaus Notabene, published.

Aug. 31 *Four Upbuilding [Edifying] Discourses,* by S. Kierkegaard, published.

Oct. 16 Moves from Nørregade 230A (now 38) to house at Nytorv 2, Copenhagen.

1845

Apr. 29   *Three Discourses on Imagined Occasions,* by S. Kierkegaard, published.

Apr. 30   *Stages on Life's Way,* edited by Hilarius Bogbinder, published.

May 13–24   Journey to Berlin.

May 29   *Eighteen Upbuilding [Edifying] Discourses* (from 1842–43), by S. Kierkegaard, published.

Dec. 27   Article "The Activity of a Travelling Esthetician . . . ," containing references to P. L. Møller and *The Corsair,* by Frater Taciturnus, published in *Fædrelandet* [*The Fatherland*].

1846

Jan. 2   First attack on S.K. in *The Corsair.*

Jan. 10   S.K.'s reply by Frater Taciturnus in *Fædrelandet.*

Feb. 7   Considers qualifying himself for ordination (VII^1 A 4).

Feb. 27   *Concluding Unscientific Postscript,* by Johannes Climacus, published.

Mar. 9   "Report" (*The Corsair*) begun in first NB Journal (VII^1 A 98).

Mar. 30   *Two Ages: the Age of Revolution and the Present Age. A Literary Review* [*The Present Age* is part of this work], by S. Kierkegaard, published.

May 2–16   Visit to Berlin.

June 12   Acquires Magister A. P. Adler's books: *Studier og Exempler, Forsøg til en kort systematisk Fremstilling af Christendommen i dens Logik,* and *Theologiske Studier.*

Oct. 2   Goldschmidt resigns as editor of *The Corsair.*

Oct. 7   Goldschmidt travels to Germany and Italy.

1847

Jan. 24   S.K. writes: "God be praised that I was subjected to the attack of the rabble. I have now had time to arrive at the conviction that it was a melancholy thought to want to live in a vicarage, doing penance in an out-of-the-way place, forgotten. I now have made up my mind quite otherwise" (VII^1 A 229).

Date of preface to *The Book on Adler* [*On Authority and Revelation*], not published; ms. in *Papirer* (VII^2 B 235–70; VIII^2 B 1–27).

Drafts of lectures on communication (VIII^2 B 79–89), not published or delivered.

Mar. 13 *Upbuilding Discourses in Various Spirits,* by S. Kierkegaard, published.

Sept. 29 *Works of Love,* by S. Kierkegaard, published.

Nov. 3 Regine Olsen marries Johan Frederik Schlegel.

Dec. 24 Sells house on Nytorv.

1848

Jan. 28 Leases apartment at Tornebuskegade and Rosenborggade 156A (now 7) for April occupancy.

Apr. 19 S.K. notes: "My whole nature is changed. My concealment and inclosing reserve are broken—I am free to speak" (VIII^1 A 640).

Apr. 24 "No, no, my inclosing reserve still cannot be broken, at least not now" (VIII^1 A 645).

Apr. 26 *Christian Discourses,* by S. Kierkegaard, published.

July 24–27 *The Crisis and a Crisis in the life of an Actress,* by Inter et Inter, published.

Aug. Notes that his health is poor and is convinced that he will die (IX A 216).

Reflections on direct and indirect communication (IX A 218, 221–24).

Sept. 1 Preaches in Vor Frue Kirke (IX A 266–69, 272).

Nov. *The Point of View for My Work as an Author* "as good as finished" (IX A 293); published posthumously in 1859 by S.K.'s brother, Peter Christian Kierkegaard.

"Armed Neutrality," by S. Kierkegaard, "written toward the end of 1848 and the beginning of 1849" (X^5 B 105–10) but not published.

1849

May 14 Second edition of *Either/Or;* and *The Lily of the Field and the Bird of the Air,* by S. Kierkegaard, published.

May 19 *Two Minor Ethical-Religious Essays,* by H. H., published.

June 25–26 Councillor Olsen (Regine's father) dies.

July 30 *The Sickness unto Death,* by Anti-Climacus, published.

Nov. 13 *Three Discourses at the Communion on Fridays,* by S. Kierkegaard, published.

1850

Apr. 18 Moves to Nørregade 43 (now 35), Copenhagen.

Sept. 27 *Practice [Training] in Christianity*, by Anti-Climacus, published.

Dec. 20 *An Upbuilding [Edifying] Discourse*, by S. Kierkegaard, published.

1851

Veiviser (directory) listing for 1851: Østerbro 108A (torn down).

Jan. 31 "An Open Letter . . . Dr. Rudelbach," by S. Kierkegaard, published.

Aug. 7 *On My Work as an Author;* and *Two Discourses at the Communion on Fridays*, by S. Kierkegaard, published.

Sept. 10 *For Self-Examination*, by S. Kierkegaard, published.

1851–52

Judge for Yourselves!, by S. Kierkegaard, written. Published posthumously, 1876.

Veiviser listing for 1852–55; Klædeboderne 5–6 (now Skindergade 38).

1854

Jan. 30 Bishop Mynster dies.

Apr. 15 H. Martensen named Bishop.

Dec. 18 S.K. begins polemic against Bishop Martensen in *Fædrelandet.*

1855

Jan.–May Polemic continues.

May 24 *This Must Be Said; So Let It Now Be Said*, by S. Kierkegaard, advertised as published.

First number of *The Moment.*

June 16 *Christ's Judgment on Official Christianity*, by S. Kierkegaard, published.

Sept. 3 *The Unchangeableness of God. A Discourse*, by S. Kierkegaard, published.

Sept. 25 Ninth and last number of *The Moment* published; number 10 published posthumously. S.K. writes his last journal entry (XI^2 A 439).

Oct. 2 Enters Frederiks Hospital.

Nov. 11 Dies.

Nov. 18 Is buried in Assistents Cemetery, Copenhagen.

Translators' Preface

With Volumes 5 and 6, the work on the text of *Søren Kierkegaard's Journals and Papers* is completed—eighteen years after the task was undertaken. We are deeply grateful to the many persons who in various ways have given encouragement and assistance from the fifties on into the seventies.

Dr. Gregor Malantschuk of the University of Copenhagen has continued to share with us the fruits of his lifetime of penetrating study of all of Kierkegaard's works. For the support of this international collaboration we acknowledge the assistance of Rask-Ørsted Fondet and Carlsberg Fondet. The translations of Kierkegaard's letters included in this volume are the collaborative work of the editors and of Dr. Henrik Rosenmeier, University of Copenhagen, who is presently preparing a full volume of letters and documents.

The year 1972–73 was a year of concentration on Volumes 5 and 6. We acknowledge with thanks a sabbatical leave granted by St. Olaf College, as well as the quarters arranged by the college for the Kierkegaard Library, a research and publication grant from the National Endowment for the Humanities, the courtesies and facilities of the Kierkegaard Bibliotek of the University of Copenhagen, and guest-scholar quarters at Nyhavn 18 provided by Danmarks Nationalbank. This superb contributive constellation made possible an unprecedented year of undispersed time and effort, resulting in a certain quality of work, we trust, and in an earlier completion of the whole task. We are also indebted to Gyldendal Forlag of Copenhagen for permission to use the text of the *Papirer* and to absorb the editors' notes, and to Munksgaard Forlag of Copenhagen for similar permission regarding *Breve og Aktstykker vedrørende Søren Kierkegaard.*

Dr. Rune Engebretson has generously provided translations of the German passages in the text and Professor Emeritus Bert Narveson the translations from Greek and Latin. Nathaniel Hong has meticulously checked the apparatus, and Todd Nichol and John Hendricks have carefully read the entire manuscript. Grethe Kjær has again given valuable counsel and assistance in numerous ways. Dorothy Bolton and Ann Søvik had a share in the typing. Members of the Indiana University Press have consummated their part in this long publication process. To all these colleagues and to friends and son we are permanently and gratefully beholden.

Kierkegaard Library   H.V.H.
St. Olaf College   E.H.H.
Northfield, Minnesota

A history of Kierkegaard's journals and papers and a full account of the principles of this selection from them are given in the translators' preface to Volume 1. Briefly, the entries in the first four volumes of this edition are arranged topically, and chronologically within each topic. Volumes 5 and 6 contain the autobiographical selections. Volume 7 will contain a complete index and composite collation.

The entries in Volumes 5 and 6 are arranged in as rigorous a chronological order as possible, given the many undated and loose items. This has required an interleaving of entries from sections A, B, and C in the Danish edition of the *Papirer*. A collation of entries in the present volume with the standard designations in the *Papirer* is provided at the end of the volume.

Within the entries, a series of five periods indicates omissions or breaks in the Danish text as it stands. A series of three periods is used in the few instances of the translators' omissions.

Brackets are used in the text to enclose certain Danish terms just translated or to enclose references and formulations supplied by the translators.

Footnote numbers in the text refer to the editors' notes, which appear in serial order at the end of the volumes. Kierkegaard's notes and marginal comments appear at the bottom of the particular page, at the end of the entry, in a following entry, or in a few special cases as a bracketed insertion within an entry.

Kierkegaard's consciously developed punctuation (VIII^1 A 33–38) has been retained to a large extent. This is evident in the use of the colon and the dash and a minimal use of question and quotation marks. Pedagogical-stylistic characteristics (change of pace, variation of sentence-length, and the architecture of sentences and paragraphs) have also been carried over in the main. They are intended as an invitation to reflection and rereading—ideally, aloud.

Søren Kierkegaard's Journals and Papers

I. THE EARLY YEARS
1829–1837

« **5051**

Dear Brother,[1]

Your reply arrived long before I had expected it. I waited for your letter for less time than you had to be in suspense for mine, and I am pleased that you liked it. As to your belief that I have read Cicero's letters, this is not so at all; I have not read a single one of them. I suppose that I shall get to read them next year. It is true that the *artium* has not yet become particularly difficult, but it may become so by the time I have to take my exams, for a man by the name of Asp,[2] *cand. theol. et juris,* has written a book about increasing the *artium* requirements.[3] He demands, for example, that solid geometry and trigonometry be made mandatory subjects for this examination, and he demands that there be written translations in German and French and that the English language not be neglected as it has been until now, but that it be taught and that there be written translations in this language as well. He also proposes that anyone who fails any subject pass another exam[4] in that discipline the following spring. One thing he complains of in his book is the slighting of the university-trained graduates in medicine in favor of apprentice barbers. I really hope that his proposals are not adopted, as it would be extremely unpleasant for me to have to tackle the English language[5] in my last year of school.[6] It was already decided at the time of the last exams that I not be examined until 1830 because I am, after all, a bit young. Bindesbøll[7] teaches religion and New Testament; Warncke[8] is my history teacher, of course; Marthensen[9] is my mathematics teacher; and Ursin[10] has left the school for good. I am studying Greek with the Professor,[11] something I did not expect, inasmuch as he became quite fed up last year with teaching Greek to the A section of the first class.

Incidentally, you must not think that the Professor's sickness has been a particularly dangerous one, for he has in fact been teaching us for a long time now, and his leg has healed completely. When you write to him, do not go into too much detail about the cause of his being laid up, for, as you know, I only heard about it from his servant.

If you could find something out about Fritz Lange,[12] whether his eyes are better or even worse, I would appreciate it. What I have heard here is that where he was staying he started wearing thick glasses on doctor's advice but that he fell in the street and got splinters in his eyes so he is completely blind, but this I neither credit nor hope.

I have indeed found the book you requested, and Father has also fulfilled your wish and bought you a Danish Bible. These books will, as you request, be sent along, tied and sealed in a small canvas-covered box. Greetings have been conveyed to Mrs. Fenger,[13] as you requested in your letter, and she returns most loving greetings to you. She had obtained one of the books, P. Hald's dissertation,[14] and it has already been sent. She promised to see if she could get hold of the other, the Bishops' Pastoral Letter of 1817,[15] and if she does, it will be sent with the others.

I hope you are as well as are most of us here, with the exception of Petrea[16] who has been unwell for some time. Nicoline[17] is mending, and her finger is nearly cured, but it is still somewhat sore.

Everybody sends you greetings: Father,[18] Mother,[19] Nicoline, Lund,[20] Petrea, Niels,[21] Mrs. Lund,[22] and Ole Lund's daughters,[23] but above all, greetings

from
Your affectionate brother,
Søren

Copenhagen, March 25, 1829
[In M. P. Kierkegaard's handwriting:] Probably Ferdinand[24] will write a few words on the back of this.
P. S. Just as Søren is about to enter this letter in the copy book, Lorentzen[25] is paying me a visit, and he asks most emphatically that his warmest greetings be sent to you. I (Søren) will soon write to you so that I may be able also to gainsay Father.[26]

Herrn	[Postmark]
Cand. Theol. P. C. Kierkegaard	Hamburg
Unter Linden 20 drey Treppen	13/3
in	N. 15/3 2.
Berlin	

Hiermit 1 Kastchen in Leinen, mit 2 gedruckte Bücher gemerkt P. C. K. Franco Hamburg den Werth 8 Rbthl Silber.

Letters, no. 2   March 25, 1829

« 5052

[Reading notes[27] on Philipp Marheineke, *Geschichte der teutschen Reformation,* part 1 (Berlin: 1816).]

I C 1   *n.d.,* 1831–32

« 5053

[Reading notes on J. C. Lindberg, *Historiske Oplysninger om den danske Kirkes symboliske Bøger.* (Copenhagen: 1830).]

I C 2   *n.d.,* 1831–32

« 5054

[Reading notes on S. J. Stenersen, *Udsigt over den Lutherske Reformation,* part 1. (Christiania: 1818).]

I C 3   *n.d.,* 1831–32

« 5055

[Interpretations[28] of various passages from the synoptic Gospels: Luke 3:1, 11:39; Mark 4:27, 7:11; Matthew 13:36, 15:5, 15:32, 18:15, 18:24; Luke 10:26, 12:54; Matthew 16:14; Luke 17:16, 17:20, 17:24; Matthew 19:7; Luke 17:19, 19:1; Matthew 16:16, 16:21, 16:27, 17:24, 16:18, 21:33, 21:44; Luke 20:16, 22:48; Matthew 23:16, 24:24; Matthew 26:3; Luke 22:48; Matthew 26:61, Luke 23:30.]

... Luke 17:19. ἡ πίστις σου σέσωκέ σέ. It seems odd that Christ adds this, for he always made faith a condition for their being saved; but how, then, were the others saved who did not manifest their faith, indeed, seemed not even to have it, since they did not return to give God the honor?

In margin: *See p. 1 [i.e., I C 9]. ...

I C 7   *n.d.,* 1832–33

« 5056

In margin of 5053 (I C 7):

*In his sermon Grundtvig[29] observes that it was indeed necessary for truth to be present, for if the words "Lord Jesus, save us" had been only idle talk, he would not have been saved; but in the first place the faith mentioned is immediate, spontaneous faith, which is called forth by suffering, and in the last place, and if I may call it that, an intensified faith.

I C 9   *n.d.,* 1832–33

« 5057

[Latin translation by Kierkegaard of Acts 1–4[30] and of Acts 24–27[31].]

I C 11–12   *n.d.*, 1833–34

« 5058

Lectures on Dogmatics
by
H. N. Clausen[32]

[. . .]

I C 19   *n.d.*, 1833–34

« 5059

[A schematic analysis,[33] based on A. Neander, *Geschichte der Pflanzung und Leitung der Christliche Kirche durch die Apostel,* I–II (Hamburg: 1832), I, pp. 168 ff., of the Greek expression for the "gifts of the spirit" in I Corinthians 12. Reading notes[34] on A. Neander, *Geschichte der Pflanzung* . . . , I, pp. 332 f., 342, 364 ff.]

I C 16, 18   *n.d.*, 1834

« 5060 *The Path of Fate*[35]

p. 31 . . . . . the young man shouted lustily, his heart leapt into life, and he assumed a manly stance.

Matthew 5:45 Luke 15:11 Ephesians 2:7
Titus 3:4 John 3:16 I John 4:10, 16, 19
Romans 5:8

I C 17   *n.d.*, 1834

« 5061

I am amazed that (as far as I know) no one has ever treated *the idea of a "master-thief,"*[36] an idea that certainly would lend itself very well to dramatic treatment. We cannot help noting that almost every country has had the idea of such a thief, that an ideal of a thief has hovered before all of them; and we also see that however different Fra Diavolo may be from Peer Mikkelsen[37] or Morten Frederiksen,[38] they still have certain features in common. Thus many of the stories circulating about thieves are attributed by some to Peer Mikkelsen, by others to Morten Frederiksen, by others to someone else, etc., although it is impossible to decide definitely to which of them they really belong. This shows that men have imagined a certain ideal of a thief with some broad general features which have then been attributed to this or that actual thief. We must especially bear in mind that wickedness, a propensity for stealing, etc. were not considered to be the one and only core of the idea. On the contrary, the master-thief has also been thought of as one endowed with natural goodness, kindness, charitableness, together with extraordinary bearing, cunning, ingenuity, one who really does not steal just to steal, that is, in order to get hold of another person's possessions, but for some other reason. Frequently we may think of him as someone who is displeased with the established order and who now expresses his grievance by violating the rights of others, seeking thereby an occasion to mystify and affront the authorities. In this respect it is noteworthy that he is thought of as stealing from the rich to help the poor (as is told of Peer Mikkelsen), which does indeed indicate magnanimity, and that he never steals for his own advantage. In addition, we could very well imagine him to have a warm affection for the opposite sex, for example Forster[39] (Feuerbach, part II), something that on the one hand indicates a bright spot in his character and on the other gives him and his life a romantic quality which is required in order to distinguish him from the simple thief—whether he steals in order to provide, if possible, a better future in his beloved's arms (like Forster) or whether in his activity as a thief he is conscious of being an opponent of the established order or an avenger against the authorities of some injustice perhaps committed by them against him. His girl walks by his side like a guardian angel and helps him in his troubles while the authorities are in pursuit to capture him, and the populace, on the other hand, regards him suspiciously as one who is, after all, a thief, although perhaps an inner voice sometimes speaks in his defense, and at the same time he finds no encouragement and comfort among the other thieves since they are far inferior to him and are dominated by viciousness. The only possible association he can have with them is solely for the purpose of using them to achieve his aims; otherwise he must despise them.

I A 11   September 12, 1834

‹ **5062**

Such a master-thief (Kagerup,[40] for example) will also boldly and candidly confess his crime and suffer punishment for it as a man who is conscious of having lived for an idea, and precisely thereby he acknowledges the reality [*Realitet*] of the state and does not, as one might say, disavow it in his life; he opposes only its abuses. We could also imagine him as one who would make fools of a court, but we must regard this as a kind of jest about the whole thing and an expression in deed of a vanity entirely consistent with his idea. He will never abandon candor, and he will come with his own confession as soon as he has demonstrated how he *could* hoodwink a court.

                                    I A 12   September 17, 1834

« **5063**

The difference between an author who picks up his material everywhere but does not work it up into an organic whole and one who does that is, it seems to me, like the difference between mock turtle and real turtle. The meat from some parts of the real turtle tastes like veal, from other parts like chicken, but it is all together in one organism. All these various kinds of meat are found in mock turtle, but that which binds the separate parts is a sauce, which still is often more nourishing than the jargon which takes its place in a lot of writing.

                                    I A 32   November 22, 1834

« **5064**

It seems that the part of the watchman's song for ten o'clock that says "Be wise and clever," in contrast to what follows: "Tend your light and fire," must be said to thieves, for cleverness and wisdom ought to be recommended to those who are awake rather than to those who are sleeping.

                                    I A 39   November 27, 1834

« **5065**

[Reading notes[41] on P. Marheineke, *Die Grundlehren der Christlichen Dogmatik als Wissenschaft* (2 ed.; Berlin: 1827). *ASKB* 644.]

                                    I C 25–26   n.d., 1834–35

« **5066**

[Reading notes,[42] together with comments, on F. Baader, *Vorlesungen über spekulative Dogmatik,* I (Stuttgart, Tübingen: 1828), II (Münster: 1830). *ASKB* 396.]

                                    I C 27–33   n.d., 1834–35

« **5067**

With respect to actions they accused religion of:
(1) prompting improper, ghastly acts against the common civil-moral life.——

I do not understand his[43] argument, for he aims to show that a man may easily be religious and also immoral, because the one belongs to feelings, the other to action.

(2) actions that have no meaning for the sensate life, none for morality.

But we are supposed to believe that those actions that are the more or less spontaneous movement of the feelings out into life must be good, since, after all, feelings themselves are good, are true.—

Some are of the opinion that when the imagination must submit to being used for the work of carrying the reduced images to their full magnitude, this *Erschöpfung*[44] is the feeling of the great and majestic in nature.

I C 34   *n.d.*, 1834–35

« 5068

[Exegesis[45] of Ephesians on the basis of L. J. Rückert, *Der Brief Pauli an die Epheser erläutert und vertheidigt* (Leipzig: 1834).]

I C 35   *n.d.*, 1834–35

« 5069

[Kierkegaard's Latin translations[46] of Philippians, Colossians, and I and II Thessalonians in their entirety.]

I C 36   *n.d.*, 1834–35

« 5070

[Kierkegaard's Latin translations[47] of Colossians 1:14, 24; 2:11, 22.]

I C 37   *n.d.*, 1834–35

« 5071

One frequently sees examples of how the magnetized[48] come to the knowledge, with respect to man's condition after death, that everything centers in Christ, that one who has not thoroughly believed according to the gospel is given up to external torment etc.—; in this connection it could be very interesting, as Tutti Frutti[49] mentions somewhere (vol. III), to make a magnetic experiment with a person of the Mohammedan religion and see if the same result is achieved.

I A 41   January 22, 1835

« 5072

We must, of course, imagine him [the master-thief] well-equipped with a very good sense of humor,* which can very well be reconciled with his discontent, which is precisely what will make him satirical and

—even though he must not be thought of as always being discontented
—can still be readily reconciled with his lowly origin at the grassroot
level of the nation. In some cases he will resemble an Eulenspiegel.

I A 13   January 29, 1835

« 5073

Addition to 5072 (I A 13):

*I cite as an example a Peer Mikkelsen[50] who informs the authority
concerned that he wants to leave town. Or that such a fellow, when a
policeman encountering him for the second time observed: I think we
know each other, would answer: Yes, we taken a walk together
(the first time the policeman had been obliged to chase after him way
out to Vibenshuus). Or that a Cartouche[51] appears in person to get the
reward placed on his head.

I A 14   January 29, 1835

« 5074

He [the master-thief] is not a man who tries to lead others astray;
on the contrary, he dissuades them from leading such a life. He has
tasted its bitterness, and he endures it only because he lives for an idea.
He scorns base thieves, and yet fate always drives him together with
them. The one who is closest to him, his true friend in life and in death,
is no thief, loves him, and will sacrifice everything for him. He is eager
to lead him away from the wrong path he has taken, but knowing his
vehemence, he does not dare to speak to him about it. Frequently the
master-thief also feels extremely unhappy about his position, about his
being regarded by many as branded; he feels *misunderstood* (tragically).

I would prefer to think of such a master-thief as someone who had
lost his father early in life and now has only an old mother whom he
loves dearly and she him. While the mother is shocked by her son's
errant ways, however, his beloved completely overlooks his bad side,
happy to possess his love, although she perhaps scarcely dares talk
about his love lest she betray him. I would want to emphasize particularly this relationship to his mother and to his beloved in order to
indicate his geniality.

I A 15   January 29, 1835

« 5075

For one scene I could imagine him [the master-thief] in a wooded
area with the moon shining. He addresses the moon: "Thanks, moon,
you silent witness to the lovers' rendezvous, the robber's lurking, the

miser's anxiety, the policeman's drowsiness—yet you are especially partial to the thief, you who are a thief yourself and steal your light from the sun!"

Perhaps my comment on the policeman's insignia could appropriately be put in his mouth. See the appended slip [i.e., I A 17].

I could also imagine him encountering in a tavern a tramp (an unsuccessful government clerk or perhaps a title-bearing secretary who also tried to cut a figure with his title and his education—all in all, a low comedy character) who tried to incite the peasants by talking about the deficiencies of the management etc., and who would thus be a sharp contrast to the master-thief's earnest discontent with much of the system.

I A 16   February 9, 1835

« 5076

Attached to 5075 (I A 16):

Probably the reason the police use an insignia picturing a hand with an eye in the center[52] is to indicate thereby that they have an eye in every finger, but the fact that this eye does not extend to the thumb as well indicates that they also have a finger to put over the eye, if necessary.

I A 17   December 16, 1834[53]

« 5077

Fausts Leben, Thaten und Höllenfahrt in fünf Büchern, neue verbesserte Auflage. 1799.

This book is by a man named Klinger;[54] see encyclopedia. Faust is presented as the inventor of printing (see p. 3), and Satan vows that this invention is going to saddle the world with a heap of troubles (see his lines, pp. 28–37). Thus the idea of having the world be destroyed by books, found in Andersen's *Walking Tour*,[55] chapter 1, comes from the legend of Faust.

p. 65. Faust: "ich wollte einen Teufel haben und keinen meines Geschlechtes."[56]

p. 221. Here we find the description of a visionary: Ueber dem sog er (that is, the visionary) gleich einem Trocknen Schwamme die Thorheiten und Charlatanerien ein, die andre ausheckten, ein Umstand, wodurch sich die Schwärmer von den Philosophen gänzlich unterscheiden; denn diese hassen und verachten die Hypothesen eines andern, da jene allen Unrath des menschlichen Geistes annehmen, und sich zu eigen machen.—[57]

It is also quite remarkable how Satan (see p. 378 etc.) shows Faust the horrible and widespread consequences of his acts, and how Klinger in a note (p. 385) develops the idea that the whole human race, from king to beggar, each according to his ability, is collectively the creator of the so-called moral world. Klinger promises to develop this in greater detail in his *Giafar*.

I C 46   *n.d.*, 1835

« 5078

Faust im Gewande der Zeit—Ein Schattenspiel mit Licht von Harro Harring dem Friesen von Ibenshof an der Nordsee. Leipzig: 1831.

I C 47   *n.d.*, 1835

« 5079

Szenen aus Fausts Leben, von Schr., Offenbach: 1792 (presumably the same one v. Raumer mentions, p. 196, and calls Schreiber).*

He points out in his preface that there is an aspect of Faust that is suitable for dramatic treatment: "dass nämlich der Mensch nicht gemacht ist für den Umgang mit höhern Wesen, und dass er es nicht ungestraft wagen dürfte, aus dem Kreise heraus zu treten."[58]–.....
His taking leave of his father is moving. His meeting the traveler (see p. 24) is comic.—He then has him continue his journey and encounter life's various characters, both the friendly and genial and the ludicrous —for example, p. 28, his encounter with the young man. . . . . The scene with the young man in the hut is excellent. The scene in the learned society is really funny. Faust's observations (p. 41) at the Baltic Sea are also really notable. . . . .

Of the particular beautiful things I point out only the fisherman's song, p. 108.

[Song transcribed.][59]

*This book belongs to the University Library.

I C 48   *n.d.*, 1835

« 5080

Der Faust der Morgenländer oder Wanderungen Ben Hafis. Erzählers der Reisen vor der Sündfluth.[60] Bagdad; 1797. . . . [Reading notes and excerpts.[61]]

I C 49   March 7, 1835

« 5081

If we compare the master-thief with the Italian robber, we see an essential difference in that the social element is dominant in the latter.

We cannot very well imagine him except as the head of a robber band in whose midst, when the dangers and difficulties of plundering are passed, he gives himself over to reveling; whereas in the master-thief something far deeper is operative, a touch of melancholy, an encapsulation within himself, a dim view of life-relationships, an inner dissatisfaction.

I A 18   March 15, 1835

« 5082

Eulenspiegel seems to represent the satyr-like in Northerners.[62]

I A 51   March 16, 1835

« 5083

Historisches Taschenbuch, herausgegeben von Friedrich v. Raumer. Fünftes Jahrgang. Leipzig: 1834. Pp. 128–210.[63]

[P. 129, 133] Did Faust[64] actually exist? . . . . . All this is far too shrouded in legend, something like the story about his dog, in which an evil spirit is supposed to have been hidden.—. . . . . [P. 144] He was in Leipzig, and there are two pictures of it here. They are printed in Raumer. . . . . .[65]

I will cite only some of the literature. Raumer gives it in great detail.

Neumann et C. C. Kirchner, *auctor et respondens, dissertatio historica de Fausto praestigiatore.* Wittemberg: 1683.4.1742, 1743, 1746.

Bouterwek, *Geschichte der Poesie und Beredsamkeit*, Band IX, p. 422.

Ueber Calderons wunderthatige Magus ein Beitrag zum Verstandniss der Faustischen Fabel, v. Dr. Rosenkrantz. 1829.8.

[P.203 f.] **Schriften über Göthes Faust.**
1. *Ueber Göthes Faust und dessen Fortsetzung nebst einem Anhange vom ewigen Juden.* Leipzig: 1824.8.
2. *Aestetische Vorlesungen über Göthes Faust, als Beitrag zur Anerkennung wissenschaftlicher Kunst Beurtheilung.* Herausgegeben von Dr. H. F. W. Hinrichs. Halle: 1825.8.
3. *Vorlesungen von Wolf über Göthes Faust,* 1829 in Jena gehalten, nicht gedruckt.
4. *Vorlesungen über Göthes Faust* von K. E. Schubarth. Berlin: 1830.
5. *Heroldstimme zu Göthes Faust, ersten und zweiten Theils mit besondre Beziehung auf die Schlussscene des ersten Theils,* v. C. F. G. G–l. Leipzig: 1831.8.

6. L.B. (Bechstein) *die Darstellung der Tragödie Faust von Göthe auf der Bühne. Ein zeitgemässes Wort für Theater Directionen, Schauspieler und Bühnenfreunde.* Stuttgardt: 1831.12.

7. *Ueber Erklärung und Fortsetzung des "Faust" im Allgemeinen und insbesondre über "Christliches Nachspiel zur Tragoedie Faust,"* von K. Rosenkranz. Leipzig: 1831.

8. *Vorlesungen über Göthes Faust,* von F. A. Rauch. Büdingen: 1830.

9. *Sehr treffende Bemerkungen und Erlaüterungen über Göthes Faust gibt Falk in seinem Buche, "Göthe aus näherem Umgang dargestelt."–*

[P. 206] **Erzählungen.**

Doctor Faust, eine Erzählung, von Hamilton, frei übersetzt, v. Mylius. Im zweiten Bande der Bibliothek der Romane. Das französische Original führt den Titel: *l'enchanteur Faustus.*

Fausts Leben, Thaten und Höllenfahrt in fünf Büchern, v. Klinger.*

Faust, v. Mainz, Gemälde aus der Mitte des funfzehnten Jarhunderts, v. I. M. Kamarack. Leipzig: 1794.

Der umgekehrte Faust oder Froschs Jugendjahre, v. Seybold. Heidelberg: 1816.

Fausts Lehrling eine kleine Erzählung, v. Gerle. *Im dritten Theile von des Verfassers Schattenrisse und Mondnachts Bilder.* Leipzig: 1824.8.

Faustus ein Gedicht in lyrischer Form, v. Ludvig Bechstein. Leipzig: 1832.4.–†

[P. 205] **Opern.**

Dr. Fausts Mantel ein Zauberspiel mit Gesang i zwei Akten, v. Adolph Baüerle. Wien: 1819.8.

Faust Trauerspiel mit Gesang und Tanz, v. Julius v. Voss. Berlin: 1824.8.

Faust Oper in vier Aufzügen, v. Bernard. Musik v. Spohr.

Fausto, opera seria, in drei Akten in Paris zum ersten Male gegeben im März. 1831. Die Musik v. Fräulein Louise Bertin.

I C 51   n.d., 1835

« 5084

Faust und D. Juan, Tragoedie in fünf Akten, [66] v. Grabbe. Frankfurt: 1829.8.

I C 52   n.d., 1835

In margin: *In Student Association Library.
In margin: †In the Athenæum. See 1834 catalog, p. 156.

« **5085**

[Pp. 159 ff.] It is related in the so-called *Dr. Joh. Faustens Miracel, Kunst und Wunderbrech,* how Faust made contact with the devil, and not until the devil Aziel came, who, in reply to Faust's question how fast he was, said: As fast as human thought—not until then did he become involved with him. Lessing[67] has made use of this in having the spirit say he was as fast as the transition from evil to good. —

See v. Raumer,[68] p. 161. —

[P. 196.] See Lessing,[69] his letters on the most recent literature, pt. 1, p. 103, and *Analekten für die Litteratur,* pt. 1, p. 210, also pt. 2 of his *Theatralischem Nachlasse.*

I C 53   *n.d.,* 1835

« **5086**

It is indeed curious that the legend has provided Faust with a dog in which the devil conceals himself (see v. Raumer,[70] p. 133). It seems to me that the legend thereby wants to suggest that for a man like Faust, for whom all conditions of life were so utterly askew and who had such a canted stance toward everything, that for him, I say, the dog, this usually faithful companion to man, here did in fact retain his character as faithful but also became an evil spirit who, in line with his faithfulness, never deserted him.

I C 54   March 16, 1835

« **5087**

(The Wandering Jew[71] seems to have his prototype in the fig tree that Christ commanded to wither away.)

I C 65   March 28, 1835

« **5088**

Just as a consistent development from the Protestant view of the Bible as constituting the Church led to the establishment of a new branch of knowledge, namely, introductory scientific scholarship in which one sought to prove that by having its origin in the apostles it had the right to constitute the Church, so also the theory about the apostolic symbols[72] leads to an introductory scientific scholarship.

I A 59   *n.d.,* 1835

« 5089 *Some Observations on Grundtvig's Theory of the Church*[73]

1. Grundtvig[74] believes that the Church is based on the sacraments and that whoever changes them changes the Church and has *eo ipso* withdrawn from it. But in this connection I beg to remark: In his attack[75] why did not Grundtvig emphasize the Lord's Supper as something already instituted rather than baptism, something that was still to come, for, after all, it had not yet been introduced into the Church. —(No change in the words of institution. —Commentary—the opposition party insists upon only the evil[76]—dilemma: either both are heretics or both are Christians.)—

2. Nevertheless, something has always been regarded as essentially Christian, something as less essentially Christian, and in this respect the belief has been that the Bible contains the essentially Christian—in what, then, is Grundtvig's theory different from the others? The others let it be less definite, whereas Grundtvig believes that he has found an expression that once and for all decides what is Christian faith and what is not. This he now is obliged to maintain as essential and, of course, must most stringently insist upon it, which Lindberg[77] has also done very consistently; he must insist on every letter, yes, every thousandth part of a jot, for otherwise the door is immediately opened for determinations from man's side as to what is Christian and what is not, and in that case he must reasonably grant the same right to every other man, and in that case his theory comes to be on the same level as the others. —But if we look now at the expression of Christian faith upon which he believes the Church to be based, we must admit that viewed in and of itself it is impossible for an idea to find completely adequate expression in words—even if Deity himself spoke the words, there would always be a little snag as soon as man set about to understand them. Here I would concede something that I am temporarily willing to concede—that it was given by inspired men—but if we insist on the idea of inspiration in this way, as we are obliged to do here according to Lindberg's theory, then we must also certainly limit this activity to the language in which it was originally given, but at present all the churches that have essentially the same creed have it in translation, and it is precisely the Greek Church that differs in its creed from the others (which is why Grundtvig declares somewhere in *Theologisk Maanedsskrift*[78] that it is like a withered branch). But must we now concede a miracle with respect to the translation? Nothing warrants

our doing that. (If it is assumed, then what was mentioned above holds true.) —But, of course, with translation many more snags arise etc.— consequently the more consistently that theory is maintained, the more it diverges from the truth, but if it is not consistently maintained, then we are just where we started, and Grundtvig's theory has no significance whatsoever.—

3. In which capacity[79] did the Apostles give this creed—(over–under–heretics–belonged itself to the Church).

To me it appears far more natural to think that the Lord's Supper as the originally true center in the Church has been kept genuinely alive, and that out from this center the external outlines have gradually been drawn. Which is why Christianity is far more detailed in the institution of the Lord's Supper as described in the New Testament than in baptism.* (Mystery for both the gentile Christians and the Jewish Christians.)

Grundtvig has been asked to prove that the present creed was the original one, but on that point the Magister[80] [Lindberg] held that it was up to the others to prove that it was not the original. In a sense this cannot be denied, for Grundtvig can always appeal to the fact that we have it now and he does not know how it was previously; so it is up to the others to make their proof. Meanwhile the whole matter gets to be awkward for Grundtvig, for he himself has said that it does not depend on the dead letter (that is, books) but on the Living Word,[81] and it is not particularly reasonable to think that we can now muster up a Living Word from 1800 years ago; thus it appears that Grundtvig invites refutation of his theory but at the same time says that you had better not do that, for by my very theory I have deprived you of every possibility of proof. —But not so with the Magister [Lindberg], for in order to make something out of the Altar Book he has called attention to the fact that 300 years ago it did not exist; consequently he has gotten himself involved in arguing on the basis of dead letters, and thus we could demand, if not legally at least with a certain fairness, that he prove that this creed was the original one.

The opposition[82] has pointed out that the creed is not found in the N. T. (to what extent is it proper in principle to attack him in that manner??). To that Lindberg[83] and Grundtvig etc. answered: (1) Well, it was natural, for he [Paul] was writing to Christians, and they knew

*and if there should be reason for concealment anywhere, it would much more likely be here than in baptism.

the creed so well that he did not need to quote it. But it is still an awkward matter, for the Christians also knew the Lord's Supper as well, and yet Paul quotes the words of institution in I Corinthians 11.[84] Now it cannot be denied that the Christians also often transgressed against the articles in the Apostles' Creed—why then do the Apostles never quote it, if not in its entirety then at least in part. But please note, with the weight attributed to the words of institution as a confession of faith, as he specifically says in I Corinthians 11: ἐγὼ παρέλαβον ἀπὸ τοῦ κυρίου, ὃ καὶ παρέδωκα ὑμῖν etc. (2) On the point that it is not found in the oldest Church Fathers, Magister Lindberg observed that they kept it secret. But suppose it was so—that would still not be reason enough to keep the Apostles from quoting it, since, after all, there was far more reason for a person to have considered the Lord's Supper as something of a mystery (which in fact they did), and this is discussed completely in I Corinthians 11. But suppose it was the case, this much is certain—that we do find it recorded from about the fourth century, and although it is not quite like ours, we can say that here (with reference to Lindberg, who argues from the dead letter) we do have something which we know exists; how it was previously we do not know, but we assumed that it had been just like this and quite consistently claim that if you believe the opposite the burden of proof lies with you. But inasmuch as the present creed and that of the fourth century are not exactly the same, since, on the contrary, the fourth century creed lacks certain articles and yet, if you want to be consistent, you must acknowledge that according to your train of thought I can say that the one is just as original as the other, then you must acknowledge that we do not have the original. This conclusion is unsatisfactory only for you who believe that if we do not have it, then the Church is sunk—then the Covenant is broken and no happiness can come to man, but this conclusion is not unsatisfactory for us who believe that the Church essentially expresses itself at the concrete moment in its confessions, and that they consequently are to be regarded as mileposts on the way of Christian development.

Grundtvig also believed that this theory should be of theological assistance in determining what is Christian and what is not. He believed that the Bible was deaf and dumb, that it could be interpreted every which way, but he believed that these words were so simple that no one could misunderstand them. But in the first place it is, properly speaking, ridiculous to maintain that an exposition such as we find in the Bible, drafted by the same Apostles, should be confusing, as if the clarity of a matter were lessened by being illuminated from many sides, especially by the same men. The next thing to note is that nowadays the Bible is continually under attack, but—suppose now that this theory about the creed was just as universally accepted as the view of the Bible —I would still like to know if an opponent would find it more difficult to attack just the single phrase—the forgiveness of sins—than the entire teaching in the Bible, as if the single phrase did not involve far greater possibilities for interpretation than the complete exposition, where the individual expression is illuminated within the whole.[85]

N.B. It seems to me that Clausen[86] has erred in this controversy by going into an investigation of whether or not there was an essential change, because from Grundtvig's position there can be no question of that, for the theory has been advanced (see above) precisely to prevent human determinations as to what is Christian or not. —But on the other hand Grundtvig, Lindberg,[87] Engelbrecht,[88] etc. have also erred, of course, by replying as to the authenticity of it, for in all consistency they ought to have utterly repudiated the investigation.

I A 60   May 28, 1835

« 5090

Addition to 5089 (I A 60):
The misunderstanding in the theory of the "λόγος" as carried over to the word, since no matter how living the Living Word is, it still is not creative in that sense, for the very reason that it is not absolutely creative, does not come forth in its fullness, and therefore there is no absolute difference between the living and the written Word.

The same objections could be made against the creed as they themselves make against the Bible[89]—the whole external way in which conclusions are reached—an introductory science[90] made into the creed—the altered Lord's Supper.

I A 61   *n.d.,* 1835

« 5091

It seems to me that Grundtvig[91] regards the development of Christian knowledge as advancing not along a difficult road but on a railroad track like a steam engine, with steam fired up by the Apostles; consequently one comes to Christian knowledge in closed machines.

I A 62   June 1, 1835

« 5092

Copenhagen, June 1, 1835

You know how very enthusiastically I listened to you[92] in the past, how interested I was in your description of your stay in Brazil, although not so much in the mass of detailed observations you made, enriching yourself and your scholarship, as in your first impressions of those natural wonders, your paradisiacal joy and happiness. Something like this always appeals to any man of warmth and feeling, even if he intends to find his satisfaction and work in an entirely different field; it is especially appealing to the young, who as yet only dream about their destiny. Our early youth is like a flower at dawn, cupping a lovely dewdrop, reflecting pensively and harmoniously its surroundings. But soon the sun rises over the horizon and the dewdrop evaporates; with it vanish life's dreams, and now the question is (to use once again a flower metaphor) whether one is able, like the oleander, to produce by his own effort a drop that can stand as the fruit of his life. This requires, above all, that a person find the soil where he really belongs, but that is not always so easy to discover. In this respect there are fortunate temperaments so decisively oriented in a particular direction that they go steadily along the path once assigned to them without ever entertaining the thought that perhaps they should really be taking another path. There are others who let themselves be so completely directed by their environment that they never become clear about what they are really working toward. Just as the former class has its internal categorical imperative, so the latter has an external categorical imperative. But how few there are in the former class, and to the latter I do not wish to belong. The majority will get to try out in life what the Hegelian dialectic really means. Incidentally, it is altogether proper that wine ferments before it becomes clear; nevertheless the particular aspects of this condition are often unpleasant, although regarded in its totality, of course, it has its own pleasantness, inasmuch as it still has its relative results in the context of the universal doubt. It is especially significant for the person who through this comes to realize his destiny, not only because of the contrasting tranquility that follows the preceding storm but also because then *life has* an entirely different meaning than previously. This is the Faustian element that for a time asserts itself more or less in every intellectual development, which is why I have always been of the opinion that world-significance ought to be attributed to the idea of Faust. Just as our forefathers had a goddess of longing, so, in my opinion, Faust is doubt personified. More he should not be, and it certainly is a sin against the idea when Goethe allows Faust to be converted in the same way as Mérimée[93] lets Don Juan be converted. Do not raise the objection that the moment Faust addressed himself to the devil he made a positive step, for right here, it seems to me, is one of the most profound elements in the Faust legend. He approached the devil for the express purpose of becoming enlightened on things about which he was previously unenlightened, and precisely because he addressed himself to the devil, his doubt increased (just as a sick man falling into the hands of a quack is likely to get even worse). Admittedly Mephistopheles let him look through his spectacles into the hidden secrets of man and the world, but Faust could still not avoid having doubts about him, for he could never enlighten him about the most profound intellectual matters. In accordance with his idea he could never turn to God, for once he did that, he would have to say to himself that here was the true enlightenment, and at the same moment he would, in fact, deny his character as a doubter.

But this kind of doubt can also show itself in other spheres. Even if a man has come to terms with himself on several such main issues, there are still other important questions in life. Naturally every man desires to be active in the world according to his own aptitudes, but this again means that he wishes to develop his aptitudes in a particular direction, namely, in the direction best suited to his individuality. But which direction is that? Here I stand before a big question mark. Here I stand like Hercules, but not at the crossroads—no, here there are a good many more roads to take and thus it is much more difficult to choose the right one. It is perhaps my misfortune that I am interested in far too much and not decisively in any one thing; my interests are not subordinated to one but instead all stand coordinate.

I will try to indicate how things look to me.

1. *The natural sciences.* If I look first of all at this whole movement (including in this classification all those who seek to clarify and interpret the runic inscriptions of nature: from those who calculate the course of the stars and, so to speak, stop them in order to inspect them more closely, to those who describe the physiology of a particular animal; from those who survey the countryside from the heights of the mountains to those who descend to the depths of the abyss; from those who follow the development of the human body through its countless nuances to those who examine intestinal worms), I would of course see examples along this road, as on every other road (but principally on

this one), of people who have made a name for themselves in the literature by their enormous assiduousness in collecting. They know a great many details and have discovered many new ones, but nothing more. They have merely provided a substratum for others to think about and work up. These men are satisfied with their details, and yet to me they are like the rich farmer in the gospel:[94] they have collected a great deal in the barn, but science can say to them: "Tomorrow I will demand your life," insofar as that is what decides the significance each separate finding is to have in the whole picture. To the extent that there is a kind of unconscious life in such a man's knowledge, to that extent the sciences can be said to demand his life; to the extent that this is not the case, his activity is like that of the man who contributes to the upkeep of the earth by the decomposition of his dead body. This, of course, is not the case in other instances, with the kind of scientific researchers who through their reflection have found or are trying to find that Archimedean point which is nowhere in the world and from that point have surveyed the whole and have seen the details in their proper light. As far as they are concerned, I do not deny that they have had a very salutary effect on me. One rarely finds tranquility, harmony, and joy such as theirs. Here in Copenhagen we have three worthy representatives: An Ørsted,[95] whose face to me has always resembled a Chladni figure that nature has touched in the right way; a Schouw,[96] who provides a study for an artist wanting to paint Adam giving names to all the animals; and finally a Hornemann,[97] who, intimate with every plant, stands like a patriarch in nature. In this respect I also remember with joy the impression *you* made upon me, you who stood as the representative of a great nature that also should have its voice in parliament. I have been enthusiastic about the natural sciences and still am, but I do not think that I will make them my principal study. The life by virtue of reason [*Fornuft*] and freedom has always interested me most, and it has always been my desire to clarify and solve the riddle of life. The forty years in the wilderness before I reach the promised land of natural science seem too costly to me, all the more since I believe that nature can also be observed from a side that does not involve insight into the secrets of science. What difference does it make whether I view the whole world in a single flower or listen to the many hints that nature offers about human life, whether I admire the bold freehand sketches in the firmament or the nature-sounds in Ceylon[98] remind me of those sounds in the spiritual world or the departure of the migratory birds[99] reminds me of the deeper longings in man's breast.

2. *Theology.* This seems to be my most immediate choice,[100] but here also there are great difficulties. Christianity itself has such great contradictions that a clear view is hindered, to say the least. As you well know, I grew up in orthodoxy, so to speak, but as soon as I began to think for myself the enormous colossus gradually began to totter. I call it an enormous colossus deliberately, for taken as a whole it actually is very consistent and through the many centuries the separate parts have fused together so tightly that it is difficult to get at it. Now I could very well accept particular parts of it, but then these would prove comparable to the seedlings often found in rock fissures. On the other hand, I could probably also see the distortions in many separate points, but for a time I was obliged to let the main foundation stand *in dubio.* The moment *that* was changed, the whole thing took on an entirely different cast, and thus my attention was drawn to another phenomenon: rationalism, which on the whole looks rather second-rate. As long as reason [*Fornuften*] consistently follows its own nature and, by analyzing the relation between God and the world, again comes to look at man in his deepest and most inward relation to God and in this respect also from its own viewpoint considers Christianity to be that which has satisfied man's deepest needs for many centuries, as long as this is the case, there is nothing objectionable, but then it is no longer rationalism, for rationalism then acquires its own special coloring from Christianity and consequently is in a completely different sphere and does not construct a system but a Noah's ark (to use an expression Professor Heiberg[101] used on another occasion) in which the clean and the unclean animals lie down side by side. It creates just about the same impression our National Guard of the old days would make alongside the Potsdam Guard. That is why it virtually tries to attach itself to Christianity, bases its formulations on scripture, and sends a legion of Bible passages in advance of every single point, but the formulation itself is not penetrated by it. They conduct themselves like Cambyses,[102] who in his campaign against Egypt sent the sacred chickens and cats ahead, but they are also prepared, like the Roman consul,[103] to throw the sacred chickens overboard if they will not eat. The fallacy is that they use scripture as a basis when they agree with it but otherwise not, and thus they rest on two alien positions.

Nonnulla desunt.[104]

—As far as little annoyances are concerned, I will say only that I am starting to study for the theological examination, a pursuit that does not interest me in the least and that therefore does not get done very fast. I have always preferred free, perhaps therefore also indefinite, studying to the boarding house where one knows beforehand who the guests will be and what food will be served each day of the week. Since it is, however, a requirement, and one scarcely gets permission to enter into the scholarly pastures without being branded, and since in view of my present state of mind I regard it as advantageous, plus the fact that I know that by going through with it I can make my father happy (he thinks that the real land of Canaan[105] lies on the other side of the theological diploma, but in addition, like Moses of old, ascends Mount Tabor and declares that I will never get in—yet I hope that it will not be fulfilled this time), so I had better dig in. How lucky you are to have found an enormous field of investigation in Brazil, where every step offers something new, where the screaming of the rest of the Republic of Scholars does not disturb your peace. To me the scholarly theological world is like *Strandveien*[106] on Sunday afternoon during the Dyrehaug season*—they dash by each other, yelling and shouting, laugh and make fools of each other, drive their horses to death, tip over and are run over, and when they finally come—covered with dust and out of breath—to Bakken—well, they just look at each other, turn around, and go home.

As far as your coming back is concerned, it would be childish of me to hasten it, just as childish as Achilles' mother[107] trying to hide him to avoid a quick, honorable death.—Best wishes!

I A 72   June 1, 1835

« 5093

In margin of 5092 (I A 72):

*There is something strangely ironic in Copenhageners' excursions to Dyrehaug.[108] They are trying to shake off the bourgeois dust of the city, flee from themselves—and find themselves again at Bakken.

I A 73   January 14, 1837

« 5094 *Gilleleie*[109]

During my stay here at *Gilleleie* I have visited Esrom, Fredensborg, Frederiksværk, Tidsvilde. The last village is known chiefly for its [St.] *Helen-Spring*[110] (see Thiele, *Danske Folkesagn*,[111] *Samling* I, pp. 29 ff.), to which the whole countryside goes on pilgrimage around Midsummer's Eve. Just outside the village one's attention is immediately drawn to a fairly tall three-cornered column with the inscription that shifting sand once devastated this locality and buried the whole village of Tibirke under its drifts, but that it was checked by the tireless efforts of our excellent government. After being informed about the nature of the terrain by the inscription on the column and the lush buckwheat growing on both sides, if one looks down from this high point into the valley where *Tidsvilde* lies, his eyes meet a friendly, smiling nature: the small but very neat houses lie separately, surrounded by fresh greenery (if I may put it this way, it is like individuals reaching a friendly hand to each other in a smiling totality and not like larger cities which, when we approach, impress upon us the sharp outlines of the whole mass of buildings), for the whole area where the sand drifted most is now planted with fine trees—so one is almost tempted to believe that the whole thing was fiction, a strange fiction: that right here where people come to seek their health so many have found their graves. In the twilight the whole thing looks like an illustrated legend, a kind of Job's story in which *Tibirke Church* plays the main part. Alone on a great sandy hill, it stands like a gravestone over the unfortunate village but also as an example of a church built on a rock over which storm and sand cannot prevail, but since the church held its own, a forest sprang up there where the drifting sand had been. —Upon entering the village one is distressed to find—instead of peaceful rural tranquility, perhaps mixed with a little melancholy here because of the circumstances— boisterous noise, tents and tables, where, strangely enough, almost all the vendors are German, just as if to say that only foreigners could conduct themselves in such a manner here, that only a foreign tongue could profane the place in this way. On leaving the village one comes to a field, where the *grave* of [St.] Helen lies. There it stands—quiet, simple, surrounded by a fence of granite boulders; the gate leading to the slightly elevated grave stands open. But here, too—in order that every solemn impression may be disturbed—right beside it a tent has been set up; a bunch of men have chosen this as their place for boozing and making a racket and for mocking those who come to visit it [the grave]. A strange sort of discourse is going on here. Since these men are from this vicinity, they have imbibed with their mother's milk a considerable awe for this grave and the cures to which it is presumed to have contributed.* These they cannot completely deny, but now they want to convince themselves and others that they can disregard them and choose this way of jeering at the whole thing. There is a

---

*The cure employed consists of sleeping on the grave every St. John's Eve three years in a row and of providing oneself with some earth from the grave, for which purpose there was a special scoop. In addition one must not forget the poor, for whose benefit a money box has been placed in the village.

curious contrast to their behavior in the conversation and behavior of
a man who functions as a kind of caretaker and carries a key to the
wooden shed that contains the springs (there are, in fact, three,[112]
which is why they do not say locally: go to the spring, but to the
springs), whereby he earns a little money. He declares that he has been
there twenty years now and has seen many who have been cured. One
soon detects that he, too, does not put much trust in the whole thing
but for his own good eulogizes the place. Just as I, upon my arrival,
did not need to fear becoming an object of their derision—for they
would expect a man dressed in modern clothes, wearing spectacles,
and smoking a cigar to be just as loftily enlightened as they themselves
rather than someone coming there with pure intentions—so also the
keeper of the key just mentioned was disconcerted, for he was afraid
that his interest might possibly clash with the impression his remarks
would make upon me. He therefore snatched at the expedient commonly used, as I have noticed—namely, that those concerned had been
healed through these means "by the help of God." It is quite characteristic of such folk to come to that conclusion, for where they are unable
to explain the cure by way of these means, they shift over to something
more remote to dispose of the whole thing, but precisely in this way
they make the whole matter remarkable, for after all it would be remarkable that the help of God would have linked itself to this channel.
To be consistent with their rational position, they either had to deny
the whole thing and insist upon a perfectly evident fact or, if they were
more modest, postpone the explanation indefinitely.

Upon entering the site of the burial mound, a certain melancholy
mood comes over one, evoked by the strange mysteriousness, by the
dark side that superstition carries with it, elusive to the observer and
nevertheless suggestive of a whole system or nexus. One sees himself
surrounded by hanks of hair, rags, crutches, hears the shrieks of the
suffering, their prayers to heaven, hears the individual's desperate
laments at not being able to fall asleep (on the whole it seems a
beautiful thought that it is made a condition that one must *sleep* in this
holy place, as if to signify the quiet, devoted-to-God peacefulness), and
all this at midnight on a burial mound, surrounded by nothing but
small pieces of wood in the form of mementos placed on graves and
bearing testimony to the happily cured sufferings of the healed. And
now day is breaking, dawn with its strangely animate mobility and
clammy dampness disappears; the sun in its majesty illuminates the
landscape and perhaps hears the jubilant hymns of the healed. —Some

of the boards mentioned give briefly and simply the name and birth-
place of the healed and their gratitude to God—for example: "Johanne
Anders' Daughter, 1834, suffered much with headaches, Miracle June
23, 1834"; "Sidse Anders' Daughter, *sola gloria.*" —A few are much
larger and more detailed; some have not written their names in full;
some have written in the first person; others tell about the person
concerned—for example, "Such and such a girl was cured here" etc.*
On the whole it is noteworthy that the majority are women. In the
middle of the site is the grave proper, with a stone, or more correctly,
a piece of stone, lying upon it; the inscription is not legible; the
springs, in a wooden shed, are right on the beach a short distance a-
way. The land slopes quite steeply to this point. Charles W. Schröder
has composed a report memorializing Crown Prince Frederick's visit
here.† —Down on the beach there is a stone upon which Helen is
supposed to have come sailing; it is said to be visible at low tide. The
legend[113] has it that when they were going to carry her body to the
graveyard they were unable to go beyond the place where her burial
mound is now, and at the same time three springs gushed forth from
the earth.

I A 63   *n.d.,* 1835

« **5095**

On July 5 I visited *Gurre Castle,* where excavation of the ruins is
now in progress. The castle itself (see Thiele, *Danske Folkesagn,*[114]
Samling I, pp. 90 ff. —Another one at Vordingborg? built by Valdemar
Atterdag, destroyed in the Feud of the Counts?[115] "God may keep
paradise if I may keep Gurre Castle"; his wild hunt in the air on the
white horse; the black hen with the black chicks) has had a beautiful
location, surrounded on all sides by forest. A very large area [of forest]
still remains, and the region indicates that at one time there was more.
In addition, there is Lake Gurre, which is fairly long and relatively

---

*It is also interesting to read the many names on the markers in Normandsdalen
in Fredensborg; each one combines to tell a whole history.

†"Anno 1774, June 18. The honor and the favor bestowed on [St.] Helen-Spring
by being paid a gracious visit by Crown Prince Frederik when he was shown the great
work in this region, for which his great father will be eternally praised. The spring indeed
pleased him, but what impressed him more was that the district is now free from the
disturbance of shifting sand. What can the kingdom not expect in time from him who
in his youthful years wants to find out for himself what can be to the benefit and interest
of his state, his people and country. —Erected most humbly by the present caretaker at
the sand dunes.

Chr. Wilhelm Schröder"

narrow and has a forest of good-sized beech trees on one side and a
forest of smaller, stunted trees on the other. The lake itself is overgrown with rushes in many places. When one views this landscape in
the afternoon light, when the sun is still high enough to give the
friendly landscape the necessary sharp contours, like a melodious
voice that is sharply enough accented not to lisp, the whole environment seems to whisper: It is good to be here. It is the kind of cozy,
intimate impression a lake surrounded by forest (large enough to
separate and unite at the same time) can produce, but the sea cannot.
A special feature of this view is the waving rushes along the beach.
While the sighing of the trees makes us hear King Valdemar's hunt,
the sound of the horns, and the baying of the hounds, the rushes seem
to exhale applause—the blonde maidens admiring the knights' swift
riding and noble poise. How different in this respect the view around
Lake Søborg! The mighty canes also bow before the wind, but their
rustling proclaims struggle and power. The sea, which like a mighty
spirit is always in motion, still gives intimations of intense mental
suffering even when it is most quiet. Here around Lake Gurre there
rests a quiet melancholy; the region lives, so to speak, more in the past.
This is also why it is overgrown. The sea, on the other hand, captures
the land—they face each other like two hostile powers. The coastline
is barren and sandy; the land rises as if to make vigorous resistance.
The sea is greatest when the storm strikes up its bass, when its distinctive deep roar is pierced by heaven's thunder and the whole scene is
illuminated by lightning. Lake Gurre is most beautiful when a soft
breeze ruffles its blue surface and the song of birds accompanies the
soughing of the reeds; the sea is accompanied only by the hoarse
shrieking of the solitary seagull. The former (the sea) is like a Mozart
recitative; the latter like a melody by Weber. —From here the road goes
to *Hellebæk*. The last mile goes through a lovely woods offering views
of a different kind. The woods itself is fairly large and wild, and only
the rut (not a road) reminds us that we still have any connection with
the human world. Here and there leaps up a wild animal which has
been hiding in the shadow of the bushes from the rays of the midday
sun. The birds fly up screeching. The countryside is quite hilly and
forms many ponds in the forest. The slope of the land and the darkness
created by the leaves convey the impression that the ponds are very
deep. In contrast to their dark mirrors, one single flower grows and
blooms on the surface of the water, a *nymphaea alba* (white waterlily),
swimming around with its great broad green leaf; pure, white, and

innocent, it has bobbed up out of the depths of the sea. Not far from Hellebæk lies Odin's Hill, where Schimmelmann[116] is buried. The view has been praised and talked about so much that it, regrettably, is not very impressive. People still do not grow weary of gadding about busily pointing out the romantic settings (for example, K——[117] at Fredensborg). From there the road goes to Esrom and then to Gilleleie.

I A 64   n.d., 1835

« 5096

On July 8 I made an excursion to Esrom. The road along the lake from Esrom to Nøddebo is one of the loveliest I have seen for a long time. On the left side [is] Solyst, which is built almost on the lake, and farther along Fredensborg. On the right is a continuous forest, alternately beech and spruce. Here and there are beautiful tracts of three- and four-year old spruce trees. A thunderstorm overtook me along the way. I rejoiced to see such a storm come up over Lake Esrom and Grib Skov,[118] but it turned out to be just rain. Meanwhile it was interesting to see the preliminaries to such a drama. I have seen the sea on such an occasion turn blue-gray and become agitated, and I have watched the gusts of wind that announced the approach of the storm swirl the grass and sand upward along the coast, but I have never seen a performance in which not only the grass but a whole forest is set in motion by these gusts of wind (these trumpet calls that announce the judgment). However, since it turned out to be nothing but rain, I decided it was best to turn in somewhere. Such a place came into sight. Although I searched a long time for a roadway, I found none. Seeing a figure in the window, I waved, but she probably did not see fit to take the trouble of going out in such a rain, and as is generally the case with farmers, opening the window was out of the question. Consequently I was obliged to stop the carriage under some trees that leaned over the road as if to give me shelter. Clad in my enormous overcoat, I entered the front room and found myself in the presence of three persons about to eat their supper. The furniture included, of course, the great long table at which farmers like to eat and a towering four-poster [*Himmelseng,* heaven-bed] in the literal sense of the word, for I imagine that in order to get into bed one would have to climb up to the loft and fall in—a fall of some distance, as is the habit of farmers. The next room, to which the door stood open, was a storeroom for linen, duck, damask, and the like, in great disorder, prompting one to think that this was a little band of thieves, an idea that seemed to be supported by the location of the place (Lake Esrom on one side and Grib Skov on the other and no house within a mile) and the appearance of the people. Let us now look at them a bit. At the farther end of the long table just mentioned sat the man, with his sandwiches and bottle of aquavit. He listened impassively to the tale of my sad fate, taking an occasional sip from his glass, something the cubic volume of his nose seemed to indicate he did quite frequently. Yet the frequent indulgence had in no way diminished its pleasure, and I am certain that he still drank his schnaps with the same relish as one who has just resigned from the Temperance Society. The woman was not very tall and had a broad face with an ugly upturned nose and crafty eyes. With regard to their way of making a living (custom bleaching), she maintained that one had to earn his morsel some way. There was also a little round-shouldered girl, the same person who had appeared at the window and whom I had taken for a child.

Soon the rain stopped, and I hastened on. But this was only the beginning, and when I entered Grib Skov it really began to storm. Now the lightning and thunder began in earnest. We were soon drenched with rain and had no need to hurry as far as that was concerned; but the lad (Rudolph) who was with me was thoroughly frightened. There I sat soaked to the skin amid thunder and lightning and pouring rain in the heart of Grib Skov, and beside me sat a boy who trembled at the lightning. At full trot we finally reached a house where we took shelter, wretched and dilapidated. Poor people. Housewifely woman. Sat and spun. Snuffling husband. The first thing I noticed upon entering was a sort of door to a closet; it was made of an old slab on which was painted a girl in simple rural costume and the following inscription: "My fields feed me, my sheep clothe me; here I take my nourishment as the house is able to provide." I asked for a little bread for my horse, which they were not very willing to give as they had only half a loaf. But they were persuaded, and when I paid them quite well the woman answered that she could not take that much, but she consented to accept it when I said I could spare it and she needed it.

I A 65   n.d., 1835

« **5097**

Hillerød, July 25, 1835

After a considerable walk through the forest, where I became acquainted with several of the little lakes I am so fond of, I came to *Hestehaven* and Lake Carl. Here is one of the most beautiful regions I have ever seen. The countryside is somewhat isolated and slopes steeply down to the lake, but with the beech forests growing on either side, it is not barren. A growth of rushes forms the background and the lake itself the foreground; a fairly large part of the lake is clear, but a still larger part is overgrown with the large green leaves of the water lily, under which the fish seemingly try to hide but now and then peek out and flounder about on the surface in order to bathe in sunshine. The land rises on the opposite side, a great beech forest, and in the morning light the lighted areas make a marvelous contrast to the shadowed areas. The church bells call to prayer, but not in a temple made by human hands. If the birds do not need to be reminded to praise God, then ought men not be moved to prayer outside of the church, in the true house of God, where heaven's arch forms the ceiling of the church, where the roar of the storm and the light breezes take the place of the organ's bass and treble, where the singing of the birds make up the congregational hymns of praise, where echo does not repeat the pastor's voice as in the arch of the stone church, but where everything resolves itself in an endless antiphony—?[119]

I A 66   July 25, 1835

« **5098**

On July 27 and 28, together with the cousin of Pastor Lyngbye,*[120] I went over to *Sweden* to Mølleleie. At Krabberup manor [we] visited Baron von Gyldenstjerne[121] and saw his fish collection, climbed the highest points, Östra Högkull and Vestra Högkull, drove through a not so little beech forest (small lakes), even up to Kullan to the lighthouse, made a little botanical excursion on Kullan, and Pastor Lyngbye was so kind as to give me a few plants collected there—dried and wrapped in paper.

*N.B. "Young Inger swings to Askelund's peak,"–
"Wind, waft gently!"[122]

I A 67   *n.d.,* 1835

« **5099**

July 29. As one walks from the inn[123] over Sortebro[124] (so-called because at one time the bubonic plague is supposed to have been checked here) to the bare fields along the beach, about a mile north one comes to the highest point around here—*Gilbjerg.* [125] This spot has always been one of my favorite places. One quiet evening as I stood there listening to the deep but quietly earnest song of the sea, seeing not a sail on the enormous expanse of water but only the sea enclosing the sky and the sky the sea, while on the other side the busy hum of life became silent and the birds sang their evening prayers—then the few dear departed ones rose from the grave before me, or, more correctly, it seemed as if they were not dead.[126] I was very much at ease in their midst, I rested in their embrace, and I felt as if transported out of my body and floating about with them in a higher ether—but then the seagull's harsh screech reminded me that I stood alone, and everything vanished before my eyes, and I turned back with a heavy heart to mingle with the world's crowds—without, however, forgetting such blessed moments. —I have often stood there and pondered my past life and the various influences that have been important to me, and the pettiness that so often creates animosity in life, the many misunderstandings that so often separate persons of various temperaments, who, if they really understood one another, would be knit together with indissoluble bonds, vanished before my eyes. When the whole, looked at in perspective this way, displayed only the larger, more vivid outlines, and I did not lose myself in the detail as I often do but saw the whole in its totality, I was empowered to perceive things differently, to understand how often I had made mistakes, and to forgive others. —As I stood there, free from the depression and despondency that would make me see myself as an enclitic of the men who usually surround me, or free of the pride that would make me the constituting principle of a little circle—as I stood there alone and forsaken and the brute force of the sea and the battle of the elements reminded me of my nothingness, and on the other hand the sure flight of the birds reminded me of Christ's words: "Not a sparrow will fall to the earth without your heavenly Father's will,"[127] I felt at one and the same time how great and how insignificant I am; then those two great forces, pride and humility, joined compatibly. Fortunate is the man for whom *this* is possible at all times in his life, in whose breast these two factors have not only come to terms with each other but have reached out a hand to each other and have been married—a marriage that is neither a marriage of convenience nor a marriage of misfits, but a truly quiet marriage, performed in a person's heart of hearts, in the holy of holies, with not many witnesses present, but where everything takes place alone before the eyes of *him* who was the only one who attended the first wedding in the Garden of Eden and blessed the pair—a marriage that will not be barren but will have blessed fruits visible in the world to the eye of the experienced observer, for these fruits are like cryptogams[128] in the plant world: they avoid the attention of the masses and only the solitary searcher discovers them and rejoices in his find. His life will flow on calmly and quietly, and he will drain neither the intoxicating glass of pride nor the bitter cup of despair. He has found what that great philosopher—who by his calculations was able to destroy the enemy's implements of war—desired but did not find: that Archimedean point[129] from which he can lift the whole world, that point which precisely for that reason must lie outside the world, outside the restrictions of time and space.

From this spot I have seen the sea rippled by a soft breeze, seen it play with pebbles; from here I have seen its surface transformed into a massive snow cloud and heard the low bass of the storm begin to sing falsetto; here I have seen, so to speak, the emergence of the world and its destruction—a sight that truly calls for silence. But what is the meaning of this expression, which is so often profaned? How often do we not meet sentimental blondes who, like nymphs in white gowns, with armed eyes* watch such phenomena in order to break out in "silent admiration"? How different from the wholesome, exuberant natural girl who watches such things in manifest innocence. Furthermore, *she* remains silent and like the Virgin Mary[130] of old hides it deep in her heart.

In order to learn true humility (I use this expression to describe the state of mind under discussion), it is good for a person to withdraw from the turmoil of the world (we see that Christ[131] withdrew when the people wanted to proclaim him king as well as when he had to walk the thorny path), for in life either the depressing or the elevating impression is too dominant for a true balance to come about. Here, of course, individuality is very decisive, for just as almost every philosopher believes he has found the truth, just as almost every poet believes he has reached Mount Parnassus, just so we find on the other hand many who link their lives entirely to another, like a parasite to a plant, live in him, die in him (for example, the Frenchman in relation to Napoleon). But in the heart of nature, where a person, free from life's often nauseating air, breathes more freely, here the soul opens willingly to every noble impression. Here one comes out as nature's master, but he also feels that something higher is manifested in nature, something he must bow

---

*Something Gynther[132] said on a different occasion holds true of them: "People who come with armed eyes but also with armed hearts."

down before; he feels a need to surrender to this power that rules it all. (I, of course, would rather not speak of those who see nothing higher in nature than substance—people who really regard heaven as a cheese-dish cover and men as maggots who live inside it.) Here he feels himself great and small at one and the same time, and feels it without going so far as the Fichtean remark (in his *Die Bestimmung des Menschen*[133]) about a grain of sand constituting the world, a statement not far removed from madness.

I A 68   *n.d.*, 1835

« 5100

Gilleleie, August 1, 1835

As I have tried to show in the preceding pages,[134] this is how things actually looked to me. But when I try to get clear about my life, everything looks different. Just as it takes a long time for a child to learn to distinguish itself from objects and an equally long time to disengage itself from its surroundings, with the result that it stresses the objective side and says, for example, "me hit the horse," so the same phenomenon is repeated in a higher spiritual sphere. I therefore believed that I would possibly achieve more tranquility by taking another line of study, by directing my energies toward another goal. I might have succeeded for a time in banishing a certain restlessness, but it probably would have come back more intense, like a fever after drinking cold water.

What I really need is to get clear about *what I must do*,* not what I must know, except insofar as knowledge must precede every act. What matters is to find a purpose, to see what it really is that God wills that *I* shall do; the crucial thing is to find a truth which is truth *for me*,†[135] to find *the idea for which I am willing to live and die*. Of what use would it be to me to discover a so-called objective truth, to work through the philosophical systems so that I could, if asked, make critical judgments about them, could point out the fallacies in each system; of what use would it be to me to be able to develop a theory of the state, getting details from various sources and combining them into a whole, and constructing a world I did not live in but merely held

---

*How often, when a person believes that he has the best grip on himself, it turns out that he has embraced a cloud instead of Juno.

†Only then does one have an inner experience, but how many experience life's different impressions the way the sea sketches figures in the sand and then promptly erases them without a trace.

up for others to see; of what use would it be to me to be able to formulate the meaning of Christianity, to be able to explain many specific points—if it had no deeper meaning *for me and for my life?* And the better I was at it, the more I saw others appropriate the creations of my mind, the more tragic my situation would be, not unlike that of parents who in their poverty are forced to send their children out into the world and turn them over to the care of others. Of what use would it be to me for truth to stand before me, cold and naked, not caring whether or not I acknowledged it, making me uneasy rather than trustingly receptive. I certainly do not deny that I still accept an *imperative of knowledge* and that through it men may be influenced, but *then it must come alive in me,* and *this* is what I now recognize as the most important of all. This is what my soul thirsts for as the African deserts thirst for water. This is what is lacking, and this is why I am like a man who has collected furniture, rented an apartment, but as yet has not found the beloved to share life's ups and downs with him. But in order to find that idea—or, to put it more correctly—to find myself, it does no good to plunge still farther into the world. That was just what I did before. The reason I thought it would be good to throw myself into *law* was that I believed I could develop my keenness of mind in the many muddles and messes of life. Here, too, was offered a whole mass of details in which I could lose myself; here, perhaps, with the given facts, I could construct a totality, an organic view of criminal life, pursue it in all its dark aspects (here, too, a certain fraternity of spirit is very evident). I also wanted to become a lawyer so that by putting myself in another's role I could, so to speak, find a substitute for my own life and by means of this external change find some diversion. This is what I needed to lead a *completely human life* and not merely one of *knowledge*,* so that I could base the development of my thought not on—yes, not on something called objective—something which in any case is not my own, but upon something which is bound up with the deepest roots† of my existence [*Existents*], through which I am, so to speak, grafted into the divine, to which I cling fast even though the whole world may collapse. *This is what I need, and this is what I strive for.* I find joy and refreshment in contemplating the great men who have

---

*[See I A 76.]

†How close men, despite all their knowledge, usually live to madness? What is truth but to live for an idea? When all is said and done, everything is based on a postulate; but not until it no longer stands on the outside, not until one lives in it, does it cease to be a postulate. (Dialectic–Dispute)

found that precious stone[136] for which they sell all, even their lives,*
whether I see them becoming vigorously engaged in life, confidently
proceeding on their chosen course without vacillating, or discover
them off the beaten path, absorbed in themselves and in working
toward their high goal. I even honor and respect the by-path which lies
so close by. It is this inward action of man, this God-side of man, which
is decisive, not a mass of data, for the latter will no doubt follow and
will not then appear as accidental aggregates or as a succession of
details, one after the other, without a system, without a focal point. I,
too, have certainly looked for this focal point.[137] I have vainly sought
an anchor in the boundless sea of pleasure as well as in the depths of
knowledge. I have felt the almost irresistible power with which one
pleasure reaches a hand to the next; I have felt the counterfeit enthusiasm it is capable of producing. I have also felt the boredom, the
shattering, which follows on its heels. I have tasted the fruits of the tree
of knowledge and time and again have delighted in their savoriness.
But this joy was only in the moment of cognition and did not leave a
deeper mark on me. It seems to me that I have not drunk from the cup
of wisdom but have fallen into it. I have sought to find the principle
for my life through resignation [Resignation], by supposing that since
everything proceeds according to inscrutable laws it could not be
otherwise, by blunting my ambitions and the antennae of my vanity.
Because I could not get everything to suit me, I abdicated with a
consciousness of my own competence, somewhat the way decrepit
clergymen resign with pension. What did I find? Not my self [Jeg],
which is what I did seek to find in that way (I imagined my soul, if I
may say so, as shut up in a box with a spring lock, which external
surroundings would release by pressing the spring). —Consequently
the seeking and finding of the Kingdom of Heaven was the first thing
to be resolved. But it is just as useless for a man to want first of all to
decide the externals and after that the fundamentals as it is for a cosmic
body, thinking to form itself, first of all to decide the nature of its
surface, to what bodies it should turn its light, to which its dark side,
without first letting the harmony of centrifugal and centripetal forces
realize [realisere] its existence [Existents] and letting the rest come of
itself. One must first learn to know himself before knowing anything

*Thus it will be easy for us the first time we receive that ball of yarn from Ariadne
(love) and then go through all the mazes of the labyrinth (life) and kill the monster. But
how many there are who plunge into life (the labyrinth) without taking that precaution
(the young girls and the little boys who are sacrificed every year to Minotaurus)—?

else (γνῶθι σεαυτόν). Not until a man has inwardly understood *himself* and then sees the course he is to take does his life gain peace and meaning; only then is he free of that irksome, sinister traveling companion—that irony of life*† which manifests itself in the sphere of knowledge and invites true knowing to begin with a not-knowing (Socrates[138]),‡ just as God created the world from nothing. But in the waters of morality it is especially at home to those who still have not entered the tradewinds of virtue. Here it tumbles a person about in a horrible way, for a time lets him feel happy and content in his resolve to go ahead along the right path, then hurls him into the abyss of despair. Often it lulls a man to sleep with the thought, "After all, things cannot be otherwise," only to awaken him suddenly to a rigorous interrogation. Frequently it seems to let a veil of forgetfulness fall over the past, only to make every single trifle appear in a strong light again. When he struggles along the right path, rejoicing in having overcome temptation's power, there may come at almost the same time, right on the heels of perfect victory, an apparently insignificant external circumstance[141] which pushes him down, like Sisyphus, from the height of the crag. Often when a person has concentrated on something, a minor external circumstance arises which destroys everything. (As in the case of a man who, weary of life, is about to throw himself into the Thames and at the crucial moment is halted by the sting of a mosquito.) Frequently a person feels his very best§ when the illness is the worst, as in tuberculosis. In vain he tries to resist it but he has not sufficient strength, and it is no help to him that he has gone through the same thing many times; the kind of practice acquired in this way does not apply here. Just as no one who has been taught a great deal about swimming is able to keep afloat in a storm, but only the man who is intensely convinced and has experienced that he is actually lighter than water, so a person who lacks this inward point of poise is unable

*[See I A 79.]

†It may very well in a certain sense remain, but he is able to bear the squalls of this life, for the more a man lives for an idea, the more easily he comes to sit on the "I wonder" seat[139] before the whole world. —Frequently, when one is most convinced that he understands himself, he is assaulted by the uneasy feeling that he has really only learned someone else's life by rote.[140]

‡There is also a proverb which says: "One hears the truth from children and the insane." Here it is certainly not a question of having truth according to premises and conclusions, but how often have not the words of a child or an insane person thundered at the man who would not listen to an intellectual genius?

§[See I A 80.]

to keep afloat in life's storms. —Only when a man has understood
himself in this way is he able to maintain an independent existence and
thus avoid surrendering his own *I*. How often we see (in a period when
we extol that Greek historian because he knows how to appropriate an
unfamiliar style so delusively like the original author's, instead of cen-
suring him, since the first prize always goes to an author for having his
own style—that is, a mode of expression and presentation qualified by
his own individuality)—how often we see people who either out of
mental-spiritual laziness live on the crumbs that fall from another's
table or for more egotistical reasons seek to identify themselves with
others, until eventually they believe it all, just like the liar through
frequent repetition of his stories. Although I am still far from this kind
of interior understanding of myself, with profound respect for its significance I have sought to preserve my individuality—worshipped the
unknown God. With a premature anxiety I have tried to avoid coming
in close contact with those things whose force of attraction might be
too powerful for me. I have sought to appropriate much from them,
studied their distinctive characteristics and meaning in human life, but
at the same time guarded against coming, like the moth, too close to
the flame. I have had little to win or to lose in association with the
ordinary run of men, partly because what they do—so-called practical
life*—does not interest me much, partly because their coldness and
indifference to the spiritual and deeper currents in man alienate me
even more from them. With few exceptions my companions have had
no special influence upon me. A life that has not arrived at clarity about
itself must necessarily exhibit an uneven side-surface; confronted by
certain facts [*Facta*] and their apparent disharmony, they simply halted
there, for, as I see it, they did not have sufficient interest to seek a
resolution in a higher harmony or to recognize the necessity of it.
Their opinion of me was always one-sided, and I have vacillated between putting too much or too little weight on what they said. I have
now withdrawn from their influence and the potential variations of my
life's compass resulting from it. Thus I am again standing at the point
where I must begin again in another way. I shall now calmly attempt
to look at myself and begin to initiate inner action; for only thus will

---

*This life, which is fairly prevalent in the whole era, is manifest also in big things;
whereas the past ages built works before which the observer must stand in silence, now
they build a tunnel under the Thames (utility and advantage). Yes, almost before a child
gets time to admire the beauty of a plant or some animal, it asks: Of what use is it?

I be able, like a child calling itself "I" in its first consciously undertaken act, be able to call myself "I" in a profounder sense.

But that takes stamina, and it is not possible to harvest immediately what one has sown. I will remember that philosopher's[142] method of having his disciples keep silent for three years; then I dare say it will come. Just as one does not begin a feast at sunrise but at sundown, just so in the spiritual world one must first work forward for some time before the sun really shines for us and rises in all its glory; for although it is true as it says that God lets his sun shine upon the good and the evil and lets the rain fall on the just and the unjust,[143] it is not so in the spiritual world. So let the die be cast—I am crossing the Rubicon! No doubt this road takes me *into battle,* but I will not renounce it. I will not lament the past—why lament? I will work energetically and not waste time in regrets, like the person stuck in a bog and first calculating how far he has sunk without recognizing that during the time he spends on that he is sinking still deeper. I will hurry along the path I have found and shout to everyone I meet: Do not look back as Lot's wife[144] did, but remember that we are struggling up a hill.

                                                     I A 75   August 1, 1835

« **5101**

In margin of 5100, p. 35 (I A 75):
This explains a not uncommon phenomenon, a certain avarice concerning ideas. Precisely because life is not healthy but knowledge is too dominant, ideas are not regarded as the natural flowers on the tree of life, are not adhered to as such and as having significance only if they are that—but are regarded as separate flashes of illumination, as if life became richer because of a crowd, so to speak, of such external ideas (*sit venia verbo*[145]—aphoristically). They forget that the same thing happens to ideas as to Thor's hammer—it returns to the point from which it was thrown, although in a modified form.

                                                            I A 76   n.d.

« **5102**

Addition to 5101 (I A 76):
*A similar phenomenon is the erroneous view of knowledge and its results in regarding the objective results and forgetting that the genuine philosopher is to the highest degree sub-objective. I need only mention Fichte.[146] Wit is treated the same way; it is not regarded

as Minerva, essentially springing from the author's whole individuality
and environment, therefore in a sense something lyrical,* but as flowers one can pick and keep for his own use. (The forget-me-not has its
place in the field, hidden and humble, but looks drab in a park).

I A 77   n.d.

« 5103

Addition to 5102 (I A 77):
*And this also accounts for the blushing which usually accompa-
nies a certain type of witticism, suggesting that it came forth naturally,
new-born.

I A 78   September 20, 1836

« 5104

Addition to 5100, p. 37 (I A 75):
*A curious kind of irony is also to be found in an Arabian tale
"Morad the Hunchback" (in *Moden Zeitung, "Bilder Magazin,"* no. 40,
1835). A man comes into possession of a ring which provides everything he wishes but always with a "but" attached—for example, when
he wishes for security he finds himself in prison etc. (this story is found
in *Riises Bibliothek for Ungdommen,* II, 6, 1836, p. 453). I have also heard
or read some place about a man who, standing outside a theater, heard
a soprano voice so beautiful and enchanting that he promptly fell in
love with the voice; he hurries into the theater and meets a thick, fat
man who, upon being asked who it was who sang so beautifully, answered: "It was I"—he was a castrato.

I A 79   n.d.

« 5105

Addition to 5100, p. 37 (I A 75):
§"Es ist, wie mit den anmuthigen Morgenträumen, aus deren eins-
chläferndem Wirbel man nur mit Gewalt sich herausziehen kann, wenn
man nicht in immer drückender Müdigkeit gerathen, und so in krank-
hafter Erschöpfung nachher den ganzen Tag hinschleppen will." Novalis, *Schriften.* Berlin: 1826. I, p. 107.[147]

I A 80   n.d., 1835

« 5106

The fourth of August I visited Pastor Lyngbye[148] in his parsonage
and took an excursion out on *Lake Søborg.*[149] This previously immense
lake is now about to disappear. We worked our way through the outlet

of the lake with much difficulty; the water is so shallow and silted that like a whale among herring we pushed mud ahead of us. But apart from this the nature round about us was very interesting; the heavy growth of six-foot rushes and the lush vegetation of all kinds of lake plants led us to indulge in the fantasy that we were in an utterly different climate. Eventually we came out on the lake itself. Here, too, the water is scarcely a foot deep and overgrown with seaweed, which Lyngbye gathered for the mollusks. The loud clamoring of wild ducks, sea gulls, cranes, etc., and the floating islands made a pleasant impression.

I also inspected the ruins of the castle but did not see anything new (Becker[150] covers just about everything in his description of Danish castles). —The three rows of closed pews clearly indicate that this is no ordinary country church. On the wall up near the altar is a register of the pastors since the Reformation, and it was really awe-inspiring to reflect on these men—they were court chaplains—who according to the information often had remained thirty to forty years (yes, one even forty-eight years) in the same call, in the same congregation. – In the graveyard Lyngbye had found a tombstone, now sent to Copenhagen to be placed in the Round Tower, on which was written "Ave Maria" in intertwined runic letters. He believed that it could be an epitaph for Queen Helvig, who is known to have lived here.

I A 69   n.d., 1835

« **5107**

As a fishing hamlet and the northernmost point in Sjælland, and for that reason somewhat isolated from the surrounding countryside, *Gilleleie* is unique. This is apparent, for example, in the inhabitants' "Gable Assemblies" and in the "repast," as it is called, shared by all the men after every catch, a dinner for which every man puts in his two cents worth. Furthermore, they are almost all related to each other and are like one big family. Therefore, during my stay, when a boat on its scheduled run to the Island of Hessel was somewhat overdue in rather stormy weather, there was universal anxiety in the village and they frequently hurried to Gilbjerg to see if the boat was visible.

I A 70   n.d., 1835

« **5108**

Among the farmers here in this region I have met one who really stands out—Jens Andersen of Fjellenstrup. He is well read not only in the Bible but also in historical works—for example, in Saxo, Snorre, and the Icelandic sagas published by the Old Norse Society (he had borrowed them from the pastor). He discussed them very intelligently —yes, I could almost say unctuously—but unfortunately he had the defect of drinking, and then I will not deny that his conversation was disgusting, for he carried on the same as when he was sober.

I A 71   *n.d.*, 1835

« **5109**

Hoffmanns Schriften,[151] X, *"Meister Floh,"* p. 287.

"Wie sprach er zu sich selbst ein Mensch, der die geheimsten Gedanken seiner Bruder erforscht, bringt über den diese verhängnisvolle Gabe nicht jenes entsetzliches Verhältnitz, welches den ewigen Juden traf, der durch das bunteste Gewühl der Welt, ohne Freude, ohne Hoffnung, ohne Schmerz, in dumpfer Gleichgültigkeit, die das caput mortuum der Verzweiflung ist, wie durch eine unwirthbare trostlose Einöde wandelte?"[152]

I C 60   September 1, 1835

« **5110**

It is also remarkable that Germany has its Faust, Italy and Spain their Don Juan, the Jews (??) the Wandering Jew, Denmark and north Germany, Eulenspiegel.

I C 61   October 1, 1835

« **5111**

The legend about the Wandering Jew is told in its entirety in *Ein Volksbüchlein.* Munich: 1835.

(The Student Association[153] has it.)

This legend, which has an altogether Christian coloration, excludes the ascetic-religious aspect, just as with Faust.

I C 62   October 13, 1835

« **5112**

Concerning the Wandering Jew.

(Ahasverus. Shoemaker. Cartophilus. Doorman.[154])

See *Almindelig Morskabslæsning i Danmark og Norge* by Nyerup. Copenhagen: 1816.

Literature:

particularly dissertations, one by Prof. Christopher Schulz in Königsberg, 1689; one by Prof. Carl Anton in Helmstad, 1755. These are in the University Library, also one *sub praesidio* Gotfried Thilonis, *de*

Judaeo immortali, Wittemburg, 1672; one under Prof. Sebastian Niemann's chairmanship, *de duobus testibus vivis passionis dominicae,* Jena,
1668; the third, defended in Regensen, by Caspar Kildgaard, Hafniæ,
1733: *de Judaeo non mortali.* —

I C 64   n.d., 1835

« 5113

The beautiful thing about *Lemming's* playing (he is a Danish musician; I heard him at the Student Union[155]) was that he *stroked* the
guitar. The vibrations became almost visible,[156] just as waves become
almost audible when the moon shines on the surface of the sea.

I A 103   n.d., 1835

« 5114

We often deceive ourselves by embracing as our own many an idea
and observation which at the moment either springs forth vividly out
of a time when we read it or lies in the consciousness of the whole age
—yes, even now as I write this observation—this, too, perhaps, is a fruit
of the experience of the age.

I A 109   November 13, 1835

« 5115

Presumably there is scarcely anyone among the gentlemen[157]
present who has not vividly experienced that in every intuition there
is something, the ultimate and the best, which is so light, so ethereal,
so evanescent, that it constantly disappears between the fumbling
hands and, frolicking innocently, evades the searching eye—a truly
inviolable *noli me tangere.*[158] But just as most of you, gentlemen, have
experienced how difficult it is to keep the mind free of every profane
impression, you will no doubt concede that within the true humanistic
charmed circle—*procul o procul este profani*[159]—I have ventured to express
what every student feels and ought to feel, but which, proclaimed and
trumpeted in the streets and lanes, is thereby betrayed, misunderstood, and mutilated. What better forum could I wish for, what more
competent assembly, than the humanistic society: the Student Association, which, no doubt vigorous and incorruptible in its judgment, also
possesses what to me is most important, that intellectual ear which
with creative sympathy gives the words the inexpressible fullness they
have in the speaker's breast but not upon his lips.

I B 1   n.d., 1835

« **5116** *Our Journalistic Literature*[160]

A study from nature in noonday light.
Talk given to the Student Association
November 28, 1835

Gentlemen!

Before I go into my subject proper, may I make a few prefatory observations.

When I as one of the younger members, perhaps unacquainted with many of the conventions, without a practiced eye for the, may I say, theory of perspective in oration, which promptly enables one to see how that which has been worked out in the study will appear when it steps forth into a large assembly, how that which is spoken in a smaller circle must be modified when it lays claim to a wide audience —when I, I say, stand before you here, it is as much in the confidence of your humanity as it is in the conviction that the person who mounts this podium is not thereby made assembly chaplain but as an individual in the totality of the Student Association perhaps expresses what is already shared by many other members, so that, without claiming to say anything new, he hopes he will not be unwelcome if he repeats something partially familiar, much more so in this matter, which another member has recently attempted to stress from another point of view, and illuminate something which is already in part a given in the consciousness of most members—in any case I did not wish a point of view, if not the opposite of that position at least a modification of it, to lack a spokesman in this forum where the subject has already been introduced. Therefore I must request the forebearance especially of the gentlemen present who perhaps share my point of view, insofar as my presentation may be faulty; the others can at most complain about a wasted hour and about the tediousness of such an indirect proof of the correctness of their point of view.

It is certainly not without reason that artists seldom or never paint a landscape at midday but more frequently by morning light. The distinctive freshness, the wonderful quivering, the exuberant changeableness of light and shadow evoke a particularly propitious total impression which does not permit any single point to be emphasized and, even though it were merely for the moment of discernment, to be divorced from the whole. Something similar happens in other spheres as well. We like to dwell on an idea's first appearance in world history;

we would like to have people from East and West come and worship it in its swaddling clothes, and I by no means deny the significance of such a poetic consideration, but just as entire races as well as particular individuals eagerly turn from the perhaps somewhat Novemberish flowering of life to the fresh bud in order with the help of imagination to visualize the blossoms that were denied in life, so man also is inclined, when it is a matter of a new life which is supposed to break through, to give imagination free play and let a mighty tree spring forth from the factually given mustard seed. Whether their hopes will be dashed, only time will tell, but reflection can and ought to get involved in investigating only the factually given and to inspect it in the noonday light. And if the result of these reflections should become a little frosty, one also knows, since at this point I abandon the position of observation, that early frost does not harm the seed, that is if it is winter seed and not the quick-to-shoot-up and just as quick-to-be-harvested mature spring grain. In general I believe that it is beneficial, for the individual man as well as in every individual life, to stop the wheel of development, to look back over the past, and to see how far one has come, whether dirt and other such things have caused detrimental frictional resistance to quicker progress. May I now also heartily approve brisk action as well as the reflection which collects and in the instant secures the often dissipated energies and thereby, like the significant silence before the battle, conditions new and vigorous activity; yet may I just as heartily disapprove of a phenomenon that often assumes the shape of reflection, a certain morbid imagining that hinders action as well as true reflection, and if it does allow it to take place and then, if there has been any movement at all, reveals the past period more as an approximation of caricature than of the ideal, it promptly lets a person fall into the same old daydreaming. It is certainly good and encouraging for a man to become conscious of having achieved something, but to fancy that one has achieved more than he really has is and remains harmful and easily leads to that kind of daydreaming.

Let us consider those with whom we compare ourselves, and let the liberal newspapers remember—this has already been said here—that even if they do more and better than the conservative papers they are not thereby doing anything so great, especially for the liberals themselves, who so profoundly despised those papers. Just as I do not at present share many of our contemporary age's excessively sanguine hopes, so I also along with many hypochondriacs dissuade people from climbing Tabor[161] in order to assure them that they will not come into the promised land: both positions because at least this evening I want to grant reflection the first voice. And even though I must disapprove of the daredevilry that boldly mounts Odin's throne and in the tranquility of the gods' eternal contemplation smiles down on men's fighting and foolishness, and I must rejoice that just as the time is long vanished which let people seek the company of wild animals instead of building and living among human beings, so is the time also past which transformed men in the middle of life's clamorous noise into hermits, whether as moralists they were solely occupied every minute of their lives with drawing bills on heaven without paying any attention to what went on close at hand—or whether as indifferentists they first felt of the wall to see if it was warm when they heard the fire alarm— but in action I must disapprove of one of the age's beautiful, to be sure, but also among us rather busy efforts (after bringing men to work jointly for one goal by setting aside the narrow-hearted bourgeois mentality and moonshiny family-sentimentality), a full-blown misapplication of effort, namely that one promptly has a party name at hand for that which somewhat approximates one or another of the current views, without remembering the countless number of gradations and shadings that have to be taken into account, just as it is true that a natural and sound life does not have its confession of faith all worked out, which is usually a sign of one of the last stages of life—in action I must disapprove of it, I say, since I stand here simply as a *réflecteur*.

Moving on to my real subject, I shall first of all attempt a historical recapitulation.*

Mr. Ostermann[162] begins his comments with Winther's *Raketten*. I completely share Mr. Ostermann's appreciation of Winther's talent, the main characteristic of which is the distinctive style that marks and gives every one of his pieces its color. But when we want to find in it one of the seeds of the later development, I must protest. *Raketten* with all its good and bad points was the most beautiful, most individual flower on *Politvennen*'s stem, and it is certainly true that most of his imitators completely lacked his talent and adopted his weak points. But the position was nevertheless the same. On the whole he was contented with the existing state of things; he criticized only the supposedly illegal conduct of individual public officials: the Public Assistance administrative devil, outpost skirmishing, Hannibal Sehested. His suc-

---

*I owe it to myself to mention that part of the historical section was written before I came into possession of Ostermann's manuscript.

cessors follow in his tracks, and I do not remember finding in a single paper of this kind an attack upon a larger function of the body politic, on the organization itself and not its misuse by a concrete individual; the only exception perhaps is *Sandhedsfaklen* and it is also naive enough to believe that it walks hand in hand with *Kjøbenhavnsposten.* Or does Mr. Ostermann believe that *Raketten* is to be regarded as the seed, inasmuch as it acted the critic? Or did not *Raketten* coexist all this time with *Kjøbenhavnsposten* without influencing the latter in any way? Or did not *Raketten* maintain its tone after the change in the tone and character of *Kjøbenhavnsposten?* Or was there not some rather conspicuous reason for calling forth such a change in principle? I look upon liberal journalism as a new development which no doubt may have many connections, for example, showing, as Mr. Ostermann himself points out, the extent to which the freedom of the press ordinance permitted one to go in a certain direction polemically without necessarily designating the direction—in relation to a previous one, but what really has made it what it is no doubt is a number of new factors that have come into existence. In this respect may I just cite as proof the acknowledged fact that, if I may put it this way, people greeted each other with a "Happy New Year" or, as the favorite poet of this new life says: "Denmark's May and Denmark's morning."

And now I will attempt to show where these new factors are to be found.

The *July revolution* of 1830.[163] Revolutions follow the same course as illness. When cholera was endemic in Europe, the attacks were not very violent. The July revolution was distinguished, by, among other things, its elegance and refinement; it was a successful operation by an experienced surgeon. All the violent episodes that accompanied the revolution of '89 were not present here, and thus the July revolution stands as a remarkable example of a clean, pure revolution, free of extraneous elements. Meanwhile the rest of Europe stood like spectators to see, to use an expression children use, what was what. The news about it was played in every key, but since there was nothing but the name and few scarcely saw how well-balanced it had come off by and large, naturally such a folk-recitative with choir could not fail to influence the other governments and nations. Here, too, it was not without influence, and although I cannot agree with a view expressed in an address of thanks—a view that also makes it unclear how the order to the chancellery concerning provincial consultative chambers could find the people prepared in any way—yet I may point out, since I am dealing only with journalistic literature here, that I am unaware of any Danish publications having expressed any wish or opinion on the matter prior to the official announcement of the order to the chancellery about provincial chambers. Whether a number of people prior to that time had wanted such things clarified or whether it was rather something vague and obscure, one of those vibrations by which the French revolution agitated men all over, I do not know and am not concerned about here, but I doubt that such a wish got journalistic expression prior to that order. From then on the trail is clearer, in life —the Society of May 28—as well as in journalism and in literature proper. But just as we cannot deny here that the government was the active agent and that that order was the sunshine that called forth the flowers of literature, and just as, generally speaking, nothing in the world appears without two factors, so also the liberals, as I characterize them here, with an amused receptivity for such institutions, had their share in this; but I nevertheless believe that prior to that order the government and the liberals faced each other as two entities which, because of the July revolution, had a great deal to say to each other but did not know how to begin until the government broke the silence. To avoid misunderstanding, I repeat that I am speaking only about *literature*.

And now I am at the point where the new development has its beginning, and therefore, in order to avoid intrusion later in the development, I will set up a milestone with the following inscription:

> "By means of a natural elasticity, the July revolution and its echoes in many places in Europe kept the people and the government apart in at least a literary, if not a total, silence, until the government gave the signal."*

Mr. Ostermann has made the transition to the genuinely new development by discussing the well-known publication by Lornsen and the frank treatment of it in *Maanedsskrift for Litteratur*. As for the former, while I cannot refrain from pointing out that it does not immediately concern me since it is German and is not journalism, I do call attention to the fact that for one thing it must be regarded as a result of the July

---

*Mr. Ostermann, of course, also emphasizes the government's step, and it is to emphasize even more this point in time and the government's activity that I permit myself this exposition.

revolution, exerting an influence mainly through the Polish ditto,[164] and second—and this is the crux of the matter—that our journalistic literature (I have *Kjøbenhavnsposten* in mind) does not give it much of a recommendation* or draw any further conclusions from it. Thus you understand that this book did not get a very favorable reception in the journals, and as far as other literature is concerned, you will remember that here as well as in Holstein, which really does not concern me, it evoked some counterblasts, even sermons against it, I believe. Apropos of that, I may point out that in *de slesvig-holsteenske Prælaters og Ridderskabets Adresse* it states that "according to their most humble opinion (. . . . . "while still being convinced that intrigues of individual malice by no means correspond with public opinion" . . . . .) the needs of the times require ever more insistently a consideration of expressed wishes." May I also point out that, if anything, the whole document must be regarded as a result of the July revolution exerting an influence mainly through the Polish [revolution] (my first thought), also that it is German, and finally that—my main point—the Danish journalists quite tersely repeat the whole thing without blinking an eye. —As far as the latter (the treatment in *Maanedsskriftet*) is concerned, you remember what Mr. Ostermann himself correctly pointed out, that it is even more recent than that order.

For the sake of completeness I shall now do my best with respect to the Danish journals and base the foregoing more on a general consideration of the Danish development, in relation to the supporting European views pertaining to the determination of this point in time. I will show, for one thing, that prior to that order no such wish was expressed in the journals (this then becomes the negative side), and second, switch over to the positive side, that there can never be a mistake about the point in time because of the remarkable fertility in contrast to the previous sterility.

*"Chancellor Lornsen's Rebellion and Arrest" (*Kjøbenhavnsposten*,[165] no. 282, November 29, 1830). "From a publication printed and published in Kiel, *Ueber das Verfassungswerk in Schleswigholstein,* written by Chancellor Lornsen, and many articles referring to the same that have come out in the duchy, all of which may be had along with Lornsen's book in the bookshops of the capital city, we have learned something of the rebellious aims and the proceedings which the aforementioned Chancellor L., appointed a little over a month ago as sheriff of Sylt, disclosed not only by the publication and circulation of the above-mentioned book but also by other illegal actions." —His arrest and later his sentencing and imprisonment in Rendsborg prison are reported quite briefly and tersely, without even the exclamation and question marks the press customarily uses when it does not dare say more.

I shall now go through *Kjøbenhavnsposten* for 1829,* 1830, and 1831 to February 12 to substantiate my first point.

1829. It plays around with esthetics (Master Erik[166] is not to be seen) but does not ignore patriotic themes: praises the wedding ceremonies of Prince Ferdinand and Princess Caroline and the illumination, the smallpox service, also foreign news, for example, in Riise's *Archiv,* even Mohammed II and Emperor Alexander, Turkish jurisprudence; Migueliana. The news section contains esthetic and cultural news, anecdotes, and other literary confection. Thus the paper is not political.

1830. Liunge continues to be the esthete and as such prepares for confirmation with Heiberg; from September on special attention is paid to the unusual volcanic eruptions all over Europe, yet always theoretically, not practically.

1831. Up to February 12 it generally maintains the same tone. To point up the contrast even more, I will compare the months of the first half of the year, for example, up to May, with a few of the following months. At the beginning of the year (the first month and a half) there is foreign news, but it is dealt with simply as history. The news is chosen from an artistic point of view. From here on the newspaper is more attentive to domestic news—for example, the many items about censorship, some taken from larger works, some from foreign papers, and from March on a man who signs himself T (in the previous month and a half, as NB, he produced only one piece, and this a translation) begins to write something almost every single day. In a series of articles under the heading *Miscellany* he tries to show what flattery is, etc., elaborates on what a good heart is ("put up with every thing, let oneself be spit in the eye"), what it is to be "malicious," the nature of egotism—arousing feelings by means of fables; he talks about the national economy, about the meaning of the terms "aristocrats" and "democrats"—and finally gets started on the ordinance of April 14, 1831. Here there is an extraordinary change; the pulse, which previously was calm, now begins to speed up a little. A striking productivity appears inside the journals as well: even before the end of March writings about the provincial assemblies by David and by the two Tschernings come out. From now on *Maanedsskrift for Litteratur* also begins to carry some political treatises which, as the editor himself observes in a note, the times seem to require now.

---

*I need not pay any attention to 1827 and 1828, since Mr. Ostermann has correctly observed that during that period *Kjøbenhavnsposten* for the most part estheticized; I would not need 1829, either, but use it merely for sake of completeness.

I have tried to show that with respect to the origins of the new development the government incited the journalists, not the journalists the government. Here I owe it to Mr. Ostermann to discuss in a few words his view of *Raketten* as one of the seeds of the new development. I look upon it as an attempt to make journalism out to be more the active factor in this whole development. I hope what I have just said helps answer the question whether this is the situation at present.

I now proceed further with my historical development of the activity of our liberal journalism—that I have only *this* to deal with ought to be suggested by the circumstances of the times, and the relation between Mr. Ostermann's presentation, which deals practically only with this, ought to put it beyond question. My previous remarks may seem to presume that just as the government has set the tone of journalistic literature, it will also continue to do so. What has been said does not mean, as I have already suggested above, that journalism has not been active at all, but only that the government is the *primus motor.* Just as when two resilient bodies, one at rest and the other in motion, collide, this collision occasions a reaction from the body previously at rest, and this reaction in turn produces a primary impact but in such a way that we always regard the reaction as conditioned by the primary impact—so also do I consider this relationship, yet with the modification that in the meanwhile it happens that the reaction was too weak at the moment to evolve a new impulse from body no. 1, so that this body, if all activity is not to cease, must put itself in motion anew. To substantiate what I have said, I shall refer to the nodal points where, so to speak, the two powers come together and show whether the energy of journalism gives rise to action by the government or whether the government by its action causes journalistic activity, just as much when it encourages and promotes the new development as when it repressively keeps the creek of journalism from becoming stagnant water and forces it to become a stream. That not much in the way of results can be expected until 1834 can reasonably be concluded from the fact that it was only in 1834 that a question of great significance for journalism arose, freedom of the press, and instead of practical experiments in this respect, as one would have expected, theoretical investigations were undertaken.

I go on with my historical recapitulation.

In 1831 the government's next step was the provisional ordinance of May 28; it does not create much of a stir in the journal. From now on the news section is preoccupied with cholera and the paper itself with investigations into Denmark's national defense.

In 1832 there is the first convocation of the wise men; in April, I believe, there are a few items about that institution, and later in May there is news about the May-Society, which can be linked, not altogether incorrectly, to that convocation.

In 1833 the government takes no step. The influence of the Ordinance of April of that year about censorship will be discussed later. Several items from the *Hamburger Korrespondent,* the *Kieler Korrespondent,* the *Zeitung für die elegante Welt,* the *Eremit,* etc., are found in the news early that year. Research into the Latin language. Tscherning goes traveling. The King goes traveling; his illness.

In 1834 investigations into the Ordinance of April 1833 just discussed lead to a big fight, and Ussing does a fair job of showing that on the whole we do not have censorship. Here follow the well-known articles on the management of the Society for Moral Delinquents—the Ordinance of May 15 on the assemblies. From now on the theoretically acknowledged freedom of the press begins to be used *in fact.* From now on there is a constant battle between *Kjøbenhavnsposten* and the censor, beginning with the article on political guarantees; then comes the controversy about the Norwegian *Morgenpost,* and finally formal legal proceedings are initiated against *Kjøbenhavnsposten.* In connection with this, I continually remind you that the Ordinance of May 15 *precedes* this action. There also appears the first journalistic seed of the liberal chaos, but in the beginning an attempt was made to provide for the seedling the supporting stake of a few familiar theorems.

From now on the government's steps, as well as journalism's— which prior to this had been somewhat "piano"—begin to be somewhat more "forte." As we approach the times in which we are living, I must call attention to the enormous difficulties bound up with such a vivisection and I must discuss the positive steps by the government: the elections and the convening of the provincial consultative chambers, and its repressive steps: the proceedings against Prof. David,[167] the familiar recitative, "We, we alone,"[168] and the ban against publicity of the provincial consultative chambers. From the popular point of view, I regard the petition as being a most emphatic step; but at the same time I must point out that, regarded as a literary document, it floats without any anchor if one forgets that it was occasioned by fear of a tightening up of the freedom of the press. But since it did not proceed from the journals I shall not discuss it further; on the contrary, it was that government's recitative which first set the journals in motion here and even in England. Now the government's negative and positive steps speedily follow each other, and as a result, the reaction in journalism as well, so a great deal of difficulty is involved in showing which side provided the primary thrust. But if one recalls the nature of the government's positive steps and the big role of elections and the convening of the provincial consultative chambers, and also the nature of negative steps, then one remembers that the David case occasioned Haagen's contribution. If I were to draw conclusions, I would say that since the government provided the first impulse, the connection between the government and journalism may be described as follows: the government was active-passive (or affected through an activity); journalism was passive-active (or acting through a passivity).

Having finished my historical recapitulation, in which I have attempted to show how our journalism performed in relation to the government, I shall now consider more closely its weaker aspects. Since I am chiefly dealing with Mr. Ostermann, I will discuss only *Kjøbenhavnsposten* and *Fædrelandet*.

Kjøbenhavnsposten. Our whole age is imbued with a formal striving. This is what led us to disregard congeniality and to emphasize symmetrical beauty, to prefer conventional rather than sincere social relations. It is this whole striving which is denoted by—to use the words of another author—Fichte's and the other philosophers' attempts to construct systems by sharpness of mind and Robespierre's attempt to do it with the help of the guillotine; it is this which meets us in the flowing butterfly verses of our poets and in Auber's[169] music, and finally, it is this which produces the many revolutions in the political world. I agree perfectly with this whole effort to cling to form, insofar as it continues to be the medium through which we have the idea, but it should not be forgotten that it is the idea which should determine the form, not the form which determines the idea. We should keep in mind that life is not something abstract but something extremely individual. We should not forget that, for example, from a poetic genius' position of immediacy, form is nothing but the coming into existence of the idea in the world, and that the task of reflection is only to investigate whether or not the idea has gotten the properly corresponding form. Form is not the basis of life, but life is the basis of form. Imagine that a man long infatuated with the Greek mode of life had acquired the means to arrange for a building in the Greek style and a Grecian household establishment—whether or not he would be satisfied would be highly problematical, or would he soon prefer another

form simply because he had not sufficiently tested himself and the
system in which he lived. But just as a leap backward is wrong (something the age, on the whole, is inclined to acknowledge), so also a leap
forward is wrong—both of them because a natural development does
not proceed by leaps, and life's earnestness will ironize over every such
experiment, even if it succeeds momentarily.

Now after these preliminary comments to my reflections on the
career of *Kjøbenhavnsposten,* I hope, inasmuch as I diligently tried to
state the reasons behind *the whole striving in our time* because a single
illustration here is futile, that you, my listener, will agree when I characterize it as jittery busyness. But I already hear one or another of you
saying: You are contradicting yourself, since you previously maintained that the government had the active role. It merely seems so, for
it is by no means my intention to deny that in *Kjøbenhavnsposten,* especially in the news columns, a certain petty exasperation is to be found,
but I did not want to discuss that earlier, since at that point the discussion was simply about the progress of the new development through
journalism and the service of journalism in that connection, and I
cannot regard it as any sort of step. It is this whole striving I have tried
to describe as jittery busyness, for jittery busyness is not action but a
fitful fumbling. To use the words of a poet employed in another connection, jittery busyness is "a restless rambling—from castles in Spain
—to mouse-traps—and home again." Authentic action goes hand in
hand with calm circumspection. Most likely you have all been in the
situation of having traveled along a road in a carriage and arriving half
asleep at your destination, and then when you ask about the road in
the unfamiliar area the farmer tells you: "First turn right and then left
and then left again at the willow lane by the village pond, and then you
will have about half a mile left; then turn right, and you are there"—
but you have all certainly experienced that one never arrives at his
destination that way. One must first drive to the nearest village and
there inquire the way to the next one, and so on. And here, where the
subject is a new development, here we diligently pay attention to the
compass. And although development and progress in other nations
can help us considerably and give us many cautionary points, one
should remember that it does not do to travel in Sjælland with a map
of France.

There is always something Quixotic about such striving; one
sounds the alarm every minute, gives Rosinante the spurs, and charges
—at windmills; at the same time there is no lack of discernment which

makes one aware that some evil demon or other has changed the giants into windmills, although Sancho Panza most solemnly swears that they were, are, and will remain windmills.

That a striving like this can easily unsettle life, I dare assume to be *in confesso* since common experience indicates that nervousness is something very harmful.

How this jittery busyness and the disturbing activity resulting from it can be inferred from the fundamental character of the *Kjøbenhavnsposten* I shall now attempt to show by pointing out that *Kjøbenhavnsposten* lacks unity. Natural scientists maintain that a heavenly body is formed from a cloud mass through the harmony of centrifugal and centripetal forces combining with the rotation around an axis—and to me *Kjøbenhavnsposten* seems to be just like such a fog mass, but one whose existence as a planet has still not been realized through the uniting of centrifugal and centripetal forces combined with rotation around an axis. Therefore we are not surprised that during an earlier period there has been a certain instability in the articles, as at one time the centrifugal and at another the centripetal tendency dominated, and recently there has been an imbalance of the centrifugal tendency. That I understand a competent editor to be the axis around which the planet turns and that I have intended the centrifugal and centripetal tendencies to designate what up to now have been popularly given the party names liberals and conservatives scarcely needs to be pointed out. It is quite natural and can hardly be denied that *Kjøbenhavnsposten* has become somewhat more unified recently, and that the center of our political solar system, the Assembly in Roskilde, has exercised upon it some power of attraction and thereby helped it find its track and regulate its course, and that on the other hand the centrifugal force which usually had control has done its best to keep it. Meanwhile, to repeat, since the harmony of the forces has not taken place as yet nor the rotation about the axis, either, it runs the risk of being easily drawn into another solar system, since—seen from our solar system—the centrifugal direction in another must appear as centripetal.

Mr. Ostermann has also mentioned some complaints against *Kjøbenhavnsposten* and has tried to justify it. He divides them into two classes: (1) the charge of bitterness and crude tone and (2) untruthfulness and dishonesty. I shall venture to pinpoint them a little more explicitly. After saying that he is by no means a blind worshipper of every utterance that bears the liberal label and that, on the contrary, he frequently is compelled to concede the truth and justification of these complaints, and then after examining the source of these charges and showing that they are advanced by forthright, honorable, and truth-loving men, Mr. Ostermann proceeds to consider the charge in category no. 1.[170] He points out that the opposition party can hardly be expected "to sprinkle sugar on wormwood"; he uses a metaphor to show how innocent abusive expressions can be. "It is a truth"—so go his words—"we must never forget that when an energetic and forceful character expresses himself, his words have a distinctive color, for the thought is distinctive, and however unimportant it may seem to many to omit a word here and there, yet one ought to consider how essential this little word, as it is called, is for the writer, how the thought contained in it is totally and completely rooted in the writer's individuality and how precisely this word is for him a most important thing"—etc. I do not believe that the Danish ear is so spoiled that it is unable to bear a frank word or two; I do not believe that the Danes are so unfeeling that they do not know how to forgive this or that bitterness spoken in indignation. But, gentlemen, I believe the discussion *is not about this!* When an author heatedly and emotionally writes words which he perhaps is unable to substantiate, one is perhaps far more willing to be carried away by him than inclined to judge him harshly, for what comes from the heart as a rule goes to the heart. But it should be remembered that our authors have a battery which they must beware of—I mean the existing ordinance on the freedom of the press. The result of this is that, in the belief that one has the right to speak, one cuts as closely as possible to the ordinance on the freedom of the press, and the result of that, again, is that in order to avoid the punishment of the law, authors must use extreme caution so that the expression one previously could excuse because of emotion and blood circulation now comes out cool and premeditated. I do not blame an author at all for trying to say as much as it is permitted to say; but what is more natural for him, trying to dance on the narrow line between the legally allowed and not allowed, discouraged by some of his predecessors' desperate somersaults into the Siberia of freedom of the press, what is more natural for him than to move as adroitly as possible. Yes, when he has stepped forward perhaps a bit rashly, yet for that very reason with fire and force, and let himself be carried away and exposed himself to criticism—well, then we would judge otherwise. But recollect, too, that these tightrope dancers most often are masked (pseudonymous or anonymous). And if it were in otherwise good and vigorous pieces that one allowed himself such adroit acrimonies—well, it might be better that they not be there, but then others most likely would not really be so sensitive about the matter. It should also be remembered that these acrimonies actually are concealed in notes and footnotes, in question marks and exclamation marks.

Mr. Ostermann now moves on to the heart of the matter and tries to show that a little rancor in a daily paper is not so dangerous. I do not think it is, either. But it is a mistake, all the same. I would never have discussed this whole abuse if attention had not already been drawn to it. I take exception to it first and foremost because it is not *action,* and next, because it is a *cowardice.* The fact that *Kjøbenhavnsposten* has more subscribers than *Fædrelandet* may be assumed to be due mainly to the fact that it comes out every day, partly to the variety of its interests, and also to its practice of summarizing the most important domestic newspapers.

Mr. Ostermann now takes up the second charge of untruthfulness and dishonesty. On this occasion I must state that I have never heard *Kjøbenhavnsposten* categorically accused of untruthfulness and dishonesty; that it has been charged now and then with having spoken falsely in a particular article is quite a different matter. Mr. Ostermann attempts to show how someone who believes he has truth on his side, yet is lacking valid legal proof, has no trouble using the press to get his opinions expressed. Since Mr. Ostermann generally recommends great caution in this regard, I will make only a few remarks. In the first place, every such accuser can very well be required to sign his name, because hardly anyone wants to appear before a secret court, and fairness also seems to demand that such an accuser must be branded a liar in public when the accused has cleared himself. In the next place, since, on the one hand, the charge must be expressive enough to be understood, and, on the other hand, not too expressive, lest he get a slander suit hung on him, the accuser will recollect how easily he could step on *lots of toes* and how much he would be inclined to do this if an innocent person actually replied and justified himself, even though not saying so directly but hinting that he nevertheless just possibly felt himself the object of attack since he defended himself. He will remember that and will be even more deterred from using such means.

I now go on to *Fædrelandet,* and here we have a happier situation. After withstanding the storm over the David trial, *Fædrelandet* got on its feet with rejuvenated energy and especially of late has achieved a vigorous and sound existence. *Fædrelandet* seems to have found the direction in which it wants to move and in a competent editor a hand that will prevent every kind of eccentricity. It seems to have understood that myth—I am almost tempted to call it that—about the battle of freedom of the press in this country, from which one learns among other things to investigate more closely what freedom of the press there is before sounding the alarm.

My presentation is now finished.

I have discussed our liberal journalism and thereby dealt mainly with *Kjøbenhavnsposten* and *Fædrelandet* (of the other periodicals the one that perhaps most deserves mention is the *Dansk Ugeskrift*, which, possibly more unobtrusive and quiet than others, has produced many interesting articles); however, I shall not go into that further. I have attempted to show that on the whole it (liberal journalism), perhaps with the exception of the most recent past, has *not* been *as active* as one is perhaps inclined to believe, that *Kjøbenhavnsposten* in particular has often used a substitute for genuine activity. —I have not discussed the conservative papers since I did not believe that time allowed them to be included in one talk. Whether my presentation has been successful, the honored assembly can best judge—and however this judgment may turn out, it will always be a joy to me if the assemblage will acknowledge my endeavor to stand this evening simply as a *réflecteur*.

I B 2   *n.d.*, 1835–36

« 5117

Often when reading a good poem or some other work[171] that bears the mark of genius, I have thought that it was good that I myself was not its author, for then I would not be allowed to express my joy without the fear of being accused of vanity.

I A 118   January, 1836

« 5118

It should be noted that a riddle a person must solve was one of the characteristic ways in which the dialectic of life was conceived in an earlier age (see another scrap of paper [i.e., I A 113] which may be found in my desk). See for example, *Erzählungen und Märchen,*[172] by F. H. von der Hagen. II, pp. 167, etc.

I A 120   February, 1836

« 5119

People understand me so little that they do not even understand my laments over their not understanding me.[173]

I A 123   February, 1836

« 5120

Goethe's Werke,[174] XVIII. Stuttgart, Tübingen: 1828.–

Wilhelm Meisters Lehrjahre, 1, 2, 3 . . . [reading notes and quoted passages from pp. 51, 175, 191, 220, 221, 226].

Lehrjahre, 5, 6 . . . [reading notes and quoted passages from pp. 73, 90 ff., 255 ff.].

Lehrjahre, 7, 8 . . . [reading note].

Wilhelm Meisters Wanderjahre oder die Entsagenden, 1 . . .

[Reading notes and quoted passages from pp. 49, 52, 55. For text see I C 72 and *Pap.,* XII, pp. 212–13.]

I C 72   n.d., 1836

« 5121

Goethe aus näherm persönlichen Umgange dargestellt. Ein nachgelassenes Werk von Johannes Falk. Leipzig: 1832.

[Reading notes and quoted passages from pp. 1, 4, 8, 11, 13, 20, 22, 23, 24, 25, 26, 50 ff., 66, 77, 78, 207, and 209. For text see I C 74 and *Pap.,* XIII, pp. 214–17.]

I C 74   n.d., 1836

« 5122

Goethe's Leben von Dr. Heinrich Döring, zweite ergänzte Ausgabe. Weimar: 1833.

[Reading notes and quoted passage from p. 16.]

I C 75   n.d., 1836

« 5123

Addenda to my previous excerpts from Falk, pp. 79 ff. [i.e., I C 74]. . . .

[Quotations; for text see I C 76 and *Pap.,* XII, pp. 218–19.]

I C 76   n.d., 1836

« 5124

Generally speaking, it is rather amazing that Goethe was not free from a certain superstitiousness. See *Anhang zu J. W. Goethe's Leben* by Döring. Weimar: 1833 . . . [quotations from p. 28].

I C 77   n.d., 1836

« **5125**

Baggesens samtlige Værker. [175]
V, p. 472 (*"Gjengangeren og han selv"* . . . [quotation from poem].

I C 78   *n.d.,* 1836

« **5126**

There is a very remarkable passage in a poem of the Middle Ages which I have never read or seen any mention of but have only heard. It is called "The Dance of Death" or something like that, and death is represented as dancing[176] with various people and carrying on a dialogue with them. Finally, Death comes to a cradle in which a baby is lying; Death bows over the cradle and invites the child to dance, but the child answers:

> Hr. Todt, dass kann ich nicht verstahn:
> Ich soll tanzen und kann noch nicht gahn.[177]

I C 79   *n.d.,* 1836

« **5127**

Volkslieder der Serben, metrisch übersetzt und historisch eingeleibet v. Talvi. Zwei Bände, zweite Auflage. Halle, Leipzig: 1835.

I C 81   *n.d.,* 1836

« **5128**

Erzählungen und Märchen, herausgegeben v. Friedrich Heinrich v. der Hagen. 1ster Band. Prenzlau: 1825.

In volume II of this collection (Prenzlau: 1826), p. 325 ff., there is a Serbian tale with the title *"Bärensohn. "* . . . . . There is a striking similarity between this story and what is told here in the north about Thor and his adventures. . . . . . Now he comes to a farmer and once again he wants to enter an eating match, but the farmer recommends that before touching the food he should cross himself and say "In the name of the Father and of the Son and of the Holy Spirit"; when he had done that he was surfeited before he had eaten half the food placed before him. . . . . .

A very singular, naive, childish tone runs through the whole story,* which is characterized by numerous contradictions in the determination of the size of the persons appearing in the poem. In other respects, as mentioned, there is a striking similarity to the Scandinavian, which can be reserved perhaps for a convenient time.

In margin: *See Mag. Hamerich on Ragnarok,[178] p. 93 note.

I C 82   *n.d.,* 1836

« **5129** *Esthetic Miscellany No. 2*

See preceding part, i.e., volume, in I C 82.

In volume I of the *Erzählungen* cited there are also some Arabian tales (pp. 1–48[49]), Italian (pp. 48–66[51–77]), etc., a very interesting ghost-story, *"der heilige Drei Königs Abend"* [pp. 111–26], one with more of a moral aspiration, *"Erkenne Dich selbst, so erkennen Dich die Andern"* [pp. 129–37]. The story about *"Virgilius der Zauberer"* is extraordinary. There are two pieces about him, one [pp. 147–52] from an ancient manuscript, the other (pp. 156–209) from an old Dutch chapbook.

In volume II there are many Arabian tales, some of them familiar, but I wish to emphasize one, "Harun Arreschyd und die beiden Bettler" [pp. 87–89], one of the most delightful short stories I have read in a long time, and which contains a fine irony upon those who trust not in providence but in men and who at first glance are successful but later lose. There follows a long romance under the title *"Geschichte des Prinzen Kalaf und der Prinzessin Turandokt"* [pp. 90–221], which was very tiresome because of the odd contrast between an overabundance of action and the drawn-out, dull, trivial dialogue alongside. I found nothing I cared for even in the details. Nevertheless I will refer to a very interesting situation [p. 139]. The cruel princess (T.) has given every suitor the condition that he solve a riddle or lose his head. A young prince has been executed just recently, and at that very execution Kalaf meets a man who is desperate about it. In his despair, this man, who is the prince's steward, throws away a picture. A picture of the cruel beauty, which, of course, Kalaf picks up. But since, unfortunately, he loses his way and it is dark, he must wait all night, burning with the desire to see this beauty. —As for the rest, there is in this whole collection really nothing notable for my enterprise.[179] The whole thing is all too trivial and there is nothing of the splendor which folk-life expresses in a special way.

I C 83   *n.d.,* 1836

« **5130**

In margin of 5129 (I C 83):

*Really poetic, too, is the ending the legends attribute to several people—for example, see volume I, p. 138[–41], *"der Höllenjäger."* It tells that at the time Donatus was the Roman emperor there lived a knight named Laurentzius, whose land was coveted by the emperor, who therefore commanded him to go out and find (for the emperor) a black horse, a black dog, and a black falcon, and if he were unable to do so he was never to come back. The knight went away and actually got what he was after (incidentally, the manner in which he gets it is very interesting; his wife advises him to go to his confessor and confess all his sins etc.); he returns, and now the emperor goes hunting with the black dog, the black horse, and the black falcon, but he is never seen again.

See *Nordiske Kæmpehistorier*[180] by Rafn, II, p. 628, about Didrik of Bern (but here it seems to be with a positive result).

With reference to this see some appended observations under the designation A [i.e., I C 85].

I C 84   *n.d.*, 1836

« 5131

A.

Such a sudden disappearance—which, following an otherwise conspicuous and distinguished life (whether good or evil), sets the imagination in motion in a way calculated to make that life as grandiose as possible in order to keep that life, elevated above all and everything in other respects, from being eclipsed by death as everyone else's is —such a disappearance is not uncommon, whether I think of an Elijah or a Romulus or the ultimate in this respect, Christ's Ascension. But what I particularly want to point out here is how consistent the mode of disappearance is within the whole view which is affirmed in this kind of literature. Whereas the dominant thought in connection with a heavenly ascension is obviously the splendor that the person enters so that in a sense everything is over, at least the mood of the reader is one of peace and rest in the thought of this splendor and is not concerned about a conception of what he now in his glory is going to do (since his glory is thought of as essentially passive, as a rest in a shady region, in ambrosial fragrance, etc.)—here is the idea of letting him undertake a host of adventures (see Rafn,[181] p. 627), and in vain does one call out to him that he should stop, but he goes off like a *wandering Jew,* yet with this difference that all his accoutrements (dog, horse, falcon) are reminiscent of the mighty hunter who at every moment meets a new animal, each one more remarkable than the last. As a continuation of such stories are the tales heard in many regions about the *wild hunt,* and the farmer familiar with such stories (it is certainly a very erroneous view that such legends supposedly have a harmful effect on the farmer; on the contrary, he is not at all fearful because of them but is at home with them) hears the barking of dogs and the galloping of horses etc. at night, all the relics of the time when the whole world was a forest inhabited by dragons, lions, etc. It is the consistent development of their whole view of life, and whereas classical antiquity, as a fitting symbol of all its striving, had Sisyphus roll the stone up until it came down again and so on over and over (the Danaides scoop water into a vat as it continues to overflow), the romantic period has the knight hold his own in the folk tale. It has been said that Christianity really developed the romantic, but if it was Christianity that did that (which, after all, is doubtful, for Christianity admittedly lures thought out beyond the earthly to something on the far side and to that extent is romantic, but that far side is a judgment or a sleep-like dormant state prior to a judgment), it was only through contact with the northern [culture], which precisely by its marriage with Christianity produced chivalry and—precisely by the conception of life and death so characteristic of northerners, a conception of life as a battle, here as well as beyond, and of death as downfall in this life parallel to downfall in the other life as a transition to standing again—gave rise to the genuinely romantic.

I C 85   March, 1836

« 5132

The historical aspect of stones and trolls.

I A 143   n.d., 1836

« 5133

Since it was, after all, reasonable, I am not at all surprised that that great era might be affected in an essential way by every external circumstance, that even something like a huge stone might be an influence. This perhaps accounts for the belief that the trolls lived under stones, and in order to extort some gift from a troll it was only a matter of getting in between when the troll wanted to go down under. But the really remarkable thing is the nemesis that was likely to follow when someone became involved with them, for how often we hear of someone's having gotten the good sword, the bow, the arrow, etc., he asked for, and yet there usually was a little "but" that went with it in that he often thereby became an instrument in the hands of fate to wipe out his own family etc., how many tragic consequences resulted from the

minor circumstance that this sword once drawn cannot be put in its
sheath unless it has been dipped in warm human blood.

/   I A 144   March, 1836

« **5134**

Forelæsninger over den nyere danske Poesie, [182] by Molbech. Part I.
Copenhagen: 1832.

They begin with Evald. After some more general observations about
the relation of poetry to the life of a people and linked to this observations about our Danish poetry, on p. 18 he says that poetry should bear
a distinctive mark of national life, but not art, however: "Art works
. . . . . are everywhere equally accessible for everyone endowed with an
eye for art. When we stand before an Apollo Belvedere, before a holy
family by Raphael, or a landscape by Claude Lorrain, it makes no
difference if the beholder is a Spaniard or Englishman."

But surely this is not the case, for just as one who is proficient in
the language in which a poetic work is written but has never lived in
the country of its origin would always lack something, the national
individuality by which the poet was essentially nurtured, so also one
can contemplate a work of art but can never get the characteristic
impression, the inner understanding of, for example, a Raphael, which
we must imagine to be present for a contemporary generation. For us
beholders a certain historical aspect is more prominent—which consists in contemplating that such and such was the case with that people
—and a differentiating gradation in the "to what extent" one is able to
live into that nationality is indeed conceivable, but one still never gets
a perfectly adequate impression as does one who has imbibed with his
mother's milk the ideas constitutive of that nationality. Therefore it
seems somewhat narrow to want to maintain this view only with respect
to poetry just because of language, for it is self-evident that if one is
to understand the poem he must know the language, and therefore at
the outset I specified proficiency in the language.

P. 220. Here the discussion is about "The Fisherman," and the
error is pointed out in the objection that Evald's fishermen do not
speak the way common people do. Evald did not aim to present only
the single gallant and noble action of Hornbeck's fishermen but the
whole occupation whose chores and way of life in themselves suggest
a more poetic character than that of a farmer or craftsman. In his
drama there is also the idea of a poetic image of the Danish sailor. . . . .
[p. 221] a poetic aim which could not but raise Evald's spirit, inflamed

by love of the fatherland, to a more lofty lyrical enthusiasm than that required by a merely idyllic-emotional subject.

P. 228. "The Romance of 'little Gunvert'. . . . . ." After that [pp. 228–29] a parallel is drawn between it and Goethe's *"Der Fischer."*

P. 247 has some observations about how the prose of ordinary life has been used in poetic rendering. . . . .

P. 262. ". . . . . Jens Immanuel Baggesen . . . . . Baggesen was a rare Proteus in his poetry, and the keynote of his poetry is a constant hovering on the border between earnestness and irony. Thus it can be said that his life and fate were also an everlasting surging motion without rest. . . . . ."

Forelæsninger by Molbech, II.

ɪ ᴄ 87   March, 1836

« 5135

Forelæsninger, by Molbech. Part II. Copenhagen: 1832.

P. 15. "To limit the bounds of elegaic poetry to the love-relation alone is as wrong, we think, as to assume it to be only unhappy love [p. 16] whose lament is to be heard in the elegy. . . . . . In the secret depths of feeling the chords of joy and sorrow are so close to each other that the second resonates all too easily when the first is moved. In the midst of his happy heaven of love the poet can discern presentiments of the vain character of earthly joy or in the possession of bliss feel the influence of a clandestine fear of losing it."–[*]

P. 91. "In going through the whole store of lyric poetry collected in his (Baggesen's) works, we shall find that, both in content and in execution, most of it centers upon wholly subjective states in which, again, the main role is played by evanescent erotic moods and in part by an elegant and witty gallantry or that uncultivated relation to the other sex in the superficial forms of the modern period, a remnant of the chivalric spirit playing upon the surface of life, a kind of half ironic jest with the situations in which inclination can test how far it dares to go in this instance without becoming earnest, without overstepping the boundary where it expresses itself as passion."–

An explanation of the concept "romantic" is found in the twenty-first lecture, but some of it is not new. P. 81: "Since this (the dominant

[*] P. 84. In passing the author mentions the hymn in the early Greek and Roman churches and in this connection [p. 85 note] Herder, *Briefe zur Beförd. der Humanität, VII, Sämtl. W.,* pp. 21 ff., *Preisschrift über die Wirk. der Dichtkunst, Sämtliche Werke zur Sch. Lit., IX,* pp. 419 ff. The whole thing may be of interest to me, must investigate.[183]

tendency to draw the eternal and the infinite, that whose measure and bounds no earthly flight can approach, down into the world of phenomena) remains eternally unattainable, even for the most powerful imagination, the most profound reason, and the ardent enthusiasm of the most ardent love, so must that which we called [p. 182] the romantic, the eternal yearning, the wistful, the infinite and unfulfilled bliss in feeling, the presentient and supraterrestial in imagination (the foundation of the whole world of the fabulous), the mystical and the profound in thought, which simultaneously seeks to be identified with feeling and imagination—This, I say, must serve to fill in the broad chasm between idea and essence, between the eternal, the divine, the supernatural, which human striving seeks to assimilate or to bind in the various forms of art or form-kingdoms, and these forms themselves. Thus it is not the sentimental or the chivalrous or the marvelous element that constitutes the essential or necessary substance of the romantic—it is rather the infinitude, the freedom without physical barriers in the working of the imagination, in the intuiting of the ideal, in the fullness and depth of feeling, in the idea-oriented power of reflection to which we must look for that fundamental condition for the romantic and also for a large and significant share of modern art. The romantic, declares Jean Paul, is the beautiful without boundaries or the beautiful infinite, just as there is a sublime infinite."

Jean P.[184] [p. 183] likens the romantic to the illumination of an area by moonlight or to the tone waves in the echo of a ringing bell, of a stroked string—a trembling sound that swims as it were, farther and farther away and finally loses itself in us and still sounds within us although outside of us it is quiet. —Furthermore [p. 183] "all poetry writing is a kind of truth-saying art, and romantic poetry writing is a presentiment of a greater future." [P. 184] Therefore the romantic has been called the poetry of presentiment.— [P. 186] But if we were to consider in toto each of the various arts with respect to its affinity to the romantic and the capacity to assume the character of the spiritually unlimited, we would find that in the graduation of this affinity they appear in an order in which tonal art takes first place, for it exceeds all other art in dealing with the infinite, the inexhaustible, the unfathomable in the soul, but here only through feeling, immediately intuited; after that come poetry, painting, sculpture. . . . . Music as the most romantic of all the beaux arts is also the most recent; yes, we could say that genuinely musical composition, the discovery of theory of harmony and its practical application in music, belongs wholly to our period (modern painting is distinguished by chiaroscuro and the full range of color)—whereas sculpture belongs to the ancient period. —P. 189. Here it may be necessary to recall that the romantic as such is not an exclusive possession of Christian Europe; there is much romantic material in Oriental (Indian), Scandinavian, and Celtic mythology. — P. 198. Another observation which we join to that (that a poetic spirit closely related to the classical can still belong to our modern period) is this: the romantic, which we contrast to the classical, must not be confused with an exclusively spiritual or mystical striving for a union with the higher, the extrasensory. Besides its ideal foundation or essential power which gives it a predominantly spiritual, imaginative, emotional character, the romantic has an aspect oriented to the sense-world, whereby it is capable of developing and presenting its distinctive art world. This use of romantic material occurs poetically in various ways, but on the whole they can be said to have in common the characteristic of seeking and presenting a beauty in the manifold, a combination of the most motley, marvelous, fabulous [p. 199], and imaginative forms and images, a comprehensible whole to the assimilating imaginative power and the beholding artistic taste. This manifoldness, which is the dominant feature of romantic artistic perception, is just as characteristic of it as the singularity, unity, and simplicity of the great, of the sublime, are characteristic of classical art. But in modern poetic works we find romantic manifoldness in many very different expressions. In the Middle Ages, for example, it appears for the most part only as rich material or incomplete elements for the poetic works in which very often move the most glorious, the noblest, and most vivacious spirit, the purest religious faith, and the most ardent feeling, but because of a lack of background and artistic skill, they were unable to shape and treat the extraordinarily rich poetic stuff which they had acquired. Medieval poetry, which on the whole has a predominantly epic character, is therefore extremely rich in content but nonetheless frequently formless. —[P. 200] Another later expression of the romantic in poetry was less authentic and less elevated than that in which the spirit is preoccupied with the mysteries of the marvelous and a living faith in the sacred and the extrasensory. Instead it clings more closely to the sense-world and to everyday life and summons the marvelous down from the religious sphere of faith and presentiment to a lower, more motley, and imaginative stage where the prodigiously marvelous, magic, and witch-arts play their game, where fairies, gnomes, elves, and a host of other supernatural creatures and dark powers intrude upon human fate and the course of events.

I C 88   March 24, 1836

« 5136

It would be really interesting to make a comparison between our Danish heroic ballads and the kind of drinking songs current here a half century ago; simply because both have the essential color of folk life, it could be very important in order to discern the musical tone rooted in the people. (Beranger.)[185]

I A 147   March, 1836

« 5137

Die Poesie der Troubadors,[186] nach gedruckten og handschriftlichen Werken derselben, dargestellt v. Friedrich Diez. Zwickau: 1826....

I C 89   April 22, 1836

« 5138

Ludvig Tiecks Schriften,[187] IV, *Phantasus,* part I. Berlin: 1828. p. 129...... Es giebt vielleicht keine Erfindung, die nicht die Allegorie, auch unbewusst, zum Grund und Boden ihres Wesens hätte. Gut und böse ist die doppelte Erscheinung, die schon das Kind in jeder Dichtung am leichtesten versteht, die uns in jeder Darstellung von neuem ergreift, die uns aus jedem Räthsel in den mannichfaltigsten Formen anspricht und sich selbst zum Verstandniss ringend auflösen will. Es giebt eine Art, das gewöhnlichste Leben wie ein Mährchen anzusehn, eben so kann man sich mit dem Wundervollsten, als wäre es das Alltäglichste, vertraut machen. Man könnte sagen, alles, das Gewöhnlichste, wie das Wunderbareste, Leichteste und Lustigste habe nur Wahrheit und ergreife uns nur darum, weil diese Allegorie im letzten Hintergrunde als Halt dem Ganzen dient, und eben darum sind auch Dantes
                                                                Allegorien
so überzeugend, weil sie sich bis zur greiflichsten Wirklichkeit durchgearbeitet haben. Novalis sagt: nur die Geschichte ist eine Geschichte, die auch Fabel sein kann. Doch giebt es auch viele kranke und schwache Dichtungen dieser Art, die uns nur in Begriffen herum schleppen, ohne unsre Phantasie mit zu nehmen, und diese sind die ermüdenste Unterhaltung.–
See in this connection Heyne (*Romantische Schule,*[188] p. 20).

I C 95   *n.d.,* 1836

« 5139

Ueber Goethe's Faust.[189] Vorlesungen von Dr. K. E. Schubarth. Berlin: 1830....

I C 96   *n.d.,* 1836

« **5140**

When I notice that my head is beginning to act up. —The poet should have what the Northmen expected in Valhalla—a pig from which a piece can always be cut and which always restores itself.

Shoot a bullet in the head: three, two, one, now my tale is done; eight, nine, ten, now another can begin.[190]

I A 156   *n.d.*, 1836

« **5141**

I have just now come from a gathering where I was the life of the party; witticisms flowed out of my mouth; everybody laughed, admired me—but I left, yes, the dash ought to be as long as the radii of the earth's orbit _____

_____

and wanted to shoot myself.[191]

I A 161   *n.d.*, 1836

« **5142**

Blast it all, I can abstract from everything but *not from myself*; I cannot even forget myself when I sleep.

I A 162   *n.d.*, 1836

« **5143**

Conversation with J. Jürgensen,[192] April 18, 1836.

He was drunk, as was noticeable primarily by watching the corners of his mouth. He was of the opinion that poetry is actually of minor importance, a superfluous development, and he praised philosophy. He praised memory, envied me my youth, talked about the falling of leaves, about the whistling and gusting of the wind. "Half of life is for living, the other half for repenting, and I am fast entering the second half." "In youth one is able to make a lot of very bad mistakes and make them good again." —"I have lived a very active life, have been connected with everything that is worth anything nowadays, have a "Du" relationship[193] with all the gifted people— just ask me about them."—

I A 166   April, 1836

« **5144**

A wandering musician played the minuet from *Don Juan* on a sort of reed pipe (since he was in another courtyard, I could not see what it was), a pharmacist pounded his medicine, and the maid scrubbed in

the court* etc., and they did not notice a thing, and perhaps the flutist
did not either, and I felt so wonderful.

June 10, 1836

*And the groom currying his horse knocked the currycomb
against a stone, and from another part of the city came the voice of the
shrimp seller.[194]

I A 169   June 10, 1836

« 5145

The wonderful releasing power that children have.
12 [June, 1836]. A wonderful assurance, like the wind—no one
knows whence it comes or where it goes.—

I A 173   June 12, 1836

« 5146

A strange apprehensiveness—every time I woke up in the morning
after having drunk too much, what it was about eventually came true.

I A 179   n.d., 1836

« 5147

Someone who went insane because he was constantly aware that
the earth was going around.

I A 182   n.d., 1836

« 5148

Don Juan[195] by Hoffmann. (The melancholy as soon as the theater
lights are extinguished—sensitive—)—

I A 184   n.d., 1836

« 5149

Children who remember their mother—[196]

I A 186   n.d., 1836

« 5150

Letter from Wilhelm.[197]

I A 187   n.d., 1836

« 5151

My situation when I borrowed money from Rask[198] and Monrad[199]
came.

I A 188   n.d., 1836

« 5152

P. E. Lind.[200]

I A 189   *n.d.,* 1836

« 5153 *Situation*

Someone wants to make a confession of the utmost importance, but the one to whom he wants to open up does not come right away, and then he tells something quite different.

I A 194   *n.d.,* 1836

« 5154

Grundtvig[201] regards the Apostles' Creed as the *countersign*[*] which Christ whispered in man's ear and which he wants to hear again from the *last one* on Judgment Day.

July 6, 1836

[*] Password (also related to the fact, as Grundtvig so often relates, that in the earliest Church they did not dare say it aloud; one person whispered it in the ear of another and so on).

I A 202   July 6, 1836

« 5155 *Situation*

Two individuals, each of whom conceitedly relates to the other a brilliant incident from his own life, but neither of whom pays any attention to what the other says; yet at the end each makes the same observation about the other—that he was boring, for he always wanted to talk about himself.

I A 204   July 11, 1836

« 5156

The conflict between the orthodox and the rationalists can be interpreted as a conflict between the old and the new soap-cellars,[202] which in common with religious conflicts develops a considerable terminology, resulting in: (1) The Old Soap-Cellar, where the New Soap-Cellar folk live (the rationalists who have bought the building from under the Old Soap-Cellar people, that is, taken over the Church); (2) The New Soap-Cellar, where the Old Soap-Cellar people live (the orthodox, who are progressive (Grundtvig), abandon Luther, etc.).

I A 220   August 10, 1836

« 5157

Heyne's *(Romantische Schule)*[203] potent criticism of W. Schlegel's curious practice of always using an earlier work as his standard, and with the result that he continually retrogresses, is completely true, but Heyne himself and his consorts have gone to the opposite extreme and judge everything by the duodecimo standard which the very earliest contemporaries supply, and here again in this brief span they always have a work one year or a half year older to use for comparison.

I A 223   August 12, 1836

« 5158

From an earlier excerpt, most likely from 1835 [i.e., I C 53], Lessing's treatment of Faust, a fragment in *Gothold Ephraim Lessings sämtliche Schriften,*[204] Berlin: 1794, XXII, pp. 213–231. . . .

I A 100   September 7, 1836

« 5159

Doctor Faust
fliegendes Blatt aus Cöln.[205]
See *Knaben Wunderhorn,* I, p. 214.

I C 101   September 8, 1836

« 5160

To what extent is Faust *a drama of immediacy,* as J. L. Heiberg[206] says *(is there such a thing?).*

To what extent is it proper to let Faust, on his first encounter with Mephisto, construe him as humorous (Lessing,[207] Klinger,[208] folk-tales, *Knaben Wunderhorn,*[209] I, 214—similar to the passage in Goethe,[210] p. 85: Was willst du armer Teufel geben etc.). Incidentally, Goethe did this before in another passage, on p. 69: "das also war des Pudels Kern, Ein fahrender Scolast? Der Casus macht mich lachen." This is the first time Mephisto appears. Is it perhaps Goethe's intention to distinguish between *der Geist* (p. 34) and Mephisto (the whole nonphysical—and [p. 71] "bescheidne Warheit sage ich Dir").

*What is the nature of Goethe's irony and humor—*it is like thunder and lightning viewed by someone who is on a mountain and elevated above it—he has *outlived* them, to that extent it is more than classical (romantic-classical).

Faust is at home in the ebb and flow of irony. This is why in the first scene [pp. 29 ff.] he runs through the whole climax. He wants to embrace the macrocosm, is repulsed, then charges at the microcosm, and, repulsed there also, falls in the arms of Wagner (irony), but this irony must give rise to his humor, which now also expresses itself with respect to Wagner, p. 36 following.

Incidentally, I cannot omit mentioning here that in an earlier reading of this poem I misunderstood line 3 from the bottom of page 35: *nicht einmal dir*,[211] because I had overlooked *einmal* and taken this passage to mean that the devil would tempt Faust with the idea of his God-likeness, which consequently elevated him far above the devil. Now I see that this is not at all Goethe's meaning, even if there could be something quite right about letting Mephisto enter into such a relationship with Faust on his first appearance.—

Irony is humorously construed by Faust himself ("meine Schüler an der Nase herum"[212] [p. *29*]). Wagner's whole relationship to him is ironical, but then, the very moment he has decided to let the senses be everything, a new disciple (profound irony) comes along. There is irony when the peasants receive him with jubilation because he had once saved them; irony, when Wagner rejoices over this but immediately looks upon the peasants' jubilation humorously. The whole scene with the dog is irony.

P. 57, *top of page, is an authentic prophetic insight into the soul of every profoundly religious doubter.* He personally feels how important it is for men to have such a religious point of departure, and therefore he does not think of trying to deprive them of it by mockery.

P. 64. Jehovah was not in the storm; the tranquility, however, which is poured out over Faust is *nothing more than relaxation.* He is already too involved with the devil, and therefore he misunderstands the gospel. The persuasions of the Kingdom of God cease. Similarly a certain tranquility is inevitable the moment the Commandant lets go of Don Juan's hand,[213] since the struggle between the conflicting powers ceases after a fashion.

What significance is there to Mephisto's [p. *79*] *insistence that Faust repeat "herein" three times before he comes.*

Compare Goethe's *Faust* with the poem in *Knaben Wunderhorn*, for example, *F.,* p. 75, where he lulls him to sleep so he cannot steal away, with the change in *Knaben Wunderhorn*,[214] when he paints Venus instead of Christ, whom he cannot paint.

It is curious to see the younger generation, which certainly has something Faustian about it, attach itself to the Goethean version, which in no way has anything seductive about it as Don Juan does in some aspects (in Faust

none at all); it is rather as if Goethe were the gray man in Peter
Schlemihl[215] who took out of his pocket Faust's shadow, which said:
justo judicio Dei damnatus sum.[216]

September 8, 1836

Should there not also be a few moments * of inspiring cognition* (is it not
compatible with the idea of the devil's assistance or with the stage prior
to contact with him); how much of this comes in the second part? And
are they not then of an entirely different kind?

Probably Lord Byron's Manfred[217] is Faust without a Goethean
educating Mephisto?

*At least a striving in that direction, as is suggested in its own way
in the popular book[218] in Danish that I have. See p. 10.

I C 102   September 8, 1836

« **5161**

Everything ends with hearing[219]—the rules of grammar end with
hearing—the command of the law with hearing—the figured bass[220]
ends with hearing—the philosophical system ends with hearing—therefore the next life is also represented as pure music, as a great harmony
—would that the dissonance of my life would soon be resolved in it.

I A 235   September 11, 1836

« **5162**

*What actually is the source of the comic that can be produced simply by
clothing the same idea in other dress?* For example, I believe it is in *Claras
Skriftemaal*[221] (from *Hverdagsforfatterens Historier*) that a woman[222] is
described as so ethereal that she, as it says, does not walk but floats,
with every step at the point of rising from the earth; she was formed
of the mists of the mountain—one thinks of Hoffmann's tailor[223] who
was given balloon gas and who then began to rise toward the ceiling
of the drugstore, but stopped there, descended again, etc. *Or,* instead
of saying: Like the reaper with his scythe going over the field, one says:
Like the barber with his razor going over the heavily bearded cheek.

I A 244   September 19, 1836

« **5163**

In Tieck's *Schriften,*[224] vol. IV, p. 462, there is a remark on Goethe's work with the theater in Weimar, declaring that on the whole it

was very negative and thereby no doubt forestalled the bad, but on the other hand often cut out the work of splendid genius as well.

I C 103   September 19, 1836

« 5164

Crazy Peter in Kallundborg, when warned not to stand too close to the fire: "Isn't a piece of fine rye bread with roast beef on it better than a dry piece of rye bread?" (From A. Lund)[225]

I A 249   September 26, 1836

« 5165

In Tieck's *Schriften*,[226] vol. IV, Berlin, 1828, pp. 199 f., in the second portion of "der getreue Eckart und der Tannenhaüser," the Faustian principle appears in the nature of the sensate that wants to be gratified (for example, p. 202); likewise the story about the Mount of Venus[227] and the life lived therein. Some passages and expressions are reminiscent of Goethe's *Faust*,[228] for example, p. 210 bottom.

I C 104   October 22, 1836

« 5166

In margin of 5166 (I C 104):
It is Don Juanian, the musical-sensuous[229] (see the scene in Lenau's *Faust*[230] where Mephisto strikes up–). See *Irische Elfenmärchen*[231] by Grimm, 1826, p. 25 etc., "Der Kleine Sackpfeifer," especially pp. 28, 29, 30.

I C 105   September 29, 1837

« 5167

Literature on Faust[232]
This is found rather extensively in Raumer, *Historisches Taschenbuch*, fifth year. Berlin: 1834. Pp. 183–206.
Volksbücher....
Schriften über Faust, und die ihn erwähnen....
Dichterische Behandlungen....
Französische Uebersetzungen....
Englische Uebersetzungen....
Schriften über Göthes Faust....
Opern....
Erzählungen....

I C 106   n.d., 1836

« 5168

The World-Famous
Master of the Black Arts
and
Sorcerer

Doctor
Johan Faust

and

the Pact He Made with the Devil,
His Amazing Life and
Horrible Death

———

Copenhagen [*n.d.*][233]
On Sale at 107 Ulkegaden

[. . .]

I C 107   *n.d.,* 1836

« 5169

On page 10.[234] It is extremely interesting to see how from another
scholarly viewpoint other scholarly efforts have been attributed to
Faust. See Raumer, *Historisches Taschenbuch,*[235] fifth year, p. 134.
(Manuscripts of the non-extant plays of Plautus would reconstruct
Aristotle if he had been lost. Moehsen and Trithem.)

I C 108   October 28, 1836

« 5170

It is remarkable to note the naïveté with which the legend given
here[236] treats Faust's relation to Mephistopheles. The inability to rise
to the conception of absolute mastery over nature's powers, riches,
glory, etc., is constantly manifest, and for that reason Faust gets into
many scrapes, gets hold of money in all kinds of ways, accepts bribes,
etc., but this of course is not conceived humorously (as it was in a
certain sense in the case, for example, of Molière's *Don Juan* and, if I
am not mistaken, Heiberg's *Don Juan;* the humor lies precisely in
seeing a hero like that in such a scrape). Inasmuch as the folk-con-

sciousness has been unable to detach itself from life's barriers, to that extent its position is a kind of humorous commentary on the folk-consciousness itself, which, wanting to understand such a striving, has been unable to understand it clearly.

I C 109   October 29, 1836

« **5171**

Addition to 5170 (I C 109):
Well, this is true not only of Faust but also of Mephistopheles, who, after all, must try all sorts of expedients; in a way, then, this lies in the past, since Faust in fact completely dominated Mephistopheles.

A counterpart to this is the enchanted shields, weapons, shirts, etc., with which those virile and most eminent warriors, with a span of one foot between the eyes, are supplied.—

I C 110   *n.d.,* 1836

« **5172**

A humorous touch, although unconscious, is the mortgaging of different parts of his body, although in the past he did pledge himself to the devil with his skin and hair.—[237]

I C 111   *n.d.,* 1836

« **5173**

To illuminate individual national differences in the conception of the legend of Faust, he might be compared with the magician Virgilius[238] told about in *Erzählungen und Märchen,* herausgegeben von F. H. von der Hagen (Prenzlau: 1825), I believe in the first volume. Görres tells about him in his work *Die teutschen Volksbücher,*[239] pp. 225–229.

I C 112   *n.d.,* 1836

« **5174**

It cannot be denied that the picture of Faust's life in Auerbach's basement, where he is sitting at the table with the students (see Raumer, *Historisches Taschenbuch,*[240] V, opposite the title page) is very reminiscent of Don Juan, as is the big goblet he is holding.

I A 266   October 29, 1836

« **5175**

"My God, my God. . . . ."[241]

I A 271   November 11, 1836

« 5176

The bestial sniggering. . . . .[242]

I A 272   *n.d.*, 1836

« 5177

The bourgeois mentality. Hoffmann's *Meister Floh.*[243] The story of the tailor who got a dose of balloon gas. This in itself is not at all humorous; but when it is told that he had squeezed so much out of his customers that his wife had gotten a new dress, when it is related that every Sunday upon coming home from church he was allowed to go to the pharmacy, in short, when this commensurable finiteness in all conditions of life is placed in relation to anything so extraordinary and when Hoffmann with the painstaking profundity of a scientist then tells how he first of all ascended to the ceiling and plunged down again and finally was abruptly carried out the window by a breeze—the humor emerges.

I A 280   *n.d.*, 1836

« 5178

Is there not something of parody in the overwhelming predominance of prose? It is very interesting to see how metrical form and everything pertaining to it gradually disappear. With the troubadours the romance was in verse, and to my knowledge only the novel was in prose (a contribution to clear up the concept of the novel); most of the books popular today were originally written in verse.

I A 286   November, 1836

« 5179

What are the limitations of opera? Our opera, that is, as we give it here, is close to vaudeville.

I A 296   *n.d.*, 1836

« 5180

An encounter on November 30, when *The Two Days*[244] was presented, with an unfamiliar but beautiful woman (she spoke German) —she was alone in the orchestra section with a little brother—she understood the music.

I A 297   *n.d.*, 1836

« 5181

At the moment the greatest fear is of the total bankruptcy toward which all Europe seems to be moving[245] and men forget the far greater danger, a seemingly unavoidable bankruptcy in an intellectual-spiritual sense, a confusion of language[246] far more dangerous than that (typical) Babylonian confusion, than the confusion of dialects and national languages following that Babylonian attempt of the Middle Ages[247]—that is, a confusion in the languages themselves, a mutiny, the most dangerous of all, of the words themselves, which, wrenched out of man's control, would despair, as it were, and crash in upon one another, and out of this chaos a person would snatch, as from a grab-bag, the handiest word to express his presumed thoughts.* In vain do individual great men seek to mint new concepts and to set them in circulation—it is pointless. They are used for only a moment, and not by many, either, and they merely contribute to making the confusion even worse, for one idea seems to have become the fixed idea of the age: to get the better of one's superior. If the past may be charged with a certain indolent self-satisfaction in rejoicing over what it had, it would indeed be a shame to make the same charge against the present age (the minuet of the past and the galop of the present). Under a curious delusion, the one cries out incessantly that he has surpassed the other, just as the Copenhageners, with philosophic visage, go out to Dyrehaugen[249] "in order to see and observe", without remembering that they themselves become objects for the others, who have also gone out simply to see and observe. Thus there is the continuous leap-frogging[250] of one over the other—"on the basis of the immanent negativity of the concept," as I heard a Hegelian say recently, when he pressed my hand and made a run preliminary to jumping. —When I see someone energetically walking along the street, I am certain that his joyous shout, "I am coming over," is to me—but unfortunately I did not hear who was called (this actually happened); I will leave a blank for the name, so everyone can fill in an appropriate name.† If older critics[251] have been charged with always seeking in their retrogression an older writer whom they could use as a model in order to censure later writers, it would be wrong to charge contemporaries with this, for now when the critic sets about to write there is hardly a writer left to provide the ideal, and instead of this the publisher who is supposed to promote the critic's work sees in amazement a counter-criticism of the criticism not yet written.‡ Most systems and viewpoints also date

---

*One would speak according to the association of ideas (the words *Selbstsucht*[248]).

†Just as some people, with an instinctive vehemence, rub writing paper to flatten it, so too there are those who, having heard a name, promptly forget it.

‡[See I A 329.]

from yesterday, and the conclusion is arrived at as easily as falling in love is accomplished in a novel where it says: To see her and to love her were synonymous* —and it is through curious circumstances that philosophy has acquired such a long historical tail from Descartes to Hegel, a tail, however, which is very meager in comparison with that once used from the creation of the world and perhaps is more comparable to the tail that man has, according to the natural scientists. But when one sees how necessary it has become in a later age to begin every philosophical work with the sentence: "There once was a man named Descartes,"[252] one is tempted to compare it with the monks' well-known practice.[253] But now if only a few gifted men can more or less save themselves, it seems all the more dangerous for those who must be dependent on others for their living. They must clutch at the drifting terminology rushing by them, with the result that their expression becomes so mixed and motley (a kind of Blumenlese[254]) that, just as in French a foreigner may say something with a double meaning, they say the same thing throughout a whole book, but with different expressions from different systems. As a result of this, a phenomenon† has arisen that is quite similar to the famous dispute between a Catholic and a Protestant who convinced each other, inasmuch as men can very easily convince one another because of the vague and indefinite meanings of the words. But in this wild hunt for ideas, it is still very interesting to observe the felicitous moment when one of these new systems achieves supremacy.‡ Now everything is set in motion, and usually this also involves making the system popular—per systema influxus physici[255] it lays hold of all men. How Kant was treated in his time is well known, and therefore I need only mention the infinite mass of lexicons, summaries, popular presentations, and explanations for everyman, etc. And how did Hegel fare later, Hegel, the most modern philosopher, who because of his rigorous form would most likely command silence? Has not the logical trinity been advanced in the most ludicrous way? And therefore it did not astound me that my shoemaker had found that it could also be applied to the development of boots, since, as he observes, the dialectic, which is always the first stage in life, finds expression even here, however insignificant this may seem, in the

---

*[See I A 330.]

†Which, together with barenecked Danish bluffness, has made the polemic equally useless and nauseating.

‡The result presumably is that philosophy is put up for auction; at the moment there really seem to be no buyers.

squeaking, which surely has not escaped the attention of some more profound research psychologist. Unity, however, appears only later, in which respect *his* shoes far surpass all others, which usually disintegrate in the dialectic, a unity which reached the highest level in that pair of boots Carl XII wore on his famous ride, and since he as an orthodox shoemaker proceeded from the thesis that the immediate (feet without shoes—shoes without feet) is a pure abstraction and took it [the dialectical] as the first stage in the development.[256] And now our modern politicians! By veritably taking up Hegel, they have given a striking example of the way one can serve two masters, in that their revolutionary striving is paired with a life-outlook which is a remedy for it, an excellent remedy for lifting part of the illusion which is necessary for encouraging their fantastical striving. And the actuality of the phenomenon will surely not be denied if one recalls that the words "immediate or spontaneous unity" occur just as necessarily in every scientific-scholarly treatise as a brunette or a blonde in every well-ordered romantic household. At the happy moment everyone received a copy of Holy Scriptures, in which there was one book which was almost always too brief and sometimes almost invisible, and this was, I regret—the Acts of the Apostles. And how curious it is to note that the present age, whose social striving is trumpeted quite enough, is ashamed of the monks and nuns of the Middle Ages, when at the same time, to confine ourselves to our own native land, a society[257] has been formed here which seems to embrace almost the entire kingdom and in which a speaker began thus: Dear Brothers and Sisters. How remarkable to see *them* censure the Jesuitry of the Middle Ages, since precisely the liberal development, as does every one-sided enthusiasm, has led and must lead to that. And now Christianity—how has it been treated? I share entirely your disapproval of the way every Christian concept has become so volatilized, so completely dissolved in a mass of fog, that it is beyond all recognition. To the concepts of faith, incarnation, tradition, inspiration, which in the Christian sphere are to lead to a particular historical fact, the philosophers choose to give an entirely different, ordinary meaning, whereby faith[258] has become the immediate consciousness, which essentially is nothing other than the *vitale Fluidum* of mental life, its atmosphere, and tradition has become the content of a certain experience of the world, while inspiration has become nothing more than God's breathing of the life-spirit into man, and incarnation no more than the presence of one or another idea in one or more individuals. —And I still have not mentioned the concept

that has not only been volatilized, like the others, but even profaned:
the concept of redemption, a concept which journalism in particular
has taken up with a certain partiality and now uses for every one, from
the greatest hero of freedom to the baker or butcher who redeems his
quarter of the city by selling his wares a penny cheaper than the others.
And now what is to be done about this? Undoubtedly it would be best
if one could get the carillon-clock of time to be silent for an hour, but
since this presumably will not be achieved, we shall at least join with
our banking people[259] and cry out to them: Savings, hefty and sweep-
ing economies. Of course, to over-bid one's predecessors can be of no
help, and instead of following the novelist who, in his indignation that
a full facial blush of a girl in a novel was not a sign of her being a decent
girl, swore that every girl in his novels should blush far down her back
—instead of following him in making such an attempt, we wish rather
to bring to mind a happier phenomenon: the move from cursing to
simple statements. —We would also wish that powerfully equipped
men might emerge who would restore the lost power and meaning of
words, just as Luther restored the concept of faith for his age. In
everything there is the trace of the invention so characteristic of the
period: the speed-press, even in the curious reflection the age has
gotten into, with the result that the age, continually limiting its expression by reflection, actually never manages to say anything. This curious
prolixity has also crowded out time-and-talk-saving pithy aphorisms
and in their place has allowed the appearance of a certain oratorical
jabbering which has taken over even our mealtimes. Only when this
economizing, together with the restoration of the language's prodigal
sons, has been introduced, can there be hope for better times. And
here it occurs to me, to touch again upon your letter,[260] that there
really is merit in Grundtvig's attempt to vivify the old Church-language
and to advance his theory of the Living Word,[261] although I still cannot
omit reminding you that just as we use the word "scribbling" to designate bungled writing, we also have a particularly good expression to
characterize muddled speaking: "hot air"—and that this should really
be more effective than writing. I do not maintain, despite Pastor
Grundtvig's claim that the written word is powerless and dead, despite
the court judgment[262] confirming his theories by a strange irony of
fate: that his (written) words were dead and powerless—I still do [not]
believe I dare maintain that.

I A 328   *n.d.*, 1836-37

« **5182**

Addition to 5181, p. 79 (I A 328):

‡Because of this rush, the generation does not get much solid content; in spite of all its efforts it becomes a kind of *Schattenspiel an der Wand*[263] and thereby it becomes a myth, yes, not even criticism, as Görres rightly observes (see *Die christliche Mystik,*[264] I, preface, p. vii, bottom—the passage should be quoted[265]). —Finally the theater becomes actuality and actuality comedy.

I A 329   n.d., 1836–37

« **5183**

Addition to 5181, p. 80 (I A 328):

*Thus the talk that suicide is cowardice is for most men nothing but a leap over a stage—those shrewd and proud fellows who have never known that it requires courage! Only he who has had the courage to commit suicide can say that it was cowardly to have done it.[266]

I A 330   n.d., 1836–37

« **5184**

Sorrow has come to me since I last wrote to you.[267] You will note this from the black sealing wax I am obliged to use—although as a rule I hate such external symbols—since there is nothing else to be had in this tragic family. Yes, my brother[268] is dead, but oddly enough I am not actually grieving over *him;* my sorrow is much more over my brother[269] who died several years ago. On the whole I have become aware that my sorrow is not momentary but increases with time, and I am sure that when I get old I will come to think rightly of the dead,[270] not—as it says in the rhetoric of consolation—to rejoice over the thought of meeting them yonder, but properly to feel that I have lost them. As far as my brother is concerned, I am sure it will take a long time for my grief to awaken. —At first there are so many ridiculous situations that I find it impossible not to laugh. For example, today my [brother's] brother-in-law, the business agent—I have spoken of him before and will describe him in more detail some day—makes a visit to console his sister. In his aristocratic, strangely grating voice, a superb parody of the gentlemanly, he tries to ingratiate himself by his formalities and bursts out: *Ja! Was ist der Mensch?*[271] A clarinet, I answered; whereupon he immediately fell out of his role and tried to explain to me that the proper gentleman does not have a voice like a bear but a sonorous and melodious voice. All this time he stood before the mirror

and smoothed his hair or plucked out the occasional hair that had
become a little gray or reminded him a bit too much of its original
color—red—and for this he had a special instrument, a pair of tweezers,
on his dressing table—and I really believe that it can truthfully be said
of the hairs of his head what the gospel says of all hair, that they are
numbered.[272] The undertaker came then to inquire if they wished to
have more than ham, salami, and Edam cheese to be served, and
offered to make all the arrangements; my brother-in-law the business
agent declined, explaining that it would be good for his broken-
hearted sister to have something to think about so as to forget the
emptiness and stillness prevailing around her now that her "sainted
husband" was gone. (It is terrible how quickly people learn to say *that,*
that is, the husband who is sainted no longer needs me, and it naturally
follows that I do not need him either. I always notice how speedily
people begin to say "my sainted husband, my sainted wife." Similarly,
the quicker a woman is to scold, the less modesty she has. Consider
how in the beginning children respond to the question "What does the
child want?" (one of the questions put to every child in the concise
epitome of knowledge inflicted upon them) by saying "Da-Da," and
with such melancholy observations the child's first and yet most innocent period begins—and yet people deny original sin![273]

Since it was, in fact, moving time, he advised her to move to
another place and the sooner the better, in order "to avoid sorrowful
memories"! That fits the pronouncement in the newspaper that "We
have lost everything." —Not so, for the memories of one who has lost
everything are precious, gratifying, for he can never, after all, live more
happily than in the past.[274] One thing is sure, that on such an occasion
what most people lose is memory. —I shall pass over the intervening
days. Then came the day of the funeral. Great quantities of the already
mentioned cheese, sausage, and ham are served; there is no lack of a
variety of wines and cakes—No one is seen eating anything—alas, *so
great is the grief!* Here the rule of the book "about good manners"[275]
—that no one is to begin to eat before his neighbor—is carried out
literally. God help us, what if it were carried out literally at every meal!
In the old days the natural association of ideas led one on such occasions to recall the true dictum that without beer [*Øl*] and food the hero
is nothing, and therefore there was a funeral feast [*Gravøl*], but nowadays this has become a gravediggers' feast [*Graverøl*], for the funeral
director, the pallbearers, the gravediggers, etc., are the ones who eat
for all of us. On such occasions I always develop a fearful appetite and

despite good manners I begin first—but no one follows my example anyway.

I A 331   *n.d.*, 1836–37

« **5185**

On the wedding day[276] came a letter from her brother; he was a captain in the Brazilian army. It was handed to her, and since we were eager to hear from him, I read it aloud:

"Dear Sister! What he was to you I will not speak of; you yourself know it too well. I will just say that although over here I see 100 die daily, I nevertheless truly feel that death is a universal fate, but also that I have had only one brother-in-law, just as you no doubt also feel that he was your first and last love.

Your Brother $\frac{+}{1}$

Postscript
Excuse the short reply: you no doubt have had to put up with enough tedious talk, and I have just received orders to battle and must take off. Take care of yourself and remember that the short time was the visible pole and thank God that it lasted as long as it did; as is the visible pole, so is the quotient of the true.[277]

Your ———"

I A 332   *n.d.*, 1836–37

« **5186**

December 2[278]

I will no longer converse with the world[279] at all; I will try to forget that I ever did. I read of a man who lay abed[280] for 50 years, never speaking to anyone; like Queen Gudrun[281] after she had quarreled with O——, I shall go to bed after quarreling with the world. Or I will run away to a place where no one knows, no one understands my language, or I theirs, where, like a Caspar Hauser[282] the Second, I can stand in the middle of a Nürnberg street without really knowing how it all happened.

The trouble is that as soon as one has thought up something, he becomes that himself. The other day I told you[283] about an idea for a Faust, but now I feel that *it was myself* I described; I barely read or think about an illness before I have it.

Every time I want to say something, someone else says it at the same time. It is just as if I were a double-thinker and my other *I* continually anticipates me, or while I stand and talk everyone believes it is someone else, so that I may justifiably raise the question the bookseller Soldin[284] put to his wife: Rebecca, is it I who is speaking? —I will run away from the world, not to the monastery—I still have vigor —but in order to find myself (every other babbler says the same thing), in order to forget myself, but not over there where a babbling brook meanders through the grassy glen. —I do not know if this verse is by some poet, but I wish some sentimental poet or other would be compelled by inexorable irony to write it, but in such a way that he himself would always read something else. Or the echo—yes, Echo,[285] you grand-master of irony, you who in yourself parody the loftiest and the most profound on earth: the word that created the world, since you give only the outline, not the fullness—yes, Echo, away with all the sentimental rubbish that hides in woods and fields, in churches and theaters, and that every once in a while breaks away from *there* and drowns out everything for me. I do not hear the trees in the forest tell old legends and the like—no, they whisper to me about all the stuff and nonsense they have witnessed so long, beseech *me* in God's name to chop them down and free them from the babbling of those nature worshippers. —Would that all those muddled heads sat on one neck; like Caligula,[286] I know what I would have to do. I see that you are beginning to fear that I will end on the scaffold. No, mark well, the muddle-head (I mean the one who embraces them all) would certainly like to have brought me there, but you forgot that such a wish does no actual harm in the world. Yes, Echo—you whom I once heard chastise an admirer of nature when he burst out: Listen to that infatuated nightingale singing its solitary flute-like notes in the light of the moon —and you answered: —oon—loon—lunatic[287] (revenge, yes, you took revenge)—*you* are the man![288]

No, I will not leave the world—I will go into an insane asylum,[289] and I will see if the profundity of insanity will unravel the riddle of life. Fool, why didn't I do it long ago, why has it taken me so long to understand what it means when the Indians honor the insane, step aside for them. Yes, into an insane asylum—do you not believe that I will end up there?

—However, it is fortunate that language has a section of expressions for chitchat and nonsense. If it did not, I would go mad, for what would it prove except that everything said is nonsense. It is lucky that language is so equipped, for now one can still hope to hear rational discourse sometimes.

It is called a tragedy when the hero gives his whole life to an idea
—folly! (Then I commend the Christians for calling the day the martyrs
died their birthdays, because in this way they anathematize the festive
notion men usually have about birthdays.) —No, a misunderstanding!
On the contrary, I grieve when a child is born[290] and wish that at least
it may not live to be confirmed! I weep when I see or read *Erasmus
Montanus;*[291] he is right and succumbs to the *masses.*[292] Yes, that is the
trouble. When every confirmed glutton is entitled to vote, when the
majority decides the matter—is this not succumbing to the masses, to
fatheads? —Yes, the giants, did they not also succumb to the masses?
And yet—and this is the only comfort remaining!—and yet every once
in awhile they terrify the Hottentots trotting over them by drawing in
their breath and giving vent to a flaming sigh—not to complain—no, all
condolences declined—but to frighten.

I want—no, I don't want anything at all.[293] Amen!

And when one meets at twentieth-hand and more an idea that has
sprung fresh and alive from an individual's head—how much truth
remains? At most one can reply with the old saying: "But at least it
does taste like fowl," said the old crone who had made soup out of a
branch on which a crow had sat.

I A 333   *n.d.,* 1836–37

« **5187**

It is these trifling annoyances[294] that so often spoil life. I can
cheerfully struggle against a storm until I almost burst a blood vessel,
but the wind blowing a speck of dust into my eye can irritate me so
much that I stamp my foot.

These small annoyances—they are like flies—just when a person is
about to carry out a great work, a tremendous task, crucially important
to his own life and the life of many others—a fly lands on his nose.[295]

I A 335   *n.d.,* 1836–37

« **5188**

One thought succeeds another; just as it is thought and I want to
write it down, there is a new one—hold it, seize it—madness—demen-
tia![296]

I A 336   *n.d.,* 1836–37

« **5189**

If there is anything I hate it is these smatterers—often when I go
to a party I deliberately sit down to talk with some old spinster who

lives on telling news of the family, and I listen most earnestly to everything on which she can hold forth.[297]

I A 338   n.d., 1836–37

« 5190

I prefer to talk with old women who chatter about their families, next with demented people—and least of all with very sensible people.[298]

I A 339   n.d., 1836–37

« 5191

How very unfortunate we human beings are, how few the things that give us enduring and solid pleasures. I had hoped by this time through my perseverance to have come into "possession of the virgin"—. O, excellent Holberg![299] How delightful to see a phraseologist like S. T. Leander parody himself with a single phrase—his solid pleasures—his—"possession of the virgin"![300]

I A 341   n.d., 1836–37

« 5192

The following outline on the development of comedy is in the *flyvende Post*[301] of 1828, although not in the same form as this.

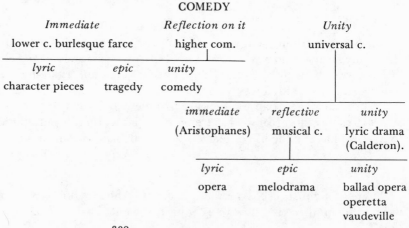

COMEDY

Immediate	Reflection on it	Unity
lower c. burlesque farce	higher com.	universal c.

lyric	epic	unity
character pieces	tragedy	comedy

immediate	reflective	unity
(Aristophanes)	musical c.	lyric drama (Calderon).

lyric	epic	unity
opera	melodrama	ballad opera operetta vaudeville

Inspiration—illusion.[302] Why does not Heiberg have a third position here.

Caprice; irony; humor??

I C 124   January 16, 1837

« **5193**

Literature about the Wandering Jew. [303]

See *Almindelig Morskabslæsning i Danmark og Norge* by Nyerup. Copenhagen: 1816.

Particularly dissertations: one by Prof. Christopher Shulz in Königsberg, 1869; one by Carl Anton in Helmstad, 1755. These are in the University Library, also one *sub praesidio Gotfried Thilonis, de Judaeo immortali,* Wittenberg: 1672; one under Prof. Sebastian Niemann's chairmanship, *de duobus testibus vivis passionis dominicae,* Jena: 1668; one in Regensen[304] by Caspar Kildgaard, Hafniæ: 1733: *"de Judaeo non mortali."*—

See Görres,[305] pp. 201–3.

See *Ein Volksbüchlein,* Zweite Ausgabe. Munich: 1835, pp. 267–74.

Blade af Jerusalems Skomagers Lommebog, [306] Copen¹agen: 1833.

I C 116   *n.d.,* 1836–37

« **5194**

The romance by A. W. Schlegel, *"die Warnung,"* is in *Auswahl deutscher Gedichte* v. Dr. K. E. P. Wackernagel, Berlin: 1836, zweite Auflage, pp. 407 [ff.].

I C 117   *n.d.,* 1836–37

« **5195**

In Goethe's *"aus meinem Leben,"*[307] part 3, there is also his idea of an adaptation of the Wandering Jew, in which, true to himself, he seeks to motivate the Wandering Jew's despair.

I C 118   *n.d.,* 1836–37

« **5196**

Den evige Jøde, translated from the German. Copenhagen: Stadthagen Publishing Co., 1797. 246 pp.

A miserable production, unless one wants to use the book as a guide in teaching history, yet a very poetic foreground: four young people from four different nations who meet at the Leipzig Easter Fair —one is an enthusiast of Lavater's *Physiognomical Fragments*[308] and practices successfully until he meets this man. Yet it is remarkable that such a connoisseur of faces does not recognize a Jew's superb, pronounced physiognomy, but this unexplained ignorance nevertheless does provide the occasion for a very interesting scene in which each one asks him in his own language what nationality he is, and replying in the language of each one, he refuses to tell. —On the whole, devoid of any significance. Who is speaking is completely forgotten, and the various disappointments—for example, that he informs a number of quarreling critics of the existence of the work whose spuriousness has been asserted, or the way he regards himself as disadvantageously presented on the stage—are very badly utilized. On the whole, there is only a frame, not content. Because it is easier, he is here conceived, as in most adaptations, more as the *temporal* Jew than as the *eternal* Jew,[309] that is, completely atomized time is presented in its multiple, variegated forms, but on the whole, instead of the more inwardly turned eye, signifying the deepest, most silent despair, there is the perception of external objects in and for themselves, and he is endowed with a good bit of garrulousness (ἀλαζονεία), characteristic of an adventurer. Those involved do not understand what he says [p. 4]: that the Wandering Jew may stay only three days in one place, and it is a *poetic* fate which the Wandering Jew cannot cheat (for that would be the suicide of the idea) by satisfying their curiosity for three days and three nights. The only way such a thing could be done would be by emphasizing, as a contrast, how little this interested him, how little everything was compared to the sorrow he bore, which he could never alleviate by expressing it at some moment, inasmuch as there would never be moments enough—simply because he was eternal.

I C 119   February 29, 1837

« **5197**

In margin of 5196 (I C 119):
The Wandering [eternal] Jew[310] is the petrified wife of Lot brought to consciousness.

I C 120   n.d.

« **5198**

I will merely quote the profound words in A. W. Schlegel's romance about the Wandering Jew:[311]

> Ich bin nicht jung, ich bin nicht alt,
> Mein Leben ist kein Leben.[312]

and
der ewige Jude v. Wilhelm Müller, *Taschenbuch zum geselligen Vergnügen,* 1823, p. 10:

> So zieh' ich Tag und Nacht einher,
> Das Herz so voll die Welt so leer,

Ich habe Alles schon gesehn
Und darf doch nicht zur Ruhe gehn.[313]

I C 121   August 28, 1837

« 5199

When the artistry of conception and execution is lacking, half the pleasure is lost, no matter how piquant and interesting the situation. This can readily be seen, for example in *Mittheilungen aus dem Tagebuche eines Artzes,*[314] von C. Jürgens, I–III, Brunswig: 1833. . . .

I C 123   *n.d.,* 1836–37

« 5200

The article by Martensen[315] in *Maanedsskriftet*[316] is of a very curious kind. After leap-frogging[317] over all his predecessors he has progressed out into an indeterminate infinity. Because his position is not given—this he specifically announces—his criticism of Hegel is external and his existence is equivocal, and since the article, itself not characterized by a very individualized presentation and tone, does not bear his likeness, so that one was obliged to say when it appeared: Give to Caesar that which is Caesar's,[318] and because of his relation to a certain learned man[319] in Munich, his article could be *ein fliegendes Blatt aus München,*[320] which has now been nailed down in *Maanedsskriftet.* — (By this likeness I do not mean a facsimile of his handwriting or his features carved in stone, but rather something like a watermark in paper, which both is and is not and which brands as a liar everyone who ventures to pass it off as his own.)

II A 7   *n.d.,* 1837

« 5201

The episode Poul Møller[321] includes in his essay on the immortality of the soul in the latest issue of *Maanedsskrift* is very interesting; perhaps it will become the usual thing to mitigate the more strictly scholarly-scientific tone with lighter portions which, however, bear forth life much more fully, and in the area of knowledge will be somewhat comparable to the chorus, to the comic portions of romantic dramas.

II A 17   February 4, 1837

« 5202

[Excerpts from Rheinwald, *Reportorium,*[322] XVII, on the Alexandrians and the Scholastics.]

II C 11   *n.d.,* 1837

« **5203**

It could be very interesting to show up the falsity in all kinds of expressions—for example: "Something could be made of this" (yes, quite right, for anyone who can make something of anything at all can make it of nothing).
"I was in a hurry"
"To disparage the former."

II A 582   *n.d.,* 1837

« **5204**

There are books in which some borrowed idea or notion comes back again and again in a wholly extrinsic way, so that it is almost the same as the refrains in old ballads, N.B., those that pop up in the middle of the stanza and do not have the slightest relation to the poem itself.

II A 585   February 5, 1837

« **5205**

I was appalled the first time I heard that *letters of indulgence* stated that they absolved from *all* sins: *"etiam si matrem virginem violasset."*[323]
I still remember how I felt when a few years ago, in my youthful, romantic enthusiasm for a *master-thief,* I said he was merely misusing his talents, that such a man could no doubt change, and my father very earnestly said: "These are crimes that can be fought only with the constant help of God." I hurried to my room and looked at myself in the mirror (see F. Schlegel's *Samtl. W.,*[324] VII, p. 15, bottom). —Or when father frequently declared that it would be good to have "an elderly and revered confessor to whom one could really confide."
Or what romantic terror, what a wealth of possibilities for nameless horror in the departed spirit's asking Christian Eisengrün to come to the graveyard at a stipulated time in 21 days and to pray these words, *just these words:*
I Corinthians 2:11: "For what person knows a man's thoughts except the spirit of the man which is in him? So also no one comprehends the thoughts of God except the Spirit of God." (Kerner, *Eine Erscheinung aus dem Nachtgebiete der Natur.*[325] 1836. P. 217.)

II A 20   *n.d.,* 1837

« **5206**

On looking through a volume of *Aftenposten*[326] for the year 1782, I see that it tried from its more restricted point of view to do the same

as *Flyveposten*[327] did from its (N.B. *Flyveposten* has wings)—to understand the strange conflict between normal everyday life and the poetic.
Incidentally, *Aftenposten* is more permeated with a cozy family atmosphere.

II A 21   n.d.,   1837

« 5207

When Grundtvig[328] on the basis of a later position retracts a prior
position, he does it not in humble recognition of his mistake but out
of proud satisfaction over the present position.

II A 27   n.d.,   1837

« 5208

There are men who, with their horrible officious way of poking
their noses into everything, play a very comical role. I cannot think of
a better illustration of such people than the one Baggesen provided in
Jens Skovfoged (in *Kalundborgskrøniken*):[329]

> Here comes Jens Skovfogd so snoopy and snippy
> Riding a horse so clippity clippity.[330]

II A 35   n.d.,   1837

« 5209

Hero legends are permeated by a very remarkable self-contradiction, an utterly naïve lie (which is why these stories are so easily
parodied). I shall take only one example from the saga of Hervor and
King Heidrek found in Rafn's *Nordiske Kæmpehistorier,*[331] III. It is not
simply forgetfulness of what was said previously which accounts for
reporting practically every hero as the strongest etc., but something of
a quite different kind. Thus on p. 8 it tells that Svafurlame gets Tyrfing
from the trolls, a sword with the special characteristic that every time
it was drawn it proved fatal to the one who drew it; he now proceeds
to draw the sword, attacks the trolls, but he does not touch them and
consequently should actually have killed himself. Farther along on
page 8, where Angantyr is about to do battle with Hialmar, but Odd
advises him to let him go instead, because he had a silk shirt with which
no steel could make contact (consequently a sword that cuts everything
—and on the other hand a shirt that cannot be cut up by any sword).[*]
Another contradiction in all such tales is in the conception of the way

---

[*] *In margin:* Similarly in Ørvarodd's Saga,[332] in the third part of *Kæmpehistorier* by
Rafn, on p. 118, where he battles with Øgmund and says: I smote your arm, but it was
not cut, although I have a *sword which stops at nothing.*

the warriors live; the stories dwell upon their great courage, passion
for fighting, etc., and at the same time portray them most anxiously
taking care to have not only good weapons but even enchanted weapons which would give an otherwise wretched warrior the advantage
over the proudest warrior.[*] At the same time, in the story about the
battle it is overlooked that only one of the warriors had this auxiliary
help, and it takes a terribly long time for the victory to be decided—
yes, he is just barely victorious. —In this romantic life there is an irony
still slumbering in and with its immediacy. —Also related to this is the
splendid naïveté in the story about the chain that bound the Fenris
wolf;[333] five things that are not to be found in this world are named,
and it is said of them: thus they are not to be found in the world. —
Thor, when he is fishing for the Midgaard serpent, thrusts his legs
through the boat (no doubt physically impossible) and ends up standing on the bottom of the sea.

                                                    II A 36   n.d., 1837

« 5210

Many a poet should say with an old German poet:[334]

> O starker Gott! O gerechter Richter
> Erbarm dich über mich armen Richter.

(*Altdeutsche Lieder* by Görres, p. 159.)

                                                    II A 40   n.d., 1837

« 5211

I have read Andersen's novel *Improvisatoren*[335] and find nothing in
it, just one good observation. In saying good-bye at night, the Italian
says: *felicissima notte,* and Andersen observes—"the Scandinavian
wishes: 'Good night, sleep well'; the Italians wish: 'The most blissful
night! The southern nights have more than—dreams.'" (Pt. I, p. 102.)
This makes me think of those simple-hearted watchmen who always
appear in old German songs[336] with their *"Wach uff, wach uff,"* reminding lovers that day is dawning.

                                                    II A 42   n.d., 1837

« 5212

Generally speaking, it is almost impossible to read hero legends
without smiling. One has only to picture how comical it would be to

---

[*] *In margin:* or a precious ointment which heals every wound.

see a hero such as Holger the Dane "come running,"[337] a thoroughly trite expression, and sometimes it says that they run after each other a few miles[338]—then Carl Magnus[339] comes running and smites him etc. There is a curious naïveté also in their not remembering what was said previously. Holger the Dane (see Rahbeck,[340] pt. 2, p. 289) comes to Morgana, who sets a crown upon his head, whereupon he forgets everything but her and her love, and yet on page 292 it says that he meets King Artus and speaks with him about their exploits and then again farther on [p. 293] that he does not remember the past until Morgana removes the crown. An eccentric morality makes the heroes essentially immoral, and it is curious to see the confidence they place in the verdict of a duel as to who is right, and at the same time that they are not embarrassed over fighting for the one each of them favors, whether or not he is right. —The theological disputes[341] they carry on during the battle are also extremely comical. —The narrator has so little dramatic vision that he has a Mohammedan[342] say: O God, Mohammed and *our other false gods* (see p. 45 in Holger[343]).[*]

Incidentally, I have noted in my copy several things in the same vein.—

[*] *In margin:* It is just about as bad a line as Papageno's in *The Magic Flute:*[344] "I am a child of nature."

                                                              II A 43   *n.d.,* 1837

« 5213

In margin of 5212 (II A 43):
Nor does the narrator have a particular eye for placing the actual battle in proper relation to the enormous masses of troops we frequently hear mentioned—sometimes in the millions. As to the battle itself, we hear that Oliver, Roland,[345] or someone like that came running and smote a king; but when one of the enemy saw it, he came running and attacked Roland, and Roland said: God help me, poor man that I am. Thereupon they win the battle and Roland alone slays 1,000. God knows how he found time to do it since the first engagement was so dangerous.—

Also comical is the long recitation of the countries[346] someone has conquered, the warriors he has vanquished, since the quantitative magnitude has a spontaneous negative influence on the reader's impression of the person's quality.

Holberg[347] has perceived this in an exceptional way. The more frequently something is said to be extraordinarily great, the less so it becomes.—

II A 44   n.d.

« 5214

Presumably Holger the Dane[348] was written originally in French, translated into Latin, and translated from Latin into Danish by Christen Pedersen; in any case Pedersen got the original from a Catholic country. Thus in speaking of Holger the Dane's wonderful last days,[349] he says on page 252: The person who believes or disbelieves this does not sin thereby, for it is not found in the creed. —However on page 272 it reads: (obviously an observation made by Christen Pedersen, even though he says it as if the Chronicle reported it) Which however is not believable and ought not to be believed by us, for it is not to be found in Holy Scripture.

II A 45   n.d., 1837

« 5215

Quite true! Everything I touch suffers the fate depicted in a poem[350] *(Knaben Wunderhorn):*

Ein Jäger stiess wohl in sein Horn,
wohl in sein Horn,
Und Alles, was er bliest, das war
verlorn.

II A 51   n.d., 1837

« 5216

It is touching to go past the most ordinary of book stores and see *Den Ærke Troldkarl Faust,*[351] etc., see the most profound [books] offered for sale to the most ordinary people.

II A 54   n.d., 1837

« 5217

The Wandering Jew [. . .].[352]

II A 61   n.d., 1837

« 5218

It is curious that the Italian blue-violet shade, which we usually do not have here in our country, can be seen on a clear evening by looking at the air through a window if one has a light between oneself and the window.

II A 625   May, 1837

« 5219

O God, how easy it is to forget such intentions! Dethroned in my own inner being, I have once again returned to the world in order to prevail there for some time yet. But what good is it to win the whole world and lose one's own soul.[353] Again today (May 8) I tried to forget myself, not in the boisterous tumult (that surrogate does not help) but by going out to Rørdam[354] and by talking with Bolette and by getting (if possible) the devil of my wit to stay home, the angel with the flaming sword (as I have deserved) who places himself between me and every innocent girlish heart—since you overtook me, O God, thank you for not letting me immediately go mad—I have never been so fearful of it —thank you for once again inclining your ear to me.

II A 67   May 8, 1837

« 5220

Today the same episode again—but I got out to Rørdam[355]—good God, why should the inclination begin to stir just now—how alone I feel —confound that proud satisfaction in standing alone—everyone will now hold me in contempt—but you, my God, do not let go of me—let me live and reform—

II A 68   n.d., 1837

« 5221

During this time I have read various things by A. v. Arnim, among others *Armuth, Reichthum, Schuld und Busse der Grafinn Dolores,*[356] 2 volumes.

II, p. 21, where he speaks of her seducer.[357] . . .

II A 70   May 16, 1837

« 5222

Eine Parallele zur Religionsphilosophie, von Karl Rosenkranz (Bauer's *Zeitschrift,*[358] II, 1, pp. 1–32)

He shows that if the different religions are reduced to the simplest terms, three positions can be laid down.

(1) der Mensch ist Gott
(2) Gott ist Gott
(3) Gott ist Mensch.[359]

The first, of course, is ethnicism; [p. 2] it does not posit unity as *den sich vermittelnde* [that which mediates itself], but as immediate and spontaneous, and forgets where a *vermittelnde* process has taken place, namely, in the conclusion. It is an assertive proposition. Thus in pagan religions the *Zauberer* [magicians] are themselves the power to which the elementary powers yield. [P. 3] In the *Indian* religion it is *Brahma*, or whoever rises by penitence to it, immediately one with God (therefore it is not necessary for his *Erscheinung* [manifestation] to be congruent with his essence—just like the Catholic clergy in another direction); in the *Buddhist* religion the *Lama* is God directly. [P. 5] In *dualistic* religions man is the intermediate being for realizing that process; the two powers need him for their completion. Here instead of quietism there is reciprocal action between the positive and the negative substance; from this comes (1) the heroic; (2) [P. 6] the tragic (since action is the main thing, but death sets the boundary to it). With the *Greeks* it was the *religion of art* or the beautiful individual. [P. 7] The heroic and the tragic come more to the front (Heracles) with the enlarged definition of individual freedom but thereafter switch over to the opposite. The hero, who in action makes himself God, has his opposite in the atheist, who by the dialectic of thought denies the gods; [p. 8] the tragic in the comic, which absolutizes the idiosyncratic individuality (Aristophanes). The Romans [P. 9] Hegel describes their religiousness as *"Ernsthaftigkeit."* The R. went mad [p. 10] in the Roman emperor, who made himself God: Er hat nicht, wie der chinesische Keiser, seinem Willen eine bestimte Richtung zu geben; er lebt nicht, wie ein Lama, in einem monchischen Quietismus; er ist kein Held wie Rostem; er ist kein Künstler, der wie ein Phidias, Skopas Götterideale schafft und dadurch sich endlich als die Macht der Religion erfährt; durch den Titel, durch den Namen weiss er sich als die unbedingte Macht. Diese Apotheose ist die Carricatur der hellenischen Apotheose, die immer als Resultat erscheint.

[P. 11] Monotheism. [P. 12] appears historically in *Judaism* and *Mohammedanism,* and the more isolated *Deism.* Judaism develops in the first books, where God appears in his omnipotence as lawgiver, [p. 13] (Moses stays completely in the background); then in Job the detached individuality appears in a kind of opposition to God, and [p. 14] in the Psalms sets his mind at rest by [acknowledging] that God is God, the Almighty, against whom man must not strive. [P. 16] Mohammedanism develops a caricature; God's omnipotence becomes arbitrariness, and [p. 17] his governance becomes fatalism. [P. 19] Deism basically reverses the relationship, for while monotheism as such presupposes that God is God and therefore man is man, it presupposes that man is man and therefore God is God (as a necessary accessory to realizing man's deserved bliss).

[Pp. 21 f.] Christianity. Paganism was poetic, monotheism prosaic; the former eventuated in madness; only by means of numerous separate, limited individualities could a unity in essence emerge, but where the primordial forces are not tamed by individual limitation, there is the imperfect, and the ugly and the unnatural emerge. The *Vitae Imperatorum* of Suetonius gives examples of it. Hegel: "Sich so als den Inbegriff aller wirklichen Mächte wissend, ist dieser Herr der Welt das ungeheure Selbstbewusstsein, das sich als den wirklichen Gott weiss, indem er aber nur das formale Selbst ist, das sie nicht zu bändigen vermag, ist seine Bewegung und Selbstgenuss die eben so ungeheure Ausschweifung." [Pp. 23 f.] Christianity is the negative identity of the two separate and traceable-only-to-each-other positions in monotheism, but is also the abrogation of paganism's immediate assertive position. Monotheism's position is categorical. Paganism's position is problematic, and monotheism's hypothetical. Christianity's position is apodictic, since it contains the disjunction of the divine and the human in concrete unity. Weil Gott an sich Mensch ist so wird er es auch. [P. 25] It is not like the incarnations in Indian pantheism, all of whom have the marks of accidental character in both form and intention. [P. 26] But neither is it a human becoming as if God needed man in order to achieve consciousness. [Pp. 30 f.] Therefore Christianity contains the most glorious life-view. The tragic element for the religion of art was der Schmerz des unbegriffenen Todes, der den Genuss der schönen Heiterkeit zwar nicht negirte, wie in Ægypten, aber unangenem störte. Das Traurige im Monotheismus war die Last des Gesetzes, welches der Mensch zwar als das des heiligen Gottes, aber nicht als sein eignes anerkannte. Selbst die Autonomie der theoretischen und Autokratie der praktischen Vernunft im Deismus ist nur eine secondäre.

II A 92   June 8, 1837

« 5223

The phrase ἀποκαραδοκία τῆς κτίσεως,[360] in Romans 8:19 tallies with some poetic glimmerings in the legends, for example, about mermaids who are redeemed by human love,[361] about gnomes etc. (F. de la Motte Fouqué, Hoffmann, Ingemann, who reproduced the old legends, the other side of which is that these spirits are able to plunge men into destruction.)

II A 98   June 26, 1837

« 5224

Guldkorset[362]–Gudrun[363]–

Falsehoods in stories.

At the same time they are eulogized for heroic courage—they get the weapon which safeguards them—

II A 590   *n.d.*, 1837

« **5225**

How unhappy I am—Martensen has written an essay on Lenau's *Faust.* [364]

II A 597   *n.d.*, 1837

« **5226**

The Don Juanian life is really musical,[365] and thus it is very proper for Lenau[366] in his *Faust,* at the moment Faust begins to portray Don Juan, to have Mephistopheles start the music.

—Martensen[367] has not seen the deeper significance of this circumstance.

II A 598   *n.d.*, 1837

« **5227**

The idea, the philosophy of life, of knowing all evil, which a sect of gnosticism[368] embraced, is profound; only one must have a predisposition for it, which is suggested in legends by the ability of the baptized to see things that others do not see.

II A 599   *n.d.*, 1837

« **5228**

Metaphysical lectures by the publican Zacchaeus in a sycamore tree, tediously compiled for the diversion and reassurance of troubled consciences in dark and sorrowful hours, by his grateful colleague, the former assistant customs officer. Along with a young philologist's immortal commentary, in order to increase the saleability of the book there is included a brief résumé of the topics *belieblich* arranged *zum Gebrauch für Jedermann.* [369]

Drone House. Printed this year.

A list of abusive words one can use without being sued for libel is included.[370]

II A 600   *n.d.*, 1837

« **5229**

Why is there so much talk about—or, more correctly, what after all is the source of the idea of talking about the devil's **great-grandmother.**[371]

II A 601   *n.d.*, 1837

« 5230

Someone dies just as he has proved that there is eternal damnation, trapped in his own theory. Remarkable transition from theory to practice.

II A 602   *n.d.*,   1837

« 5231

Yes, I believe I would surrender to Satan so that he could show me every abomination, every sin, in its most dreadful form—it is this penchant, this taste, for the secret of sin.[372]

II A 603   *n.d.*,   1837

« 5232

Although I rail against others for studying compendiums instead of the sources, I myself live a compendium—although I am able to win every argument, I am saddled with a ghost from my own imagination which I cannot argue away.—[373]

II A 607   *n.d.*,   1837

« 5233

Now and then I see myself hemmed in by an appalling, phrase-laden figure—I would call it a compendium of a human being—a brief résumé of emotions and ideas—a *belieblich*[374] long, thin man whom nature, however, has arrested, so to speak, in every development—he should have long arms, but the upper arm is extremely long and the lower arm very short, the same with his fingers, face, etc.; every communication begins with a very promising introductory phrase so that one hopefully applies a prodigious criterion, but then it comes to nothing.—[375]

II A 609   *n.d.*,   1837

« 5234

All of us walk this road over the Bridge of Sighs into the peace of eternity.—[376]

II A 611   *n.d.*,   1837

« 5235

The Hottentots always cut off the head of a snake they have killed, fearing that someone may accidentally step on it and be bitten, since they believe that even after its death the snake can do injury with its poison.[377]

II A 613   *n.d.*,   1837

« **5236**

Why does a dog howl . . . . .[378]

II A 614   *n.d.*, 1837

« **5237**

I feel like the poor parrot who is always asked: What do you want?
You want sugar? —Yes, ... You shall have sh———![379]

II A 616   *n.d.*, 1837

« **5238**

Like a lonely spruce tree, egoistically exclusive and pointing toward the higher, I stand and cast no shadow, and only the wood dove
builds its nest in my branches.

Sunday, July 9, in Frederiksberg
Park, after visiting Rørdam[380]

II A 617   July 9, 1837

« **5239**

I cannot help being amazed that Justinus Kerner[381] (in his *Dichtungen*) is able to interpret so conciliatingly the phenomenon which has
always shocked me since my very first experience of it—that someone
says just exactly what I say. To me the phenomenon[382] seemed to be
the most confusing, almost Punch-and-Judy, disorder: the one would
begin a sentence which the other would finish, and no one could be
sure who was speaking.

II A 115   July 11, 1837

« **5240**

In margin of 5239 (II A 115):
Justinus Kerner has interested me so much just now because,
although he is far more gifted, I see in him the same artistic barrenness
I see in myself. But I also see how something can be done even though
essential continuity is lacking and can be fulfilled only by continuity of
mood, of which every single little idea is a blossom, a kind of novelistic
aphorism,[383] a plastic study. While his own *Dichtungen*[384] are full of
excellent imaginative ideas, his reports *aus dem Nachtgebiete der Natur*[385]
are so dry that we could almost take that to be indirect proof of their
truth.

II A 116   July 13, 1837

« 5241

[*] I have often wondered how it could be that I have had such great reluctance to write down particular observations;[386] but the more I come to know individual great men in whose writings one does not detect in any way a kaleidoscopic hustling together of a certain batch of ideas (perhaps Jean Paul by his example has given me premature uneasiness in this respect) and the more I recall that such a refreshing writer as Hoffmann has kept a journal and that Lichtenberg[387] recommends it, the more I am prompted to find out just why this, which is in itself innocent, should be unpleasant, almost repulsive, to me. Obviously the reason was that in each instance I thought of the possibility of publication, which perhaps would have required more extensive development, something with which I did not wish to be bothered, and enervated by such an abstract possibility (a kind of literary hiccoughing and squeamishness), the aroma of fancies and mood evaporated.[†] I think, instead, that it would be good, through frequent note-writing, to let the thoughts come forth with the umbilical cord of the original mood, and to forget as much as possible all regard for their possible use, which would not happen in any case by referring to my journals; rather, by expectorating myself as in a letter to an intimate friend, I gain the possibility of self-knowledge and, in addition, fluency in writing, the same articulateness in written expression which I have to some extent in speaking, the knowledge of many little traits to which I have given no more than a quick glance,[‡] and finally, the advantage, if what Hamann[388] says is true in another sense, that there are ideas which a man gets only once in his life. Such practice backstage is certainly necessary for every person who is not so gifted that his development is in some way public.[389]

[*] *In margin:* Resolution of July 13, 1837, made in our study at six o'clock in the evening.

                                              II A 118   *n.d.*, 1837

« 5242

[†] *In margin of 5241* (II A 118):
And therefore the entries I have are either so completely cryptic that I no longer understand them or are entirely occasional, and I can also see why usually many entries are from one and the same day, which suggests a sort of day of reckoning, but this is crazy.

The apparent wealth of fancies and ideas which one feels in ab-

stract possibility is just as unpleasant and it brings on uneasiness
similar to that which a cow suffers when it is not milked at the proper
time.[390] Therefore one's best method, if external conditions are of no
help, is, like the cow, to milk oneself.

II A 119   n.d., 1837

« **5243**

[‡] *In margin of 5241* (II A 118):
Something like this is also to be found in scholarship. There are
men who read only the most important works on the most important
developments, and therefore they do know a little about the scholarly
King's Highway but absolutely nothing about the lanes and by-ways
and their unsung glories and vistas; somewhat like Englishmen they
take the transcontinental highway, but this is also the reason that their
knowledge is so *compendieus.*[391]

II A 120   August 26, 1837

« **5244**

Addition to 5243 (II A 120):
Those abbreviated men!

II A   November 4, 1837

« **5245**

What a wonderful expression Lichtenberg[392] proposes, "the simple phrase, 'graduate student prose,' to describe the writing pattern of
those who write in a fatuous popular style ordinary everyday thoughts
which at best express what sensible people have already thought."

II A 124   n.d., 1837

« **5246**

Everyone sees material for parody in small-town life, but no one
sees that the *capital city* is a *parody* of a world-historical metropolis;
people do talk together, and yet the one immediately reprints in
cramped *duodecimo letters* the other's *uncial letters;*[393] the world's tragedies are simultaneously produced in the largest theaters and in vaudeville houses, scene for scene and with identical words.

II A 126   July 14, 1837

« **5247**

I have also united the tragic with the comic: I crack jokes and
people laugh—I cry.[394]

II A 132   July 14, 1837

« **5248**

Excerpt from Wilhelm Lund's review of Hauck's book in *Maa-nedsskrift for Litteratur*[395]

[P. 311]		An existence *by itself*	
		An existence *for itself* (Individuality)	
[Pp. 312f.]		Receptivity	Spontaneity
	1.	*Crystal*	
		(Production)	
[Pp. 313f.]	2.	*Plants*	
		(Reproduction)	
[Pp. 315f.]		Absorption	Secretion
			a) for nourishment
			b) mediate, secretion proper
			c) Excretion
[Pp. 316ff.]	3.	*Animals*	
		Veins	Arteries
		Nerves	
		Sensory organs	Muscles
		Feeling	Will
		(Instinct)	
[P. 321]	4.	*Man*	
		Reason	Freedom

II A 154 *n.d.*, 1837

« **5249**

Situation

A person wants to write a novel in which one of the characters goes insane; during the process of composition he himself gradually goes insane and ends it in the first person.[396]

II A 634   *n.d.*, 1837

« **5250**

What a wonderful prelude to a visit to a cemetery—a pretty little girl at the window of the sexton's house, peeking out curiously.

II A 635   *n.d.*, 1837

« **5251**

I don't feel like doing anything. I don't feel like walking—it is tiring; I don't feel like lying down, for either I would lie a long time, and I don't feel like doing that, or I would get up right away, and I don't feel like that either[397]—I don't feel like riding—the motion is too vigorous for my apathy; I don't feel like doing anything except just taking a drive, indolently, smoothly undulating along, letting objects in abundance glide by, pausing at every beautiful spot merely to feel my listlessness—my ideas and impulses are just as barren as a eunuch's desire. —I seek in vain for something to stimulate me—not even the pithy language of the Middle Ages is able to destroy the emptiness that prevails in me—now I really feel the meaning of the expression about Christ's words:[398] that they are life and spirit—to be brief: I do not feel like writing what I have written here, and I do not feel like erasing it either.

II A 637   n.d., 1837

« 5252

Would to God that I were a fiddler[399]—a farmers' woodland festival after all, they are the happiest class of people, the farmers and farm girls. But right now I have no way of expressing all my feelings. Would that out there I had one person to whom I could communicate—one of the few to cling to now more than ever—and be rid of these philistines and cadets who do not childishly and goodnaturedly see the mote as most men do, but aristocratically overlook the good.

II A 640   n.d., 1837

« 5253

Every flower of my heart turns into a frost flower.

II A 641   n.d., 1837

« 5254

My ideas suffer the same fate as parents who do indeed bear healthy children but forget to have them baptized in time; along come the subterranean spirits and put a changeling in their place (native gifts are not lacking, but solicitous care and nurture).

II A 642   n.d., 1837

« 5255

It seems as if I were the hero in a story, a *wild* shoot who should be displayed in a novel.

II A 644   n.d., 1837

« 5256

It seems as if I were a galley slave chained together with death; every time life stirs, the chain rattles[400] and death makes everything decay—*and that takes place every moment.*

II A 647   n.d., 1837

« **5257**

Everything human lies, hope as well as despair—I read this as a quotation in an old devotional book.

II A 648   *n.d.*, 1837

« **5258**

Each one takes his own revenge on the world. I get mine by carrying my sorrows and afflictions shut up inside me while the laughter entertains everybody. If I see anyone suffering, I am sorry for him, console him as well as I can, listen calmly when he assures me "that *I* am happy." If I can keep on doing this until I die, I will be avenged.[401]

II A 649   *n.d.*, 1837

« **5259**

The fate of my ideas and their fulfillment is much like fishing during certain months of the year—the fish nibble—there are plenty of nibbles, but no fish.

II A 653   *n.d.*, 1837

« **5260**

I am a two-faced Janus: with one face I laugh, with the other I cry.[402]

II A 662   *n.d.*, 1837

« **5261**

Unfortunately my real spirit frequently is present in me only κατὰ κρύψιν.[403]

II A 164   September 20, 1837

« **5262**

Now I know a suitable subject for a dissertation: concerning the concept of satire among the ancients, the reciprocal relation of the various Roman satirists to each other.[404]

II A 166   September 25, 1837

« **5263**

Holberg's *E. Montanus* remains a comedy (although in so many other respects it is a tragedy), because in the end madness wins by laying a punishment upon E. and *forcing* him to *knowledge of the truth* by a means (beating him) that is even more demented than the madness of all the others.

II A 167   September 27, 1837

« 5264

..... this is why the Chinese have neither light nor shadow in their painting.

II A 670   *n.d.*, 1837

« 5265

The Lord's Prayer, also in its separate parts, corresponds to the Ten Commandments as the sole command.

II A 673   *n.d.*, 1837

« 5266

Fantasy: An insane man who answered every question with a grade rating—when asked how he was, he answered: B+ etc.

II A 677   *n.d.*, 1837

« 5267

Unfortunately my life is far too subjunctive; would to God I had some indicative power.

II A 171   October 7, 1837

« 5268

If the Romans were egotists in their highly developed use of the *pronomen reflexionum*[405] and the conspicuousness with which they knew how to refer this *pronomen* to the principal idea, then I believe Grundtvig[406] is right.

II A 182   October 24, 1837

« 5269

The reason I prefer autumn to spring is that in the spring one looks at the earth—in the autumn[407] at heaven.

II A 185   October 29, 1837

« 5270

There is really something nonsensical about writing for the times and the gratification of the times; that is not the way it goes. It begins with one or more, in proportion to the greatness of the idea, going mad (I am convinced that there were Copernicians in all the insane asylums before Copernicus)—then comes a great mind who comprehends the idea but is not understood by the contemporary age. Then all at once it magically appears in various people and ends as sheer triviality. —We are not living in that beautiful age in which Minerva springs out of Jupiter's head—here she bursts the head of her original father and then wanders irresolutely around until she finally ends in an asylum.

II A 189   November 4, 1837

« **5271**

[Excerpt from Johan Eduard Erdmann, *Vorlesungen über Glauben und Wissen*[408] (Berlin: 1837). Lectures 1–7 (pp. 1–70).]

II C 38   November, 1837

« **5272**

Continuation of 5271 (II C 38):

Lecture 8

[Pp. 70 f.] We have now reached the point that the true is defined as the opposite of the "I" and it must be true just because it is the opposite of the "I." Every other definition of truth is accidental; essentially it is just the opposite of the "I." But that which makes truth the truth is nothing other than the "I itself." And for its content, truth has only that which the "I" gives it. —Now it switches over to the opposite.[*]—

[P. 73] the coinciding of religious superstition with its opposite, the very domination of the "I" over the contents of belief, can also be shown empirically. A hovering enters in here between the greatest superstition, consequently slavish fear, and the greatest arbitrariness and independence (fetishism).

[*] The reason that it is so difficult to get people to perceive this dialectical movement and that they imagine it to be much easier by means of the phenomenal analogies Erdmann uses [pp. 71 f.] is that such a transition seems to involve the incommensurability of *life,* which is inaccessible to the abstract dialectic developing through the thought-knots of necessity.

Kierkegaard

II C 39   November 7, 1837

« **5273**

Continuation of 5271 (II A 38), *lectures 9–15.*

II C 40   November, 1837

« **5274**

See how Erdmann[409] develops religious irony in *"Wissen und Glauben,"* lecture ten, where irony in one respect is construed quite properly and where he, for example, has correctly perceived the difference between it and unbelief, which is simply what it is and is open to any influence.

II A 193   November 9, 1837

« **5275**

Original sin—redemption—angels—"You shall be like the angels" —eternal damnation.

II A 629   *n.d.*, 1837

« **5276**

About eternal damnation
eternal, continuous development (*contrad. in adjecto*[410]) the eternal as the opposite of time, not an infinite succession of moments in time.
Children who die early—
Pagans—
See Gynther,[411] II, p. 118, bottom.

II A 630   *n.d.*, 1837

·« **5277**

Lectures on Introduction to Speculative
Dogmatics
by
Martensen[412]
Winter Semester '37 & '38

Lecture 1   November 15
[. . .]
Lecture 10   December 23
[. . .]

II C 12–24   November 15–December 23, 1837

« **5278**

[Excerpts and reading notes,[413] continuation of 5271 (II C 38–40):]
Part Two

[. . .]   Nov. 16
[. . .]   December 12, 1837
II C 42–48   November 16–December 14, 1837

« **5279**

I would like to write a novel in which there would be a man who every day walked past the plasterer on Østergade, took off his hat, and stood in silence, and then said as he had done regularly every day: O you wonderful Greek nature, why was I not allowed to live under your heaven in the days of your prime.

II A 200   11:30   December 7, 1837

« 5280

I think that if I ever do become an earnest Christian my deepest shame will be that I did not become one before, that I had to try everything else first.[414]

II A 202   December 8, 1837

« 5281

I would like to write a novel in which the main character would be a man who had gotten a pair of glasses, one lens of which reduced images as powerfully as an oxyhydrogen microscope[415] and the other magnified on the same scale, so that he perceived everything very relatively.[416]

II A 203   December 10, 1837

« 5282

I am utterly dismayed upon reading the essay with which Fichte[417] begins his journal. When we see a man with his abilities arm himself for battle with such earnestness, such "fear and trembling" (Philippians[418]), what is there for the rest of us to say? I think I will give up my studies, and now I know what I will be—I will become a witness in the office of a notary public.

II A 204   December 12, 1837

« 5283

On the Relation between Kant and Fichte . . .
[Reading notes on Erdmann, *Vorlesungen über Glauben und Wissen.*][419]

II C 49   December 12, 1837

« 5284

Once in a while, just after I have gone to bed and am ready to fall asleep, a rooster crows at midnight; it is unbelievable how much that can stimulate the imagination. I remember how just last night there poured in upon me vivid childhood recollections of Fredriksborg, where the crowing of the rooster announced a happy new day, how I had it all again: the chill morning air, the dew on the grass which kept us from frolicking about as we wished.

II A 205   December 16, 1837

« 5285

Addition to (II A 205):
And I was mistaken, for it was not the morning-crowing, but the *midnight-crowing.*

II A 206   April 4, 1838

« 5286

Zeitschrift für Philosophie und spekulative Theologie,[420] v. Dr. J. H. Fichte . . .

II C 50   December 18, 1837

« 5287

Why does the reading of fairy tales provide such fortifying relaxation for the soul? When I am weary of everything and "full of days,"[421] fairy tales are always a refreshing, renewing bath[422] for me. *There* all earthly, finite cares vanish; joy, yes, even sorrow, are infinite (and for this reason are so enlarging and beneficial). One sets out to find the blue bird,[423] just like the Crown Princess who lets someone else take care of the kingdom while she goes to look for her unhappy lover. What infinite sorrow is implied in her wandering about dressed as a peasant girl and saying to the old woman she meets: "Ich bin nicht allein, meine gute mutter; ich habe ein grosses Gefolge bei mir von Kummer, Sorgen, und Leiden."[424] One completely forgets the particular private sorrows which every man can have, in order to plunge into the deep-seated sorrow common to all, and is easily tempted to wish that he could meet an old woman to whom he could say, "Meine gute Mutter"—or a young girl roaming the world in search of her lover, in order to join her pilgrimage. —Or what strong and eternal friendship is implied in the same story by the Wizard, the guard and protector of "Huldreich," who goes around the world eight times and then, according to custom, first blows a long blast on the trumpet and thereupon shouts five times with all his might, "O Huldreich, König Huldreich! Wo bist du?"[425] —Or the story of the king and queen who had but one daughter—there was no question of finances, etc. etc. They do not summon parliament—no, they call together all the nursemaids.

II A 207   11:30   December 26, 1837

« 5288

I was in a strange mood the other day, collapsed within (as an old ruin must feel), abstracted from myself and my *I* in a pantheistic state of dissolution, and I read an old folk song (published by Sneedorf-

Birch),[426] which tells of a girl who waited for her lover one Saturday evening, but he did not come—and she went to bed "and wept so bitterly"; she got up again "and wept so bitterly." Suddenly the scene expanded before my eyes—I saw the Jutland heath[427] with its indescribable solitude and its lonely lark—and now one generation after another arose before me, and the girls all sang for me and wept so bitterly and sank into their graves again, and I wept with them.

Strangely enough, my imagination works best when I am sitting alone in a large assemblage, when the tumult and noise require a substratum of will if the imagination is to hold on to its object; without this environment it bleeds to death in the exhausting embrace of an indefinite idea.

II A 679   December 30, 1837

II. THE AUTHORSHIP BEGINS
1838–1839

« 5289

Nulla dies sine linea.[428]
1838

II A 208   n.d., 1838

« 5290

I would like to write a novella with my own mottoes.
Motto: Fantasy for a post horn.

A man who is writing his biography—his childhood has made no impression on him at all, and in his narrowmindedness he sees only the ludicrousness of it—until he begins to teach children, discovers the meaning of childhood, and reproduces his own.

I would choose for my motto the Italian text of the words in *Don Juan:*[429] But they wither and soon fade away.

Prompted by the song[430] "My Brimming Glass" and its gay tune, he will experience total recollection of his childhood.

It is strange that the view of life articulated here (and the fact that it contains a view of life makes it interesting) caused people to enjoy wine, etc., moderately when with friends—fear of Christian restraint led them to become addicted (the latter occurs far more frequently in our day).

* *

Winter is summer's *abbreviatur.*[431]

The book should be published with occasional refrains by an insane man.

The prototype in his predilection for the stock exchange (its ruinous decline) because of his relation to utterly reduced families.

II A 683   January 2, 1838

« 5291

How strange it is that one day I walk in cothurni[432] and the next —in boots.

II A 684   n.d., 1838

« 5292

The other day I met a woman (Mrs. Ross) who really belongs in a hospital ward; all she talks about is illnesses and medicines and health precautions—but the main point she really wants to talk about is the extent to which the closest relatives should be allowed to visit a sick person who is practically lying at death's door.

II A 685   January 3, 1838

« 5293

If I am a literary weed—well, then at least I am what is called "Proud Henry."[433]

II A 686   n.d., 1838

« 5294

Vaudeville is a musical association of ideas.

II A 688   n.d., 1838

« 5295

I was just searching for an expression to designate the kind of people I would like to write for, convinced that they would share my views, and now I find it in Lucian: παράνεκροί[434] (one who like me is dead), and I would like to issue a publication for παράνεκροί.[435]

II A 690   January 9, 1838

« 5296

Lucian[436] has an excellent dialogue between Charon and the Cynic Menippus, which begins with Charon's demanding an obol for the trouble of taking him across the Styx, but Menippus declaring that he does not have one.

II A 691   January 10, 1838

« 5297

When I read a book, what gratifies me is not so much what the book itself is as the infinite possibilities there must have been in every passage, the complicated history, rooted in the author's personality, studies, etc., which every phrase must have had and still must have for the author.

II A 693   January 13, 1838

« 5298

It is strange that no one ever thought of having a man at the point of dying say to Death—If you do not die, then I am going to kill you

—and what confusion there would be in the world if it happened, how awkward for those waiting for a rich man's death.

II A 696 January 18, 1838

« 5299

Speculative Dogmatics[437]
by
Martensen . . .

II C 26–28 *n.d.*, 1838–39

« 5300

The emphasis on head-aptitude nowadays is just as unreasonable and unjust as the levy of a head-tax.

II A 700 February 6, 1838

« 5301

When at times there is such a commotion in my head that the skull seems to have been heaved up, it is as if goblins had hoisted up a mountain a bit and are now having a hilarious ball in there.

In margin: God forbid!

II A 702 February 9, 1838

« 5302

April.

Such a long period has again elapsed in which I have been unable to concentrate on the least little thing—now I must make another attempt.

Paul Møller is dead.[438]

II A 209 April, 1838

« 5303

This morning I saw a half dozen wild geese fly away in the crisp cool air; they were right overhead at first and then farther and farther away, and at last they separated into two flocks, like two eyebrows over my eyes, which now gazed into the land of poetry.

II A 210 April 1, 1838

« 5304

I sat with little Carl on my lap and talked about how much I really liked the old sofa in the new apartment into which I was moving. He said that he also liked it very much. When I asked him why, he of course could not answer. But is it not curious that I muse with a strange sadness on reminders from a time I have never experienced, and now again I see him going in the same direction.

II A 212   *n.d.,* 1838

« 5305

I went over to hear Nielsen[439] give a reading of *"Glæde over Danmark"* and was strangely moved by the words:
Remember the traveler far away.
Yes, now he has gone far away—but I at least will surely remember him.[440]

II A 216   April 2, 1838

« 5306

With me everything is "wandering":[441] wandering thoughts—wandering rheumatism.

II A 222   *n.d.,* 1838

« 5307

What is man, this stamen in everlasting flowers[442] (the transfiguration of history).

II A 712   April 12, 1838

« 5308

That the earth is in the center may also be seen from Christ's being in heaven, descending into the abyss, but remaining on earth, so that no one needs to climb up to heaven to bring him down—or into the underworld to bring him up; therefore the Church, without being able to comprehend him, correctly teaches that Christ is in it, although it also teaches that he is in heaven.

II A 714   *n.d.,* 1838

« 5309

A *fantasy:* a mad school teacher with a Mardi Gras whip[443] in his hand; he insists that it is Aaron's priestly staff bearing mature almonds.—

II A 717   *n.d.,* 1838

« 5310

In the spiritual sense there prevails no respect at all for the right of property—they shout: crucify him, crucify him, and then they cast lots for his clothes.[444]

II A 720   *n.d.,* 1838

« 5311

Our age heralds and announces, and yet no John the Baptist is
born any more.

II A 723   n.d., 1838

« 5312

If Gjødwad[445] (licentiate I shall call him because he exercises so
much license) is convicted, he could be called "the one-time idol in the
office of *Kjøbenhavnsposten.*" —Incidentally, it will be easy for *Kjøbenhavnsposten* to get a new editor, since they take for granted occasional
incarnations of Brahma—or Rosenhoff[446] could take over the post and
also become county barber with three shaving basins: *Kjøbenhavnsposten, Den Frisindede, Concordia.*

II A 728   April 15, 1838

« 5313

If Christ is to come and live in me, it will have to be according to
the Gospel[447] for the day[448] given in the almanac: Christ enters
through closed doors.

II A 730   n.d., 1838

« 5314

I would like to write a novella which begins with an unqualified
still life, until through the medium of the Don Juan music a new light
is suddenly ushered in, and then the whole thing is drawn into an
utterly fantastic world.

II A 732   n.d., 1838

« 5315

There are several absolutely wonderful great ideas in Grabbe's
Don Juan, [449] each one of which shoots up like an enormous spruce at
a given moment and stands before us.

II A 733   n.d., 1838

« 5316

Equal strokes,
Pause not long,
Pull now, steady,
Danish lads.[450]

II A 736   n.d., 1838

« 5317

Die Ironien in den Reden Jesu, by F. Joseph Grulich. Leipzig: 1838.

                                    II A 737   *n.d.,* 1838

« 5318

An author should always give something of his personality, just as Christ feeds us with his body and blood.

                                    II A 739   *n.d.,* 1838

« 5319

This morning I met an odd procession in Lovers' Lane—some young girls dancing with each other along the path—at first I thought what giddyheads, but then as I came closer I saw that they were dancing to the music of two young men behind them playing flutes—I almost began to dance with them—so there is still that kind of poetry in the world. —If I encounter more such phenomena, I will certainly become a Don Quixote who sees such things in everything.

                                    II A 740   *n.d.,* 1838

« 5320

My life these days is more or less like a duplicated copy of an original edition of my own self.

                                    II A 742   *n.d.,* 1838

« 5321

I have been reading Görres's *Athanasius*[451] these days—not only with my eyes but with my whole body, with the solar plexus.

                                    II A 745   *n.d.,* 1838

« 5322

For a dedication copy of my treatise:[452]
Since I know that you probably will not read it, and if you did would not understand it, and if you understood it would take exception to it, may I direct your attention only to the externals: gilt-edges and Morocco binding.

                                    II A 749   *n.d.,* 1838

« 5323

A midnight hour
Satan—the devil—fly specks, etc. You have tricked me, cheated me

of the moments I should have enjoyed. —The watchman cries: There is no other Savior.[453]

II A 753   n.d., 1838

« 5324

There is an *indescribable joy* that glows all through us just as inexplicably as the apostle's exclamation[454] breaks forth for no apparent reason: "Rejoice, and again I say, Rejoice." —Not a joy over this or that, but the soul's full outcry "with tongue and mouth and from the bottom of the heart":[455] "I rejoice for my joy, by, in, with, about, over, for, and with my joy"—a heavenly refrain which, as it were, suddenly interrupts our other singing, a joy which cools and refreshes like a breath of air, a breeze from the trade winds which blow across the plains of Mamre to the everlasting mansions.[456]

II A 10:30 A.M. 228   May 19, 1838

« 5325

In many ways my yearnings and thoughts are like Nebuchadnezzar,[457] who not only asked the soothsayers to interpret his dreams but also to tell him what he had dreamed.

II A 757   n.d., 1838

« 5326

When God had created the world . . . . .[458]

II A 229   June 4, 1838

« 5327

Ueber die Præexistents Christi oder
die Voraussetzung der menschlichen
Persönlichkeit
by
Pfarrer Conradi
(Bauer's journal, III, 2, pp. 348 ff.)[459]

II C 53   n.d., 1838

« 5328

How I thank you, Father in heaven, for having kept an earthly father[460] present for a time here on earth, where I so greatly need him; with your help I hope that he will have greater joy in being my father the second time than he had the first time.

II A 231   July 9, 1838

« **5329**

I am going to work toward a far more inward relation to Christianity, for up until now I have in a way been standing completely outside of it while fighting for its truth; like Simon of Cyrene (Luke 23:26), I have carried Christ's cross in a purely external way.

II A 232   July 9, 1838

« **5330**

I hope that my contentment with my life *here at home* will turn out to be like that of a man I once read about.[461] He, too, was fed up with home and wanted to ride away from it. When he had gone a little way, his horse stumbled and he fell off, and as he got up on his feet he happened to see his home, which now looked so beautiful to him that he promptly mounted his horse, rode home, and stayed home. It depends on getting the right perspective.

II A 233   July 10, 1838

« **5331**

When I stand and look far out over Røyen's[462] old place into Hestehaven, and the thick forest condenses in the background, accentuating the darkness and mystery in its depths even more by the crowns that top single isolated trunks—then I seem to see myself very vividly as a little boy running along in my green jacket and gray pants—but unfortunately I have grown older and cannot *fetch myself.* Contemplating childhood is like contemplating a beautiful region as one rides backwards; one really becomes aware of the beauty at that moment, that very instant, when it begins to vanish, and all I have left from that happy time is *to cry like a child.*

Fredriksborg, July 30, 1838
II A 238   July 30, 1838

« **5332**

It could be interesting to trace Chiliasm through its historical modifications right up to the present, at which time it is obviously beginning to be heard again somewhat, for example, in the younger Fichte[463] et al. It could be a contrast to Baur's Gnosticism,[464] together with which doctrine it would provide the way to the true Christian-dogmatic categories. (A factor here could, for example, be the doctrine of Holy Communion, Luther's interpretation, etc.) (Of course, the specifically Jewish element in the doctrine must be eliminated first.)

II A 240   August 2, 1838

« **5333**

In margin of 5331 (II A 240):
I think there is a work called Corrodi, *Geschichte der Chiliasmus,* in three volumes. See Münscher's *Kirkehistorie,* p. 353, note 23.[465]

II A 241   *n.d.*

« **5334**

Copyist Exegesis
or
The Relation between the Old and the New Testament

After Hierax or Hierakas[466] had nourished himself in Christianity by *copying* Holy Scripture, he found in his wisdom that the difference between the Old and the New Testament is that celibacy is not taught in the former—such a conception is possible only for people who stand in an external relation to the object the way a copyist does.

II C 3   August 6, 1838

« **5335**

My father[467] died on Wednesday (the 8th) at 2:00 A.M. I so deeply desired that he might have lived a few years more, and I regard his death as the last sacrifice of his love for me, because in dying he did not depart *from* me but he died *for* me, in order that something, if possible, might still come of me. Most precious of all that I have inherited from him is his memory, his transfigured image, transfigured not by poetic imagination (for it does not need that), but transfigured by many little single episodes I am now learning about, and this memory I will try to keep most secret from the world. Right now I feel there *is* only *one* person (E. Boesen[468]) with whom I can really talk about him. He was a "faithful friend."

II A 243   August 11, 1838

« **5336**

My good mood, my tranquility, soars upward like a dove, pursued by Saul's evil spirit,[469] by a bird of prey, and it can save itself only by mounting higher and higher, by getting farther and farther away from me.

II A 760   August 17, 1838

« 5337

There is a curious continuity running through the series of names
used to describe the first four centuries: *apostolicum, gnosticum, novatia-
num, arianum.* [470] The Church ends, as it were, with the first century,
since its history after that is designated by the names of heretics.

II A 255   August 28, 1838

« 5338

sub rosa [471]

to S. S. Blicher
On the occasion of his nature concert [472]
Wenn ich ein Vögelein wär,
Und auch zwei Flüglein hätt,
Flög ich zu Dir;
Weils aber nicht kann sein,
Bleib ich allhier. [473]

II A 259   September 11, 1838

« 5339

An esthetic thought-bridle on Knight Andersen's wild hunt
through the shadowed valley of self-contradiction. [474]

II A 768   *n.d.,* 1838

« 5340

Even if *Kjøbenhavnsposten* were published in imperial folio, this
would not make it a *magna charta.*

II A 769   *n.d.,* 1838

« 5341

My position is armed neutrality. [475].

II A 770   *n.d.,* 1838

« 5342

Sir Knight, so many a path is in decay
But open and broad is the *graveyard*-way.
eia! eia! eia!
eia! eia! eia! [476]

II A 771   *n.d.,* 1838

« 5343

Take off your shoes, for the place where you are standing is
holy. [477] . . . . . It does not help, of course, that many of them are—
trouserless.

II A 772   *n.d.,* 1838

« **5344**

The liberal is related to *Kjøbenhavnsposten*[478] the way Niels Klim's caraway kringles are related to him.[479]

II A 777   *n.d.,* 1838

« **5345**

There are many means of self-defense. It is well-known that the musk-ox exudes such a strong odor that no one can come near it.

II A 778   *n.d.,* 1838

« **5346**

Kjøbenhavnsposten[480] is wind-warped (it twists with the wind).

II A 779   *n.d.,* 1838

« **5347**

One must be careful with my preface, for the same thing happens to it as happened to the treasure:

> but if you say one word
> it disappears again.
>   Oehlenschlaeger's *"Skattegraveren"*[481]
>   II A 780   *n.d.,* 1838

« **5348**

But Andersen[482] is not so dangerous, after all; from what I have experienced, his main strength is an auxiliary chorus of volunteer arrangers and invitation distributors, a few vagabond esthetes, who perpetually protest their honesty, and this much is certain, they can by no means be charged with any *reservatio mentalis,* for they have absolutely nothing *in mente.*[483]

II A 781   *n.d.,* 1838

« **5349**

My witticisms, he says, are far-fetched; his[484] are not—they are culled.

II A 782   *n.d.,* 1838

« **5350**

Christliche Polemik,[485] Dr. Karl Henrich Sack. Hamburg bei Perthes: 1838.

According to what I have read in this book so far, there are many very good things in it, but it is more popular than scholarly; frequently it is even devotional, and besides this it is curiously laid out, somewhat like a textbook.

In the preface there is nothing particularly notable, but the analysis of indifferentism, with which the book itself begins, is interesting in many ways and could be developed with much greater scholarly significance.

The two main forms of indifferentism are naturalism and mythologizing (depending on whether the indifferentism takes a factual or ideal turn, but the basis of this division is again one of those miserable scholastic bits that are of no importance). . . .

Gnosticism . . .

> Sack's remark on p. 278 about Gnosticism is superb and agrees entirely with what I have thought and to which there are also allusions in this book in connection with Schaller.[486] . . .
>
> II C 60   September 30, 1838

« **5351**

An author's works should bear the imprint of his likeness,[487] his individuality, as did the portrait Christ is supposed to have sent to King Abgarus of Edessa; it was not an artistically elaborated painting but a kind of inexplicable, miraculous emanation on canvas.

II A 270   October 6, 1838

« **5352**

After the ancient world's greatest tyrant, Dionysius, the new world's greatest ditto inherited the ear—with which he heard secret confession (just as Dionysius heard even the faintest sound in his notorious prison).

II A 275   October 11, 1838

« **5353**

[Notebook on "The History of Philosophy from Kant to Hegel,"[488] lectures by H. L. Martensen, University of Copenhagen, first semester 1838–39.]

II C 25   *n.d.,* 1838–39

« **5354**

[Reading notes and excerpts,[489] K. Rosenkranz, *Encyclopedie der theologischen Wissenschaften* (Halle: 1831).]

II C 61   November 9, 1838

« 5355

[Excerpt[490] from B. Bauer, *Die Urgeschichte der Menschheit nach dem biblischen Berichte der Genesis, kritisch untersucht.*[491]

II C 62   *n.d.*, 1838–39

« 5356

There are times in the spiritual life when the adjective "match-less" acquires, contrary to the intention of the persons using it, the same meaning conveyed if one were to praise a glove or a stocking by saying that it was *matchless.*[492]

II A 300   November 22, 1838

« 5357

[Reading notes and excerpts,[493] Johann Adam Möhler, *Athanasius der grosse und die Kirche seiner Zeit, besonders im Kampfe mit Arianismus* (Mainz: 1827).]

II C 29   *n.d.*, 1838
II C 30   11 o'clock, December 6, 1838
II C 31   December 9, 1838

« 5358

[Reading notes and excerpts, Johannes Voigt, *Ueber Pasquille, Spottlieder, und Schmähschriften aus der ersten Halfte des sechzehnten Jahrhunderts.*[494]]

II C 63   *n.d.*, 1838–39

« 5359

Dichtungen v. Ulrich v. Hutten, didactisch-biographischen und satyrisch-epigrammatischen Inhalts. Zum erstenmal vollständig übersetzt und erläutert, herausgegeben v. E. Münch. Stuttgart: 1828.–.

II C 64   *n.d.*, 1838–39

« 5360

[Reading notes and excerpts, *De impostura religionum breve compendium seu liber de tribus impostoribus,* Genthe (Leipzig: 1833).]

II C 65   *n.d.*, 1838–39

« 5361

So much in the novel depends essentially on the total effect produced by the detailed manifoldness of the presentation, because here also it holds true that: What is sown is perishable, what is raised is imperishable.[495]

II A 312   11 o'clock, evening, Christmas Day, 1838

« **5362**

At just this moment I feel the dreadful truth in the words:
Psalm 82:6: "I say, 'You are Gods, sons of the Most High, all of you; nevertheless, you shall die like men and fall like a tyrant.' "

II A 319   January 3, 1839

« **5363**

[Reading notes and excerpts, *Die christliche Lehre von der Versöhnung in ihrer geschichtlichen Entwicklung von der ältesten Zeit bis auf die neueste.* [496] By Dr. Ferd. Chr. Baur (Tübingen: 1838).]

II C 32   *n.d.*, 1838–39

« **5364**

The trouble with me is that my life, my state of mind, always follows two declensions, in which not only the suffixes become different but the whole word is changed.

II A 328   January 17, 1839

« **5365**

1 8 3 9
ad se ipsum[497]

II A 340   *n.d.*, 1839

« **5366**

[Quotation from Chateaubriand.][498]

II A 341   *n.d.*, 1839

« **5367**

There must have been many who had a relationship to Jesus similar to that of Barrabas (his name was Jesus Barrabas). The Danish "Barrabas" is about the same as "N.N." [Mr. X or John Doe], בַּר אַבָּא , *filius patris,* his father's son. —It is too bad, however, that we do not know anything more about Barrabas; it seems to me that in many ways he could have become a counterpart to the Wandering Jew. The rest of his life must have taken a singular turn. God knows whether or not he became a Christian. —It would be a poetic motif to have *him,* gripped by Christ's divine power, step forward and witness for him.

II A 346   February 1, 1839

« **5368**

You, sovereign queen of my heart, *"Regina,"*[499] hidden in the deepest secrecy of my breast, in the fullness of my life-idea, there where it is just as far to heaven as to hell—unknown divinity! O, can

I really believe the poets when they say that the first time one sees the beloved object he thinks he has seen her long before, that love like all knowledge is recollection, that love in the single individual also has its prophecies, its types, its myths, its Old Testament. Everywhere, in the face of every girl, I see features of your beauty, but I think I would have to possess the beauty of all the girls in the world to extract your beauty, that I would have to sail around the world to find the portion of the world I want and toward which the deepest secret of my self polarically points—and in the next moment you are so close to me, so present, so overwhelmingly filling my spirit that I am transfigured to myself and feel that here it is good to be.[500]

You blind god of erotic love! You who see in secret, will you disclose it to me? Will I find what I am seeking here in this world, will I experience the conclusion of all my life's eccentric premises, will I fold you in my arms, or:

Do the Orders say: March on?[501]

Have you gone on ahead, you, my longing, transfigured do you beckon to me from another world? O, I will throw everything away in order to become light enough to follow you.

II A 347   February 2, 1839

« 5369

What is said about the Messiah is true of every idea: it is ἀπάτωρ, ἀμήτωρ, ἀγενεαλόγητος, μήτε ἀρχὴν ἡμερῶν μήτε ζωῆς, τέλος ἔχων[502] (Hebrews 7:3).

II A 361   February 10, 1839

« 5370

Philo says somewhere: "ὁ ἄθεος ἀπάτωρ ἐστί, ὁ δὲ πολύθεός ἐστι ἐκ πόρνης."[503]

II A 364   February 11, 1839

« 5371

I am strangely alarmed when I note the extreme melancholy with which Englishmen of an earlier generation have spotted the ambiguity basic to laughter, as Dr. Hartley has observed:* What if laughter were completely misunderstood, what if the world were so bad and existence so unhappy that laughter really is weeping?[504] What if it were a misunderstanding—a misunderstanding caused by a compassionate genius or a mocking demon—?

*"Dass wenn sich das Lachen zuerst bey Kindern zeiget, so ist es ein entstehendes weinen, welches durch Schmerz erregt wird, oder ein plötzlich gehemmtes und in sehr kurzen Zwischenraumen widerholtes Gefühl des Schmerzens." (See *Geschichte der komischen Literatur*,[505] by Flögel, I, p. 50.)

II A 373   February 21, 1839

« 5372

The sad thing about me is that my whole life is an interjection[506] and has nothing nailed down (everything is movable—nothing immovable, no real property)—my sorrow is a despairing wail—my joy an overly lyrical tra-la-la.

II A 382   March 13, 1839

« 5373

The other day I heard a conversation between some farm girls and farm lads. One of the fellows, the kind commonly called a ladies' man, asked a very beautiful girl with a strong mark of mysteriousness about her, which Goethe[507] discusses in his *römische Elegien:* Do you have a sweetheart?—to which she replied: No. Whereupon he answered: "Well, then, you are also a bad girl."

II A 386   March 23, 1839

« 5374

I do have one advantage over most authors in that my ideas are always made out in someone's name and are not payable to the bearer; they are made out in someone's name even though I remain anonymous.

II A 389   April 3, 1839

« 5375

The higher criticism
See Hebrews 4:12, κριτικὸς διαλογισμῶν καὶ ἐννοιῶν.[508]

II A 395   April 23, 1839

« 5376

Christ is the true *magister matheseos.*[509]
ἔμαθεν ἀφ' ὧν ἔπαθε.[510] Hebrews 5:8.

II A 397   April 23, 1839

« 5377

Categories are the shewbread of our modern age—digestible only by the clergy.

II A 398   April 25, 1839

« 5378

And I who by nature am a quiescent-letter[511] [*Hvile-Bogstav*] have not yet found something in which I can rest [*hvile*];[512] if only I might soon find it so that I could really become full-toned.

II A 406   *n.d.,* 1839

« 5379

Most of what is written is nothing more than *asserta*[513] on plain paper—I, however, write on a stamped paper.[514]

II A 413   *n.d.,* 1839

« 5380

Cornelius Nepos tells of a general who was kept confined in a fortress with a considerable cavalry regiment; to keep the horses from getting sick because of too much inactivity, he had them whipped daily to put them in motion—in like manner I live in my room as one besieged—I prefer to see no one, and every moment I fear that the enemy will try an assault—that is, someone will come and visit me. I would rather not go out, but lest I be harmed by this sedentary life—I cry myself tired.[515]

II A 414   May 10, 1839

« 5381

I am so unhappy at present that in my dreams I am indescribably happy.[516]

II A 415   *n.d.,* 1839

« 5382

When I open my eyes these days they lift a great load of weights (launch a mass of "flies") which promptly settle down again; so too it is with my hope, for the door through which it is granted me at times to look into brighter regions (my daily environment and atmosphere are like the view and climate in a Greenland cave, and for that reason I receive very few visits in this my winter residence, since only missionaries have the courage to creep on all fours into such a cave—hope, the missionary of heaven—rarely sends out a gleam) is not a door that stays open once it is opened, nor is it a door that shuts again slowly so that one still might have the hope of peeking through it a few times before it shuts, no, it shuts promptly again, and the dreadful thing about it is that one almost forgets what he saw.

II A 416   May 11, 1839

« 5383

All existence [*Tilværelsen*] makes me anxious, from the smallest fly to the mysteries of the Incarnation; the whole thing is inexplicable to me, I myself most of all; to me all existence is infected, I myself most of all. My distress is enormous, boundless; no one knows it except God in heaven, and he will not console me; no one can console me except God in heaven, and he will not take compassion on me. —Young man, you who still stand at the beginning of your goal, if you have gone astray, turn back to God, and from his upbringing you will take along with you a youthfulness strengthened for manly tasks. You will never know the suffering of one who, having wasted the courage and energy of youth in insubordination against him, must begin to retreat, weak and exhausted, through devastated countries and ravaged provinces, everywhere surrounded by the abomination of desolation, by burned-out cities and the smoking ruins of frustrated hopes, by trampled prosperity and toppled success—a retreat as slow as a bad year, as long as eternity, monotonously broken by the daily repeated sigh: These days—I find no satisfaction in them.[517]

II A 420   May 12, 1839

« 5384

I say of my sorrow what the Englishman says of his house: My sorrow *is my castle.*[518] —But there are many men who, when they have occasion for sorrow (wear crepe around the hat), ask for sympathy not so much to alleviate the sorrow as to be petted and pampered a bit, and thus basically look upon having sorrow as one of life's conveniences.

II A 421   May 12, 1839

« 5385

I have no alternative than to suppose that it is God's will that I prepare for my examination[519] and that it is more pleasing to him that I do this than actually coming to some clearer perception by immersing myself in one or another sort of research,[520] for obedience is more precious to him than the fat of rams.[521]

II A 422   May 13, 1839

« **5386**

Somewhere in an Indian book I have read these words: Whoever disbelieves this will be condemned to hell and reborn as an ass.

II A 431   May 17, 1839

« **5387**

Preface[522]

Whether this preface is going to be long or short, I simply do not know at this moment. My soul is filled with but one thought, a longing, a thirsting, really to run wild in the lyrical underbrush of the preface, really to rumble about in it, for just as the poet at times must feel lyrically stirred and then again relishes the ethical, so I as a prose writer feel at present an indescribable joy in surrendering all objective thinking and really exhausting myself in wishes and hopes, in a secret whispering with the reader, a Horatian *sussuratio*[523] in the evening hours, for the preface always ought to be conceived in twilight, which also is undeniably the most beautiful; no wonder, therefore, that we read that the Lord God walked in the cool of the evening (Genesis),[524] an evening hour when the pressure of reflection is a somber distant sound, like the laughter of the harvesters.

II A 432   May 17, 1839

« **5388**

I live and feel these days somewhat as a chessman must feel when the opponent says: That piece cannot be moved[525]—like a useless spectator, since my time has not yet come.

II A 435   May 21, 1839

« **5389**

Hamann, VI, p. 144.[526]

II A 438   *n.d.,* 1839

« **5390**

Something very strange that has often disquieted me has been the thought that the life I lived was not my own but, without my being able to prevent it, was completely identified with another particular person, and each time I did not become aware of this until it had been partially lived through.

II A 444   May 24, 1839

« 5391

The trouble with me is that while other authors usually think less of what they have written in the past, I am just the opposite and always think better of what I have written prior to what I am writing at present.

II A 476   July 14, 1839

« 5392

The imagination leaps particularly when one reads or hears about something that *vanished long ago* and is so vividly interested in it that one can only say what is sometimes said of ready-made clothing—it is as if stitched to one's body.

II A 480   July 17, 1839

« 5393

I would like to write a dissertation[527] on suicide dealing with statistical information on suicide and its relation to the ancient world-view and the modern, its pathological Chladni figures, etc.

II A 482   July 20, 1839

« 5394

It is with me as with Sarah: $\nu \epsilon \nu \epsilon \kappa \rho \omega \mu \acute{\epsilon} \nu o s$,[528] I will come up for examination $\pi \alpha \rho \grave{\alpha} \kappa \alpha \iota \rho \grave{o} \nu \ \dot{\eta} \lambda \iota \kappa \acute{\iota} \alpha s$.[529]

II A 490   *n.d.*, 1839

« 5395

My unhappiness with the present is that I am jealous of the past.[530]

II A 492   *n.d.*, 1839

« 5396

It is dreadful that I am obliged to purchase every day, every hour —and the price is so variable![531]

II A 495   *n.d.*, 1839

« 5397

For the period of a year, a mile in time, I will plunge under-ground[532] like the river Guadalquibir—but I am sure to come up again!

II A 497   *n.d.*, 1839

« 5398

In the present age I with my aptitudes am like the beautiful little spots one sees occasionally, too far for a walking tour and too close for

an expedition, and for that reason never visited or given any attention
—similarly I appear neither on the present horizon nor on the tele-
scopic horizon of the generation.[533]

II A 503   n.d., 1839

« 5399

Now I can understand why H. Hertz was so eager to talk with me,
now that I have read his latest handiwork[534] with its political outbursts
and forays. It is just a shame that he omitted the Translator's satirical
sallies, which he no doubt believes can be done without impairing the
main content, but I find it to be the best, and it definitely should not
be left out, simply because of the dramatic interest in the Translator's
character, but there presumably are good reasons for it—for this Hertz
is not the man.

II A 508   July 21, 1839

« 5400

The trouble with me is that I immediately use up in one single
desperate step the tiny bit of happiness and reassurance I slowly distill
in the dyspeptic process of my toilsome intellectual life.

II A 509   July 22, 1839

« 5401

My journey through life is so unsteady because in my early youth
my forelegs[535] (expectations etc.) were weakened by being overstrained.

II A 510   July 22, 1839

« 5402

The reason I find so little joy in life is that when a thought awakens
in my soul it awakens with such energy, larger than life, that I actually
overstrain myself, and for me the ideal anticipation is so far from
explaining life that instead I am debilitated when I depart from it to
find something equivalent to the idea. I am too disturbed and, so to
speak, nerve-shattered to rest in it.

II A 512   July 25, 1839

« 5403

I have felt anxious and distressed these days because of the talk
by my singing-master Basil,[536] Pastor Ibsen,[537] on the attractiveness of
a position at the Prince's Court[538]—I who was sure that I had broken
with the world to the extent that every prospect in that direction was

destroyed (in a worldly sense, for God will surely make more and more definite for me the prospect of a higher Royal Household through it), I who believed that my whole life devoted to the service of God[539] would scarcely be enough to atone for the dissipations of my youth. I hear once again the old sirens' song; with someone walking politely alongside me to show me the way, I might very well take the first step on a path where all is lost if one cannot glitter. —No, thank you, Herr Pastor! When I sit alone like a Greenlander in my kayak,[540] alone on the great ocean, sometimes above water, sometimes under, always in God's hands, I may on occasion harpoon a sea monster if it seems appropriate—but I am not cut out for an Admiral.

II A 520 July 28, 1839

« **5404**

I can tell that my religious life of late has lost some of its energy from the fact that I no longer find the stirring rhythm of hymn-singing as invigorating as the dwindling lulling of the liturgy, the Extreme Unction of the Christian life.

II A 521 July 28, 1839

« **5405**

. . . . . if my witticisms are far-fetched, as some say, theirs certainly cannot be charged with that, for they are culled.[541]

II A 533 August 8, 1839

« **5406**

If only I could have my examination soon so that I could become a *quodlibetarius*[542] once again.

II A 534 August 8, 1839

« **5407**

. . . . . I am as timorous as a *Scheva*,[543] as weak and muted as a *Dagesch lene;*[544] I feel like a letter printed backward in the line, as uncontrollable as a pasha with three horsetails.* Yes, if thinking about one's miseries removed them just as those who are conscious of their good deeds lose their reward, how happy a hypochondriac of my format would be, for I take all my troubles in advance and yet they all remain behind.

August 24, 1839

In margin: as solicitous of myself and my scribblings as the National Bank is of its own, generally as reflexive as any pronoun.[545]

II A 540 August 24, 1839

« **5408**

All of Grundtvig's[546] preaching is nothing but a perpetually repeated exodus of the imagination so that it is impossible to follow along, a weekly evacuation. He continually says the reason the Church up until now has not appeared in its full radiance is that it suffers under external pressures; when these are gone, it will be seen—yes, then it will be seen whether this Church of his is the perfect Church or whether in many ways it does not need a preacher like Mynster,[547] who always leads everything back to the individual; that is where the battle must be and must not lose itself in such historical ramblings.

II A 542   August 26, 1839

« **5409**

Rasmus Nielsen's Robust and Faithful Moral Philosophy[548]
Found in Mads Madsen's Coffin[549]
or
The World Seen from a Cellar Door

II A 546   n.d., 1839

« **5410**

Like Mohammed's tomb, my soul hovers between two magnets and as yet has not found a unifying point of direction, but both of them tear and pull at it the best they can.

II A 548   August 30, 1839

« **5411**

At times my consciousness is far too spacious, far too universal; whereas it usually is able to contract convulsively and sensitively about each of my thoughts, at such times it is so huge and slack that it could very well serve several of us.

II A 549   August 30, 1839

« **5412**

I know of no better epigram for my childhood than the lines of Goethe's *Faust:*[550]

"Halb Kinderspiele,
Halb Gott im Herzen!"

II A 557   September 9, 1839

« **5413**

I read it[551] the first time I stayed at Gilleleie; I usually spent most of my time there strolling in a woods, and I read it aloud to the animals.

I spoke louder than the birds sang and they did not understand me. What could be more natural, then, that I began thinking of my last country holiday, when I did not need to go out for a walk to escape misunderstanding and to secure at least non-understanding for myself, and that is already something; one is actually tempted to establish a kind of freemasonry, because, after all, to be totally misunderstood by others ought to be regarded as a happy fate.

II A 817   *n.d.*, 1839

« **5414**

Venerable Sir
I went for a walk this afternoon at 6 o'clock

Get up, dear, put on your boots and cover yourself from the bottom up with leather and wander away from your home and your ancestral city and for a brief hour be a foreigner in Reitzel's shop. And he put on his boots and was away from his home, and he said: Dear, if I found favor in your eyes.[552] . . . . .

II A 818   *n.d.*, 1839

« **5415**

Addition to 5414 (II A 818):
my style *non solum claudicat*
like the progenitor of the Jews,

prorsus
sed omnino judaizat.[553]

II A 819   *n.d.*, 1839

« **5416**

Addition to 5414 (II A 818):
I do not suffer merely as Tantalus[554] did—at every moment I am not only faint from hunger but at the very same moment I am almost *surfeited.*

II A 820   *n.d.*, 1839

« **5417**

What is truth—that is the question which for me still continues to stand as a heading of a very thick, very well-bound book—with blank
                                                                                        only   unhappy
pages. Up until now the truth I have found has not had happy results for me. After my houseman by entering my bedroom had intimated that it was already day, after he had given me a brief summary of the

events of the day and the night (unfortunately there was nothing like a fire, for example, and I could well understand that I had slept so soundly, because the night had been so unusually boring), had *prepared* my mind (waked it from its slumbers) for the question of the day, one of the most difficult and important and crucial problems for just about the whole internal economy—procuring the necessary store of fire-wood for the winter—after I had listened to my highly trusted houseman's report on the preliminary investigation of the weather, an investigation I listened to sitting up in bed because of its unusual importance and interest as well as the *Umsicht* with which it was treated (for less important matters I usually lie stretched out), he thought with all certainty that he dared propose that the wood purchase take place today. Meanwhile, since I was unable advantageously and profitably to contemplate the heavens from my prone position, I decided to get up and scan the sky.

I decided not to buy it as I could see that it was definitely going to rain.

I went out for a walk and got sopping wet.

II A 821   *n.d.*, 1839

« **5418**

[Notes[555] on the doctrine of the Lord's Supper, also on the power of the keys (confession, penance, absolution), and Church government, in the early Church, Catholicism, and Protestantism.]

II C 33   *n.d.*, 1839–40

« **5419**

[Texts[556] in Danish from the Prophets, Psalms, and the Book of Tobit.]

II C 36   *n.d.*, 1839–40

« **5420**

While the one great world-historical development (the pagan) relaxes or takes pride in its *nil admirari,*[557] the other (the Jewish) begins with "*admirari,*" with אֱלֹהֵן (from an Arabian *radix admirari*).[558]

II A 560   September 11, 1839

« **5421**

The expression "at last,"[559] which appears in all our collects, is the most epically momentous and most lyrically impatient expression, the truly Christian Watchword.

II A 561   September 11, 1839

« **5422**

I am good at keeping secrets, because I forget them just as soon as I hear them.

                                                    II A 565   *n.d.*, 1839

« **5423**

Of my relation to my surroundings here at home, I can *now* say with Jacob:[560] I saw Laban's face, and, lo, it was not disposed toward me as it was yesterday or the day before yesterday.

                                                    II A 567   *n.d.*, 1839

« **5424**

The Old Testament "Jehovah" is the true παιδαγωγός[561] and pedagogical bedrock: "I am that I am, go and lead my people Israel out of Egypt";[562] we with our officious talkativeness can all benefit from a period of being subordinate.

                                                    II A 572   September 17, 1839

« **5425**

I feel utterly shattered these days, so that my relationship to Christianity seems destined to become altogether agonizing: ἵνα φανερωθῇ τὰ ἔργα τοῦ θεοῦ ἐν αυτῷ[563] (John 9:3), just as with the *man blind from birth.*

                                                    II A 574   September 23, 1839

« **5426**

See page 9 at bottom [i.e., II A 385].

The great poetic power of folk literature is expressed in various ways, also in the intensity of its craving and coveting (in comparison with which the covetousness of our age is simultaneously so sinful and tedious because it always craves and covets *what belongs to the neighbor*); this covetousness, on the other hand, is very conscious that the neighbor no more possesses what it seeks than it does itself, and therefore it does not need to desire what is his, and if it gets what it desires, it will have a superabundance for the whole world, and if eventually it covets sinfully, it will nevertheless tower so imposingly over the chicken-thieves of our time, since it is so scandalous and titanesque, that it inevitably must at least shake people up, and in its descriptions it does not allow anything to be scaled down by the cold calculation of probability and pedestrian understanding. D. Juan still glides across the stage with his 1,003 mistresses and no one smiles at it, but if this were created in our time it would be laughed to scorn; no one dares do it, out of respect and deference for tradition no one dares do it; indeed, one is carried away by it *momentant,* although in the next moment he is ashamed that this enthusiasm has "made a fool of him".[564]

II A 575   *n.d.,* 1839

« 5427 *Childhood*

> Halb Kinderspiele,
> Halb Gott im Herzen.[565]
>   Goethe

II A 802   *n.d.,* 1838

« 5428 *Youth*

> Begging—that is not our way!
> Youth on the road of life
> Lustily seizes the treasure.
>   Christian Winther[566]

II A 803   *n.d.,* 1838

« 5429 *Twenty-five Years Old*

> ..... So lass uns leben,
> Wir beten, sing'n, erzählen uns Geschichten
> Und lachen über goldne Schmetterlinge;
> Wir hören Neuigkeiten von dem Hof
> Aus armer Schlucker Munde, schwätzen mit,
> Wer wohl gewinnt, verliert, wer steigt, wer fällt,
> Wir sprechen von geheimnissvollen Dingen,
> Als ob wir in das Tiefste sie durchschauten;
> Und so in unserm Kerker überleben
> Wir alle Secten und Partei'n der Grossen,
> Die mit des Mondes Wechsel sich verändern.
>   King Lear[567]

II A 804   *n.d.,* 1838

« 5430

Addition to 5429 (II A 804):
Then it was that the great earthquake occurred, the frightful upheaval which suddenly drove me to a new infallible principle for interpreting all the phenomena. Then I surmised that my father's

old-age was not a divine blessing, but rather a curse, that our family's exceptional intellectual capacities were only for mutually harrowing one another; then I felt the stillness of death deepen around me, when I saw in my father an unhappy man who would survive us all, a memorial cross on the grave of all his personal hopes. A guilt must rest upon the entire family, a punishment of God must be upon it: it was supposed to disappear, obliterated by the mighty hand of God, erased like a mistake, and only at times did I find a little relief in the thought that my father had been given the heavy duty of reassuring us all with the consolation of religion, telling us that a better world stands open for us even if we lost this one, even if the punishment the Jews always called down on their enemies should strike us: that remembrance of us would be completely *obliterated,* that there would be no trace of us.[568]

II A 805   n.d.,   1838

« **5431**

Addition to 5430 (II A 805):

Inwardly shattered as I was, with no prospect of leading a happy life on this earth ("that it might go well with me and I might live long on this earth"), devoid of all hope for a pleasant, happy future—as this naturally proceeds from and is inherent in the historical continuity of home and family life—what wonder then that in despairing desperation I seized hold of the intellectual side of man exclusively, hung on to that, with the result that the thought of my eminent mental faculties was my only comfort, ideas my only joy, and men of no importance to me.[569]

II A 806   n.d.,   1838

« **5432**

Much of my suffering occurred because the doubt, concern, and restlessness, which my real self wanted to forget in order to form a view of the world, my reflective self seemed to try to impress upon me and sustain, partly as a necessary and partly as an interesting feature of transition, in the fear that I might have shammed a result.

For example, now when my life has shaped up in such a way that it seems that I am destined to study for the examination[570] *in perpetuum* and that no matter how long I live I will never get beyond the point where I once voluntarily stopped (just as one occasionally sees mentally deranged people who forget their whole intermediate life and remember only their childhood, or forget everything but one single moment in their lives)—it seems that the very thought of being a student of theology must remind me simultaneously of that happy period of possibilities (which might be called one's preexistence) and of my stopping there, feeling somewhat like the child who does not grow because he had been given alcohol. Now when my energetic self tries to forget it in order to act, my reflective self wants very much to hang on to it, because it seems interesting, and, as reflection raises itself to the power of a universal consciousness, abstracts from my personal consciousness.[571]

II A 807   *n.d.*, 1838

« **5433**

[Almost word for word the piece incorporated among the *"Diapsalmata"* in *Either/Or*, I: "How strangely sad I felt"—etc.][572]

II A 824   December 20, 1839

« **5434**

And you, too, my *lucida intervalla*,[573] I must bid farewell, and you, my thoughts, imprisoned in my head, I can no longer let you go strolling in the cool of the evening, but do not be discouraged, learn to know one another better, associate with one another, and I will no doubt be able to slip off occasionally and peek in on you—Au revoir![574]
S.K.
formerly Dr. Exstaticus[575]

II A 576   December 20, 1839

« **5435**

[Exegesis[576] in Danish and Latin of Romans 9–16, based partially on F. A. G. Tholuck, *Auslegung des Briefes Pauli an die Römer.* Berlin: 1824.]

II C 9   *n.d.*, 1839–40

« **5436**

[Exegesis[577] in Danish of parallel passages from the Pentateuch, the Prophets, Psalms, and Acts 1–4, 7, 8.]

II C 10   *n.d.*, 1839–40

III. CRISIS AND DECISION
1840–1842

« 5437 *Fantasies for a Coach Horn**

Goodbye, you, my home
Goodbye, accept my greetings.

Greetings to you, mighty nature, with your fugitive beauty. It is not you I want, it is the memory of you. In vain do you stop me along my way. You must bow beneath the mighty power of destiny, which rolls over you and with every turn of the wheel gives birth to the fate that for you is irresistible.[578]

III A 15   n.d., 1840

« 5438

Addition to 5437 (III A 15):

*I am not especially musical, and it is the only instrument I sometimes play, and since there now seems to be a desire to replace the coach horn with a regular trumpet and to have the mail-coach driver take an examination in performance, it is high time to give a valedictory. It is a shame that the transportation authorities cannot get birds to perform certain soulful pieces instead of this ridiculous chirping and cocky chattering from which no one can learn a thing or get any genuine and elevating satisfaction—moreover, retired journalists and other has-beens could be placed in the various forest districts as echoes. No doubt a consequence of this would be that it would not always be so punctual, for example, when Echo is somewhere else on a visit, but one could at least hear something worth hearing, for each district ought to have certain characteristic renditions, and since one would know beforehand what would be performed in a particular district, everyone could travel according to his own taste. But I do not deny that it would be an inconvenient job to have to leap out of bed whenever some hare-brained German wanted to make sure that there was an Echo. Then, too, they would have to be very competent linguistically, lest they be asked questions in a language they did not under-

stand, very attentive, too, lest there be confusion as to meaning and
it be all too frequently necessary to say: I beg your pardon—.

III A 16   *n.d.,*   1840

« **5439**

Addition to 5437 (III A 15):
Greetings and salutations, you village beauty, [you] young girl,
inquisitively sticking your head out the window; fear not, I will not
disturb your peace; just look straight at me so that I will not completely
forget you.

III A 17   *n.d.,*   1840

« **5440**

Addition to 5439 (III A 17):
Greeting and salutations, you winged tenants of the sky, you who
so easily ascend to regions the rest of us strive with all our might and
main to reach—

III A 18   *n.d.,*   1840

« **5441**

Addition to 5439 (III A 17):
Superficiality is so characteristic of travelers; that is why, when the
coachman blows his horn, they usually say he is blowing the fat off the
soup.

III A 19   *n.d.,*   1840

« **5442**

Addition to 5437 (III A 15):
Wake up, arise, dress up in all your glory! It is not you who in fickle
flight will rush past over our heads; you will remain; it is we who swiftly
will glide past you.

III A 20   *n.d.,*   1840

« **5443 *Melodrama for the Coach Horn***

But do spare me
the perpetual tooting.

III A 21   *n.d.,*   1840

« **5444**

There is no one I would rather have fall down or be blocked by
the drawbridge Knippelsbro[579] than those bustling businessmen who

have so exceedingly much to do in the world; whereas the rest of us, if Knippelsbro is raised, find it a convenient opportunity to meditate—

III A 22   *n.d.*, 1840

« **5445**

Those who are called in the eleventh hour—[580]

III A 31   *n.d.*, 1840

« **5446**

I have always been charged with using long parentheses. Studying for my final examination[581] is the longest parenthesis I have experienced.

III A 35   *n.d.*, 1840

« **5447**

Somewhere in England there is a gravestone with only these words on it: The Unhappiest.[582] I can imagine that someone would read it and think that no one at all lies buried there but that it was destined for him.

III A 40   *n.d.*, 1840

« **5448**

Troels Lund[583] told that once as a lad, during a visit with an older Lund, he wanted very much to get hold of a pipe before going for a walk in the woods and was able to borrow one. At that time the object of all his desires was to own a pipe. Twenty years later he received the same pipe as a gift—alas, how much he had wished for since that time!

III A 42   *n.d.*, 1840

« **5449**

Unfortunately I am too intelligent not to feel the anguish of knowledge, too deficient to feel its blessedness—and the knowledge which leads to salvation and the salvation which leads to knowledge of the truth have so far remained a secret to me.

III A 44   *n.d.*, 1840

« **5450**

Nyhavn 282,[584] the Charlottenborg side—

III A 50   *n.d.*, 1840

« **5451**

July 17[585]

Kallundborg—

On board the smack.[586] How dreadfully boring the conversation usually is when one has to be together with others this way for such a long time; just as toothless old people have to turn food over and over in the mouth, a certain comment is repeated again and again until finally it has to be spit out. There were four clergymen along, and although the crossing lasted eight or nine hours (for me an eternity), the experienced passengers found it to be unusually swift, and this gave all the clergymen the occasion first to comment individually that skippers usually did not care to have clergymen on board because their presence brought headwinds and that the truth of this observation was now demolished, and then at the end of the crossing to join in full chorus to establish it as a principle that all this about headwinds was not so. Vainly did I stretch the sails of my organs of hearing to capture a light breeze; a dead calm prevailed. From all four directions one heard only that skippers did not care to have clergymen on board (which shows what a dubious good the dissolution of parish bounda-ries[587] is, for the fact that there was complete parish freedom on board the smack and I could listen to whichever clergyman I wanted to did not help in the least). Since each of the clergymen seemed equally interested and justified in being the owner of this story, none of them of course would grant another a *privilegium exclusivum*.[588] —I had hoped that I would become seasick, or, failing that, that all the other passen-gers would be seasick. There is something special about watching people go on board for a sea journey. A journey at sea is like a minia-ture of all human life. People come on board from the most varied circumstances and occupations, but one common danger confronts them all (I am not thinking of the possible sinking of the ship): becom-ing seasick. The thought of it is the sounding board for the whole thing, the keynote that sounds in everything, whether it is expressed in a certain solemn taciturnity or in a forced liveliness or in an over-bearing cheerfulness; the specific in all these moods is their relation to this one thought, and this accounts for the tragi-comedy. Just as death is the infinite humorist who takes in everything (while man's humor, on the other hand, is always limited, because even in its most desperate form it always has a line beyond which it cannot go, the greatness of which it must acknowledge)—digests everything with equal ease: a king and a beggar, one who shrieks and howls and one who bears his cross in silence—just so does the comic element in seasickness consist in the fact that all earthly relativity, from which no one can completely emancipate himself, is here suspended, and the greatest contrasts lie alongside each other without any petty jealousy. But precisely because death has this enormous earnestness, it is itself the illumination in which great passions, both good and evil, are transparent, no longer limited by the external; this explains the love which expresses itself so touchingly because it is present in its extreme opposite, in separation. C. Boesen[589] told me of a young girl who accompanied her married sister and her children on the ship; the married sister suffered the cramps of seasickness; the young girl was seasick herself but tried to keep going in order to help the children. Here love was certainly present, and perhaps just as strong as it was true, for it certainly takes great strength to overcome the tedium of seasickness so that one can concern himself about others; but love moved in an imperfect medium, for precisely in its transitory character seasickness is so trivial that it is impossible to remain properly serious when one thinks of a young girl constantly interrupted in her loving solicitude by—vomiting.

III A 51 July 17, 1851

« **5452**

Aarhuus,[590] July 18[591]
Life in these country towns is just as wretched, ridiculous, and *abgeschmakt*[592] as the gait assumed in walking the streets. It is useless to try to appear dignified (for to walk and meditate is absolutely impossible; the meditation itself would turn out to be nothing but dashes) —and then when one considers that he is the object of this typical country-town curiosity—

III A 52 July 18, 1840

« **5453**

N.B. Anders[593] at the review of the troops.[594]—Kalløe Castle and Marsk Stig.[595] ("King Mastix")—Knebel:[596] the three hills. —The visit to Aarhuus Cathedral; the organ. —The ravenous hunger of market towns for "news from the capital"; they have no independent life like that of the country, which is especially attractive to someone like me who travels in order *to forget.*

III A 53 *n.d.*, 1840

« **5454**

I am so listless and dismal that I not only have nothing which fills my soul, but I cannot conceive of anything that could possibly satisfy it—alas, not even the bliss of heaven.

III A 54   *n.d.,* 1840

« **5455**

To you, O God, we turn for peace . . . . . but give us also the blessed assurance that nothing shall be able to take this peace from us, *not we ourselves,* not our foolish, earthly desires, my wild lusts, not my heart's restless craving![597]

III A 55   *n.d.,* 1840

« **5456**

My total mental and spiritual impotence at present is terrible precisely because it is combined with a consuming longing, with an intellectual-spiritual burning—and yet so formless that I do not even know what it is I need.

III A 56   *n.d.,* 1840

« **5457** *The Tramp; the Vagabond*

A young man born in Christiansfeldt of a prosperous father who brought him up very strictly; he became dissolute; the father finally washed his hands of him; he went to Germany and took to the highways as a vagabond. Came back in a few years, went to Fyn where a venerable clergyman exhorted him to see the error of his ways; this helped; he stayed with him for a time, was treated very kindly, if not as a member of the family still not as a domestic servant, ate in his own room, etc. Handsome fellow that he was, as he worked in the garden one day he attracted the attention of an old colonel who was visiting the pastor. He wanted to have him as a servant. Prevailed upon him to do so. Now a new life began for the young man. The colonel was a bachelor and, as is not unusual for the elderly, became very fond of him, and it was not long before the young man became everything to him and altogether indispensable. —Two years went by in this way.

One morning the colonel rings as usual, but no one comes; the old man becomes uneasy, goes to the young man's room, where he finds a letter addressed to him, begging his forgiveness: "but my walking stick has once again become too warm in my hand and I yearn for the German highways." No one has heard anything from him since then.

In connection with this I have a mind to use as a final episode the incident from Viborg prison that Mrs. Boesen[598] told to me in Knebel.

She and her husband visited the prison. In a separate cell they found five or six adult gypsies (about 25 to 30 years old) who were being taught the alphabet in order to be prepared for confirmation. C. Boesen asked the teacher who was the smartest of them, and he pointed to one of them, whereupon C. encouraged him to persevere in his efforts "since, after all, he had nothing on his conscience and the prospect of becoming a useful citizen was now opening up for him in so many ways." They left the cell and wondered a little when the jailer locked up again and shut the teacher up with his pupils. They asked the jailer why and learned to their amazement that the teacher was also a prisoner who formerly had been a private tutor but had stolen money from a safe. C. B. now realized the significance of his words, since they must have been very mortifying to the teacher, who, seen from this standpoint, must have had a good deal on his conscience.– I will now try to imagine that this teacher was my tramp.

III A 57   *n.d.*, 1840

« **5458**

On Mols [. . . . .][599]

III A 58   *n.d.*, 1840

« **5459**

The consciousness of sin ought not to be volatilized by careless observations about a *commune naufragium*[600] anymore than it ought to be constricted into a despairing stare at what for the individual is self-inflicted; it should not degenerate into self-torment as if therein lay a kind of perfection. Just as the mind ought to be ready and willing to bear the dispensations of fate also when they appear as self-inflicted consequences, so a person ought to be assured that power will be given to him to bear them—but how can the individual be convinced that he will get power to bear a burden when it is one he has laid upon himself with his own hand and he therefore must strive *proprio marte*[601]–?

III A 59   *n.d.*, 1840

« **5460**

Socrates [. . . . .][602]

III A 60   *n.d.*, 1840

« **5461**

The trouble with me is that when I was pregnant with ideas I was hypnotized by the ideal; that is why I give birth to deformities, and actuality does not conform to my burning longings—and may God grant that this will not be true also of love, for there too I have a secret anxiety that an ideal has been confused with an actuality.[603] God forbid! As yet this is not so.

But this anxiety makes me eager to know the future and yet I fear it!—

III A 64   *n.d.*, 1840

« **5462**

Sailing down the Gudenaa[604] to Albæk; visiting Støvringgaard Manor;[605] the evening light.

III A 65   *n.d.*, 1840

« **5463**

I have been considering preaching for the first time in the church at Sæding, and it would have to be next Sunday.[606] To my surprise I see that the text is Mark 8:1–10 (feeding the 4,000), and the words "How can one feed these men with bread here in the desert?" struck me, since I will be speaking in the poorest parish on the Jutland heath.

III A 66   *n.d.*, 1840

« **5464**

The visit at Hald;[607] the carefree old man I met who lay on his back in the heather with only a stick in his hand. He accompanied me to the Non Mill. We came to a stream called Koldbæk; he assured me that it was the most delicious water in the whole region, whereupon he went down to it, lay full length on his stomach and drank from it. We continued on our way, and he confided to me that he actually had started out with the intention of begging.

What a happy fellow! So unconcerned as he slept there in the heather, so content refreshing himself there with the cold water. Suppose he slept a little too long, what of it, he was not playing the stock market . . . . . and when he arrives at his destination, he will greet the family, talk about the hard times, lament "that he did not get to talk to the king[608] in Viborg, since there was no one who got less than two rix-dollars";[609] he is then ushered into the servants' hall. People come home from the fields and food is served. The conversation centers on all that has taken place in the household, and while he satisfies his hunger he skims for an hour the cream of that meager stock of events (for compared to more complicated historical lives the still life is like Swiss cows compared to Holstein cows: they give less but better tasting milk—what aroma lingers over the sparse events of quiet domestic life). After that he rambles home, perhaps lying down to sleep along the way.

And this is the life we are brought up to disdain! And what a life the rest of us lead, whether we toil and moil[610] or whether by sleeping we have more than we need! The earth no longer yields by itself what human life needs for sustenance, but nevertheless does not such a life remind us most of our paradisal origin? Even the motto under which life goes: "In God's Name." Is it not an incantation which gets in a supernatural way what cannot be gotten in a natural way? And is not the soul precisely by means of this way of life set free and emancipated from the tyranny in which superfluity binds us, no less than poverty?

Moreover, there are several stages in this life. This is the simplest. Others represent more individual features of the poetic: fiddlers, masters in story-telling, in currying favor, etc. These give recompense, as it were, for *usus fructus*.[611] After all, is it not this life in all its forms which has pledged to possess nothing but which retains only *usus fructus*—?

I did not like it that the good fellow wanted to kiss my hand because I gave him a mark. I would have preferred more bold confidence.—

(On the way I met an old woman carrying a cradle on her back. I could not help thinking of those old creatures who are poetry's dry nurses for children, dispensing to them the mother's milk of poetry. But I was mistaken, for although she seemed to know Hald from the old days, it turned out that she was acquainted with only a seventy- to eighty-year period.)

My beggar, however, was well-informed. When I asked him who had owned Hald long ago, he answered that it went back to very old times. I already had some misgivings and was afraid that this, too, would turn out to be seventy years, but then he told the story of Mr. Bugge[612] who for seven years was besieged in Hald and at last had but one cow left, which was led out to water every day covered with a different hide. A poor old woman was admitted into the stronghold and came back with abundant gifts and assured the enemy that Hald could last out seven more years of siege without being starved out.

III A 67   *n.d.,* 1840

« 5465

Hundrup[613] told me about a luckless genius, a poor, addicted elementary school teacher named Andresen,[614] who went around to the most common, ordinary places and showed off his mathematical proficiency. One time in just such a place he met a traveler, whom he promptly nabbed, and exhibited his skills in a number of sharp mathematical calculations on the condition of free board as his reward. When he had finished and the traveler, who actually had enjoyed his performance, asked how much he should pay him for his board, he answered: four shillings, two shillings for beer and two shillings for brandy.

III A 69   *n.d.,* 1840

« 5466

Everywhere when I arrive in a country town the first one I meet is a man beating a drum and loudly proclaiming some important news or other—for example in Aarhuus: that because of the torrential rainstorm the streets are to be swept. How important everything is in these small towns. In Holstebro there was target-shooting, which had already gone on for one day. I wish the honorable inhabitants of Holstebro success so that this rare entertainment might last at least eight days. The bird did seem to be very tough and tenacious, for although the wing was shot off (at least the prize was bestowed upon the lucky winner), it still sat there. The town judge was present in all his high distinction and made microscopic observations by means of a telescope. The only thing the town lacked was an official newspaper to publish the results. Anders[615] was just as highly entertained by the review of the troops in Aarhuus as by the Shooting Society in Holstebro, since they marched out onto the field with drums beating and flags flying. The king arrived in Viborg too late one night and therefore the assembled inhabitants did not go to bed but sat up like the wise virgins. The queen arrived at 2:30 A.M., and then the torches were lighted. Up till now in each of the country towns where I have been after the king's visit, the inhabitants have maintained they know from a very reliable source that nowhere had he enjoyed himself as much as with them.

In Holstebro,[616] the Jerusalem of drygoods merchants, I of course thought of father.[617] I met the old man Fell[618] who had been in partnership with Troels Lund.[619]

When we passed the church in Idum[620] the coachman told me that the pastor's name was Giedde,[621] whereupon I got off to greet him. My reception was somewhat cool, and although I did not know his family I had by no means expected anything like this. It proved, however, to be a mistake, for the pastor's name was *Gjeding*.[622]

III A 71   n.d., 1840

« **5467**

The girls here in the Ringkjøbing region go around in men's hats. It looks very affected. As I passed by I saw one of them run out into the field. She could have been taken for a man, but her walk betrayed that it was a woman. In the afternoon I met one of them and expected to have the pleasure of her taking off her hat to me so that I could take mine off in return.

III A 72   n.d., 1840

« **5468**

I sit here all alone (I have frequently been just as alone many times, but I have never been so aware of it) and count the hours until I shall see Sæding. I cannot recall any change in my father, and now I am about to see the places where as a poor boy he tended sheep, the places for which, because of his descriptions, I have been so homesick. What if I were to get sick and be buried in the Sæding churchyard![623] What a strange idea! His last wish[624] for me is fulfilled—is that actually to be the sum and substance of my life? In God's name! Yet in relation to what I owed to him the task was not so insignificant. I learned from him what fatherly love is, and through this I gained a conception of divine fatherly love, the one single unshakable thing in life, the true Archimedean point.

III A 73   n.d., 1840

« **5469**

I would like to know what a young girl [. . . . .][625]

III A 74   n.d., 1840

« 5470

Here in Sæding parish there is a house in which it is said there lived a man who at the time of the plague survived everyone else and buried them.[626] He dug deep furrows in the heather and buried the bodies in long rows.

III A 75   *n.d.,* 1840

« 5471

Just as it is customary to say: *nulla dies sine linea*,[627] so can I say of this journey: *nulla dies sine lacryma*.[628]

III A 77   *n.d.,* 1840

« 5472

The cows in Aarhuus, Randers, etc., are actually much more cultured than in Copenhagen (they know how to find their way home by themselves and the like). This accounts for the fact that people speak of them with a certain deference, as did my coachman from Salten. When I asked about the kind of cattle grazing there, he answered: "Those are all Aarhuus cows."

III A 79   *n.d.,* 1840

« 5473

It seems as if I really must experience opposites. After staying for three days with my impoverished aunt,[629] almost like Ulysses' cronies with Circe, the very first place I visited after that was so overcrowded with counts and barons that it was terrible. I spent the night in Them[630] and the evening as well as the morning in the company of Count Ahlefeldt,[631] who invited me to visit him at Langeland. The only acquaintance I met today was my noble old friend Rosenørn.[632]

III A 80   *n.d.,* 1840

« 5474

The parish clerk[633] in Sæding made a very solemn farewell speech to me, assuring me that from my father's gift[634] he perceived that he must have been a friend of education and I could rest assured that *he* would work for it in Sæding parish.

III A 81   *n.d.,* 1840

« **5475**

There is, however, an equilibrium in the world. To the one God gave joys, to the other tears and permission to rest every once in a while in his embrace—and yet the divine reflects itself far more beautifully in the tear-dimmed eye, just as the rainbow is more beautiful than the clear blue sky.

III A 83   *n.d.*, 1840

« **5476**

How glorious the sound of the dragoons blowing assembly; it seems as if I already heard the hoofbeats as they charged—listen, they are victorious, the cry of victory whistles through the air! —And yet, what are all other calls compared to the one the archangel will someday blow: "Awake, you who sleep, the Lord is coming!"[635]

III A 84   *n.d.*, 1840

« **5477**

My Regine!

To

Our own little Regine

S.K.

Such a line under a word serves to direct the typesetter to space out that particular word. To space out means to pull the words apart from one another. Therefore, when I space out the words above, I intend to pull them *s o   v e r y   f a r   a p a r t* that a typesetter presumably would lose his patience and very likely would never set type again in his life.

Your S.K.

[Address:[636]]
To
Miss Regine Olsen[637]

Letters, no. 15   *n.d.*

« **5478**

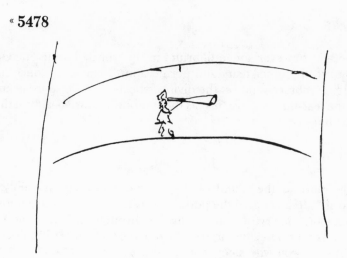

My Regine!

This is the Knippelsbro.[638] I am that person with the spyglass. As you know, figures appearing in a landscape are apt to look somewhat curious. You may take comfort, therefore, in the fact that I do not look quite that ugly and that every artistic conception always retains something of the ideal, even in caricature. Several art experts have disagreed as to why the painter has not provided any background whatsoever. Some have thought this an allusion to a folk tale about a man who so completely lost himself in the enjoyment of the view from Knippelsbro that at last he saw nothing but the picture produced by his own soul and which he could just as well have been looking at in a dark room. Others have thought that it was because he lacked the perspective necessary for drawing—houses. But the spyglass itself has a unique characteristic about which tradition tells us the following: the outermost lens is of mirror glass[639] so that when one trains it on *Trekroner* and stands on the left side of the bridge at an angle of 5° off Copenhagen, one sees something quite different from what is seen by all the other people about one; thus, in the midst of a friendly chat about the view of the ships, one sees or thinks that one sees, or hopes to see, or wishes to see, or despairs of seeing that which the secret *genie* of the spyglass reveals to him who understands how to use it correctly. Only in the proper hands and for the proper eye is it a divine telegraph; for everybody else it is a useless contrivance. Yesterday your brother scolded me for always speaking of *my* cobbler, *my* fruit dealer, *my* grocer, *my* coachman, etc., etc., etc. By this means he seems to have accused me of a predominant use of the first-person possessive pronoun. Only you know of *your* faithful friend that I am not extensively but intensively much more given to the use of the second-person possessive pronoun. Indeed, how could he know that, how could any person at all—as I am only yours

Yours eternally

In testimony whereof I permit my *eternalized* P. Møller[640] to stand as witness.

Granted in *our* study.

[Address:]
To
Miss R. Olsen

Letters, no. 17   *n.d.*

« **5479**

My Regine!

Es endet Schmerz
So wie der Scherz
So wie die Nacht
Eh' man's gedacht.[641]

The other day when you came to see me you told me that when you were confirmed your father had presented you with a bottle of lily of the valley (*Extrait double de Muguet*). Perhaps you thought that I did not hear this, or perhaps you thought that it had slipped by my ear like so much else that finds no response within. But not at all! But as that flower conceals itself so prettily within its big leaf, so I first allowed the plan of sending you the enclosed to conceal itself in the half-transparent veil of oblivion so that, freed from every external consideration, even the most illusive, rejuvenated to a new life in comparison with which its first existence was but an earthly life, it might now exude that fragrance for which longing and memory ("from the spring of my youth")[642] are rivals. However, it was nearly impossible for me to obtain this essence in Copenhagen. Yet in this respect there is also a providence, and the *blind* god of love always finds a way. You happen to receive it at this very moment (just before you leave the house), because I know that you, too, know the infinity of the moment. I only hope it will not be too late. Hasten, my messenger, hasten my thought, and you, my Regine, pause for an instant, for only a moment stand still.

Yours eternally,
S.K.

[Address:]
To
Miss R. Olsen

Letters, no. 18   *n.d.*

« **5480**

My Regine!

I have now read so much by Plato[643] on love, but still there is one encomium on it that I value more highly than the *summa summarum* of all those by the competitors in the *Symposium*, [644] or, rather, there is a love upon which I will deliver an encomium, not at any symposium but in the stillness of the night when everybody sleeps or in the midst of noisy uproar when nobody understands me. —In the stillness of midnight, for the day does begin at midnight, and at midnight I awoke and the hours grew long for me, for what is as swift as love? Love is the swiftest of all, swifter than itself.

> *Zwei Musikanten ziehn daher,*
> *Vom Wald aus weiter Ferne,*
> *Der eine ist verliebt gar sehr,*
> *Der andre wär' es gerne.* [645]

What is here separated in two, love unites; he is in love, and yet at the same time he is constantly wishing to be so: a restiveness, a yearning, a longing make him wish at every moment to be what he already is at that very moment. It constantly outbids itself without taking notice of the fact that the only other bidder is itself, so that in a manner of speaking, it is the only bidder. In a state of blissful impatience it bids higher and higher all the time, because possession of its object is incommensurable with any worth. Like that merchant, it sells everything in order to buy the field in which the precious pearl[646] lay buried, and it wishes always to possess more in order to pay more dearly for it. Just as the merchant sighs to himself each time he contemplates his treasure: "Why could not the whole world be mine, so that I might give it away in order to acquire the treasure I won?"—so love never possesses its object in a dead and impotent way but strives at every moment to acquire what it possesses at that very moment. It never says, "Now I am safe, now I will settle down," but runs on forever, more swiftly than anything else, for it outruns itself. But this haste, this hurry, this restiveness, this yearning, this wishing, what is it but the power of love to drive out forgetfulness, stupor—death? And what would even heavenly bliss be without wishing, without the wish to possess it, for only sober understanding thinks it foolish to wish for what one possesses. But this wish is also clamoring or whispering, depending on circumstances, but never many-tongued; for if I dared to wish, then I certainly know what I would wish for, and if I dared to wish for seven things, yet I would have only one wish, notwithstanding the fact that I would gladly wish it seven times, even though I knew that it had been fulfilled the first time. And that wish is identical with my deepest conviction: that neither Death, nor Life, nor Angels, nor Principalities, nor Powers, nor the present, nor that which is to come, nor the Exalted, nor the Profound, nor any other creature may tear me from you, or you from me.[647]

> Die stehn allhier im kalten Wind
> Und singen schön und geigen:
> Ob nicht ein süssvertraumtes* Kind
> Am Fenster sich wollt' zeigen?[648]

Your
S.K.

Postscript: When you have forgotten everything that lies between, I would only ask you to read the salutation and the signature, for as I myself have become aware, it has the power to calm or to excite[649] as have but few incantations.

    *I hope this adjective may be applied to you and that you have not become too anxious at the thought that I might suddenly measure one foot between the eyes.

Letters, no. 21   n.d.

« 5481

My Regine!

    This letter has no date nor will it get one, for its principal content is the consciousness of a feeling that probably is present in me at every moment, albeit in all the different musical keys of love, and that is precisely why it is not present at any particular moment as opposed to others (not exactly at ten o'clock, not even at eleven sharp, nor on November 11 as opposed to the tenth or the twelfth). For this feeling is constantly rejuvenating itself; it is eternally young, like those books transmitted to us from the Middle Ages, which, although several hundred years old, are always "printed this year." —Today I stood on the Knippelsbro,[650] and this day does not have a date either, as there is no day when I do not undertake that expedition.

On St. Martin's Eve[651] when I failed to come at eight o'clock, I was at Fredensborg, but I cannot say yesterday or the day before yesterday, for I have no today as a point of departure. People were surprised that I drove alone. Formerly, as you know, I never drove alone, for sorrow, worry, and sadness were my faithful companions. Now those in the traveling party are fewer in number. They are memory and recollection of you when I drive out, and longing for you when I drive home again. And at Fredensborg these companions of mine meet, embrace, and kiss.[652] This is the moment I love so much, for you know that I love Fredensborg indescribably for a moment, for one moment, but only for one moment that is priceless to me.

As this letter is undated and consequently might have been written at any time, it also follows from this that it may be read at any time, and if any nocturnal doubt should assail you, you may read it even at night; for truly, if I ever doubted for a moment that I dared call you "mine" (you know how much I associate with this expression; you know this, you who wrote me yourself that your life would be *concluded* with me if I were to become separated from you; Oh, do then let it be *included* in me as long as we are united, for until then we are not truly *united*), I have never doubted for a moment, no—I write this out of the deepest conviction of my soul—indeed not even in the most obscure corner of the world shall I doubt that I am yours,

Yours eternally,
S.K.
Letters, no. 23   *n.d.*

« **5482**

My Regine!

Am I dreaming, or "comes a dream from the spring of my youth here to my easy chair"?[653] —This picture[654] belongs to you, and yet it is here now. But it finds no rest, no abiding place with me *any longer;* it yearns impatiently to take the message to you and to remain with you. She holds a flower in her hand. Is it she who gives it to him, or has she received it from him only to return it to him in order to receive it once more? No outsider knows. The wide world lies behind him; he has turned his back upon it. Stillness prevails throughout as in eternity, to which such a moment belongs. Perhaps he has sat like this for centuries; perhaps the happy moment was only a brief one and yet sufficient for an eternity. With the picture my thought also returns to its beginning, and I tear myself away, flee from everything that would imprison me in chains of sorrow, and I cry out louder than the sorrows . . . . . yet, yet, yet in all of this I am happy, indescribably happy, for I know what I possess. And when it storms and roars in the workshop of my thoughts, I listen for your voice; and when I stand in a crowd amidst noise and uproar that do not concern me, then I see the open window, and you stand in your summer dress—as once at the Schlegels —and you look and look, and the surroundings become alien to you and only contribute towards directing your attention, your soul to one point, unwaveringly with no thought for anything else, and the distance between us vanishes and you are mine, united with me, though a whole continent were to separate us.

I am enclosing a scarf. I ask you to accept it and desire that *you alone* may know that you own this trifle. When you are festively dressed (you know my opinion of that) and you sit alone waiting for me, then please indicate to me that you own it and that possession of it is not unwelcome to you.

Your
S.K.

[On the back of the enclosed picture:]

> *Es vergeht keine Stund in der Nacht,*
> *Da mein Herze nicht erwacht,*
> *Und an dich gedenkt,*
> *Dass du mir viel tausendmal*
> *Dein Herze geschenkt.*

des Knaben Wunderhorn[655]

[In Regine Olsen's handwriting:]

> And if my arm doth give such pleasure,
>   Such comfort and such ease;
> Then, handsome merman, hasten;
>   Come take them both—oh, please.[656]

Letters, no. 27   *n.d.*

« **5483**

Wednesday,[657] December 30

My Regine!

In order to convince you that your box is not used for tobacco but rather serves as a sort of temple archive, I send you the enclosed document.[658]

Today I reminded you of that Wednesday[659] when I *approached* you for the second time in my life. Even the weather recalled that memory to my soul, just as a winter day occasionally may evoke the thought of a summer day quite vividly by virtue of a certain similarity that has its basis in dissimilarity. I felt so unspeakably lighthearted. I drove to Lyngbye,[660] not as I usually do, somber and dejected, carelessly flung in a corner of the carriage seat. I sat in the middle of the seat, uncommonly straight, not with my head bent low, and looked about me happily and confidently. I was immensely pleased to see everybody. I greeted them with mingled feelings, as if each person possessed at once both the sacred solemnity of old friendship and the seductive charm of new acquaintance. In the parsonage I heaped flattery on everybody; we swam in a surfeit. I enjoyed being extravagant, because I felt myself stirred by something far exalted above flatter. . . . . . But today this recollection affected you painfully. You misunderstood me. Allow me then to relate another tale that also took place on a Wednesday. The event occurs in historical time, and therefore I shall date it. It was on Wednesday, November 18, 1840, that you told me that you had expected a letter from me. At first I only wanted to reply in kind by saying that it was really more appropriate for me to receive than to write a letter. Your remarks about the difficulty in getting to write and having your letter posted came as pure and good seed sown in soil that had been properly weeded (for you remember that I said that the thought of those difficulties had suddenly occurred to me and that this thought instantly became my best, most faithful companion who would never leave my side), and now a rich (the Latinist says *laeta*, that is, joyful) abundance bloomed where formerly a cold wind had swept across naked fields. You told me that you had thought of bringing the letter yourself. Then I saw you, and I see you just as clearly, just as vividly at this moment. You walk quietly and meekly, your eyes on the ground, and only occasionally do you lift your gaze filled with peace and bliss to heaven. You walk unperturbed and undisturbed by your worldly surroundings with your thought focused on only one object, as a devout pilgrim in the service of love. Unnoticed you make your way (I see everything in the mind's eye), nobody bows respectfully to the halo around your head, but neither does anyone compassionately pity you (perhaps you remember that you spoke about Alberg's family);[661] only one person sees you, only one understands you, but neither will he permit you to undertake this pilgrimage, not even in the spirit. And when you sometimes bow your head sadly, then he knows that the spirit is willing, then he hastens to meet you, then he feels, my Regine, that you have conquered him, then he wishes to try you no more; and although the struggle was very brief and although he may with a slight change say like Caesar, "I came, I saw, *she* conquered,"[662] the joy shall be no less long-lasting.

Your
S.K.

The enclosed manuscript represents a wreath and an eye that looks at that wreath.

Letters, no. 29   December 30, 1840

« 5484 *Preface*

Its significance. Probably it is irrelevant to the dissertation[663] but it is a necessary factor in the personality.

See EE, p. 18 [i.e., II A 432]

I have worked on this dissertation with fear and trembling lest my dialectic swallow too much. . . .

III B 2   n.d., 1840–41

« 5485

We read: And God tested Abraham,[664] and he said to him: Abraham, and Abraham answered: Here I am. We ought to note in particular the trusting and God-devoted disposition, the bold confidence in confronting the test, in freely and undauntedly answering: Here I am. Is it like that with us, or are we not rather eager to evade the severe trials when we see them coming, wish for a remote corner of the world in which to hide, wish that the mountains would conceal us, or impatiently try to roll the burden off our shoulders and onto others; or even those who do not try to flee—how slowly, how reluctantly they drag their feet. Not so with Abraham, he answers undauntedly: Here I am. He does not trouble anyone with his suffering, neither Sarah, who he knew very well would be grief-stricken over losing Isaac, nor Eliezer, the faithful servant in his house, with whom, if with anyone, he certainly might have sought consolation. We read: He arose early in the morning. He hurried as if to a jubilant festival, and by daybreak he was at Moria, the place designated by the Lord. And he cut the wood for the fire, and he bound Isaac, and he lighted the fire, and he drew the knife. My listener, there was many a father in Israel who believed that to lose his child was to lose everything that was dear to him, to be robbed of every hope for the future, but there was no one who was the child of promise in the sense Isaac was to Abraham. There was many a father who had had that loss, but since it was always, after all, God's almighty and inscrutable governance, since it was God who personally obliterated, as it were, the promise given, he was obliged to say with Job:[665] The Lord gave, the Lord took away. Not so with Abraham—he was commanded to do it with his own hand. The fate of Isaac was laid in Abraham's hand together with the knife. And here he stood on the mountain early in the morning, the old man with his one and only hope. But he did not doubt; he looked neither to the right nor to the left; he did not challenge heaven with his complaints. He knew it was the weightiest sacrifice God could ask, but he also knew that nothing was too great for God. Of course, we all know the outcome of the story. Perhaps it does not amaze us anymore, because we have known it from our earliest childhood, but then the fault does not really lie in the truth, in the story, but in ourselves, because we are too lukewarm genuinely to feel with Abraham and to suffer with him. He went home happy, confident, trusting in God, for he had not wavered, he had nothing for which to reproach himself. If we imagine that Abraham, by anxiously and desperately looking around, discovered the ram that would save his son, would he not then have gone home in disgrace, without confidence in the future, without the self-assurance that he was prepared to bring to God any sacrifice whatsoever, without the divine voice from heaven in his heart that proclaimed to him God's grace and love.

Nor did Abraham say: Now I have become an old man, my youth is gone, my dream has not been fulfilled; I became a man and what I yearned for you denied me, and now that I am an old man you fulfilled everything in a wonderful way. Grant me now a quiet evening; do not summon me to new battles; let me rejoice in what you gave me, in the consolation of my old age.[666]

III C 4   *n.d.*, 1840–41

« **5486** *The Upbuilding Implications of the Thought That before God We Are Always in the Wrong*[667]

Otherwise we might be tempted to despair of providence.

For if there were one man, one single man, no matter if he were the most powerful who ever lived in the world or the most humble, a man who on judgment day could justifiably say: I was not provided for, in the great household I was forgotten, or even if he put much of the blame at his own door yet could justifiably say: I acknowledge that I went astray in the world, I departed from the way of truth, but I did repent of my sin, I honestly intended and strove to the uttermost for the good, I lifted up my voice and shouted to heaven for help, but no one answered, there was no constructive solution, not even the remotest relief . . . . . if there were such a man, then everything would be foolishness, where then would the limit be.

—Anyone who has ever yielded to temptation must confess, however, that there was a possibility that in the next moment help was already at hand, and this is an observation, not a sophism, as it might seem to a despairing mind inclined to say: One can always say that.[668]

III C 5   *n.d.,* 1840–41

« **5487**

You complain about mankind, about the world's corruption. We will not decide whether or not you are right, we will admit that a far more saintly person than we are has made the same charge with far greater authority:

> There is no ground
> in act and word
> on which we now can build
> every heart is a snare
> every vow is dung
> every rogue like a child
> every promise like a shadow.[669]

But a lot depends on you yourself, for there still is a battle no one else can fight for you, a doubt that no one else can put to rest, a care that no one else can put to rest, a care and concern about God. As soon as you have found assurance about this, you will find the world to be much better, for then you will not seek in the world or demand of it what it cannot give—then you yourself will be able to comfort and reassure others.[670]

III C 8   n.d.,   1840–41

« 5488 *God's Fatherly Love*[671]

..... and if it seems to you, as your thoughts wander off from the paternal home and stray about in the wide world in order to rise to the concept of him as the almighty creator of all things and yet also the common father of all, if it seems that you still are missing some of the preferential love that was bestowed on you in your paternal home because he, your earthly father, was your only father and you were his only child, and if as a result it seems to you that the metaphor is not completely satisfactory, if you feel that such earthly representations ought not be included, well, then we admit that the metaphor falls short somewhat.

But when you yourself were anxious and troubled and went to your earthly father for consolation and assurance and found him to be downcast and sorrowful himself, so that his sorrow only augmented yours and did not alleviate it even if you momentarily forgot your own in your sympathy for his sufferings, and on the other hand when you, weak and crushed, turned your mind and your thoughts to him who cares for all and found him always powerful in weakness, the more powerful the weaker you yourself became, then, my listener, the metaphor does not quite fit, either, and you feel all the more that it does not fit you. But if in the preceding lines you felt a certain sadness about taking the best there is on earth to express the divine and it still did not reach up to heaven but along the way dissolved and disappeared before your eyes, this is now not the case, for now you have perceived that God is not called father according to the earthly designation, but that it is the other way around, that it is as scripture[672] says, that all fatherhood in heaven and on earth is named after him, the heavenly father, that the name of father does not strive upward from earth to heaven but descends from heaven to earth, so that even if you had the best father there could be on earth, he is still only your step-father, only a reflection of the father-love after which he is named, only a shadow, a reflection, a picture, a metaphor, a dim expression of the fatherliness from which all fatherhood has its name in heaven and on earth. O, my listener, I trust that you have apprehended this blessedness, or rather that my presentation has managed to make you mindful

of what you possess better, more richly and blessedly, or rather that
I have disturbed nothing for you.[673]

III C 12   *n.d.,* 1840–41

« 5489 *The Congregation as the Bride of Christ*

On the Gospel about a king who gave a wedding feast for his
son.[674] . . . . . When we think of the blessed moment when, after the
many separations, the many trials, they who love each other are finally
united.

But we must, after all, use metaphors—why not the best?[675]

III C 24   *n.d.,* 1840–41

« 5490

The only consoling thought I have is that I could lay me down to
die and then in my last hour do what I dare not do as long as I live
—confess the love which makes me just as unhappy as it makes me
happy.[676]

III A 90   *n.d.,* 1841

« 5491

O Lord, my God, give me again the courage to hope. Merciful
God, let hope once again make fertile my sterile and barren mind.

III A 91   *n.d.,* 1841

« 5492

Der heilige Franciscus ein Troubadour,[677] by J. Görres.

III A 93   *n.d.,* 1841

« 5493

Next to taking off all my clothes, owning nothing in the world, not
the least thing, and then throwing myself in the water, I find most
pleasure in speaking a foreign language, preferably a living one, in
order to become *entfremdet*[678] to myself.

III A 97   *n.d.,* 1841

« 5494

My doubt is terrible. —Nothing is able to stop me—it is an accursed
hunger—I am able to devour every argument, every consolation, and
reassurance—I rush past every obstacle with the speed of 10,000 miles
a second.

III A 103   *n.d.,* 1841

« 5495

I feel like writing a novel about a man who deals in jewels. He would have to be a Jew. His reluctance to part with these precious objects (he loves them so much that sometimes he hesitates to sell them), an immense insight into decayed prosperity and the secrets of the affluent life—this diamond has belonged to a man who at the time had over two casks of gold at his disposal. I will not identify him; he is still living, a man of prestige, but his money is all gone. The extremely painful scenes when a person like that disposes of such objects. The otherwise humble Jew feels his superiority—the malicious glimpse into his plight, the secret whispers among the Jew's associates about whether the man is totally ruined or just temporarily, etc., etc.

III A 105   *n.d.*, 1841

« 5496

In addition to my other numerous acquaintances, with whom, on the whole, I have a very formal relationship, I do have one intimate confidante—my melancholy, and in the midst of my joy, in the midst of my work, she beckons to me, calls me aside, even though physically I remain on the spot. It is the most faithful mistress I have known—no wonder, then, that I must be prepared to follow at any moment.[679]

III A 114   *n.d.*, 1841

« 5497

There is a rambling of *raisonnement*[680] which in its interminability has the same relation to the result as the incalculable lists of Egyptian kings have to the historical outcome.[681]

III A 115   *n.d.*, 1841

« 5498 *Lines for a Girl Who Has Been Seduced*

. . . . . spare me your pity—you understand neither my sorrow nor my joy—I still love him so much that I have but one wish: to be young again and to be seduced by him once again.[682]

III A 116   *n.d.*, 1841

« 5499

I journeyed to Fredensborg with two absolutely incredible horses —when they were supposed to stand, they fell down; when they were supposed to get up, they needed support; when they went slowly, they limped; but when they set off in a fast trot, they were the best runners

imaginable—it is the same with me, once I get started no one can keep
up with me.

III A 121   n.d., 1841

« **5500**

Addition to 5499 (III A 121):
On the floor of the empty carriage lay five or six kernels of oats
which danced to the vibrations and formed the strangest patterns—I
fell to pondering over it.

III A 122   n.d., 1841

« **5501**

R
..... and I loved her so much, she was light as a bird, as bold as
an idea, I let her ascend higher and higher, I reached out my hand and
she rested on it and fluttered her wings, and she called down to me:
It is glorious up here. She forgot, she did not know, that it was I who
made her light, I who gave her boldness of thought, that it was faith
in me that made her walk upon the water, and I paid tribute to her and
she accepted my tribute. At other times she fell to her knees before me
and wanted only to gaze up at me and forget everything.

III A 133   n.d., 1841

« **5502**

My girl—the Latinist says of an alert listener: *pendet ex ore
alicujus.* [683] He is thinking particularly of the ear which picks up what
it hears, carries it through the secret passage of the ear, and hides it
deep within. We say it with a completely different meaning, for how
I do hang continually on your lips, how alert I am, yes, an exceptionally
alert listener, so that even if nothing is said, I still hear the beating of
your heart.

III A 134   n.d., 1841

« **5503**

I live constantly on the border between felicitous Arabia and
desert Arabia. [684]

III A 142   n.d., 1841

« **5504**

[Petition to the King, requesting permission to submit the dissertation, "The Concept of Irony," in Danish rather than in Latin. [685]]

Letters, document XV   June 4, 1841

« **5505**

My Regine!

You may remember that about a year ago I sent you a bottle of this essence,[686] adding that I had deliberately let some days go by after you had mentioned your fondness for it in order to conceal that fine flower in the veil of recollection. Now I recollect this once more. In other words, I recollect that you then mentioned that which I recollect, that I recollected that you mentioned it. Thus the recollection of it has become even more precious to me, not retrospectively but progressively. That is the blessing of time. I send you then a bottle of it enveloped in an abundance of leafy wrappings. But these leaves are not the kind one tears off hastily or throws aside with annoyance in order to get to the contents. On the contrary, they are precisely of that kind which gives pleasure, and I see with how much care and solicitude you will unfold every single leaf and thereby recollect that I recollect you, my Regine, and you will yourself recollect.

Your

S.K.

[Address:]
To
Miss Regine Olsen

Letters, no. 42   *n.d.*

« **5506**

De vita. E. vita[687]
Steamship cabin.[688]

III A 146   *n.d.,* 1841

« **5507**

..... You say, "What have I lost[689] or, more correctly, robbed myself of"—what have I lost, alas, how would you know or understand. If the question is raised, it is best for you to be silent—and how could anyone know it better than I, who had put my whole extremely reflected soul into a mounting of the best possible taste for her pure, deep [soul]—my somber thoughts—my gloomy dreams, my scintillating hopes—and besides all this, all my instability, in short, all that scintillation alongside her depth—and when I then became dizzy from looking deep into her infinite givingness, for nothing is as infinite as love—or when her feelings did not sink into the depths in the same way but danced on the surface in the buoyancy of love—

What have I lost, the one and only thing I loved; what have I lost in the eyes of man, my chivalrous word; what have I lost—that in which I have placed and, without fearing this blow, will always place my honor, my joy, my pride: in being faithful. . . . . . . Yet right now my soul is as uneasy as my body, a cabin shaken by the double movements[690] of the steamship.

III A 147   n.d., 1841

« **5508**

In margin of 5507 (III A 147):
And how difficult it is for me in this case, when I want so much to act, to find that the only activity allotted to me is what is usually left to women and children—to pray.

III A 148   n.d., 1841

« **5509**

> Why do you rub so vehemently
> See, I obey your very hint
> If you need me and call
> I come like lightning.[691]

Not I alone, my Ⓡ, but every other genie of the ring.[692] Please note that by the various genii of the ring I mean all the various willing servants within me that respond to your beck and call, a servant for your every wish, and if possible ten for every one; but all these are collected within me in one genie of the ring, who, unlike the one who appeared before Aladdin, is not linked to you by an external and accidental bond, but with the longing of my whole soul, for did I not myself bring you the ring I obey.

In another sense both you and I united together are the genie of the ring.

III A 149   n.d., 1841

« **5510**

You say: She was beautiful. O, what do you know about it: I do know it, for her beauty has cost me tears—I myself brought flowers to adorn her, I would have hung all the ornaments in the world upon her, but of course only insofar as they would have accentuated her loveliness—and when she stood there dressed in all her finery—I had to leave —when her delighted, exuberant glance met mine—I had to leave—I went out and wept bitterly.[693]

III A 150   n.d., 1841

« **5511**

She did not love my shapely nose, she did not love my eyes, my small feet—she did not love my good head—she loved just me, and yet she did not understand me.

III A 151   *n.d.,* 1841

« **5512**

I can really see how important language was to me for hiding my melancholy—here in Berlin it is impossible for me; I cannot deceive with language.[694]

III A 155   *n.d.,* 1841

« **5513**

Dear Emil,[695]

I have arrived in Berlin as you may already have learned from my letter to Peter,[696] which I wrote very quickly but mailed somewhat late. It is still my unalterable opinion that travel is foolish. But I hope that my stay will not be without significance for me when I have settled down a bit. I have much to think about and am suffering from a monstrous productivity block. I have as yet no occasion to let its *nisus* wear off (and it has already for some time been true of my countenance what was said about that emperor,[697] *"vultus erat nitentis"*[698]). I have begun to attend lectures. I heard one by Marheineke[699] with which I was quite pleased, for although it did not contain anything new, it was very nice to hear much of that which one is accustomed to seeing in print. Schelling[700] has not yet begun.

How are things with you at home?—and how is that person whose name I will not mention, although I hope your letters will contain something enlightening for me? Provide me with news. But the deepest secrecy must prevail. Do not let anybody suspect that I want it. Hitherto I have firmly adhered to the principle according to which I have decided to act. In this I had the encouragement, if you please, and I think of it mostly from that point of view, of having Professor Sibbern[701] look for me the day before I left "in order to give me a thorough dressing down," since he too had now become convinced that I was an egotistical and vain man, an ironist in the worst sense. When he did not find me, Peter became the victim; he grew angry and replied that it was none of Sibbern's business. I suppose Sibbern has spoken with the family. I could only wish that he had also spoken with her, for then I would have attained my goal. Meet her without being observed. Your window can assist you. Mondays and Thursdays from 4:00 to 5:00 P.M., her music lessons. But do not meet her in the street except Monday afternoons at 5:00 or 5:30, when you might meet her as she walks from Vestervold via Vestergade to Klædeboerne, or on the same day at 7:00 or 7:30, when she and her sister are likely to go to the Exchange by way of the arcades. But be careful. Visit the pastry shop there, but be careful. For my sake practice the art of controlling every expression, of being master of any situation, and of being able to make up a story instantaneously without apprehension and anxiety. Oh, one can fool people as much as one wants, as I know from experience, and at least with respect to this I have unlimited recklessness. But she must not suspect that I am concerned about her, for she might misunderstand and become dangerously ill. Also, sound out Peter a little. I wrote nothing at all to him, or at least I did so very guardedly. I trust nobody. He used the opportunity provided by Sibbern's visit to try to penetrate my shell but met only my ironic laughter. For I am afraid that somebody or other might take it upon himself to tell her that I am still thinking about her. That would be quite a rewarding role which might be tempting.

I can well imagine that many of my good friends will use my absence to malign me, but do not defend me—I beg of you. Still, write to me so that I may surmise whence animosity comes.

As for yourself: work—write—forget. Those stubborn thoughts must be made to obey. Acquire a wider circle of acquaintances in order to learn better how to be self-contained. I am sitting here in a hotel at a noisy dinner table where every possible language is spoken, where everybody is very busy, and for a moment I am silent in order to allow this noise to compel my thought inwards. "Cheers for me and you,"[702] say I; that day will never be forgotten. And so I live every day. I have in fact decided to eat at the hotel. It is not much more expensive. The food is good, and I do not care to eat with the Danes[703] (this last is a secret note for you alone). In case anyone asks you where I eat, reply that the hotel keeper had offered me such reasonable rates before I had spoken with the Danes that I preferred to eat here. Incidentally, I feel inner strength within me,[704] and so, period.

Take care of yourself!
Your
S. Kierkegaard

Please do me the favor of sending a little note of greeting to
Henrich, Michael, Carl, Sophie,[705] Jette, Wilhelm.[706] You can send it
to 7 St. Kjøbmagergade.
My address is:
Mittelstrasse 61
eine Treppe hoch

[Address:] *an dem Herrn, Cand. der Theologie*
E. Boesen
Copenhagen
Philosophgangen

[Postmarks:]
Berlin   Hamburg
31/10   3–4   2/11

Letters, no. 49   October 31, 1841

« **5514**

[Extended notes[707] on lectures by Phillip K. Marheineke on "Dogmatic Theology with special Reference to Carl Daub's System," Berlin,
October, 1841–February, 1842.]

III C 26   *n.d.,* 1841–42

« **5515**

And do you not think, then, that I long to give her this proof of
my love, this reparation for all the humiliation she must have suffered
from commiserating relatives and friends (God knows it was not my
fault that it happened this way*[708]) by once again rushing forth, by
demonstrating that it was not a sense of duty, not fear of public opinion, which made me stay with her—but that I, the most unstable of all
men, nevertheless came back to her. How disappointed they would be,
how the toothless female gossip with which they were able to discon-
cert the girl would have to stop once I had staked my honor in calling
[her] mine. In fact, if I did not abominate suicide, if I did not feel that
all such virtues were glittering vices, I would go back to her—and then
end my life, a plan I am sorry to say I have entertained for a long time,
and which would make separation from me doubly hard for her, for
who loves like a dying man; and this is actually the way I have felt about
it every time I embraced her—it never occurred to me to live with her
in the tranquil, trusting sense of that word. It is truly heartbreaking.
My only desire was to remain with her, but from the moment I felt that
it would inevitably come to grief, and unfortunately that moment came

all too soon, I resolved to make her think that I did not love her; and now here I am, hated by everybody for my faithlessness, the apparent cause of her unhappiness, and yet I am as faithful to her as ever. However painful it might be to my human pride, I would even rejoice to see her happy with another, but at present she is consumed with grief, because I, who could make her happy, would not. And truly I could have made her happy, were it not etc.

And although it is unwise for my peace of mind to think about it, I nevertheless do think about the ineffable moment when I would go back to her. And although I generally consider myself able to take suffering which I regard as God's punishment, this, however, some-times gets to be too severe. I also believe that I have done her wrong in not letting her know how much I am suffering. And when at times I remember having once said that science and scholarship would lose a devotee in me, I have a strong feeling that this was incorrect, for precisely because I am leaving her, science and scholarship have lost what it can lose in me, for I think only of her, and I am convinced that she is not suffering as much as I am. God grant that some good may still come to her from my suffering.

III A 159   n.d., 1841

« 5516

You must know that you will find your happiness in never having loved anyone but her, that you will stake your honor upon never loving another.[709]

III A 160   n.d., 1841

« 5517

How great is a woman's devotion. —But the curse which hangs over me is that I never dare let any person become deeply and inti-mately attached to me. God in heaven knows the many times I have delighted like a child in planning something that would please her and then was obliged to make it a principle, for fear of drawing her closer to me, never to do anything in momentary joy but to wait until com-mon sense and prudence forbade it. I believe that my relation to her can truly be called unhappy love—I love her—she is mine—her only wish is [for me] to remain with her—the family implores me[710]—it is my supreme desire—I must say no. To make it easier for her, I will try to lead her to believe that I was a downright deceiver,[711] a wanton person, in order if possible to get her to hate me, for I believe it will be even harder for her if she suspects that it was melancholy—how much melancholy and wantonness do resemble each other.

III A 161   *n.d.*, 1841

« **5518**

..... and when I feel unhappy like this, it is my consolation, my only consolation, that she is not suffering with me. It is difficult to experience having the one you love break faith, but this daily suffering, ...
and if I did remain with her, I would have to be cheerful, and if despite all that she happened to see me suffer ..... when I am happy it is my constant sorrow that she cannot share it.

III A 163   *n.d.*, 1841

« **5519**

I cannot extricate myself from this relationship, for I cannot write about it, inasmuch as the instant I want to do that I am invaded by an anxiety, an impatience, which wants to act.[712]

III A 164   *n.d.*, 1841

« **5520**

And perhaps you lament that men are faithless to you—perhaps you are wrong, for who knows so intimately another man's deepest secret—perhaps you are right, you perhaps have experienced it in action. —O, there is still one who is not faithless to you—and if it seems to you that men were closest to you, and if it seems hard to you that you have to learn to know the faithfulness of God by first learning to know the faithlessness of men, and if it seems far more beautiful to you possibly to learn to make out the faithfulness of God from the faithfulness of men—O, you would never have perceived it in the same way as you do now. —You would never have perceived that God is your neighbor, your nearest, the one closest to you.[713]

III A 165   *n.d.*, 1841

« **5521**

..... and this terrible restlessness—as if wanting to convince myself every moment that it would still be possible to return to her—O God, would that I dared to do it. It is so hard; my last hope in life I had placed in her, and I must deprive myself of it. How strange, I had never really thought of getting married, but I never believed that it would turn out this way and leave so deep a wound. I have always ridiculed those who talked about the power of women, and I still do, but a young, beautiful, soulful girl who loves with all her mind and all her heart, who is completely devoted, who pleads—how often I have been close to setting her love on fire, not to a sinful love, but I need merely have said to her that I loved her, and everything would have been set in motion to end my young life. But then it occurred to me that this would not be good for her, that I might bring a storm upon her head, since she would feel responsible for my death. I prefer what I did do; my relationship to her was always kept so ambiguous that I had it in my power to give it any interpretation I wanted to. I gave it the interpretation that I was a deceiver. Humanly speaking, that is the only way to save her, to give her soul resilience. My sin is that I did not have faith, faith that for God all things are possible, but where is the borderline between that and tempting God; but my sin has never been that I did not love her. If she had not been so devoted to me, so trusting, had not stopped living for herself in order to live for me—well, then the whole thing would have been a trifle; it does not bother me to make a fool of the whole world, but to deceive a young girl. —O, if I dared return to her, and even if she did not believe that I was false, she certainly believed that once I was free I would never come back. Be still, my soul, I will act firmly and decisively according to what I think is right. I will also watch what I write in my letters. I know my moods. But in a letter I cannot, as when I am speaking, instantly dispel an impression when I detect that it is too strong.

III A 166   n.d., 1841

« 5522

This very moment there is an organ-grinder[714] down in the street playing and singing—it is wonderful, it is the accidental and insignificant things in life which are significant. I think of the ship-boys, of the Laplanders who played in the moonlight on board ship—a Laplander: ordinarily who would pay any attention to him.

III A 167   n.d., 1841

« 5523

There is a church near her home,[715] and I can still remember and clearly hear its dull beat. At the appointed time, the signal sounded in the midst of our small talk in the living room, and then the nocturnal whispers began. It was a church bell that suggested their time.[716]

III A 168   n.d., 1841

« **5524**

And this I know, that even now when I feel all too acutely the value of money, all that I have would be at her service if she wished it, and I would thank God that she gave me this chance to prove how much she means to me.

III A 169   *n.d.*, 1841

« **5525**

And when the sun shuts its vigilant eye, when history is past, I will not only wrap myself in my cloak but I will throw the night around me like a veil, and I will come to you—I will listen as the savage listens—not for your footsteps but for the beating of your heart.[717]

III A 170   *n.d.*, 1841

« **5526**

As agreed, I am returning the flowering plant[718] which for eight days now has given me joy, has been the object of my tender loving care. But this is a small thing, for it is you yourself, after all, who loved it forth[719] [*opelsket*]—loved it forth, what a beautiful and rich expression, what a treasure the language possesses—loved it forth, and should not your ardent gaze, which has rested on this tender plant again and again, should not the warmth of your love be more than adequate to make it blossom in a very short time. It is unbelievable that the ardor of your eyes has not consumed it, but is it not true, is it not regrettably true, that there were also times when you despaired of my love or had fearful intimations that our happiness would not last, and a gentle dew of tears refreshed it, and look, it doubled its growth, became twice as beautiful; in this way, too, it was loved forth.

III A 171   *n.d.*, 1841

« **5527**

My dear Jette,[720]

Although I am well aware that the enclosed flower picture by no means can stand comparison with that marvelous fruit picture with which you surprised me on my birthday, still I do not hesitate to send you my modest work as a gift, adding that you must not, as seems so probable, scorn it. It makes no claim on you to be of artistic value; it desires only to be worthy of your affection, for I can assure you that all the time I was working on this flower picture you were constantly in my thoughts. It is all the more deplorable that I began a week late, for despite my having sat up the whole night before last, I have just now finished the picture. Although the blossom itself did not take me much time, the leaf did, even though one might believe that the whole thing had been done with a single stroke. But of course I do not need to tell all this to an artist like you.

Please accept, then, my little gift, a late flower in the month of November, which thus has arrived one day late.[721] But fair is fair: I promised to hide your picture so that nobody would see it; in turn you must promise me not to put my picture on display anywhere, nor show it to anyone, nor mention my name in connection with it—"for that is so embarrassing."

Your uncle,
S.K.

A birthday flower
respectfully
planted
by
N.N.

[Address:]
To
Henriette Lund

Letters, no. 71   *n.d.,* 1841 or 1842

« **5528**

How it does humble my pride not to be able to go back to her. I had so prided myself on remaining true to her, and yet I dare not. I am not in the habit of bringing disgrace on my honor—faithfulness has always been a matter of honor to me. And yet in her eyes I must appear as a deceiver, and it is the only way I can make good my mistake. I have maintained my position with a dreadful consistency, in spite of all my own deepest wishes. As for the external attacks by men who want to pressure me, I do not pay much attention to them. And yet I am still plagued by anxiety. Suppose that she really begins to believe that I am a deceiver, suppose she falls in love with someone else, something which in many respects I naturally wish would happen—suppose that she then suddenly comes to know that I have really loved her, that I did this out of love for her, out of a deep conviction that it would never work, or in any case that with the greatest joy in the world and gratitude to God I would share all my joy with her, but not my sorrow—alas, the last can be worse than the first.

III A 172   n.d., 1841

« **5529**

I enjoy no pleasures any more; I do not enter into them with abandon as in the old days; I do not want to be happy if she is sad.

III A 173   n.d., 1841

« **5530**

. . . . . again today I checked myself in an attempt to let her know, to let her suspect in some way, that I still love her. My mind is so resourceful and there is a certain satisfaction in thinking a clever plan has been found. I would like to write a letter home which would be printed. The heading should be: My Ⓡ [722]—that would be enough for her. The letter itself could be full of subtle hints. But I must not do it; I humble myself beneath God's hand. Every time I get an idea like that, and it usually happens many times a day, I transform it into a prayer for her, that it will all be for the best for her, which is my wish.

III A 174   n.d., 1841

« **5531**

Today I saw a beautiful girl—I am not enthralled by that any more —I do not want it—no husband can be more faithful to his wife than I am to her. It is also good for me, for those little infatuations were very disturbing.[723]

III A 175   n.d., 1841

« **5532**

If it were she who had broken the engagement[724] with me, it would have been easy to forget her, no matter how much I loved her; I would have dared hoist all sails in order to forget her; I would have dared write[725] about her—but now I cannot persuade myself to do it. I remind myself of it often enough, and frequently the memory comes without my calling it forth. Because of all this my soul is becoming more earnest; alas, I hope it may be for the best for me.

III A 176   *n.d.*, 1841

« **5533**

My thoughts are continually hovering between two images of her[726]—she is young, exuberant, animated, unsophisticated, in short, as I perhaps have never seen her—she is pale, withdrawn, waiting for the hours of solitude when she can weep, in short, again as I perhaps have never seen her.

III A 177   *n.d.*, 1841

« **5534**

Now the affair has been settled once and for all, and yet I will never be through with it. She does not know what an advocate she has in me. She was clever. Her parting words were the plea that I remember her once in a while. She knew very well that as soon as I remembered her there would be the devil to pay. But I would have done it anyway, without her asking it.

III A 178   *n.d.*, 1841

« **5535**

I am so happy to have heard Schelling's second lecture[727]—indescribably. I have been pining and thinking mournful thoughts long enough. The embryonic child of thought leapt for joy within me as in Elizabeth,[728] when he mentioned the word "actuality"[729] in connection with the relation of philosophy to actuality. I remember almost every word he said after that. Here, perhaps, clarity can be achieved. This one word recalled all my philosophical pains and sufferings. —And so that she, too, might share my joy, how willingly I would return to her, how eagerly I would coax myself to believe that this is the right course. —O, if only I could! —Now I have put all my hope in Schelling —but still, if I knew that I could make her happy, I would leave this very evening. It is very hard to have made a person unhappy, and it is very

hard that to make her unhappy is almost the only hope I have of
making her happy.

III A 179   n.d., 1841

« **5536**

[Extended account[730] of F. W. J. Schelling's lectures on "Philosophie der Offenbarung," Berlin, November, 1841–February, 1842.]

III C 27   November 22, 1841–February 4, 1842

« **5537**

[Notes[731] on K. Werder's lectures on "Logik und Metaphysik,"
Berlin, first semester, 1841–42.]

II C 28–29   n.d., 1841–42

« **5538**

At times the idea comes to me: When I return [from Berlin],
perhaps she will have decided for sure that I was a deceiver. Suppose
that she had the power to crush me with a look (and outraged innocence can do just that)—I shudder to think of it, it is terrible—not the
suffering, for that I would certainly go through if I knew it was for her
good—but the humble game of playing with life implied here, pushing
a person around this way wherever one wishes.

III A 180   n.d., 1841

« **5539**

My
    Solomon[732] says: A good answer is like a sweet kiss. You know that
I am well-known, yes, almost unpopular, because I am always asking
questions. Ah, they do not know what I am asking about. Only you
know of what I ask, only you can answer. O, give me an answer. Only
you can give me a good answer, for a good answer, says Solomon, is
like a sweet kiss.

Your[733]

III A 183   n.d., 1841

« **5540** *Situation*

A seducer who already has the love of several girls on his conscience becomes enamored of a girl whom he loves to the extent that
he does not have the heart to seduce her, but neither can he really
decide to take up with her. He happens to see someone with a striking
resemblance to her; he seduces her in order that in this pleasure he
can enjoy the other.[734]

III A 187   n.d., 1841

« 5541

Here in Berlin, a Demoiselle Hedwig Schulze, a singer from Vienna, performs the part of Elvira.[735] She is very beautiful, decisive in bearing; in height, in the way she walks and dresses (black silk dress, bare neck, white gloves), she strikingly resembles a young lady I knew. It is a strange coincidence. I must make proper use of a little power against myself in order to dislodge this impression.

III A 190   n.d., 1841

« 5542

December 14

My dear Emil,[736]

Thank you for your letter, and shame on you for letting me wait so long. After all, it has been almost a month. Furthermore, as my bootblack had mailed it for me, I was afraid that he had been responsible in some manner for its not reaching you. But when he assured me repeatedly that he had indeed taken care of it, I was left in my solitude to pour out my faithful Danish heart in Danish on the subject of Danish faithlessness; I would even have written you a sermon upon this text: "I have learned to have abundance and to do without."[737] This sermon would presumably have contained a multitude of lies, in which all preternatural moods abound, among them the fundamental lie that I had learned to do without a letter from you. True enough, a letter is not a conversation, and the only thing I can say I miss now and then are my *colloquia.* How good it was to talk myself out once in a while, but, as you know, I need a rather long time for that even though I talk fast. Still, a letter always means a lot, especially when it is the only means of communication.

Should I tell you that you are fortune's child in finding news that is of interest to me, or should I admire your talent? Bærentzen,[738] the painter, must be a good source. One of the daughters there was also engaged; her fiancé left and let it be rumored that he had died (but be very discreet with this story, for the person in question probably still knows no better than that he is dead). But inasmuch as that young girl, whose name I will not mention, declines an invitation, then perhaps I ought to see genuine tact in this, proof that she fears to walk arm in arm with companions in misfortune, and that is good. That her family hates me is good. That was my plan, just as it was also my plan that she, if possible, be able to hate me. She does not know how much she owes me on that score, and I have left nothing untried (from which you may conclude that a good deal of what the family says is true), and I intend to go on leaving nothing untried. Even here in Berlin, my unfortunately all too inventive brain has not been able to refrain from planning this or that. She must either love me or hate me; she knows no third way. Nor is there anything more corrupting for a young girl than the stages in between. If she suspected how subtly everything was planned,[739] after I had convinced [her] that it had to be broken, well then—then she would probably be right in seeing proof in it that I loved her. I have almost sacrificed my good name and reputation for her sake. For that was why I was defiant, that was why I spent two weeks in Copenhagen outdoing myself in effrontery, that is why I shall always try to appear in such a light that she may truly succeed in having me in her power. Believe me, I know how to be consistent. —But meanwhile please continue to provide me with whatever news you can find out about her.—

You seem to be afraid that I want to consign you to the idyllic, not as a place for frolicking but for grazing and grubbing[740] about in the pond. How could you get such an idea? Have I not said and written that you are consigned to yourself, which is precisely why you can frolic about lyrically on your own, do whatever you want with the world, forget it, remember it, hate it, love it. Be glad that no other human destiny is tied to yours. Get into your kayak[741] (surely you know those Greenland boats), put on your swimming suit, and be off with you to the ocean of the world. But that is certainly no idyll. If you cannot forget her, cannot write poetry about her, all right then, set all sails.[742] Become all attentiveness. Let no opportunity to meet her pass you by. Always be on the lookout for the accidental; make use of it. You must be the one who makes it meaningful or the one who reduces it to nothing. If you sense that she wants to draw nearer, then break off, brush her aside; but next time you meet, cast her a meaningful glance. Death and Pestilence! Why all this fuss for the sake of a girl? Still, I want in no way to deny that your position is awkward. In that respect we are opposites. I always seem to behave actively, you passively. You lack one thing which I possess: you have not learned to despise the world, to see how trivial everything is: you break your back lifting its copper coins.

You write that you are gathering material for a new treatise. Last time you were working on a short story. What is the meaning of this? How will it all end? Please be good enough to keep yourself in check a little. You know that I usually say of myself that I rummaged around in the folder a little too soon, but what are you doing right now? Finish your short story whatever the cost. Or, and this would be my advice, write some critical essays first, for those are jobs you can finish quickly. I am writing[743] furiously. As of now I have written fourteen printed sheets. Thereby I have completed one part of the treatise which, *volente deo*, [744] I shall show you some day. This last week I wrote nothing. I am lying fallow, gathering strength, but already I feel something stirring within me. Please show me that you are careful about your tempo,[745] which consists of *ein, zwei, drei*, etc. (Of course the deepest secrecy must prevail about my writing activity. You must not say a word about it.)

Schelling[746] is lecturing to an extraordinary audience. He claims to have discovered that there are two philosophies, one negative and one positive. Hegel is neither one nor the other; his is a refined Spinozaism. The negative philosophy is given in the philosophy of identity, and he will now present the positive and thereby assist scholarship to its true eminence. As you see, there will be promotions for all those with degrees in philosophy. In the future not only the lawyers will be the *doctores juris utriusque*. [747] We, the magisters, are now the *magistri philosophiae utriusque*, [748] now, but not quite yet, for he has not yet presented the positive philosophy.

By the way, what I write to you concerning this young girl must remain between us, and you must not with a single word in any way interfere with my tactics. What does it matter if people believe that I am a deceiver? I am just as able to study philosophy, write poetry, smoke cigars, and ignore the whole world. After all, I have always made game of people, and why should I not continue to do so to the last? —Of course I have my painful moments when I regret that I became engaged, not that I broke the engagement. For only by virtue of the fact that I did become engaged to her did she gain any power over me. Had this not been the case, then my philosophy would soon have swept this actuality aside, however beautiful and interesting it was. Now in the event she does gain sufficient strength truly to hate me, it would be an exceedingly curious relationship if I should ever meet her again in this life. If so, I shall take care not to rob her of the sole benefit, which I have done my best to provide her with, for without my assistance she would never have had the strength to hate me. From the remarks you quote in your letter I gather that she must have confided in her sisters. That was what I wanted. For they will now fan the flames, and, while every remark I make is always of such a nature that I may give it another meaning whenever I choose, now that her sisters are her tutors in reading, everything will necessarily be understood as I want it to be understood.

With this, God speed. Please write soon. My regards to your father and mother.[749] Greetings to Henrich, Michael, Carl, Sophie, Jette, Wilhelm.[750] N.B. Please send me *The First Love*[751] in Heiberg's translation as soon as you can. It is in the theater repertoire and is available at Schubothe's;[752] but do not let anyone suspect it is for me.

> Your sincerely devoted
> S. Kierkegaard
> [Deleted: Farinelli][753]

[On an enclosed slip:]

I have no time to get married. But here in Berlin there is a singer from Vienna, a *Demoiselle* Schulze.[754] She plays the part of Elvira and bears a striking resemblance to a certain young girl, so deceptive that I was extraordinarily affected to see her in the very part of Elvira. When my wild mood sweeps over me, I am almost tempted to approach her and that not exactly with the "most honorable intentions." Usually it does not matter much about a singer, and she does look like her. It might be a small diversion when I am tired of speculation or sick of thinking about this and that. She lives nearby. Well, probably nothing will come of this. You know so well how I talk that you know what such stuff means, and it means no more now that I am writing about it. But meanwhile I do not want you to mention to anybody that there is such a singer in Berlin, or that she is playing Elvira, or etc.

[Address:]
An dem Herrn Cand. Theol. E. Boesen
Copenhagen
Philosophgangen

[Post marks:]
Berlin   Hamburg
12/16 2–3   12/17 4–6
Letters, no. 54   December 14 [1841]

« **5543**

December 15 [added in pencil: 1841]

Dear Professor:[755]

Today, through my nephew Henrich Lund,[756] I received the greetings you expressly requested him to convey. I am so pleased to have those greetings that it would never occur to me to return my own greetings by the same medium. On the contrary, I consider them a poetic summons (*poscimur*)[757] to reply in what may be a rather discursive manner.

Even now when I cannot personally ascertain it for myself every day, I have never doubted that you would maintain some of that interest with which you have always honored me, especially after Poul Møller's death.[758] Therefore, when I did not receive greetings of any kind from you until now, I easily explained this to myself by saying that circumstance had not brought you into contact with anybody whom you knew to be writing to me.

So here I am in Berlin going to lectures. I am attending lectures by Marheineke,[759] Werder,[760] and Schelling.[761] I have heard Steffens[762] a few times and have also paid my fee to hear him, but oddly enough, he does not appeal to me at all. And I, who have read with such great enthusiasm much of what he has written, *Karrikaturen des Heiligsten,* to mention just one example, I, who had really looked forward to hearing him in order to ascertain for myself what is usually said about him, that he is matchless when it comes to monologue—I am utterly disappointed. His delivery seems so uncertain and hesitant that one begins to question what progress one is making, and when a flash of genius transfigures him, I miss that artistic awareness, that oratorical brilliance I have so often admired in his writings. He lectures on anthropology, but the material is essentially the same as that contained in his published book. So I prefer to read him. But his anthropology will always make fairly heavy reading for anybody not well versed in the natural sciences. —I am, by the way, sorry to find myself disappointed in this respect. That's why I have not called on him either. On the whole I live as isolated as possible and am withdrawing more and more into myself.

Werder is a virtuoso; that is all one can say about him. I suspect that he must be a Jew, for baptized Jews always distinguish themselves by their virtuosity and of course do participate in all fields nowadays. Like a juggler, he can play and frolic with the most abstract categories and with never so much as a slip of the tongue even though he talks as fast as a horse can run. He is a scholastic in the old sense; as they did in Thomas Aquinas,[763] so he has found in Hegel not only the *summa* and the *summa summae* but the *summa summarum.* In this respect he is almost a psychological phenomenon for me. His life, his thought, the richness of the outside world almost seem meaningful to him only when they have reference to Hegel's *Logic*.[764] It is, however, very advantageous for the young people studying at the University to have such a man.

Schelling lectures to a select, numerous, and yet also *undique conflatum auditorium*.[765] During the first lectures it was almost a matter of risking one's life to hear him. I have never in my life experienced such uncomfortable crowding—still, what would one not do to be able to hear Schelling? His main point is always that there are two philosophies, one positive and one negative. The negative is given, but not by Hegel, for Hegel's is neither negative nor positive but a refined Spinozaism.[766] The positive is yet to come. In other words, in the future it will not be only the lawyers who become the *doctores juris utriusque*,[767] for I venture to flatter myself that without submitting another dissertation I shall become a *magister philosophiae utriusque*.

The longer I live here in Berlin the more I realize the truth of the advice you have given me again and again out of regard for both me and my dissertation:[768] that it be translated into German. I will wait and see about that. If it does happen, I can honestly say that you are responsible. If any good comes of this, it will be a pleasure for me to think that in this I have once more an occasion to thank you.

Berlin is probably the only place in Germany worth visiting for scholarly reasons. Therefore I really hope to benefit from this semester. The stay here is helping me to concentrate and limit myself. Otherwise, God be praised, I am fairly well. From my native country I hear little. The Danes here do get the newspapers, but I do not read them as I do not have enough time, yet time enough and time sufficient to think about a man like you, dear Professor, who by your conduct towards me have always obliged me and entitled me to call myself

Your devoted
S. Kierkegaard

[Address:]
An dem Herrn Prof. Dr. Sibbern
Ritter der D. O., *und* D. M.
Copenhagen

[Postmark:]
Berlin
16/12–3

Letters, no. 55   December 15, 1841

« **5544**

My dear Jette,[769]

You hope that I will forgive you your silence, and your hope shall not be in vain, all the more so because in the letter in which you tell me of that hope, in that very letter, you assure yourself of it and make impossible for me what would otherwise have been impossible anyway.

I am glad the little scarf pleases you. You may thank Miss Dencker[770] for its being a "pretty little scarf," and you may thank Henrich[771] for its coming as an agreeable surprise. From this you will see, my dear Jette, not only how much I want to do you a favor but also how willingly everyone lends me a helping hand. I know that you would do the same if I were in need of your assistance to surprise any of the others. Perhaps you would almost prefer to be the one to assist me in giving pleasure to somebody else rather than be the object yourself of the combined efforts by me and the others. And that is as it should be, and it is indeed a beautiful secret when everybody may thus be made happy at the same time, even though in different ways.

A letter from Michael[772] informs me that you have not been altogether well, but as you yourself do not mention this, I conclude that it cannot have been very serious.

My time is pretty well taken up, especially since *Geheimeraad* Schelling[773] is pleased to lecture for two hours every day, giving me much to attend to. That is why you are getting a brief reply from me. If this seems to you to be a change, yet that which I consider the principal object of a correspondence will remain unchanged: my greetings. My dear Jette, please convey my greetings to H., M., C., S., W.,[774] and accept my greetings for yourself.

Your Uncle

Letters, no. 56   *n.d.* [near end of 1841]

« **5545**

[Reading notes[775] on G. W. F. Hegel, *Vorlesungen über Æsthetik,* III.]

III C 34   *n.d.,* 1841–42

« **5546**

It is very remarkable that the wrath of the gods pursues the family of Labdakos; it is evident in Oedipus' fate; the daughters of his unhappy marriage are Antigone and Ismene. Meanwhile, as we see, Antigone is engaged to Creon's son. The family develops very tranquilly. This is Greek tragedy. Romantic tragedy could be joined to it if, for example, I had Antigone fall in love with all the energy of love, but in order to halt the vengeance of the gods she would not get married, she would regard herself as a sacrifice to the wrath of the gods because she belonged to the family of Oedipus, but she would not leave behind any family that could again become the object for the angry gods' persecution.[776]

III C 37   n.d., 1841–42

« **5547**

As well as being interesting, *Philoctetes* does border on being drama. Philoctetes' mounting bitterness and the progressive self-contradiction in his behavior connected with it are profoundly true psychologically, but the whole thing is not classical.

III C 40   n.d., 1841–42

« **5548**

Jan. 16, 1842

My dear Emil,[777]

Your letter arrived and was welcome, as is everything that comes from you. However, there is something in it that I do not understand, something that shows that you do not understand me. You say that there was conflict and discord in my letter, but in what way I do not know. My view is unchanged, inflexibly unchanged, the same as it was that day, the date of which I do not remember, and even long before then. If you can succeed in showing me any deviation in my compass or demonstrate that any faint puff of air, any squall, or any mood has rippled the surface of my soul, let alone stirred its depths, then I will pledge myself to give you not only the gold of Peru but the girl you love into the bargain. The matter remains unchanged. Just as strongly as I feel that I am an exceptional amorist, I also know very well that I am a bad husband and always will remain so. It is all the more unfortunate that the former is always or usually in inverse proportion to the latter.[778] I am capable of tempting a girl, of making an impression on her, and that I have done altogether too often here [*may be read as:* formerly]. Her soul must have acquired resilience through contact with me, and I daresay that for a young girl it cannot have been a joking matter to have contended with me. Either this resilience must elevate her higher than she would ever have risen otherwise—and that will happen if she is able to hate me; everything has been directed towards that—or it will bring her down. If so, I stand prepared, even if I am a bad husband and even if my soul is preoccupied with far too many other things, for then she will be just as well off with me. In saying this I am not underestimating myself, but my spiritual life and my importance as a husband are irreconcilable entities.

But you go on to ask if her image looms before me again. Death and Pestilence! Would you make me a child once more as if I did not know what I want, one who sits and sings in the dark and sees ghosts and is afraid? Did I not tell you in my very first letter that forgetting her is still out of the question?[779] As yet I have neither taken out the stylus of oblivion in order to efface, nor have I mixed the colors on my poet's palette in order to paint a portrait of recollection for myself. That I will not do; that would be irresponsible. I am not the issue. I realize very well what I have possessed, and my spirit is not yet extinct, my soul is not yet powerless, my thoughts still abound. I will certainly persevere, but she is the issue and how she takes it. That remains to be seen before I place the final period. And what is it you want now? Should I now vacillate, should I now fear that the effect of the broken engagement could not be overcome if she were to return to me? I do not fear that kind of thing, and moreover I am not permitting her to return because of promises of gold and greenwoods. There will always be enough pain, but I am only saying that she will be better off than by standing alone. I do not ask for more than that. I have far too much sense of and reverence for what stirs in a human being not to guard it with just as much esthetic as ethical earnestness. Therefore, get thee far behind me with such notions as that of her image probably looming before me again. You are not (I think you will agree with me and not be offended by my saying it) accustomed to holding your life poetically in your hand the way I am. So far I have managed that, and I still do so. Until now there has been no deviation. Everything has been so directed that she will come to see me as a deceiver; if this succeeds, then she has been helped, then she is afloat once more. But if she cannot do so, then I always have a ship at sea with a captain who knows his duty very well. I do not regret what has happened, and if you are able by the harshest torture to wring a single groan of that kind out of my letter, then in the future you may smile at my childishness. I do not regret it, least of all for my own sake. You ought to know enough about my relationship to be able to see the consistency with which I have steered towards the point where I now am. My life divides itself into chapters, and I can provide an exact heading for each as well as state its motto. For the present it proclaims: "She must hate me." No human being has been permitted to probe too deeply, and in the unanimous condemnation of the town you also see that I have proof that I acted correctly. I shall only give you one little example to convince you that I am the same. In the company of the Danes here in Berlin I am always cheerful, merry, gay, and have "the time of my life," etc. And even though everything churns inside me so that it sometimes seems that my feelings, like water, will break the ice with which I have covered myself, and even though there is at times a groan within me, each groan is instantly transformed into something ironical, a witticism, etc., the moment anybody else is present. I do this partly because I never became used to grabbing other people by the arm, and partly because my plan demands it. Here, a groan which might, after all, possibly mean something entirely different, might reach the ear of a Dane, he might write home about it, she might possibly hear it, it might possibly damage the transitional process, the result of which I intend to ascertain for myself in the fullness of time. Do you already see the great difficulty here? I must decide when that time is, however difficult it may be here once more to steer between the esthetic and ethical in the world. I have been ill; that is to say, I have had a lot of rheumatic headaches and have often not slept at night. I could call a doctor; perhaps something might be done about it. But if I called a doctor, the Danes would know about it at once. Perhaps it might occur to one of them to write home, it might reach her ear, it might be disturbing—ergo, I do not call a doctor, and I feel better because I remain faithful to my principle, and in spite of all his skill a doctor might do me harm because I would come into conflict with my principle. Do I need to feel ashamed when I compare myself with other people? Do I need to blush when I claim to know how to act and how to act consistently? What is more, I lack diversion. Absence from home practically always makes an impression on a person, and especially so under such utterly singular circumstances. The last day before I left, you accompanied me and got some idea of the many kinds of enjoyment always at my disposal. In Berlin I have nothing of the kind. I miss my hired coachman, my servant, my comfortable landau, my light-hearted flight through the lovely regions of our Sjælland, the merry smiles of the young girls, which I knew how to turn to my advantage without doing them any harm. I am working hard. My body cannot stand it. So that you may see that I am the same, I shall tell you that I have again written a major section of a piece "Either/Or."[780] It has not gone very quickly, but that is due to its not being an expository work but one of pure invention, which in a very special way demands that one be in the mood. I hold my life poetically in my hand, but from this follows that which I cannot get away from: that between two poetic possibilities[781] there lies a third, that of actuality and contingency. Suppose she were taken ill. I have weighed that eventuality carefully, and obviously illness cannot be taken into account when it is a question of an entire life, but still this is a very special matter. But please note once more how faithful I am to my principle. I thought this matter over before I left home; a golden key opens all doors, and I believe you know that I understand the uses of money. For a moment it occurred to me that here again I might attempt bribery. It would have been easy for me. Moreover there was one person who I was certain could provide me with absolutely reliable information, but then I would have had to show him my hand. I dare not do that, and accordingly I remained faithful to my principle. You are the only one from whom I get an occasional bit of information, and surely you cannot complain that I am impatient in demanding it of you. And yet it is the only thing of importance to me at the moment. As to the rest, only I myself can gather the intelligence.

I hope you see that it provides an occasion for misunderstanding when you bring your own love affair into this. I know nothing of these sentimental palpitations. My relationship with her has a far different reality from that and has been appealed to a far more exalted forum, and if I had not had the courage myself to bring the case before that forum, I would consider myself a soft, esthetic semi-human person, a worm. For it would be terrible to play for such high stakes merely because of a whim. Apparently you are a novice: you have feeling, I have passion. But my understanding is enthroned above my passion; yet, at the same time my understanding is passion. Here let me draw my sword from its scabbard. Is it seemly to devote oneself in this manner to feeling? I do not understand you. Once a girl has made such a strong impression on me as she has on you, then I declare war, and then I am in my element, for the war itself is my delight. That a girl should be unconquerable, that thought has never yet been entertained in my recalcitrant, if you will, or proud head. Do you not hear martial music, is not your soul all emotion? —It is incomprehensible. And moreover, is not the world open to you? My Emil, do learn a little from my example. Or do you have the *idée fixe* that this girl can only be happy with you?—*eh bien!* Still, you have no responsibility. Imagine what it means to have lured a girl out into the mainstream and now to be sitting and waiting to see how it will end. Should I not have sunk deep into the earth; and yet I carry my head high. And what are you doing to banish [*may be read as:* change] it? Are you working, writing poetry, exposing your breast to danger? You want to get away. There is no worse way. I knew that before I went abroad, and I would not have gone if it had not been out of consideration for her. I would have spent the winter in Copenhagen. In the first place I wanted to meet public opinion head on, and I believe that my presence would have meant a lot, and second, I was aware of that which we already spoke about at the time, that such a stay might well have its own difficulties. But if the whole thing was to have any meaning for her, I had to leave; ergo, I left. I keep watch over myself. No miser could brood more anxiously over his treasure. I watch every word, every facial expression, every *Anspielung.*[782] Moreover, I keep up my interest in scholarship, in art, and even—with God's help—in my own productivity. That is the way things stand with me, and so they must remain until the moment arrives. As far as I am concerned, then, it cannot be a question of my calming down, for I am calm; but, as there is a point outside myself, I must wait for it to be clarified. I could of course fling myself into my carriage at once and travel to Copenhagen and see for myself, but I will not do that. It makes it all the worse that Schelling's most recent lectures have not been very important.[783] That being so, I could very well do it, but I will not do it because I do not want to, because it would only make me lose confidence in myself if I were to do it prior to the moment I determined when I left home. In this respect as well I have special signs to go by. Incidentally, I could wish I had my papers with me, for I do miss them also. What I have written here[784] up to now is probably not bad, and I believe it will find favor in your eyes. So I also long, as Paul[785] says, to present my charismatic gift to you. My Emil, would that I could shout these words so loudly that I might summon you from the hyperborean twilight of soul in which you live. And if you were to lose this girl now, is there then nothing else for you to do? That is the way it usually is for a young girl, but you, you can work, can bring joy to others, can fetch old and new things from your storeroom, can comfort; in short, you can become a pastor, and that is the only thing worth the trouble in this world. Note in this also my own misfortune, imagine the tempests that I have to endure, now more than ever, and now more than ever without having deserved them. For I have wanted to keep her out of this, too, not because of excessive stress, but for far more profound reasons.

Here you have my contribution in this matter. It will have to suffice; I can say no more. When that moment arrives when I say "Period," I shall tell you more, but I never communicate what does not belong to me. I know my own nature, and I have betrayed to her how one gains power over me. I did it painstakingly, and it would have been easy to prevent. But I do not want to steal away from it, for I have not wanted to provide myself with an opportunity for self-deception.

So you want to become a missionary? And you do not wish me to dismiss the matter lightly. All right then, why do you want to be one? If it is for your own peace of mind, I daresay that would be a most indefensible reason, and it does not exactly give one an idea of what is called "the call," for then one ought rather to say, "Physician, heal thyself."[786] Or is it for the sake of the others? To be honest, I do not believe it. You are still suffering from such an affair, you would hardly be up to that. If you want to get away, all right then, travel, but do not take upon yourself such a serious responsibility. Or is it a legitimation, as though one could do no less? Am I right? If it offends you to have me speak like this, please forget it is I, imagine an older person, think of everything that might distort the impression of my words as separate from me, and retain only my friendship and its influence. Travel, if you want to; my purse is always open to you. But above all, work, set yourself a definite goal, and stick to it. If you so desire, I shall be happy to renounce my authority to say this, but it is nonetheless true.

You are getting a fairly long letter from me. I wanted to correct your ideas about me. I am glad to learn from your letter that she is well; that she is cheerful is an ambiguous matter. The Olsen household has great ability in dissimulation, and surely association with me has not diminished that virtuosity.

And now, my dear Emil, my greetings, my friendship, my devotion to you. I sing that little song from *The White Lady*[787] (the tenant farmer's lines to the officer at the very beginning): "Take my hand, take my hand; in this breast dwells honesty."

Greetings to your father and mother.[788]

Your
S.K.

I do not need to tell you that in regard to all my letters the deepest secrecy must prevail.

[Address on a separate envelope:]
An dem Herrn Cand. Theol. E. Boesen
Copenhagen
Philosophgangen

[Postmarks:]
Hamburg   Berlin
1/18   1/17 2–3
                        Letters, no. 62   January 16 [1842]

« **5549**

I must include hypochondria in "Either/Or" in order to characterize the isolated elements in isolated subjectivity.[789] This I should like
to do in "Either Or"—and then mediate in B's papers in part two.

                                        III B 130   *n.d.,* 1842

« **5550**

[Final draft of "Ancient Tragedy as Reflected in the Modern,"[790]
part of *Either/Or,* I.]

                                        III B 132   January 30, 1842

« **5551**

                                                Feb. 6 [1842]

My dear Emil,[791]
I did receive your letter. You seem to hint in it that there is some
inconsistency between my last and next-to-last letters, inasmuch as in
the earlier one I urge you to be seated in the council, and in the later
one become a little vehement, almost as if I wanted to dismiss you
again. You are not completely wrong about that. The fact is that when
I assured you in my first letter that you held a seat in the council of
my thoughts, that was true enough, but that means primarily that I
often include you in my thoughts, that you really do have a seat and
a vote in many aspects of my life, but especially with respect to all of
my modest production. However, in this matter I feel that I must rely
wholly upon myself, and there it was apparent to me at once that I had
said too much and all the more so when I read your letter. You miss
the point, but you do so because you do not know the true situation,
primarily because you do not know my motives. This became even
more apparent to me in your letter and perhaps I did react a bit
vehemently. It must have seemed especially so to you, although there

really was not an untrue word in anything I said. I have often said that I am born to intrigues, but in another sense I can say that I am born to intrigues, entanglements, peculiar relationships in life, etc., all of which perhaps would not be so peculiar if I had not been so peculiarly constituted, primarily if I had not possessed what I might call that passionate coldness with which I rule my moods, that is, every determination of them *ad extra*.[792] From the development of this argument you will see that I cannot add much to my previous letter. The affair, which by now has been dealt with often enough, has two sides: an ethical and an esthetic. Were she able to take the affair less to heart, or, if it might even become an impetus for her to rise higher than she otherwise would have, then the ethical factor is cancelled—then only the esthetic remains for me. Then I am your man, then I am in my element, equally much whether it is a question of forgetting or of conquering. She was an exceptional girl, as I have always said, and in that sense I have never cooled towards her. Nor do I believe that she would in that sense have been hurt by having been engaged to me. What is then to be done: I open the gates of oblivion, I fling myself into the stream[793] of life, and I believe that I am too good a swimmer to go under just because I am tossed by a little rolling swell. The esthetic is above all my element. As soon as the ethical asserts itself, it easily gains too much power over me. I become a quite different person, I know no limit to what might constitute my duty etc. There you see the difficulty: if I had broken the connection for my own sake because I believed that the esthetic factor which constitutes something so essential in every character and required it in mine chiefly because I felt that my whole spiritual life was almost at stake (which would have been a most respectable reason and something quite different from the reason people usually have for breaking up, that there is somebody they like better, etc.)—then the ethical would have crushed me. I have been rather ill while I have been in Berlin, but now I am quite well again. Nobody will be told what goes on inside me, and now I am of course quite pleased with the thought that I held back about this. The cold is not so bad in Berlin, but the East wind is awful when it gets going, and often I have had the experience of not once being warm, for a whole week in a stretch, not even at night. Cold, some insomnia, frayed nerves, disappointed expectations of Schelling,[794] confusion in my philosophical ideas, no diversion, no opposition to excite me—that is what I call the acid test. One learns [to] know oneself. It was a godsend that I did not break the engagement for my own sake; then it would have overwhelmed me. All that I wanted to save by breaking the engagement was in the process of fading away like a phantom anyway, and I would have remained as one who for a phantom had thrown away her happiness as well as my own. I broke it for her sake. That became my consolation. And when I suffered the most, when I was completely bereft, then I cried aloud in my soul: "Was it not good, was it not a godsend that you managed to break the engagement? If this had continued, you would only have become a lifelong torment for her. Even if she now learns," so I continued, "that I have gone out like a candle, she will see God's just punishment of me in this, she will not grieve for me, and that is the only thing I do not want to allow her to do." These are not over-wrought feelings, and that prattle about how she will always be glad to stay with me because she loves me cannot be thought about. I am too old to talk that way. I know myself, I know what I can endure; what she can endure, I do not know. These are not overwrought feelings, and I know this best because they are able to quell the upheavals of my soul. Now I am calmer, and I do not anticipate such spiritual trials. Moreover I could have been exposed to humiliations in a quite differ-ent manner. Suppose that she had had the strength to forget me, had recovered in a way that might have surprised the world (something I had my reasons for expecting), then I would have been stuck. Those who only considered the esthetic in the affair would have laughed at me; those who considered the ethical would still have called me a deceiver and a scoundrel. Is it not infuriating? I pass through this world, and I harbor healthy and powerful emotions in my breast, so many that I believe ten people might make themselves into honest citizens with them, and I—I am a scoundrel. But I laugh at mankind as I have always done; I am taking a terrible revenge on them, for the worst revenge is always to have the right on one's side. That is why I show my hand so reluctantly. I do not want to have their insipid praises. But it is a dangerous path, as I know very well, and were it not that I had so much else to humiliate me, then I would consider continu-ing to follow it.

    You say she is sick. Does this mean that she is provided with news about me from the Lunds?[795] Does she get it from the children or from Miss Dencker[796] who visits the Tiedemanns, where she also visits? I hope she has not fallen into the hands of Miss Dencker. I hope she is not mired in gossip. In truth she is too good for that. And I who could not tolerate her by my side because I found it too humiliating for her, for in some way she would vanish because of my singularity, I who had worked out that plan in order really to elevate her, either so that she recovered or so that she might have the triumph that I—who even though in public opinion am nothing but the most unstable and egotistical person inside the walls of Copenhagen—that I would almost become a laughing stock by returning to her! That would be sweet-smelling to my nose, for even though I would not be a fool in her eyes, it would please me to be so in those of the world, provided that she could ascend thereby. What do I care about myself? I have myself. And now this too will disturb me, for it will after all seem as though I am returning to her out of pity. However, I refuse to be discouraged. Whenever I get to Copenhagen, I have a considerable influence on public opinion, and surely I can thumb my false nose at them once more. —For safety's sake I want you to make it generally known that as soon as Schelling has finished I am coming home. That was always my plan. My intention was to have another look at the affair then. Please say that the reason for my return is that I am extremely dissatisfied with Schelling, which by the way is only all too true. Then I shall see what is to be done. I dare not attempt anything until I am back in Copenhagen myself. There are difficulties of quite another kind that I must first straighten out. This whole affair is boundlessly complicated. But with God's help I keep up my courage. She will probably hear that I am returning in the spring. That is all I can do now; I dare do no more, although God knows that I would like to. And I do this also because I believe that I may be justified in doing it for my own sake, for I regard the relationship as broken only in a certain sense. You see how carefully I have guarded her interest. If I should return to her, then I would wish to include those few creatures whom she has learned to love through me, my four nephews and two nieces.[797] To that end I have kept up, often at a sacrifice of time, a steady correspondence with them.[798] Naturally, in order to divert attention, I have given this the appearance of something bizarre on my part. But like everything else, this remains between us. Therefore, you see, in returning to her I fear no danger from the same quarter that you do. Indeed, had I left her for my own sake, then everything would have been lost. But I have not done so. In my own eyes I do not return as the Prodigal Son, I am no less proud than before, her trust in me cannot be weakened by my return. But as I have said, there are other things to take into consideration.

Do you now see the difference between my relationship and yours? You have only esthetic considerations, or do you believe that on the Day of Judgment you will have to render an account because you have not become engaged to a girl to whom you would very much like to become engaged? If so, one would have to say that on the Day of Judgment you may demand an accounting for why you did not get her. There is a yawning abyss between yours and mine. Therefore I am pleased that you are thinking better of it. Anyway, when I do get to Copenhagen I shall do my humble bit to give more support.

It is absolutely imperative that I return to Copenhagen this spring. For either I shall finish Either/Or[799] by spring, or I shall never finish it. The title is approximately that which you know. I hope you will keep this between us. Anonymity is of the utmost importance to me. Only in one case would I not have come if I had thought it necessary for her sake. For her I do everything; I am profligate with myself more than with money, and that is saying a lot. In this connection I long to see you. You are used to seeing my works in the making; this time it is different. When I now take out my scrolls and read to you some fourteen to twenty sheets, what do you say to that? Courage, Antonius![800] In a certain sense these are difficult times, and some of the chapters I am working on do indeed need all my sense of humor, all my wit, wherever I get it from. I have completely given up on Schelling.[801] I merely listen to him, write nothing down either there or at home.

I suppose my stock is pretty low in Copenhagen. Even my brother Peter wrote with some reservation. All that does not worry me; I am almost more worried, if it should come about that I return to her, that people will say, "He has something decent about him after all." That contemptible rabble! Of course I might have remained with her, let her suffer all that which it was then impossible to prevent, and told her that she herself had after all wanted it—and would have been extolled and honored as a good husband. That is how most husbands are. I refuse to do that. I would rather be hated and detested.

Either/Or is indeed an excellent title. It is piquant and at the same time also has a speculative meaning. But for my own sake I will not rob you prematurely of any enjoyment.

This winter in Berlin will always have great significance for me. I have done a lot of work. When you consider that I have had three or four hours of lecture every day, have had a daily language lesson, and have still gotten so much written (and that regardless of the fact that in the beginning I had to spend a lot of time writing down Schelling's lectures and making fair copies), and have read a lot, I cannot complain. And then all my suffering, all my monologues! I feel strongly that I cannot continue for long; I never expected to; but I can for a short while and all the more intensively. Greetings to your father and mother.

Take care of yourself, my dear Emil,

Your
S.K.

[Address:]
An dem Herrn E. Boesen
Candidat der Theologie
Copenhagen
Philosophgangen

[Postmarks:]
Berlin   Hamburg
2/7 2–3   2/8 4–5
                              Letters, no. 68   February 6 [1842]

« **5552**

My dear Emil,[802]

Schelling[803] talks endless nonsense both in an extensive and an intensive sense. I am leaving Berlin and hastening to Copenhagen, but not, you understand, to be bound by a new tie, oh no, for I feel more strongly than ever that I need my freedom. A person with my eccentricity should have his freedom until he meets a force in life that, as such, can bind him. I am coming to Copenhagen to complete Either/Or. It is my favorite idea, and in it I exist. You will see that this idea is not to be made light of. In no way can my life yet be considered finished. I feel I still have great resources within me.

I do owe Schelling something. For I have learned that I enjoy traveling, even though not for the sake of studying. As soon as I have finished Either/Or I shall fly away again like a happy bird. I must travel. Formerly I never had the inclination for it, but first I must finish Either/Or[804] and that I can do only in Copenhagen.

What do you think of that? Probably you have missed me at times, but have a little patience and I shall soon be with you. My brain has not yet become barren and infertile, words still flow from my lips, and this eloquence of mine, which you at least appreciate, has not yet been stilled.

Really, I cannot understand how I have tolerated this servitude here in Berlin. I have taken off only Sundays, have been on no excursions, have had little entertainment. No thank you! I am Sunday's child,[805] and that means that I ought to have six days of the week off and work only one day.

I have much, very much, to tell you. I suppose that now and then you have not understood me very well. That will now be taken care of. Besides, I am not very good at writing letters. Usually I have written to you quite literally at the very moment I received yours. This makes my letters lively, but accordingly, by and large they do not say any more than a spoken conversation would. Afterwards I am often troubled by this. I may have forgotten most of it, but one thing I do remember, and now I do not think it matters. Of course you are the only person to whom I write in this manner. I am accustomed to considering you as an absolutely silent witness to the most momentous movements of my soul. Yet I manage to keep my perspective.

I hope that it will also mean something to you that I am coming. Surely it is not presumptuous to say that there is one person to whom I mean something. Then we shall once more open our *fiscus*. I have not been extravagant; on the contrary I have saved a lot, and on this we may have many happy days. Then, when I once more walk arm in arm with you, when the cigar is lit, or when "the Professor"[806] sits on the coachbox proud and straight and scornful of the whole world, proud that he is driving for me, who am also scornful of the whole world, and we stop, and you have friendship enough to let yourself be truly influenced by what I have to recite to you: "Hurrah for me and you,[807] I say, this day will never be forgotten."

I have no more to say to you in writing. I hope you are taking strict precautions against any third party's seeing my letters or reading them, and also that your facial expression betrays nothing. This caution you do understand. You know how I am, how in conversation with you I jump about stark naked, whereas I am always enormously calculating with other people.

My dear Emil,
please take care of yourself,
your
S.K.

[Address on the envelope:]
An dem Herrn Cand. Theol. E. Boesen
Copenhagen

Philosophgangen

[Postmarks:]
Berlin   Hamburg
2/27   2–3   3/1
Letters, no. 69   February 27, 1842

« **5553**

[Final draft of "The Seducer's Diary," concluding part of *Either/ Or*, I.⁸⁰⁸]

III B 168   April 14, 1842

« **5554**

The older one gets, the more he feels at certain times like shouting: Allah is great, somewhat as the Arabs do on almost every occasion in life. Today a paper was missing; it was extremely important for me to know whether or not it still existed; if it did, it could completely eliminate the need for a very elaborate piece of work—looking for some other things, I opened a secret drawer, and there it was—and I shouted: Allah is great.⁸⁰⁹

III A 220   *n.d.*, 1840–42 (?)

« **5555** *My Umbrella, My Friend*

It never forsakes me; it did that only once. It was during a terrible storm; I stood all alone on Kongens Nytorv, forsaken by everybody, and then my umbrella turned inside out. I was at a loss as to whether or not I should abandon it because of its faithlessness and become a misanthrope. I have acquired such an affection for it that I always carry it, rain or shine; indeed, to show it that I do not love it merely for its usefulness, I sometimes walk up and down in my room and pretend I am outside, lean on it, open it up, rest my chin on the handle, bring it up to my lips, etc.⁸¹⁰

III A 221   *n.d.*, 1840–42 (?)

« **5556**

If I did not know that I am a genuine Dane, I could almost be tempted to explain my self-contradictions by supposing that I am an Irishman. For the Irish do not have the heart to immerse their children totally when they have them baptized; they want to keep a little paganism in reserve; generally the child is totally immersed under water but with the right arm free, so that he will be able to wield a sword with it, embrace the girls.⁸¹¹

III A 223   *n.d.*, 1840–42 (?)

« 5557

My head is as empty and dead as a theater when the play is over.[812]

III A 224   n.d., 1840–42 (?)

« 5558

. . . . . after one has lived a dozen years in this appalling still life, this wretched, meager life has yielded just about as much cream as one can swallow in one single instant without overeating. I cannot march to that tempo.[813]

III A 225   n.d., 1840–42 (?)

« 5559

Where is the comic in the following incident. Today a man from the workhouse[814] approached me out on the green and handed me a letter which he asked me to read. It began like this: In deepest submission I throw myself on my knees before you, etc. —I looked up from the paper involuntarily to see if he was doing that, but he was not. Would it have been more comic if he had? Does the comic lie in this contradiction between an idiomatic phrase and actuality?[815]

III A 198   n.d., 1842

« 5560

"Schreibe" sprach jene Stimme und der Prophet antwortete "für wen?" Die Stimme sprach "für die Todten, für die Du in der Vorwelt lieb hast." "Werden sie mich lesen." "Ja, denn sie kommen zurück als Nachwelt."

See Herder, Zur Literatur und Kunst,[816] XVI, p. 114.

In margin:
See also the same volume, pp. 8, 9, 10, regarding a poem worth reading by Bishop Synesius.

III A 203   n.d., 1842

« 5561

May, 1842

Disjecta Membra[817]

III A 227   May, 1842

« 5562

. . . . . and if the bitter cup of suffering is handed to me, I will ask that, if possible, it be taken away, and if it is not possible, I will take it cheerfully, and I will not look at the cup but at the one who hands it to me, and I will not look at the bottom of the cup to see if it is soon empty, but I will look at him who hands it to me, and while I trustingly empty the goblet I will not say to any other man: Here's to your health, as I myself am savoring it, but I will say: Here's to my health, and empty its bitterness, to my health, for I know and am convinced that it is for my health that I empty it, for my health, as I leave not one drop behind.[818]

III A 228   n.d., 1842

« 5563

. . . . . and it was the delight of his eyes and his heart's desire. And he stretched out his arm and took it, but he could not keep it; it was offered to him, but he could not possess it—alas, and it was the delight of his eyes and his heart's desire. And his soul verged on despair, but he preferred the greater anguish, losing it and giving it up, to the lesser of having it wrongfully, or, to speak more exactly, as one should do in this holy place, he chose the lesser anguish to avoid the greater one of possessing it with a soul at strife . . . . . and oddly enough it turned out to be the best for him.[819]

III A 229   n.d., 1842

« 5564 *Page from a Street Inspector's Diary*[820]

It was April 1, 1830, that I became district inspector below the stock exchange.
  (a) Reflections on a fish tank in one of the fishing boats, the enormous horizon, still life in contrast
  (b) A Laplander—idyll
  the coal market   the old market
  the straw market
       the tale of a gutter plank
       deluge
The editor has been unable to restrain himself from slipping in a few observations.

It is Sunday afternoon—all so quiet—a shrimp-seller cries his wares—
  A man with plantain—the out-of-the-way place where it grows—
  A woman selling oranges—harbinger of spring—
  A little love story in the district—[821]

III A 245   n.d., 1842

« **5565**

The tale of the rat that became a misanthrope.[822]

III A 246   *n.d.,* 1842

« **5566**

[The final draft of "The Immediate Stages of the Erotic or the Musical Erotic."[823]]

III B 172   June 13, 1842

« **5567**

[The final draft of "Silhouettes."[824]]

III B 173   July 25, 1842

« **5568**

[The final draft of the "Preface" by the editor, Victor Eremita.[825]]

III B 189   November, 1842

« **5569**

No doubt I could bring my Antigone[826] to an end if I let her be a man. He forsook his beloved because he could not keep her together with his private agony. In order to do it right, he had to turn his whole love into a deception against her, for otherwise she would have participated in his suffering in an utterly unjustifiable way. This outrage enraged the family: a brother, for example, stepped forward as an avenger; I would then have my hero fall in a duel.

III A 207   November 20, 1842

« **5570**

Plot. Someone publishes a novel, he uses fictitious names to draw attention away from the historical aspect of it. It so happens that he uses the name of an actual girl, one who has many little traits that fit the fictitious girl. The girl in the novel is portrayed unsympathetically; the actual girl is disgraced. The author can extricate himself only by confessing the truth. But he cannot—collision.

III A 208   November 20, 1842

« **5571**

In margin of 5570 (III A 208):

Aeschylus' life could be the occasion for such a tragedy, since he unknowingly reveals the mysteries.

See Aristotle, *Ethics,*[827] 3, 2.

III A 209   *n.d.*

« 5572

Copenhagen

The Stoics' four categories: τὰ ὑποκείμενα, τὰ ποῖα, τὰ πῶς ἔχοντα, τὰ πρός τι ἔχοντα (Tennemann).[828]

Quantity.

totality

Unity–plurality–universality

allness

Quality

Reality; negation; limitation

Relation

Inherence and substance; causality and dependence; interaction.

Modality

Possibility, impossibility–being, non-being; necessity, chance.

Judgments

According to quality: affirmative, negative, infinite.

According to quantity: singular, particular, general.

According to relation: categorical, hypothetical, disjunctive.

According to modality: assertive, problematic, apodictic.

Conclusions

According to quality: of individuality, of particularity, of universality

Quantity: of totality, analogy, induction.

Relation: categorical, hypothetical, disjunctive.

IV C 2   *n.d.,* 1842

« 5573

"Inter accidentia sola, non autem inter formas substantiales individuorum ejusdem speciei, plus et minus reperitur."

See Cartesius, *De methodo,*[829] p. 1.

IV A 1   *n.d.,* 1842

« 5574

For the most part Descartes has embodied his system in the first six meditations. So it is not always necessary to write systems. I want to publish "Philosophical Deliberations"[830] in pamphlets, and into them I can put all my interim reflections. It perhaps would not be so bad to write in Latin.

IV A 2   *n.d.,* 1842

« 5575

I would like to write a piece which would be called: *Life Put to the Test.* It must be very imaginative. A hypochondriacal anxiety together with an egotistic self-indulgence could here take shape in all sorts of with an egotistic self-indulgence could here take shape in all sorts of forms in such a way that the piece would annul itself, because all the forces which had withdrawn from one another in this way finally find themselves captured in an actuality which they themselves had hypothetically posited, but which now, as a result of the power actuality always has, would give birth to an actuality which they had not suspected at all.

For example, a hypothetically contracted marriage, in which the children would make a dash in the calculations.

A hypothetical civil service appointment which involved one in actuality.

A hypothetical state that got into a lot of trouble with actuality.

IV A 197   *n.d.*, 1842 (?)

« **5576**

If one modernized it a little, it could very well be used as a motif for a tragedy—the story which is told in Aristotle's *Politics,* Book V, 4,[831] about the origin of the political disturbances in Delphi arising out of a marriage-match affair. The bridegroom, for whom the auguries prophesy misfortune originating in his marriage, suddenly changes his plan when he comes to fetch the bride. The family, regarding this as ridicule, is insulted, and in order to take revenge they plant a sacred vessel from the temple among his kitchen utensils, and he is condemned as a temple-thief.

IV A 8   *n.d.*, 1842–43

« **5577**

Ritter and Preller[832] have included a good selection of quotations from Plato in their history of Greek philosophy. They are noted in my copy.

IV A 201   *n.d.*, 1842–43

« **5578**

Darwin, *Zoonomie,*[833] überstzt v. Brandis. Baroque as well as original or primitive thoughts are found in this book.

IV C 6   *n.d.*, 1842–43

« **5579**

Erdmann, *Geschichte der Philosophie.*[834] Two volumes of this work have been published in many parts. Part two of volume two contains Leibniz and Idealism before Kant.

IV C 8   *n.d.*, 1842–43

« 5580

In Gottscheden's translation of Leibniz, *Theodicee*[835] (1763 edition, Hannover and Leipzig), in a note on p. 80[836] about Malebranche's theory of passivity, there is mention of a work by a Professor Gabriel Fischer: *Vernünftige Gedanken von der Natur; was sie sey? dass sie ohne Gott und seine allweise Beschränkung unmächtig sey; und wie die einige untheilbare göttliche Kraft in und durch ihre Mittelursachen nach dem Maasse ihrer verliehenen Wirkbarkeit oder Tüchtigkeit, hier in der Welt alles wirke.*[837] 1743, no city or publisher. The book was confiscated, he says [p.81].

In Gottscheden's translation of Leibniz's *Theodicee* (1763 ed.), p. 81,[838] there is mention of a work by a Jesuit, Thomas Bonartes, *De concordia scientiae cum fide.*

The Jesuit Friedrich Spee (the one who has written *Cautio criminalis*)[839] has also written in German a work on the Christian virtues and argues the power of God's love to forgive sins even without the sacraments and the intervention of the Christian Church. See Leibniz, *Theodicee*, 1, para. 96.[840]

Franciscus v. Sales, *De amore Dei.*[841]

Cardanus, *De utilitate ex adversis capienda*   Quoted in
Novarinus, *De occultis Dei beneficiis.*   L., para. 215.[842]

Theagenes and Chariklea,[843] a romance by Heliodor, Bishop of Larissa, which is mentioned in Gottscheden's translation of Leibniz's work on King, *De origine mali*[844] (1763 edition); he refers to Huetius, *De l'Origine des Romans.*[845] There are two German translations, an old one without date and city, a new one by the Protestant pastor, M. Agricola, in the Jena of Mannsfeld, 1750.

IV C 9   *n.d.*, 1842–43

« 5581

Gregorius Rimini, general of the Augustinian order, accepted the dogma of the damnation of infants and therefore received the nickname of *Tortor infantum.*[846]

See Leibniz, *Theodicee*, 1, para. 92.[847]

IV A 14   *n.d.*, 1842–43

« 5582

A Jesuit, Johan Davidius, has written a book, *Veridicus Christianus*, which is a kind of bibliomancy; one can open it up and be seized by the sudden and unexpected and thereby become a Christian.

See Leibniz, *Theodicee*, 1, 101.[848]

IV A 15   *n.d.*, 1842–43

« 5583

A satirical book against the Gomarists,[849] *Fur praedestinatus,* has been published. See Leibniz, *Theodicee,* para. 167.[850]

IV A 16   *n.d.,* 1842–43

« 5584

What kind of novel is the book Leibniz mentions in his *Theodicee,* para. 173[851] under the title: *Mademoiselle de Scudery?* As a matter of fact, Hoffmann's well-known story[852] has the same title.

IV A 17   *n.d.,* 1842–43

« 5585

> Cantantur haec, laudantur haec,
> Dicuntur, audiuntur.
> Scribuntur haec, leguntur haec.
> Et lecta negliguntur.[853]

IV A 22   *n.d.,* 1842–43

« 5586

In section 4 of the fifth chapter of King's book, *De origine mundi* [*mali*][854] there are unquestionably a good many paragraphs which from an ethical point of view would be really useful.

IV A 25   *n.d.,* 1842–43

« 5587

πάντως γὰρ οὐδεὶς Ἔρωτα ἔφυγεν ἢ θεύξεται μέχρι ἂν κάλλος ᾖ καὶ ὀφθαλμοὶ βλέπωσιν.—
See the last words of the preface to Longus, *Pastoralia.* [855]

IV A 30   *n.d.,* 1842–43

« 5588

Descartes[856] (in his essay, *De passionibus*) observes correctly that *admiratio*[857] has no opposite (see Article LIII). Similarly, that *cupiditas* ought not have its opposite in *aversio* but ought to have no opposite (see Article LXXXVII). This is important for my theory of anxiety. See JJ,[858] page 3 from back [i.e., III A 233].

IV C 10   *n.d.,* 1842–43

« 5589

τὸ γὰρ κακὸν τοῦ ἀπείρου, ὡς οἱ Πυθαγόρειοι εἴκαζον, τὸ δὲ ἀγαθὸν τοῦ πεπερασμένου.
ἐσθλοὶ μὲν γὰρ ἁπλῶς, παντοδαπῶς δὲ κακοί.
See Aristotle's *Ethics,*[859] II, 5.

IV C 15   *n.d.,* 1842–43

« 5590

Aristotle[860] distinguishes three aspects of the soul: πάθη, δυνά-
μεις, ἕξεις. (Garve[861] translates the last one as "skills"; see chapter
5 in Aristotle. Chapter 4 in book II.)

IV C 18   n.d., 1842-43

« 5591

The identity of virtue and beauty is also seen by Aristotle (3:10):
φοβήσεται μὲν οὖν καὶ τὰ τοιαῦτα, ὡς δεῖ δὲ καὶ ὡς ὁ λόγος
ὑπομένει τοῦ καλοῦ ἕνεκα·τοῦτο γὰρ τέλος τῆς ἀρετῆς.[862]

IV C 22   n.d., 1842-43

« 5592

With respect to the concept of poetry it would be good to point
out how Aristotle distinguishes ποιεῖν and πράττειν[863] and defines
art. See 6, 4.[864]–

IV C 24   n.d., 1842-43

« 5593

Epicurus has already abolished the principle of contradiction: his
dispute with Chrysippus. See Leibniz's *Theodicee*,[865] para., 169. The
dispute between Diodorus and Chrysippus. Diodorus maintained that
what had not existed and would not exist was impossible; Chrysippus
denied it and maintained that it was possible,[866] para. 170.[867]

IV C 34   n.d., 1842-43

« 5594

Leibniz's comments on King's book,[868] para. 4.[869] Even though
the matter is altered as much as possible, these qualities still remain:
extension, motion, divisibility, resistance.

IV C 41   n.d., 1842-43

« 5595

The distinction that Bonaventura, following certain Church Fathers, makes between συντήρησις and *conscientia.*[870] See Tennemann,
Geschichte der Philos.,[871] VIII, pt. 2, p. 532.

IV C 42   n.d., 1842-43

« 5596

Abelard has written a work [entitled] *De praedicamentis.* See Tennemann,[872] VIII, pt. 1, p. 186.

IV C 43   n.d., 1842-43

« **5597**

In margin of 5596 (IV C 43):
Also Leibniz in his German letter to Wagner, the only German in
Erdmann's edition.[873]

IV C 44   *n.d.*

« **5598**

Tennemann, *Geschichte der Philosophie,*[874] III.

Aristotle

Up to p. 120 I have underlined in my copy everything that was
striking.
The whole inquiry into πρώτη φιλοσοφία,[875] the ambiguity in it;
at times it is ontology, at times theology. This confusion seems to me
to be repeated in modern philosophy. See p. 67.[*]
In his classification all things are

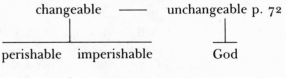

changeable —— unchangeable p. 72

perishable   imperishable   God

heaven

Where is there a place for man?
He does not classify dichotomously as Plato does:
substance—accident
He has a trichotomy:
matter—form—deprivation (στέρησις).
That is, matter has an original form.
There are four kinds of causes (see p. 120). Matter, form and
prototype, effecting cause, *Endzweck.*[876]
P. 121. Luck and chance.

IV C 45   *n.d.,* 1842–43

« **5599**

[*] *In margin of 5598* (IV C 45):
In Berlin Schelling maintained that logic ought to be πρώτη
φιλοσοφία.[877]
See my manuscript.[878]

IV C 46   *n.d.*

« 5600

What is implied in Antisthenes' position that nothing can be defined by what it is and any attempt at such a definition is a tautology.
Only the characteristics of things can be stated. Aristotle opposed this.
See Tennemann, *Geschichte der Philosophie*,[879] III, p. 235. Also II,
p. 97.

IV C 83   *n.d.*, 1842–43

« 5601 *Lectures*[880] *on the Greek Sophists According to the*
         Sources

Introduction
Concerning the significance of the primary sources—concerning
Greek philosophy in particular.—
This lecture will not be without significance for the problems that
preoccupy our age. The category to which I intend to trace everything,
and which is also the category lying dormant in Greek Sophistry if one
views it world-historically, is motion (κίνησις), which is perhaps one
of the most difficult problems in philosophy. In modern philosophy it
has been given another expression—namely, transition and mediation.

IV C 97   *n.d.*, 1842–43

« 5602

Addition to 5601 (IV C 97):
I will also go through each primary source book philologically.
Among those I include: Plato's *Theaetetus, Euthydemus, The Sophist,
Gorgias, Protagoras*—Aristotle's work on Protagoras and περὶ τῶν
σοφιστικῶν ἐλέγχων.[881] However, what is known of them from Sex-
tus Empiricus, from Athenaeus, etc., is simply to be consulted and
must not be presented directly.

IV C 98   *n.d.*, 1842–43

« 5603

A.
Das Wesen als Grund der Existents
(a) Die reinen Reflexions Bestimmungen
         (α) Identitæt (β) Unterschied (γ) Grund
(b) die Existents
(c) das Ding

B.
Die Erscheinung
(a) Die Welt der Erscheinung
(b) Inhalt und Form
(c) Das Verhaltniss

C.
Die Wirklichkeit[882]

IV C 101   *n.d.*, 1842–43

« **5604**

How does ideality become alive for the lyrical poets—the epic poet has the subject matter and the muse, for the lyrical poet the muse itself is the subject matter; the epic poet invokes the muse, the lyric poet is infatuated with the muse whether it is a happy love affair or not.

IV C 107   *n.d.*, 1842–43

« **5605**

The epical lies in continuity, the lyrical in discreteness. The originality of the epical is therefore different from that of the lyrical.

IV C 123   *n.d.*, 1842–43

« **5606**

A remarkable definition of the beautiful: τὸ γὰρ καλὸν ἐν μεγέθει καὶ τάξει ἐστί, διὸ οὔτε πάμμικρον ἄν τι γένοιτο καλὸν ζῷον (σύγχειται γὰρ ἡ θεωρία ἐγγὺς τοῦ ἀναισθήτου γενομένη), οὔτε παμμέγεθες· οὐ γὰρ ἅμα ἡ θεωρία γίνεται, ἀλλ' οἴχεται τοῖς θεωροῦσι τὸ ἕν καὶ τὸ ὅλον ἐκ τῆς θεωρίας, οἷον εἰ μυρίων σταδίων εἴη ζῷον. See Aristotle, Ch. 7.[883] Curtius[884] remarks on this passage that Aristotle did not acknowledge that there are beautiful children. It presumably was not worth the trouble of finding out whether or not this was so. At the end he quotes book 4 of Aristotle's *Ethics,* but this is a very careless reference.*

In margin:*The passage is 4, 7, where he speaks of μεγαλοπρέπεια and observes *en passant:* ἐν μεγέθει γαρ ἡ μεγαλοψυχία ὥσπερ καὶ τὸ κάλλος ἐν μεγάλῳ σώματι. οἱ μικροὶ δ'ἀστεῖοι καὶ σύμμετροι, καλοὶ δ' οὔ.[885]

IV C 124   *n.d.*, 1842–43

« **5607**

On the theme of the comic significance of evil, comparison can be made with a passage in Leibniz's *Theodicee,* [886] in which he refers to an English book which has conceived of hell as comic. See para. 270. (The English prelate he talks about presumably is King?)

IV C 126   *n.d.,* 1842–43

« **5608**

The Plan for My Lectures [887]

1.

On the Concept of Poetry

2.

The Movement through Esthetics

3.

The Comic

Esthetics Abrogated
Cultus des Genius [888]

IV C 127   *n.d.,* 1842–43

IV. THOUGHTS LIKE NATIONS IN MIGRATION
1843–1844

« 5609

Abelard[889] lends himself superbly to dramatic treatment. In Bossuet's *Geschichte*, [890] VI, pp. 315 ff., I have underlined several hints concerning his life. The situations would be extremely interesting; Heloise not only had fallen in love with Abelard but was philosophically infatuated with him, proud of his renown, jealous of his philosophical distinction.

IV A 31   n.d., 1843

« 5610

If I should ever be accused of something, I would petition His Majesty the favor of promptly receiving the most extreme (relative to the incident) sentence, even if it were execution, and that it be carried out immediately. I would make the petition for the following reasons: (1) because the trial costs money, (2) it costs time, and I have no time to wait for men to decide what is just, which is a matter of indifference to me, anyway, if I can just get it over with, (3) because all the talk about justice is drivel, and one may just as well have himself be executed outside the law and without being sentenced as by the verdict of three courts.[891]

IV A 34   n.d., 1843

« 5611

Quod vero (perdix) supervolante masculo, vel audita solum voce ejus, vel etiam solo halitu oris concepto concipiat, Aristoteles[892] refert.[893]

Hieronymi Cardini, De rerum varietate, [894] p. 375.

IV A 36   n.d., 1843

« 5612

Philosophical terminology and its usage simply degenerate to the ridiculous. I wonder what someone would say if I were to speak of an earthquake in the old terminology.

"Inter terrae miracula est motus ejus, de quo alias dictum est. Quatuor ejus differentiae, ab effectu. *Chasmatichus, Brasmatichus, Clitimachus, Micematichus.*"[895]

Everyone would understand the difference but not the terminology.

See Hieronymus Cardanus, *De rerum varietate,*[896] p. 57.

IV A 37   *n.d.,* 1843

« **5613 *My Opinion of "Either-Or"*[897]**

There was a young man as favorably endowed as an Alcibiades. He lost his way in the world. In his need he looked about for a Socrates but found none among his contemporaries. Then he requested the gods to change him into one. But now—he who had been so proud of being an Alcibiades was so humiliated and humbled by the gods' favor that, just when he received what he could be proud of, he felt inferior to all.

IV A 43   *n.d.,* 1843

« **5614**

Even if I proved nothing else by writing *Either-Or,* I proved that in Danish literature a book can be written without needing the warm jacket of sympathy,[898] without needing the incentive of anticipation, that one can work even though the stream is against him, that one can work hard without seeming to, that one can privately concentrate while practically every bungling student dares look upon him as a loafer.[899] Even if the book itself were devoid of meaning, the making of it would still be the pithiest epigram I have written over the maundering philosophic age in which I live.

IV A 45   *n.d.,* 1843

« **5615**

When I was very young, I could not understand how one went about writing a book. Now I understand it very well, but now I do not see how anyone would want to do it.[900]

IV A 53   *n.d.,* 1843

« **5616**

All infinite knowledge is negative ("always to be in the wrong"[901] is also an infinite relation), and yet the negative is higher than the positive.* Thus Pythagoras also taught that the even number is imperfect, the uneven number perfect.[902]

* The Pythagoreans also regarded the finite as higher and more perfect than the infinite.
See Tennemann,[903] I, p. 115.
In margin: As a rule the Pythagoreans did not regard as perfect that from which something arises, but that which arises from something.
See Tennemann, I, p. 119.

IV A 56   *n.d.,* 1843

« **5617**

If they say that what I say is the same as what all the others say, I have no objection if they mean the same as what Leucippus meant when he declared that a tragedy and a light comedy have the same letters, except that the order is different.
See Tennemann, *Gesch. d. Ph.,*[904] I, p. 264, bottom.

IV A 61   *n.d.,* 1843

« **5618**

If anyone wants to call my fragment of wisdom Sophistic, I must point out that it lacks at least one characteristic according to both Plato's and Aristotle's definitions: that one makes money by it.[905]
See Tennemann's *Gesch. d. Ph.,*[906] I, p. 355, note 6 b.

IV A 63   *n.d.,* 1843

« **5619**

I will say to myself what Socrates says to Theaetetus: Ὠδίνεις γάρ, ὦ φίλε Θεαίτητε, διὰ τὸ μὴ κενὸς ἀλλ' ἐγκύμων εἶναι.[907]
See Ast,[908] II, p. 22.

IV A 64   *n.d.,* 1843

« **5620**

As soon as I[909] state the immediate, the statement is essentially untrue, for I cannot state anything immediately but only mediately.
Repetition

Doubt, then, does not arise from and advance with truth; on the contrary, as long as doubt is not present everything is true. Doubt comes through ideality and ideality through doubt.

The ideas are always dichotomous
[*In pencil:* in reflection every-   In ideality everything
thing is dichotomous.]   is dichotomous
        to know—truth

to love——the beautiful
to will——the good

The principal pain of existence is that from the beginning I have been in contradiction to myself, that a person's true being comes through an opposition. —It may be that one does not perceive this contradiction, for in ideality by itself, just as in reality [*Realiteten*],[910] everything is true. But it cannot remain hidden from a person when he submits everything to ideality—he then discovers that reality is a fraud. It is usually through an illusion that one realizes this. But it is easy to see that if all sense perception is not a fraud, then there would be no illusion at all. That men persist in the mixed position that sense perception as a rule is true but now and then deceives proves nothing, because the fact that something appears to be different under other conditions is, after all, not a deception by sense perception, but on the contrary the opposite would be a deception by sense perception. An eye can be so lazy that it does not detect the change, but in that case it is the particular eye that deceives the individual.

> All this demonstrates the possibility of doubt per se. Now he wanted to try to determine more definitely what it is to doubt, for the language had many different expressions to describe this situation, and it is not properly called doubt.

When a judge is uncertain, he conducts an interrogation, pursues every clue, and then pronounces a judgment—that is, he comes to the conclusion: guilty or innocent; but now and then he dismisses the charge. Is then nothing accomplished by that judgment? Indeed there is—the uncertainty is determined. He was uncertain as to how he should judge; now he is no longer uncertain, now his verdict is ready: he judges that he is uncertain. He rests in that, for one cannot rest in uncertainty, but one can rest when one has determined it.

    IV B 10 a (Suppl., XI³, pp. xxxvii–xxxviii)   *n.d.*, 1842–43

« **5621**

[The completed manuscript of "Johannes Climacus or *De omnibus dubitandum est.*"[911]]

                                    IV B 1   *n.d.*, 1842–43

« **5622** *Outline*

Once in his early youth a man allowed himself to be so far carried away in an overwrought irresponsible state as to visit a prostitute. It is all forgotten. Now he wants to get married. Then anxiety stirs. He is tortured day and night with the thought that he might possibly be a father, that somewhere in the world there could be a created being who owed his life to him. He cannot share his secret with anyone; he does not even have any reliable knowledge of the fact. —For this reason the incident must have involved a prostitute and taken place in the wantonness of youth; had it been a little infatuation or an actual seduction, it would be hard to imagine that he could know nothing about it, but now this very ignorance is the basis of his agitated torment. On the other hand, precisely because of the rashness of the whole affair, his misgivings do not really start until he actually falls in love.[912]

IV A 65   *n.d.,* 1843

« 5623

. . . . . a kiss which was something more than a peck.[913]

IV A 67   *n.d.,* 1843

« 5624 *Outline*

A man who for a long time has gone around hiding a secret becomes mentally deranged. At this point one would imagine that his secret would have to come out, but despite his derangement his soul still sticks to its hideout, and those around him become even more convinced that the false story he told to deceive them is the truth. He is healed of his insanity, knows everything that has gone on, and thereby perceives that nothing has been betrayed. Was this gratifying to him or not; he might wish to have disposed of his secret in his madness; it seems as if there were a fate which forced him to remain in his secret and would not let him get away from it. Or was it for the best, was there a guardian spirit who helped him keep his secret.[914]

IV A 68   *n.d.,* 1843

« 5625

Un sot trouve toujours un plus sot, qui l'admire.

Boileau.[915]

IV A 69   *n.d.,* 1843

« 5626

When I am not *reus voti,*[916] nothing happens for me. Because of it I passed my theological examination,[917] because of it I wrote my dissertation,[918] because of it I was all through with *Either/Or*[919] in eleven months. If anyone were to find out the actual incentive. . . . . .

Good Lord, they no doubt are thinking, such a big book as that must
certainly have a very profound incentive . . . . . and yet it is exclusively
concerned with my private life—and the purpose—well, if this were
discovered, I would be declared stark raving mad. I perhaps would be
excused for personally regarding it as an interesting piece of work, but
for me to look upon it as a good deed, that for me this is the most
appealing aspect of the whole thing. . . . . .

IV A 70   n.d., 1843

« 5627

Probably no one suspects that *Either/Or*[920] has a plan from the
first word to the last, since the preface[921] makes a joke of it and does
not say a word about the speculative.[922]

IV A 214   n.d., 1843

« 5628

Some think that *Either/Or* is a collection of loose papers I had
lying in my desk. Bravo! —As a matter of fact, it was the reverse. The
only thing this work lacks is a narrative, which I did begin but omitted,
just as Aladdin left a window incomplete. It was to be called "Unhappy
Love."[923] It was to form a contrast to the Seducer. The hero in the
story acted in exactly the same way as the Seducer, but behind it was
melancholy. He was not unhappy because he could not get the girl he
loved. Such heroes are beneath me. He had capacities comparable to
the Seducer's; he was certain of capturing her. He won her. As long
as the conflict went on, he detected nothing; then she surrendered, he
was loved with all the enthusiasm a young girl has—then he became
unhappy, went into a depression, pulled back; he could struggle with
the whole world but not with himself. His love made him indescribably
happy at the moment; as soon as he thought of time, he despaired.[924]

IV A 215   n.d., 1843

« 5629

The first διάψαλμα[925] is really the task of the entire work, which
is not resolved until the last words of the sermon.[926] An enormous
dissonance is assumed, and then it says: Explain it. A total break with
actuality is assumed, which does not have its base in futility but in
mental depression and its predominance over actuality.

The last διάψ.[927] tells us how a life such as this has found its
satisfactory expression in laughter. He pays his debt to actuality by
means of laughter, and now everything takes place within this contra-

diction. His enthusiasm is too intense, his sympathy too deep, his love too burning, his heart too warm to be able to express himself in any other way than by contradiction. Thus A[928] himself would never have come to a decision to publish his papers.[929]

IV A 216   *n.d.*, 1843

« 5630

I resist in vain. My foot slips. My life nevertheless remains a poet-existence. Can anything worse be imagined? I am predestined; fate laughs at me when it suddenly shows me *how everything I do to resist becomes a factor in such an existence.*[930]

IV A 217   *n.d.*, 1843

« 5631

If I had not decided when publishing *Either/Or* not to use any old material,[931] I would have found in going through my papers some excellent aphorisms I could have used. Today I found a little scrap of paper with the following written on it: "I am so tired that I feel that I need an eternity to rest, so depressed that I feel that I need an eternity to forget my troubles; I wish that I could sleep so long that I wake up an old man and then lie down again to sleep the eternal sleep."[932]

IV A 221   March 15, 1843

« 5632

An actual love affair could not be used in the first part, for it always affects a man so profoundly that he enters into the ethical. What I could use was a variety of erotic moods. These I was able to link to Mozart's *Don Juan.* Essentially they belong in the world of fantasy and find their satisfaction in music. In such cases a girl is much too little, precisely because she is infinitely much more.[933]

IV A 223   *n.d.*, 1843

« 5633

In a review in *Forposten*[934] I see that it is quite properly pointed out that this narrative is not called a seducer's diary but *the* seducer's, suggesting that the method really is of prime importance, not the portrayal of either Johannes or Cordelia.[935]

IV A 231   *n.d.*, 1843

« 5634

P. 336, "that it is every man's duty to become revealed" actually says the opposite of what the whole first part says, as the lines just quoted do in fact say. The esthetic is always hidden: if it expresses itself at all, it is exploitive. Therefore it would have been wrong to have A express his interior nature directly or, indeed, even in B's papers. In A's papers there are intimations of his interior being; in B's papers we see the exterior with which he is accustomed to deceive people—that is why A can come up with the statement about what would be the most derisive remark about existence (p. 334).[936]

The aim of the sermon[937] is not to lull, not to win a metaphysical position, but to motivate to action. That I can in fact do at every moment.

Healing and reconciliation take place essentially by means of compassion. It is a blessing for a man that there is something that he cannot, despite his freedom, will. He cannot will to destroy all existence. Arid morality would merely teach man that he is incapable, would mock his impotence; the upbuilding lies in seeing that one cannot will it.

The second part begins with marriage, because it is the most profound form of the revelation of life. It is ingenious to have Jupiter and Juno called *adultus* and *adulta*, τελειος, τελεια,[938] in connection with tracing marriage back to them.—[939]

IV A 234   *n.d.*, 1843

« 5635

Autopathetic and sympathetic doubt are identical.[940]

IV A 236   *n.d.*, 1843

« 5636

"To choose oneself" is no eudaimonism, as one will readily perceive. It is quite remarkable that even Chrysippus sought to elevate eudaimonia as the highest aim by showing that the basic drive in everything is to preserve and maintain itself in the original condition, and pleasure and happiness appear insofar as it succeeds.[941]

See Tennemann, *Ges. d. Ph.*,[942] IV, pp. 318–19.

IV A 246   *n.d.*, 1843

« 5637

But where is the boundary between worldly wisdom and religiousness. Mynster's[943] preaching is far from being wholly religious at all times. He gives consolation by saying that everything will perhaps turn out all right again, that better days are coming, *etc.*, which after all is not even a genuinely religious consolation; one shrinks from going out into the current—one tries to wade as long as possible. As long as this is not definitely decided, there always remains a doubt about the importance of actuality in one's whole train of thought.[944]

IV A 71   n.d., 1843

« 5638

That woman who was worshipped during the French Revolution as "the goddess of reason" would be a good subject for a drama. It is well-known that she died sometime later in the most pitiable state in a hospital.

IV A 74   n.d., 1843

« 5639

Theodorus Atheos said: He gave his teaching with his right hand, but his listeners received it with their left.[945]

See Tennemann, *Ges. d. Phil.,*[946] II, p. 124, note 39.

IV A 75   n.d., 1843

« 5640 *Outline*[947]

Let us assume (something neither the Old Testament nor the Koran reports) that Isaac knew the purpose of the journey he was going to make with his father to Mt. Moriah, that he was going to be sacrificed—if the present age had a poet, he would be able to relate what these two men talked about along the way.* I imagine that Abraham first of all looked at him with all his fatherly love, and his crushed heart and venerable countenance made what he said more urgent; he admonished Isaac to bear his fate patiently, he vaguely led him to understand that as a father he was suffering even more because of it. —But it does not help. I imagine that then Abraham turned away from him for a moment and when he turned back to him again he was unrecognizable to Isaac—his eyes were wild, his expression chilling, his venerable locks bristled like furies upon his head. He grabbed Isaac by the chest, drew his knife, and said: "You thought I was going to do this because of God, but you are wrong, I am an idolater, and this passion has again stirred in my soul—I want to murder you, this is my desire; I am worse than a cannibal. Despair, you foolish boy who fancied that I was your father; I am your murderer, and this is my desire." And Isaac fell on his knees and cried to heaven: "Merciful God, have mercy on me." But then Abraham whispered softly to himself: "So must it be, for it is better that he believes I am a monster, that he curses me and the fact that I was his father, and still better, that he prays to God—than that he should know that it was God who imposed the test, for then he would lose his mind and perhaps curse God."

—But where indeed are the contemporary poets, who have intimations of such conflicts? And yet Abraham's conduct was genuinely poetic, noble, more noble than anything I have read in tragedies. — When the child is to be weaned, the mother blackens her breast, but her eyes rest just as lovingly on the child. The child believes that it is the breast which has changed, but the mother is unchanged. And why does she blacken her breast? Because, she says, it would be a shame for the breast to appear attractive when the child must not have it. — This collision is easily resolved, for the breast is only a part of the mother herself. Fortunate is he who has never experienced more dreadful collisions, who did not need to blacken himself, who did not need to journey to hell to find out what the devil looks like so that he could make himself look like him and in this way possibly save another human being, at least in that person's God-relationship. This would be Abraham's collision.

—He who has explained this riddle has explained my life.[948]

But who of my contemporaries has understood this?

IV A 76   n.d., 1843

« **5641**

In margin of 5640 (IV A 76):

* One could also have Abraham's previous life be not devoid of guilt[949] and have him secretly ruminate on the thought that this was God's punishment, perhaps even have him get the melancholy thought that he must ask God's help to make the punishment as severe as possible.

IV A 77   n.d.

« **5642**

The nature of my love-relationship is very singular. The usual procedure for theological students is to begin by being teachers, that is, minor spiritual advisers to their chosen ones, and end by becoming lovers and married men. I began by being a lover and ended being a spiritual adviser. If worst comes to worst, my conduct is still far better and I have not debased the holy in the service of my love; I submit myself to the religious just as much as I seek to get another to submit.[950]

IV A 79   n.d., 1843

« **5643**

There is a place out in Gribs-Skov[951] which is called the Nook of Eight Paths.[952] The name is very appealing to me.

IV A 81   *n.d.,* 1843

« **5644**

It is very curious. I had decided to change that little preface[953] to the "Two Sermons,"[954] because it seemed to me to harbor a certain spiritual eroticism, and because it is extraordinarily hard to devote myself so ironically that the polemical contrast is not clearly present. I hurry to the printer. What happens. The printer asks for that preface. I did laugh at him a little, but secretly I thought: He may in fact be "the single individual." Rejoicing in the thought I at first decided to have only two copies printed and to present one to the typesetter. There was really something very beautiful about his movement. A typesetter —who one would surely think would become as weary of a manuscript as an author.

IV A 83   *n.d.,* 1843

« **5645**

After my death no one will find in my papers the slightest information (this is my consolation) about what really has filled my life;[955] no one will find the inscription in my innermost being that interprets everything and that often turns into events of prodigious importance[956] to me that which the world would call bagatelles and which I regard as insignificant if I remove the secret note[957] that interprets them.

IV A 85   *n.d.,* 1843

« **5646**

It seems to be my destiny to discourse on truth, insofar as I discover it, in such a way that all possible authority[958] is simultaneously demolished. Since I am incompetent and extremely undependable in men's eyes, I speak the truth and thereby place them in the contradiction from which they can be extricated only by appropriating the truth themselves. A man's personality is matured only when he appropriates the truth, whether it is spoken by Balaam's ass or a sniggering wag or an apostle or an angel.[959]

IV A 87   *n.d.,* 1843

« **5647**

Little by little, being an author has become the most contemptible profession of all. Usually one has to come forward like the gardener's apprentice in the vignette in *Addresseavisen*, [960] hat in hand, bowing and groveling, recommending oneself with good references. How stupid: the one who writes should understand what he is writing better than the one who reads; otherwise he should not write.—

Or one has to become a clever shyster who knows how to lead the public by the nose. —That I will not do, I will not, I will not, no, no, [961] the devil take it all. I write as I want to, and here the matter rests—the rest can do as they wish, refrain from buying, reading, reviewing, etc.—

IV A 88   *n.d.*, 1843

« **5648**

It is remarkable how rigorously, in a certain sense, I am being educated. Now and then I am placed down in the dark hole; I creep around there in agony and pain, see nothing, no way out. Then suddenly there stirs in my soul a thought so vivid that it seems as if I had never had it before, even though it is not unfamiliar to me, but previously I had been married to it, so to speak, only with the left hand and now I am married to it with the right. Now when it has established itself in me, I am cared for a bit, I am taken by the arms, and I, who had been scrunched together like a grasshopper, now grow up again, as sound, thriving, happy, warm, and lithe as a newly born infant. Then I must give my word, as it were, that I will follow this thought to the uttermost; I pledge my life and now I am buckled in the harness. I cannot pause and my powers hold out. Then I finish, and now it all starts over again.

IV A 89   *n.d.*, 1843

« **5649**

Addition to 5648 (IV A 89):

When I have God's disfavor, I am more miserable than a wobbly calf; when he nods approval to me, I am prouder than the whole world.

IV A 90   *n.d.*, 1843

« **5650**

I know very well that right now I have the best brains among the younger generation, but I also know that tomorrow this can be taken

away from me—yes, even before I dot this with a period. When someone else discovers that he has a good head he believes himself to be
taken care of for a lifetime. I do not believe this. I cannot build upon
the finite in this sense.

IV A 91   *n.d.*, 1843

« **5651**

I sit and listen to the sounds in my inner being, the happy intimations of music, the deep earnestness of the organ. To synthetize them
is a task not for a composer but for a man who in the absence of larger
demands upon life restricts himself to the simple task of wanting to
understand himself. —To mediate is no art when one has no elements
within himself.

IV A 93   *n.d.*, 1843

« **5652**

It is unbelievable what naïveté is to be found even in a full-fledged
author like Heiberg, what frivolous nonsense with regard to the category of time, what conventional drama talk, for example in *De Danske
i Paris,*[962] act I, scene 12. The major briefly relates the story of his life.
He ends by saying that people in Copenhagen will open their eyes
when they see him, whom they have always been pleased to call a
confirmed bachelor, return with a wife and daughter seventeen years
old. Consequently he has been married for eighteen years, and no one
has suspected it. He has had no moments of anxiety, no suffering, no
fearful presentiments, etc., or he has had them but no one has
managed to penetrate him. It is really a shame that the man has not
become more than a major, and that just recently; he ought to be a
lieutenant-colonel at least. My dear major, my dear professor, I would
like to know a little bit about this dexterous feat, that I would like, and
in return I present you with the whole vaudeville as a gift—just a few
pages [would be enough], for he who is occupied with what is important does not need so many scenes. Even if I were paid 100 rix-
dollars,[963] even if I would be declared a genius, I would never have
written such rubbish in earnest.* The major talks nonsense (at Heiberg's request) in all seriousness, quite as if he could be Holberg's
Ulysses, who is also the man for the times.

In margin: *To write this way is what I call letting the pen gossip
on paper.

IV A 96   *n.d.*, 1843

« **5653**

At vespers on Easter Sunday[964] in Frue Kirke[965] (during Mynster's sermon) she nodded to me. I do not know if it was pleadingly or forgivingly, but in any case very affectionately. I had sat down in a place apart, but she discovered it. Would to God she had not done so. Now a year and a half of suffering and all the enormous pains I took are wasted; she does not believe that I was a deceiver, she has faith in me. What ordeals now lie ahead of her. The next will be that I am a hypocrite.[966] The higher we go the more dreadful it is. That a man of my inwardness, of my religiousness, could act in such a way. And yet I can no longer live solely for her, cannot expose myself to the contempt of men in order to lose my honor—that I have done. Shall I in sheer madness go ahead and become a villain just to get her to believe it—ah, what help is that. She will still believe that I was not that before.

Every Monday morning between nine and ten she met me. I made no effort to have it happen.[967] She knows the street I usually walk, I know the way she

[A page torn from the journal]

I have done everything in order that she may not suspect that she perhaps bears a little bit of the guilt herself. A young girl should, after all, have calmness and humility. Instead, it was she who was proud;[968] it was I who had to teach her humility by humbling myself. Then she took my depression wrong; she believed that I was so meek and humble because she was such a matchless girl. Then she took a stand against me. God forgive it—she awakened my pride. That is my sin. I ran her aground—she deserved it, that is my honest opinion—but not what happened later. Then it was that I became depressed; the more passionately she clung to me, the more responsible I felt. It would never have been so difficult if that conflict had not taken place. Then the bond broke.

IV A 97   *n.d.*, 1843

« **5654**

Berlin, May 10, 1843[969]

The day after my arrival I was in very bad shape, on the point of collapse.

In Stralsund I almost went mad hearing above me a young girl playing the piano, among other pieces Weber's[970] last waltz. The last time I was in Berlin it was the first piece I heard in the Thiergarten, played on a harp by a blind man.[971]

It seems as if everything existed merely to bring back memories.[972] My pharmacist, who was a confirmed bachelor, has married. With reference to that, he offered several explanations: one lives only once, one must have one person who understands him. How much there is to that, especially when said without any pretension, hit home to me.

My room in the Hotel Saxon looks out upon the water where the boats are. Good Lord, how it reminds me of the past. —In the background I have the church, and the sound of its bells when it gives the time penetrates my bones and marrow.

IV A 101   May 10, 1843

« 5655

May 15

Dear Emil,[973]

The enclosed letter to you was written just after I arrived. My health was somewhat affected, but so be it. Now I am afloat again.[974] In a certain sense I have already achieved what I might wish for. I did not know whether I needed one hour for it, or one minute, or half a year—an idea—a hint—*sat sapienti,*[975] now I am climbing. As far as that goes, I could return home at once, but I will not do so, although I shall probably not travel any farther than Berlin.

When one does not have any particular business in life, as I do not, it is necessary to have an interruption like this now and then. Once more the machinery within me is fully at work,[976] the feelings are sound, harmonious, etc. As soon as I feel the law of motion truly within me, I shall return, for then I am working again, and my home becomes dear to me and my library a necessity for me.

As to my internal state in other respects, I will not say much, or rather nothing, for I will not tell lies.

My address is Jägerstrasse und Charlottenstrasse an der Ecke, my old address, but the owner has married[977] and therefore I am living like a hermit in one room, where even my bed stands.

I do not want to bother speaking the German language, and therefore I live as isolated as possible.

[Address:]
An dem Herrn Cand. E. Boesen
Copenhagen
Philosophgangen

[Postmark:]
Berlin 5/16   5-6

Letters, no. 80   May 15, 1843

« **5656**

The only person with whom I have ever had obscene talk is the old China-captain I converse with in Mini's Cafe[978] and who thinks I am forty years old. But our conversation is rather more humorous. When he begins to tell me how in Manila everyone has a tart or about the fun he has had with tarts (it is his pet expression) in London, whom one treats with a glass of grog, "for they are so fond of it"—the situation is humorous enough, an old China-captain (seventy-four years old) talking with me in that way about such things. But he certainly was not particularly involved himself, for there is still a purity in him which testifies for him; as a consequence what he says is more humorous than obscene.

IV A 105   *n.d.*, 1843

« **5657** *Repetition*

A Fruitless Venture
        A Venture in Discovery
A Fruitless Venture
        A Venture in Experimental Philosophy
A Venture in Experimental Philosophy Psychology
                by
Victorinus Constantinus *de bona speranza*
        Constantin Walter Constantius[979]

IV B 97:1   May, 1843

« **5658**

Problemata[980]
        by
S. Kierkegaard

IV B 60   *n.d.*, 1843

« **5659**

Between Each Other[*][981]
        by
Simon Stylita
Solo Dancer and Private Individual

---

edited
by
S. Kierkegaard

[*] *In margin:* Movements and Positions

IV B 78   n.d., 1843

« **5660**

In margin of 5659 (IV B 78):

Fear and Trembling
dialectical lyric
by
Johannes de silentio

a poetic person who exists
only among poets.

IV B 79   n.d., 1843

« **5661**

What is the happiest life? It is [that of] a young girl sixteen years old, pure and innocent, who possesses nothing, neither a dresser nor a tall cupboard,[982] but who makes use of the lowest drawer of her mother's bureau to hide her treasures—a confirmation dress and a hymnbook. . . . . . Fortunate is he who owns no more than that he can live drawer to drawer with her.

What is the happiest life? It is [that of] a young girl sixteen years old, pure and innocent, who indeed can dance but who goes to a party only twice a year.

What is the happiest life? It is [that of] a young girl sixteen years old, pure and innocent, who sits by the window busily sewing, and all the while she sews she steals glances toward the window of the ground floor apartment opposite, where the young painter lives.

What is the happiest life? It is [that of] that rich man of twenty-five years, who lives opposite on first floor.

Is one equally old if he is thirty summers old or thirty winters.[983]

IV B 140   n.d., 1843

« **5662**

Why did I not thrive as other children do, why was I not wrapped around in joy, why did I come to look into that region of sighs so early, why was I born with a congenital anxiety which constantly made me look into it, why were nine months in my mother's womb enough to make me old so that I was not born like other children but was born old.[984]

IV B 141   *n.d.*, 1843

« 5663

If my honor were not at stake, if my pride were not violated—I wanted it but was incapable of it. If she had abandoned me—what then —then it all would have amounted to nothing.—[985]

IV B 142   *n.d.*, 1843

« 5664

May 17

If I had had faith, I would have stayed with Regine.[986] Thanks to God, I now see that. I have been on the point of losing my mind these days. Humanly speaking, I was fair to her; perhaps I should never have become engaged, but from that moment I treated her honestly. In an esthetic and chivalrous sense, I have loved her far more than she has loved me, for otherwise she would neither have treated me proudly nor unnerved me later with her pleas. I have just begun a story entitled "Guilty—Not Guilty";[987] of course it would come to contain things that could amaze the world, for I have personally experienced more poetry in the last year and a half than [is contained in] all novels put together, but I cannot and will not do it, for my relationship to her must not become poetically diffused; it has a completely different reality [*Realitet*]. She has not become a kind of theatrical princess;* so, if possible, she will become my wife. Lord God, that was my only wish, and yet I had to deny myself that. Humanly speaking, in doing that I was perfectly right and acted most nobly toward her by not letting her suspect my agony. In a purely esthetic sense I was generous. I dare congratulate myself for doing what few in my place would do, for if I had not thought so much of her welfare, I could have taken her, since she herself pleaded that I do it (which she surely should not have done; it was a false weapon), since her father asked me to do it; I could have done a kindness to her and fulfilled my own wish, and then if in time she had become weary, I could have castigated her by showing that she herself had insisted on it. That I did not do. God is my witness that it was my only wish; God is my witness how I have kept watch over myself lest any memory of her be effaced. I do not believe that I have spoken to any young girl since that time. I thought that every rascal who happened to be engaged regarded me as a second-rate person, a villain. I have done my age a service, for in truth it was certainly [here some illegible words].

In margin: * How would anyone have suspected that such a young girl could go about nursing such ideas. Then, too, it was a very immature and merely vain idea, as the future showed; for if the constituents had actually been present, then the manner in which I broke the engagement would have been absolutely decisive. Such things must give a kind of elasticity. But so my girl was—first coy and beside herself with pride and arrogance, then cowardly.

[A page torn from the journal]

it would surely have happened. But with respect to marriage it is not true here that everything is sold in the condition "as is" when the hammer falls; here it is a matter of a little honesty about the past. Here again my chivalry is obvious. If I had not honored her higher than myself as my future wife, if I had not been prouder of her honor than of my own, then I would have remained silent and fulfilled her wish and mine—I would have married her—there are so many marriages which conceal little stories. That I did not want, then she would have become my concubine; I would rather have murdered her. —But if I were to have explained myself, I would have had to initiate her into terrible things, my relationship to my father, his melancholy, the eternal night brooding within me, my going astray, my lusts and debauchery, which, however, in the eyes of God are perhaps not so glaring; for it was, after all, anxiety which brought me to go astray, and where was I to seek a safe stronghold when I knew or suspected that the only man I had admired for his strength was tottering.[988]

IV A 107   May 17, 1843

« 5665

May

Dear Emil,[989]

[*Deleted:* Dear *Justitsraad*]

Again a little while and you will see me.[990] I have finished a work[991] of some importance to me, am hard at work on another,[992] and my library is indispensable to me, as is also a printer. In the beginning

I was ill, but now I am well, that is to say, insofar as my spirit grows within me and probably will kill my body. I have never worked as hard as now. I go for a brief walk in the morning. Then I come home and sit in my room without interruption until about three o'clock. My eyes can barely see. Then with my walking-stick in hand I sneak off to the restaurant, but am so weak that I believe that if somebody were to call out my name, I would keel over and die. Then I go home and begin again. In my indolence during the past months I had pumped up a veritable shower-bath, and now I have pulled the string and the ideas are cascading down upon me: healthy, happy, merry, gay, blessed children born with ease and yet all of them with the birthmark of my personality. Otherwise I am weak, as I said, my legs shake, my knees ache, etc. This is inadequate; instead I shall choose an expression used by my favorite actor, Herr Grobecker,[993] a proverb he used effectively with every fourth word, *"Ich falle um und bin hin,"* or with a slightly better variation, *"Ich falle hin und bin um."* When I have arranged everything at home, I shall travel again. Perhaps. *Gott weiss es.*[994]

Everything remains between us. You know I do not care for gossip.

Your
S. Kierkegaard

If I do not die on the way, I believe you will find me happier than ever before. It is a new crisis, and it means either that I now commence living or that I must die. There would be one more way out of it: that I would lose my mind. God knows. But wheresoever I end, I shall never forget to employ the passion of irony in justified defiance of non-human pseudo-philosophers, who understand neither this nor that and whose whole skill consists in scribbling German compendia and in defiling that which has a worthier origin by talking nonsense about it.

[Address:]
An dem Herrn Cand. E. Boesen
Copenhagen
Philosophgangen

[Postmark:]
Berlin 5/25   12–1

Letters, no. 82   May 25, 1843

« 5666

I am going to try to get rid of the gloomy thoughts and black moods that still live in me by writing something which will be called:

A Leper's Self-observation.[995]

IV A 110   n.d., 1843

« 5667

In margin of 5666 (IV A 110):

It will be a scene between two lepers—the one is compassionate and does not wish to be seen lest he disquiet people; the other wants to revenge himself by horrifying people. The one has brothers and has discovered only recently that they are in the same situation, that the whole family had incurred leprosy.

IV A 111   n.d.

« 5668

I have thought of adapting [the legend of] Agnes and the Merman from an angle that has not occurred to any poet.[996] The Merman is a seducer, but when he has won Agnes's love he is so moved by it that he wants to belong to her entirely. —But this, you see, he cannot do, since he must initiate her into his whole tragic existence, that he is a monster at certain times, etc., that the Church cannot give its blessing to them. He despairs and in his despair plunges to the bottom of the sea and remains there, but Agnes imagines that he only wanted to deceive her.

But this is poetry, not that wretched, miserable trash in which everything revolves around ridiculousness and nonsense.

Such a complication can be resolved only by the religious (which has its name[997] because it resolves all witchcraft); if the Merman could believe, his faith perhaps could transform him into a human being.[998]

IV A 113   n.d., 1843

« 5669

I must get at my Antigone[999] again. The task is a psychological development and motivation of the presentiment of guilt. With that in mind I have been thinking of Solomon and David,[1000] of the relation of Solomon's youth to David, for no doubt both Solomon's good sense (dominant in him) and his sensuality are the result of David's greatness. He had had earlier intimations of David's deep agitation without realizing what guilt might rest upon him, and yet he had seen this profoundly God-fearing man give such an ethical expression to his repentance, but it would have been a quite different matter if David had been a mystic. These ideas, these presentiments, smother energies (except in the form of imagination), evoke reflection, and this combination of imagination and reflection, where the factor of the will is lacking, is sensuality proper.

IV A 114   *n.d.*, 1843

« **5670**

N.B.

"But what is the flattering voice of fame
to a sigh from a maiden's breast."[1001]

Schack Staffeldt

IV A 118   *n.d.*, 1843

« **5671**

Idea:

Reminiscences of My Life
by
Nebuchadnezzar
Formerly Emperor, Recently an Ox
Published
by
Nicolaus Notabene[1002]

IV A 119   *n.d.*, 1843

« **5672**

Was Tarquinius Superbus in seinem Garten mit den Mohnköpchen sprach, verstand der Sohn, aber nicht der Bote.[1003]

See Hamann,[1004] III, p. 190 mid.

IV A 122   *n.d.*, 1843

« **5673**

N.B.

periissem nisi periissem.[1005]

IV A 123   *n.d.*, 1843

« **5674**

The motto for "Fear and Trembling" should have started with "Write"—"For whom"—"Write for the dead, for those you love in some past"—"Will they read me?"—"No!"[1006]

IV A 126   *n.d.*, 1843

« **5675**

In Shakespeare's *Ende gut* [. . . . .][1007]

IV A 127   *n.d.*, 1843

« **5676**

I have half a mind to write a counter-piece to "The Seducer's Diary." It would be a feminine figure: "The Courtesan's Diary." It would be worth the trouble to depict such a character.

IV A 128   *n.d.*, 1843

« **5677**

The sequel to "The Seducer's Diary" must be in a piquant vein, his relation to a young married woman.

IV A 129   *n.d.*, 1843

« **5678** *Pages from the Notebook of a Street Commissioner*[1008]

Under this title I would like to describe particular districts of the city that have a certain poetic atmosphere about them, such as Kultorvet (this is the marketplace with the most atmosphere), street scenes, a gutter plank, etc., fishing boats. What splendid contrasts—at one moment have his thoughts sweep that boundless view over the water at Knippelsbro, the next become immersed in contemplation of God and flounder in a tank. Characters would constantly be thrown in —love stories, maidservants, etc. It is remarkable what a healthy sense of humor is often to be found in maidservants, especially when they are criticizing the frippery of elegant ladies.

—At present I am making an effort to get every child I meet to smile.[1009]

IV A 132   *n.d.*, 1843

« **5679**

June 29, 1843

Dear Peter,[1010]

Quite some time has already gone by since I returned from Berlin,[1011] and in all that time I have heard nothing at all from you. So it is easy to explain the fact that when the miracle of your writing to me fails to take place, then the even greater miracle takes place: the prophet goes to the mountain.[1012]

How are you doing down there? How is Jette?[1013] I have practically no contact at all with the Glahn[1014] family and therefore hear nothing whatsoever. It would really make me very happy indeed if Jette were in fairly good health, for if that were so I believe you might even be able to lead a pleasant life in the country, for you like being a pastor, as far as I can judge, and besides, you have acquired some skill in dealing with life's trivialities in such a way that they do not become completely unbearable for you. This is something I understand very well; perhaps few understand it as well as I do, precisely because I am and will remain a swimmer who both *nolens* and *volens*[1015] stays out in the mainstream.

If a brief visit from me would please you in any way, I would be glad to come, even though I go for drives less frequently nowadays, at least not for such long ones, and on the whole am prepared to remain in Copenhagen and put up with the heat. My room is my *Rhodus,*[1016] and although I am not exactly leaping about in the heat, I will nevertheless remain there.

I really have nothing to write to you about, for you know that I am reluctant to write to anybody about my affairs; even in conversation I am rather taciturn. I have written to tell you that I am, as I have always been—even though appearances are mostly against me, as they may be *in specie*[1017] at this very moment when it occurs to me that Jette may not be better—happy to assure you that I am

Your devoted
Brother

You know that there is in town a Magister Adler,[1018] who became a pastor on Bornholm, a zealous Hegelian. He has come over here to publish some sermons in which he will probably advocate a movement in the direction of orthodoxy. He has a good head on him and has considerable experience in many *casibus*[1019] of life, but at the moment he is a little overwrought. Nevertheless it is always possible that this is a phenomenon worth paying attention to. —Otherwise everything is as usual, trivial, although one can get along provided one knows how to laugh—and to work. —Have you seen Martensen's book?[1020] How can people go on claiming that M. is a thinker! Let him wrestle with philosophy; that makes sense, but this kind of stuff is nothing but thoughtless self-aggrandizement.

[Address:]
To
Dr. Kierkegaard, Pastor
Pedersborg
via Sorøe

Letters, no. 83   June 29, 1843

« **5680**

. . . . . her. If she but knew all my sufferings during the past year. She should never have discovered anything. But then my whole outlook is immediately changed. In the marriage ceremony I must take an oath —therefore I do not dare conceal anything. On the other hand there are things I cannot tell her. The fact that the divine enters into marriage is my ruin. If I do not let myself marry her, I offend her. If an unethical relationship can be justifiable—then I begin tomorrow. She has asked me, and for me that is enough. She can depend on me absolutely, but it is an unhappy existence. I am dancing upon a volcano and must let her dance along with me as long as it can last. This is why it is more humble of me to remain silent. That it humbles me I know all too well.[1021]

IV A 133   *n.d.,* 1843

« **5681**

He could turn out to be a fine dramatic character: a man with a profound sense of humor who has established himself as a fashion designer and exerted all his influence and financial resources in making women ridiculous, meanwhile being as insinuating as possible in relation to them, charming them with his flattery and conversation, not because he wanted any favors (he was much too intellectual for that) but in order to get them to dress as ridiculously as possible and thus satisfy his contempt for women, and especially when a fine lady like that found a man who was just as much a fool. —In order to chastise him it could be dramatically planned so that everybody actually considered his malevolently introduced styles to be in excellent taste so that he was the only one who laughed, and yet with perfect right. —Then he fell in love with a girl. He wants to make an exception of her, cannot bear to see her wear the ridiculous clothes he himself has made fashionable in order to prostitute the sex. But he cannot convince her and has to bear the sight of his beloved dressed just like the others.[1022]

IV A 135   *n.d.,* 1843

« 5682

Addition to 5681 (IV A 135):

He gets the women to want to indicate in their dress the group differences that distinguish their husbands; this wins their husbands' approval and thus all are prostituted.[1023]

IV A 136   *n.d.,* 1843

« 5683

In margin of 5681 (IV A 135):

For example, he designs a new costume for women to wear to church in order to prostitute them there also.[1024]

IV A 137   *n.d.*

« 5684

In margin of 5681 (IV A 135):

Lines: what is everything in life but fashion—piety is a fashion as well as love and hoop skirts and rings in the noses of savages—I am different from the others only in that I have realized it and come to the aid of that sublime genius in every way until I roar with laughter at the most ridiculous of all animals—man. But there comes the Baroness von der Vüe; she probably will buy herself a new fool's costume.[1025]

IV A 138   *n.d.*

« 5685

In margin of 5681 (IV A 135):

I do not cheat my customers. I always use the best fabrics, pure gold, genuine Brussels lace. My only joy is to spoil everything in the cutting and making something tasteless out of it, for I scorn gold and silver and genuine shawls as profoundly as I scorn the women who swaddle themselves therein.[1026]

IV A 139   *n.d.*

« 5686

Addition to Printer's copy of manuscript of "Three Upbuilding Discourses":[1027]

(which is called "discourses," not sermons, because its author had no authority *to preach,* "upbuilding discourses," not discourses for upbuilding, because the speaker does not claim to be a *teacher*)[1028]

IV B 159:6   August 9, 1843

« **5687**

Under the title: Slices of Ordinary Life (or perhaps: Crisscrossings), I would make a somber sketch of life as it is at certain hours of the day in Copenhagen. Nine o'clock: the children going to school; ten o'clock: the maidservants; one o'clock, the fashionable world. As a rule, life at these different times has different colors, just as does the water where different schools of fish are to be found—it should start out with a lyric about my dear capital city and place of residence, Copenhagen.[1029]

IV A 140   *n.d.*, 1843

« **5688**

There is something curious about my little secretary, Mr. Christensen.[1030] I wager that he is the one who in various ways is scribbling pamphlets and things in the newspapers, for I often hear the echo of my own ideas, not in the way I am accustomed to writing them but in the way I casually toss them out orally. And I who was so kind to him, paid him well, conversed with him for hours, for which I also paid for the simple reason that he should not feel mortified and humiliated because his poverty made it necessary for him to be a copyist, I made him an initiate in the whole affair, cast a veil of mystery over the whole thing, made the time as pleasant as possible in every way. —The little article in *Portefeuillen*[1031] a few days before *Either/Or* was published is certainly by him. It really was not very nice of him. After all, he could have confided in me and told me that he hankered to be an author, but his authorship does not have a good conscience. He no doubt notices that I have changed a little toward him, although I was just as polite and considerate as before. On the other hand I have stopped his inquisitive snooping around my room; he must be kept at arm's length; I hate all plagiarizing pirates.

IV A 141   *n.d.*, 1843

« **5689**

My notes about Regine are oddly reversed, for what is first in time is always jotted down last, simply because what happened first made such a decisive impression on me that I did not need to be afraid of forgetting it. For example, I still have not recorded some of the most important things, that she herself declared many times that if I could only convince her that I was a deceiver she would be reconciled to everything. Incidentally, when I think of it, this remark was once again a display of her overweening pride, as if she had such an ethical nature; therefore not much importance should be attached to it. Life, in fact, is not so simple. I showed the girl the confidence of believing all the impressive things she let me know about herself and I act on the strength of that—and then it all turns out to be the worst for her. Here one sees how disastrous it is when a girl has had no religious upbringing.[1032] When I consider that it was some time before my reading of Mynster's sermons[1033] to her once a week made any impression on her. It is odd that a girl can think of herself so highly, odd that her having (*qua* single individual) favored me with her love or, more correctly, becoming engaged, should shake me up in this way. If it were a matter of differentiating characteristics, I am sure I could measure up to her.

IV A 142   n.d., 1843

« 5690

I could perhaps reproduce in a novel called "The Mysterious Family" the tragedy of my childhood, the terrifying, secret elucidation of the religious which a fearful presentiment[1034] gave me, which my imagination hammered out, and my offense at the religious. At the outset it should be thoroughly patriarchal and idyllic, so that no one would have any inkling before the words suddenly appeared and gave a terrifying explanation of everything.

IV A 144   n.d., 1843

« 5691

A mentally deranged person who went around scanning all children, for he believed that he had once made a girl pregnant but did not know what had become of her and now had but one concern—to find the child. No one could understand the indescribable concern with which he would look at a child.[1035]

IV A 147   n.d., 1843

« 5692

There are men who measure out their speech just as deliberately and abstractly as a relative's clock measured the time. It no doubt thought something like this: How unreasonable to strike twelve times at one time and the next time only once. Therefore it spaced equally long intervals between each stroke; when it was twelve o'clock it struck once and thereafter once every quarter hour, and it was three o'clock before it had finished striking twelve o'clock.[1036]

IV A 151   n.d., 1843

« 5693

Lines:

A person with a sense of humor meets a girl who had once asserted that she would die if he left her; when he meets her now she is engaged. He greets her and says: May I thank you for the kindness you have shown me. Perhaps you will allow me to show my appreciation (he takes from his vest pocket two marks and eight shillings and hands it to her). She is speechless with indignation but continues to stand there and tries to intimidate him with her glance. He continues: It is nothing—just a trifle to help with the trousseau, and the day you hold the wedding and first crown your kindness, I promise by all that is holy, for God's sake and your eternal salvation, to send you another two marks and eight shillings.[1037]

IV A 152   *n.d.,* 1843

« 5694

Instead of the plot in *Repetition*[1038] I could imagine something like this. A young man with imagination and a lot more, but who hitherto has been otherwise occupied, falls in love with a young girl—to use an experienced coquette here is not very interesting except from another angle. This young girl presumably is pure and innocent but very imaginative in an erotic way. He comes with his simple ideas. She develops him. Just when she is really delighted with him, it becomes apparent that he cannot remain with her. A prodigious desire for multiplicity is awakened and she must be set aside. In a way she herself had made a seducer of him, a seducer with the limitation that he can never seduce her. Incidentally, it could be very interesting to have him sometime later, at the peak of his powers, improved by experience, proceed to seduce her as well, "because he owed her so much."

IV A 153   *n.d.,* 1843

« 5695 *Plot*

A genius equipped with all possible capacities, with power to dominate all existence and to make men obey him, discovers in his consciousness one little sticking point, one bit of lunacy. He becomes so indignant over it that he decides to kill himself, for to him this one little point makes him a serving spirit, a human being. Moreover, this little point is not any externality (for example, being lame, one-eyed, ugly, etc.; such things would not concern him) but has an element of spirit and thus would seem capable of being removed in freedom—therefore it goads him.

IV A 154   *n.d.,* 1843

« **5696**

This is an example I can use. In volume 7, Steffens[1039] reminisces about a mayor named Benda, a generally talented and energetic man who wore a wig. As soon as he took it off, everything became muddled and confused for him. —The thralldom of being bound to a wig. Not merely that like some others he caught a little cold, but that he became insane. See pp. 215 and 216.

IV A 158   n.d., 1843

« **5697**

Heiberg[1040] remarked in his outcry over *Either/Or* that it was really hard to tell whether some of the observations in it were profound or not. Professor Heiberg and his consorts have the great advantage that what they say is known in advance to be profound. This is partly due to the fact that not a single primitive thought is to be found in them, or at least rarely. What they know they borrow from Hegel, and Hegel is indeed profound—ergo, what Professor Heiberg says is also profound. In this way every theological student who limits his sermon to nothing but quotations from the Bible becomes the most profound of all, for the Bible certainly is the most profound book of all.

IV A 162   n.d., 1843

« **5698**

I reject all reviews, for to me a reviewer is just as loathsome as a street barber's assistant who comes running with his shaving water, which is used for all customers, and fumbles about my face with his clammy fingers.[1041]

IV A 167   n.d., 1843–44

« **5699**

The Banquet,
instead, perhaps: *In vino veritas*[1042]
or: Evening
(The basic mood will be different from the mood of the title.)
The narrator goes to the Nook of Eight Paths[1043] seeking solitude. There he meets a friend, "although he had rather expected to find a frightened bird." He tells him all about the banquet. The contrast of the deep silence of the forest[1044] makes the story about the night of pandemonium better, more fantastic.
The talk on Eros.[1045]

The characters:[1046] Johannes with the nickname The Seducer, Victor Eremita, recollection's unhappy lover, Constantin Constantius, and "a young man." The last, a very young man, gives a talk[1047] in which he proves that erotic love, physical desire, is the most ludicrous of all (its frightful consequences[1048]—getting children, plus the fact that a person deceives himself in this lust and merely serves existence). He uses an essay by Henr. Cornel. Agrippa, *De nobilitate et praecellentia foeminei sexus*[1049] (which I have). By using its naïveté a comic and humorous effect is assured.

The condition is that each one is to base his talk on a definite and personal experience of love.[1050] —The young man, however, declares that he cannot provide anything like that since he has always been smart enough to stay clear of it. "One can make a fool of himself by joining up with a girl who by nature is always a silly flirt." If one is to have anything to do with them, he must only seduce!

The banquet begins with a situation.[1051] They are assembled in a festively illuminated hall where dinner music (from *Don Juan*) is being played; they themselves are dressed to the hilt and each one has a personal waiter. While the dinner music is being played, Victor Eremita rises and proposes that they sing the ditty:

My Brimming Glass and the Lusty Sound of Song.[1052]

This has an immediate effect upon the gentlemen present, who readily perceive the humor in the singing of a drinking song by such a company of dinner guests, so thoroughly out of keeping with the drinking song period.

IV A 170   *n.d.*, 1844

« 5700

Albertus Magnus . . . . .[1053]

IV A 174   *n.d.*, 1844

« 5701

Mathaeus Parisiensis . . . . .[1054]

IV A 175   *n.d.*, 1844

« 5702

"Denn wovon man frühzeitig als Kind sehr viel weiss, davon ist man sicher, später hin und im Alter nichts zu wissen, und der Mann der Gründlichkeit wird zuletzt höchstens der Sophiste seines Jugendwahns."

See *Kants vermischte Schriften,* [1055] v. Tieftrunk, II, p. 253.

"Welcher Philosoph hat nicht einmal, zwischen den Betheurungen eines vernünftigen und festüberredeten Augenzeugen, und der innern Gegenwehr eines unüberwindlichen Zweifels, die einfältigste Figur gemacht, die man sich vorstellen kan?"

Same book, p. 250.

IV A 176   n.d., 1844

« **5703**

I must use Abelard sometime. He must be completely modernized. The conflicts in his soul must not be between the authority of the Pope and Church and what he himself knows, but between his own sympathies, which are inclined to uphold the established—and then Heloise.

See p. 13 in this book [i.e., IV A 31].

IV A 177   n.d., 1844

« **5704**

Constantin Constantius's journey to Berlin[1056] is not something accidental. He generates in particular the mood for the *Posse* and here approaches the extreme point of the humorous.

IV A 178   n.d., 1844

« **5705**

The Seducer's Diary
No. 2[1057]
An Essay on the Demonic
by
Johannes Mephistopheles

N.B. It is what the age wants, to get dizzy over the abominable and then fancy itself to be superior. They will not get that from me.

Foreword

I am indebted to what Victor Eremita[1058] has published, and I can only lament that this author has not pursued the excellent ideas at his disposal but instead has become an upbuilding writer.

The scene is in the house of Cordelia,[1059] who is married to Edward;—in her house there is a young girl who is the object; the fact that it is in Cordelia's house is a subtle refinement.

He heightens his pleasure by constantly clinging to the thought that this will be his last adventure and by parceling it out, as it were, into the enjoyment. Moreover, he heightens the enjoyment by reproducing, from everything erotic in the particular situation, a compendious memory of the girl who went to ruin on this side of the idea of femininity; he heightens the enjoyment by reproducing all of his own life, and in this way the psychological presuppositions of his soul come to light.

He gets to know a courtesan and establishes a psychological union with her to explore the relation between the seduction which originates with a man and that which originates with a woman—eventually he decides to throw her over.

He runs into a Don Juan with the same girl. This throws light on the method, but he knows how to put Don Juan to good use in his plan.

IV A 181   *n.d.*, 1844

« 5706

It could be amusing to have a play begin in this way (the scene is in a man's living room out in the country, and he is talking with his neighbor):

"Yes, my friend and neighbor, it is just as I said, our relationship remains unchanged even if I have become a Councillor."

IV A 182   *n.d.*, 1844

« 5707

Unused

New Year's Gift[1060] by
Nicolaus Notabene

If I had not had more important things to do, it would have been very amusing, since it now appears that this New Year everything has become exceptionally elegant and dainty as well as banal and trivial.[1061]

IV B 125   *n.d.*, 1844

« 5708

New Year's Gift
edited
by
Nicolaus Notabene

Published for the benefit of the orphanages
Copenhagen 1844

Dedicated to every purchaser of this book
—and to the orphanages
Contents

Preface
Inter et Inter[1062]

IV B 126   *n.d.*, 1844

« **5709**

Interjectional Comments
Concerning
The Review of *Fear and Trembling* in Scharling
and Engelstoft's Journal[1063]
by
Johannes de silentio[1064]

———————

As soon as I had read this review I said to myself: This is it. I said:
This author is the man; he explains everything, explains all problems,
and does not waste time on a provisional understanding of them. May
I therefore take the occasion to wish this author every possible good
fortune and success: joy in Denmark, honor to the author, satisfaction
with the journal.

Respectfully,
Joh. d. s.
IV A 193   [February 24,] 1844

« **5710**

Post-Scriptum
to
Either/Or
by
Victor Eremita . . .[1065]
March, 1844
IV B 59   March, 1844

« 5711

Dear friend,[1066]

Will you eat with me this evening? I have already made a reservation. If so, I will come at 6:00 or 6:30. Will you be in your room at that
time?

Yours
S. Kierkegaard

Reply requested.

[Address:]
To
Mr. E. Boesen, C.T.

Letters, no. 101   *n.d.* [1844?]

« 5712

The journal[1067] will be divided as follows:

Praemonenda
1. *Examinatio*

How does a new quality emerge through a continuous quantitative
determination?[1068]

2. *Contemplatio*

de omnibus d.[1069]

3. *Exaedificatio*

concerning the expectation of faith[1070]

Miscellanea[1071]

The question to Prof. Martensen[1072] regarding the Aristote-
lian doctrine of virtue.

V A 100   *n.d.,* 1844

« 5713

Addition to 5712 (V A 100):

Second Number

1. *Examinatio*

to what extent is being a category—a quality.[1073]

2. *Contemplatio*
P. Møller[1074] poetically diffused.

3. *Exaedificatio*
a.) on the upbuilding in always thanking God.[1075]
b.) on the advantage of studying the sources.[1076]
their significance for the personality.

Miscellanea
Question to Prof. Heiberg,[1077] what is poetry.
The hidden (a young girl has said it.)
Weisse,[1078] something similar at the beginning of part one.

V A 101   *n.d.*, 1844

« **5714**

Vocalizations[1079]
to
The Concept of Anxiety[1080]

loquere ut videam te[1081]

Examples of the consequence of the relationship of generation[1082]

Högne (in the Scandinavian tales by Rafn[1083])

Robert *le diable* (Schwab, *Geschichten und Sagen*[1084])

Merlin (Fr. Schlegel, *Samtl. W.*[1085]).

The addiction to liquor transmitted from parents to children.
    Addiction to stealing
    Unnatural vices
    Melancholy
    Insanity which appears at a certain age.

V A 102   *n.d.*, 1844

« **5715**

Addition to 5714 (V A 102):
Some Shakespearean characters.[1086]

V A 103   *n.d.*, 1844

« **5716**

Addition to 5714 (V A 102):
        Cenci by P. B. Shelley[1087]

V A 104   *n.d.*, 1844

« 5717

Addition to 5714 (V A 102):
Here will be used the plan found in No. 5 of the original note-books[1088] about anxiety and in the journal, p. 62 [*i.e.,* IV A 121].

V A 105   *n.d.,* 1844

« 5718

Addition to 5714 (V A 102):
For p. 64 [i.e., IV A 128].
The prostitute who, without having been seduced, made up her mind when she was a girl to be a prostitute because that is what her sisters were.[1089]

V A 106   *n.d.,* 1844

« 5719

Addition to 5718 (V A 106):
She was called Frels. (Police-inspector Götzher.)

V A 107   *n.d.,* 1844

« 5720

Addition to 5714 (V A 102):
A father-son relationship in which the son secretly discovers everything at the bottom of it all and yet does not dare let on. The father is an important man, devout and strong; only once in a drunken condition did he let fall some words that intimated the worst. The son does not find out any more and does not dare ask the father or any other man.[1090]

V A 108   *n.d.,* 1844

« 5721 **Continuation of the Preface**

All of us have a little psychological insight, some powers of observation, but when this science or art manifests itself in its interminable amplitude when it abandons minor transactions on the streets and in dwellings in order to scurry after its favorite: the person closed up within himself—then men grow weary.[1091]

V B 147   *n.d.,* 1844

« 5722

In margin of V B 148:4:[1092]
My interest is not to be a poet[1093] but to make out the meaning

of the religious. That it will not be thought that the religious is for striplings* and stupid people—that is my aim in this story.[1094]

In margin: *and unshaven.

V B 148:5   n.d., 1844

« 5723

He [is] essentially* closed up within himself—she could not be that even if she wanted to (why not? A woman cannot express dialectical reduplication, just as she cannot express many consonants preceding one vowel but only the vowels).[1095]

*The significance of the portions entered the fifth of each month.[1096]

V B 148:25   n.d., 1844

« 5724

What his self-inclosing reserve contains he never says.
> Let us simply assume that his melancholy has no content at all. He who is melancholy can name many cares which hold him in bondage, but the one which binds him he is unable to name. Or let it be guilt. Or mental instability.[1097]

V B 148:29   n.d., 1844

« 5725

I was born in 1813,[1098] in that bad fiscal year when so many other bad banknotes were put in circulation, and my life seems most comparable to one of them. There is a suggestion of greatness in me, but because of the bad conditions of the times I am not worth very much.

A banknote like that sometimes becomes a family's misfortune.

V A 3   n.d., 1844

« 5726

. . . . . has taken and is taking only an inland journey from his own consciousness to the presupposition of original sin in his own consciousness. . . . . .[1099]

V B 47:13   n.d., 1844

« 5727

Dear Professor,[1100]

When you recommend somebody[1101] and when I have at my disposal that which is desired, then my wilfulness is your guarantee that your wish is my command. Unfortunately, however, I am not in the position of looking for, nor can I use, the person you recommend. At the moment I employ an old woman with whom I am in every way as satisfied as possible. She will be with me until this fall, when I move to the family house at Nytorv,[1102] where I have arranged things differently, so that I will have no need of such a person, and in fact will have no room for her. Even if I did, I could hardly dismiss my old woman, since she suits me in every way, and although she has been with me for only a year, she has known how to make her dismissal almost a matter of conscience for me.

So much for the content of your letter; but now a little about something entirely unrelated which nevertheless has made your letter —which I cherish as I do everything from you—most particularly welcome in its own way. Yesterday was my birthday, a day which I am very averse to celebrating and as far as possible even keep secret. But that your letter should happen to come on just that day, the only letter I have ever received from you, that the familiar handwriting should so vividly recall to me one of my most beautiful memories, that the affectionate closing should assure me of that which I certainly believed and knew yet am always happy to hear repeated, that time, which changes so much, in this respect has changed nothing—how could I do anything but consider all this as the work of a friendly fate who sent me a birthday greeting so welcome that I myself could almost have elicited it! This is why I thank you for your note and for the impression it made on me, for it allowed me to forget completely that the last time I saw your name was in that official notice announcing your resignation as principal of the Borgerdyds School. Well, it was inevitable; but all the same, not everyone has the strength to take the step himself and the strength to resign himself to taking it. If anyone should have self-confidence, rashness, and boldness enough to want to offer you consolation, then truly it is not I. But with your permission I should prefer to be the one who is no good at consoling, understood in the same sense as Cicero understands it when he writes to Titius: *unus ex omnibus minime sum ad te consolandum accommodatus, quod tantum ex tuis molestiis cepi doloris, ut consolatione ipse egerem.*[1103]

> With gratitude and affection
> your completely devoted
> S. Kierkegaard

Letters, no. 107   May 6, 1844

« 5728

Next time I will call myself Petrus Ramus and for a motto use the historical report that he was censured, *dass er gegen die Observants mit der Philosophie Beredsamkeit verbinde.*[1104]

(See Jacobi, *Smtl. W.,*[1105] IV, part 1, the preface.)

V A 21   *n.d.,* 1844

« 5729

I have half a mind to write some "wedding discourses" in the same style as my upbuilding discourses, treating the relationship of the parties concerned from a purely poetic point of view.[1106]

V A 27   *n.d.,* 1844

« 5730

In a way it has always seemed remarkable to me that the story of Eve has been completely opposed to all later analogy, for the expression "to seduce" used for her generally refers in ordinary language to the man, and the other related expressions all point to the woman as weaker (easier to infatuate, lure to bed, etc).* This, however, is easy to explain, for in Genesis it is a third power that seduced the woman, whereas in ordinary language the reference is always only to the relationship between man and woman and thus it must be the man who seduces the woman.[1107]

*Note. If anyone has any psychological interest in observations related to this, I refer him to "The Seducer's Diary" in *Either/Or.* If he looks at it closely, he will see that this is something quite different from a novel, that it has completely different categories up its sleeve, and, if one knows how to use it, it can serve as a preliminary study for a very serious and not merely superficial research. The Seducer's secret is simply that he knows that woman is anxiety.

V B 53:26   *n.d.,* 1844

« 5731

As far as I am concerned, I am safeguarded in this respect by my own experience in another direction; for although I have never been accustomed to making little summaries in order to carry all my scholarly learning in my head, although I always read widely and then turn this over to my memory, although I can be totally engrossed in my own production, and although together with all this I am doing seventeen other things and talk every day with about fifty people of all ages,[1108]

I swear, nevertheless, that I am able to relate what each person with whom I have spoken said the last time, next-to-the-last time, not to mention someone who is the object of particular attention—his remarks, his emotions are immediately vivid to me as soon as I see him, even though it is a long time since I saw him.[1109]

VB 72:22   n.d., 1844

« 5732

Some people may be disturbed by my sketch of an observer in *The Concept of Anxiety*.[1110] It does, however, belong there and is like a watermark in the work. After all, I always have a poetic relationship to my works, and therefore I am pseudonymous. At the same time as the book develops some theme, the corresponding individuality is delineated. For example, Vigilius Haufniensis delineates several, but I have also made a sketch of him in the book.

VA 34   n.d., 1844

« 5733

[Copy of F. H. Jacobi, *Werke*,[1111] IV, pt. 1 (Leipzig: 1819), with underlining and marginal marking by Kierkegaard.]

VC 13   n.d., 1844

« 5734

To the typesetter. The entire book is to be printed in the same types used in 1843 for *Two Upbuilding Discourses* and with the same number of lines per page.[1112]

VB 232:1   n.d., 1844

« 5735

Perhaps my upbuilding discourses could be made even more specific: Upbuilding Discourses for Kings and Queens—for Beggars—etc.—[1113]

VA 39   n.d., 1844

« 5736

In a section about Periander[1114] in Fenelon's *Lebensbeschreibungen und Lehr-Satze*,[1115] Frankfurt and Leipzig, 1748, I read something which I had never read before and which is extremely interesting and poetic.

The passage is from pp. 80 bottom–87 bottom.

VA 45   n.d., 1844

« 5737

I have been so indolent these days that I have not cared about anything, and the only thing I have wanted to do while groaning in my melancholy was to sit on a steed with "a lady in view who stands on the balcony of the castle and waves with her veil." My idea was that the castle should be in a forest but situated so that the balcony was visible from a distance; there would be a meadow in front of the woods, a clover field separated by a little ditch, and I would ride over the meadow—and the lovely lady at the castle would be so indistinct that she could almost be confused with the veil. This would take place in the afternoon when the soft blending of the sun—or in late evening when the sky communes with the sea. Then, breaking this connection, to cut through the water and see her standing on the coast waving her shawl, but in such a way that she and the shawl could be mistaken for phantoms of evening mist.

V A 48   *n.d.,* 1844

« 5738

Where feelings are involved, my experience has been like that of the Englishman who had financial troubles; even though he had a hundred pound note, there was no one around who could change it.[1116]

V A 52   *n.d.,* 1844

« 5739

How impatient I am basically is best seen from the fact that I am appalled by the state of pregnancy, simply because it has to last for nine months and all one's will power, all one's feelings, the most extreme efforts—avail nothing.

V A 54   *n.d.,* 1844

« 5740

If anyone wanted to challenge the truth of the theory that our age is an age of movement, then let him consider that Pastor Grundtvig[1117] is alive, a man who is far superior to Archimedes and does not even need or dream of needing a fixed point in order to move heaven and earth—no, he does it without a foothold. He needs so little—or more correctly, he literally needs nothing—to produce this tremendous effect, and since it is a familiar fact that he is able to become furious over nothing, it is easy to see not only that the age is one of movement[1118] but that it is terribly harrowing to be a contemporary of this Ale-Norse[1119] warrior.

V A 58   *n.d.*, 1844

« 5741

Now I am going to write occasional discourses instead of upbuilding discourses, wedding addresses and communion addresses or funeral addresses.[1120]

V A 62   *n.d.*, 1844

« 5742

[Copy of F. A. Trendelenburg, *Elementa Logices Aristotelicae,*[1121] 2 ed. (Berlin: 1842) with underlining and notations by Kierkegaard.]

V C 11   *n.d.*, 1844

« 5743

These days I suffer very much from a mute disquietude of thought. I am enveloped in an anxiety; I cannot even say what it is that I cannot understand. Like Nebuchadnezzar,[1122] I must ask not only for an explanation of the dream but that someone tell me what it was I dreamed.

V A 71   *n.d.*, 1844

« 5744 *Report*

"In vino veritas"[1123] is not going well. I am constantly rewriting parts of it, but it does not satisfy me. On the whole I feel that I have given far too much thought to the matter and thereby have gotten into an unproductive mood. I cannot write it here in the city; so I must take a journey.[1124] But perhaps it is hardly worth finishing. The idea of the comic as the erotic is hinted at in *The Concept of Anxiety.*[1125] The fashion designer is a very good figure, but the problem is whether by writing such things I am not deferring more important writing. In any case it must be written in a hurry. If such a moment does not come, I will not do it. At present the productivity has miscarried and makes me constantly write more than I want to write. August 27, 1844

V A 109   August 27, 1844

« 5745

Much of the content of "In vino veritas"[1126] will no doubt seem to be terribly sensuous; already I hear an outcry, and yet what is this compared to Goethe, for example, Philine in *Wilhelm Meister.*

V A 82   *n.d.*, 1844

« **5746** *At Esrom*[1127]

The sun in the foreground, the clouds gather over Gribs-Skov[1128] (toward Nøddeboe). The clouds creep down toward Esrom, the trees bow to them (with the wind). The whole scene looks like an army, like a nation in migration,[1129] flanked by light cavalry, the clouds.

V A 84   *n.d.,* 1844

« **5747**

The Seducer's talk[1130] is like what is called shower clouds.

V A 87   *n.d.,* 1844

« **5748**

In connection with what I read in Rötscher[1131] about the accent on the ethical, it occurs to me that in my personal life I, too, used it properly, as both a poet and a speaker, inasmuch as I said with reference to my relation to Regine and breaking the engagement and her certain death:[1132] She chooses the shriek, I the pain.[1133] Now I can say that she did choose the shriek and I did choose the pain.

V A 88   *n.d.,* 1844

« **5749**

I would like to apply to Professor David[1134] the words of Baggesen:[1135] Everything eventually has an ending, even the dress coat Mr. N. had reversed three times: even Jesper Morten's[1136] sermon at vespers last night eventually ended.

V A 91   *n.d.,* 1844

« **5750** *Lines by an Individual*

"As a girl my wife taught me to write short sentences, for at times she sat with me and promised me a kiss at the end of each sentence. Then when I had learned to write short sentences, for which my critic commended me, I was married, and then my wife taught me that writing books was not worth the trouble."

In margin: Originally intended for the Judge in "The Wrong and the Right."[1137]

V A 92   *n.d.,* 1844

« **5751**

In the old days cloth must have been such good quality that the nap grew out again on the reverse side. That was why a dress coat could be reversed twice (my father had this done with his fine woolen dress coat), and not until then was it both reversed and scraped.

VA 93   n.d., 1844

« 5752

The stupidity of Grundtvig[1138] (who has now gone completely into vaudeville, toward which he has always had a leaning, for example, his featherbrained desire to be a prophet and seer without any intuition of how such a figure must be tempered in accordance with all the crises of Christianity) is that he always wants to have spiritual security. This accounts for his insipid outspokenness and wittiness à la Lars Mathiesen.[1139] Luckily he selected the words: "Ladies and Gentlemen,"[1140] strongly reminiscent of Dyrehavsbakken.[1141] Just like his wittiness are the Ohs! and Ahs! and Eees! of the barenecks, a bodyguard of interjections, the only class of people Grundtvig has won for himself.—He hopes to produce a great effect by talking, yes, particularly in the vein of the vague. But he perhaps could also produce an effect by standing on his head. Eventually the proof of a doctrine's truth will be to sweat, knit one's brows, thump one's head, smile confidently, visibly swoon under the power of the spirit, etc. It is something like Helveg's[1142] jumping up and down in the pulpit to the honor of Christianity, probably wanting to prove its truth by the fact that he could leap a foot into the air.

VA 94   n.d., 1844

« 5753

In margin of 5752 (VA 94):
It seems just as ridiculous as for a Hercules of a pastor to take gladiator positions when he prays in order to demonstrate by the rippling muscles of his arms how fervently he is praying etc. It is not muscles that are needed in order to pray and to pray fervently—nor is this the kind of trembling that is of the spirit and inwardness.

VA 95   n.d.

« 5754

N.B. I must once again put out a little polemical piece like the *Prefaces* by Nicolaus Notabene. I am thinking it could be done under the title: Models, or Experiments in Various Kinds of Writing. [*In margin*: N.B.] The particular types will be parodied. This is so the irony will also appear to better advantage.

VA 99   n.d., 1844

« **5755**

The purpose of the five speakers in "*In vino veritas,*"[1143] all of whom are *Karikaturen des Heiligsten,* [1144] is to illuminate women essentially but nevertheless falsely. The Young Man understands women solely from the point of view of sex; Constantin Constantius considers the psychic aspect: faithlessness—that is, of frivolousness; Victor Eremita conceives of the female sex psychically as sex, her significance for the male, i.e., that there is none; the fashion designer considers the sensate aspect, outside the essentially erotic, of the vanity which is more pronounced in a woman's relationship to women, for as an author[1145] has said, women do not adorn themselves for men but for each other; Johannes the Seducer considers the purely sensate factor with respect to the erotic.

V A 110   *n.d.,* 1844

« **5756**

It is three years now since I got the notion to try my hand at being an author. I remember it quite clearly, it was a Sunday; no, wait a minute—yes, that is positively right, it was a Sunday afternoon; I sat as usual in the café in Frederiksberg Gardens[1146] and smoked my cigar. When I went out for no reason at all and with no destination in mind, the path, as usual, led me out here where it seems so good to be, so cozy, where my mood is pitched to a certain melancholy elevation over the world and what is of the world, where even the envied glory of the throne is—as indeed it is out here: a queen's memorial to her deceased lord. For the native Copenhagener, Frederiksberg Gardens is likely to be tinged with melancholy since the old king's death; and his successor, by not taking up residence in the summer palace here, has permitted his subjects to feel the loss of their king in the beautiful way, just as a good subject misses one departed, for a surly grump never rightly appreciates anyone living or worthily misses anyone departed. —But what compensates for childhood's unforgettable impression that the king is the king and that Frederik VI is the king, that an *appellativium* in this case is a *proprium* and a *proprium* an *appellativum.* [1147] What other age in life is able to adorn the picture of the king to the point of being a superhuman as does the childlike ignorance which still has not experienced a change of kings, which knows nothing *in concreto!* Devoid of all envy, with no intimation of the pain of being king, uncritical of reputed good or weak qualities, whether he is a good or a wise king, every child has in the king an almost inescapable figure and without having read the royal constitution[1148] he involuntarily does what it asks: thinks as affectionately as possible of His Majesty the King. Such a king, of course, lives in an ivory-towered castle with balconies—and so Frederik VI sailed here on Sundays, and he himself was the pilot—and the towers and the swans and the reproduction in actuality of what the child knew from Nürnberg prints, assisted by his own imagination, and the king and the queen, who sailed in a boat, and the swans sailed behind them. And how true this reproduction is. For what the powerful cannot persuade the man of, the child with his cunning is able to persuade him of, and what the adult with all his might is unable to torment out of actuality, the child gets from it richly and in superabundance.

Yes, Frederik VI on Sunday in Frederiksberg Gardens, and he piloted himself and the rowers and the swans as well—it is over, only the fragrance of flowers at the entrance, only the memory remains—and even the best subject is still not such a subject as a child is, and the best subject has a concept of the pains of being king and that to be a king is nothing to desire, but the child sees the king as the one and only happy one, but alas, it is a misunderstanding—for it was the child who was the one and only happy one.

Now the king lives here no more; boisterous life is left behind; the child did not go to the hilarity of Vesterbro,[1149] no, he went to Frederiksberg. The contrast makes it quieter. On coming out there one finds the place uncrowded; even at the fountain there is no crush of people. But the joyful mood, despite its inwardness and beauty, is like the worship of a tolerated sect; the leaf-canopied garden and the darkling water make it a sanctuary for a pair of lovers who know life's passion, and for a lonely unhappy man who consorts with melancholy thoughts. My eyes rested at times on the pair of lovers looking for a remote spot in the gardens down a narrow path in order to get away from the noise and find themselves, and at times I discovered the opposite, the more distant sailors, as it were, who from far away sought the crowd in order to lose themselves in the crowd.

But over there at the café there is a small group. When one has withdrawn within the fortress of the café, he feels at a distance from the happy communal life, and this distance manifests a heterogeneity which is perceived with mixed feelings, composed partly of nobility which wants to transcend the separation and partly of a melancholy longing (which wants to yield to the separation), for the wholesome contentment of common life which must avail itself of the moment and dressed up in Sunday clothes must make the most of the holiday moment.[1150]

V A 111   *n.d.*, 1844

« **5757**

Dear Peter,[1151]

I am sorry that your visit to me yesterday was in vain. I would have enjoyed spending an hour talking with you. But please do not give up on me for that reason, or give up thinking of me or the thought of visiting me. Do believe in repetition—but no, for I have, after all, proved that there is no repetition![1152] But then please doubt repetition and please come again. For of course in this case repetition would mean that your visit would be in vain a second time. And there is no repetition (cf. *Repetition*)[1153]—so in all human probability you will find me at home next time.

Your devoted cousin,

S.K.

Letters, no. 113   1844

« **5758**

Lavendelstrædet

83, facing the courtyard

Hansen.[1154]

V A 112   *n.d.*, 1844

V. THE PSEUDONYMOUS AUTHORSHIP
CONCLUDED 1845–1846

« **5759**

Writing Sampler

Apprentice Test Pieces
by
Willibald, Alexander, Alexius, Theodor,
Holger Rosenpind or Rosenblad
Prospective Author
Apprentice Author[1155]

VI B 194 *n.d.*, 1844–45

« **5760**

Additions to 5759 (VI B 194):

No. I
Speculative-heralding Style

No. II
Historical-prophetic Style
of a Seer and Bard

No. III

Memoir Style . . .

VI B 199–201 *n.d.*, 1844–45

« **5761**

An experiment in highly polished, elegant writing, an opus turned out solely as a New Year's gift:

On the Migration of Birds[1156]
with tables and sketches

That our age is an age of mental depression, there is no doubt and no question; the only question is what can be done about it and what the age demands in this respect, for the age is a fashionable patient who is not given orders but is asked what he wants. In this case it seems inadvisable to prescribe what physicians usually prescribe for depression, that is, activity, because it most likely has motion enough, one would think, since it is an age of ferment. As a matter of fact, the depression is the very result of the unrest and fermentation, which will end in yeasty bloating, for sick it is, even though some think it is too hale and hearty. As a rule horseback riding is the activity prescribed, but since our age is in fact a personification and not an actual person, it would be impossible to get it up onto an actual horse. But riding a hobby-horse is no activity at all, as we learn from the experience of all ages, since every age does have its own hobby-horse.[1157]

Because of this need I venture to suggest a closer relationship to nature as a provisional analgesic until we see what comes of this ferment.* For what is as recreating as watching migratory birds: this apparent lack of any laws and yet a perfect law. Even watching the stars and their measured course across the sky must, especially in this connection, be acknowledged as a significant remedy for the depression of our age. But this is only the classical and lacks the romantic.

> Here Faber's book[1158] on our migratory birds is to be used.

*convinced that this is what the age demands.[1159]

VI B 222   n.d., 1844-45

« **5762**

A Program of Innocent and Inexpensive Diversions
A result of many years of experience

I get up in the morning—look out of the window to see if the weather is fine or just the sort of weather I happen to want. If such is the case,* I express my supreme approval with a nod and a gracious smile. As a matter of fact, my principal diversion is assuming that everything revolves around me[1160] and that the whole world exists for my sake alone. This diversion is both very amusing and exceedingly innocent, for of course I do not ask that it produces results for any other man; on the contrary, like everyone else, I am swindled by the merchants etc. A child can quarrel with another child about a horse trotting by, even come to blows, by saying: That belongs to me, and the other says: No, it belongs to me.

* If this is not the case, I divert myself thinking about what kind of weather I would rather have had and what I would have done if it had turned out that way.[1161]

VI B 224   n.d., 1844–45

« 5763

Addition to 5762 (VI B 224):
In the morning I go right away to the market place and find out the market prices—the servant girls—Knippelsbro.[1162]

The special point about my diversions is that they are varied. Here are two principal variations. I regard the whole city of Copenhagen as a great social function. But on one day I view myself as the host who walks around conversing[1163] with all the many cherished guests I have invited; then the next day I assume that a great man has given the party and I am a guest. Accordingly, I dress differently, greet people differently, etc. I am sure those who know me have frequently observed that my manner may be somewhat different, but they probably do not dream that this is the reason. —If an elegant carriage goes by with four horses engaged for the day, I assume that I am the host, give a friendly greeting, and pretend it is I who has lent them this lovely carriage.
I also vary my diversions by sometimes regarding Copenhagen as a large city and sometimes as a little one.[1164]

VI B 225   n.d., 1844–45

« 5764

For: My Innocent Diversions
in "Writing Sampler"

Sometimes I turn away from men completely and take a fancy to the clouds; this is an innocent and very legitimate infatuation, especially if one is careful to go to solitary places where one does not encounter anyone and is painfully reminded that one lives among men.[1165]

VI B 226   n.d., 1844–45

« 5765

For the piece on "My Innocent Diversions"

The Battle between the Crows and the Sea Gulls
on the Commons

The Diversion of Fighting with the Wind

For this I have a big umbrella with a strong frame. I go out to one of the most gusty spots, open the umbrella, and hold it in front of me against the wind, just as in a bayonet skirmish against the cavalry. The grips are as follows: the one hand grasps the handle, the thumb of the other hand is on the release button above so I can trick the wind if it gets too powerful by closing the umbrella. —Now we close it.

This diversion is also a very beneficial motion because one must make the most curious leap.[1166]

VI B 227   *n.d.*, 1844-45

« **5766**

For "Writing Sampler"

Something about the night watchman's song
or about night watchmen as
untaught singers

The various circumstances are to be examined.[1167]

VI B 229   *n.d.*, 1844-45

« **5767**

For "Writing Sampler"[1168]

What is not used about Grundtvig in "Concluding Postscript" can be used here, somewhat reworked. The title will be—The Danish Pantheon: Portrait of Pastor Grundtvig.[1169]

VI B 231   *n.d.*, 1844-45

« **5768**

I have returned a little book Reitzel[1170] sent me but am jotting down the title:
Über die Aesthetik der Hegelschen Philosophie,
by Wilhelm Danzel. Hamburg, 1844.

VI A 4   *n.d.*, 1844-45

« **5769**

When Father[1171] died, Sibbern[1172] said to me, "Now you will never get your theological degree," and then I did get it. If Father had lived, I would never have gotten it.[1173] —When I broke the engagement, Peter[1174] said to me, "Now you are lost." And yet it is clear that if I have indeed amounted to something, I did it through that step.

VI A 8   *n.d.*, 1844-45

« 5770 *The Police Agent*

Should be treated dramatically.[1175]

A demonic figure, who could just as well have become a carouser, yes, even a murderer, etc., but is now a servant of justice. (A frustrated childhood and youth have made him hostile toward the human race.)

The conception of police-justice as only a defense against poverty, just like the Spartans' relation to the Helots. (Contradiction of the idea.)

The contradiction that a character like this serves justice and yet does it so well that he is the most prominent.

VI A 10   n.d., 1844–45

« 5771

In margin of 5770 (VI A 10):

There should be something shifty in his demeanor which would have its roots in his inner instability but which he himself, lying to himself and to others, would explain as craftiness. His instability was not a lie; the lie was that he later explained it as subtlety. It is true that he sometimes said what he did not wish to say, but afterwards he lied and explained that the purpose of it had been to discover something about others.

VI A 11   n.d., 1844–45

« 5772

Under the title "Private Tutorials" and keeping it as delicate as possible, I would like to depict a feminine character whose greatness would lie precisely in her shy, loving, unassuming resignation (for example, a somewhat idealized Cornelia Olsen,[1176] the most admirable woman I have known, and the only one who has compelled my admiration). She would go through the experience of her sister's marrying the one she herself loved. This is a collision for resignation.

VI A 12   n.d., 1844–45

« 5773

To the typesetter:[1177]

The entire work is to be printed in large format, like that of Erslew's *Lexicon.*[1178] Medium-sized type the size of that in the lexicon is to be used. The other prefaces found in the work are to be set in brevier. The preface to the entire book [is to be set in type] larger than that of the text.

January 1845
VI B 8:1–2 January, 1845

« **5774**

Three Moral Tales[1179]
for children, adults, but especially for childlike souls
respectfully
sent out into the world
by
Hilarius Bookbinder[1180]
by order.

(1) Once does not count.
   The one who fell from the mast[1181]—did it again, and so it was said:
   It is nothing at all.
(2) The fairy tale about the Big Tease.
   Maybe you do not know what a Big Tease is; he is not really a
   human being, he has a big head, thin legs, carries his head askew
   on his shoulders.
(3) The hunter.
(4) Gossipmonger-Mary. A ghost story.

VI A 142   *n.d.,* 1845

« **5775**

Addition to 5774 (VI A 142):
   A number of Big Teasers are found in the various occupations in
life; this one was an author. He construed things in such a way that
what stupid people said as criticism simply was praise. Therefore, it is
all the same. —He even has one of the characters say that this is the
real trick.

VI A 143   *n.d.,* 1845

« **5776**

Addition to 5775 (VI A 143):
   These Big Teasers are not really human beings; this is noticed
especially by their contemporaries, for they are more mentally-spiritu-
ally qualified; therefore they make out best after death.

VI A 144   *n.d.,* 1845

« **5777**

A counterpart to the parable about the sower and the seed.[1182]
It would deal with preachers.
   The owner of a wheat farm gave each of his servants an equal
share of equally good wheat seed.
   But one stored the seed in a damp place where it sprouted too
soon and was spoiled.

And one mixed it with ordinary seed.

And one thought: the seed now belongs to me, why should I sow it, and he sold it for money.

And one did sow it but scattered it so carelessly that it was worthless.

One sowed it but put too high a price on it.

This is poorly worked out, for the unity of the idea is not preserved, but it may be used; the notion is a good one and lends itself especially well as a conclusion to a discourse or as an opening in order to exclude malpractices.

VI A 13   n.d., 1845

« 5778

Six Discourses on Imagined Occasions[1183]
by
S. Kierkegaard

VI B 100   n.d., 1845

« 5779

Aristotle's Rhetoric[1184]

The enthymeme[1185] is a rhetorical syllogism.

Ch. II

Rhetoric[1186] is the capacity, the rhetorical ability, to consider in everything that which is suitable for awakening belief ($\pi\iota\theta\alpha\nu\acute{o}\nu$).

Every other [art[1187]] will either instruct or awaken conviction ($\delta\iota\delta\alpha\sigma\kappa\alpha\lambda\iota\kappa\acute{\eta}-\pi\iota\sigma\tau\iota\kappa\acute{\eta}$[1188]).

$\pi\iota\sigma\tau\iota\varsigma$,[1189] in the plural, the means whereby conviction is awakened (consequently active).

Three kinds of $\pi\iota\sigma\tau\epsilon\iota\varsigma$ in speaking:[1190] (1) that which is constituted by the character of the speaker ($\mathring{\eta}\theta o\varsigma$[1191]), (2) that which puts the hearer in a particular mood, (3) that which lies in the speech itself in that it proves or seems to prove.

Rhetoric becomes an off-shoot of dialectic and of that part of morals which can be called politics.[1192]

VI C 2   n.d., 1845

« 5780

$\alpha\H{\iota}\tau\iota o\nu-o\H{\upsilon}\ \alpha\H{\iota}\tau\iota o\nu$[1193]

Rhetoric,[1194] ch. III

There are three kinds of hearers, therefore [three kinds of] speakers:[1195]

(1) to θεωρὸς (the knowledgeable), the artful speech (ἐπιδεικτι-
κὸς[1196])
the present
praise and censure
the praiseworthy—the vicious
(2) to deliberative assemblies (ὁ ἐκκλησιαστὴς)
the future
persuading—dissuading
benefit—harm
(3) to the judge
the past
accusation—defense
justice—injustice

VI C 3   *n.d.*, 1845

« **5781**

(1) The character of the speaker (ἦθος).[1197]
(2) The listeners are brought into a certain state.
(3) The speech proves or seems to prove.

(1) in deliberative conclusions.
(2) before courts.
(3) eulogies.[1198]

VI C 4   *n.d.*, 1845

« **5782**

Addition to 5781 (VI C 4):
In his *Rhetoric*
Aristotle does not consider
the "listener" at all.—
Only in Book I, ch. 3,[1199]   See Book III, ch. 1
at the very beginning, is   marked in my copy of
there a little bit.   the translation.[1200]

VI C 5   *n.d.*, 1845

« **5783**

That one makes the movement of infinite reflection and then
suddenly ends up with categories that speak of the endearing goodness
which does not know how good it is itself, the purity which is ignorant
of sin. (The first of which is within the category of immediacy; the
second is pure nonsense.)[1201]

VI B 130   *n.d.*, 1845

« **5784**

Sections[1202]

(1) Subject of the Address
(2) The Listener
(3) The Speaker

VI B 131   *n.d.*, 1845

« **5785**

Report

This[1203] was laid aside for the present. Would get to be too discursive to serve as a kind of introduction to my fragmentary discourses. Must be worked out separately and deal essentially with religious address.

VI B 132   *n.d.*, 1845

« **5786**

(1) Logical Problems[1204]
by
Johannes Climacus.
First a preface about *Philosophical Fragments.*

(2) Something about the Art of Religious Address[1205]
With Some Reference to Aristotle's *Rhetoric*
by
Johannes de Silentio[1206]
with the motto from Aristotle's *Rhetoric,*[1207] II,
chapter 23 (in the little translation,[1208]
p. 197), about a priestess who forbade her
son to become a public speaker.

(3) God's Judgment[1209]
A Story of Suffering
Psychological Experiment

(4) Writing Sampler[1210]
Apprentice Test Pieces
by
A.W.A.H.   Rosenblad
                                        Apprentice Author
                                    VI A 146   *n.d.*, 1845

« **5787** *Logical Problems*[1211]

No. 1. What is a category. What does it mean to say that being is a category.

      Is it an *abbreviatur* which world history gradually deposits.

No. 2. On the historical significance of the category.

No. 3. How does a new quality appear through a continued quantitative increase.

No. 4. On the leap.

No. 5. On the difference between a dialectical and a passion-filled transition.

No. 7. [changed from: 6] Conclusion–Enthymeme–resolution a trilogy.

No. 6. All historical knowledge is only approximation.

No. 8. What is existence?

VI B 13   n.d., 1844–45

« **5788**

A.

The Truth of Christianity as an Objective Issue[1212]

(a) The Historical Point of View[1213]

1.

The Bible[1214]

2.

The Church[1215]

3.[1216]

Speculation

(b) The Speculative Point of View[1217]

VI B 14   n.d., 1844–45

« **5789**

B.

The Subjective Issue[1218]

1.

An Expression of Gratitude to Lessing[1219]

VI B 15   n.d., 1844–45

« 5790

B.
The Subjective Issue[1220]

1.

An Expression of Gratitude to Lessing[1221]
Madvig[1222] is somewhat like him.
(His whole style.[1223] That he ventured to say: I.)

2.

Whether the Approximation of Probability[1224] (just as great for the contemporary and the latest) can be of interest (1) in order to gain faith—or (2) when one has faith.

No! (1) Illusion. —(2) Spiritual trial unto relapse.

In order to dispel the illusion which has gained a foothold during eighteen centuries,[1225] the piece made it all contemporary with the appearance of the god and maintained the distinction between the contemporaries and the last disciple.[1226]

VI B 16   n.d., 1844–45

« 5791

Addition to 5790 (VI B 16):

Positions

(1)

    (a) Objectivity stresses: the one spoken to, for example, to God, to pray[1227] means to speak to God.

    (b) Subjectivity stresses: what [1228] is said; one does not stand and talk with one of the other cellar-merchants even though God's name is spoken.

(2)

    (a) Objectivity stresses: what[1229] is said; the summary of thought-determinants.

    (b) Subjectivity stresses: *how*[1230] it is said; infinite passion[1231] is crucial, not its content, for its content is in fact itself.

VI B 17   n.d., 1844–45

« 5792

*This is also dialectical with respect to time,[1232] the pure repetition which is just as difficult as the first appropriation. This is because

man is a synthesis of the temporal and of the eternal, every moment
out upon "70,000 fathoms."[1233]

> In the moment of decision it appears as if the decision
> were in the present moment, and with that it changes into
> a striving. For example prayer—it was quite right once to
> sink into God and then remain there, but since man is a
> finite being, to pray means continual striving to achieve
> the true inwardness of prayer.[1234]

VI B 18   n.d., 1844–45

« 5793

In his idea-relationship to truth, Lessing is just as negative as he
is positive, equally as much, has just as much of the comic as he has
pathos, equally as much, and in his idea-relationship is always in a state
of becoming—that is, striving.[1235]

VI B 35:14   n.d., 1845

« 5794

[Nothing historical can become infinitely certain to me, except
that I] exist [er til], which is not something historical, because as one
who knows himself in relationship to God I am more than historical,
I am eternal; or the illusory result.[1236]

VI B 35:15   n.d., 1845

« 5795

The subjective existing thinker who has the categories of infinitude in his soul has them always, and therefore his form is continually
negative. Suppose such a person devoted his whole life to writing one
single book, suppose he published it, suppose he assumed there was
a reader—he would then express his relationship to a reader negatively
and without qualification; whereas a positive assistant professor who
scribbles a book in fourteen days blissfully and positively addresses
himself to the whole human race. That negative thinker, on the other
hand, could never achieve any kind of direct relationship to his reader.
He therefore would probably say: I can just as well recommend the
reading of this book as advise against it, because, bluntly speaking,
there is no direct gain from reading and no direct loss from not having
read it.*

The subjectively existing thinker is therefore just as negative as he
is positive. Among the negative ones there are a few. . . . . .[1237]

* Note. For the sake of caution I must beg everyone not to be bothered about what he reads here. It is written for idle people; yes, the serious reader will easily perceive that it is a joke to tease Lessing.[1238]

VI B 35:19   *n.d.,* 1845

« 5796

This is what Socrates develops in the *Symposium.* In his dissertation, Magister Kierkegaard was alert enough to discern the Socratic but is considered not to have understood it, probably because, with the help of Hegelian philosophy, he has become super-clever and objective and positive, or has not had the courage to acknowledge the negation. Finitely understood, of course, the continued and the perpetually continued striving toward a goal without attaining it means rejection, but, infinitely understood, striving is life itself and is essentially the life of that which is composed of the infinite and the finite. An imaginary positive accomplishment is a chimera. It may well be that logic has it, although before this can be regarded as true, it needs to be more precisely explained than has been done up to now, but the subject is an existing [*existerende*] subject, consequently is in contradiction, consequently is in the process of becoming, consequently is, if he is, in the process of striving.[1239]

VI B 35:24   *n.d.,* 1845

« 5797

. . . . . that, like the Wandering Jew in a beautiful legend, I should lead the pilgrims to the promised land and not enter myself, that I should guide men to the truth of Christianity and that as my punishment for going astray in my younger days I myself would not enter in but would venture only to be an omen of an incomparable future. . . .[1240]

VI B 40:33   *n.d.,* 1845

« 5798

The distinction between τὸ εἶναι—and τὸ ὄν.[1241] The confusion in Hegelian philosophy; a fitting observation on this by R. Nielsen in his *Propedeutiske Logik.* [1242]

VI C 1   *n.d.,* 1845

« 5799

That heavy breathing in the organ's breast.

VI A 28   *n.d.,* 1845

« **5800**

The contradiction: the driver of the modest hearse who had only half-covered the single horse with the horse-blanket so as to whip it better . . . . . the profundity in death . . . . . the prosaicness in this.

VI A 29   *n.d.*, 1845

« **5801**

A New Book
God's Judgment[*][1243]
A Story of Suffering
A Psychological Experiment
by
. . . . . de profundis

Here the categories of sin are used. His inclosing reserve is due to his not daring to let anyone know that it is a punishment he is suffering.

[*] *In margin:* A married man.

VI A 31   *n.d.*, 1845

« **5802**

In margin of 5801 (VI A 31):
It would be easy enough for him to find release if he would initiate her into his suffering, but he fears to do this for the very reason that the frightfulness of it will completely destroy her or make her sympathetic[1244] in such a way that she will follow him like Cain's wife,[1245] and this is precisely what he does not want. —On the other hand, he thinks he owes it to God to be silent erotically this way about his sufferings.
See p. 185, bottom [i.e., VI A 47].
See p. 194 [i.e., VI A 55–59].

VI A 32   *n.d.*, 1845

« **5803**

Now is the moment, now is the time, to write a dialectical guide to pseudonymous books by all the pseudonymous authors.[1246]

VI A 40   *n.d.*, 1845

« **5804** *The Relation between* **Either/Or** *and the* **Stages**[1247]

In *Either/Or*[1248] the competing components were the esthetic and the ethical, and the ethical was the choice. For this reason there were only two components, and the Judge was unconditionally the winner, even though the book ended with a sermon and with the observation that only the truth that builds up is the truth for me (inwardness—the point of departure for my upbuilding discourses).

In the *Stages*[1249] there are three components and the situation is different.

(1) the esthetic-sensate is thrust into the background as something past (therefore "a memory," for after all it cannot become utterly nothing).

The young man (thought—melancholy); Constantin Constantius (hardening of the understanding). Victor Eremita, who can no longer be the editor (sympathetic irony); the fashion designer (demonic despair); Johannes the seducer (damnation, a "marked" individual). He concludes by saying that woman is merely a moment. At that very point the Judge begins: Woman's beauty increases with the years, her reality [*Realitet*] is precisely in time.[1250]

(2) The ethical component is polemical: the Judge[1251] is not giving a friendly lecture but is grappling in existence, because he cannot end here, even though with pathos he can triumph again over every esthetic stage but not measure up to the esthetes in wittiness.

(3) The religious comes in a demonic approximation (Quidam[1252] of the experiment) with humor as its presupposition and its incognito (Frater Taciturnus).[1253]

VI A 41   *n.d.*, 1845

« 5805

A story of *suffering;*[1254] suffering is the religious category.

In *Stages* the esthete is no longer a clever fellow frequenting B's living room—a hopeful man, etc., because he still is only a possibility; no, he is existing [*existerer*].

"It is exactly the same as *Either/Or.*"

Constantin Constantius and the Young Man placed together in Quidam of the experiment. (Humor advanced.)

    as a point of departure for the beginning
        of the religious.—
    just as the tragic hero was used to bring out faith.

Three Stages and yet one Either/Or.

VI B 41:10   *n.d.*, 1845

« **5806**

Dear Sir:

As I have sent Mr. Philipsen, the bookseller, what remains of the edition of my *Upbuilding Discourses*, would you please be so good as to deliver to him upon request the copies that you have left.[1255]

May 10, 1845

Respectfully,
S. Kierkegaard

To
Mr. Bianco Luno, printer

Letters, no. 119   May 10, 1845

« **5807**

May 14, 1845
On arriving in Berlin[1256]

The only utilizable character on board the ship was a young fellow (a jaunty student) wearing a velvet cap fastened with a handkerchief, a striped tunic over a coat, a cane hanging by a looped string from one of the buttons. Guileless, open, much traveled, alert to everything, naive, bashful, and yet cheerful. By combining him with a gloomy traveler (like Mr. Hagen[1257]) a mournful effect could be produced.

VI A 42   May 14, 1845

« **5808**

The Secrets of a Heart
See p. 163 in this book [i.e., VI A 12].
(Private Tutorials)
or
Close to unhappiness and yet the unhappiest

In life there are many such situations in which the one who stands alongside, and consequently on the outside, nevertheless suffers the most.

In margin by the title: Sophie Beaumarchais[1258]
(*Clavigo*)

VI A 44   *n.d.*, 1845

« **5809** *A Character*

An old man sitting in the Royal Gardens or Cherry Lane or Philosopher's Way (Contrast: the warm summer air, the bracing freshness of the greenery—and the old man). He is an old widower, has no children, dines occasionally with a relative who is better off. He sits there regularly on certain days.

VI A 45   *n.d.,*   1845

« **5810**

For p. 171 bottom [i.e., V A 32]:

The dialectical contradiction must be maintained in such a way that it is uncertain whether he is closed up solely because of an erotic love affair with God, or out of pride toward men.

Even in David's psalms there are examples of the kind of self-encapsulation or closedupness which seeks to avoid every human relationship in order to remain *Du und Du* with God.[1259]

VI A 47   *n.d.,*   1845

« **5811**

Some place in *Biblische Legenden der Muselmänner aus arabischere Quellere,*[1260] by Dr. G. Weil, Frankfurt/M., 1845, it says of one of the characters that God himself personally accompanied him to the grave and walked in front of the coffin, and the four angels walked behind. —The out-and-out humor in this.

VI A 53   *n.d.,*   1845

« **5812**

The same book[1261] tells of the many times the saintly personages ask God to put them to a severe test to prove their devotion to him —and then they fail.

VI A 54   *n.d.,*   1845

« **5813**

It perhaps would be appropriate to carry out a psychological experiment at another point: a prospective clergyman, for example, who has fears about becoming a clergyman (due to a guilt situation he goes to a remote place, because he does not dare do even this at home for fear of being surprised, and reads law to see which sins are forbidden by the church—*de occultis non judicat ecclesia*[1262]). And yet his only wish is to become a clergyman, because it seems to him to be the only way possible to make some compensation for his sin. —The dialectical contradiction: whether he is benefiting others by being silent about his sin and seeking to be effective in a more quiet manner, or whether it would be better to divulge everything.

In margin: de occultis non judicat ecclesia could be the title.

VI A 55   *n.d.,*   1845

« **5814**

Addition to 5813 (VI A 55):

A situation where in a rustic setting he hears the merry sounds of children playing in a creek running into a little freshwater lake, later sees them come laughing and marching along the road, all of which makes him urgently feel the incongruity between being a child that way and living as he does with this enormous responsibility, whereas the mature periods of animals and of plants and of everything else correspond to what childhood is.

VI A 56   *n.d.,*   1845

« **5815**

In margin of 5813 (VI A 55):

And one of his lines would be: Would that it were not the case that the Church does not judge what is hidden—would that it did. That which consoles many is for me a prolongation of my suffering. Should I inform on myself? Then my work would be hindered. Do I dare not do it?

VI A 57   *n.d.,*   1845

« **5816**

In margin of 5813 (VI A 55):

Lines: What I miss most is my pulpit: This is the situation where one has sufferings and the deathbed and the sickbed.

VI A 58   *n.d.,*   1845

« **5817**

In margin of 5813 (VI A 55):

I have bought a new copy of canon law to study it again to see whether I dare to be a pastor—but just buying the copy makes me shudder, because it is as if the book dealer might notice in me what a painful study I am making of it.

VI A 59   *n.d.,*   1845

« **5818**

This must now be done: A person closed up within himself is pictured in a third stage, where he himself discovers that his guilt is nothing more than that he has been closed up within himself. –The dialectic: whether, demonically understood, he is not greater at this moment than if he had talked right away; the closedupness therefore returns, and although he has made this discovery, he again keeps it to himself in his self-incapsulation.

VI A 61   *n.d.,* 1845

« **5819**

The little band of enthusiasts[1263] that is formed in Pastor Grund-tvig's Ale-Norse[1264] taproom.

VI A 73   *n.d.,* 1845

« **5820**

Today I wanted to visit Father's grave,[1265] felt an unusual compulsion to do so, was more than usually withdrawn within myself–and what happens–when I arrived at the entrance near the turn, a woman came running, with hat and shawl and parasol, a really silly sort of woman. The sweat poured down her face, and she addresses an old woman walking a few feet away from me, a basket on her arm: What can be keeping you, we have been waiting for half an hour now (the talk flowed on, but in her flurry she ran back and forth like a dog)–we have waited for half an hour, my sister is ready to cry, the hearse has already arrived, and the whole funeral party, and the trumpet players–and so it went on and on. Therefore the sister who was about to cry was on the verge of tears because the trumpet players had come but the lady with the basket had not. –I walked down another path, and fortunately they were not to be in the vicinity of Father's grave. But it is strange how the comic insinuates itself, particularly into the most momentous moods.

June 10, 1845

VI A 75   June 10, 1845

« **5821**

Vertically in margin of 5820 (VI A 75):
This could be worked up with a touch of irony under the title: Tears at a Grave.

VI A 76   *n.d.,* 1845

« 5822

New Zealanders kiss each other with their noses. Engel[1266] in his *Mimik* quotes a passage from a travel account which he reports.

VI A 77   *n.d.*, 1845

« 5823

William Afham's part (in the *Stages*) is so deceptively contrived that it is praise and high distinction to have stupid fuss-budgets pass trivial judgment on it and say that it is the same old thing. Yes, that is just the trick. I never forget the anxiety I myself felt about not being able to achieve what I had once accomplished, and yet it would have been so very easy to choose other names. This is also the reason Afham states that Constantius said that never again would he arrange a banquet, and Victor Eremita, that he would never again speak admiringly of Don Juan.[1267] But the Judge declares that he will keep on repeating.* As the author himself suggested, wherever it is possible and wherever it is not possible.

*"That only thieves and gypsies say that one must never return where he has once been."[1268]

VI A 78   *n.d.*, 1845

« 5824

The *Stages* will not have as many readers as *Either/Or*, will barely make a ripple. That is fine; in a way it rids me of the gawking public who want to be wherever they think there is a disturbance. I prophesied this myself in the epilogue to "Guilty?/Not Guilty?"[1269]

VI A 79   *n.d.*, 1845

« 5825

There is something that grates on me in being a teacher—it would be best if a pastor were to read another pastor's sermon aloud so that he himself could really become a listener to the exhortation.

VI A 82   *n.d.*, 1845

« 5826

They think it is so easy; they attack my presentation as mistaken in maintaining a doubleness[1270]—they should try it themselves. The vociferous, assertive direct method is much easier.

VI A 83   *n.d.*, 1845

« 5827

The review of my *Fragments* in the German journal[1271] is essentially wrong in making the content appear didactic, expository, instead of being experimental by virtue of its polar form, which is the very basis of the elasticity of irony. To make Christianity seem to be an invention of Johannes Climacus is a biting satire on philosophy's insolent attitude toward it. And then, too, to bring out the orthodox forms in the experiment "so that our age, which only mediates etc., is scarcely able to recognize them"* and believes it is something new—that is irony. But right there is the earnestness, to want Christianity to be given its due in this way—before one mediates.

*In margin: (these are the reviewer's words.)

VI A 84   n.d., 1845

« 5828

*A Possible Concluding Word
to All the Pseudonymous Writings*[1272]
by
Nicolaus Notabene[1273]

I will tell the esteemed public how it happened that I became an author.[1274] The story is quite simple, for I can by no means attribute it to my having had a vision, a dream, a stroke of genius, or some such thing. In a sense I had more or less loafed away some of my student years, reading and thinking, it is true, but my indolence had been thoroughly dominant. Then one Sunday afternoon four years ago I was sitting in the cafe in Fredericksberg Gardens, smoking my cigar and watching the waitresses, and suddenly the thought overwhelmed me: You are wasting your time and doing no good; all around you one first-rate genius after the other pops up and makes life and existence and world-historical traffic and communication with eternal happiness easier and easier—*What are you doing?* Should you not also hit on some way of helping the age? Then it occurred to me—what if I were to settle down to making everything difficult. Thus one may seek to serve in all kinds of ways. Even if the age did not need a little ballast, I would still be loved by all those who make everything easy, for if there is no one willing to make it hard, it becomes all too easy—to make it easy.[1275] From that moment on I found my entertainment in this work, that is, the work has been entertaining, but it certainly has not been maintaining, for I have put money into it.[1276] After all, one cannot insist that people must pay to have everything made hard—that in fact would make it still more difficult. But those who make it easy really should support me, for they are the gainers. They have definitely made use of me and simply assumed that I did it for their sakes, just so they could have something to make easy.

VI A 85   n.d., 1845

« **5829**

It might be an appropriate dramatic contrast to present a sooth-sayer who lived at the same time as Socrates and prophesied about a hero who would come. The hero was Socrates and he did in fact exist, but the soothsayer was aware of this and Socrates was the one who least of all seemed designated thereby. What merit would the prophecy of such a soothsayer have—and yet he was right.

VI A 86   n.d., 1845

« **5830**

It could be a very funny plot for a vaudeville play to have a Swedish family, having read in the papers[1277] about the matchless Danish hospi-tality (that barbers give shaves gratis, that prostitutes operate gratis (see *Either/Or*[1278]) etc.), take off for Copenhagen for a fortnight in the firm conviction that this is the way it always is in Copenhagen—and then develop it in situations. To compensate for the misunderstand-ing, the play could end with a happy love affair, germinating from sympathy with the situation of misunderstanding.

VI A 87   n.d., 1845

« **5831** *A Surprising, Surprising Surprise*[1279]

The King of [Prussia[1280]] has come—it is absolutely certain. We have our information from a maid servant who saw him and recognized him and from a man who was so close to him that he could have spoken with him if His Majesty had been prepared with what he should say on such an opportunity and occasion. But on festive occasions, just as in public defense of doctoral dissertations, one is prepared with only a limited number of answers and courtesy phrases.* The whole event has something so oddly surprising about it that the editorial office staff must be excused for not having spies out and ministry-reports to

---

In margin: *Our reporter explains that he did not get the honor of talking person-ally with His Majesty or of showing him about the town, which no one knows as well as he does.

submit to its public. But it is certain that he has come, and since he has been seen and recognized, as far as facts are concerned it makes no difference by whom he is seen and recognized—our witnesses are not to be scorned.

The maid servant is an unusually clever chambermaid with unusually good and unusually numerous recommendations from the many places where she has worked (there has been such a demand for her). She has been engaged seven times but has been very prudent about it and with none of the beloveds ever let things reach the point of ultimate protestations; she came out of it all right—a little innocent jest, and then the gifts. She is really clever. When she is supposed to do errands in the city, she does not slouch and drag along as the other maid servants do—no, she runs like the wind—but not to get home early —she just wants to make sure of the time she has at her own disposal. Thus she assumes that an ordinary Wednesday or Saturday expedition to the market takes, as a rule, two to two and a half hours. The days when there is so much traffic, as on Vimmelskaftet and Amagertorv, that a trading ship must ride at anchor more frequently, she runs through the secondary streets and counts on having exactly two hours in which to visit someone or other. This morning she was sent out to the custom house with her master's lunch—he is a customs officer. What happens? Well, she described it, but the one who saw her excitement when she told it . . . . . she recognized the King immediately. He was a young man in a white uniform; she saw him quite clearly, so clearly that she is convinced that he also saw her, of which she is not a little proud. It amazed her no end that our King walked over and embraced someone else, but a servant girl standing there, who also took the man in white to be none other than the King, explained that it must be a foreign custom, a strange way of showing courtesy, that the Chief Marshal or someone like that should represent the King so that the King himself could stand calmly as an onlooker and see how much was made of the King.

Ceremonies were hurriedly outlined (we go on with the story) for the three days the King would be Denmark's guest—but only the ceremonies for the first day are decided; we state it here and admire the wisdom of not deciding things too long in advance when one is dependent on wind and weather. Immediately after disembarking considerable changing of clothes—that is, undressing—and then to bed to sleep. This entertainment is planned to last twelve hours. Curious! Anyone who has read anything about ceremonies certainly must marvel because they are always planned as if royalty and the highest royalty did not need to sleep. It is the same with little people. Mr. and Mrs. Burmann's ceremony for a Sunday in Dyrehaven is an excellent [example]: they ride out, eat lunch, eat dinner, spend the whole day in the bosom of the family and of nature—but no one has given any thought to sleep—and therefore Malle and Klister must seek solitude.[1281]

The entertainment lasts twelve hours. At eight o'clock in the evening they get up, renewed and refreshed, completely new and different people. But the visit is not an official one, nor is it purely personal, but a mixture of the two. The ceremony has focused on this and is specifically arranged in painterly tableaus. So they get up. For a quarter of an hour, after a signal from the Chief Marshal, the two kings walk back and forth arm in arm and affectionately pat each other many times; this diversion lasts a quarter of an hour. Then they sit down at a great green table, for now the negotiating begins. This is the reason the Chief Marshal thought it best to provide and implement a familiar tableau. When Napoleon and Talleyrand had worked together for many days and nights, they both fell asleep. The first part of this was not painterly and cannot be depicted, only the last part. They both fell asleep, and the ceremony, which also is the program, explains that it is after many days and nights of strenuous effort. Therefore a man-in-waiting goes in and calls the King, just as in that tableau. They get up.

Since the King of ——— is supposed to have the intention of learning to know the Danish state, and since, in reliance on his military power, he fears only the intelligence of this country, he especially wishes to get to know this. This has been prepared for. All the male and female teachers of German have been gathered together hastily, and these are grouped in such a way that they are enough for the whole nation which is to be presented to the foreign monarch.[*] As if at random, our King, while walking arm in arm with the foreign King down the row, as if at random addresses one of his subjects and now another—and look, to the foreign monarch's amazement they all answer in German. They permit him to remain ignorant of the fact that they are language teachers, and our King does not get too involved with any of them for fear that one of the language teachers might betray that he was only a phrase-book and not a man. Our queen, too,

[*]*In margin:* And in order to guarantee his observations, he wishes to see them by night, has them summoned in order that they should not have time to prepare themselves.

in passing, occasionally drops a word now to one, now to another of the women; it appears to be quite at random and yet she always chances upon a language teacher, and the foreign monarch is more surprised than ever. But it is Nathanson,*[1282] the wholesaler, who attracts the foreign King's particular attention. He has offered his services as one who speaks perfect German and who is also expert in politics. He is also supposed to have proposed that during the time the foreign King was here he might publish the *Berlingske Tidende*[1283] in German, but this was refused since it was assumed that the numerous diversions would leave no time for any of the monarchs to read this paper.

*Everything is built around him; a nation fortunate enough to have such a man must also show him off. Our King holds forth with him much longer, discusses Denmark's prosperity, and gives him the chance also to shine in mental arithmetic. In addition, the wholesale grocer is relied upon to use the utmost discretion in satisfying the royal visitors. The intention is to get the foreign monarch himself to enter into discussion with Nathanson, and behold, he can answer much faster than he is asked, and that is why he is given a medal which he wears around his waist—it is so heavy that it cannot be carried any other way.

VI B 233   *n.d.,* 1845

« 5832 *The Scandinavian Idea*[1284]

Wherever there are good people they are joined by good people. The King of P.[1285] is here, and now the Scandinavian Brothers arrive, I do not mean those greeted with catcalls[1286] but those greeted with applause.[1287]

At this point we should take the example of Sallust's story of the three brothers who had themselves buried alive in order to decide boundary disputes: in like manner they express this symbolically by three of them getting drunk.

Hans Povelsen, a graduate student, is the central figure here. His motto is: Now or Never. It is two weeks now since he first let his sweetheart listen critically to the speech he intends to give, but he is not satisfied with it and with her assurance that he does it very well, and now he goes around with a copy which he hands to passersby with the request that they stop and listen to him. The author of this article was fortunate enough to listen to him at a gateway to Vimmelskaftet[1288] and must testify to the fact that Mr. P. knows his job very well; his gestures perhaps could be somewhat more expert, but his voice and facial expressions were evidence of an unmistakable effort, which may in fact go on three or four days yet, unless the Swedes do not show up at all, and in that case it can go on longer—if his strength holds out. But this is the trouble. For fourteen days and nights he has not closed his eyes, and the resulting exhaustion is evident in his alarming absent-mindedness. If the Swedes actually do arrive and P. actually does get to give his speech,[1289] there is no doubt that a union will result. The danger is from another direction. There is supposed to have been a pastor so absentminded that he married two completely strange and incompatible people. There was nothing to object to in the act itself. The wedding discourse was unusually fine; the speaker inspired the two to be joined together uncommonly well—the trouble was simply that they were wrong for each other. There were many unpleasant consequences involved in getting separated. Thus it is not to be feared that Mr. Povelsen is likely to forget his talk on that day (although that has already happened many times in the daily practice), but that he will unite us Danes, perhaps not with the Swedes, but with another race— and after having been so fervently united it will be difficult to be separated.

The ceremony at this festivity is designed to be especially mean-ingful—as Povelsen says: Now or Never. First of all 500 Swedish stu-dents will be placed *vis-à-vis* 500 Danish students, and they will gaze romantically at each other and then soulfully. This entertainment will last a quarter of an hour.

The ceremony is planned for just one day, since in these three days the spirit will be so active that, as the prophet[1290] declares, your maidens and young men will have visions; thus one always must be prepared for a sudden marvelous proposal which then would be put into action.

In St. Peter's Church in Rome four sermons are preached in four places at the same time; in the same way it has been resolved that four speeches should be delivered here at the same time, but since there are not as many orchestras as speakers, they must be satisfied with a common fanfare. A list of the different songs and speeches is laid at each place-setting like a menu, so each one may choose.

(The young people's gaiety in the words has an amusing side— which has a value of its own—but not the Ale-Norse.[1291])

In conclusion, an apotheosis.

Grundtvig[1292] appears on an elevation in the forest background, supported by Barfod[1293] and Povelsen. He is artistically draped in a great cloak, has a staff in his hand, and his face is concealed by a mask with one eye (deep and profound, so as to see into world history) and a mossy beard with birds' nests in it (he is very old—about 1,000 years); he has a hollow voice melodramatically accompanied by a few blasts on a conch (as at a town meeting); he speaks in dithyrambic rhythm. When he has finished his speech (that is, when the committee in charge of the festivities says "Enough," for otherwise he would never finish), a bell rings, a cord is pulled, the beard falls off, followed by the enormous cloak, and we see a slim young man with wings: it is Grundtvig as the spirit of the Scandinavian idea, he says: Ladies and Gentlemen.*

—This was on a Sunday. Strangely enough, Bishop Mynster[1294] preached that same Sunday. There was not a soul in church; nevertheless, just as the great congregation had inspired him to give a glorious sermon, so too the empty church inspired him. When he was through, he gazed in front of him in silence, and if there is a transfiguration when the dead go behind the curtain, then he was transfigured in the same way—and like one who is dead.[1295]

*This is what I have been prophesying for half a century now. Shoemaker Mathiesen can testify that I said it to him one Sunday afternoon forty-five years ago when we met in the barber shop of district barber Biberak, now deceased. What I have suffered for the sake of this idea, how often I have been close to despair for old Denmark, how many tears it has cost me—this only shoemaker Mathiesen knows, he who first accepted my teaching, and that is why he shall also be my successor in the tyranny.

VI B 235   n.d., 1845

« 5833

. . . . . as fervent as the dying prodigal's last yearning for the salvation of his soul—as painful as the drunkard's first dim consciousness as he awakens.

VI A 88   n.d., 1845

« 5834 *Situation*

With modification it could [have] be[en] used in the psychological experiment " 'Guilty?'/'Not Guilty?' "[1296]): Quidam[1297] of the experiment, for example, was a theological candidate who became a pastor, lived in the country, came to the capital, at the request of one of his friends, preaches at the morning service, delivers a good sermon, takes out a piece of paper which is a list of those for whom wedding banns are to be read from the pulpit—and reads [the banns]: followed by the name of the girl to whom he had been engaged—and now another name.[1298]

VI A 94   n.d., 1845

« **5835**

If I am totally occupied with something and I want to talk about it to people who regard it as foolishness, what then? Well, if I am a* genius who feels called to remake the world, then I will rant and shout in the conviction that I will surely get people to see that this is terribly important. But if I have any sense and reflection, I will not make such assumptions about myself and will express the discrepancy by placing the comic between us and talk about it in the form of the comic. Thus, simply by comprehending the comic myself, I will avoid what the ranting genius always ends up with—becoming comical.[1299]

In margin: *roaring

VI A 95   n.d., 1845

« **5836**

The well-dressed lady who Sunday afternoon sailed around in the canal in one of Eskildsen's boats all alone by herself.

VI A 97   n.d., 1845

« **5837 *Lines for a Humorous Individual*[1300]**

"Just as it is most pleasant to trudge through the world without being known by His Majesty the King, Her Majesty the Queen, Her Majesty the Crown Princess, His Royal Majesty the Crown Prince—so, too, it seems to make life immensely troublesome to be known by God. Wherever he is, each and every half-hour becomes *infinitely* important. It is not possible to endure living like this for sixty years, any more than one could endure preparing for the comprehensive final examination [for sixty years], which, after all, one endures for only three years and is not nearly so strenuous. Everything disintegrates into contradiction. You are promptly lectured not to go on dozing but to live with the highest passion of infinity. So you shape up, turn up all spick-and-span for the parade*, as we say—yes, you must learn to shorten the sails. What does it mean—in the end everyone gets just as far, and it all is not worth much. Here things go as they go with me and my physician. I complain about feeling indisposed. He answers, "You drink too much coffee and walk too little." Three weeks later I talk with him again and say: I really do not feel well at all, but now it cannot be because of drinking coffee for I do not drink coffee at all, or lack of movement, for I walk all day long. He answers, "Yes, that must be the reason; you do not drink coffee and you walk too much." Consequently my indisposition continues to be the same, but when I drink coffee, my indisposition comes from drinking coffee, and when I do not drink coffee, then my indisposition comes from not drinking coffee. So it is with us men. All earthly existence is a kind of indisposition; for some it is because of too much effort, for others because of too little, and if anyone asks the cause, the first question put to him is: Are you exerting yourself too much? If one answers "yes," then he is told: You are exerting yourself too much. If one answers "no," he gets the opposite answer, sticks his tail between his legs and slinks away. Even if I were paid ten dollars I would not presume to explain the riddle of life. Why should I? If life is a riddle, then the outcome will be that the one who has posed it will himself explain it when he perceives that there is no great traffic in solutions

I did not invent the riddle, but in the *Frisindede, Freischütz,* and other papers where riddles are run, the explanation follows in the next issue. The distinction of being named in the paper as the one who solved the riddle on the same day as we all get to know the solution does not interest me.

An old maid or pensioner who solves riddles.

VI A 98   *n.d.,*   1845

« **5838**

Addition to 5837 (VI A 98):
If God can do everything effortlessly, then his presence prevents men from slowing their pace.

VI A 99   *n.d.,*   1845

« **5839**

In margin of 5837 (VI A 98):
*They come running with a passion such as no one had during the bombardment.

VI A 100   *n.d.,*   1845

« **5840** *Lines*

Just as the sick man longs to cast off the bandages, so also my healthy spirit longs to throw off this physical exhaustion.* Just as the conquering general shouts as his horse is shot from under him: A new horse—O that the victorious healthiness of my spirit might shout: A new horse, a new body.†

Just as someone in peril at sea violently pushes away another drowning man who tries to grab his legs, so my body hangs like a heavy weight on my spirit, until it is destroyed in death. Like a steamship in which the machinery is too large for the construction of the ship, so do I suffer.[1301]

In margin: *this fusty, perspiring mush-envelope which is the body and the body's exhaustion.

In margin: †for only the body is worn out.

VI A 103   *n.d.*, 1845

« **5841**

Something about Cows Stampeding[1302]
A Study

> An especially detailed description of the appearance of individual cows in their performances of genius, a description of how they flourish their tails, of their oblique canter, of the expression in their eyes—of the one that was embarrassed when I stared at it and promptly put its tail between its legs again.

In margin: "All of nature makes happy gestures"[1303]—cows, too, even if there is a question about the extent to which a little irony forms the basis of that statement.

VI A 104   *n.d.*, 1845

« **5842**

Fortunately I am not one of fortune's favorites, nor am I one of the much admired ones, for my willingness to rejoice with them and to offer them my tribute is matched by the meagerness of my desire to be such a one myself, because a life like that is contentious in relation to the universal, devoid of consolation in relation to the unhappy.

There is a bird called a "rain-warner,"[1304] and such am I—when a storm is brewing in a generation, then individualities like me show up.

VI A 119   *n.d.,* 1845

« 5843

I had a strange experience leaving Vesterport[1305] tonight. It was dark; I passed a couple of boys in one of the narrow sidestreets. I scarcely noticed them and had passed them when I heard one of them, telling the other a story, say: "And then they came to the old fortune-teller." The same thing happened to me once this summer at twilight out at Peblingesø.[1306] There were two little girls, and the one said: "And then a long way off he saw an old castle." I believe that the greatest poet could scarcely produce such an effect as these stirring reminders of the fairy story: "the old castle far away," "and then," or "they walked a long way *until,*" etc.

VI A 125   *n.d.,* 1845

« 5844

Grimur Thomsen must be a very learned man; this is apparent in the many books he quotes in his dissertation,[1307] and yet the dissertation indicates that he has read still more books, for example, *Fear and Trembling, The Concept of Anxiety, Either/Or*, which he does not quote.—

VI A 128   *n.d.,* 1845

« 5845

In margin of 5844 (VI A 128):
He seems to divide the literature into two unequal parts: the books he uses, and those he uses for quotation—therefore it cannot be denied that he has used the literature. —He cannot be blamed for putting his light under a bushel, but on the other hand it can also be misleading to place a light on a mountain when at best it is suitable only for lighting the lower places.

VI A 129   *n.d.,* 1845

« 5846 *Situation*

An old falcon, one of those whose ancestors were used for hunting, sits in a solitary tree and tells himself stories about how it was in those proud days (developed with an element of fanaticism). In a swamp below, concealed by rushes, sit two frogs in deepest amazement at what the falcon is telling; they were just about to tell their own life-stories to each other when they became aware of the falcon and now are too embarrassed to begin.

VI A 130   n.d., 1845

« **5847**

It could be amusing to run, without context or explanation, this question in one of the papers: Why does everyone, at least at certain times, have such an indescribable longing to be a bird? Not a word more. This could be used in a novel as a pre-arranged message among thieves or as a wager.

The novel would begin by saying: One day the citizens of the city of M—— were amazed to read in *Speideren,* their local newspaper, the following lines under the heading "A Question."

VI A 131   n.d., 1845

« **5848**

Peter Rørdam[1308] is a very sanguine and childlike person (he says: I am angry, and then is no longer angry, and then is angry again; he wants to do something and intellectually is in the phase when, like children, one does it all in one's pants). But it is too bad that seventy years is the maximum age; if it were customary to live on the average to be 250 years, R. would be normal, since he is now in his fortieth year.

VI A 134   n.d., 1845

« **5849**

The theme remains continually the same, but every time he wearily shouts: What time is it?—the answer is: Eternity.

(There is an Italian folk-tale[1309] of a poor wretch who woke up in hell and shouted: What time is it?—and got the answer: Eternity.) Used somewhere in *Either/Or.*[1310]

VI A 135   n.d., 1845

« **5850**

Logical Problems[1311]
by
Johannes Climacus
Edited
By
S. Kierkegaard

VI B 89   n.d., 1845

« **5851**

Concluding Simple Postscript[1312]
(Detailed yet superfluous Postscript)
to
Philosophical Fragments
by
Johannes Climacus

—————

edited
by
S. Kierkegaard
Copenhagen 1845
Available at Reitzel's

VI B 90   *n.d.*, 1845

« **5852**

Sept. 30, 1845

Dear Sir:[1313]

With all my searching, as I told you, I could only come to the flattering conclusion that the broken and lost or lost and broken cup could not be matched. Fortunately, as you now know, it had the distinction in your household also of being the only one of its kind. Why fortunately? Well, usually it is assumed quite properly that to lose the only one of its kind is the heaviest loss of all, but when it comes to coffee cups an exception is made, and one finds it a consolation that the lost cup was the only one of its kind and finds lightest what is usually the heaviest loss of all—losing what is matchless.[1314]

So let the accompanying pair of cups take the place of the one that is lost, and on the same condition: that if it is lost, it will not be of great consequence.

S. Kierkegaard

[written on the back of the envelope:] To Mr. Kold
in Fredensborg
Together with a package marked K

Letters, no. 120a   September 30, 1845

« **5853** *A Request to The Corsair*[1315]

Sing sang resches Tubalcain—which translated means: Cruel and bloodthirsty *Corsair,* high and mighty Sultan, you who hold the lives of men like a plaything in your mighty hand and as a whim in the fury of your invective, O, let me move you to compassion, curtail these sufferings—slay me, but do not make me immortal! High and mighty Sultan, in your quick wisdom consider what it would not take long for the paltriest of all those you have slain to see, consider what it means to become immortal, and particularly to become that through the testimonial of *The Corsair*. O, what cruel grace and mercy to be forever pointed to as an inhuman monster because *The Corsair* inhumanly had spared him! But above all not this—that I shall never die! Uh, such a death penalty is unheard of.* I get weary of life just to read it. What a cruel honor and distinction to have no one be moved by my womanly wailing: This will kill me, this will be the death of me—but everybody laughs and says: He cannot die. O, let me move you to compassion; stop your lofty, cruel mercy; slay me like all the others.

Victor Eremita[1316]

(Here perhaps could be added the words at the end of the postscript to *Either/Or*, which are in the tall cupboard closest to the window.)

In margin: *Slay me so I may live with all the others you have slain, but do not slay me by making me immortal.

VI B 192   n.d., 1845

« **5854**

Addition to 5853 (VI B 192):

Have no fear—why spare me, I have no wife to sigh for me, perhaps to grieve . . . . . over the husband you slay, no beloved to feel the drubbing more devastatingly, no children whose tenderness makes the blow heavier for them than for the father—I have no legitimately acquired distinction in society that can be temporarily embittering to see wasted, I have no famous family name so that an entire family will suffer by the attack upon one single member—spare instead everyone who has anyone who perhaps cannot help but feel violated even though the one who is wounded disdains the attack. . . . . .

VI B 193   n.d., 1845

« **5855**

Somewhere in the book *Concluding Postscript*[1317] I quoted some words of Luther (on the Babylonian captivity). It reads: *"in diesen Sacramenten,"* and without a doubt Luther meant thereby the five Catholic [sacraments]. Now someone rushes forward and protests, etc. Well, go ahead. That is just what I wanted. I did not wish to begin a scholarly investigation in the book or use my best weapons. Now I am tempted to write a little foreword, a eulogy, and then I can quote the far more significant lines in the same book which I have noted in my copy (Gerlach's edition[1318]).

VI A 141   *n.d.*, 1845

« 5856 *Situation*

Behind me: the organ; my place in the pew in Freslers Kirke; in the foreground a window, outside it a tree with branches stirring in the summer breeze.

VII[1] A 231   *n.d.*, 1845–47

« 5857 *Lines and a Situation*[1319]

(could be used in an idyllic operetta)

A *low-comedy character* (a jaunty fellow in not the worst sense) sits outside an inn at a well-supplied table—a schoolmaster enters.

Schoolmaster: Why in the world did you come out here and what are you doing here? You seem to be leading the life of the rich man in the gospel.[1320]

Character: O, don't you know, you who are the school teacher out here. It's good that I came so that I can arrange something with you—I am out here on behalf of the Temperance Society.

Schoolmaster: You know that I am a member in good standing and keep your pledge.

Character: Don't you know that I am not a member of the Temperance Society, damned if I will be, but you know from our youth that I've always had the gift of gab and so the Temperance Society has hired me to travel around and get members. And may I congratulate the Society for doing it. I write everything on the expense account: four schnapps per day and two glasses of punch every day I hold an inspiring meeting and an extra swig for every member I get. I help the Society with my talent, and the Society helps my talent with countless well-brewed egg nogs. —And you should hear me talk. —Yes, I'm really enthusiastic about the Society; every time I talk I always think of the four schnapps.

Schoolmaster: But is this any help to the Society?

Character: Why not? If one is going to gather money, he doesn't smell of the money,[1321] and what does the butter care about what fattens up the cabbage? Besides, the Society has still another lecturer, the traveling paragon, he follows after me wherever I have been and convinces those who have been won over by my lecture: but I will not work for the Society in that way—it is so sacrificial—but now to the matter at hand, if you would like a glass of punch, then I am the man who can treat you to it.

VII¹ A 233   *n.d.,* 1845–47

« **5858**

If I ever write about marriage, I shall have to look into Fischart. I find something of his quoted in Flögel, *Geschichte der komischen Literatur,*[1322] III, p. 339, etc.

VII¹ A 241   *n.d.,* 1845–47

« **5859** *Writing Sampler*[1323]

Apprentice Test Pieces
by
A. B. C. D. E. F. Rosenblad
[*changed to:* Godthaab]
Prospective Author

N.B. The book must be done up with all possible elegance: a border around every page (as in *Urania*),[1324] each section with a distinctive type, ornamental and clamorous initial letters—in short, everything *à la* catchpenny books. Some letters in red (as in old books), others in green, blue, etc., so that the book might appeal to the public and thoroughly have the appearance of a sampler, corresponding to the motto: "Delightful ribbons, gold, green, and blue."[1325]

N.B. Perhaps it could come out in serial form and be offered in advance as a suitable New Year's gift.[1326] . . .

Preface . . .
No. 1
The Theater . . .
No. 2
Literature . . .
No. 3
[Politics] . . .

No. 4
Criticism and Taste . . .
No. 5
News . . .
No. 6
Morals . . .
No. 7
Arrival of Swedish Students . . .
No. 8
Society of Watchmen . . .
Postscript . . .

VII² B 274:1-22   *n.d.*, 1846–47

« **5860**

. . . Finally, one wish: if only I might appear in *The Corsair* soon. It is very difficult for an author to stand singled out in Danish literature as the only one (assuming that we pseudonyms are one) who is not abused there. Yes, even Victor Eremita has had to experience the hitherto unheard of disgrace—of being attacked?*—no, of being immortalized[1327]—by *The Corsair*. No doubt it would be highly desirable that this disgrace to literature did not exist at all, that there be no literary publication making money by prostitution, for what is a woman's loveliness if it is for sale for money,† and what is a bit of talent when it is in the service‡ of vile profit, but if it does exist then it is highly desirable to be in the company of, or in agreement with, what one respects even though one disapproves of some particulars, than to sit in the place of honor among the despicable.[1328]

In margin: *it is an honor.
In margin: †without such an author's talent.
In margin: ‡without a whore's beauty. . . .

VII¹ B 1   *n.d.*, 1845

« **5861**

ubi spiritus ibi ecclesia
ubi P. L. M. [Møller] ibi "The Corsair."[1329]

VII¹ B 5   *n.d.*, 1845

« **5862**

Hilarius Bookbinder, my chief, has been flattered in *The Corsair*.[1330]

Frater Taciturnus
In charge of part 3 of
Stages on Life's Way.[1331]

VII[1] B 6   *n.d.,*   1845

« **5863 *Some Good-natured Gossipy Remarks***

It is a matter of common knowledge that a trifle, a nothing, and especially gossip, create the biggest sensation. I have been pleased to corroborate this by having an insignificant pseudonymous little article in *Fædrelandet*[1332] create much more of a sensation—because it dealt with Mr. P. L. Møller—than all my writing put together. I am positive that my whole life will never be as important as my trousers[1333] have come to be. Yes, one might almost think that my trousers have become what the age demanded, and, if so, I sincerely hope that the demand of every age may be as moderate for the person concerned, for, good Lord, it does not demand trousers from me, after all, it merely demands that I wear them, and this demand really does not embarrass me, inasmuch as I have made a practice of wearing trousers since I was four years old, but it never really occurred to me that it would become so extraordinarily important to others. But since my writing has never been so fortunate as to satisfy the demands of the age, I thought to myself: If you can do it in such an easy way by means of your trousers, then everything is fine again. I always have to make some self-sacrifice, but what is that compared to being important. Just yesterday my servant reminded me to put on a new pair, but I thought to myself: That won't do; perhaps the new ones will not satisfy the demand of the age. But the old ones certainly do. Innumerable ladies and gentlemen have personally made sure that I am wearing them, and according to what I could discern from their facial expressions, they did completely satisfy the demand of the age. To accommodate the demand of the age I have candidly and freely replied to everyone who asked if they *actually* were the trousers—presumably so that he could relate that he personally had *actually* seen them—I have answered him solemnly, as is seemly in this important matter: Yes. —Whether they are my trousers or someone else's makes no difference to me, but for someone ardently trying to hold to a concept of the greatness in or potential to every man there is something sad about having an abundance of observations which seem only to bear witness to irresponsibility, silliness, crudity, and the like.

But to move on—I now go from my trousers to something just as unimportant: Literatus P. L. Møller. The manuscript of my latest book was ready by the middle of December, 1845, and a few days before Christmas I delivered the manuscript in its entirety, as I am in the habit of doing, to the printer. Thus I was finished and at leisure, had the time and opportunity to do what I otherwise could not do, and in my joy and gratitude over being finished I felt like doing somebody a little service. Then came P. L. Møller's brilliant *Gæa.*[1334] Among other things it contained a little attack (after praising the pseudonyms) on one of the pseudonyms. Usually I pay no attention to such things, but this was different. Mr. P. L. Møller is sufficiently well-known to Danish literature, and for that reason I knew very well that I would make some people happy by challenging him—therefore the article in *Fædrelandet* included the lines: "obtrusive as he (P. L. M.) is and known to many, I really believed I would be doing some people a service by challenging him for once."[1335] It is so seldom that P. L. M. shows his true colors that I could not let the opportunity pass. So, far from being an article responding in self-defense to an attack, it was a service I wanted to do for others. The main point of the article was to get Mr. P. L. M. out of literature and the respectable company of famous Danish authors into the dance hall of *The Corsair,* to which, according to an article he himself revised for the *Who's Who of Authors,* he has already contributed both poetry and satire. What a real psychological satisfaction it was for me to see how quickly* Mr. P. L. M. took the hint. He came right out and bowed very deferentially in *Fædrelandet*[1336]—and then off he went, that is, he disappeared. Where he went I do not know, but he vanished[1337] like a sneeze—and from that time on, according to my barber, things have been very busy in *The Corsair's* dance hall.

Further—for now I go on to something just as unimportant as Mr. P. L. M.—to *The Corsair.* They are all paltry—my trousers, Mr. P. L. M., and *The Corsair*—and thus are subjects only for gossip, which goes against my grain, for although I have a Greek enthusiasm and love for conversation, gossip has always been repugnant to me. But in saying this I do not want to wrong anyone for the sake of a whim by lumping three paltry things together in order to round off a phrase, for I feel that I must make an exception—I owe my trousers the apology that they are altogether innocent in all this gossip.

I shall write more briefly about *The Corsair.* It is my private opinion that such a disproportionate and immoral phenomenon does great

In margin: *and how perfectly.

harm by inveigling the unstable and tempting the semi-educated; to me it is a national disgrace that such a phenomenon flourishes on such a scale. But you see, *The Corsair* has immortalized and flattered me.[1338] Occasionally I do take notice of such things, for, looking at it polemically, I believe that one cannot get finished with the incompetent criticaster who wants to throw his weight around if one does not go to the bottom of it and adduce examples when one is praised by the incompetent.* I wanted to do something, and just today I found among some old papers a rudimentary article[1339] written in my days of immortality, even if I did not have the time and opportunity then, being fully occupied as an author with my own ideas. Add to that the fact that it was a difficult thing to do effectively. Since that paper, according to my barber, is supposed to be ironic and extremely witty, I was afraid it would manage to make a joke of the matter, even benefiting by it, as if it were my intention to say something witty at its expense and thereby prompt it to be witty also. As I see it, that would have been the most dreadful responsibility to assume. So time went on, and my leisure commenced, during which the matter presumably would come up again. And what happens—along comes Mr. P. L. M., most opportunely for me. Precisely because I could now start from a kind of attack, I might be able to prevent the dreadful falsification that my little *inserat*[1340] became a compliment, and I might be able to make it so emphatic that that paper would have to abandon every hope of maintaining a kind of relationship to me as a high-ranking ally by continuing to pamper me and my immortality, for I too am supposed to be ironic and witty—how close lies the loathsome copula of misunderstanding! And I succeeded all right, for, according to my barber, no one has been as abused as I have been.

That is the whole story. . . .

VII[1] B 69   *n.d.*, 1846

« **5864**

A First and Last Declaration[1342]

Announcement
For the sake of form and order [essentially the same as *Postscript*, p. 551,11.10–30], the voice of the one speaking comes from me but it

---

In margin: *Note. This is why I also did this earlier on the occasion of an article in *Berlingske Tidende*,[1341] an otherwise decent and respectable paper.

is not my voice; the hand writing is mine, but it is not my handwriting. Juridically and literarily the responsibility is mine* [essentially the same as p. 552,11.15–26] that my personal actuality in relation to the pseudonymous writers is a burden of actuality which they may want removed† in order to live unconstrained.‡ Only when the relationship is like that is it ironical enough so that I, as the hidden source dialectically reduplicated—yes, it is ironical enough—may be called§ the authors' author; yet this relation is different from the unseemly one of an *actual* author's having another behind him, one who is really the author, not of the book, for this really belongs to the first one, who precisely by the book *actually* became the author, but is the author of the author. The poetized author has his definite life-outlook [essentially the same as pp. 552, 1.38–553,1.6] dance‖ with—then this cannot be truly charged to me, who properly and in the interest of the purity of the relation have done everything from my side to prevent what the curious part of a small reading public has done everything to achieve —God knows in whose# interest!

With gratitude to Governance who in multiple ways—even though often in spiritual suffering—through independence, through health, through undiminished strength of mind, through a balanced discernment despite a productivity that advanced by leaps and bounds—has favored my enterprise continuously in that through labor I found the rest I needed for labor, and granted me much more than I had expected—the performance appears to others to be verbose folderol—I lay down the pen which in my author's hand was to me my mandatory work but also the satisfaction of my need, the pen which has been so dear to me despite the repeated fines‡‡ I have had to pay so that the pseudonyms could be authors.

---

*Note. For this reason my name as editor was placed on the title page of *Fragments*
** as early as 1844 [essentially the same as p. 552 note, 11.2–4].
In margin: **as crucial to the whole effort.
In margin: †or made as insignificant as possible.
In margin: ‡So my likeness, my picture, my figure, as conceived by a passport issuer would have a wholly disturbing effect and have very little ironical significance if such a thing became the object for the profundity of an ingenious researcher.
In margin: §the author's or
In margin: ‖If someone in judging has‡‡ deceived himself by taking for indiscretion that which not only is not mine but has even been placed by the pseudonymous writers in the deceptive indirect form of revocation.
††has been busy deceiving himself.
In margin: #from the very beginning.
In margin: ‡‡instead of honoraria.

The opportunity seems to invite it, yes, to demand it. Well, then, I will use the opportunity afforded by the end of this story to bid farewell to my reader, if I dare speak of such a one. If so, I request of him a forgetting-remembering, as the relationship requires, just as appreciation of the inwardness derived thereby is sincerely offered now in the moment of farewell, when I, with all good wishes for their future, am being separated from the pseudonyms, and courteously thank everyone who has kept silent, and with deep respect thank the Kts[1343] company—that it has spoken.

There is only one thing a limited person, acting, can understand and strive to understand to the point of compliance: what Governance demands of him as duty, what use it will make of him, [and he is not to be concerned about] when, how, or perhaps none at all, about what is going to happen to him, perhaps this, perhaps that; one who learns to obey has no right to raise these questions, but neither does he have responsibility for the outcome, he who in obedience is humorously released from embarrassing illusions about an extraordinary importance in regard to the demands of the times, who in *self*-concern is ironically released from governing-solicitude for the masses, who, indeed all, each one individually, are able only in self-concern to seek and find the truth, if they are going to find it at all in the only place where it is to be sought. If there is to be no disturbing, apparently great but deceitful, middle term which falsifies a man's relation to the divine, then, according to what I have learned from my elders and sought to understand on my own, then the only reasonable thing to do is earnestly and inwardly to pledge oneself in unconditioned obedience and care-freely, if possible, hilariously, to let the outcome be God's affair and no concern of one's own, coveting* assurance in God that just as a doubtful result is powerless to make something doubtful, so also the most brilliant result is powerless to prove something and a catastrophic result is powerless to refute something with regard to truth as inwardness.

Copenhagen, February, 1845

In margin: *inner strengthening and

VII[1] B 75   February, 1846

« **5865**

For p. 217.[1344]   A note which was not printed because it was prepared later, although it was rough-drafted, and for certain reasons I did not want to change or add the least thing to the manuscript as it was delivered lock, stock, and barrel to Luno[1345] the last days of December, 1845.

Note. This experiment (" 'Guilty?'/'Not Guilty?' ")[1346] is the first attempt in all the pseudonymous writings at an existential dialectic in double-reflection. It is not the communication which is in the form of double-reflection (for all pseudonyms are that), but the existing person himself exists in this. Thus he does not give up immediacy, but keeps it and yet gives it up, keeps erotic love's desire and yet gives it up. Viewed categorically, the experiment relates to "The Seducer's Diary" in such a way that it begins right there where the seducer ends, with the task he himself suggests: "to poetize himself out of a girl." (See *Either/Or*, I, p. 470.[1347]) The seducer is egotism; in *Repetition* feeling and irony are kept separate, each in its representative: the young man and Constantin. These two elements are put together in the one person, Quidam of the experiment, and he is sympathy. To seduce a girl expresses masculine superiority; to poetize oneself out of a girl is also a superiority but must become a *suffering* superiority if one considers the relationship between masculinity and femininity and not a particular silly girl. Masculinity's victory is supposed to reside in succeeding; but the reality [*Realitet*] of femininity is supposed to reside in its becoming a story of suffering for the man. Just as it is morally impossible for Quidam of the experiment to seduce a girl, so it is metaphysically-esthetically impossible for a seducer to poetize himself out of a girl when it is a matter of the relationship between masculinity and femininity, each in its strength, and not of a particular girl. The seducer's egotism culminates in the lines to himself: "She is mine, I do not confide this to the stars . . . . . not even to Cordelia, but say it very softly to myself." (See *Either/Or*, I, p. 446[1348]). *Quidam* culminates passionately in the outburst: "The whole thing looks like a tale of seduction."[1349] What is a triumph to one is an ethical horror to the other.

VII[1] A 83   *n.d.*, 1846

« **5866**

Addition to 5665 (VII[1] B 83):   The experiment, however, is precisely what is lacking in *Either/Or* (see a note in my own copy[1350]); but before it could be done absolutely right, an enormous detour had to be made.

The experiment is the only thing for which there existed [*existeret*] considerable preliminary work[1351] before it was written. Even while I was writing *Either/Or* I had it in mind and frequently dashed off a lyrical suggestion. When I was ready to work it out, I took the precaution of not looking at what I had jotted down in order not to be disturbed. Not a word escaped, although it came again in a superior rendering. I have not gone through what I had jotted down, and nothing was missing, but if I had read it first, I could not have written it. The experiment is the most exuberant of all I have written, but it is difficult to understand because natural egotism is against adhering so strongly to sympathy.

VII[1] B 84   *n.d.,* 1846

« 5867

Inasmuch as what I first wrote contained a little review[1352] or, more correctly, a little effusive discourse on these novels,[1353] so, too, in the role of reviewer I wish to end with the same. If the author deigns to read these lines, I trust he will find me unchanged, for I surmise that he read the little piece at the time. I trust he will find me unchanged and changed only in the repetition: a bit more clarity, a bit more lightness in style, perhaps also somewhat more gentle and forbearing, therefore also changed in the repetition. . . .[1354]

VII[1] B 95   *n.d.,* 1845–46

« 5868 *Preface*[1355]

This article actually was written to appear in *Nordisk Literatur-Tidende*—but became too long for that publication—and moreover we have no journal here. Only catchpenny writing seems to thrive in Denmark and then so amazingly that what is contemptible in literature will soon begin to rival financial dominion. I find myself so indebted to the author of *A Story of Everyday Life* that I would willingly pay a little fine to be the author of a review. It could also be asked whether it is seemly for a nation to reverse things in such a way that only vilification is remunerated, whether it is not an outrageous injustice to all impecunious authors, and even to those with means, inasmuch as the laborer is worthy of his hire. So first of all a little fine is in order to publish a little book, and then the next step, for when an author is not paid in money, he is certainly paid some other way. Without a doubt he is paid in another way, although it nevertheless does bear some resemblance to paying the fine. As soon as the little book is published, there is an uproar on the dance floor of literary vilification; and while the little review is noticed by only a few as it steals like a forlorn, godforsaken soul along the short, short road to oblivion, crudity and ignorance and licentiousness gloat in the support of numerous subscribers and go on and on making money on the circumstance, which no one at all cared about—until vilification got it besmirched.

I do not say this for my own sake, my outlook on life is essentially polemic, but because some discrepancies have placed me in a most peculiar and awkward position. As a rule reviewing a book is considered a courtesy, even if a critical journal is in a position to pay a respectable fee for the work, but nowadays things have gotten so out of hand that I almost fear that it will be taken as an attack on the author of the book, for no doubt vilification, in its zeal, will embrace also the book under review. This book should consider itself fortunate to have escaped abuse until now when a bungling reviewer—innocently to be sure—prompts abuse when everything else has been forgotten, perhaps even prompts abuse by a slanderer who pursues one up and down the street like a beggar.

Finally, when the public at large, which, to be sure, declares every time there is a group consisting of two: We despise the official organ of literary prostitutes, but in the role of the public, manifests this in a curious manner by subscribing to it on the largest possible scale and reads it—finally, when the public at large has been gratified and is probably tired of the man and the constant mention of the book, the man and the book will have become a boring subject—a new remuneration, for it becomes a guilt which spills over on the innocent man and book, whose guilt was—being obliged to tolerate a gross slander, keeping on with the abuse until the public was sick and tired, not of the slander, but of the man and the book, not making the distinction that the man and the book had no responsibility at all for the continual commentary.

No matter how much one loves a family, it is not at all strange if someone gets tired of coming to visit when none of the lovable members of the family says a word, but a rude child dominates the conversation. That is just about the situation in Danish literature. Seldom do we hear a significant word from a legitimate author; no literary organ champions decorum and order—no, all the good elements are silent— but the element loudly celebrating vilification's proudest triumphs so dominates the prostituted order that one can hardly hear himself speak. Even if an author remains attached to the lovable family of

Danes, loves the mother tongue above all—is it seemly for such a situation to keep on this way?

VII[1] B 132   *n.d.*,   1845–46

« **5869**

Introduction[1356]
Two Ages
Novel
by
The Author of "A Story of Everyday Life"
edited by Johan Ludvig Heiberg. Reitzel 1845

VII[1] B 135:5   *n.d.*

« **5870**

Today I heard a cabdriver say of a drunken driver who drove by at a rather fast pace: "He has got hold of some of the sort of thing that leads one straight to the gutter."

VII[1] A 1   *n.d.*,   1846

« **5871** *Concluding Postscript*

The entire manuscript, lock, stock, and barrel, was delivered to the printer *medio* December, or thereabouts, 1845. —"A First and Last Declaration" was dashed off on a piece of paper in the original manuscript but was laid aside to be worked out in detail and was delivered as late as possible lest it lie around and get lost in a print shop.[1357] I would not permit a note[1358] to a portion about the pseudonymous books to be printed simply because it was written during the printing. The lies and gossip and vulgarity that encompass one make a person's position difficult enough, perhaps make me too tensely anxious to have the truth on my side down to the most minute thread—what's the use?

VII[1] A 2   *n.d.*,   1846

« **5872**

In margin of 5871 (VII[1] A 2):
Because of the present situation (the unpleasantness with *The Corsair* and the town gossip), I was momentarily unable to make up my mind whether or not I should leave out the acknowledgment of my authorship, whether I should not indicate in the printed material by specifying the dates that the whole thing was older than all this unpleasantness. But, no! I owe it to the truth to pay no attention to all this and to do everything as had been decided, leaving the outcome

up to God and accepting everything from his hand as a good and perfect gift, refusing to act shrewdly, trusting that he will give me a steady and wise spirit.

VII¹ A 3   n.d.

« 5873

It is now my intention to qualify as a pastor.[1359] For several months I have been praying to God to keep on helping me, for it has been clear to me for some time now that I ought not be a writer any longer, something I can be only totally or not at all. This is the reason I have not started anything new along with proof-correcting[1360] except for the little review of *The Two Ages*,[1361] which, I repeat, is final.[1362]

VII¹ A 4   February 7, 1846

« 5874

How appalling for the man who, as a lad watching sheep on the Jutland heath, suffering painfully, hungry and exhausted, once stood on a hill and cursed God—and the man was unable to forget it when he was eighty-two years old.[1363]

VII¹ A 5   n.d., 1846

« 5875 *De occultis non judicat ecclesia*[1364]

See p. 268 [i.e., VI A 31].

See pp. 194, 185, and 171 [i.e., VI A 55–59, 47, and 31–32] in this book.

Do I dare keep my guilt secret? And yet do I dare declare it myself.

If God wants it out in the open, then he can indeed do it; this self-denunciation can, after all, be playing providence.

Today an accusing memory came along. Suppose the accusation got out. I could travel far away from here, live in a foreign country, a new life far removed from the memory, far removed from any possibility of its being revealed. I could live in hiding—no, I have to stay where I am, doing everything unchanged, without one single rule of prudence, leaving everything to God. It is terrible how remaining where one is, educated only by possibility, can develop a person.

VII¹ A 6   n.d., 1846

« 5876

In margin of 5875 (VII¹ A 6):

Here the German saying could also be used: *Gott richt't, wenn niemand spricht*[1365] (that is, when everybody is silent, when no one thinks of accusing, no one dreams that there is a complaint, or when the accuser is dead). See *Deutsche Märchen und Sagen,*[1366] v. J. W. Wolf, Leipzig, 1845, p. 213.

VII[1] A 7   *n.d.*

« 5877

Up until now I have made myself useful by helping the pseudonyms become authors. What if I decided from now on to do the little writing I can excuse in the form of criticism. Then I would put down what I had to say in reviews, developing my ideas from some book or other and in such a way that they could be included in the work itself. In this way I would still avoid becoming an author.[1367]

VII[1] A 9   February, 1846

« 5878

Professor Nielsen[1368] said to Sager[1369] when the latter, upon seeing his apartment out in Fredriksberg, expressed the opinion that it was wonderful for the professor to be able to live out there and study at leisure: "No (*sinne, sinne*[1370]), Sager, I shall not be reading any more; now I am going to die." In contrast to Director Sager's no doubt courtly conception of what it means to study, old Mikkel's "reading" is delightfully impressive; the whole story is an excellent indication of Nielsen's noble simplicity—and then these words of resignation: Now I am just going to die.

VII[1] A 11   *n.d.,* 1846

« 5879

Even for famous authors the royalties in Danish literature these days are very small, but the tips that go to the literary swine are considerable. The more contemptible a man of letters is these days, the more he makes.

VII[1] A 18   *n.d.,* 1846

« 5880

Let us be especially happy that this name[1371] has lasted twenty years and not precipitously overrate the work of a couple of years but rejoice in the perseverance, that seventy years are the highest honor.

If I may be allowed to give an example, what makes Bishop Mynster the noble paradigm from whom anyone can learn, what keeps him steadfast through all these impetuosities called the demands of the times? And how rash to be unwilling to accept that every year he lives makes him more significant instead of less so. To be eloquent in the first ardor of youth, O, that is beautiful, but to be an upbuilding witness at seventy, that is great.[1372]

VII[1] B 131   n.d., 1845–46

« 5881

Only after the publication of the last big book, *Concluding Postscript*, have I dared give myself time to look around and be concerned about my external existence.

> My financial condition no longer permits me to be an author.[1373] General observations on the literary situation in Denmark.

I will make application to the state, for I shall, with God's help, continue proudly and calmly to maintain an ironical position against chimerical magnitudes such as the public, against the importunate tyranny of the daily press, etc. And just as fittingly I shall, with God's help, continue to be what I have always been, submissive. By accommodating myself I could perhaps become popular with the public, but that I do not want—so I shall not be an author at all.[1374]

Commendatory points:

(1) My efforts as an author must be in agreement with the interests of the state.

(2) I have shown that I can make use of leisure.

(3) I am young and rigorously cloistered in order to work.

(4) I am unmarried and have nothing else to occupy me.
> This is different from the usual state support of a man as an author who also has many other things to do or has a family.

And all the more I hope to be considered since other authors do earn a small royalty on their books (even though this may be little enough), whereas I actually put out money, so that my proofreader literally makes more than I do.

VII[1] B 211   n.d., 1846

« 5882 *De occultis non judicat ecclesia*[1375]

> See pp. 256, 194, 185, 171 [i.e., VII[1] A 6; VI A 55–59, 47, 31–32].

The tragic story of an unhappy lover could be interwoven here with a correlation in dates but without otherwise having the least thing to do with each other.

The editor came into possession of both in a very strange way.

VII[1] A 21   n.d., 1846

« 5883 An Arithmetic Problem

If I were a clergyman and could preach in such a manner that the individual would go home from church wanting to hear me again, extolling me and exulting over me—however, if by studying his individuality I learned the way influence should be brought to bear with him and then proceeded to thrust him away so that he finally almost became angry with me and went and shut his door and prayed to God —in which case would I benefit him the most. In the one case my very deception would have assisted him to the truth; and in the other my assistance to the truth would have become the deception; in the one case he would have ended with the truth and begun with the deception, and in the other he would have ended with the deception and begun with the truth.

But such a one does, nevertheless, need men, if not in the second sense, then in the meaning of the Stoics when they said: *Sapientem nulla re indigere, et tamen multis illi rebus opus esse. —Ergo quamvis se ipso contentus sit sapiens, amicis illi opus est, non ut habeat, qui sibi aegro assideat, sed ut habeat aliquem, cui ipse assideat, pro quo mori possit.* [1376]

This is quoted from a little essay by Dr. Bayer in Fichte's journal,[1377]XIII, 1844, p. 86.

VII[1] A 23   n.d., 1846

« 5884

And so I am criticized[1378] because I am for Mynster[1379] and find pleasure in a little expression of his approval. Did I not say the same thing in *Fædrelandet*[1380] in 1845 when I declined the commendation of the *Berlingske Tidende;* have I not said the same thing all along, from the first book to the last.

As for the preface[1381] to "Concluding Postscript": (1) it is by Johannes Climacus, and here again what appears at the end of the book[1382] holds true, namely, that I am not the pseudonym, who permits himself a recklessness which I neither am able nor wish to do; (2) what expressions of approval and censure are meant? The analogies to the hurrah of the mobs and *pereat.* [1383] As a consequence of his disdaining and rejecting mob-approval, does he therefore disdain the truly distinguished single individual? What foolishness. If a paper like the *Corsair* were not utterly lacking in self-knowledge, it would readily see why I do not want its approval; and if it had any self-knowledge, it would perceive why I even want to be abused by that contemptibleness which is concealed only from its own eyes.

VII[1] A 26   *n.d.,*   1846

« 5885

The way I see it, to be victorious does not mean that *I* am victorious, but that the idea is victorious through me, even though I am sacrificed.

VII[1] A 27   *n.d.,*   1846

« 5886

Report[1384]

VII[1] A 97   *n.d.,*   1846

« 5887

March, 1846

the ninth

The *Concluding Postscript*[1385] is out; the pseudonymity has been acknowledged;[1386] one of these days the printing of the "Literary Review"[1387] will begin. Everything is in order; all I have to do now is to keep calm, be silent, depending on *The Corsair* to support the whole enterprise negatively, just as I wish. From the standpoint of the idea, I am at present as correctly situated in literature as possible, and also in such a way that to be an author becomes a deed.[1388] In itself it was a most capital idea to make a break with *The Corsair*[1389] in order to prevent any direct advances* at the very moment I was through with the authorship[1390] and, by assuming all the pseudonyms, ran the risk of becoming an authority of sorts. This is why right now, when I am advancing polemically against the age,[1391] I owe it to the idea and to irony to prevent any confusion with the ironical bad brandy *The Corsair* serves in the dance halls of contemptibleness. Incidentally, it has happened here, as it frequently does, that despite all my deliberation, a something more eventuates which is due not to me but to Governance. It always happens this way, that to which I give the most thought I

In margin: Prior to that time nothing could be done; my work for my idea demanded all my time, every minute, and undisturbed as possible. It is really superb that just when someone supposes and is spitefully pleased that I am taking a rash step (and this perhaps evokes some malicious glee) I am just then being most calculating and level-headed. But the best support for all action is—to pray, that is actually the true genius; then one never comes out on the short end.

always understand far better afterwards, both as to its ideal significance and the fact that it was precisely what I should have done.[1392]

But this existence is exhausting; I am convinced that not a single person understands me. The most anyone, even an admirer, would concede is that I bear all this unpleasantness with a certain poise, but that I want it—of course no one dreams of that. But then on the other hand it would again be hasty human thoughtlessness to conclude, if it were understood why I, by virtue of the idea of double-reflection, must wish it, that ergo he is not suffering at all, is insensitive to all this vulgarity and the brazen lies. Just as if one could not voluntarily decide to take upon himself all tribulations if the idea enjoins it. The article against P. L. Møller[1393] was written in great fear and trembling; I did it during the holidays, but for the sake of forming a regulating resistance I did not neglect going to church or reading my sermon. So also with the article against *The Corsair*.[1394] On the other hand they were properly written, for if I had evinced passion, someone along the way would have found occasion for a direct relation to me. It was amusing and psychologically superb to see the haste with which P. L. Møller got the hint given about withdrawing into *The Corsair*. He came forward, bowed politely,[1395] and then withdrew to the place where he is at home.

What pains me most, however, is not the vulgarity of the rabble but the secret participation in it by the better people. I, too, would like to make myself comprehensible to one single person, to my reader. But I dare not, for then I defraud the idea. It is precisely when I am succeeding most, when brutality is at its most shameless peak, that I dare not speak. Finally, it is my responsibility to be consistently unyielding so that I will not be responsible for several people going completely astray. So be it, I must be silent.

The last two months have been very rewarding for my observations. What I said in my dissertation[1396] about irony making phenomena stand revealed is so true. First of all, my ironic leap into *The Corsair* goes a long way toward making it perfectly clear that *The Corsair* is devoid of idea. Seen from the point of view of idea, it is dead, even if it did get a few thousand subscribers.[1397] It wants to be ironical and does not even understand irony. Generally speaking, it would have been an epigram over my whole life if it might ever be said: Contemporary with him there existed a bungling ironic journal that sang his praises; no, hold on—he was abused, and he himself asked for it. —Secondly, my ironic leap into *The Corsair* shows up the self-contradiction of the environing world. Everyone has been going around saying: It is nothing; who cares about *The Corsair* etc. What happens, when one does it, is that he is charged with being rash; they say he has deserved all this (now, you see, it is "all this") because he prompted it; they hardly dare walk in the street with me—fearing they too will be in *The Corsair*. The self-contradiction, however, has a deeper basis; in their Christian envy they half wish that the paper may go on, each one hoping that he will not be attacked. They now say that the paper is despicable and nothing; they enjoin the persons under attack not to dare become angry or make any protest, ergo, the paper must flourish. And the public has first the stimulation of envy and then the shameless pleasure of watching the victim of the attack—whether it affects him.* And this phenomenon in such a little country as Denmark, this phenomenon as the one and only prevailing—and this is supposed to be nothing! How well cowardice and contemptibility suit each other in the bond of shabbiness! And when the whole thing bursts some day, Goldschmidt will be the one who suffers; and it is absolutely the same public—and then the world has become such a splendid world!

Furthermore, my observations abundantly strengthen my conviction that when a man consistently expresses one idea, every objection to him contains a self-contradiction of the one who makes it.† They say I am the one who cares about *The Corsair*. What happens? The "concluding Postscript" was delivered lock, stock, and barrel to Luno before I wrote against P. L. Møller. Now in the preface[1398] to it (which, incidentally, was written in May of 1845) there was something which could be regarded as pointing to the latter (this shows among other things how early I was aware of it). Now if I had cared about *The Corsair*, I would have made some changes in it simply to avoid the appearance of being so. I know how I fought down the temptation to do it, because it pained me to think of Bishop Mynster, for example, saying: And Kierkegaard refers to such a thing even in a book. But I was true to myself in not caring about *The Corsair*—and then what happens? Well, just as expected—allusions to *The Corsair* are found in everything I write. Here is the dead giveaway, for it must be "they" themselves who had *The Corsair in mente,* since they find it even in something written prior to that time.

In margin: *And now has the chance to lie about him: that he is affected, that he is able to hide it but is affected just the same. The latter formula is especially convenient for scandal mongers.

In margin: †Who thereby is not talking about him but about himself.

Two things in particular occupy me: (1) that whatever the cost I remain intellectually true in the Greek sense to my existence-idea; (2) that in the religious sense it becomes as elevating and ennobling to me as possible. I pray God for the latter. Solitary I have always been; now I really have the opportunity to practice again. My solitary secret is not my grief but is precisely that I have the upper hand, that I transform what is hostile into something that serves my idea without its having any intimation of this itself. Yes, this life is certainly satisfying, but it is also terribly strenuous. From what a tragic side one learns to know men, and how sad that what will look so good at a distance is always misunderstood by contemporaries. But again it is the religious which redeems; here there is sympathy for all, not the garrulous fellow-feeling of cliques and henchmen, but infinite sympathy for each and all—in silence.

But without a doubt it is educational to be placed as I am in so small a city as Copenhagen to work almost to despair with all one's capacities, with deep agony of soul and much inner suffering, to put money into publishing books—and then literally not to have ten men who read them through properly, while on the other hand students and other authors find it almost ridiculously easy to write a big book, and then to have a paper which everyone reads, which has the license of contemptibleness to dare say anything, the most lying distortions—and it is nothing, but everybody reads it; and then the whole pack of envious people who lend a hand by saying just the opposite in order to minimize in that way. Day after day to be the object of everybody's conversation and attention, and then the business of defending me against an attack in order to attack me still worse themselves. Every kitchen boy feels justified in almost insulting me in accordance with *The Corsair*'s orders; young students titter and grin and are happy to see a prominent person trampled on; professors are jealous and secretly sympathize with the attacks, and spread them, too, with the appendage, of course, that it is a shame. The slightest thing I do, if it is merely to pay a visit, is twisted and distorted into lies and told everywhere; if *The Corsair* finds out, it is printed and read by everybody, the man I visited is embarrassed, gets almost angry with me, for which he cannot be blamed. Eventually I will have to withdraw and associate only with people I do not like, for it is, after all, almost a wrong against the others. And so it continues, and sometime when I am dead, men's eyes will be opened; then they will admire what I wanted to do and will simultaneously treat in the same way a contemporary who probably is

the only one who understands me. God in heaven, who could endure
this if there were not an interior place in a man where all this can be
forgotten in communion with you.

But my activity as an author is finished[1399]—God be praised. It has
been granted me to conclude it myself, to understand myself when it
ought to stop, and next to publishing *Either/Or* I thank God for that.
I know very well and find it quite in order that people will not see it
this way and that it would in fact take but two words from me to prove
it so. This has hurt, it seems that I still could have desired that recognition, but let it be.

If I only could make myself become a pastor. Out there in quiet
activity, permitting myself a little productivity in my free time, I shall
breathe more easily, however much my present life has gratified me.

VII[1] A 98   March 9, 1846

« **5888**

But nothing must be written, not one word; I dare not. Were I to
write, I would give the reader a hint and throw the whole thing out of
gear. He must not find out anything secretly. I have tossed off a few
things[1400] during this time which are not bad but which can be used
only in a completely different situation.

I have thought of the last version as being like this:

Short and Sweet

In my opinion an editor is literarily responsible when there is no
author. The editor of *The Corsair* is Mr. Goldschmidt,[1401] university
student, a bright fellow, without an idea, without scholarship, without
a point of view,[1402] without self-control, but not without a certain
talent and a desperate esthetic power. At a critical moment in his life
he approached me.[1403] I tried indirectly to help him negatively. I praise
him for his self-assurance in getting himself established. I believe he
has succeeded in what he wanted to do. I had hoped that he would have
chosen an honorable way to earn a name for himself; to be honest, it
pains me that as the editor of *The Corsair* he *continues* to choose the way
of contemptibility to earn money. It was my desire to snatch, if possible, a talented man from being an instrument of rabble barbarism, but
I certainly had no wish to be shamefully rewarded by being immortalized[1404] by a paper of contemptibility which ought never exist and by
which I can only wish to be abused. It is expedient for my life as an
author to be abused and that is why I wished it and asked for it as soon

as I was finished, for by the time Frater Taciturnus[1405] wrote, Johannes Climacus[1406] had already been delivered to the printer a few days before. I had also hoped to benefit others by this step; they do not want it—well, I will go on asking for abuse because it suits my idea and in order to get some good, after all, out of the existence of a paper like that. It is sad to see the pack of fools and the fatuous who laugh and yet, at least in this case, they do not know what they are laughing at. God alone knows whether or not I am playing for too high stakes with respect to my contemporaries. My idea requires it; its consistency satisfies me beyond measure—I cannot do otherwise, I beg forgiveness of all the better people who are undialectical or do not have the presuppositions to understand that I must do as I am doing—and then forward: Would that I might be abused. However important or unimportant my life as an author, this much is certain: because of my dialectical relation, I am the only Danish author who is so situated that it can serve the idea to have every possible lie and distortion and nonsense and gossip come out, confusing the reader and thus helping him to self-activity and preventing a direct relationship. No other Danish author can possibly benefit from the reading of lies and distortions by 1,000 readers* when he addresses himself to 100. But he serves me every time he serves me with abuse, and that he will certainly do; he cannot get away from me, and his inability to pursue the good expresses itself in the defiance of an unhappy infatuation and a self-stifling through abusive words, all of which I regret inasmuch as I meant him well. But his abuse is irrelevant; I could just as well be absent.

If Mr. Goldschmidt will reply in a decent paper and sign his name to it, I will read it; I no longer read *The Corsair;* I would not even commend it to my servant, for I do not believe it lies within a master's authority to be able to order his servant to go to an obscene place.

S.K.

VII[1] A 99   *n.d.,* 1846

« **5889**

What really distresses me in the whole affair is to see all of the conceited ones who want to play the loftiest game of intellectuality, and then I am practically the only one who has the Greek mentality and the education of independence for it, and then I am the very one who

---

*No other Dane can benefit from rabble barbarism's having a widely read organ which has him in its power, when it so pleases a literary tramp.

wanted to work toward something like that, which is directly related to my whole task.

VII[1] A 101   n.d., 1846

« **5890**

Listen here, little *Corsair!* Be a man for once! It is womanish to nag a man about his love affair, it is womanish to express rejected love by running after a man and abusing him;[1407] be a man and keep still. Only woman as the weaker sex can be forgiven for manifesting her weakness first in the devotion of importunate erotic love and then, rejected, in the devotion of dirty spite; a man must be able to be himself, must be able to keep silent when he perceives that it is a confession of weakness to continue to scold, just the way a prostitute runs after a man or a pestering beggar pursues one up one street and down the other.

VII[1] A 103   n.d., 1846

« **5891**

March 16

Given the conditions in the world as it is, to be an author should be the extraordinary employment in life, an employment which escapes the dialectic of the universal (office and whatever pertains to that; a living and whatever pertains to that). Therefore not only should the author's production be a testimony to the idea, but the author's life ought to correspond to the idea. But, alas, of all categories the category of actuality is the most mediocre. To be an author is to be in a fraternity and is just as cluttered up with finiteness as anything else. Authors are supposed to be of mutual help to each other, criticize each other's writings, talk about what one is going to do, etc. Your intimate friends in particular are supposed to profit from the relationship and have little scraps of news to run around with: "that they personally saw the manuscript, heard part of it, talked with the author, etc."

By taking advantage of my pseudonymity, I have stayed completely clear of this. In the finite sense I have thereby done irreparable damage to myself, have offended people, have shirked the salutary tradition of small talk, and have given my whole enterprise the appearance of chance and caprice; and even if I were now to show how everything hangs together, what exceedingly rigorous ordering formed the basis, no one would believe it—for it would be inconceivable that anyone should have such a plan and keep quiet about it. Fools, only the person who can keep quiet is one who has such a plan.

When I had finished,[1408] I tried to do a little for others. I wrote the two articles against P.L.M. and *The Corsair*.[1409] After that I was happy to review *Hverdags Historien*.[1410] The end result will be, I am sure, that people will be led to believe that I am doing it in order to gain favor. Ah, if I wanted to have power and prestige in Danish literature—which I easily could—I would have done just the opposite. I would not have broken so emphatically with *The Corsair*, for its continual nonsense still exerts an influence on mass opinion, and to be commended by it[1411] would still be a titillating ingredient. Very quickly I should have put myself at the front as the awaited one, deigned to recognize one or two of the younger ones, taken a negative position toward the older ones—this is how to get ahead in Danish literature, and this is what the younger ones want, and anyone who wants to have power must always line up with the younger ones. But I did exactly the opposite instead—precisely because I do not wish and am too melancholy to want to have status and recognition in the world. I irritate the younger ones, for none of them stands so high that he can slip past me and what I do—I bow to the older writers. The minute I stop I will be happy to leave everything unchanged in Danish literature, to get Professor Heiberg[1412] esteemed as in the past, Bishop Mynster[1413] venerated as absolutely as possible—then everything will again be in order. And then I am accused of ambitious vanity. Would that he who accuses might first reflect for a moment. For example, *The Corsair* no doubt fancies that it has enormous power—how then can a person who breaks with it be seeking power?

How fundamentally polemic I am by nature I can best see in the fact that the only path by which the attacks of men can affect me is the sadness I feel on their behalf. As long as I am embattled, I am imperturbable, but when I have supremacy, then I become sad at seeing human folly and contemptibleness. My author-existence is truly as pure as new-fallen snow, removed from all worldly avidity, is in the service of the idea; therefore the masses, who actually do not understand me, still ought to have a gratifying impression of it. But that is not to be. Well, let them tell lies, let them slander and misrepresent. But certainly every older generation of authors, insofar as they have the innocent and admissible desire to enjoy recognition, must always wish for a successor like me, who, like a woman, desires nothing himself but desires only to elevate the elders.

Meanwhile everyone has a special license to taunt and attack me in all sorts of ways. They profit in a strange way from my supposed intelligence. They say what they like, and if it is refuted by the facts, then they say: Well, one can't figure it out, for he is so intelligent and cunning and clever. They maintain that I do this and that out of vanity; the facts contradict this, and so they say: Yes, he is so intelligent—that is, he is intelligent enough to do the opposite, but just the same he is vain. A curious argument! If I do the opposite of what vanity bids me do, either I must be stupid, or if I am intelligent, then I must not be vain. Now if I am conceded to be intelligent—ergo, I am not vain. But see, they arrive at the opposite conclusion. Ultimately it all comes down to this, that men are not able to conceive of an intelligent man not coveting status and power. They assume this (for good and stupidity are identical) and consequently draw the conclusion: Even if we cannot prove it, he must be vain because he is so intelligent—intelligent enough to do the opposite of what vanity bids him do. But their presupposition contains a veritable confession.

But how many lives are wasted in this confounded garrulousness about others.

VII¹ A 104   March 16, 1846

« **5892**

At best, well-meaning people will no doubt find my habit of walking the streets etc. excusable as an eccentricity. The majority will regard it as vanity! Good Lord, as if I were so stupid not to know that much self-exposure etc. simply reduces one's importance, that men love the illusion involved in keeping concealed—for then one must be somebody. As if I were such a poor student of Shakespeare that I have misinterpreted and forgotten those lines[1414] by the old king to Henry V as prince, in which he reprimands him and commends another who appears in public only rarely—those lines which have always seemed to hover before me when, in the service of the idea, I decided to do the imprudent thing and disdain the appearance of being somebody, which Socrates develops so beautifully in the *Republic*,*[1415] saying that one ought to shun the appearance of being good. But that all this is in the service of the idea, is my highest interest, my artistic exertion in order to sustain my productivity, something I could scarcely dare confide to Spang,[1416] that my only justification is that I acted against the understanding, that without it I would have been a prolific word-gusher as authors these days are, to whom it never occurs to realize [*realisere*] one jot of what they write—ah, yes, who of those who think about it will not say that it is foolishness or a lie! Never mind, all the greater my art. For to do this and then secretly let people understand it—that would be bungling. My production has been maieutic, my life has supported it by being the stumbling block. —There is, however, one who knows it, and even if my thoughts almost run wild before me in the tremendous strain, he remembers it, he reminds me once again: God in heaven!

In margin: *(The passage as marked in my copy of Schleiermacher's translation,[1417] book II.)

VII¹ A 105   n.d., 1846

« 5893

My concern was to present the various stages of existence in one work if possible—and this is how I regard the whole pseudonymous productivity. For that purpose it was a matter of *keeping oneself unchanged in equability*[1418] so that, for example, the religious should not first appear when I was so old that my style had lost some of the opulence present in the esthetic. This did not mean that the religious should have this opulence but that the one writing should be able to produce it simultaneously, thus making it clear that the religious did not lack it for some fortuitous reason—namely, that the author lacked the necessary youthfulness.

Another author would be able to do the same work, but if he were not able to do it in the course of five or six years, he would be unable to do it. The whole venture stands rather isolated, not only because of what it is in itself but also because of its good fortune.

I had another reason for having to hurry, even though I used the strictest discipline[1419] to keep from neglecting the most insignificant comma—my financial situation no longer makes it possible for me to continue serving the judicial-maieutic idea on the scale I have been serving it. It has not been judicial in the direct sense, by thundering and all that—no, indirect by action and thereby providing an epigram on the age.

It is my consistency which actually has put me on this collision course. Had I been just half as consistent, I would be much better understood by now. But obedience is dearer to God than the fat of rams[1420] and consistency is dearer to the idea than worldly recognition for gossip and humbug.

It is said that I am a slipshod writer. Well, that is a matter of opinion. I am fully convinced that there is not a Danish writer who pays

as much attention to the most insignificant word as I do. I write everything in my own hand twice, some parts three and four times, and in
addition, something no one knows anything about, there is my medi-
tating as I walk; before I write I have said everything aloud to myself
many times—and this they call being a slipshod writer! And why? Because they have no conception of it at all, because to them an author
is someone who at most spends a certain number of hours a day sitting
in a room and writing and otherwise has nothing to do with his ideas.
Therefore, that kind of an author needs time when he comes home to
get into the spirit again—whereas I come home with the whole thing
thought through and memorized, even in its stylistic form—when people read a few pages of my writing they are almost always amazed at
my style—but a big book—well, how is that possible—ergo: I must be a
slipshod writer. No, when one wills only one thing, wills one thing with
every sacrifice, every effort—then it is possible.

In a way I can become nauseated by life, for I, who love but one
thought—which a person can really be if he wills it—I constitute an
epigram upon men, because their judgment of me, the fact that they
cannot really understand my consistency, is tragic proof of the categories, the mediocrity, in which they live.

VII[1] A 106   n.d., 1846

« 5894

And yet my ironic powers of observation and my soul derived such
extraordinary satisfaction from gadding about on the streets[1421] and
being a nobody in this way while thoughts and ideas were working
within me, from being a loafer this way while I was clearly the most
industrious of the younger set and appearing irresponsible this way
and "lacking in earnestness" while the earnestness of the others could
easily become a jest alongside my inner concerns. Now this is all upset;
the rabble, the apprentices, the butcher boys, the school boys, and all
such are egged on. But I will not play to such a public. I have nothing
to do with it; it lacks the requisite condition for manifesting my irony
or its significance for the idea. It was in the encounter with people who
because of their education, I might say, were able to grasp something
more profound in me or to have some conception of it—it was in the
encounter with such people that my irony was gratified by posing the
enigmatic problem and my wrath found satisfaction in seeing how they
disparaged me. But the completely uneducated class, the school boys
and the butcher boys, of course have no requisite conditions; this

terrain is unsuitable, irony cannot be used here. —It is sad to see that
there actually are papers written for school boys, that already at such
an early age they are plunged into the confusion of ambiguity. I will
give only one situation, yet it is typical. It was with Lieutenant
Bardt,[1422] Adjutant of the Hussars. He came walking along with his
little son. The father greeted me with his usual almost excessive attention, stepped aside to allow me the flagstones—if the lad had not known
who I was, he might have gotten a notion that I was somewhat extraordinary—but the boy obviously knew me, he was a reader of *The Corsair*.
What a combination! Must it not be harmful to children at one moment
to read about a man being mistreated in this way, practically inviting
the whole bunch of school boys to whistle at him on the streets—and
then the next moment to see him treated in this manner by his father,
or read samples of his writing in Danish school readers.—[1423]

And now that I have remodeled my external life, am more withdrawn, keep to myself more, have a more momentous look about me,
in certain quarters it will be said that I have changed for the better.
Alas, but my idea is not being served as it was then. But then, after all,
my writing days are over.[1424]

VII[1] A 107   *n.d.,* 1846

« 5895

I cannot make up my mind to write down anything about her.[1425]
I distrust paper; it could fall into the hands of an outsider and upset
her now when everything is more or less all right. As far as I am
personally concerned, I hope that God will remember everything and
remind me of it. There is not one single day since that day when I have
not thought of the affair morning and night. Her last request to me was
that I would think of her once in a while—she certainly did not need
to ask me that. Her appalling question—whether I had any intention of
ever getting married—was fortunately answered banteringly. It was
dreadful; I could have given her a little comfort, and God knows how
I wanted to, and God knows how much I needed to mitigate the affair
for myself. But it was good that my consistency triumphed. I answered:
"Well, maybe in ten years, when I have sowed my wild oats and am
tired out, then I may have me a little young girl again to rejuvenate
me." It was cruel; it was also cruelly hard to have to do it. And if I had
not done it and everything else as well, would she now be engaged?
No. If I had solemnly spoken what was in my heart: No, I will never
marry anyone but you—she would have acted according to that. Then

if a new engagement were proposed to her, she would only have been irresolute, and if she had consented, she would have done it with a divided soul—now, however, with her total self, because I alienated her.

VII[1] A 108   n.d., 1846

« **5896**

The idea that I expressed existentially in order to support the pseudonymous writings was in utmost consistency with this productivity. If with such an enormous productivity I had lived withdrawn, concealed, seldom seen in public and then with a somber mug as becomes a philosopher, a professorial countenance—by Jove, every Tom, Dick, and Harry, every silly girl, college student, and the like would have found me to be profound. It would have been extremely inconsistent with what I was writing; but what do fools care about consistency—and how many wise men are found in each generation. —That it was very strenuous I do not deny; every man can have weak moments when he snatches at finite consolations closer at hand, but consistency is still the salvation. Being inconsistent wins a man honor, status, money, etc.—but at death one regrets having been inconsistent. It is different with consistency. Just as the fox lured the lice to the tip of his tail and then threw them off, so does consistency treat the stupid who instead of wanting to learn something from someone or teach someone something—have nothing to offer but money, status, and hurrahs. In the beginning it looks as if they could be included, but then consistency proceeds farther and farther out into the deep, and they get dumped off. If these were my last words, I know they are truth in me: Everyone who *truly wills something* will always find an admirer in me, or if necessary, assistance;—but these fools, this crowd, this whole jumble of men and women who only want to waste their own lives and help others to waste theirs: well, in me they will find their man. Look at little Goldschmidt;[1426] he plays the hypocrite to himself with the fancy that he was called by God to be a scourge for us poor wretches —then the condition is offered him to abuse what he himself had immortalized![1427] He did it. Consequently there was no truth in him; his divine wrath was a sham, for otherwise he would have been faithful to the truth and persecuted the wicked but not what he himself admires —because it will not admire him.[1428]

VII[1] A 109   n.d., 1846

« **5897**

Gossip and garbage instead of action is what people still want, and so they find it interesting. Goethe relates in *Aus meinem Leben*[1429] that *Werthers Leiden* made such a big sensation that from that time on he never again had the peace and absorption he once had, because now he was plunged into all sorts of connections and acquaintances. How interesting and titillating to chatter and prattle! Nothing would have been easier to prevent if Goethe really had had the courage, if he truly had loved the idea more than acquaintances. One with Goethe's powers can easily thrust people aside. But he is soft and sentimental and does not want to—but then he wants to tell it as an incident. But people like to hear it, because it excuses them from action. If someone were to hold forth something like this: Once in my youth I really did have faith in peace and guilt, but then I became busy in the world, made many acquaintances, and I got to be councillor, and since then I have not really had the time or the concentration—people would be very moved by this kind of talk and would eagerly listen to it. The secret of life if one wants a good standing is: clever rubbish about what one wants to do and how one is frustrated—and then no action.

One day Councillor Molbech[1430] was here. He congratulated me on my eccentricity, on my strange way of life, because it benefited my work. "I would like to do the same," he said, then he went on to say that the same day he had to go to a dinner and "There I have to drink wine, which I cannot tolerate, but one cannot get out of it, for then begins the: Ah, just one little glass, Councillor; it will do you good." I answered: "Nothing is easier to prevent. Do not say a word about not being able to tolerate wine, for then you yourself egg on the foolish sympathy. Sit down at the table; when you are served wine, smell of it and then say or express with a look that the wine is not good. Then the host will become angry and will not press you." To which Molbech answered: "No, I cannot do that; why should I fall out with people?" I answered: "In order to get your own way. Is that not sufficient reason?" But so it goes: first of all to chatter about it to me for an hour and make a fool of me with all that wind, then go to dinner and chatter about it—and drink, then go home and feel bad from it—and chatter about it all night long with his wife: this is living and being interesting.

VII[1] A 110 *n.d.*, 1846

« 5898

Unpleasant as it is to have a mentally disturbed person around every day, it is far more disgusting to be contemporary with a man who has sold out once and for all to contemptibleness, this utter unpredictability, this loathsome absence of bounds, since after all he has contempt for himself and has nothing at all to lose.

VII[1] A 111   *n.d.*, 1846

« 5899

It was a Greek principle that I existentially expressed; now it is disarranged. And what has disarranged it? The fact that the press is used on such a great scale. It is the press that actually destroys all personality, that a cowardly wretch can sit in hiding and write and print for the thousands. All personal conduct and all personal power must run aground on this. It would be most interesting to talk with Socrates about the matter.

VII[1] A 112   *n.d.*, 1846

« 5900

In the next to the last scene in *Hamlet,* when Hamlet dies, his sorrow, almost to despair, is that no one will come to know his life. And this is most certainly true, for anyone who has had one single idea, but by desperate efforts has concealed it in the form of a deception,[1431] becomes aware of this contradiction in the moment of death, for now in death he dares to speak, and now death comes so suddenly. There is also something sad, something truly tragic, in the fact that a man like that, who all his life has borne the full hundred-weight of misunderstanding, will lead the same life after his death, that some clumsy rag-picker or other, who nevertheless has become aware that he did amount to something, will probably put up his picture—alas, it no more resembles him than the clumsy rag-picker resembles the departed one.

But he who has willed to endure such a martyrdom in order to sense the idea of truth ought never be inconsistent, he must never secretly provide people with an explanation. The more consistent he is in this respect, the more true he is to his idea, which will reward him with inner happiness. Just as in life he repudiated the world's honor, so should he also do it in death and after his death continue to be the riddle he was in life, for precisely in this is the epigrammatic-judicial nerve of his life, and precisely in this his faithfulness to the idea.

But one thing may truthfully be said, that men have no conception these days of what it means to act and to think and, thinking, to act consistently to the uttermost. Even an apparently consistent beginning always ends in chatter.

VII¹ A 113   n.d., 1846

« 5901

The only thing that really pains me is that anyone can imagine that the cessation of my being an author[1432] can be linked to this latest unpleasantness. Obedient to the idea, to me it was a joy to keep on working this way without entering into personal relations with any man, without any earthly concerns, serving only the idea. And I was so glad that the last would be like the first, that I knew how to stop and renounce completely that kind of activity. I was entirely successful. Perhaps it would have been detrimental if people had really under-stood this—so let them fancy that I could be motivated by some petty consideration.

VII¹ A 114   n.d., 1846

« 5902

The contemporary public cashes in on every more exceptional person in this way—because he, too, is a human being and looks some-thing like the others and perhaps lacks some of the skills others have, they seem to be completely equal; in contemporaneity a spruced-up store clerk and a genius are peers. On the whole an exceptional person gets ahead of others only enough so that it becomes titillating to the contemporary public to sniff at him, chatter about him, smear his whole intellectual-spiritual life, if possible make his name odious sim-ply because it is in every dunce's mouth.[1433]

VII¹ A 115   n.d., 1846

« 5903

As long as I live I will never and can never be recognized simply because I apply half of my energies to preventing it. The moment I begin to be recognized in this life, the same moment I will tend to become an authority, and in that very same moment my mission is over —not only that, but perhaps my earlier mission will be utterly ruined. Unquestionably no one understands my resignation, some because they have not the time and opportunity or desire to think about such things, others because they could not even understand it if they wanted to.

VII¹ A 116   n.d., 1846

« **5904**

However unjustly I am actually treated here at home, because my whole productivity does not really show up well in so small a theater, although a foolish, curious, envious, and spiteful contemporary public would like essentially to constrain me because they think that after all I am confined by the limits of language, nevertheless the smallness of the country still has the advantage that all the drama contained in my activity as an author over the 4½ years shows up in a totally different way. It could not be produced in Germany, for the country is too large; there no one can imagine being a maid-of-all-work. My writings show up to advantage in recollection, in poetic recollection, and the time will come when girls will color with excitement when a poet recounts the whole design of my life.

VII¹ A 117   *n.d.*, 1846

« **5905**

My contemporaries cannot grasp the design of my writing. *Either/Or* divided into four parts or six parts and published separately over six years would have been all right. But that each essay in *Either/Or* is part of a whole, and then the whole of *Either/Or* a part of a whole: that, after all, think my bourgeois contemporaries, is enough to drive one daft.

VII¹ A 118   *n.d.*, 1846

« **5906**

If I lived in an ordinary market town, it would be still worse. Generally speaking the majority have a secret notion that I am a competent, capable man, but they speculate something like this: If we all get together and tease him, he will have to give in. A negative conspiracy like that is possible only in a small country.

There is also a kind of envy in a small country, simply because everybody knows everybody else and almost involuntarily thinks of himself in relation to each of the others. They do not want to take everything away from me, just a little—as if anyone had the right to rob a man of even the slightest.

VII¹ A 119   *n.d.*, 1846

« **5907**

In spite of all my poverty before God in my personal mortification for what I personally have committed, it would still be possible that I may be for my nation "a gift from God"; God knows they have treated me poorly, indeed, mistreated me as children mistreat a valuable present.

VII¹ A 120   *n.d.*, 1846

« 5908

The artistry in my whole undergirding life was not merely my not talking about what totally concerned me, or about the books into which I step by step put my whole effort, but it was especially that I was always ready to talk about everything else, crack jokes, banter, etc., just like a loafer having a thoroughly good time.

VII¹ A 121   *n.d.*, 1846

« 5909

The injustice in Denmark's small proportions is the obtrusiveness and conformity which thereby develop. A little country such as Denmark naturally can have but one genuinely outstanding person in each particular area, but this person must live in continual contact and association, also in continual literary skirmishes among those of reputation, with various nonentities—who also are somewhat alike. Christian Winther[1434] is a lyrical poet, Holst[1435] also, Barfoed,[1436] too; perhaps each one of the three writes a poem for a festive occasion: ergo, all three are poets. The one who loses out in this situation is Christian Winther. Denmark is such a little country that to be the greatest in a particular area in the country cannot be an essential expression for the essentially extraordinary. Christian Winther would be outstanding in Germany as well, whereas the others would disappear. To be the greatest philosopher in Denmark borders on satire—just about like being the greatest—yes, just imagine it—the greatest among all the traveling theatrical companies one has seen—in Odense, or like P. L. Møller's eulogy[1437] of what I wrote in my polemic against Heiberg[1438]: "It was the wittiest of all the things written against Heiberg"—alas, may I not request Heiberg as the standard, for to use as the standard those who have written against him certainly makes a fool of me. In somewhat the same way *Den Frisindede*[1439] (Rosenhaab) informed me that I ought to be just as popular as such a profound philosopher as H. C. Ørsted.[1440] *Pro dii immortales*[1441]—only "on the mountain"[1442] is it possible for one to say anything like that in earnest.

VII¹ A 124   *n.d.*, 1846

« 5910

March 29, 1846

Dear Professor:[1443]
Please pardon my causing you a small inconvenience. As you are the editor, I must turn to you concerning the author of *A Story of Everyday Life*. May I ask you to take the trouble to send him one copy of the accompanying little book.

As you will gather from the first page, the other copy is intended for you yourself, Sir, as the immediate recipient. It is a pleasure for me to be able to send you a copy of what I write, and thus it cannot become a habit with me.

Yours respectfully,
S. Kierkegaard

To Professor Heiberg

[Address:]
To
Professor J. L. Heiberg
Knight of Dannebrog
Accompanying parcel

Letters, no. 134   March 29, 1846

« 5911

April 6

Dear Professor,[1444]
When I arrived home rather late Thursday evening I received your note of April 2. On Friday morning I was to leave for a visit to my brother[1445] near Sorøe; now that I have returned I immediately take the first opportunity for a brief reply.

Thank you for your welcome note. When one has written a little esthetic review[1446] and he who possesses absolute esthetic authority applies it in praise, it is of course always nice to be the one whom that distinguished person distinguishes. There is an ingenious Oriental proverb that wisely declares that only the deaf sage can resist flattery wisely, because simple-mindedness would regard either of these elements as sufficient: deafness or sagacity. And I, who am neither deaf nor sage, how would I fare in such a dilemma! Therefore it is fortunate that it is impossible for me to be led into such temptation by your note. For when he who has authority praises or approves, then this is after all not flattery, nor would it be wise to turn a deaf ear to it, but indecorous and vain conceit not to heed it gratefully. The reverse is likewise true. If he who admiringly subordinates himself expresses, in his very utterance of admiration, a tolerably clear awareness and idea of what it is he admires, then neither is this flattery. In the former case, authority (reposing in the arbiter), and in the latter case, truth (reposing in the subordinate), are the essentials of that sincerity which precludes the emptiness of flattery.

Thank you also for the possibility you mention of a comment from the author of *A Story of Everyday Life*. What I said in my review[1447] about those stories with reference to the reading public, I may here repeat about that friendly comment with reference to my unworthy self: "I think this is a welcome present in any season; looking forward to it is in itself a pleasure; receiving what has been looked forward to is no less a pleasure."

You are, indeed, the editor of these stories. But an editor has it within his power, whenever he wishes, to consider himself as dissociated from the book and the author. I had applied to you in your capacity as editor and begged pardon for causing you any small inconvenience. On the assumption that this unknown author might honor me with a note, you could have waited until the note was finished, and then you could have enclosed in a business envelope that which already constituted adequate attention to me. As I see it, you would have been fully justified in so doing. All the more, then, do I appreciate your note. The contents are indeed the judgment of him who has authority, and I have thanked you for that. But the note itself is a courtesy which in a welcome manner places me in your grateful debt.

Yours most respectfully,

S. Kierkegaard

To Professor Heiberg
Knight of Dannebrog

[Address:]
To
Professor J. L. Heiberg
Knight of Dannebrog

Letters, no. 136   April 6 [1846]

« 5912

For anyone who is a nobody or even less, Copenhagen is the most pleasant city imaginable in which to live, because, since we are all of no consequence, but there still are a few of some magnitude, there is upward movement. When I was a young man and a nobody, I enjoyed my freedom, I dared live as I pleased, driving alone in my carriage,[1448] keeping the windows shut in public places—it never occurred to anybody to pay any attention to it. But now, now envy watches my every step in order to say: That is pride, that is arrogance, that is vanity. The laughable thing about it is that most likely no one in any country lives as unaltered a life as I have lived since the time I was a student: consequently the change does not lie in me, as if I were now putting on airs—no, I am doing everything the same, but now envy has gotten its eye on me. Why should he have the right to ride alone, says a spruced-up store clerk; it would suit me capitally to ride with him, but it is pride. Of course it never occurs to anyone to reflect on why I live as I do; no, they brazenly, shamelessly, and obtrusively want to force me, if possible, to take the store clerk along.

VII[1] A 125   n.d., 1846

« 5913 *The Way I Have Understood Myself*
in All My Literary Work[1449]

I am in the profoundest sense an unhappy individuality, riveted from the beginning to one or another suffering bordering on madness, a suffering which must have its deeper basis in a misrelation between my mind and my body, for (and this is the remarkable thing as well as my infinite encouragement) it has no relation to my spirit, which on the contrary, because of the tension between mind and body, has perhaps gained an uncommon resiliency.

An old man[1450] who himself was extremely melancholy (why, I will not write down) gets a son in his old age who inherits all this melancholy—but who also has a mental-spiritual elasticity enabling him to hide his melancholy. Furthermore, because he is essentially and eminently healthy of mind and spirit, his melancholy cannot dominate him, but neither is he able to throw it off; at best he manages to endure it.

In the most solemn moment a young girl[1451] (who with girlish self-assurance manifests prodigious powers which suggest to me a way of escape from something begun through a tragic mistake, a way out, to break an engagement, for at first her powers made it seem as if she would not be troubled at all) lays a murder on my conscience; a worried father solemnly repeats his conviction that it will be the death of the girl. Whether or not she was flirting does not concern me.

From that moment I dedicated my life humbly to serve an idea to the best of my ability.

Although no friend of confidants, although absolutely disinclined to speak with others about my innermost concerns, I nevertheless thought and still think that it is a man's duty not to bypass the court which is available in talking things over with another person, just so this does not become a frivolous confidence but is an earnest and official communication. I therefore asked my physician whether he believed that the structural misrelation between the physical and psychical could be dispelled so that I could realize the universal. This he doubted. I asked him whether he thought that my spirit could convert or transform this misrelation by willing it. He doubted it; he would not even advise me to set in motion all the powers of my will, of which he had some conception, since I could blow up everything.[1452]

From that moment I made my choice. I have regarded that tragic misrelation, together with its sufferings (which no doubt would have driven to suicide most of those lacking sufficient spirit to comprehend the utter wretchedness of the agony) as my thorn in the flesh,[1453] my limitation, my cross; I have looked upon it as the high price at which God in heaven sold me a mental-spiritual capacity unequalled among my contemporaries. This does not inflate me, *for I am crushed;* my desire has become a daily bitter pain and humiliation for me.

Without daring to appeal to revelations or anything like that, I have seen it as my task in a warped and demoralized age to affirm the universal and make it lovable and accessible to all others who are capable of realizing it but are led astray by the age to pursue the exceptional, the extraordinary. I have considered my task to be like that of one who himself became unhappy in loving men but wishes to help others who are capable of happiness.

But since my task was also for me (in all humility) a devout attempt to do something good to compensate for what I had done wrong, I have been especially careful so that my efforts would not be in the service of vanity, above all that I would not serve the idea and the truth in such a way that I received earthly or temporal advantages from it. This is why I am positive that I have worked with true resignation [*Resignation*].

Throughout all my work I have also continually believed that I understood better and better God's will for me: that I bear the agony with which God keeps me in check and thus perhaps perform the extraordinary.[*]

If I were to describe in greater detail an inward understanding of the particulars of the task, this would become a whole folio which few would have the capacity and earnestness to understand. But I do not have time for anything like that either.

I may truthfully say that I possess my capacity in weakness and frailty. It could never occur to me that a girl, for example, would not have me if only I were sure enough myself that I dared do everything to win her; it could never occur to me that I would not accomplish the most amazing things if only I were sure enough of myself that I dared attempt it. My misery is rooted in the second; my almost suprahuman feeling of power, in the first. Most men are the opposite—they fear external opposition and do not know the dreadful suffering of interior opposition. I have no fear of any external opposition, but there is an interior opposition when God lets me feel the thorn which gnaws—this is my suffering.

VII[1] A 126   *n.d.*, 1846

« **5914**

[*] *In margin of 5913* (VII[1] A 126):

My service through literature is and will always be that I have set forth the decisive qualifications of the whole existential arena with a dialectical acuteness and a primitivity not to be found in any other literature, as far as I know, and I have had no books to consult, either. Secondly, my art of communication, its form and its consistent execution. But at present no one has time to read seriously and to study; this being the case, until a later time my productivity is wasted, like delicacies served to yokels.

VII[1] A 127   *n.d.*, 1846

« **5915**

With respect to the crucial features of my life, the fate reserved for me seems to be that of never being able to be understood by others. No one would ever dream of that which is the determining factor in my life. In a certain sense the total misunderstanding is a torment when one lives as intensely as I do.

When I left her—what was the reason. Yes, no one would even suspect that.

Now when I stop being an author,[1454] everyone will feel he knows all about it and will explain that it is because I have become fearful and am tired of all this unpleasantness.[1455] Well, let's look at that. When I decided before all this trouble began to end with *Concluding Postscript* (something I had to decide for many reasons, partly financial), I wanted to have the satisfaction of being an author who could work on an enormous scale and then stop, without ever exchanging ten words with anyone as to the reasons why. When all this trouble began, I understood at once that this would be linked to my stopping. This has irritated me, it is true. If I dared to advise myself, I would unreservedly keep on writing for some time. But precisely because the situation is as it is, I dare not give up my resolution, for then I would be cowardly. But what other man besides me understands this.

How sad it is to have anything at all to do with this riffraff (who otherwise may be good-natured, inoffensive, and lovable, only not when they want to judge ideas and thinkers), who cannot think two thoughts together and are able to understand only what is shallow and paltry.

VII[1] A 128 *n.d.*, 1846

« **5916**

Out in the cemetery a widow has placed the following line over her departed one:

Man! You have fought.

But "man" used emphatically this way signifies a hero; it does not mean a married man (for only in a low style does one say: man, my man, her man), much less an undertaker.[1456] Alas, the deceased was an undertaker.

VII[1] A 40 *n.d.*, 1846

« **5917**

..... *Der Neidige ist ein Martyrer, aber des Teufels.*

See Abraham a St. Clara
Coll. Works,[1457] X, p. 392
VII[1] A 41 *n.d.*, 1846

« **5918**

Hebrews:

10:39: But we are not of those *who shrink back to their own destruction.*

VII[1] A 42 *n.d.*, 1846

« 5919

"Three Occasional [*changed from:* Confessional] Discourses"[1458]
by
S. Kierkegaard

VII^1 B 136   *n.d.*, 1846

« 5920

In an old devotional book (Arndt, *Sande Christendom*[1459]) there is a beautiful comment on the verse: "God shall wipe away our tears."[1460] He adds this excellent catechetical question: But how is God going to wipe them away if you have not wept at all? —What truth in this simple statement, what stirring eloquence.

VII^1 A 43   *n.d.*, 1846

« 5921

Anaxagoras is supposed to have said: The senses are limited, the mind is feeble, life is short.
Indeed, it is in Cicero, in *Quaestiones academicae,*[1461] 1, 12.

VII^1 A 44   *n.d.*, 1846

« 5922

Little by little as education and refinement increase and demands become greater and greater, a philosopher will naturally find it increasingly difficult to satisfy the demands of the age. In former days the requirement was spiritual-intellectual capacities, freedom of mind, and passion of thought. But compare that with the present; at present in Copenhagen it is required that a philosopher shall also have sturdy or at least shapely legs, and his clothes must be fashionable. It becomes more and more difficult, unless one is content with just the last requirement and assumes that everyone who has sturdy or shapely legs and whose clothes are fashionable is a philosopher.

VII^1 A 50   *n.d.*, 1846

« 5923

When there is thunder in the air and one looks at the expanse of water and the one solitary tree, the whole thing is similar to the Chladni sound-figure formed when a glass sheet is played upon. There is still something vibrating in the figure.

VII^1 53   *n.d.*, 1846

« 5924

>Berlin, May 5–13
>1846[1462]
>VII[1] A 129   *n.d.*, 1846

« 5925

>*To the typesetter*
>the smallest possible brevier
>Preface . . .[1463]
>May 5, 1846
>S.K.
>VII[1] B 150   May 5, 1846

« 5926

Just as every lodger has a bootblack, so every great author has some bungling windbag or other who serves him by abusing him, who, every time the author writes anything, regularly pronounces in a paper that it is the most cantankerous rubbish etc. For example, Madvig[1464] has Baden,[1465] and P. L. Møller[1466] is also a bungling windbag like that. A bungling windbag like that resembles the odd-job men who hang around the market; when the farmers come to market, each one picks out a wagon where he thinks he may earn something, and in the same way the bungling windbag selects an author he can make a profit on, inasmuch as the author's name guarantees that the public will surely read—something bad about him.

>VII[1] A 55   *n.d.*, 1846

« 5927

As a polemicist, H. Hertz[1467] impresses me as being like an officer who as a volunteer in foreign service has been a spectator at a battle, comes home, and then out on the common organizes a maneuver which is supposed to be the battle: Hertz organizes a battle after it is all over.

>VII[1] A 66   *n.d.*, 1846

« 5928

There is really a deceptive turn by Bishop Mynster when in his sermons[1468] (the one on "Give us this day our daily bread" and the one on miracles) he says concerning the forgiveness of sin: *Some day* (that is, in eternity) it shall be said to him who in repentance has humbled himself and believed, "Your sins are forgiven you." "Some day," i.e., in eternity—but the nub of the forgiveness of sin is precisely to make it valid in time. It is the new creation, and the pastor does say at confession: "I declare unto you the gracious forgiveness of all your sins." Is this forgiveness only for the future? Once again this is using immanence (this *some day*) instead of transcendence.

VII[1] A 78   *n.d.*, 1846

« **5929**

One who like me has had a polemic view of all existence since childhood and for a while recently has received first-class service in *The Corsair* can be regarded as having good prerequisites for the world of time. Such [prerequisites] are worth a lot of money.

VII[1] A 85   *n.d.*, 1846

« **5930**

Regrettably I must say that my life has been wasted. If I lived anywhere else than in Copenhagen, this would no doubt be interpreted to mean that I had dissipated the best years of my youth in reckless living, in disorganized studies, perhaps in debauchery. Alas, but it is just the opposite. I have amounted to something—and that is why my life is to be regarded as wasted here in Copenhagen, where one can live happily and very pleasantly—as long as he is nobody—here in Copenhagen where little more than bad things is said about anyone who is somebody, with the obvious result that one who is nobody can say with pride: Nothing bad is said about me. Here in Copenhagen if one is a student or a graduate but no more, a supervisory clerk in a government office, a shop clerk, a student at the art academy, but no more—when the weather is very warm, he can freely and easily go for a walk with an umbrella against the sun, although it is not customary —but if I, for example, am so audacious as to do this, it is pride. A Cerberus-envy watches every step made by anyone who is somebody in order to interpret it as pride and arrogance.

VII[1] A 90   *n.d.*, 1846

« **5931**

No doubt part of what contributed to making *Either/Or* a success has been that it was a first book and therefore one could take it to be the work of many years—and thus conclude that the style was good and well-developed. It was written lock, stock, and barrel in eleven months. At most there was only a page (of "Diapsalmata") prior to that time. As far as that goes, I have spent more time on all the later works. Most of *Either/Or* was written only twice (besides, of course, what I thought through while walking, but that is always the case); nowadays I like to write three times.

VII¹ A 92   n.d., 1846

« **5932**

Outside of Vesterport now there is a Panorama. The showman or barker says: "Here the new lucky star is displayed, here everyone finds out his full age, as well as his future bride or bridegroom."[1469] Good Lord, usually everyone knows how old he is and does not need any secret art for that—but his future bride—well, that would be worth finding out. —Incidentally, it is splendid that the announcement contains such qualitatively varied statements about what will be learned by those entering.

VII¹ A 95   n.d., 1846

« **5933**

When someone says: While this and that was taking place, something else happened, we usually think of the former as lasting longer and therefore usable in showing that the second takes up only a moment within the first while. We say: While Cicero was Consul, this and that happened; while Pitt was prime minister, etc. This is why it was so funny to read in the paper some time ago about the festivities at Skamlingsbank:[1470] *While* Grundtvig was speaking the people from Fyn arrived. Of course, the fact of the Fyn islanders' arrival is unimportant. The choice and funny aspect of it is the idea conveyed of the fantastic length of pastor Grundtvig's talk—that *while* he was speaking (while Cicero was Consul). For example, it could be said: *While* Grundtvig was speaking, a French fleet put out to sea and conquered Algeria.

VII¹ A 96   n.d., 1846

« **5934**

Upbuilding Discourses
in
Various Styles and Spirits
by
S. Kierkegaard

[*Changed from:*

Godly Discourses
by
S. Kierkegaard]
Copenhagen 1846
Available at Reitzel's   Printed by Bianco Luno[1471]

VII¹ B 192:1-2   n.d., 1846

« **5935**

[Markings in books by A. P. Adler, sketch and drafts of *Bogen om Adler,* alterations in manuscript.[1472]]

VII² B 236–70   *n.d.,*   1846–47

« **5936**

Literary Review
Magister Adler
A Psychological Study from Nature
That Is, Based on His Writings[1473]
by
S. Kierkegaard

VII² B 242   *n.d.,*   1846–47

« **5937**

Sept. 7, 1846

Report[1474]   *Result*

1.

The real vulgarity in the prevailing literary contemptibleness is not so much *what* is written as *for whom* it is written. If a paper like *The Corsair* could give us a guarantee that it would be read only by a few hundred of the most intelligent people in the country, it would do no harm at all. But to ironize the extraordinary, it is also necessary for the one who does it to be intellectually educated enough to make an evaluation and to have pathos enough to be inspired: only then is it irony to joke about a person's accidental characteristics, an author's figure, etc. But when something like that is written for the lowest classes, for shop assistants and boys, maidservants and silly women, etc., then it is *eo ipso* coarseness and slave insurrection. For that class of people has not the remotest intimation of what it means to evaluate or understand; for them an author exists [*existerer*] *qua* man just as any other man, and their evaluation of a man is whether or not he is strong and can fight, etc.

Yes, even if something like that is written for the intrinsically respectable and good, but simpler and not essentially cultivated, social class, it is still coarseness; the simplicity consists precisely of not being able to think a dialectical doubleness (in a sense this is the beauty of it). Simplicity thinks that the extraordinary is the extraordinary and nothing bad is to be said about it. If a man is an extraordinary philosopher, then he is not to be insulted. When simplicity is itself incapable of judging whether a man is an outstanding philosopher, simplicity quite properly draws the conclusion that when something like this is written about him, *ergo* the man is no great philosopher.

But the villainy in this literary contemptibleness lies in the authors, who up to a point could be respectable authors even if they are of secondary rank but stir up the rabble in order to get revenge and hurt and confuse and defile.

2.

It was really ironic of me to live so much on the streets and avenues while I was writing the pseudonymous works. The irony consisted of belonging to a completely different sphere *qua* author and spending so much time on the streets and in the markets. The irony was directed at the intellectual, affected Hegelian forces we have, or had, here at home. But as soon as there is an attempt from another corner, by literary rabble barbarism, to make it seem that I really belong on the street, then the irony quite properly disappears and I take exception to the forum. —If Goldschmidt had himself detected it and had on his own played a joke—well, then he would have amounted to something. But I had to challenge him myself—and quite properly did it only when I was ready. If P. L. Møller's[1475] article had appeared a month earlier, he would have received no reply. Then neither could I have avoided the situation nor, as long as I was actually productive, would I have dared expose myself to the disturbances that might possibly result from the fuss.

What makes my life so intensely strenuous, but at the same time full and rich in almost its most insignificant expression, is that I must have the idea everywhere, whereas other men do not seem to have the slightest need for it. But there again I also have the advantage that in the midst of all the fuss and trouble I never become an essential part of it but because of my predisposition to observation continually maintain myself as a third person to some extent.

3.

The whole affair this last half year has further confirmed for me the thesis: *mundus vult decipi.* [1476] If the supporters of this literary rabble barbarism were to be asked: But why attack Kierkegaard—they would answer as one of them answered me (in other respects he was a person of some status): "There must be no authority." Let us look at this. An author essentially educated by Socrates and the Greeks and with a grasp of irony begins an enormous literary activity; he specifically does not want to be an authority and with that in mind quite properly sees that by continually walking the streets[1477] he must inevitably minimize the impression he makes. And he was absolutely right: in all the distinguished circles frequented by authorities he was not in the remotest way regarded as an authority. What happens then—barbarism inundates him and compels him in pursuance of the idea to do what he otherwise would like to do, withdraw a little. Let him live in seclusion like this for only six months, and lo, he is an authority. His prestige is so great that he himself would be the only one who actually could reduce the impression he makes. Who was it, then, who helped make him into an authority? The very ones who began their talk and their activity on the basis that "There must be no authority."

4.

What, then, is the source of the unpleasantness, the annoyance, to me? Naturally not in *what* was said (for I have frequently said the same thing in jest about myself) but *to whom* it was said, because it has saddled me with a crowd of riffraff with whom I do not have and do not care to have any fellowship. Things I can laugh at so heartily in the company of, for example, Carl Weis,[1478] I cannot really laugh at *in the company* of Jewish peddlers, shop clerks, prostitutes, school boys, butcher boys, etc. For example, when I laugh with him at my thin legs, I am presuming thereby an essentially common intellectual background. Were I to laugh at them with the riffraff, that would imply that I acknowledge a common base with them. —Precisely because the situation is as it is, the curious state of affairs has come about that the only one here at home who is actually competent to handle wittily and with irony such dialectical problems as ironizing a proficiency cannot defend doing it—and that one person is myself. I certainly pledge myself to write witty articles about myself and my legs in quite another vein than Goldschmidt can, but then the riffraff will not be able to understand them.

VII[1] A 147   September 7, 1846

« 5938

Generally speaking, the world stays just as wise—that is, just as stupid. For example, when a man, misunderstood, ridiculed, persecuted, insulted, despised by his contemporaries, has fought for a truth, the next generation discovers that he was great—and admires him. And if there happens to be an enthusiast in the next generation who actually understands that departed one to the extent that he goes and does likewise, then this enthusiast again is persecuted, insulted, despised, etc. Consequently the distinguished one is first despised by his contemporaries and then the true admirer of the distinguished one is despised by his contemporaries, that is, the second generation, which, as they say, admires the dead and departed one. *Mundus vult decipi,*[1479] and the world is always made the fool, especially when it admires, for in order to admire it must take the best away—and then admires it but despises the one who truly admires the best in the departed distinguished one.

VII[1] A 148   *n.d.,* 1846

« **5939**

From "The Book on Adler"[1480]

. . . . . There are examples in Adler of wild constructions no doubt familiar (esthetically and artistically) to Frater Taciturnus,[1481] since he, himself using a completely different style, has Quidam[1482] of the experiment express himself in this stylistic form. To construct rhetorically upon a conditional clause and then have the main clause amount to nothing, an abyss from which the reader as it were once again shrinks back to the antecedents; to plunge into a tentative effort as if this wealth were inexhaustible and then the very same second discontinue it, which is like the trick of pulling up short at full gallop (most riders fall off—usually one first breaks into a gallop and then into a trot); to be at the head of a cavalry of predicates, the one more gallant and dashing than the other, to charge in, and then swerve; the leap in modulation; the turning to the concept in one single word; the unexpected stop etc. Just as the voice of all passionate peoples, all southern peoples (the Jews, for example), continually changes tone, just as every passionate person talks in this manner, so is it also possible to produce this effect stylistically.

But this would take me much too far afield, and how many are there, after all, who have any intimation of how prose can be used lyrically and of (what I am committed to) how prose can produce a stronger lyrical effect than verse if people would only learn how to read and to insist on thought in every word, whereas verse always has a little padding. So I cut this short; it would concern only authors anyway. In this respect all of the pseudonyms have an unqualified linguistic value in having cultivated prose lyrically. It is clear that Adler, too, has learned something from them, but what his flattering reviewer says in the *Kirketidende,*[1483] that he began just about the same time as the pseudonyms,[1484] is not true, for he began after them, and the style of his four last works is markedly different from that in his sermons,[1485] where he had not as yet been so strongly influenced. On the other hand, what his reviewer says about the presence of passages in Adler (four last books)[1486] thoroughly reminiscent of the pseudonyms is true, but I see nothing meritorious in that, neither in copying another nor in forgetting that by having had a revelation[1487] of his own one has entirely different things to think about than language exercises.

VII[1] A 150   n.d., 1846

« **5940**

Human envy will eventually do away with every essential qualification and set its own power-hungry arbitrariness in their place. If someone—humble before God but with noble pride—wants to be neither more nor less than he is, but does want to be that, envy is heaped upon him. On the other hand, if someone begins with the concession: I am a contemptible subject—then, to be sure, his talent can be acknowledged, for then he can be held down. This is why it was not inconceivable that Adler[1488] suddenly was able to be successful, for he really begins with the concession: I am half-mad—then his meager talent can very well be acknowledged; he can never become a threat, for he is half-mad. That is how all that wretched deviousness is nurtured. Someone writes a comedy for students, taking the fraternal liberty to use actual persons.[1489] Indeed, anyone who objected to this would be a poor sport. But then the play is sneaked around in the provinces[1490] —where, of course, it is not put on for the students, and finally it is staged at the Royal Theater.[1491] It is this sneaking half-officiality that makes people take to it. Whatever steps forward with the claim and consciousness of being something specific arouses envy, but this half-private and half-official business flatters the public. Such a piece of trumpery by a poet becomes popular because the public thinks it absolutely charming, that this is something private between him and them, that he is not really a poet but is speaking *en famille.*[1492]

VII[1] A 154   n.d., 1846

« **5941**

Yes, of course I am an aristocrat (and so was and is everyone who is truly conscious of willing the good—and there are never very many of them)—but I insist on getting out into the street, among men, where there is danger and opposition. I do not want (à la Martensen,[1493] Heiberg,[1494] and the like) to live cowardly and effeminately at a fashionable distance in select groups, guarded by illusion (that the masses seldom see them and therefore imagine them to be something). It is indeed true that the world wants to be deceived, that if it seldom sees a man it believes he is something—but I do not want to deceive and do not want an illusion. None of those noble ones who truly desired mankind's well-being ever did this, they never lived an effeminate life, snobbishly aloof in aristocratic circles.

VII¹ A 155   *n.d.*, 1846

« 5942

This is how I have understood myself. As long as I was pseudonymous, both the idea of the production and the illusion of the production required that I act outwardly as I did; it was absolutely important to me to do everything to support the illusion that I was not an author. The fact that people nevertheless did regard me as author does not concern me; men are like that and have no aptitude for ideas except for playing havoc with them; but among other things my idea is that this ought not to interfere. —But from the moment I assumed the authorship,[1495] decorum required that I appear less. All this trouble[1496] is of some good in that it helps me to behave in that way.

The whole pseudonymous production and my life in relation to it was in the Greek mode.

Now I must find the characteristic Christian life-form.

VII¹ A 156   *n.d.*, 1846

« 5943

Some may think that I appear in public[1497] less frequently than before because I am dependent, because I am tired of it or do not want to expose myself to insults. But what is independence. If, out of fear of being regarded as dependent because of appearing infrequently, I appear more frequently, then I am indeed dependent, then my environment does indeed control me. Many, of course, will not understand this because they are not sufficiently dialectical.

VII¹ A 157   *n.d.*, 1846

« 5944

A Note for "The Book on
Adler" that was not used.

I see that Johannes Climacus was reviewed in one of the issues of Scharling and Engelstoft's *Tidsskrift.*[1498] It is one of the usual two-bit reviews, written in "very fine language" with periods and commas in the right places. A theological student or graduate who otherwise is thoroughly incompetent in discussion nevertheless copies the table of contents and then adds his criticism, which is something like this—that J. C. is certainly justified in the way in which he emphasizes the dialectical, but (yes, now comes the wisdom) on the other hand one must not forget mediation. Historically J. C. comes after Hegelianism. J. C. without a doubt knows just as much about mediation as such a theological graduate. In order, if possible, to get out of the spell of mediation, constantly battling against it, J. C. decisively brought the problem to its logical conclusion through the vigor of a qualitative dialectic (something no theological student or graduate or second-rate reviewer can do)—and then the book is reviewed in this way—that is, with the help of a bungling laudatory review the book is ruined, annulled, cashiered. And the reviewer himself even becomes important: for the reviewer to stand loftily over the author in this way looks almost like superiority —with the help of a wretched stock phrase. The reviewer is so insignificant that he would scarcely be able to write a review if the book were taken away from him, for he copies with a suspicious anxiety, and a reviewer like that becomes so important at the end. The way an author works is to use his time and energy strenuously concentrating upon bringing the problem to its logical conclusion, and then along comes a laudatory review and assists in making the issue and the book into the same old hash. And the author is not read, but the reviewer calls attention to himself and the review is read, and the reader must involuntarily believe the review because it is laudatory, the review which by way of praise has annihilated the book. *Mundus vult decipi.* [1499] But this comes about because to be a genuine author means a sacrificed life and because an intermediate staff of fiddlers has been formed (two-bit reviewers), whose trade flourishes. And since we are accustomed to the coarsest, most boorish guttersnipe tone in the papers, a reviewer presumably thinks that when, as a bonus, he is so nice as to praise the book —he has a right to reduce it to rubbish. Johannes Climacus most likely would say: No, thank you, may I request to be abused instead; being abused does not *essentially* harm the book, but to be praised in this way is to be annihilated, insofar as this is possible for the reviewer, the nice, goodnatured, but somewhat stupid reviewer. An author who really understands himself is better served by not being read at all, or by having five genuine readers, than by having this confusion about mediation spread abroad with the help of a goodnatured reviewer, spread with the help of his own book, which was written specifically to battle against mediation. But the concept of author in our day has been distorted in an extremely immoral way.

VII[1] A 158   *n.d.,* 1846

« **5945**

Under the title:

The Gospel of Suffering[1500]

I would like to work out a collection of sermons. The texts would be partly from Christ's Passion Story,[1501] partly powerful words such as the apostles[1502] spoke when, after having been scourged, they went away rejoicing, thanking God that they were allowed to suffer something, or when Paul[1503] calls his chains a glorious honor, or when he says to Herod Agrippa: I wish that every one of you were as I, except for these chains. Or the several passages in the Epistle to the Corinthians, where there is one paradox after the other: Ourselves poor, we make all rich;[1504] or Rejoice and *again* I say rejoice.[1505] Also the passage in the Epistle of James[1506] that we should count it all joy when we are tried in various sufferings.

Alongside of this should follow three short but delightful discourses:

What We Learn from the Lilies of the Field
and from the Birds of the Air[1507]

There is a scrap of paper[1508] pertaining to this in the old case for my Bible.

VII[1] A 160   *n.d.,* 1846

« **5946**

As I have said so often, for the satisfaction of my own sense of freedom and self-control, it was my desire when I gave up being an author[1509] to communicate to others the impression of an author-existence that lived completely by its own laws. And truly it was so, but the misfortune was that this recent unpleasantness[1510] has immersed me in gossip. What I so rejoiced over: knowing myself when to stop, my triumph of freedom, which I did in fact attain—all that has now been distorted and smeared by the mean circumstances of life. And on the other hand, what I would have liked so much to do—as my independent resolution according to higher orders, which it is—that I am tempted not to do when not one or another wretch but this whole wretched life in a market town distorts it.

VII[1] A 164   *n.d.,* 1846

« 5947

November, 1846

Perhaps—I say no more, for I know very well how difficult it is to pass judgment on oneself *in abstracto*[1511] if one is going to pass judgment truthfully—if I had been successful in halting my writing[1512] and in concentrating upon taking an official appointment, if everything had gone as it should have, then it would have been clear that it was my own freedom that determined the outcome. Now this cannot be done. I face a huge obstacle in connection with becoming a pastor. If I undertook it, I would certainly run the risk of causing offense as I once did with the engagement. On the other hand, living in seclusion and quiet in the country, for example, has been made difficult, because my mood is still somewhat bitter and I need the spell of writing to forget all the petty meanness of life.

It becomes more and more clear to me that I am so constituted that I just never manage to realize my ideals, while in another sense, humanly speaking, I become more than my ideals. Most men's ideals are the great, the extraordinary, which they never achieve. I am far too melancholy to have such ideals. Other people would smile at my ideals. It was indeed my ideal to become a married man and make that my whole life. And then, despairing of achieving that, I became an author and perhaps a first-rate one at that. My next ideal was to become a village pastor, to live in a quiet rural setting, to become a genuine part of the little circle around me—and then, despairing of that, it is quite possible that I will again realize something which seems to be far greater.

When Bishop Mynster advises me to become a rural pastor,[1513] he obviously does not understand me. Of course I do wish it, but our premises do not agree at all. He assumes that in one way or another I want to take this path to get ahead, that I want to be somebody after all, and just there is the rub—I want to be as insignificant as possible, that is the very idea of my melancholy. For just this reason I have been content to be regarded as half-mad, but this was still but a negative form of being somewhat uncommon. It certainly is possible that this actually may become the shape of my life, so that I may never find the beautiful, quiet, calm life of being not much at all.

My conversation with Bishop Mynster made me aware again of the truth of what I have always privately known and why I have never spoken with anyone about what really matters to me—it amounts to nothing, for I cannot and I dare not speak with anyone else about what totally and essentially and inwardly constitutes my life; therefore on my side the conversation becomes almost a deception. In relation to a man like Mynster, I am deeply grieved about it all, for I esteem him so highly.

VII[1] A 169   November 5, 1846

« 5948

To the Dedication
"*That Single Individual*"
in the occasional discourse[1514] the
following piece should really have been added.

Beloved!

Please accept this dedication. It is offered, as it were, blindly, but therefore in all honesty, untroubled by any other consideration. I do not know who you are, I do not know your name—I do not even know if you exist or if you perhaps did exist and are no more, or whether your time is still coming. Yet you are my hope, my joy, my pride, in the uncertainty of you, my honor—for if I knew you personally with a worldly certainty, this would be my shame, my guilt—and my honor would be lost.

It comforts me, beloved, that you have this opportunity for which I know I have honestly worked. If it were feasible that reading what I write came to be common practice, or pretending to have read it in hopes of getting ahead in the world, this would not be the opportune time for my reader, for then the misunderstanding would have triumphed—yes, it would have beguiled me to dishonesty if with all my powers I had not prevented anything like that from happening—on the contrary, by doing everything to prevent it I have acted honestly. No, if reading what I write becomes a dubious good (—and if with all the powers granted me I contribute to that, I am acting honestly), or still better, if it becomes foolish and ludicrous to read my writings, or even better, if it becomes a contemptible matter so that no one dares acknowledge it, that is the opportune time for my reader; then he seeks stillness, then he does not read for my sake or for the world's sake—but for his own sake, then he reads in such a way that he does not seek my acquaintance but avoids it—and then he is *my* reader.

I have often imagined myself in a pastor's place. If the crowds storm to hear him, if the great arch of the church cannot contain the great throngs, and people even stand outside listening to him—well, honor and praise to one so gifted that his feelings are gripped, that he can talk as one inspired, inspired by the sight of the crowds, for where the crowd is there must be truth, inspired by the thought that there has to be something for everybody, because there are a lot of people, and a lot of people with a little truth is surely truth—to me this would be impossible! But suppose it was a Sunday afternoon, the weather was gloomy and miserable, the winter storm emptied the streets, everyone who had a warm apartment let God wait in the church until better weather—if there were sitting in the church a couple of poor women who had no warm apartment and could just as well freeze in the church, indeed, I could talk both them and myself warm!

I have often imagined myself beside a grave. If all the people of honor and distinction were assembled there, if solemnity pervaded the whole great throng—well, honor and praise to one so gifted that he could add to the solemnity by being prompted to be the interpreter of the throng, to be the expression for the truth of sorrow—I could not do it! But if it was a poor hearse and it was accompanied by no one but a poor old woman, the widow of the dead man, who had never before experienced having her husband go away without taking her along—if she were to ask me, on my honor I would give a funeral oration as well as anyone.

I have often imagined myself in the crucial decision of death. If there was alarm in the camp, much running in to inquire about me— I believe I could not die, my old irascible disposition would once more awaken and I would have to go out once again and contend with people. But if I lie secluded and alone, I hope to God I may die peacefully and blessedly.

There is a view of life which thinks that truth is where the crowd is, that truth itself needs to have the crowd on its side. There is another view of life which thinks that wherever the crowd is, untruth is, so that if every individual who separately and in stillness possessed truth were to come together in a crowd (in such a way, however, that the crowd acquired whatever decisive, favorable, noisy, loud significance there was), untruth would promptly be present there. But the person who recognizes this last view as his own (which is rarely pronounced, for more frequently a man believes that the crowd lives in untruth, but if they would only accept his opinions everything would be all right) confesses that he himself is the weak and powerless one; moreover, how could one individual be able to stand against the crowd, which has the power! And he could not wish to have the crowd on his side: that would be defeating himself. But if this latter view is an admission of weakness and powerlessness and thus perhaps seems somewhat uninviting, it at least has the good point of being equable–, no one insults it, not one single person, it makes no difference, not to one single person.

To be sure the crowd is formed by individuals, but each one must retain the power to remain what he is—an individual. No one, no one, not one is excluded from being an individual except the person who excludes himself—by becoming many. On the contrary, to become part of the crowd, to gather the crowd around oneself, is what makes distinctions in life. Even the most well-intentioned person talking about this can easily insult an individual. But then once again the crowd has power, influence, status, and domination—it is the distinction in life which predominantly looks down on the individual as weak and impotent.

VII[1] A 176 *n.d.,* 1846

« **5949**

I really did imagine that I had a little understanding of men, but the longer I live the more I perceive that we simply do not understand each other at all. If I had wanted to do them harm, they would have honored and esteemed me and thanked me: and the only thing I wanted was to be of benefit to them. Here is a young man, wholeheartedly willing to prostrate himself before me, he wants to go out in the world as one of my followers and proclaim my honor—and the only thing I want is least of all this. I would say to him, and it is the only thing I will say: Go home, lock your door, and pray to God, and you will have infinitely more than the fragment you can get second-hand from me. Here is a young girl.[1515] Her only desire is one thing, to kneel adoringly at my feet—and the only thing I want is least of all this. I will simply say to her: Go into your room, lock your door, pray to God, and you will have infinitely much more than the paltry fragment of admiring me. —And that is why I am called an egotist.

VII[1] A 184 *n.d.,* 1846

« **5950**

Excerpts 1–5 from C. G. Carus, *Psyche. Zur entwicklungsgeschichte der Seele*[1516]:

In the whole unconscious world the pressure of the environment and the counter-pressure of the individual are identical. The first trace of spontaneity is constituted by the mediation of this pressure and counter-pressure by a third: general sensation, feeling, self-regard [pp. 99–120].

Unconsciousness. —Then an impressionable substance must be formed (nervous system); then there must be an environment—consciousness of a world;—then a gathering and conservation of impressions (*Innerung*—or in a higher sphere *Erinnerung*), and this conservation must have reached a certain goal. Self-consciousness. God's consciousness [pp. 102–11].

Animals: natural drive; artificial drive; migratory instinct [pp. 140–41].

The understanding of a child; imagination in puberty; reason [p. 160].

And as the human organism develops by way of a uniform repetition, the set of primitive cells is repeated, so also memory, which is a repetition [p. 165]. And just as at the same time there then is a striving in the organism toward wholeness, so also there is a wholeness in the imagination. —Imagination completes the human being [p. 167].

VII[1] C 5   *n.d.*, 1846

« 5951

Right now I feel once again what I have so often felt: how difficult it is for me to understand others. I fall upon a book with ravenous passion, and as I read, it seems that I find only the utterly familiar, and when I have closed the book, it seems that I must certainly have overlooked something. On the other hand I seem to find thoughts I have never had, but I am unable to grasp and hold them. But as soon as I myself think over this or that, I am sure to get to the bottom of it whether or not I have read it.

How others manage, I do not understand. Probably the need for independent thought in them is not so great; therefore they can more easily learn by rote.

Add to this that I have developed as a poet to the point where the act of writing is itself the greatest pleasure for me.

How I would like to read and read; I think it would be a shortcut. And I still believe that I will get farther with patience—along the long road of independent thought.

VII[1] A 202   *n.d.*, 1846

« 5952

Not like the former editor, who succeeded in entering into relation with the conversation of the moment—and therefore succeeded in becoming welcome.

I will rather strive to enter into relation with silence. There are too many pages to rummage in—just as students have too many books— therefore one does not read well.

  The contents will be what, spiritually understood, could be called daily bread. Make clear what *harmony* is, the *universal.* What is common to all (the religious touch).

  Then I will choose a somewhat more difficult thought—and then it will be like the poor invited to a banquet of the distinguished —then a very simple thought, which will be like the distinguished going to a banquet of the poor.

If possible, the reader is to read aloud.[1517]

In margin: Politics in the special sense must be excluded altogether.[1518]

VII[1] B 212 n.d., 1846

« 5953

Addition to 5952 (VII[1] B 212):

No. 1

Public Opinion

No. 2

What one learns from the lilies of the field and the
birds of the air[1519]

No. 3

On being a good listener[1520]

No. 4

The misuse of laughter

No. 5

The difficult situation of distinction in a small country

No. 6

The intrinsic validity of occupation with the intellectual-spiritual

No. 7

Why Socrates compared himself to a gadfly[1521]

No. 8

Solitude and silence as essential ingredients of
personal life[1522]

No. 9

On the upbringing of children[1523]

No. 10

The corruptive and misleading aspects of the now so common use of the statistical in the realms of the spirit[1524]

VII[1] B 213 n.d., 1846

« **5954**

All the last four books[1525] are to be published in one volume under the title:

Minor Works by S. Kierkegaard

VII[1] B 214   *n.d.,* 1846

« **5955**

Addition to 5954 (VII[1] B 214):

Minor Works
by
S. Kierkegaard

VII[1] B 217   *n.d.,* 1846–47

« **5956**

Addition to 5955 (VII[1] B 217):

Contents[1526]

I.   Discourse on the Occasion of Confession
II.   Literary Review   Adler
III.   What One Learns from the Lilies of the Field and the Birds of the Air   3 Discourses
IV.   The Gospel of Suffering

VII[1] B 218   *n.d.,* 1846–47

VI. WRITINGS OF THE SECOND PERIOD
1847–MAY 1848

« **5957**

January, 1847

What I take exception to in all this trouble with literary contempt-ibleness[1527] is, of course, not its attack and its insults (I invited it myself)[1528] nor their conduct, which, after all, patronizes this con-temptibleness, no, it is their meanness, which, because they do not know how to grasp a situation, wants to be ingenious and pass judg-ment on me, that it was a rash step etc.

But the time will surely come when all these cowards will think it no longer necessary to lie. As soon as the danger is over, they will most likely dare say that I was right. What paltriness we live in! It is so characteristic that right now when Goldschmidt[1529] has gone abroad and P. L. Møller[1530] has apparently lost his nerve, they are beginning to appreciate my action. And there are those brave, bold journalists who, when it comes to criticizing a poor policeman for losing his temper, use frank, bold, outspoken language: Fie on the hypocrites! It is these loyal supporters of the government, these outspoken journal-ists, who attack the liberals for every little trifle—where no danger is involved! But where there is a bit of danger (somewhat like firemen being the only ones tried and tested in dangers during times of peace), there has not been one single hint of a word.

But this is why those who should have maintained the pathos with respect to my action are in difficulties with me. Now that the danger is over, they perhaps even want to say what they did not dare say before; but they have a bad conscience about me, they feel that I see right through them, and they are almost afraid that if the opportunity comes I will, with new recklessness and probably very good reasons, let them pay the penalty for this meanness.[1531]

VII¹ A 214   January, 1847

357

« **5958**

It can be regarded as an epigram and as a proof that books are no longer written for eternity: the paper itself on which they are printed is so poor that it will disintegrate in the course of fifty years.

VII¹ A 218   *n.d.*, 1847

« **5959**

If there lived in a market town a painter, a veritable genius—and let us assume (for otherwise the analogy does not fit, since, after all, in a small country books are circumscribed by the limitations of language) that the making of paintings was forbidden. He worked industriously night and day and finished one, yes, two large historical paintings. But the inhabitants did not like them, would rather have him paint signboards. When he refused, they banded together to deride him. There were, however, a few individuals who did essentially have sufficient insight to value his talents and work, but they were envious and therefore joined the others. —This will soon be the situation in Denmark for every person of competence who refuses to join a clique.

VII¹ A 219   *n.d.*, 1847

« **5960**

Someday I must use this theme
              I Thessalonians 2:11
"aspire to live quietly."

VII¹ A 220   *n.d.*, 1847

« **5961**

January 20, 1847

The wish to be a rural pastor[1532] has always appealed to me and been at the back of my mind. It appealed to me both idyllically as a wish in contrast to a strenuous life and also religiously as a kind of penitence, to find the time and the quiet to grieve over that in which I personally may have offended. I was convinced that I was about to be successful as an author and, this being the case, I thought it right to end that way. Meanwhile it seems perfectly clear *that the situation here at home is becoming more and more confused.*

The question now is, insofar as there is any question about the need for an extraordinary in the literary, social, and political situation —and I dare maintain this before God's judgment seat—whether there is anyone in the kingdom suitable to be that except me. When I gave her up, I gave up every desire for a cozy, pleasant life; my personal guilt makes me capable of submitting to *everything*. In this way there is an ethical presupposition here. In the next place, by accepting a specific post in the state as a teacher of religion I am committing myself to being something that I am not. Because of a guilt I carry, I would have to be prepared at every moment to be attacked on that score. Then, if I am a clergyman, the confusion will take on tragic dimensions inasmuch as I would have kept back something upon entering this profession. My position as author is different. I contract no personal relationship to any person who can make claims upon my example or upon the antecedents in my life; I ride so loosely in the setting that I can be dashed down any time it so pleases God without affecting any other person in the least. This is the second, the more important, ethical presupposition. As far as my intelligence, talents, skills, and mental constitution are concerned, there can be no doubt that I am rightly constructed in every way and I will bear a huge responsibility if I refuse a task like that. It certainly is true that it seems more humble to pull back and become a pastor, but if I do that, there can also be something vain and proud in proudly rejecting the more spectacular. On the other hand, from now on I must take being an author to be the same as being at the mercy of insult and ridicule. But to continue along this road is not something self-inflicted, for it was my calling, my whole *habitus*[1533] was designed for this.

There is no doubt that as an author in times like ours I could by strict moral discipline be of great benefit. But it by no means follows that I will win out. Rather it means that I am prepared to get the worst of it. Strictly speaking, I am not suited for the tasks of a rural pastor. Therefore, I have constantly intended simply to express the universal and that the ethical meaning should consist in my preferring that to the more spectacular. But now and from now on my career as an author is truly not spectacular. It is perfectly clear that I will be sacrificed. Out of cowardice and envy the aristocrats will continue to keep quiet, letting me push forward and then letting me fall as a sacrifice to rabble barbarism and then finally profit from the whole thing. In other words, humanly speaking, my work will be without pay. But I ask nothing else. The fact that I may be temporarily impatient does not prove a thing, for at any suitable moment I am still willing to sacrifice anything, and hope that God will give me the strength to bear everything.

If I am unwilling *à la* Mynster[1534] to idolize the establishment (and this is Mynster's heresy) and in my zeal for morality eventually confuse it with the bourgeois mentality, if I am unwilling to abolish completely the category of the extraordinary and again *à la* Mynster only understand that there have been such ones, understand it only afterward, then I cannot personally reject what has so clearly been laid upon me as a task.

Although Mynster has a certain good-will toward me and in his quiet moments perhaps even more than he admits, it is clear that he regards me as a suspicious and even dangerous person. For this reason he would like to have me out in the country. He thinks things are all right so far, but anything is to be feared from a man of character, especially in relation to the whole network in which he wants to keep life imprisoned. Therefore his advice is entirely consistent for him; from his point of view it is also well-meant for me, inasmuch as he is not particularly scrupulous about damage to a man's inner being just as long as he makes good, in his opinion, in the world. Mynster has never been out in 70,000 fathoms[1535] of water and learned out there; he has always clung to the established order and now has completely accommodated to it. This is what is magnificent about him. I shall never forget, I shall always honor him, always think of my father when I think about him, and no more is needed. But Mynster does not understand me; when he was thirty-six years old he would not have understood me, in fact, he would have resisted understanding me in order not to ruin his career, and now he cannot understand me.

But for God all things are possible.[1536] Humanly speaking, from now on I must be said not only to be running without a clear goal[1537] before me but going headlong toward certain ruin—trusting in God, precisely. This is the victory. This is how I understood life when I was ten years old, therefore, the prodigious polemic in my soul; this is how I understood it when I was twenty-five years old; so, too, now when I am thirty-four. This is why Poul Møller[1538] called me the most thoroughly polemical of men.

VII¹ A 221   January 20, 1847

« **5962**

Only when I am writing do I feel just fine. Then I forget all the disagreeable things in life, all the sufferings, then I am at home with my thoughts and am happy. If I refrain from it for just a few days, I immediately get sick, overwhelmed, depressed, and my head gets stodgy and weighed down. An urge like this, so plentiful, so inexhaustible, which after continuing day after day for five or six years still surges just as copiously, must certainly be a calling from God. To squeeze back this wealth of thoughts still lying in my soul would be torture, a martyrdom, and would render me totally incompetent. And why should it be thrust back? Because I got the idea of wanting to make a martyr of myself by penitentially forcing myself into something for which I, as far as I understand myself, am not suited.[1539] No, God forbid, and God will certainly not leave himself without witness also in the external world. It is hard and depressing to pay out one's own money so as to work harder and more intensely than any man in the kingdom! And in all this work it is hard and depressing to get out of it the persecutions of the cowardly, envious aristocrats and the insults of the rabble. It is hard and depressing to have these prospects: if I work even harder and more intensely, things will get even worse! But I would gladly and patiently put up with all this if I could only succeed in attaining inner assurance that it is not my duty to force myself into a self-chosen martyrdom by taking a position which in a certain sense I could wish for but could neither fill satisfactorily nor be happy in. But becoming an author is not self-chosen; on the contrary it is by virtue of the deepest need and urge of my whole personal being.

God, give me your blessing and assistance, and above all spiritual assurance, spiritual assurance against the doubts that arise within me, for one can always manage to struggle with the world.

The same thing will happen to me this time as earlier in my engagement. Only, God be praised, with this difference: I do not wrong anyone, I do not break any promise, but the similarity is that once again I must steer into the open sea, live in grace and out of grace, utterly in God's power. It is, after all, much more secure to have a steady job in life, an official appointment, it is not nearly so strenuous —but in God's name the other, by the grace of God, is even more secure. But at every moment it takes faith. This is the difference. The majority of people live far too securely in life and therefore get to know God so little. They have permanent positions, never strain themselves to the limit, have the comfort of wife and children—I shall never disparage this happiness, but I believe it my task to dispense with all this. Why should what we read again and again in the New Testament not be allowed. But the trouble is that men have no knowledge at all of what Christianity is, and this is why there is no sympathy for me, this is why I am not understood.

VII[1] A 222   *n.d.*, 1847

« **5963**

Now I must work out the idea of the forgiveness of sins,[1540] in rhetorical form.

VII¹ A 223   *n.d.,* 1847

« **5964**

The following passage was removed from the preface to "The Gospel of Suffering":[1541]

These are Christian discourses, for the life-expression of the discourse, as I understand it, is the essential and the essentially correlative form for Christianity, which is a matter of faith and conviction: Christianity certainly is a fact but the kind of fact that can only be believed, with the result that it can only be talked about or preached about—witness to it is not to its being true (for this is the relation of secular wisdom to its various objects), but witness to it is to the fact that one believes it is true.

VII¹ A 224   *n.d.,* 1847

« **5965**

"We endeavor to win men"[1542]
but before God we stand revealed.
To what extent this is allowed.

VII¹ A 227   *n.d.,* 1847

« **5966**

January 24

God be praised that all the assaults of rabble barbarism have come upon me. Now I have gained time to learn inwardly and to convince myself that it was indeed a gloomy thought to want to live out in a rural parish[1543] and do penance in seclusion and oblivion. Now I stand resolved and rooted to the spot in a way I have never been. If I had not been put through the mill of insults, this gloomy idea would have continued to pester me, for a certain kind of prosperity fosters gloomy ideas; if, for example, I had not had private means, I would never, with my disposition to melancholy, have reached the point I have sometimes reached.

VII¹ A 229   January 24, 1847

« **5967**

One has a superabundance; another is like a superfluity.
One has a superabundance; another is superfluous.[1544]

VII¹ A 246   *n.d.*, 1845–47

« **5968**

[Manuscript of *Bogen om Adler*[1545] (title of English translation, *Authority and Revelation*).]

VII² B 235   *n.d.*, 1846–47

« **5969**

Preface . . .
Copenhagen   January, 1847[1546]

VII² B 270   January, 1847

« **5970**

The structure of the three discourses about the lilies and the birds[1547] is as follows: the first is esthetic, the second ethical, the third religious.

VIII¹ A 1   *n.d.*, 1847

« **5971**

It is certainly fine to write pithy proverbs,[1548] but the one who is supposed to realize them has the difficult task. The particular proverb is always not only one-sided but almost epigrammatically one-sided, but the person who is to live according to it also has to take the other proverbs into consideration.

As an example I cite Jesus Sirach 4:29: Do not struggle against the stream, and 4:30: Defend the truth unto death and the Lord God will then fight for you.[1549]

VIII¹ A 2   *n.d.*, 1847

« **5972**

Despite everything people ought to have learned about my maieutic carefulness, in addition to proceeding slowly and continually letting it seem as if I knew nothing more, not the next thing—now on the occasion of my new upbuilding discourses[1550] they will probably bawl out that I do not know what comes next, that I know nothing about sociality. You fools! Yet on the other hand I owe it to myself to confess before God that in a certain sense there is some truth in it, only not as men understand it—namely, that when I have first presented one aspect sharply, then I affirm the other even more strongly.

Now I have my theme of the next book. It will be called:

"Works of Love."[1551]

VIII[1] A 4   *n.d.*, 1847

« 5973

..... And you, who even though humanly speaking cannot be charged with misusing your gifts, you still do possess fortunate advantages and no doubt sometimes have the self-satisfied feeling that you are able to win people to your side, you who perhaps rarely find anyone you cannot captivate, you who thus seem from the very beginning to have been an object of preference—have you profoundly perceived that God is unchangeable—that all your ingenuity, all your gifts, all your cleverness is not merely wasted but is also as unnoticed and overlooked as a little insect crawling on the ground.

VIII[1] A 5   *n.d.*, 1847

« 5974

The situation will soon become properly ironic again. Over against fatuous political earnestness and the appalling jollity of the speculators, I raised the jest of irony—in a changed context, such as the present one, where practically everyone has become ironic, I become, quite ironically, the most earnest of all.

VIII[1] A 13   *n.d.*, 1847

« 5975 *The Relations of the Three Parts of*
Upbuilding Discourses in Various Spirits

1. Part One[1552]

The design is essentially ethical-ironic and thereby upbuilding, Socratic.

The most ironic category (notice also that it is the absolutely moral category) is singleness, that single individual [*hiin Enkelte*]. The single individual [*den Enkelte*] can, in fact, be every man and, eminently so, any man who ethically and ideally wills to be the highest. No one is excluded by individual differences from eminently being the single individual, and yet it probably is the case that there is no single individual living. This is the relation between facticity and ideality, which is simultaneously just as much moral and ethical as it is ironical.

Incidentally, in order to give maieutic support, in the pseudonymous writings I always used "that single individual" [*hiin Enkelte*] in the sense of differentiation, for of course differential presuppositions are required in order to pursue dialectical developments completely. In the upbuilding or edifying discourses, however, the category "the single individual" [*den Enkelte*] has been used in the clear sense of equality and the moral.

The category of the single individual is just as ironic as it is ethical and definitely both, and then again it is decidedly upbuilding (in the religiousness of immanence) in that it completely abolishes the differences as illusion and establishes the essential equality of eternity.

Note. At times the tone of discourse borders on the comic, yet with ironic pathos. If anyone wants to test it, he will see that wherever in this confessional address he is moved to laughter, he laughs ironically. For example, when it says:[1553] A large number of friends of the good, or of good friends, attached themselves to him—it is true that they believed that they were also attaching themselves to the good, but that certainly must be a misunderstanding, since he himself went around outside [the good]. Or: They erected a building; it was half-timbered (there were many others like it[1554])—and so on in many passages.

This comic tone definitely belongs.

2. Part Two is humorous.

The dialectical in the concept: to learn means that the learner relates himself to the teacher as to his more ideal *genus proximum*. As soon as the teacher takes a lower position within the very same genus and stands below the learner, the situation becomes humorous. For example, to learn from a child or from a dolt, for the child or the dolt can only humorously be called the teacher.

But the situation becomes even more humorous when the teacher and the learner do not have even the same genus in common but in qualitative heterogeneity are related inversely to one another. This is the definitely humorous relation. The lilies and the birds.

The presentation is upbuilding, mitigated by the appealing jest and the jesting earnestness of the humorous. The reader will smile at many points but never laugh, never laugh ironically. The tale of the worried lily, which is also a parable, is clearly humorous. So also is the entire discussion on being clothed.[1555] On the whole, the humorous is present at every point because the design itself is humorous.

> The three discourses are again related to one
> another esthetically, ethically, religiously.

See p. 175 [i.e., VIII¹ A 1].

3. Part Three

See this book, p. 179 [i.e., VIII¹ A 6].

VIII¹ A 15   *n.d.*, 1847

« 5976 *About the Three Discourses 1847*[1556]

It is not by chance that the fairy tale is used in the first discourse, for this is the way life is, especially when habit takes over—so far from the ideal that the ideal requirement must sound like a fairy tale. —Furthermore, all comparisons are avoided this way.

Some may find that these discourses lack earnestness. They think that earnestness in this situation[1557] is to make financial contributions, think up public works, start a new collection campaign, etc., all of which may be very praiseworthy but in the strictest sense is not earnestness. Meanwhile the world has become so prosaic that the only concern conceded to be reality [*Realitet*] is concern for making a livelihood and that again in a vexatious sense as emphasized for provocative purposes by agitators who make money on the poor. Love, repentance, etc., are regarded as chimeras, but money, money, money—

I pledge myself to read these three discourses aloud sometime in eternity, and I am convinced that they will be listened to with pleasure, also by those who here object to them and perhaps insult me. Concern is here gently modified in a childlike and pious way, and this as a happy spirit will remember it. Whether a man here in time is able to act in this way, I will not decide; but if he is so vexed that he defiantly and insultingly turns away from pure evangelical gentleness, then he is not earnest at all but rebellious. Even the sufferer ought to be able to listen sympathetically to an almost childlike but moving interpretation.

Incidentally, Holy Scripture speaks far more severely. Luke 21:34: Do not be weighed down with dissipation, drunkenness, or cares of this life.

When the apostles say to the paralytic:[1558] Gold and silver have I none, but what I have I give you: Stand up and walk—it is said very exaltedly, for a miracle, after all, is more than gold and silver. But if they had said: We have only an idea, an eternal and blessed thought, to offer you: would that not have been a good way to phrase it? In the same way I have neither silver nor gold but a mitigating, moving, truly upbuilding meditation.

In the first discourse we see how the rich birds actually corrupt the poor ones. An almost comic light falls on the rich doves who strut around,[1559] and also an ethical accent, that they are the very ones who have the cares of making a livelihood.

VIII¹ A 16　*n.d.*, 1847

« 5977　*Motion*[1560] *according to Aristotle*

κίνησις in the diversity of the categories is as follows:

in substance	γένεσις–φθορὰ
in quantity	αὔξησις–φθίτις
in quality	ἀλλοίωσις
in relation	φορά.[1561]

See Trendelenburg's two treatises[1562] on the doctrine of categories, p. 188.

See p. 163.

See pp. 136–137

See p. 99　　All this is related to my thesis which is to be found among my logical theses: the difference between a dialectical and a pathos-filled transition.[1563]

Aristotle says that πάθος is the quality in consequence of which change is possible (ἀλλοιοῦσθαι).[1564]

What I have profited from Trendelenburg is unbelievable; now I have the apparatus for what I had thought out years before.

In this book by Trendelenburg there is an index[1565] which is excellent.

VIII² C 1　February, 1847

« 5978

There is no modern philosopher from whom I have profited so much as from Trendelenburg. At the time I wrote *Repetition* I had not yet read anything of his—and now that I have read him, how much more lucid and clear everything is to me. My relationship to him is very special. Part of what has engrossed me for a long time is the whole doctrine of the categories (the problems pertaining to this are found in my older notes, on quarto pieces of paper [i.e., IV C 87–96]. And now Trendelenburg has written two treatises[1566] on the doctrine of categories, which I am reading with the greatest interest.

The first time I was in Berlin, Trendelenburg was the only one I did not take the trouble to hear—to be sure, he was said to be a Kantian. And I practically ignored the young Swede travelling with me who intended to study only under Trendelenburg. O, foolish opinion to which I also was in bondage at the time.

VIII[1] A 18   *n.d.*, 1847

« 5979

"The crowd" is really what I have aimed at polemically, and that I have learned from Socrates. I want to make men aware so that they do not waste and squander their lives. The aristocrats take for granted that there is always a whole mass of men who go to waste. But they remain silent about it, live secluded, and act as if these many, many human beings did not exist at all. This is the wickedness of the aristocrats' exclusiveness—that in order to have an easy life themselves they do not even make people aware.

That is not what I want. I want to make the crowd aware of their own ruin, and if they are unwilling to respond to the good, then I will constrain them with evil. Understand me—or do not misunderstand me. I do not intend to strike them (alas, one cannot strike the crowd) —no, I will constrain them to strike me. Thus I will still be constraining them with evil. For if they strike me first—they will surely become aware —and if they kill me—then they will become unconditionally aware, and I will have won absolute victory. In that respect my constitution is thoroughly dialectical. Already there are many who say, "What does anyone care about Magister Kierkegaard? I'll show him." Ah, but showing me that they do not care about me or taking the trouble to get me to realize that they do not care about me is still dependence. It will work out just that way if one simply has enough ataraxy. They show me respect precisely by showing me that they do not respect me.

Men are not so corrupt that they actually desire evil, but they are blind and really do not know what they are doing. Everything centers on drawing them out into the area of decision. A child can be somewhat unruly toward his father for a long time, but if the father can only get the child to make a real attack, the child is far closer to being saved. The revolt of the "masses" is victorious if we step aside for it so that it never comes to know what it is doing. The crowd is not essentially reflective; therefore, if it puts a man to death, it is *eo ipso* brought to a stop, becomes aware, and deliberates.

The reformer who, as they say, fights a power (a pope, an emperor, in short, an individual man) has to bring about the downfall of the mighty one; but he who with justice alone confronts "the crowd," from which comes all corruption, must see to it that he himself falls.

VIII[1] A 23   n.d., 1847

« **5980**

For many years my depression has prevented me from saying *"Du"*[1567] to myself in the profoundest sense. Between my *"Du"* and my depression lay a whole world of imagination. This is what I partially discharged in the pseudonyms. Just as a person who does not have a happy home goes out as much as possible and would rather not be encumbered with it, so my depression has kept me outside myself while I have been discovering and poetically experiencing a whole world of imagination. Just as a person who has inherited a great estate is never able to become fully acquainted with it, so I in my depression have been related to possibility.

VIII[1] A 27   n.d., 1847

« **5981 *Something about my Punctuation***

With respect to spelling I submit unconditionally to authority (Molbech);[1568] it never occurs to me to want to rectify it, because I know that I am not equipped in that sphere and therefore I readily admit that just about any Danish author is perhaps more meticulous in his spelling than I am.

It is quite different with punctuation. Here I yield to absolutely no one, and I very much doubt that any author can compete with me here. My whole make-up as a dialectician with an unusual sense for rhetoric, all the silent conversations with my own thoughts, and my practice of reading aloud must necessarily make me superior in this field.

I make distinctions in my punctuation. I punctuate differently in a scholarly work than in a rhetorical work. For the majority, who know but one grammar, that is probably quite enough. It follows as a matter of course that I do not by any means presume to submit my books to school boys and very young men as formal patterns of punctuation, just as a good Latin teacher does not usually teach his pupils the finer nuances of the language and the many lovely little secrets of the subjunctive, but he himself uses them in his writing. But sad to say I actually do not know any Danish author who in the ideal sense really pays attention to punctuation; they simply comply with the grammatical standard.

My punctuation is especially deviant in the rhetorical writings because they are so complex. My chief concern is the architectonic-dialectical, that to the eye the shape of the sentences becomes apparent, which, again, if one reads aloud, is rhythm to the voice—and I always have in mind a reader who reads aloud. —This explains why I at times use the comma sparingly. Thus where I want to make a subdivision that formally could be indicated by a comma, I do not subdivide the sentence. For example, "What one owes another or what one owes himself." On this point I carry on a running battle with compositors who well-meaningly insert commas everywhere and disturb the rhythm for me.

It seems to me that most Danish stylists use the period altogether wrongly. They break up all their writing into nothing but short units, but with the result that logic never comes to enjoy proper respect and logically subordinated sentences are coordinated with each other by making each one a sentence.

Above all I must repeat that I have in mind readers who read aloud and who have had practice both in following every little variation in the idea and also in being able to reproduce it orally. I am quite willing to put myself to the test of having an actor or orator accustomed to modulating his voice read a little piece from my discourses as a test—and I am convinced that he will concede that much of what he usually has to decide for himself, much that is usually explained by an instructive hint from the author, is here provided by the punctuation. Abstract grammatical punctuation does not suffice for rhetorical writing, especially with the addition of irony, epigram, subtlety, malevolence with respect to the idea, etc.

VIII[1] A 33   n.d., 1847

« **5982**

In margin of 5981 (VIII[1] A 33):
Just now I note that the elder Fichte, in his correspondence with Schiller[1569] now published by his son, complains apropos of his style that people cannot read aloud with expression.

VIII[1] A 34   n.d.

« **5983**

Generally speaking the question mark is fatuously misused by formal appendage to every interrogative sentence. I often use a semicolon and then a collective question mark. This is also rhetorically correct; one cannot keep on reading numerous questions aloud and give each one the form of a question. Therefore one simply maintains the sustained pace of the question through the whole series.

VIII[1] A 35   *n.d.*, 1847

« 5984

It is also common practice to use a dash[1570] in the sense of a division-mark to begin a minor clause where a new departure would be too much.

VIII[1] A 36   *n.d.*, 1847

« 5985

Ethical accent, pithiness of concept, antithesis, lucidity of two parts of a figure on one line, rhetorical emphasis, etc.: for all this I use a colon and dash,[1571] especially for the ironical in order to make it clear. —As a rule I use the colon for speech.

VIII[1] A 37   *n.d.*, 1847

« 5986 *My Future Punctuation*

Wherever something is quoted, I will not, as previously, use a colon and quotation marks but only quotation marks. In certain cases where the logical accent falls on the single word the colon is not used but spacing or quotation marks. For example, the concept: the neighbor is now written the concept "the neighbor."

Therefore, the colon will be used to form the conclusion and wherever it should be indicated that two clauses are placed on a par with one another in a total context. The colon does this, even makes it perceptible to the eye.

- : -

The colon establishes reflexivity, perspective, and transparency in the sentence in such a way, for example, that by the colon the antecedent clause is carried through the consequent clause and the reverse. The antecedent clause and the consequent clause do not stand alongside each other but in a fundamental relation stand on a par with one another.

So it is with the relation between two clauses. But basically the same is the case with the relation between two ideas in one clause (for example, antitheses); therefore I must use the colon there also. When one clause is a remark and the other is a reply and precisely this is to be expressed, and consequently two ideas ought not be expressed one after the other but their *zugleich*[1572] in the relation of remark and reply, then I use the colon.

Incidentally, the colon ought to be used much more than is done, for example, in connection with definitions. It is one thing to construct a sentence as a simple object; it is a quite different thing also to express thereby that it is a concept. For example, it is one thing to say: what double-mindedness fears is to suffer punishment; it is a quite different thing to say: what double-mindedness fears is: to suffer punishment. This punctuation expresses that to fear punishment is constitutive of double-mindedness, is the definitional mark of double-mindedness, precisely because in it is contained a self-contradiction, a vacillation, a doubleness, which are characteristic of double-mindedness.

VIII[1] A 38   *n.d.,* 1847

« 5987

Now they can do with me what they will—insult me, envy me, stop reading me, bash in my hat, bash in my head, but they cannot in all eternity deny what was my idea and my life, that it was one of the most original thoughts in a long time, and the most original thought in the Danish language: that Christianity needed a maieutic and I understood how to be that, although no one understood how to appreciate it. The category "proclaim Christianity, confess Christ" is not appropriate in Christendom—here the maieutic is exactly right, which presupposes that men possess the highest but wants to help them become aware of what they have.

VIII[1] A 42   *n.d.,* 1847

« 5988

Andersen can tell the fairy tale about the galoshes of good fortune[1573]—but I can tell the fairy tale about the shoe that pinches,[1574] or, more correctly, I could tell it, but because I do not want to tell it but hide it in deep silence I am able to tell something quite different.

VIII[1] A 44   *n.d.,* 1847

« 5989 *Some Observations About the Song of Watchmen*

The accidental, the distinctive in each individual watchman, in his voice, in the way he begins, his intonation, how he begins when the very moment he is supposed to begin he is standing and talking with someone. The "Hau." It is well-known that this is also shouted to oxen. I remember seeing a drove of oxen one time on Vesterbro; they obviously thought that the "Hau" being shouted was for them—but it was the watchman and it almost sounded like: "Hau watchman." —Whether the watchman sings and acts with self-esteem. The variations, for example, "girls and boy" instead of "girl and boy" etc. The genuine romanticism in the watchman who shouts out at the black horse. To call out in the night; the situation out on the highway, the nocturnal stillness.

VIII^1 A 45   *n.d.*, 1847

« **5990**

Pastor Lind,[1575] who is reforming at the reformatory, is an excellent man, and assuredly no one can be happier than I am that he has been so fortunate as to get what he himself no doubt regards as the only position perfectly suited to him. For a long time now he has had a tendency and propensity to view the world around him within the category "reformatory" and by preference concentrated on an understanding of individuals, wanting to improve them. This tendency could have developed very easily into something Don Quixotic, whereas by now getting such a natural and meaningful channel it will certainly make him outstanding and his work extraordinarily significant in the reformatory.

VIII^1 A 46   *n.d.*, 1847

« **5991**

In all likelihood the wiseacres who know how to rattle off everything will charge my Christian discourses[1576] with not containing the Atonement. Consequently, after five years of having the chance to learn from me how maieutically I proceed, they have remained every bit as wise—will probably go on being that. First the first and then the next. But these confounded men muddle into one speech all that I develop piece by piece in big books, always leaving behind in each book one stinger which is its connection with the next. But the insipidness of the speculators and of some clergy is incredible.

VIII^1 A 49   *n.d.*, 1847

« **5992**

The Incorruptible Nature of
the Inward Man[1577]
A Christian Reflection

VIII^1 A 61   *n.d.*, 1847

« **5993**

Job 17:1–2, "My spirit is broken; my days are extinct; the grave is ready for me; no one is around me but mockers." This is the way to arrange it, and then omit the next clause; then it is rhetorically excellent. In the Bible there is a period before "no one."[1578]

VIII[1] A 68   *n.d.,* 1847

« **5994**

In the same book by Carriere[1579] a remarkable line is quoted on p. 214: *der Mensch steht höher, wenn er auf sein Unglück tritt.*[1580]

And on p. 215 a line by Boccaccio: "*lieber thun und bereuen als nicht thun und bereuen.*[1581]

VIII[1] A 71   *n.d.,* 1847

« **5995**

. . . . . And when I see utter confusion and sheer misunderstanding I know that there is one ally I can still call upon for help. Well do I know that your form is terror, that you are not given to men for consolation, but yet I dare find consolation in you, for behind you I find assurance; then no one prevents me anymore from striving for what is right. Happy is the man who, no matter how much the envy of men has worked against him while he lived, yet lived in such a way that as soon as he is dead everyone will envy him for having lived in that way, lived in such a way that everyone would say in the hour of his death that it was the right [for which he had lived]. What human envy and corruption use to accuse the living becomes a eulogy for him when he is dead.

VIII[1] A 81   *n.d.,* 1847

« **5996**

I now would like to give a series of twelve lectures on the dialectic of communication.[1582] After that, twelve lectures on erotic love, friendship, and love.[1583]

VIII[1] A 82   *n.d.,* 1847

« **5997**

Men do not really understand the dialectical, least of all the dialectic of inversion. Men have the same experience with this kind of dialectic as dogs have with learning to walk on two legs: they succeed for a moment but then promptly go back to walking on all fours. They understand the dialectic of inversion at the time it is being presented to them, but as soon as the presentation is over they understand it again in terms of the dialectic of immediacy. —For example, to have but one reader or very few is easily understood in terms of the dialectic of immediacy: that it is too bad for the author etc., but that it is very nice of him to make the best of it etc. But in the dialectic of inversion the author himself voluntarily works to bring this about, desires only one or a few readers—this, you see, will never be popular. — Yesterday Molbech[1584] wrote to me (in a note dated April 29, 1847) that the sell-out of *Either/Or* is "a phenomenon in the literary history of our day which may need to be studied." And why? The Councillor of State did not know that it has been sold out for a long time, he did not know that a year ago Johannes Climacus in *Concluding Unscientific Postscript*[1585] expressed his opinion in the matter, that two years ago Reitzel[1586] talked about a new edition, that I am the obstacle; he has no idea of how I work against myself in the service of the dialectic of inversion and, if possible, in a somewhat cleansing service of truth. Whether right now at this time it would be possible to sell out a book of mine, I do not know, but before I began to set teeth on edge somewhat I really did manage to do it. A few flattering words to this one and that, no more than a half or a tenth of what an author usually does to get his books sold—and they would have been sold out. And even now, when I have set people's teeth on edge so much, even now it would all begin again if I simply let up a bit, became less productive (for what actually antagonizes them the most is the extent of my productivity), write a little book or a smaller book and only one (*Upbuilding Discourses in Various Spirits*)—then it would all begin again. That I was playing a cunning game, that I had a very large book[1587] finished and ready, that in order to have a witness to refer to, I showed it to Giødwad[1588] the same day we began proof-reading the *Discourses,* that I had counted on trapping P. L. Møller[1589] or some other bandit to write a eulogy of the *Upbuilding Discourses* and say: "It is obvious that Magister Kierkegaard, if he is willing to take the time, can produce something great etc.; much greater pains than usual have been taken with this book and for that reason it has taken him longer etc." A pack of lies which, however, would be believed and would be regarded as very sensible, also that I did a botchy job with the larger books. O, what a fate to be something out of the ordinary in a market town! Then I would have had to rush ahead with the large book, with Giødwad's testimony that it was finished at the same time, etc. And then what? Then the provincials with whom I live would have become angry once again, and why?

Because they cannot bear the scale. They cannot understand working on that scale and doing it as assiduously as I do: ergo, the author is doing a botchy job.

No wonder I am nauseated time and again by the rabble one must live with, no wonder that I can keep on working only by shutting my eyes. For when I shut my eyes I am before God, and then everything is all right, then I personally am not of any importance, which, humanly and comparatively speaking, I am insofar as it is my lot to live in a small town and with nonentities.

VIII^1 A 84   *n.d.,*   1847

« **5998**

To be trampled to death by geese is a lingering death, and to be torn to death by *envy* is also a slow way to die. While rabble barbarism insults me (for what comes out in a newspaper once would not mean much if it did not give the vulgar the mandate to insult one day after day, abuse one on the public street—schoolboys, brash students, store-clerks, and all the scum yellow journalism stirs up), upper class envy looks on with approval. It does not grudge me that. And does one want to live or does one choose to live under such conditions? No, but I am nevertheless happy that I know I have *acted.* Incidentally, nibbling mistreatment like that is the most distressing kind. Everything else has an end, but this does not cease. To sit in church where a couple of louts have the impudence to sit down beside one in order to gawk at one's trousers[1590] and insult one so loudly that every word is audible. But this is what I am used to. The fact that brazenness has a mandate in the newspapers makes the smart alecks think they are justified, yes, that they are agents of public opinion. And I realize this, but in a certain sense I have been in error about Denmark, for I did not believe that rabble barbarism actually was public opinion in Denmark, but I shall gladly testify that this is the case, something that can be factually demonstrated very easily.

VIII^1 A 99   *n.d.,*   1847

« **5999**

If I were to die *now,* the world would believe that I died from mortification over persecution, and it might serve the world right, for in a certain sense it may be said that it did not contribute to prolonging my life. But otherwise the real truth about my life is something altogether different. When I left her[1591] I chose death—for that very reason I have been able to work so enormously. That she cried out in parody: I will die, while I pretended to be just beginning a frivolous life, is all in order—she is a woman, I am an ironist, and yet the cause lies even deeper. That which induced me to leave her, my deep-seated unhappiness, naturally took on an entirely different meaning for me, since because of it I had to make her unhappy and take a murder on my conscience. From then on my dejection won out over me; it could not be otherwise. To justify my behavior to her I must constantly be reminded of my basic unhappiness. So it is.

Strange that I have lived out thirty-four years.[1592] I cannot fathom it; I was so sure of dying before that *Geburtstag*[1593] or on it that I actually am tempted to assume that the date of my birth is a mistake and that I will still die on my thirty-fourth.

VIII[1] A 100   *n.d.*, 1847

« **6000**

NB[2]

1847 May 14[1594]

VIII[1] A 107   May 14, 1847

« **6001**

Naturally I could have made my life far easier, humanly speaking, and in just that way I could have been loved and highly esteemed. But do I have the right to do this to God? And God is still the one with whom I associate most. No one gives this a thought. Alas, this is why life is so strenuous for me. When God as it were withdraws himself a little from me, I have no intimate to cling to, and then there is the incessant charge that I do that—precisely what I am doing—because God is all important to me.[*]

If I had lived in the Middle Ages I dare say I would have entered a monastery and devoted myself to doing penance. In our day I have interpreted that need in me differently. All self-torturing in a monastery only leads to delusion, but I have chosen something else. I have chosen to serve the truth, and at one of the two points where it is the most thankless work of all. Here I have the unity of doing penance and doing something beneficial. If such work is to lead to anything, it is to sheer sacrifice, sheer inconvenience, and the remuneration is never anything but ingratitude, lack of appreciation, scorn. But this satisfies me in another sense, just like penance. It is sufficiently clear that I am doing something of benefit, and I am convinced that later on it will become more clear, especially after my death, for it belongs to my idea of penance just as to my idea of work: the work is of such a nature that it will not be essentially understood until after my death, but this corresponds to my idea of penance.

I know very well that God does not wish a person to martyr himself in order to please him, that precisely this does not please God; but God will permit or forgive me that way of doing penance if I do not attach any meritoriousness to it but do it only because I cannot do otherwise. —The penance of the Middle Ages was wrong in itself and wrong again in that it was supposed to be meritorious. No, penance, if it is to be tolerated and permitted, must be a need in a person and he must therefore constantly be willing to pray God for forgiveness for doing it. A young girl really in love does not regard it as meritorious to caress her beloved; it is her joy to do it, and yet she asks for forgiveness.

[*] *In margin:* Everyone who in truth has a conception of what it means to be associated with God will also understand me.

VIII^1 A 116   *n.d.,* 1847

« 6002

What strengthens me more and more is my original, my first, my deepest, my unaltered view that I truly have not chosen this life because it would be brilliant, but as a consolation of penance in all my wretchedness. I have frequently enough set forth the dialectic of the paradox: it is not higher than the universal but in fact lower. And only subsequently a little higher. But the first, the pressure, is so strong that joy over the latter cannot be taken in vain. It is the thorn in the flesh.

VIII^1 A 119   *n.d.,* 1847

« 6003

Wednesday

Dear Peter,[1595]

The birthday on which you congratulate me and about which you say that it "often and uncustomarily has been in your thoughts these days," that birthday has also frequently and for a long time preceding it been in my own thoughts. For I became thirty-four years old.[1596] In a certain sense it was utterly unexpected. I was already very surprised when—yes, now I may say it without fear of upsetting you—you became thirty-four years old.[1597] Both Father and I had the idea that nobody in our family would live past his thirty-fourth year. However little I

otherwise agreed with Father, in a few singular ideas we had an essential point of contact, and in such conversations Father was always
almost enthusiastic about me, for I could depict an idea with lively
imagination and pursue it with daring consistency. In fact, a curious
thing about Father was that what he had most of, what one least
expected, was imagination, albeit a melancholy imagination. The
thirty-fourth year was, then, to be the limit, and Father was to outlive
us all. That is not the way it has turned out—I am now in my thirty-fifth
year.

About the rest of my letter to you: you do not appear to have
understood it quite as I intended. I did not intend to sell at just this
time, but I wanted to obtain your answer to my question about whether
or not you wanted to increase your mortgage as proposed. This would,
as I remarked, also be convenient for me whenever I might decide to
sell.

It appeared to me to be quite desirable for you to be the holder
of a first mortgage of 10,000 rdl. I shall not add any more about this,
for you yourself must be able to see very well what speaks in favor of
it, and better than I what might speak against it. It is only my intention
that the wish should agree with what is in your best interest. If it does,
you might do me the favor of granting my wish, and moreover the
favor is of such a kind that I can accept it gladly because no sacrifice
is involved on your part, for your property invested in such an unconditional first mortgage is just as safe as in any stock or bond, indeed,
probably safer.

You yourself surely do see that a first mortgage of 7,000 rdl. on
my house is a very small first mortgage; but on the other hand, since
you do hold a first mortgage, I am unable to offer anybody else terms
other than those of a second mortgage, which is not very easy to
obtain, however. Thus you who hold a small first mortgage are the only
one to whom I can apply, and even if you were someone else, it would
still seem reasonable that that someone else would grant my wish,
provided he were otherwise able to do so.

Please think about doing it. In a certain sense you do not know
very much about my life, its goal and its purpose, but you do know that
it is very strenuous, which in a certain sense you may not care for—
perhaps because you are not familiar with it. There is a necessary
silence with respect to my life, and it is precisely by silence that it gains
its strength. Even if I wanted to speak, that which is most important
to me and which most profoundly determines my life would be that

about which I must be silent. From this arises a disparity in my relationship with anyone who has, or to whom I might wish to give, a claim to closer confidence. Therefore I have never wanted to make it appear as though I maintained a confidential relationship with anybody, precisely because I knew that even if he did not discover that disparity, I myself would realize it. In my relationship with those few people with whom I have had a little closer association (for in a discursive sense I have had association with countless numbers), I have myself on one occasion pointed out to them that there was a discrepancy in our relationship, and I have added that the relationship, such as mine was to them, was dear to me but that no real confidence was possible for me.

Thus now also in relation to you. I can well understand that it must offend you or seem peculiar to you that in your relationship with another human being who probably has experienced a great deal internally, you are not more intimately informed *qua* brother. Leave it at that and consider if it is not a sort of honesty on my part to have stated that this is so. I can only say this much—that from the beginning, with sufferings which perhaps few can imagine because I was given strength to conceal them, I acknowledge more and more happily that Governance has granted me infinitely more than I had ever expected. Even now, after having worked incessantly in this way for several years without the least bit of outside encouragement, and on top of this even having been for a long time the object of ugly treatment by rabble vulgarity, by coarseness, and by curiosity, day in and day out—even now I feel grateful appreciation that I work more easily and am in better health than before, indeed, that this really has worked for my own good and added one more string to my instrument instead of damaging the old strings. You see, if you would join me in taking pleasure in that, I would be pleased.

Anyway, I could wish to speak with you at greater length sometime, especially now that I am thirty-four years old, and gradually move toward a possible change in the outer circumstances of my life by assuring myself of a livelihood after all. But I do not want to be precipitate about this. So much happiness has been granted me with respect to my work that I must in no way at all disturb my mind by too much haste. Therefore I will probably come down to you some time and stay for a few days. Greetings to Jette, Poul.

Your
S.K.

[Address:]
To
Dr. Kierkegaard, Pastor
Pedersborg
v. Sorøe

[Postmark:]
Copenhagen
5/20 1847

Letters, no. 149   May [19], 1847

« 6004

In accordance with journal NB,[1598] p. 251 [i.e., VIII^1 A 82], I have recently begun to work out some lectures on the dialectic of ethical and ethical-religious communication.[1599] In the meantime it has become clear to me that I am not qualified to give lectures. I am accustomed to working things out in detail; the burgeoning fertility of my style and exposition, every line thoroughly thought out, is too essential for me. If I were to give lectures I would insist on working them out like everything else and as a consequence read them aloud from manuscript, which I do not care to do. But I cannot be satisfied with any other method.

It is quite true that a little class would contribute to my effort, create a greater ingress for my ideas, etc., at the moment. But let it go. My ideas will gain entry, all right, and then will have just the right place. The situation will change, however long I must put up with the impertinence of my contemporaries, who at most have just a few minutes to spend looking into books, or hardly that, but plenty of time to be insulting.

As a rule, contemporaries always miss the point; they cannot forget that the author, after all, looks like them and everybody else etc. But my contemporaries are particularly clever about appraising the cut of my trousers[1600]—and there my contemporaries are right, that is just about the only thing about me they understand.

VIII^1 A 120 *n.d.*, 1847

« 6005

So I once again have put the lectures[1601] away and have taken up my interrupted work (the first part of which I have finished): "Works of Love."[1602] The dialectic of communication must be done as a book.

VIII^1 A 121   *n.d.*, 1847

« **6006**

It would not be difficult for me to make my life far easier and myself loved and respected merely by making my existence dialectically much less strenuous, by not standing unconditionally alone but, instead, chattily becoming a little association of a few individuals, acquiring adherents. No enemies are more dangerous than those who really do want to become adherents. I also have a few of these. They have understood me up to a point; they have come so close that they now wish me to join—through a misunderstanding on my part—with them.

In other respects human stupidity is extremely likable. I am constantly charged with being an egotist. What, then, is egotism? It is making one's personal life as strenuous as possible, and not wanting to have a comfortable life.

But I will hold out and will hold myself to the long perspective. If, by means of an inconsistency and by surrendering, I were to win, let us make the assumption for the time being, the approval of all men so that they came over to my side—ah, then I would have failed my idea and everything is lost. On the other hand, if I have stood entirely alone, with my every sacrifice an alienation, and I die this way: then everything will be in order. The greater the tension of the bow on the bow-string, the greater the momentum of the arrow, and the farther the momentum can carry it, the better. Therefore my whole life exists for one purpose alone—to give the idea momentum into the future. I do not intend to parcel myself out and use a few years for giving the idea momentum and then in the remaining years settle down in this accomplishment. The category of "individuality" [*Enkelthedens*] is all too crucial to risk being bungled. When I am dead, then the adherents may come, but the impression I have made is unchanged. The category of individuality is the category of eternity, and therefore within temporality it is altogether the most strenuous and the most sacrificing. It will be a long time before it gets any power in temporality, where cowardice flourishes.

Although I constantly alienate and am not at all flattered by the approval of temporality, I still have a considerable rapport with men, yes, no other living author has it to the degree I have. People are busily engaged in insulting me and ridiculing me, but they are not aware at all that a card laid is a card played, that in the end I will still have made an impression on them. It is all part of the consistency of my idea, it will all contribute to give the idea momentum if I fall or am separated from it by death.

The tragedy of our time is that it is altogether momentary. If a man gets an idea, he wants to have it promptly accepted. *Ja, Glück zu!*[1603] If someone else had gotten the idea of individuality, he would immediately have supplied it with so many adherents that the whole thing would have fizzled out since the manifestation would have become the mob of followers and the idea of individuality would have been disregarded. *Qua* dialectician I am still a little better informed. At this moment there are no irregularities, not a single straw, and I hope there will be none before my death, in order that what becomes manifest will be that it was the idea of individuality, in the service of which I stood completely alone just for that reason, and yet noticed by almost all. This is correct. To live alone in an out-of-the-way place with the idea of individuality is not consistent, not the most scrupulous expression for the idea. But to stand alone and then have everyone against one is dialectically self-evident, for the very fact that all are against me helps make it conspicuous that one is standing alone—that is dialectical and that is the victory.

I dare boldly say that every man, if I were to explain this to him in a calm and quiet hour, would understand it completely, and the next second he would not understand it. I have tried, I can explain something to a man and then say to him: Watch out now, I am going to play a trick on you. And even though I have forewarned him, I can still confuse him with the deception. An essential ironist must always be inexhaustible in changing the deception. Therefore when a person has not himself completely understood something, one can take it away from him again by means of the deception. In the first few moments he says: Aha! it is deception. He relies on the direct communication. But now the deception is placed between us, and the trick on my part is to keep in character. As soon as I consistently maintain it, he is again confused. Only the person who himself understands what he understands cannot be deceived. Everyone else can be deceived, even if in no other way than by getting him to imagine that no one can deceive him. If I had said to a man: Watch out now, I am going to trick you, he would perhaps answer: That you cannot do. Then I would answer: You are right; some time must elapse, for now you are too prepared —but in a few days. And having said that, I would begin at once, for now he would have been made unwary the very first moment.

VIII[1] A 124   *n.d.*, 1847

« **6007**

With the press as degenerate as it is, human beings eventually will surely be transformed into clods. A newspaper's first concern has to be circulation; from then on the rule for what it publishes can be: the wittiness and entertainment of printing something that has no relation to communication through the press. How significant! How easy to be witty when misuse of the press has become the newly invented kind of witticism.

For example, they write that a certain well-known person (mentioned by name) wears an embroidered shirt. This is written and then read by the whole market town where the lunatic press thrives. The man is cartooned with an embroidered shirt and this treatment goes on for half a year—and naturally is the most widely read of everything read in the market town. If this is not either lunacy or idiocy, then I know of no other alternative. People are simply too immediate and momentary, but on this scale it is a *non plus ultra*—to use the circulation of the press to discuss for half a year something which, after all, the most addle-brained person ought to be sufficiently human not to talk about for more than five minutes—it can only lead to idiocy.

VIII¹ A 133   *n.d.*, 1847

« **6008**

After a laborious process of study and development and after painstaking effort continued over a long period, the most gifted intellects of a country eventually become authors—and authors of books. But books are seldom read in this country. But the daily newspaper has wide circulation and is read by everybody. Here, then, seen from the point of view of the idea, are all those hollow and bandy-legged, clumsy and flat-footed as well as clumsy-fingered, half-witted but sly, reprehensible fellows called journalists, busily operating, and their cogitations are read by all. *Pro dii immortales!*[1604] Suppose there is only one megaphone on a ship and the cook's mate has appropriated it, an act which all regarded as appropriate. Everything the cook's mate has to communicate ("Some butter on the spinach" or "Fine weather today" or "God knows if there's something wrong below in the ship," etc.) is communicated through the megaphone, but the captain has to give his commands solely by means of his voice, for what the captain has to say is not so important. Yes, the captain finally has to ask the cook's mate to help him so that he can be heard. When the cook's mate was so good as to "report" the order, by going through the cook's mate and his megaphone the order sometimes became completely garbled. In that case the captain strained his small voice in vain, because the ship's mate, aided by his megaphone, was heard. Finally the cook's mate got control, because he had the megaphone. *Pro dii immortales!*

VIII[1] A 135   *n.d.*, 1847

« **6009** *My Farewell Lines at Death:*

"Now let me see you who have been my contemporaries decorate my grave and say: If we had been his contemporaries, he would not have been treated as he was."

VIII[1] A 139   *n.d.*, 1847

« **6010**

Just when I wanted to bring down the dictatorship of Copenhagen, orders came to appear in a new role: the victim of persecution. I shall endeavor to play it equally well. It has been said that it is not possible to be persecuted in this day and age. We will see, but if I succeed I am sure that people will say: He is himself responsible—and they are the very same people who protest that no one can ever be persecuted in this day and age. O, human stupidity, how inhuman you are!

VIII[1] A 153   *n.d.*, 1847

« **6011**

With a thorn in my flesh,[1605] my life is pointed toward achieving something I never dreamed of. But the question I have to ask myself now and then is whether I should concentrate my attention on getting the thorn out of the flesh, if possible. That would make me happier in the finite sense, but I would be lost in the infinite sense. Have I the right to do it, even if it were possible, which I doubt—in my early days I did indeed try to do something like this. This explains why I am a long way from trying to become famous with high-flown ideas. The thorn in the flesh has shattered me finitely once and for all—but infinitely I leap all the more lightly. Perhaps this is the way it should be. Perhaps God would rather have a man who is unwell and licks his thorn and is neither healed nor infinitely helped. But there is a kind of pietism, a tragic spiritual asceticism, which believes that the thorn in the flesh is given to a man merely so that he may sit and whimper and look at the thorn instead of using the thorn to rise higher; for that is

how it is, however odd it is in certain sense: with the help of the thorn
in my foot I leap higher than anyone with feet in the best condition.

VIII¹ A 156   *n.d.*, 1847

« 6012

God's eye has spotted me in my conscience and now it has been
made impossible for me to forget that this eye sees me. Having been
looked at by God, I had to and have to look to God.

VIII¹ A 158   *n.d.*, 1847

« 6013

In a way I am living like a fish in water to which a disagreeable
ingredient has been added, making it impossible for fish to breathe in
it. My atmosphere has been tainted for me. Because of my melancholy
and my enormous work I needed a situation of solitude in the crowd
in order to rest. So I despair. I can no longer find it. Curiosity sur-
rounds me everywhere. I drive thirty-five miles to my beloved forest[1606] looking for simple solitude: Alas, curiosity everywhere. These
tiresome people are like flies, living off others.

I know very well that Heiberg and the like Christianly explain my
walking the streets[1607] so much as vanity—that I do it to be seen. I
wonder if it is also to be seen that I walk about even more, if possible,
in Berlin,[1608] where not a soul knows me?

VIII¹ A 163   *n.d.*, 1847

« 6014

Absolutely right. My *Upbuilding Discourses in Various Spirits* met with
approval, especially the last one,[1609] and why? Because they are short
and because the whole book, compared to what I usually come out
with, is small. This, you see, is the heart of the matter. Pamphlet
literature. I have held back the big book about Adler, and now people
have been deluded into becoming profound and perspicacious critics
—they see but one little book, ergo, I have spent all my time on that,
ergo, it has been written with painstaking care. —I am actually obliged
to disguise my capabilities. If I let them see the actual wingspread, the
gossip that I scamp my work will start all over again. Wretched market
town! And Heiberg and his kind take part in this nonsense—because
he himself is a pamphlet author, and therefore has to maintain that as
a rule a large work is slovenly, especially since it took such a short time.

VIII¹ A 164   *n.d.*, 1847

« **6015**

It will surely end with my collapse. And when I have collapsed, when they wake up to the fact that something ought to have been done for me because my severely strained existence was doubly taxed by concern about making ends meet[1610]—then I will once again be misunderstood. Then they will say: But why didn't he say anything, he who could so easily have achieved something; why did he keep still and act as if the nonsense of the world were the only external trouble he had. What do people understand anyway! No, a philosopher may die but he may not speak; a philosopher may die for his consistency, but he may not be inconsistent. The very silence that kept me in infinity was my strength—one single word, and my strength would have gone. If this is a mistake, then my greatness is in the same area as my mistake. But that is the way I have been brought up, and that is how I have understood life.

An essential part of my work was to give the appearance of living in abundance. For that very reason I am regarded as lacking earnestness—and I did not have a job either. That again indirectly condemns my life. But I have said nothing—I have simply acted by existing infinitely myself.

VIII[1] A 170   *n.d.*, 1847

« **6016**

At one time my only wish was to be a police official. It seemed to me to be an occupation for my sleepless, intriguing mind. I had the idea that there, among the criminals, were people to fight: clever, vigorous, crafty fellows. Later I realized that it was good that I did not become one, for most police cases involve misery and wretchedness—not crimes and scoundrels. They usually involve a paltry sum and some poor devil.

My next wish was to become a pastor. But is it not just the same. How really few are the men who have a true religious need. The troubles and miseries of the majority of people are purely of this world—but that is too spongy ground for using the hydraulic jack of the religious. Give us what is strictly necessary, give us money, give us a job, etc.: that is the concern—and that is the consolation sought. Here again it farcically involves a paltry sum and is a comedy of having to lift trifles with a screw-jack.

In that respect one can presuppose nothing and actually has to begin by developing the need, if possible; but again that is just as difficult, since most people do not have the need to have the need developed.

VIII¹ A 171   n.d., 1847

« 6017

The high prices and the bread riots[1611] are very supportive and resuscitating to my whole author-existence. Ten eulogizing reviews, one hundred adherents could not benefit my cause in the same way. Now it will become apparent that I have carried the future, not myself —while all have looked upon me as queer, vain, etc.

VIII¹ A 172   n.d., 1847

« 6018

No city in Europe is as demoralizing as Copenhagen. That is because Copenhagen cannot be compared to other large cities—for it is the only one in a country, the only one in a language—and in a country which is completely wrapped up in Copenhagen, for it has never had a landed aristocracy (as Sweden, for example). Any large city which has a consciousness of being a small part of a large country must, for the sake of appearance, maintain a little modesty and decorum—for, after all, the other cities may find out. But in Copenhagen demoralization can say (as the fool in David's psalm): No one sees me. That is, when everybody or the majority in the only little big-city in this country is infected and then agree to capitulate more and more to all these loathsome passions of envy, stupidity, the market-town spirit: for no one sees us.

Furthermore, if an individual living in a large city in Europe became a victim of the meanness of envy, he would, as author, artist, etc., belong to the whole country and could then go to another large city in the same country. And who would suffer thereby? Quite rightly the city where he lived previously. But one cannot leave Copenhagen without leaving Denmark, the Danish language, the nationality. But this is altogether out of proportion. Here again Copenhagen benefits —insofar as total demoralization can be said to be fortunate. Instead of perceiving for itself and considering what a little country it is and how careful it ought to be with whatever good and excellent thing it has, the country boasts that it can force people to remain here—and be mistreated.

Moreover, only in a city like Copenhagen is it conceivable that

someone can be so prominent that all are able to agree to envy him.
But this situation is the climax of envy.

VIII¹ A 174   *n.d.*, 1847

« 6019

June 9

In a certain sense all my troubles are due to this: if I had not had
private means, it would not have been possible for me to keep the
dreadful secret of my melancholy. (Merciful God, what a dreadful
wrong my father did me in his melancholy—an old man who unloads
all his depression on a poor child, to say nothing of what was even
more dreadful, and yet for all that the best of fathers). But then I would
never have become what I have become. I would have been forced
either to go insane or to fight my way through. Now I have succeeded
in making a *salto mortale*[1612] into the life of pure spirit.

But then again as such I am completely heterogeneous to men
generally. What I actually lack is the physical and the physical presuppositions.

VIII¹ A 177   June 9, 1847

« 6620

People have continually done me an indescribable wrong by continually regarding as pride that which was intended only to keep the
secret of my melancholy. Obviously I have achieved what I wanted to
achieve, for hardly anyone has ever felt any sympathy for me.

VIII¹ A 179   *n.d.*, 1847

« 6021

As stated,[1613] one must be constrained to decisions of finitude—
the joy of freedom is precisely to venture out in decisions of infinity,
and only through freedom can one make decisions of infinity. Most
people do not understand this at all, for they are constrained to venture out in decisions of finitude—and they have no acquaintance with
the infinite. It is just the opposite with me. I ventured out on the sea
of life with a major leak from the very beginning—and simply by the
enormous effort to keep my life afloat I have developed a high level
of mental-spiritual life. It has been successful. I have looked upon my
torment as my thorn in the flesh and have recognized the eminent by
the rankling of the thorn and the rankling of the thorn by the eminent.

This is how I understood myself. In any other circumstance I would have tried to get the damage more or less repaired.

In a certain respect people disgust me because their sufferings are so *nichtige*.[1614] They have no intimation either of the torment or of how it increases in relation to talent.

But if I had not been favored externally, I would have been compelled to see whether repairs could be made. It might have been successful, too, simply because I would have been constrained. But precisely because I was as free as I was, when I as well as my physician had to say the outcome of the repair job would be very doubtful (and it was doubtful precisely because I was not constrained), I did make the right choice. In such a situation constraint is the only thing that helps, for infinity is too great a power to be applied all by itself to something like that.

Paul speaks of being ἀφορισμένος[1615]—this I have been from my earliest childhood. My torment was first of all the suffering within me and then again that my suffering and misery were always regarded as pride. I am like the lord whom the poor day laborer envied—until he saw that he had no legs.

People have admired my talents and for that very reason have wanted me to participate with others, come along, etc. When I would not, they regarded it as pride and therefore they grudge me everything. Ah, the reason was suffering and torment which would have driven the average man insane in half a year. They think it is pride, and therefore, I might almost say, they hope and expect me to go mad. What saves me, again, is not pride but suffering.

VIII[1] A 185   *n.d.*, 1847

« **6022**

Diogenes is supposed to have said that he who has never made another person angry is a poor sort of man.[1616]

VIII[1] A 197   *n.d.*, 1847

« **6023**

What I lack is the physical energy—to loaf; my energies are mental-spiritual, and all one can do with them is work.

VIII[1] A 200   *n.d.*, 1847

« **6024**

This is an excellent story; a little pruning would improve it.

A clergyman passes himself off as an ordinary man of the world and looks for a frivolous woman who will have an affair with him. He makes one condition, she must guarantee that no one will find out, "for imagine what that would mean, since I am of the cloth." She takes him several places in the vicinity but none seems sufficiently safe to the clergyman. Finally she takes him to a completely lonely place and says that no one can see us here—except God. The clergyman says, "How can God see us here—and he was the very last person I wanted to see me."

Abraham of St. Clara, *Sämtl. W.*,[1617] Lindau, 1845.
Vol. 15, pp. 54–55.
VIII[1] A 204   *n.d.*, 1847

« 6025

From earliest childhood my heart has been pierced by an arrow of grief. As long as it is there I am ironic—if it is drawn out, I will die.
VIII[1] A 205   *n.d.*, 1847

« 6026

On the picture which has Commander Sølling[1618] and a pilot boat on one side, a wreck on the other, there is inscribed underneath on one side: poverty and violent death, on the other: prosperity and natural death—alas, consequently "death" on both sides.
VIII[1] A 207   *n.d.*, 1847

« 6027

Abraham of St. Clara (*S. W.*,[1619] XV and XVI, p. 200) relates that when Dominicus became very popular in Tolosa for his preaching he left and went to Carcasson. When asked the reason, he answered: In Tolosa there are many who esteem me; in Carcasson there are many who mock me and speak against me.
VIII[1] A 212   *n.d.*, 1847

« 6028

[Set of Abraham a St. Clara, *Sämmtliche Werke*, I–XXI (Passau, Lindau: 1835–47), *ASKB* 294–311, with corners folded, sidelining, and underlining by Kierkegaard.]
VIII[2] C 2:1–61   *n.d.*, 1847–48

« 6029

The following words could be used *as a motto for a "Self-Defense."*

Open your hearts to us; we have wronged no one, we have corrupted no one, we have taken advantage of no one.

II Corinthians 7:2.

VIII¹ A 217   *n.d.*, 1847

« **6030**

Dear Sir:[1620]

It is not possible for me to be more specific about *Concluding Postscript* because I lack the necessary information. According to Luno's[1621] letter of July 30, 1847, you received 250 copies in February 1846 and 244 copies on July 11. But according to your account, dated May 4, 1847, you had an unsold remainder of 89 copies. In other words, since you had a remainder of 89 copies as of May 4, 1847, and nonetheless obtained 244 copies on July 11, 1847, from Luno, a fair number must have been sold. However, from my itemized account you will see more or less how I have calculated. I have not asked for one half of the bookstore price for any remainder, and for several I have only asked considerably less than half. With respect to *Concluding Postscript,* my claim will be 40 percent of the bookstore price on the remainder.[1622]

Concerning my *Upbuilding Discourses in Various Styles and Spirits,* this particular book was published in 1847, and therefore I can have no idea how many copies have been sold. Luno's bill of March 10, 1847, was for 287 rdl., 12 mk.[1623] Of this sum I myself have paid Luno 87 rdl., because he wanted it for paper expenditures. You have very kindly allowed the transfer of 200 rdl. to your account with Luno. But you can see for yourself that before I decide anything further, I must have some idea of the sales, as well as have my 87 rdl. returned separately. But if you want to include that sum in order to settle the matter, as I myself do also, then please make an offer that conforms with my system of calculation, which you must know by now. Undoubtedly not a few have been sold. But now that I really look into this, I see that on the whole sales have not been bad, with the exception of *Two Ages.*

It is self-evident then that throughout we are speaking only about the remainder, and not about the ownership rights to a new printing.

The question of *Either/Or* may be left until some other time.

And so until Monday evening!

Yours,

S. Kierkegaard

		Bookstore retail price	My offer

(1) *Fear and Trembling*
        Remainder with you 13
               Luno . . . . . . <u>191</u>
               204 @ 1 rdl.   204 rdl.   100 rdl.

(2) *Prefaces*
        Remainder with you 195
               Luno . . . . . . <u>122</u>
               317 @ 3 mk.   158 rdl. 3 mk.   70 rdl.
NB. I have since noticed that the retail price is
3 mk., 8 sk., but I am too lazy to add it up again.

(3) *Repetition*
        Remainder with you 38
               Luno . . . . . . <u>215</u>
               253 @ 5 mk.   210 rdl. 5 mk.   100 rdl.

(4) *Stages on Life's Way*
               with you 108
        Remainder with Luno . . . . . <u>172</u>
               280 @ 3 rdl.   840 rdl.   400 rdl.

(5) *Philosophical Fragments*
               with you 96
        Remainder with Luno . . . . . <u>200</u>
               296 @ 4 mk.   246 rdl. 4 mk.   100 rdl.

(6) *Two Ages, A Literary Review*
               with you 227
        Remainder with Luno . . . . . <u>170</u>
               397 @ 3 mk.   197 rdl.   70 rdl.

(7) *Three Discourses on Imagined Occasions*
               with you 93
        Remainder with Luno . . . . . <u>226</u>
               319 @ 4 mk.   212 rdl. 4 mk.   90 rdl.

(8) *The Concept of Anxiety*
        Remainder with you . . . . . . 85 @ 1 rdl.   85 rdl.   <u>40 rdl.</u>
[*in pencil*, Reitzel's figures: 970 rdl.

(9) Climacus' *Postscript* 381 copies @ 3 mk. 14

(10) *Upbuilding Discourses* 22 1/2 rdl.

225

87

312]

Letters, no. 152   [July, 1847]

« **6031**

There is a form of envy I have often seen in which the individual wants to get something by defiance and provocation. For example, when I walk into a place where several people have congregated, it often happens that one or the other arms himself against me by laughing; presumably he feels that he is the agent of public opinion. But when I address a word to him, the same man becomes extremely docile and cordial. That is, basically he regards me as somebody important, perhaps even more important than I am, but if he cannot manage to participate, as it were, in my greatness, then he laughs at me. As soon as he becomes participant, so to speak, he boasts of my greatness.

This is because of the limited setting, but it is very interesting to observe.

One day outside the gate I met three young fellows who began to gape and grin the minute they laid eyes on me and started out with all that brazen effrontery that is *bon ton* in this market town. What happened? When I got near enough to make contact I discovered that all of them were smoking cigars; I turned to one of them and asked for a light for my cigar. All three of them snatched off their hats, and it was as if I had done them a service by lighting my cigar with them. Ergo: the same ones will be delighted to shout Bravo for me if I merely give them a friendly, to say nothing of a flattering, word; now they shout *pereat*[1624] and act provocatively.

What Goldschmidt[1625] and P. L. Møller[1626] practiced on a large scale, every individual here does on a smaller scale. If one did not want to greet Goldschmidt, refused to visit him: he was put in the paper. He wanted to gain equal footing by defiance and provocation. It is the same with the readers of his paper. If one is unwilling to flatter them, they use his paper to insult one; if one is unwilling to flatter them, their real opinion emerges.

And I, who have always been courteous, especially to the poorer class! Now the whole thing is a comedy. But it is inestimably interesting to have one's knowledge of human nature enriched in this way.

VIII¹ A 218   n.d., 1847

« 6032

August 2, 1847

I have finished *Works of Love,* final copy and all. While working on No. VIII¹⁶²⁷ I felt a little tired and thought of traveling to Berlin. I did not dare allow myself that for fear of getting too far away from the decisive mood. I stuck it out. God be praised, it went all right. God be praised. O, while people deride and ridicule all the work I do, I sit and thank God who grants success to it. Yes, take everything else I have had, the best is still an original and, God be praised, indestructible blessed conception that God is love. No matter how hopeless things have seemed to me many times, I scrape together all the best thoughts I can muster of what a loving, affectionate person is and say to myself: This is what God is every moment.

Eventually I hope to awaken similar thoughts in men, to make them hear or to stir them up so that they quit wasting their lives without ever really considering how loving God is.—

VIII¹ A 219   August 2, 1847

« 6033

I have been under some strain for a few days. Now I am once again calm and indescribably happy, God be praised! It goes with me as I read somewhere of the Jews: A remarkable people, for when they are in harmony with their God no one can defeat them; but when they are out of harmony with him: then everyone can conquer them.

VIII¹ A 220   n.d., 1847

« 6034

I once thought that Copenhagen was a great city—now I know that it is a little market town. But one cannot live in a market town as he lives in a great city.

VIII¹ A 224   n.d., 1847

« 6035

Aug. 3, 1847

For a moment I thought of going to Stettin simply for the journey. It would hardly have occurred to me but for a casual remark Nutz-

horn[1628] made. For one thing, the state of my health, my whole constitution, all my physical habits, are diametrically opposed to doing such
a mad thing as traveling in the 85 degree heat of dog days—a time when
I hardly venture out for a ride at noon—but when I feel best by keeping
very quiet. What is the sense of going at this time of the year to a desert
where the burning sun is unbearable; what is the sense of trifling with
one's sleep, for I never sleep on board ship and consequently am very
tired the next day, and then in a strange place, which always makes the
temperature [seem] 20° warmer.

Besides, August 9[1629] draws near (thus I could not even do it
except by staying in Stettin just one day and going straight home
again), and this year I do want to be in Copenhagen August 9, as is
my custom.

Furthermore, I have business to attend to. I am dealing with
Reitzel,[1630] and I know how careless he is; if I set a bad example, then
I might as well forget it. Furthermore, every day I am expecting a man
who said he would come again to talk with me about the place.[1631]

There is still one more reason. A fleeting impulse now and then
can be fine, but one must also be able to do it in another way. Instead
of taking this hurried trip, which would be an over-exertion, I have
thought instead of having a little vacation here at home. During the
time I will do little reading, allow myself lots of space in order to rest
my head. This can also be very important for the future. As everyone
knows, it is most difficult to stop a ship in motion. In the same way I
have always had a difficult time when I have finished a larger undertaking. For that reason I usually do something different and forget everything, get it off my back, as it were, by taking such a trip. But it cannot
be done this year. So I am learning another way of doing it. This year
I have no real desire for a journey, and for something like that to be
of any benefit there must be a desire for it, a high degree of motivation.
I have been very happy these days to remain completely quiet. A
change in my nature is very clearly in process, and it ought to be
respected. I am becoming more calm, do not feel the need of such
violent motions any more. True renewal, after all, is not a vehement
diversion but a welling up from within.

Of late—and this is also a change—I have frequently entertained
and found appealing the thought of making a proper journey abroad
this fall. This in itself signifies greater poise in my soul. My first journey
abroad[1632] was unhappy due to the unhappiness connected to my

engagement. In a certain sense that matter certainly has not changed, but nevertheless it is mitigated.

VIII¹ A 227   August 3, 1847

« 6036

Sometime I should read a book by Wieland: *Aristipp und seine Zeit,*[1633] also one of his latest treatises, *Euthanasia:*[1634] *"wie hat es der Mensch anzufangen um heiter und schmerzlos zu sterben."*

VIII¹ A 228   *n.d.,* 1847

« 6037

N.B.

From now on the thrust should be into the specifically Christian.

Again a pseudonym is necessary to cut loose and provide the elasticity of limitlessness. For this will be used: *de occultis non judicat ecclesia,*[1635] a *psychological experiment.* (See Journal JJ[1636] [i.e., VI A 55].)

"The forgiveness of sins" must be emphasized. Everything should concentrate on that point; it must be established again as a paradox before anything can be done. Christianity these days has become nonsense; that is why one is obliged to take on the double task of first of all making the matter beneficially difficult.

A more rigorous, scholarly work about the art of religious address[1637] with constant reference to Aristotle's *Rhetoric.* (See Journal JJ [i.e., VI A 17]—and what is in a portfolio lying in the top drawer of the lone tall cupboard.)

VIII¹ A 229   *n.d.,* 1847

« 6038

It would be a very good text for a wedding:
> "Charm is deceitful, and beauty is vain, but a woman who fears the Lord is to be praised."

Proverbs 31:30
VIII¹ A 232   *n.d.,* 1847

« 6039

Professor Heiberg[1638] and company will say something like this: "Magister Kierkegaard is himself to blame for the whole affair,[1639] why did he not attach himself to us and live in princely privacy." So I am to blame for this! Fine. But what then. If it is maintained that I am guilty, am I therefore guilty? I should think just the opposite, that I would be guilty if I cravenly and cleverly shirked speaking about a danger which it was my duty to enter into. But Heiberg and Martensen and the whole lot have absolutely no ethical backbone; for them everything revolves around prudence, an easy life, reputation, a fat living, and status. Presumably it must hold true of every one of those noble ones from whom we wish to learn that he himself was guilty of being persecuted and put to death. If he had wanted to live some other way, if he had not been true to his idea, had haggled and bargained, whored with the public, etc.–he of course would have been honored and esteemed. The amusing thing about Heiberg is that he, Heiberg, Heiberg the Wise, who tried to profit from every illusion, has nonetheless gotten into a rather awkward position. Heiberg's life is reminiscent of those scintillating lines in *Debatten i Politivennen,* [1640] where the linen merchant is so despondent about getting into the paper, he, who all his life had scrupulously avoided getting into the papers.

And it is such authorities who are supposed to judge my efforts! If H. only understood me, how I literally and deliberately work against myself in order, please note, not to serve the truth by means of illusions, he would promptly take me for mad.

And now Martensen[1641]–what a display of abjection! With Heiberg there is still the good point that he knows how to enjoy life; there is some point to his prudence. But Martensen has a strictly Christian upbringing and does not have the kind of talent Heiberg has.

As for Bishop Mynster,[1642] that is another matter. He is so competent that one must make allowance for a little heresy. There certainly is some irregularity. If the world is no better than he pictures it in his sermons, then it is rather awkward to be highly regarded and esteemed —by the world, or to have as much world as he has. It is no art to picture the world darkly, but the art is that one's life scrupulously expresses and reflects what one learns about the world, that one's personal life manifests the relationship.

The world, after all, is the medium. Just as we say that water has such and such characteristics and the test bears it out, so must the same thing be said of the world.

But Mynster is and remains a man of eminently great ability and one of the rarest government officials. His irregularity is his own responsibility before God; and one thing is certain, he is naturally destined to have power.

VIII[1] A 233 n.d., 1847

« **6040**

Perhaps there is not one person besides me who would care to live the life I live; and yet there is not one person who, if he had time to consider it at the hour of his death, would not be happy to have lived as I have *qua* author.

VIII[1] A 237   *n.d.,* 1847

« **6041**

Aug. 14

Strangely enough, the journey to Berlin is constantly in my thoughts. But I cannot. There is a man who has approached me about the sale of my house.[1643] He came so opportunely, actually so unaccountably opportunely for me that I cannot be adequately thankful for it. Under such circumstances I dare not leave. If he were to come when I am away it would be most distressing.

Previously it has been my custom to seize opportunities for necessary diversion, venturing rather than not venturing. That is why it is so difficult for me this time to make a negative decision. A negative decision is also the most difficult when one is completely free, because there is always the possibility of doing the opposite. Once I have jumped into the carriage or aboard a ship, I am there—in that there is a kind of decision. The negative decision is far more difficult.

Unfortunately, it is all too obvious to me now how unsuited I am for practical affairs. My ideality labors indescribably under the bumbling and vagueness and drivel which are the secret of practical life. That a person does not come at the time specified or comes at the wrong time or wastes my time etc. is a torment for me. I would far rather undertake all the work myself, the most tedious work of copying —if I may just take it on alone, for then I can do it methodically and with precision. But this disgusting ambiguity is to me a nightmare.

VIII[1] A 246   August 14, 1847

« **6042**

Aug. 15

When I had the urge to travel to Berlin (while working on discourse VII of *Works of Love,* part II), I did not give in. Instead I visited the King one day, something I had no desire at all to do. I must be able to forego such great distractions. Now the point is to reduce productivity and to loaf a little here at home rather than have these intense distractions which promptly make me productive again.

VIII[1] A 249　August 15, 1847

« 6043

Aug. 16

So it is decided; I will stay at home. Tomorrow the manuscript[1644] will be delivered to the printer. —To make sure that what kept me from making the journey was in no way a possible distaste for all the fuss involved, I have—with typical suspiciousness of myself—begun a bath-cure which I knew was extremely repulsive to me.

There is a far deeper reason for my staying at home, a need within me. I must learn to do without such intense distractions. If I consider committing myself to a definite external task, it does me no good after such a forced removal to have the craving come upon me suddenly and with such a melancholy cast. Therefore just as well now as later. Now I am finished with the books;[1645] if I went on a journey, I probably would begin again and would not be convinced that I could stop without needing, like a leviathan, to break away by hurling myself in the very opposite direction.

I now feel a need to find myself in a deeper sense by coming closer to God in an understanding of myself. I must remain where I am and be *renewed inwardly*. [1646] That I might be able to take a regular journey abroad for a longer time toward the end of autumn is something entirely different. But it must not in any way have an emotional cast or a concentration of emotionality such as a little Berlin expedition would have had.

I must get hold of my melancholy. Up to now it has been deeply submerged and my enormous intellectual activity has helped to keep it there. It is clear enough that my work has helped others and that God has sanctioned it and helped me in every way. I thank him again and again for having done infinitely more for me than I expected. It comforts me that just as surely as no man has any merit before God, he has nevertheless looked upon my efforts with favor, so that through this help in my terrible suffering I have stuck it out to the end. I am aware before God that my work as an author, my readiness to respond to his beck and call, to sacrifice every earthly and secular motive, will mitigate my own impression of what I personally have done wrong. Simply because I began my writing with a burdened conscience, for that very reason I have tried my utmost to make it so pure that it could be partial payment on the debt. In the eyes of the world this purity, unselfishness, and industry seem insane. I know that God looks at it differently, although it does not follow as a matter of course that in his eyes it is so pure that before him I dare congratulate myself on it.

But now God wants something else. Something is stirring within me which hints at a metamorphosis. That is why I dare not go to Berlin, for that would induce abortion; therefore I will be quiet, by no means work too hard, not even hard, and will not begin a new book, but try to find myself and, *here where I am,* to think through the idea of my melancholy together with God. In this way my melancholy may be lifted and *Christianity may come closer to me.* Up to now I have armed myself against my depression with intellectual activity which keeps it away—now, in the faith that God has forgotten in forgiveness whatever guilt I have, I must try to forget it myself, but not in any diversion, not in any distance from it, but in God, so that when I think of God I may think that he has forgotten it and in that way myself learn to dare to forget it in forgiveness.

VIII[1] A 250   August 16, 1847

« **6044**

With respect to Adler,[1647] the only mitigating thing one could do for him would be to explain that in former times it frequently happened that a religious spoke of what Christ had said to him or to her, or that a religious spoke in the name of Christ and said *I.* There are examples of this on every page of Abraham à St. Clara. But the point is that it had its place within the whole consciousness of the age. Furthermore, none of them thought of referring to such words as a special commission (unlike Adler, whom Christ asked to write it down). And then to do it in our day, when he is utterly abandoned by any corresponding notion in the contemporary consciousness, and to do it in such a way that he himself is no help at all in determining more precisely how he understands his role.

I do not like this whole business with Adler at all. Truthfully speaking, I am all too inclined to keep Adler afloat. We need dynamic personalities, unselfish persons who are not perpetually motivated and exhausted by job, wife, and children.

Perhaps for the present one could write to him and request him to recall that preface and then drop publication of the book.[1648] And yet the book deserves to be read. But the trouble is that it will hurt A., and I am almost afraid that the reaction will be too strong for him. Everyone presumably will find Adler's concern misplaced, like my concern at one time that Goldschmidt[1649] would take my article too hard. What, did he not win, he who got all the peddlers and shopkeepers, all the riffraff, brash students, and loose women to ridicule and insult me. Yes, he certainly did win. But there was something better in Goldschmidt; he honestly thought that I was the only person he actually esteemed and admired. The question now is this: That better side of Goldschmidt, what happened to it, was it not damaged? To win the way he won could be most dangerous for him personally. Through this very victory he has come to have a self-image that perhaps will plunge him into total despair. What held Goldschmidt up was that better fragment he had; because of his contempt for others it naturally did not matter what others thought of him. But the judgment of the one person he esteems usually is all the more important to one who scorns everyone that way. O, you grinning fools who do not even know what you are grinning at. If I had power over Goldschmidt before, my power from that moment is naturally far greater. One never becomes as dependent on a person as he does by getting carried away opposing the person he actually respects. He does not have at his disposal an illusion that can fool him into thinking he has been in the right against me; Goldschmidt himself knows best of all how unselfishly I acted, I who never concealed from him that he was the stronger—when it came to inciting the riffraff and the fools against me. But the point is this, Goldschmidt personally despises the legions he commands; he himself knows best that their judgment is less than nothing; but he values my judgment very highly. Yes, he was so infatuated that I am convinced that he would have given anything to find out what I thought about the articles in which he abused me. It sometimes happens that a bandit places himself at the head of a mob, or a peddler at the head of peddlers—there is something to that, for the commander believes in the reality of those he commands. But with Goldschmidt there is a ludicrous self-contradiction: he is victorious—at the head of and with the help of those he despises, and with their help he wins over the only one he respects. Thanks for the victory! And Goldschmidt understands this himself. He is like a person who despairs over being ejected from the exclusive, cultured, noble circle where he longs and craves to be, and who is now admired in a public dance hall—that is, by those whose

opinion he despises. I believe that only a Jew could endure this; for in
a Jew there is once and for all a certain despair.

VIII[1] A 252   *n.d.,*   1847

« **6045**

Men have no idea at all of what mental suffering really is. I know
how profoundly I have been pained by the conduct of people toward
me, not because of what it cost me but because I know before God how
well-intentioned I was toward them. There is no one, no one here at
home who has sympathy with the poorer classes as I do—and yet they
are incited against me. I saw that more distinguished persons were
being wronged, and I threw myself into the jaws, and for thanks they
interpret this as vanity. O, but praise God, for the memory is priceless
to my life.

VIII[1] A 254   *n.d.,*   1847

« **6046**

Dear Sir:[1650]
     When I consider what it means for a merchant, and especially for
a bookseller, to obtain a postponement of the payment of royalties for
almost one and a half years (for a publisher normally pays in advance
as a matter of course), when I consider the nature of the book, and
when I consider that we are speaking of a printing of 1,000 copies, then
it seems to me that 700 rdl.,[1651] which you yourself originally mentioned, must be a very reasonable requirement on my part.
     If we agree, I will expedite the matter as quickly as possible, which
ought to be in your interest as well.

Respectfully,

S.K.

Reply requested.

Letters, no. 154   [August,] 1847

« **6047**

August 30, '47.

Dear Sir:[1652]
     As you do not want what I want, then you—will not publish *Either/
Or.* So, thus the matter is settled—and as you desire it, completely

"without anger" on my part, for I have already quite forgotten your "vacillation."

Respectfully,
S. Kierkegaard

[No address]

Letters, no. 156   August 30, 1847

« 6048

Dear Reitzel:[1653]

You know how much I like to have everything settled and decided, and you also know how much I desire the other party to be content. And whenever you are the other party, I am confident you also consider what is to my advantage. Therefore, without further ado I accept your offer for *Either/Or*, although the royalty is small enough—but this country is a small one as well. Certainly I prefer being pleased with my confidence in you and your concern for my interests, prefer to be pleased knowing that you are content, even though I mistrustfully urged you against your wishes to give me a little bit more. In other words: accepted. —I want the printing to consist of 750 copies. As for payment, I shall not ask for that until the June term, 1849. I hope this, as they say, is all you can ask for.

Please then have the kindness to give me written confirmation, as you did last time, containing these two points: (1) the royalties for the second printing are 550 rdl. [*in margin:* with 300 rdl. payable on June 11, 1849, and the balance, 250 rdl., *ultimo* July, 1849]; (2) the printing is to consist of 750 copies.[1654]

And so, good luck with this transaction. According to my way of thinking, you have struck an advantageous bargain, and you will find that good luck is connected with the venture. If I had not in so many ways worked against my own sales in those days when I was my own publisher, they would also have been wholly different.

As you know, I am always in a bit of a hurry with business matters. Hitherto you have indulged me in this respect; please do so now. And please reply. Such a letter is soon written.

Yours sincerely,
S. Kierkegaard

Letters, no. 157   [after August 30, 1847]

« 6049 *N.B.*

"The Book on Adler"[1655] lends itself best to division into many small separate parts. It will not be understood as a whole—and the fact that it is continually about Adler will be fatiguing, which, however, in my thinking is just the point. So there will be, for example, a section about the concept "Premise-authors,"[1656] about the universal, the individual, the special individual.[1657] A second section: A revelation in the situation of contemporaneity.[1658] A third: about the relation between a genius and an apostle,[1659] etc. This can be done easily and then the book will be read in an entirely different way, and I will be spared mentioning Adler, for it is cruel to slay a man that way.

VIII[1] A 264   *n.d.,* 1847

« **6050** *The New Book*[1660] *Will Be Entitled:*   **N.B.**

How did it happen that Jesus Christ could be crucified? Or: Has a man the right to sacrifice his life for the truth?

The point is that the dogmatic discussion about Christ's atoning death has made us completely forget the event.

His death is an atoning death, a sacrifice he wills to make. Right. However, he was not himself responsible for being condemned to death. Here is the dialectic: he wants to save the world by his death; otherwise he cannot save it—but for all that he is not himself to blame for being persecuted and put to death.

As a rule we speak only of Christ's purity and innocence, but here again a problem is overlooked. That is, the good and the true can be proclaimed in such a way that men are compelled to persecute. —In his first skirmishing with the world a man actually regards the world as the stronger, but when he has really felt his strength, he actually sympathizes with men for doing him wrong. Then it may occur to him (not on his behalf, but on theirs) that he is putting the price too high. After all, one may be so conversant with the world and with men that simply by doing what is good and true he is saying very precisely: I want to be persecuted. Is this not being too hard on men. Indeed, in that way one may almost be putting a murder on their consciences. Is it not being too hard on men to structure one's own life on the most prodigious scale, to hold to it unswervingly, to compel men in a tragic kind of self-defense to put him to death? —Here I can say, as in *Fear and Trembling,* that the majority do not understand at all what I am talking about. The minute a man sees that from now on he must either pare down the truth a little in order to take men along or in a way compel them to persecute him, take this responsibility upon themselves—is it his duty to do the former or the latter?

Thus Christ at all times must have wanted to avoid persecution (not for his own sake, for he was, in fact, willing to suffer, he who had come to suffer) but for the sake of men, lest he be the one who contributed to making them "guilty."—

Then his relationship to the powers (the clique) and to the lowly will be developed. How imprudently he must have lived.

Has any man the right to hold unreservedly to the truth to such a degree that he can foresee that his contemporaries will become guilty by doing away with him? For Christ is the truth, and therefore it could not be otherwise; and furthermore his death makes it good again, since it is atoning death.

So you see I am back again as before with *Fear and Trembling.* From whom can I try to find some clarification of thoughts like these? There are not ten who can think them once I have posed them, to say nothing of before. They all think in the opposite direction, in the direction of not being afraid of risking one's life. But their thinking does not begin with that as the given in order to ask whether one has the right to do it.

See this book, p. 194 [i.e., VIII¹ A 307].

VIII¹ A 271   n.d., 1847

« 6051

If I do not have the right God-fearingly to call something ungodliness which humanly and good-naturedly I would call weakness, then I do not have the right to sacrifice my life for the truth, either, that is, to be put to death, or let myself be put to death.

VIII¹ A 276   n.d., 1847

« 6052

It must be dreadful to be made to look like a fool the way Martensen[1661] is: to preach Christianity for such an audience, a man of distinction and for the distinguished, and for fools who run with the pack simply because it is exclusive. What satire! Martensen is indeed a preacher, presumably then a disciple of the teacher, our Lord Jesus Christ, on whom the world spit—Christ is the prototype [*Forbillede*] and Martensen the disciple who resembles him. Martensen must then either be appallingly secular-minded (that the insignificant title and distinction can be so important to him) or very stupid. I prefer to think the latter. The point is that such a man never comes to think primitively about the slightest thing; he patterns himself on this one and that, always does exactly the same thing.

And the most corrupt segment of society is the world of high society. For what, indeed, are prostitutes and drunks, etc., compared to that whole game of pernicious passions, that pandering moral laxity, etc.

No, I do not wish to be made a fool of in church. That is why I desire an empty church–then God is present, and for me at least that is more than enough.

In this day and age a full church in the capital city (far out in the country it is a quite different matter if the whole parish goes to church, something quite different from all Copenhagen streaming to one church) is a satire on His Reverence or His Most Eminent Reverence.

VIII¹ A 277   n.d., 1847

« **6053**

Concerning a portion in *Christian Reflections,* II, No. 6:[1662] That to become something great in the world is a dubious matter–it must be noted here that the reference is not to the state. In that sense Mynster may well be said to have become something great, but he has a strong tendency to want to be in the minority.

VIII¹ A 298   n.d., 1847

« **6054**

Most likely no one is aware that the cue for the word "reflections"[1663] has already been given in the introduction to one of the *Christian Discourses,* No. VI.[1664]

VIII¹ A 308   n.d., 1847

« **6055**

In the reference to the people of love, there is also a fling at Grundtvig, for it is really presumptuous that a particular group will call itself "the people of love"; it is vain and self-loving.[1665]

VIII¹ A 309   n.d., 1847

« **6056**

Far be it from me to indict the present age as if the world had been so wonderful before. No, as far as I am concerned, I would have a bad time of it in any age. Socrates was right in saying that banishment would have helped him very little, since it would have gone badly for him in every country. The root of the matter was that Socrates was the inciter.

VIII¹ A 326   n.d., 1847

« **6057**

Dear Jette,[1666]

As I have seen and talked with my brother[1667] a number of times in recent days, I have had you quite vividly in my thoughts. But I owe it to truth not to make myself out to be worse than I am, and it is really true that during the long period that has gone by since I last saw you or heard anything from you, I have not ceased thinking of you. But you know how it is: when one has not been present at the beginning of an event, it is hard to enter into it properly later on; one waits instead for something new to happen in order then to make use of the moment to begin. At least that is how it is with my relationship to the events of life, the sad as well as the joyous ones—if I do not get started at once, I prefer to skip my turn in order to begin at the beginning next time.

What I want to speak about now goes far back in time. You had already been sick for a long time when I was first informed of it. The very fact that I could not begin at the beginning made me not begin at all. Time passed, several times I decided to write you, but the following scruple always got in the way to stop me: "Now that it is too late, where shall I begin?" So time passed. —"Sunday came, and Sunday went; no new boots to Hans were sent."[1668] —Finally I was so completely out of the habit, that is to say, I became accustomed to finding it impossible to overcome the difficulty of the beginning. —Alas, perhaps you went through something similar. Now and then in the beginning you probably thought: "It is strange that I do not hear from him at all; that is shameful of him, but now that it is too late, he might as well save himself the trouble."

Then my brother came to town. For me this meant a break, a breakthrough: here is a letter for you. What you get out of it will of course depend on how you read it—yet I do not believe it is in any way necessary to be practiced in the art of reading between the lines to discern the sympathy in it.

Peter told me that you are still always confined to bed. I can quite vividly imagine the burden of this in the course of time, even though I have not experienced it myself in that way. I once spoke with you about that burden, which among other things is also this: that it is almost impossible to avoid people's misunderstanding of such suffering. —"It is not fever, nor a broken arm, nor falling and hurting oneself —what is it then?" So the doctor asks impatiently, and so does ordinary human sympathy—alas, and when one suffers in this way it is precisely a question of patience, the patience not to lose courage, the patience to endure the impatience of sympathy. But we human beings and our sympathy are like that. And when one suffers as you are suffering—even though there is a person at one's side, as there surely is at yours, who faithfully shares the yoke equally with you—then one has indeed the opportunity to realize the truth that the God of Patience verily is he who can persist completely unconditionally in caring about a human being with the same eternal unchanged compassion. As the old hymn[1669] so movingly asks, "If every hour I weep and ask," that is, whence help and comfort will come—so movingly does the poet himself reply, "But God indeed still lives." And he is every day, at every hour, early in the morning, in a sleepless hour of the night, at the time of day when one feels most weak—he is unalterably the same.

Dear Jette, when I have thus taken pen in hand I could easily go on writing page upon page. I would like to do it, and perhaps you would not be displeased to read it. But I must break off this very instant, and such a letter may always be continued a day later.

Goodbye—for it seems to me as if I have been talking with you. Goodbye! Greetings to Poul;[1670] do please tell him something about me once in a while lest he grow up in complete ignorance of having an uncle. I have asked Peter to give you my heartfelt greetings. Please greet Peter once more from

Your S.K.

Letters, no. 161   [September, 1847]

« **6058**

Right away the first time I talked with him and several times later I said to Bishop Mynster,[1671] and as solemnly as possible, that what I expressed was the opposite of what he expressed and that was the reason (besides my veneration for him) that he was of importance to me. He was very attractive and answered, as we carried on a formal conversation, that he understood me. At one point he said that we complemented one another, which, however, I did not enter into, since it was more courteous than I expected, but merely reiterated very firmly my dissimilarity. I have said to him that frequently there was something I knew must displease him, but that I certainly kept him in mind and have kept him particularly in mind—without, however changing it.

So I know that my relationship to him is as pure as possible.

VIII[1] A 332   *n.d.,* 1847

« **6059**

Oct. 3, 1847

Henrich Steffens, *Religions-Philosophie,*[1672] II, p. 260 *medio:*
so spricht sich die furchtbare Gewissheit aus, dass auch innerlich, in der
Geschichte, das Böse=Masse ist.
  P. 262, *der Heiland ist für die ganze Welt gestorben, aber nur für die*
    wahren Christen auferstanden.

VIII[1] A 337   October 3, 1847

« **6060**

I would like to create a little literary mystery by, for example,
publishing something I would call "The Writings of a Young
Man";[1673] in the preface I would appear as a young author publishing
his first book.
  I would call myself Felix de St. Vincent. The contents would
include:
  1. The Crisis in the Life of an Actress
  2. A Eulogy of Autumn
  3. Rosenkilde as Hummer
  4. Writing Sampler

VIII[1] A 339   *n.d.,* 1847

« **6061** *A Word About Myself*

I am the last stage of the development of a poet[1674] in the direction
of small-scale reformer. I have much more imagination than a reformer as such would have, but then again less of a certain personal
force required for acting as a reformer. Aided by my imagination—
which, please note, is not at all prior to the dialectical, hence immediate, but follows the dialectical—I can grasp all the Christian qualifications in the most faithful and vital way. The times obviously require
this. There are certain things which must be kept in mind constantly
or the standard is lost. To be reminded of the qualifications of the
Christian life that demand the utmost is like the flight of the wild bird
over the heads of the tamed birds.[1675] —But simply because I am a poet
whose task is to jack up the price[1676] and, if possible, to whisper to each
individual what the requirement could be, I must be especially careful
not to acquire adherents.

VIII[1] A 347   *n.d.,* 1847

« **6062**

In order not to be guilty of any exaggeration in Christianity, I can apply the standard my father followed with respect to confessing Christ. But if I do that, it would soon be evident that this would not be permitted to go unnoticed. The reason my father managed to do it was that he was completely unknown. But then someone will say: Well, if you are so devoted to religion, then become a pastor. Here, you see, is an illusion. Let us be honest now; I wonder if anyone gets the impression that a man who becomes a pastor these days is ardently occupied with religion? O, no, he gets the impression that he is someone who wants a job and some kind of impressive position in the community. Because of that illusion the clergy have become essentially impotent.

VIII¹ A 352   *n.d.*, 1847

« **6063**

Dear Jette,[1677]

I am glad that you yourself have provided the occasion for sending the book[1678] that accompanies this letter. So you yourself are responsible and will all the more carefully see to it that your reading of the book or any single part of it will not in some way conflict with my brother's idea of what is beneficial or harmful reading, for it would distress me to have that happen.

Please note, therefore, that I have arranged it so that no emphasis in any way is placed on whether or not you read it, something I never oblige anyone to do, and especially not that person whom I surely would not wish to *burden* with a *complimentary* copy.

This is my own copy, originally destined for myself: thus it has a purely personal relationship to me, not in my capacity as author as with other copies, but rather as if the author had presented it to me. However, it now occurs to me that it has not fulfilled its destiny and reaches its proper destination only in being destined for you—the only copy in the whole printing suitable for that. —The bookbinder has done a beautiful job on the book (and in judging the bookbinder's craft I am after all impartial). —It has been read through by me and is to that extent a used copy. So please notice that everything is as it ought to be now. For a brief moment you may admire the bookbinder's art as you would admire any other art object; then you may—for a longer moment, if you please, take pleasure in the thought that it is a gift; and then you may put the book down (–for it has been read–), put it aside as one puts a gift aside, put it aside carefully–if it is a welcome gift.

But enough of this. I was sorry not to be able to take my leave of you. I hope this little letter in which I take my leave will find you as well as I found you when I arrived.[1679] *Above all, do not lose your desire to walk: every day I walk*[1680] *myself into a state of well-being and walk away from every illness; I have walked myself into my best thoughts, and I know of no thought so burdensome that one can not walk away from it.* Even if one were to walk for one's health and it were constantly one station ahead–*I would still say: Walk!* Besides, it is also apparent that in walking one constantly gets as close to well-being as possible, even if one does not quite reach it–*but by sitting still, and the more one sits still, the closer one comes to feeling ill.* Health and salvation can only be found in motion. If anyone denies that motion exists, I do as Diogenes[1681] did, I walk. If anyone denies that health resides in motion, then I walk away from all morbid objections. *If one just keeps on walking, everything will be all right.* And out in the country you have all the advantages; you do not risk being stopped before you are safe and happy outside your gate, nor do you run the risk of being intercepted on your way home. I remember just what happened to me a while ago and which has happened frequently since then. I had been walking for an hour and a half and had done a great deal of thinking, and with the help of motion I had really become a very agreeable person to myself. What bliss, and, as you may imagine, what care did I not take to bring my bliss home safely if possible. Thus I hurry along, with downcast eyes I steal through the streets, so to speak; confident that I am entitled to the sidewalk, I do not consider it necessary to look about at all (for thereby one is so easily intercepted, just as one is looking about–in order to avoid) and thus hasten along the sidewalk with my bliss (for the ordinance forbidding one to carry anything on the sidewalk does not extend to bliss, which makes a person lighter)–directly into a man who is always suffering from illness and who therefore with downcast eyes, defiant because of his illness, does not even think that he must look about when he is not entitled to the sidewalk. I was stopped. It was a quite exalted gentleman who now honored me with conversation. Thus all was lost. After the conversation ended, there was only one thing left for me to do: instead of going home, to go walking again.

As you see, there really is no more space in this letter, and therefore I break off this conversation–for in a sense it has been a conversation, inasmuch as I have constantly thought of you as present. Do take care of yourself!

Yours,
S. Kierkegaard

[Address:]
To
Mrs. Henriette Kierkegaard
Pedersborg
p. Sorøe
Accompanying parcel.

Letters, no. 150 [1847]

« 6064

It would be easy for me to justify my entire work as an author on the basis of Mynster's sermons[1682]–to what extent his life matches up is not so easy to decide. But no one can be angry with me for doing what has been told to me, what I have been brought up to follow.[1683]

VIII¹ A 366   *n.d.*, 1847

« 6065

Pious Phrase Book
or
Handbook for Pastors
Containing 500 platitudes
alphabetically arranged
by
A sexton who has been employed by all churches and therefore is well acquainted with platitudes.

dedicated to Councillor Hiorthöy[1684]
the expert connoisseur,
the careful collector
of platitudes.

VIII¹ A 383   *n.d.*, 1847

« 6066

Addition to 6065 (VIII¹ A 383):
by
Esaias Strandsand

VIII¹ A 384   *n.d.*, 1847

« **6067**

Addition to 6065 (VIII[1] A 383):

Of course, the idea cannot be developed; it would get to be boring. Therefore it is best to make it a subscription offer; then one can get the most important part said in the announcement.

VIII[1] A 385   n.d.,   1847

« **6068**

The book[1685] is to be dedicated to Bishop Mynster.[1686]

VIII[2] B 116   n.d.,   1847–48

« **6069**

To

His Excellency

Your Grace, Bishop Dr. Mynster
St. D., DM., a.o.[1687]
this small book
is dedicated
in deepest veneration.[1688]

VIII[2] B 118   n.d.,   1847–48

« **6070**

On almost every page of Mynster's sermons[1689] one can show how few people he himself supposes are really Christians or even care about being Christian. But what is all this talk about a state-church, a Christian nation and people, then, but an illusion? And what does it mean—this regarding his position as paid by the state, receiving honors and esteem, almost as if he were professor of Hebrew, which naturally entails no responsibility for the few or the many who want to learn Hebrew but merely for him to have the prestige of the position. Given the admission Mynster has made, it is obvious that every teacher in the church, in the state church, has *eo ipso* a kind of missionary work, risking everything to make men aware and guaranteeing the state that everything is being done so that as many as possible can become Christians. If Mynster should in the apostolic sense become the teacher of the few Christians he himself speaks of, it would be rather a poor living and without political distinction. But one moment there are only a few Christians; the next moment the state is Christian, and a pastor or bishop has nothing more to do than a bureaucrat who holds office hours in his office—this is the way he preaches in a church—and

above all carefully avoids too close contact with people—for the sake
of advancement.

VIII[1] A 388   *n.d.*, 1847

« **6071**

Nov. 4

Today I looked in on Bishop Mynster.[1690] He said he was very
busy—so I left at once. But he was also very cold toward me. Very likely
he is offended by the latest book.[1691] That is how I interpreted it.
Perhaps I am wrong. But I am not wrong on another point, that this
has given me a serenity I have not had before. I have always winced
at writing anything I knew might offend him, yes, almost embitter him.
Now I assume that it has happened. It has happened many times
before, but he has not let himself be offended. But a momentary hurt
just livens things up for me. I have never done the slightest thing to
win his favor and support, but it would have made me indescribably
happy to have him agree with me—for his sake as well, because that I
am right I know best of all—from his sermons.

VIII[1] A 390   November 4, 1847

« **6072**

I have never had a confidant. In being an author I have in a way
made the public my confidant. But as far as the public is concerned,
I must make posterity my confidant. The same people who join in
laughing at someone to scorn cannot be used very well as confidants.

VIII[1] A 394   *n.d.*, 1847

« **6073**

I was brought up on Mynster's sermons[1692]—by my father. This is
the trouble; of course it could never have occurred to my father to take
those sermons otherwise than literally. Brought up on Mynster's sermons—by Mynster: yes, a problem.

VIII[1] A 397   *n.d.*, 1847

« **6074**

It should have been perceived that my practice of walking the
streets[1693] subsequently could have been a practical means against
anonymity. It is extremely regrettable and demoralizing that robbers
and the elite agree on just one thing—living in hiding. The cowardly
wretch who sits and scribbles and personally does not have the courage

to let himself be seen also enjoys the advantage—that it is distinguished not to be seen. Yet thousands and thousands and thousands judge and judge, and God knows if there is one who has actually thought about life—not about what occupation he ought to take up or which girl he should marry, etc., in these things constantly aping the others, but about life. —To be somebody when one must live in the street all day —that is an art. To be somebody—when one is never seen—is very easy.

VIII[1] A 407   *n.d.,* 1847

« **6075**

November 20

The fundamental derangement at the root of modern times (which branches out into logic, metaphysics, dogmatics, and the whole of modern life) consists in this: that the deep qualitative chasm in the difference between God and man[1694] has been obliterated. Because of this there is in dogmatics (from logic and metaphysics) a depth of blasphemy which paganism never knew (for it knew what blasphemy against God is, but precisely this has been forgotten in our time, this theocentric age) and in ethics a brash unconcern or, more accurately, no ethics at all. The derangement has come about in many ways and has many forms, but mainly as follows. As the crowd intimidates the king, as the public intimidates counselors of state and authors, so the generation will ultimately want to intimidate God, constrain him to give in, become self-important before him, brazenly defiant in their numbers, etc. Thus what we have today, in modern times, is actually not doubt—it is insubordination. It is useless to want to bring religion to the front; it is not even possible to mount the machinery, for the soil is a swamp or a bog. "Of course, we will all be saved" etc. is approximately the refrain. This being the case, what is meant by all this about the consolation of religion!

On this frontier, where smugglers as well as rebels traffic, I have been assigned my place as an insignificant official who by any means, by cunning, by force (that is, spiritual force) must confiscate all illusions and seize those arrogant fancies based on effrontery toward God, unparalleled in either paganism or Judaism, since it is a prodigious fraud, a debasing of the doctrine of the God-man. —As a reward for my work I must be prepared, of course, to suffer all things from men, who, in the first place are by no means happy to be torn out of all those grandiloquent fancies in which sophists in abundance still continue to strengthen them.

Humbled and crushed and annihilated, I myself have had to learn as profoundly as anyone will come to learn arduously from me or through me: that a man is nothing before God. This is what I have to teach, not directly but indirectly. To be able to do that I must constantly go to school with God, who, when necessary, starts me all over again at the beginning to make me understand what I am, what a human being is, before him.

My task is in the service of truth; its essential form is: obedience. Nothing new is to be introduced, but everywhere the springs will be repaired in such a way again that the old, nothing but the old, will be like new again. As long as I live I will, humanly speaking, have nothing but trouble and will reap ingratitude—but after my death my work will stand despite the efforts of anyone. As long as I am living I cannot be acknowledged, for only a few are able to understand me, and if people began trying to acknowledge me, I would have to exert all my powers in new mystifications to prevent it.

The only contemporary I have paid any attention to is Mynster. But Mynster cares only about holding office and administering, thinking that this is the truth. He cares nothing about the truth, even if it were suffering right under his eyes. He can only understand that the truth must and shall rule—that it must and shall suffer is beyond his understanding.

VIII^1 A 414   November 20, 1847

« **6076**

According to Mynster's[1695] view, Christianity is related to the natural man in the same way as horsemanship is related to the horse, as the trained horse to the untrained horse, where it is not a matter of taking away its nature but of improving it. That is, Christianity is an educational process, being Christian is approximately what the natural man in his most blissfully happy moment could wish to be at his best: poised, harmonious perfection in itself and in himself consummately prepared virtuosity. But such talk is 100,000 miles removed from the Redeemer who must suffer in the world and who requires the crucifixion of the flesh, all that agony as the birth pangs of salvation, because under the circumstances there is in fact an infinite, a qualitative difference between God and man,[1696] and the terror of Christianity is also its blessedness: that God wants to be the teacher and wants the disciple to resemble him. If God is to be the teacher, then the instruction must begin with disrupting the learner (man). For the sake of quality it cannot be otherwise. There is not much use in speaking of God as the teacher and then have the instruction be only a purely human improvement program.

In many ways Mynster himself is the inventor of this confusion of Christianity and education. But in another sense he has done an extraordinary service and has demonstrated the deep impression made by his former days.[1697] If there is not to be any conflict between Christianity and the world, if the insignia of battle are not to be carried, if there is to be peace of that sort, then it is really something great to have a figure such as Mynster. He has resolved a most difficult problem. If a debate starts which brings the very concept of "state church" under discussion, then Mynster's position is dubious—if the concept of state church is accepted, then Mynster is the master, and it must always be remembered that in judging a man it is an outrageous wrong unceremoniously to delete all the very presuppositions within which a man is to be judged.

Let us pay tribute to Bishop Mynster. I have admired no one, no living person, except Bishop Mynster, and it is a joy to me to be reminded always of my father. His position is such that I see the irregularities very well, more clearly than anyone who has attacked him. But the nature of what I have to say should not affect him at all —if only he himself does not take it wrong. There is an ambivalence in his life which cannot be avoided, because the "state church" is an ambivalence. But now it is very possible to ascribe to him the whole element of renewal within the established order[1698]—and then he would once again stand high. If he makes a mistake, if instead of calmly sitting in lofty eminence, holding his scepter, and letting a second lieutenant decide things, he makes the mistake of believing that he should handle the battle, then no one can guarantee the results. My corps is just the support he needs. If he makes a mistake, he will have lost not only my auxiliary-corps—that is of least importance—but he will also have lost his own position.

VIII[1] A 415   n.d., 1847

« 6077

In Denmark, the promised land of paid jobs, everything revolves around a paid job, not only that everyone pursues it and is satisfied with it—no, if anyone wants to work disinterestedly for an idea but without being paid for it, he loses all the respect of these people on the mountain[1699]—because to go out after a paid job, to get it, to be lulled to sleep in it—that is morality—the other is immorality.

VIII[1] A 417   *n.d.*, 1847

« 6078

. . . . . And this is why the time will come when not only my writings but my whole life, the intriguing secret of the whole machinery, will be studied and studied. I venture also to claim that there is hardly a diplomat who has such a good overview of an age, even though he also stands on the street and perceives every detail, as I do. I never forget that God is my helper, and therefore it is my final wish that everything will serve to his glory!

VIII[1] A 424   *n.d.*, 1847

« 6079

December 1, 1847

I have now planned and drafted the book on Adler again.[1700] The arrangement now makes everything as luminous and clear as possible.

The book is very useful. The trouble is that there are very few in our age who have enough religiousness to be able to benefit from it. In the long run, Adler with all his confusion has more religiousness than most. The other trouble is that one gets involved with this confused man who has nothing to do and therefore writes and writes. But then the whole thing gets a wrong slant. In the book Adler is still a *Nebensach*,[1701] but how easy it is for the matter to turn into a cockfight between Adler and me for a curious public.

No, let Adler go his way. Then the book will be a book of essays. In that respect the book will be all laid out when the appendices are organized.

1. Something on premise-authors[1702] (that is the introduction).

It can end like this: Just as Lichtenberg has felicitiously pointed out, accurately in any case, that there is a kind of prose, a very extensive kind, which may be called "graduate student prose," so I hereby introduce the ultimate: premise-authors.

2. A premise-author on the fact of revelation[1703]

(conclusion of the introduction).

3. A revelation in the situation of contemporaneity[1704]

Hypothesis: it is assumed that a man has come forth suddenly and claimed a revelation—how would this be evident.

4. Appendix I. The dialectical relations: the
   universal, the single individual, the special individual.[1705]
5. Appendix II. On the difference between a
   genius and an apostle.[1706]
6. Magister Adler as a satire on Hegelian philosophy and
   the Christianity of our time.[1707]

VIII[1] A 440　December 1, 1847

« **6080**

P. L. Møller[1708] has had the audacity to publish all his newspaper articles (from *Kiøbenhavnsposten, Flyveposten, Figaro,* etc.) in two volumes. Of course I promptly sent them back to Reitzel. This little episode lends itself to vaudeville, for which P. L. M. would be usable. He has gotten a state subsidy. All one has to do is to write an article about it—the title "P. L. Møller" would be enough—a state subsidy!

There certainly has never been so much talk in the papers about someone who has gotten a state subsidy as there has been about P. L. M., who quite properly, in order if possible to get even more benefit from it, does not travel.[1709] One is always reading in the papers that a book is coming out by P. L. M., who is contemplating a journey to the art centers of the world, for which he has received a state subsidy. I have read something like this seven or eight times for sure, and now again on the dust jacket. The point is, which he is well aware of, that it is a kind of recommendation to have a state subsidy, and that is why he mentions it so often; he no doubt feels that his wretched life needs every possible assistance. It is just as much a swindle as those scurvy-snobby mendicant artists who appeal to His Royal Highness the Crown Prince or the King. It is indefensible to give a man like P. L. M. a state subsidy. I do not say this because of the piddling 500 rix-dollars; as far as I am concerned he could get 1,000 if it is paid to him at the workhouse, but it compromises a nation to let a man like that get a state subsidy; it insults the others who get it, and it outrages the better minds in the younger generation.

But with regard to P. L. Møller I have done enough for the sake of the public, and on my own account I do not care about anything. But this form of swindle, using a state subsidy in such a way, is perhaps worth remembering for purely poetic use at some other time.

VIII[1] A 444　n.d., 1847

« **6081**

A book could be written
      Clues to Illuminate the Modern Religious Confusion
                           in
                      Aphorisms
Perhaps this form (glints and glimmers) would be most illuminating; a rigorous development of certain concepts which the age has
completely forgotten might promote the sickness: didacticism. In any
case, I may do it myself sometime, or perhaps my successor.

These journals could be useful. Concerning "authority," the relationship between God and man, the mission in present-day Christendom, etc.

VIII[1] A 445   *n.d.*, 1847

« **6082**

As a motto for part of my life's suffering I can, with a curious
freemasonry,[1710] use these words by the poet:[1711]

Infandum me jubes R e g i n a renovare dolorem.

VIII[1] A 446   *n.d.*, 1847

« **6083**

The girl has given me enough trouble. Now she is—not dead—but
happily and well married.[1712] I said that on the same day six years ago
—and was declared the basest of all base villains. Curious!

VIII[1] A 447   *n.d.*, 1847

« **6084**

Blosius, p. 407[1713]

*Totius perfectionis verissima regula haec est: esto humilis, et ubicunque te
ipsum inveneris, te ipsum relinque.*

VIII[1] A 450   *n.d.*, 1847

« **6085**

Alas, yes, I admit it, it has concerned me very much and very
sincerely to recognize each and every poor man who recognized me,
to remember to greet each and every servant with whom I have been
related in the slightest way, to remember that the last time I saw him
he had been ill and to ask how he was. Never in my life, not even when

most preoccupied with an idea, have I been so busy that I could not
take time to stand still if a poor man spoke to me. Is that then a crime?
I would have been ashamed before God and would have distressed my
soul if I had become so self-important that I might give the impression
that "other men" did not exist for me. Do not these other men exist
before God, and before him is not the requirement even greater that
I do not conceitedly become self-important but confess in action that
obedience is dearer to God than the fat of rams.

Was that a crime—since I am derided for doing it? Yes, it was
imprudent—imprudent according to the understanding of wretched
prudence.

And now the poorer class, who are being indoctrinated by degrees
to see in me a haughty fellow who wants to muscle in on them. O, you
fools, it is easy enough for you to get catchpenny writers who steal
money out of your pocket as an honorarium for confusing your con-
ceptions, but it is much more difficult to find one who really loves you.
One has to be very unhappy and melancholy, yes, if one is a man, one
almost has to have a troubled conscience to assist in loving the neighbor in order to endure all that one thereby exposes himself to. —It is
not noticed that those who hide behind their aristocracy are the very
ones who scorn the poor.

VIII^1 A 452   *n.d.*, 1847

« **6086**

My habit of walking the streets[1714] a great deal was once regarded
as vanity and aroused anger. It was not suspected that I did it to
undermine the impression I made (the maieutic). Now it is realized
that walking the streets a great deal robs one of esteem—and so now
they are angry with me because I do not keep to myself more, because
I am not exclusive.

VIII^1 A 453   *n.d.*, 1847

« **6087**

With respect to the acceptance of Christianity it is really another
fallacy on Mynster's[1715] part (Christianly understood it regards the
soundness of the natural man a little too highly) to say of those whom
Christianity makes too melancholy and unhappy: I do not know why
I should adopt the doctrine if I do not benefit from it. For the category
is: one *shall* accept Christianity, whether it promptly makes a person
glad or sad. The Mynster theory could easily lead to analogies with the
reasoning of Job's wife: Are you still going to keep on.

But as a rule Mynster swings all too soon away from the religious to commercial life and the bustle and hustle of activities. It is very clear that with Mynster Sunday comes but once a week—the other days are still lived partly in other categories. That is precisely why he sometimes is so powerfully gripped on Sunday, but he simply does not discover the inner difficulties of putting the religious to daily use.

VIII[1] A 455   n.d., 1847

« **6088** *Contemptible Lack of Character*

Mr. Hostrup[1716] writes a student comedy, naturally as harebrained and inconsiderate as possible, using no restraints whatsoever—after all, it would be unsporting for someone to have anything against it! Fine. But then should it not keep on being a student-comedy—that is, for students. But what happens, the play travels around the whole country, is finally performed in the Royal Theater—and now, as I see today in *Flyve-Posten,* [1717] in Norway, and in *Rigs-Tidenden,* the character who supposedly represents me is named outright: Søren Kierkegaard. No doubt the billboards have already carried my name openly in order to attract interest to the play.

And this is supposed to be a student comedy! And consequently the Danish stage has been demeaned to being *The Corsair!*

How cowardly the whole thing is. Either my name should have been on the billboard outside the Student Union from the very first or the whole character should have been removed.

It is loathsome to see how the Danes disgrace themselves and eagerly do their best to exhibit our shame to neighboring countries.

VIII[1] A 458   n.d., 1847

« **6089**

I see in the papers[1718] that my full name has appeared on the billboard, that I have been put on the stage, and that the actor who plays me has done it in such a masterly way that he has been greeted with applause. This seems to me to be inconsistent—for if it had been I in person, I would scarcely have been greeted with applause but no doubt with a little *pereat*[1719]—so the similarity still does not completely disappear.

Incidentally, I have nothing against anybody earning a few tips in these difficult times by turning me into money; here too he is not like me, for I can testify to the fact that the honorarium I have earned in Denmark amounts to less than nothing.[1720]

VIII[1] A 654   n.d., 1847

« **6090**

December 22

Dear Peter,[1721]

Now I have sold the house[1722] at last. I found a good buyer, which may in a way interest you also: Madame Bützov, widow of B., the broker.

Otherwise everything will remain unchanged. You retain your first mortgage in the sum of 7,000 rdl.[1723] and half of the bank lien. I spoke with you at one time about increasing your first mortgage. You were not willing to do that. Now it is unnecessary. I myself will assume a second mortgage of 5,000 rdl.

Both these are made non-cancellable for ten years on our part. That is the way Kraft, the attorney, has drawn up the papers. I have no objections, and it has not occurred to him that you would be anything but satisfied with this, as in fact I assume you are. But if everything had not been settled so quickly when at last the right buyer came along, I would of course have written to you at once to obtain your consent, so that I might in no way seem to have acted independently, even where I could safely count on your consent. God knows that these days I am so dizzy from all these financial matters that I am all too prone to pedantry.

By the way, I do not even remember how you obtained your first mortgage, but in any event the difference is purely a formal one. You will still wish to retain a mortgage on the property because it is that property and because it is an excellent first mortgage. Hence it does not matter at all that it will be non-cancellable for ten years. But on the other hand, if you wish to regard it as cash, then it is just as simple, whether it is non-cancellable or not, to sell to another owner, for it is very easy to obtain a first mortgage by public financing. A second mortgage is not so easy in that respect, for public finances are as a rule supposed to be invested in first mortgages. Although my second mortgage is non-cancellable for ten years, I still consider it just as good as cash.

And now it only remains for me to ask you to come to town as soon as possible after New Year to sign the new mortgage papers and to collect your interest.

As I have said, I would be very sad if there should be the least difficulty on your part or if you should decide that I have acted in any manner other than you yourself would have. I am no good at practical business matters and have a fantastic anxiety about lawyers and everything about them. Please do let me know by return mail, therefore, that you are satisfied.

Besides, I am glad that this matter has been settled and that I am happily and well out of it.

I hope you are well. I have learned that Jette has been ill. Please greet her from me, greet Poul, and accept my greeting for yourself.

Your Brother

[Address:]
To
Dr. Kierkegaard, Pastor
Pedersborg
v. Sorøe
[Postmark:]
Copenhagen
12/23
1847

Letters, no. 166   December 22, 1847

« **6091**

Dear Jette,[1724]

Thank you for your little letter which, in your own words, I must have before Christmas. I hasten to reply so that you may have my answer before New Year.

The period between Christmas and New Year is usually a particularly convenient time for me to receive letters, and a fortunate season for my correspondent, that is, if he thinks it fortunate to get a reply from me.

And now you are confined to bed again. Still, it was a sound and healthy—anything but sickly—decision to write to me right away as you did, even though you had not heard from me for so long. That, you see, is a favorable sign and makes me happy. "Last year at the same time you wrote a letter to me—but it was not sent." Then, you see, you were perhaps not bedridden, and yet your condition may have been more like that of a person who was.

Hence I am pleased on your behalf as well to have received this letter from you as a sign of health. Preserve it, and take care of it in the coming year, which God will surely make a happy one for you.

There is something closely connected with physical illness—that quiet, deeply painful, and slowly consuming worry which now turns over in agony on one side and imagines itself forgotten by others "who probably never give one a thought" and now turns over on the other side and is afraid that whatever one has to say or write will not be good enough. Oh, do banish that worry, which is especially dangerous for you because you are so frequently bedridden and constantly live in monotonous quiet. The person who is actively engaged in life soon forgets such thoughts, but the person who only sees little change around him may easily find that worrying almost becomes a necessity. When one lives in small rooms—as you know very well—they need frequent airing out; in the same way, when one entertains but few thoughts and has little diversion, then it is extremely important that what one inhales, spiritually understood, be good and beneficient and gentle and soothing thoughts.

You also need diversion, but diversion is not easily made available in monotony. And yet it is perhaps easier than one thinks if only one is willing. It is generally believed that what determines the direction of one's thoughts lies in the external and is the greater or lesser probability of this or that. But that is not so. That which determines the direction of one's thoughts lies basically in one's own self. He who has a tendency to melancholy, for example, most probably always finds unhappiness. Why? Because melancholy lies within him. In this hypothetical case there would be as great a probability of the opposite, perhaps even greater, but he arbitrarily breaks off and immediately has enough to be able to conclude that something unhappy will happen to him.

But what is it then to "have faith"? To have faith is constantly to expect the joyous, the happy, the good. But is not that an extraordinary and blessed diversion! Oh, what more does one need then? What I am about to say next might almost seem like a joke, but is in fact very serious and indeed sincerely meant for you. You are in some measure always suffering—hence the task lies right here: Divert your *mind, accustom yourself by faith to changing suffering into expectation of the joyous. It is really possible.* What is required is this flexibility in the quiet of the mind, which, whenever things go wrong for one, in that very instant begins all over again and says, "Yes! Yes! Next time it will work." Oh, if one were never to see another human being again—and that is far from your case—then one could *by faith conjure* up or forth a world of diversion into the loneliest room.

In general it is probably right to warn against self-love; still, I consider it *my duty to say to every sufferer* with whom I come into contact: *See to it that you love yourself.* When one is suffering and unable to do much for others, it is easy to fall prey to the melancholy thought that one is superfluous in this world, as others perhaps sometimes give one to understand. Then one must remember that *before God every person is equally important, without reservation equally important;* indeed, if there were any distinction, then one who suffers the most must be the closest object of God's care. And also in this lies infinite Godly diversion. But I will stop; I can truthfully say I have no more room. Take care of yourself, dear Jette. Happy New Year! Thank you for concluding the old one so beautifully by thinking of me. Greetings to Peter and to Poul.[1725]

Your devoted

S.K.

Letters, no. 167 [December, 1847]

« **6092**

When I eventually publish the discourses on the Atonement, it will be best to entitle them:

"Work of Love."[1726]

VIII[1] A 472   *n.d.,* 1847

« **6093**

There has really been great effort here at home to settle if possible the question of my significance and my work as a thinker in a rather unphilosophical manner: by the rabble—with fists.

VIII[1] A 481   *n.d.,* 1847

« **6094** *Invitation*

The undersigned plans to give a little series of lectures on the organizing trend throughout my entire work as an author[1727] and its relation to the modern period illuminated by references to the past.

As auditors I have in mind particularly theological graduates or even more advanced students. It is assumed that the auditors will be well acquainted with the works, and others are requested not to consider this invitation. I would add that these lectures will in no sense be an enjoyment but rather hard work, and therefore I do not entice anyone. And this work will have times, in the understanding of the moment and of impatience, when it is plain boring, which in my opinion is inseparable from all deeper understanding, and therefore I warn everyone against participating. If I succeed in being understood, the auditor will have the benefit that his life will have been made considerably more difficult than ever, and for this reason I urge no one to accept this invitation.

As soon as ten have signed up, I will begin; the limit is twenty, inasmuch as I wish to have such a relation to the auditors that the lectures might be, if necessary, made colloquies.

The fee is five rix-dollars, registration with the undersigned.

VIII² B 186   *n.d.*, 1847–48

« **6095** *Invitation*

Gratified to learn that my upbuilding writings, addressed to the single individual, are still read by many individuals, I have considered obliging these my readers, and perhaps gaining more individuals as readers, by publishing such works in the future in smaller sections on a subscription basis.[1728] The possible advantages are, first, that the books will be read better if they are read in smaller sections, second, that a certain calmness of understanding may enter into the relation between author and reader, so that a beginning need not be made each time, and finally, that the publication can properly take place quietly and unnoticed, avoiding the attention of all those not concerned.

From July 1 of this year I plan, then. . . .

S. Kierkegaard
January, 1848

VIII² B 188   January, 1848

« **6096** *Some Discourses to be Written for Awakening*[1729]

wound
Thoughts which attack from behind—for awakening.*

"Guard your foot when you go into the house of the Lord" (Ecclesiastes).[1730] See one of the earlier journals† [i.e., VIII¹ A 256].

This will be the introduction.

In the following discourses the text is to be chosen in such a way that it appears to be a Gospel text, and is that also, but then comes the stinger.

No. 1. "What shall we have, we who have left all?" And Christ answers: You will sit on thrones[1731] etc.

The satire for us in this question—we who have not left anything at all.

No. 2. All things serve for good, *if* we love God.[1732] If we love God. (The irony.)

No. 3. The resurrection of the dead is at hand, both of the righteous and the unrighteous.[1733]

Rejoice, you are not to ask for three proofs[1734]—it is certain enough that you are immortal—it is absolutely certain—for you must come up for judgment.[1735] This is a new argument for immortality.

No. 4. It is blessed—to be mocked for a good cause.[1736] (Rejoice when men speak all sorts of evil about you.[1737])

So rejoice, then—but perhaps there is no one present to whom this discourse applies.[1738] You, my listener, rejoice perhaps because you are highly honored, esteemed, and regarded. Yes, then indeed for you it is a meal like the stork's at the fox's house.

The satirical.

"Woe to you if everyone speaks well of you."[1739] Here is not appended "and lies"; it is not necessary, for if everyone speaks well of a person, it must be a lie.

No. 5. "For salvation is nearer to us now than when we first believed."[1740] But are you sure you have become a believer.

No. 6. He (Christ) was believed on in the world[1741] (I Timothy 3:16). But this is perhaps merely a bit of historical information.

*In margin: "An assault by thoughts"

†Journal NB², pp. 147–48 [i.e., VIII¹ A 256]. Ditto, pp. 242, bottom, and 243, top [i.e., VIII¹ A 367].

VIII¹ A 486   n.d., 1847

« 6097

What is written on the subject of the hymnbook is very mediocre. The singing of hymns engages me more than anything else in the whole church service. For a good hymn, I insist on altogether simple and to a certain extent insignificant words (in this respect there are many in the evangelical hymnbook[1742] which are outright excellent, quite as they should be, and which it would be impossible for the impetuous Grundtvig[1743] to write) and then one of those fervent melodies. I know Kingo's hymns[1744] by heart, but they are not at all suitable for singing, the whole expression is too strong, the lyrics far too pretentious. Such hymns are read at home for one's own upbuilding.

But of the piety which actually is the piety of a quiet suffering person (and this is the proper piety) Grundtvig has no knowledge at all. Grundtvig is and was and remains a boisterous fellow; even in eternity he will irritate me. It is not as if Grundtvig has not gone through anything—of course he has—but always boisterously. There are a few things which bring him to a halt, but then he makes a big noise like a train pounding on its way. The deeper, inward pain which in quiet sadness is reconciled with God is unknown to Grundtvig, and precisely this is the hymn's true tone. Grundtvig is a jaunty yodeler, or a bellowing blacksmith.

What inwardness in such a song as *"Hjertelig mig nu længes."*[1745] I could no more become tired of repeating such a song than tired of looking at the sky in autumn's gray weather when the soft, gentle colors shift and change in the finest design.

VIII[1] A 487   *n.d.,* 1847

« **6098**

Should one laugh or cry over it. *Aftenbladet*[1746] apologizes because the review of my *Works of Love* is so disproportionately long. A few days later the same paper[1747] produces an article just about as long which is a police report in the trial of a thief. Here no apology is necessary, for it is enormously important.

VIII[1] A 496   *n.d.,* 1847

« **6099** *Goldschmidt*

He gives the same impression in his program[1748] as a confirmand, or someone who has to stand up next Sunday and be examined; he knows everything inside out—about what a free-state is—has done all his homework, which everyone can do. It is graduate school prose—or like an essay written for the preliminary examination for Danish law students and veterinarians.

There is an unbelievable difference between the brash bold Goldschmidt secure behind privileged contemptibleness and the self-conscious little Goldschmidt. He looks something like a person who has been key man at all the dance halls and pubs standing in elite company and picking at his scarf. As a mother says to her child who has been naughty and now is being good again: Now I cannot recognize you.

But Mr. Goldschmidt has help. The main thing is perhaps his connections, his European connections, his connections all over Europe. He himself says: They have stipulated that their articles to Mr. G. may be printed *afterwards* in foreign journals.[1749] Joy over Denmark! What the King of Denmark has barely managed through his ministers to secure for Denmark—to be the foremost state in Europe—G. has achieved by his travels "from which he has recently returned."[1750]

–If only we can keep G. here so that he is not suddenly summoned to a European Conference in Neuchatel (where he has been; see–[1751]). Alas, alas. Unless he decides not to go in person but allows himself to be represented in the usual way (as kings by cabinet ministers)–by a blackguard.[1752] –In that case we can keep him here and benefit by his powerful connections abroad, all over Europe, his friends in Germany, England, France, Italy, Switzerland, etc. Yes, we are benefited–unless those friends are counterparts of the ones Gert W.[1753] (who also has traveled abroad) encountered in his travels: a hatter's apprentice, a strapping farm hand, a hangman with whom he drank *Dus*, etc.

VIII[1] A 655   *n.d.*, 1847–48

« **6100**

I do not deny it, I am firmly convinced of it, although Bishop Mynster[1754] himself might not maintain it; it is my firm conviction that if the world one day suddenly were to be turned upside down and Bishop Mynster were threatened with death if he did not give up Christianity, he would choose death. But, but that is not the issue. If one is prudent and things are going smoothly, it is possible of course to calculate danger in advance and avoid it. As yet there is no question of sacrificing one's life; it is a negligible matter–and precisely because it is a negligible matter there are no recriminations for avoiding it–and one never enters into danger. Furthermore, one may be right, it may be true that if it were a matter of life, one would risk his life. *Aber,* Bishop Mynster dominates many by means of his prudence, but there is one thing he cannot dominate: his prudence; he does not have his prudence in the power of enthusiasm. Since life rarely provides the great scenes where it is a matter of life and death (and least of all do they come like Christmas to a spoiled child; they come in the train of not avoiding danger with the help of prudence), and since he wards off every minor decision with the help of prudence, his life is in the power of a great illusion.

VIII[1] A 503   *n.d.*, 1848

« **6101** *Instructions for "Joyful Notes in the Strife of Suffering"*[1755]

These discourses are presented in such a way as to be continually tangential to the consciousness of sin and the suffering of sin–sin etc. are another matter: these discourses come to the subject of sin. Because the consolation lyrically rises as high as possible over all earthly need and misery, even the heaviest, the horror of sin is constantly banished. Thus another theme is cunningly concealed in these discourses: sin is man's corruption.

In the ordinary sermon this is precisely the confusion: need and adversity are preached together—with sin.

Thus the category for these discourses is different from "The Gospel of Suffering,"[1756] which leaves the suffering indefinite. Here the distinction is made: innocent suffering—in order to approach sin.

VIII[1] A 504   *n.d.*, 1848

« 6102

I cannot entertain the thought of forming an alliance with anyone. It is certainly possible to get men to endure some difficulty and opposition in the hope of victory as soon as possible. But the thought of having to lose more and more (which is the essentially Christian idea), to see before one a whole life dedicated to suffering, to be compelled to renounce the advantages offered (since no earthly advantage can be won and cashed in on without corrupting the undertaking itself—just as one corrupts an unselfish, sacrificial act by taking money for it): nobody can be persuaded to accept that.

VIII[1] A 507   *n.d.*, 1848

« 6103

Mynster's[1757] religion is something like this: living essentially as an upright pagan, making one's personal life comfortable and good, enjoying its amenities—but admitting in all this that one is very far from having reached the highest. It is this admission[1758] that he essentially regards as Christianity. Those he fights against as pagans are not the ones who live this pleasant life but those who will not make this admission. —It is a rather cheap edition of Christianity; it is fairly easy to make this admission.

And yet this is the *summa summarum* of his orthodoxy. Just as zealously as he fights those who will not make this admission, he fights, perhaps even more zealously, those who want to try to raise it a bit higher, although they also willingly make the admission. He fights them most zealously of all, unless they have died—then he honors them.

VIII[1] A 508   *n.d.*, 1848

« 6104

. . . . . I may live for thirty years, or perhaps forty, or maybe just one day: therefore I have resolved to use this day, or whatever I have to say in these thirty years or whatever I have to say this one day I may have to live–I have resolved to use it in such a way that if not one day in my whole past life has been used well, this one by the help of God will be.[1759]

VIII[1] A 533 n.d., 1848

« **6105**

This is the difference. If persecution comes from the government, one shows up well; a vain person could be tempted for the sake of the cause to go too far because it looks so góod to be the object of persecution by such a power. But when one suffers persecution by the mob, the people, the public, in short, the scum which the daily press is able to dredge up, at best by an anonymous dredger: then one has to use nine-tenths of his energy in minimizing the persecution itself; one cannot very well be celebrated for talking about such things, etc. This is the difference. When one is persecuted by the government, by the powers that be, there is a focus on decisions which time and again will make an impact (a fine, a sentence, etc.), but mob-persecution or persecution by the public is sheer dailiness, day in and day out, every day the same, every moment a new arrival knowing nothing about a person except that people grin at him in the most impudent way. They know that they are *supposed to do it,* it is their duty, for the press has ordered it. Here there is no question of modesty and bashfulness–they are doing a good deed authorized by the public mind when they ridicule a person, abuse him, shout after him, etc., when they even insult his driver so that he almost becomes afraid because he cannot understand what it all means.

What I do lack is physical strength. My mind is calm. I have always thought of myself as having to be sacrificed; now I have received my orders and I will abide by the command I have been given. Ordinarily I can take it. But when, for example, seeking recreation, I take a drive[1760] of fifteen or twenty miles and sit in the carriage in the happy ferment of thought, my body gradually becomes somewhat weak, partly from the riding, partly from the purely mental exertion, and then when I get out and it so happens I am received by a smirking, grinning crowd, and some of those present are nice enough to call me names, then my physical state is powerfully affected. Or when I have taken a long walk out on some solitary path,[1761] lost in my own thoughts, and then suddenly meet three or four louts way out there where I am all alone and they start to call me names, my physical state is powerfully affected. I do not have the physical strength for a fight

—and I know nothing which makes me more depressed than such a scene. I have the ability to make any man listen to reason—except the raw boor, to say nothing of three of them who have orders from the press: there can be no discussion with him.

Yet my faith is unshaken that I will remain standing on the spot. There must be an awakening if coarse brutality is not to prevail altogether in Denmark. For me it has had a good side. I really would not have been able to illuminate Christianity the way I have been allowed to do if all this had not happened to me.

VIII[1] A 544   *n.d.*, 1848

« **6106**

My brother's petty-mindedness and envy are all my family[1762] has done for me. He has been interested only in getting a free copy of what I wrote. Then when I plunged into *The Corsair,* he was gratified, for now he found that everything that happened to me was God's punishment. God's name can be misused in many ways. Now he is commencing to write[1763] a little—he borrows a little from me but without mentioning it; he is after all a Grundtvigian, and in all likelihood he does not read what I write, as they say in his circle of acquaintants —and then one can be utilized very nicely. And when I die, then he will come sneaking up and be—my brother, my brother who with brotherly concern has followed my endeavors, who knew me so intimately, etc.

But he does lead a more fortunate life. He sets himself up against the government. And what then? He enjoys honor and status and admiration as a martyr—and what then? Then he keeps his position. No one rumples a hair of his head.[1764] You see, candidates for this kind of martyrdom can be found!

VIII[1] A 545   *n.d.*, 1848

« **6107**

If one aims to elevate a whole period, one must really know it. That is why the proclaimers of Christianity who begin right off with orthodoxy actually do not have much influence and only on a few. For Christianity goes way back. One has to begin with paganism. For example, I begin with *Either/Or.* In that way I have managed to get the age to go along with me without ever dreaming where it is going or where we now are. But men have become aware of the issues. They cannot get rid of me just because they went along with *Either/Or* so happily. Now they may want to abandon me, they could put me to death, but it is of no use, they have me for good. If one begins immediately with Christianity, they say: this is nothing for us—and put themselves immediately on guard.

But as it says in my last discourse,[1765] my whole huge literary work has just one idea, and that is: to wound from behind.

Praise be to God in heaven—I say no more; anything else a man adds is rubbish.

VIII[1] A 548   *n.d.*, 1848

« **6108**

My whole life is an epigram to make men aware. That is why I must strive to the uttermost to stand alone—when its time comes the epigram will wound all the more deeply. It is a frightful strain; many is the time I scarcely dare think of the enormous weight I carry on my head. But every day I tackle a little bit and say to myself: Obedience is dearer to God than the fat of rams.[1766]

I can be understood only after my death; while I live I can be happy in the conviction that I will be understood; I myself can understand why I cannot be understood before and that it is my task, the work of self-renunciation, but it is truly an enormous labor.

When one is in this position, he does not need three proofs[1767] of the immortality of the soul. Great God, if by faith in eternity I did not have that right at hand, I would have succumbed long ago.

VIII[1] A 549   *n.d.*, 1848

« **6109**

What a clever story it is, the one in *1001 Nights*[1768] (*Geschichte der zwei neidischen Schwestern, Nacht* 617–637, III) that tells of an expedition in search of the talking bird, the singing tree, and the golden water. The task was to climb a high mountain. But the resistance was invisible (as the dervish in fact says to the one prince who was not afraid of any danger: Have you considered what it means to do battle with the invisible); it was nothing more nor less than voices that shouted and made an uproar, scolded, shocked, whined, ridiculed, etc.—and if one looked around he became a stone.

VIII[1] A 557   *n.d.*, 1848

« **6110 *N.B.   N.B.***

A new book ought to be written entitled: **Thoughts That Cure Radically, Christian Healing.**

It will deal with the doctrine of the Atonement, showing first of all that the root of the sickness is sin. It will have two parts. Perhaps it is better to have three.

1. First comes: Thoughts that wound from behind[1769]—for up-building.[1770] This will be the polemical element, something like "The Cares of the Pagans,"[1771] but somewhat stronger; then Christian discourses should be given in an altogether milder tone.[1772]

(1) [*changed from:* (2)] On the consciousness of sin.
The Sickness unto Death
Christian Discourses
(2) [*changed from:* (3)] **Radical Cure**
[*changed from:*] *Thoughts That Cure Radically*[1773]
Christian Healing
The Atonement

VIII[1] A 558   *n.d.*, 1848

« **6111**

I almost went and upset the whole design of *Christian Discourses* and their original purpose by including in them "Thoughts Which Wound from Behind for Upbuilding"[1774] simply because these discourses were lying there ready. A polemical piece like that belongs there least of all; it will itself be weakened by its surroundings and divert all attention away from the "Friday Discourses."[1775] No, my intention is to be as gentle as possible, right after that the powerful polemic in *Works of Love*. In this way the Christian discourses are sustained. Then, too, I may take a journey, and I would like to depart in peace. Finally, the book was getting too large; the smaller, the better I am read.

VIII[1] A 559   *n.d.*, 1848

« **6112**

No, no, no, no—I did, however, almost fail to appreciate how in Part Three Governance had added what was needed. But I wanted to be a bit clever and arrange something myself.

As so often happens, so it happened here, too. I had not thought that the third part, which was written last, should go into *Christian Discourses*.* But that is precisely where it belongs. It had not occurred to me, but Governance ordained it in such a way that, sure enough, the little book was ready just when I was about to publish *Christian Discourses.*

Without the third part *Christian Discourses* is much too mild, for me not truly in character; they are mild enough as it is. And how in the world would I get a more felicitous juxtaposition than with the enormous thrust in the third part—and the hidden inwardness in the fourth, simply because it is the communion on Friday.

The book does not become too large, either; on the contrary, without this section I would even have had to have it printed in larger type in order to reach a certain number of sheets.

Then, too, without Part Three *Christian Discourses* is too repetitious.

But as I said, I wanted to be clever. That is not good. In trust and confidence in God I would rather accept from his hand whatever comes than have a comfortable situation if I have shrewdly avoided a potential danger in order to achieve it. No doubt I do need some encouragement. If God will give it to me, I accept it with fervent gratitude. But the embarrassment that would make my heart stand still, the embarrassment that comes over me at the thought that I possibly had let God call and had shrewdly stepped aside—no, this I could not endure. When the devoted teacher looks affectionately at the child and says: Come, now, make a big jump, my little friend, but if you are afraid, if you do not feel like it, well, then, don't do it—what a shame if the child were to sadden the teacher by not doing it. So also in a man's relationship to God; he compels no one, he tells one of the dangers in advance, he frightens one through scary imaginings—and then looks at one and says: Just go ahead confidently, my child, but if you are afraid, I will not force you. Truly, there is no more compelling method than this!

At your word, O Lord! When a person does something in this spirit, then, humanly speaking, he is prepared for the worst—but yet, yet I cannot do otherwise. Then he does not expect a happy ending, humanly speaking; he believes that it is possible, that it may happen just the same—but one thing is certain: God will not let him go, God will remain with him in a cheerful boldness which is worth far more than all the world's beds of roses.

It follows as a matter of course that I again have considered the possibilities which, if I had initiated a single other person into them, would have prompted him to say: For God's sake, stop. This is why I keep silent. I cannot do otherwise—Amen. However, it could also be very possible that much of what I shudder to think about is a gloomy illusion. Perhaps so. But the impression it makes is just as powerful! And it is still true—what I have always said and taught—that true action is the inner decision.

But Mynster has touched me by retaining his friendship for me in spite of *Works of Love*. I would so much like to humor him once. I know he would like *Christian Discourses* if it did not have Part Three. But I cannot do it. I would also have liked to dedicate the fourth part to him,[1776] but that cannot be done. Perhaps here again it is only a gloomy illusion that he would get angry about Part Three; it would even be unfair of him; but in any case I have acted with this pressure upon me also. O, the more pressures there are, the clearer it is that one needs God and the clearer it is that one makes decisions trusting in God.

VIII[1] A 560   *n.d.*, 1848

« **6113**

**In margin of 6112 (VIII[1] A 560):*
Part Three is the weaving of Governance—that it was finished at the right time without my really understanding how it belonged.

VIII[1] A 561   *n.d.*

« **6114** *Instructions*

First of all, publish a book of essays.[1777] For this the book on Adler can be used as I arranged it formerly. And then a new one will be added: How was it possible that Jesus Christ could be deprived of his life.* This essay must come out, particularly together with the two about the collision between the universal and the single individual and the one on the relation between a genius and an apostle, before I begin on the doctrine of sin.[1778]

VIII[1] A 562   *n.d.*, 1848

« **6115**

**In margin of 6114 (VIII[1] A 563):*
N.B. If this essay is to be pseudonymous, I must add it as a supplement; then the title will be "Essays" by S.K., with a supplement.

VIII[1] A 563   *n.d.*

« **6116** *What It Means To Fast*

To fast is to sorrow over one's sins.
            And that is done best by anointing one's head and wash-
      ing one's face so that one does not *seem* to be fasting.[1779]

VIII[1] A 570   *n.d.*, 1848

« **6117**

[Copy of *Nye Testament* (Copenhagen: 1820) with folded corners, underlining, and marginal notes by Kierkegaard.[1780]]

VIII[2] C 3   *n.d.*, 1847–48(?)

« 6118

In *Christian Discourses,* Part Three, No. 6

This discourse quite properly is constructed in such a way that it could almost just as well be a discourse about what has been interwoven as a commentary: Woe to you if everybody speaks well of you. Its polemical aim, therefore, must also be at such an existence: to be a joiner, to be a nobody, to be insignificant, etc. Anyone who has any kind of prominence must expose himself to something—but the numerical, gloating numbers, the crowd, is in the difficult position of being able to avoid all spiritual trials.

VIII[1] A 576   *n.d.,* 1848

« 6119 *Palavering*

..... Yes, in one respect I willingly confess that most of my contemporaries have a great advantage over me, something they certainly never let me forget: viewed from the standpoint of animal qualifications, as a plough horse or a beef animal to be butchered, I am far behind them. I have neither muscles and strong legs nor fat flesh. No wonder I am looked down upon by others. The same thing, after all, is true of horned cattle. The steer walks around proudly with his head high, conscious of weighing a thousand pounds and that he will make an enormous, fat roast. And on the other hand there is the poor creature that slinks around in disgrace, the poor wretch that weighs only three hundred pounds, without an ounce of fat on its bones.

VIII[1] A 577   *n.d.,* 1848

« 6120

The person I portrayed (in the first discourse on the cares of the pagans[1781]) as crudely talking about the earnestness of life is not, as one immediately sees, what is called a poor man—indeed, I could never imagine such a person talking that way. No, it is a journalist, one of those who live, perhaps luxuriously and superfluously, live by writing about—poverty.

VIII[1] A 589   *n.d.,* 1848

« 6121

The contrast between the third and fourth parts of *Christian Discourses* is as sharp as possible and very intense: first there is something like a temple-cleansing—and then the quiet and most intimate of all worship services—the Communion service on Friday.

VIII[1] A 590   *n.d.,* 1848

« **6122**

The reason behind all this conflict with the Grundtvigians is a misunderstanding. The charge is that the Grundtvigians imagine they are the only true Christians, a little flock who, to keep themselves occupied, now are busy with all kinds of trifles.

They must be reproached for something entirely different: that they do not do anything to communicate Christianity to other men. It is a kind of eudaimonism, a sort of opulence, to live on enjoying Christianity, to keep it for themselves, and their talk about tolerance is rubbish. Christianity has never been tolerant in such a way that it has let others be pagans or be lost. No, it has been so intolerant that the apostle would rather lose his life in order to proclaim Christianity. Intolerance, to be sure, is wanting to dominate others, but we forget that it certainly is not intolerance to be willing to suffer in order to help others.

VIII[1] A 591   *n.d.,* 1848

« **6123**

Goldschmidt will no doubt end up becoming a cabinet minister. He quite properly began by despising himself; that is how one gets to be somebody these days, when the waves of agitation are too violent to notice that someone reverses himself seventeen times—if he only despises himself in such a way that there is no halting induced from within, it will work.

VIII[1] A 595   *n.d.,* 1848

« **6124**

In Part Three of *Christian Discourses,* discourse six, the passage at the end: whose only concern is to achieve the *ungodliness* of having everybody everywhere speak well of them.[1782] It is altogether correct, precisely because Christianity teaches that this cannot happen to a person except through ungodliness. It is impossible for anyone with an earnest conviction (which everyone, Christianly, ought to have) to achieve this. Consequently if anyone does achieve it, it is *eo ipso* his ungodliness. Christianity does not have a frivolous idea of what happens to a man, that, for example, everyone speaks well of him. For Christianity says: Such a thing must not happen to you, any more than stealing, whoring, etc. You will not be able to defend yourself by saying that you did not covet it, that you are not responsible—for you are to live as Christianity requires you to live, and then it is *eo ipso* impossible

for it to happen to you. If it does happen, then it is *eo ipso* proof that
you are not living as Christianity requires you to live.

VIII[1] A 596   n.d., 1848

« 6125

March 27, 1848

Once again for a moment I have been concerned about my responsibility in letting *Christian Discourses,* especially Part Three, be
published.* It is outright dangerous for me to have something written
in a completely different situation be read under the current circumstances.[1783] But I cannot do otherwise. It is Governance which has
arranged it this way for me. I have not plunged myself into any danger.
My manuscript was sent in[1784] long before this latest event, which no
doubt has changed men somewhat. Every word in my discourses is true
—nothing is more certain. I have nothing to change. Should I take it
back, then, because of personal danger? No, that I dare not do. What
I am I am simply and solely by believing in and obeying God. The
moment I catch myself cravenly fleeing any danger in which he has
willed to take me, then I will have escaped the danger all right—but to
my own degradation, alas—I will collapse into nothing. With God I can
endure all things—in God I hope this; without God, nothing.

Perhaps there is considerable hypochondria in my fear, but that
makes no difference. God knows how I suffer—but God will also help
me, and my cause.

And so I sit here. Out there everything is agitated; the nationality
issue inundates everyone; everyone is talking about sacrificing life and
blood, is perhaps willing to do it as well, but shored up by the omnipotence of public opinion. And so I sit in a quiet room (no doubt I will
soon be in bad repute for indifference to the nation's cause)—I know
only one risk, the risk of religiousness, but no one cares about that—
and no one has any intimation of what is taking place in me. Well, such
is my life. Always misunderstanding. At the point where I suffer, I am
misunderstood—and I am hated.

VIII[1] A 602   March 27, 1848

« 6126

**In margin of 6125* (VIII[1] A 602):
And contrary to my custom for week-days, I opened Mynster[1785]
and read my sermon, which I otherwise would have read on Sunday,

and it was on Nicodemus.[1786] What an admonition against my beating a hasty retreat.

VIII[1] A 603   *n.d.*, 1848

« 6127

Spirit in times like these has become a superfluity; art, science, and the like have become a luxury. There was a woman the other day who passionately complained that directly across from her lived a man who had a bowling alley; she found it offensive to national feeling that anyone in these days ran a bowling alley. And just as that poor wretch of a man presumably will slink around now and not dare lift his eyes because he is not a patriot[1787] but runs a bowling alley, so we poor authors, artists as well, etc., are becoming aware that if this does not stop we will (in the earnestness of the age) come to be as detested as joy-girls.

VIII[1] A 666   *n.d.*, 1848

« 6128

At present the reality [*Realitet*] of my work as an author has become, of course, nil, less than nil, will soon be a crime. In order to get money from the state and status as a patriot, I ultimately will be compelled to offer my services to *Fædrelandet* as a paper boy to deliver papers.

VIII[1] A 669   *n.d.*, 1848

« 6129

Brorson,[1788] no. 70, verse 5:

> That heaven is my goal,
> And the way is steadfastness.

VIII[1] A 634   *n.d.*, 1848

« 6130 *Seven discourses*[1789] *could be written on these words:*

Come to me, all who labor and are heavy-laden,
and I will give you rest.[1790]

In margin: See journal NB[5] p. 26 [i.e., IX A 33].

Come to me; for he assumes that those who labor and are heavy laden really feel the burden and the labor and now stand perplexed and moaning. One person is still looking all around for a way out, another sits in his bereavement and sees no consolation in sight, etc., but all are seeking; therefore he says: Come to me. He does not invite one who has stopped seeking.[1791]

Come to me. For he assumes that those who labor and are heavy-laden are so overstrained and exhausted that, as if in a stupor, they have almost forgotten that there is consolation, however much they wanted to be helped—it is a kind of swooning of the spirit. That is why he must call to them and recall to them that there is consolation.[1792]

VIII[1] A 637   n.d., 1848

« 6131 *N.B.   N.B.*

Wednesday, April 19

My whole nature is changed. My concealment and inclosing re-serve [*Indesluttethed*[1793]] are broken—I am free to speak.

Great God, grant me grace!

It is true what my father said of me: "You will never amount to anything as long as you have money." He spoke prophetically; he thought I would lead a wild life. But not exactly that. No, but with my acumen and with my melancholy, and then to have money—O, what a propitious climate for developing all kinds of self-torturing torments in my heart.*

How marvelously timed—just when I had resolved to speak, my physician came. I did not, however, speak to him; it seemed too sud-den. But my resolution remains firm—to speak.

Maundy Thursday and Good Friday have become true holy days for me.

VIII[1] A 640   April 19, 1848

« 6132

Addition to 6131 (VIII[1] A 640): *Alas, she could not break the silence of my melancholy. That I loved her—nothing is more certain—and in this way my melancholy got enough to feed upon, O, it got a frightful extra measure.† That I became a writer was due essentially to her, my melancholy, and my money. Now, by the help of God, I shall become myself. I now believe that Christ will help me to triumph over my melancholy, and then I shall become a pastor.

In my melancholy I have still loved the world, for I loved my melancholy. Everything has been conducive to a higher tension of the relationship for me; her suffering, all my endeavor, and finally that I have had to experience derision and now am brought to the point where I am obliged to earn a living have all contributed with God's help to a break-through.

† And yet she could not become mine. I was and am a penitent and only got a frightfully intensified punishment through having entered into this relationship.

VIII[1] A 641   n.d., 1848

« **6133** *N.B.   N.B.*

Easter Monday

No, no, my inclosing reserve[1794] still cannot be broken, at least not now. The thought of wanting to break it continually occupies me so much and in such a way that it only becomes more and more chronic.

Yet I find some consolation in having talked with my physician. I have frequently been apprehensive about myself, that I might be too proud to speak to anyone. But just as I have done it before, so I have done it again. And what could a physician say, really? Nothing. But for me it is important to have had respect for this human authority.

My intellectual work satisfies me completely and makes me submit to everything gladly, if I only may give myself to it. I can understand my life in this way: that I declare consolation and joy to others while I am myself bound in a pain for which I can see no alleviation—except this, that I am able to work with my mind in this way. Ah, in this respect I truly cannot complain about the conditions of my life; on the contrary, I thank God every day that he has granted me much more than I ever expected; I pray every day that he will permit me to dare to thank him—this he knows.

But this was the situation. My future becomes more and more difficult economically.[1795] If I did not have this closedupness to lug around, I could accept an appointment. Now it is difficult. I have long pondered the possibility of a break-through, and because hitherto I have operated essentially as an escapist, trying to forget, I have frequently thought it my duty to make an attempt to take the offensive, particularly since this inclosing reserve can become an occasion of sin for me.

Had I not done this, I should always have this to reproach me. Now I have done it, and I understand myself again, better than before, for which this has been helpful.

Now I hope that God in some way or other will come to the aid of my work as a writer or will in other ways help me make a living and thus permit me to continue as a writer.

I do believe in the forgiveness of sins, but I interpret this, as before, to mean that I must bear my punishment of remaining in this painful prison of inclosing reserve all my life, in a more profound sense separated from the company of other men, yet mitigated by the thought that God has forgiven me. As yet, at least, I cannot come to such heights of faith, I cannot yet win such cheerful confidence of faith that I can believe that painful memory away. But in faith I protect myself against despair, bear the pain and punishment of my closedupness and am so indescribably happy or blessed in the activity of mind and spirit which God has granted to me so richly and graciously.

If my closedupness is to be broken, it is perhaps more likely to happen in some way or other by God's helping me into an occupation and then helping me to concentrate fully on this. But to want to break inclosing reserve formally by continually thinking about breaking it leads to the very opposite.

VIII[1] A 645   April 24, 1848

« 6134

But I am in need of physical recreation and rest. The proofreading of the last book at such a time, spiritual trial [Anfægtelse] with regard to its publication, the economic question[1796] amid the difficulties of the times, seven years of continuous work, having to move, and now that even Anders[1797] is being taken from me and I am all alone—yet constantly working and producing (thank God! This is the only thing that helps me. Even in these days I have written something on the new book about the sickness unto death)—all this has put me somewhat under a strain. I have counted on traveling considerably during the year—and now there is no place to travel to.[1798]

Out of all this a troubled spiritual trial—which nevertheless with God's help will help me and has helped me to understand myself better. God be praised; God is love—this, after all, is the happy side of my life, the up-until-now—God be praised—rejuvenating and continually renewing source of my joy.

More and more I understand that Christianity is really too blessed and beatific for us men. Just think what it means to dare to believe that God has come into the world also for my sake. Indeed, it almost sounds like the most blaphemous arrogance for a human being to dare presume to believe such a thing. If it were not God himself who had said it—if a human being had hit upon this in order to show the significance a human being has to God—it would be the most frightful blasphemy of all. But this is why it has not been invented to show how significant a human being is to God, but it is to show what infinite love God's love is. It is indeed infinite that he bothers about a sparrow, but to let himself be born and die for the sake of sinners (and a sinner is even less than a sparrow)—O, infinite love!

VIII[1] A 648   *n.d.,* 1848

« 6135

It is wonderful how God's love overwhelms me still—alas, when all is said and done I know of no truer prayer than the one I pray over and over, that God will tolerate me, that he will not become angry with me because I continually thank him for having done and for doing so indescribably much more for me than I had ever anticipated. Encompassed by derision, plagued day in and day out by the pettiness of men, yes, even those closest to me, I know of nothing else to do at home or in my innermost being but to thank and thank God, because I comprehend that what he has done for me is indescribable. A human being—and after all what is a human being before God, a nothing, less than nothing—and then a poor human being who from childhood on has fallen into the most miserable melancholy, an object of anxiety to himself—and then God helps in this way and grants to me what he has granted to me! A life which was a burden to me however much I knew at times all the happy strains but which was all embittered by the black spot which spoiled everything, a life which, if others knew its secret, I perceived would make me an object of pity and sympathy from the very outset and a burden to myself—God takes a life like that under his wing. He allows me to weep before him in quiet solitude, to empty and again empty out my pain, blessedly consoled by the knowledge that he is concerned for me—and at the same time he gives this life of pain a significance which almost overwhelms me, grants me success and power and wisdom for all my achievements, makes my whole existence a pure expression of ideas, or he makes it into that.

For now I see so clearly (again unto new joy in God, a new occasion to give thanks) that my life has been planned. My life began without spontaneity or immediacy [*Umiddelbarhed*], with a frightful melancholy, basically disturbed from earliest childhood, a melancholy which plunged me into sin and dissipation for a time, and yet, humanly speaking, almost more deranged than guilty. Then my father's death really stopped me. I did not dare to believe that this, the fundamental wretchedness of my being, could be lifted; so I grasped the eternal, blessedly assured that God is love indeed, even though I should have to suffer in this way all my life, yes, blessedly assured of this. This is the way I regarded my life. Then once again I was plunged down, and sympathetically,[1799] into the abyss of my melancholy by having to break off my engagement—and why? Simply because I dared not believe that God would lift the elemental misery of my being, take my almost deranged melancholy away, something I now desired with all the passion of my whole soul for her sake and also for mine. It was most grievous to have to reproduce my own misery. Once again I resigned myself. Thinking only of making her free, I turned away from such a life, but always assured and blessedly assured, God be praised, that God is love—nothing has been more certain to me.

And now, now when in many ways I have been brought to the breaking point, now (since Easter, although with intermissions), a hope has awakened in my soul that it may still be God's will to lift this elemental misery of my being. That is, I now believe in the deepest sense. Faith is spontaneity after reflection. As poet and philosopher I have presented everything in the medium of imagination, myself living in resignation. Now life draws nearer to me, or I draw nearer to myself, come to myself. —For God all things are possible. This thought is now in the deepest sense my watchword and has gained a meaning for me which I had never envisioned. Just because I see no way out, I must never have the audacity to say that therefore there is none for God. For it is despair and blasphemy to confuse one's own little crumb of imagination and the like with the possibilities God has at his disposal.

VIII[1] A 650   *n.d.*, 1848

« 6136

May 13, 1848

Report on "The Sickness unto Death"[1800]

There is one difficulty with this book: it is too dialectical and stringent for the proper use of the rhetorical, the soul-stirring, the gripping. The title itself seems to indicate that it should be discourses —the title is lyrical.

Perhaps it cannot be used at all, but in any case it is enriched with an excellent plan which always can be used, but less explicitly, in discourses.

The point is that before I really can begin using the rhetorical I always must have the dialectical thoroughly fluent, must have gone through it many times. That was not the case here.

VIII[1] A 651   May 13, 1848

« 6137

In margin of (VIII[1] A 651):

If it is to be structured rhetorically, it must be centralized under certain main points, each of which would become one discourse.

What must be understood by the expression "the sickness unto death."

No. 1. Its hiddenness.

Not merely that the one who has it, or that one who has it, may wish to hide it. No, the dreadfulness that it is so hidden that one may have it without knowing it.

No. 2. Its universality.

Every other sickness is restricted in one way or another, by climate, age, etc.

No. 3. Its continuance.

Through all ages—into eternity.

No. 4. Where is it situated?

In the self.

The despairing ignorance of having a self; aware of having a self, in despair not to will to be oneself or in despair to will to be oneself.

But the point is that the task is much too great for a rhetorical arrangement, since in that case every single individual figure would also have to be depicted poetically. The dialectical algebra works better.

VIII[1] A 652   n.d.

« 6138

But here it is still best to use the title "The Sickness unto Death"; it is so rhetorical.

The *doctrine of sin* perhaps could be discussed as follows.

1. The passage in James:[1801]

No one is tempted by God, everyone is tempted by himself (the self).

2. Romans 7

Flesh and blood. Another law in the flesh.

3. Ephesians[1802]

We have not contended not only against flesh and blood but against principalities and powers.

The selfishness here

in despair not to will to be oneself or in despair to will to be oneself.

4. Everyone who sins is a slave of sin.[1803]

The thralldom of sin.

VIII[1] A 653   *n.d.,* 1848

« **6139**

N.B. It is best to remove the allusions to the dogma of inherited sin which are found especially in chapter two (and anywhere else they are found). It would take me too far out, or farther than is needed here or is useful. What is appropriately stated about sin[1804]—that orthodoxy teaches that there must be a revelation to show what sin is—is not said with respect to the doctrine of inherited sin.

VIII[2] B 166   *n.d.,* 1848

« **6140** *Compounded Feelings*

Under this title I have a mind to sketch something lyrical. The point, of course, would be that by means of strictly dialectical computations and by combinations of feelings and by coursing passions one would arrive at what could be called the combined numbers. "The mixture" will therefore signify the intensity, for the greater the compounding into oneness the greater the intensity, the more contradictions, indeed, and yet all the richer harmony.

Incidentally, it would be interesting to compute the whole area of feelings and passions this way, something no one has thought of, even less that the secret is simply to do it dialectically, not lyrically, but dialectically and then lyrically.

As an example of a number of compounded feelings, use could be made of the sketch "Something about Loving."[1805]

VIII[1] A 679   *n.d.,* 1848

Bibliography
Collation of Entries
Notes

Bibliography

KIERKEGAARD'S WORKS IN ENGLISH

Editions referred to in the notes.
Listed according to the original order of publication or the time of writing.

The Concept of Irony, tr. Lee Capel. New York: Harper and Row, 1966; Bloomington: Indiana University Press, 1968. (*Om Begrebet Ironi,* by S. A. Kierkegaard, 1841.)

Either/Or, I, tr. David F. Swenson and Lillian Marvin Swenson; II, tr. Walter Lowrie, 2 ed. rev. Howard A. Johnson. Princeton: Princeton University Press, 1971. (*Enten-Eller,* I–II, ed. Victor Eremita, 1843.)

Johannes Climacus or De omnibus dubitandum est, and *A Sermon,* tr. T. H. Croxall. London: Adam and Charles Black, 1958. ("Johannes Climacus eller *De omnibus dubitandum est,*" written 1842–43, unpubl., *Papirer* IV B 1; "*Demis-Prædiken,*" 1844, unpubl., *Papirer* IV C 1.)

Upbuilding [Edifying] Discourses, I–IV, tr. David F. Swenson and Lillian Marvin Swenson. Minneapolis: Augsburg Publishing House, 1943–46. (*Opbyggelige Taler,* by S. Kierkegaard, 1843, 1844.)

Fear and Trembling (with *The Sickness unto Death*), tr. Walter Lowrie. Princeton: Princeton University Press, 1968. (*Frygt og Bæven,* by Johannes de Silentio, 1843.)

Repetition, tr. Walter Lowrie. Princeton: Princeton University Press, 1941. (*Gjentagelsen,* by Constantin Constantius, 1843.)

Philosophical Fragments, tr. David Swenson, 2 ed. rev. Howard Hong. Princeton: Princeton University Press, 1962. (*Philosophiske Smuler,* by Johannes Climacus, ed. S. Kierkegaard, 1844.)

The Concept of Anxiety [Dread], tr. Walter Lowrie, 2 ed. Princeton: Princeton University Press, 1957. (*Begrebet Angest,* by Vigilius Haufniensis, ed. S. Kierkegaard, 1844.)

Three Discourses on Imagined Occasions [Thoughts on Crucial Situations in Human Life], tr. David F. Swenson, ed. Lillian Marvin Swenson. Minneapolis: Augsburg Publishing House, 1941. (*Tre Taler ved tænkte Leiligheder,* by S. Kierkegaard, 1845.)

Stages on Life's Way, tr. Walter Lowrie. Princeton: Princeton University Press, 1940. (*Stadier paa Livets Vej,* ed. Hilarius Bogbinder, 1845.)

Concluding Unscientific Postscript, tr. David F. Swenson and Walter Lowrie. Princeton: Princeton University Press for American-Scandinavian Foundation, 1941. (*Afsluttende uvidenskabelig Efterskrift,* by Johannes Climacus, ed. S. Kierkegaard, 1846.)

The Present Age [part of *Two Ages: the Age of Revolution and the Present Age. A Literary Review*] and *Two Minor Ethical-Religious Essays* [*Treatises*], tr. Alexander Dru and Walter Lowrie. London and New York: Oxford University Press, 1940. (*En literair Anmeldelse. To Tidsaldre,* by S. Kierkegaard, 1846; *Tvende ethisk-religieuse Smaa-Afhandlinger,* by H. H., 1849.)

On Authority and Revelation, The Book on Adler, tr. Walter Lowrie. Princeton: Princeton University Press, 1955. (*Bogen om Adler,* written 1846–47, unpubl., Papirer VII² B 235; VIII² B 1–27.)

Upbuilding Discourses in Various Spirits. (*Opbyggelige Taler i forskjellig Aand,* by S. Kierkegaard, 1847.) Part One, *Purity of Heart* [*"En Leiligheds-Tale"*], tr. Douglas Steere, 2 ed. New York: Harper, 1948. Part Three and Part Two, *The Gospel of Suffering* and *The Lilies of the Field* [*"Lidelsernes Evangelium"* and *"Lilierne paa Marken og Himlens Fugle"*], tr. David F. Swenson and Lillian Marvin Swenson. Minneapolis: Augsburg Publishing House, 1948.

Works of Love, tr. Howard and Edna Hong. New York: Harper and Row, 1962. (*Kjerlighedens Gjerninger,* by S. Kierkegaard, 1847.)

[*The*] *Crisis* [*and a Crisis*] *in the Life of an Actress,* tr. Stephen Crites. New York: Harper and Row, 1967. (*Krisen og en Krise i en Skuespillerindes Liv,* by Inter et Inter, *Fædrelandet,* 188–91, July 24–27, 1848.)

Christian Discourses, including *The Lily of the Field and the Bird of the Air* and *Three Discourses at the Communion on Fridays,* tr. Walter Lowrie. London and New York: Oxford University Press, 1940. (*Christelige Taler,* by S. Kierkegaard, 1848; *Lilien paa Marken og Fuglen under Himlen,* by S. Kierkegaard, 1849; *Tre Taler ved Altergangen om Fredagen,* by S. Kierkegaard, 1849.)

The Sickness unto Death (with *Fear and Trembling*), tr. Walter Lowrie. Princeton: Princeton University Press, 1968. (*Sygdommen til Døden,* by Anti-Climacus, ed. S. Kierkegaard, 1849.)

Practice [*Training*] *in Christianity,* including "The Woman Who was a Sinner," tr. Walter Lowrie. London and New York: Oxford University Press, 1941; repr. Princeton: Princeton University Press, 1944. (*Indøvelse i Christendom,* by Anti-Climacus, ed. S. Kierkegaard, 1850; *En opbyggelig Tale,* by S. Kierkegaard, 1850.)

Armed Neutrality and *An Open Letter,* tr. Howard V. Hong and Edna H. Hong. Bloomington and London: Indiana University Press, 1968. (*Den bevæbnede Neutralitet,* written 1848–49, publ. 1965; *Foranledigt ved en Yttring af Dr. Rudelbach mig betræffende, Fædrelandet,* no. 26, January 31, 1851.)

The Point of View for My Work as an Author, including the Appendix " 'The Single Individual' Two 'Notes' Concerning My Work as an Author" and *On My Work as an Author,* tr. Walter Lowrie. London and New York: Oxford University Press, 1939. (*Synspunktet for min Forfatter-Virksomhed,* by S. Kierkegaard, posthumously published, 1859; *Om min Forfatter-Virksomhed,* by S. Kierkegaard, 1851.)

For Self-Examination, tr. Edna and Howard Hong. Minneapolis: Augsburg Publishing House, 1940. (*Til Selvprøvelse,* by S. Kierkegaard, 1851.)

Judge for Yourselves!, including *For Self-Examination, Two Discourses at the Communion on Fridays,* and *The Unchangeableness of God* (tr. David Swenson), tr. Walter Lowrie. Princeton: Princeton University Press, 1944. (*Dommer Selv!* by S. Kierkegaard, 1852; *To Taler ved Altergangen om Fredagen,* by S. Kierkegaard, 1851; *Guds Uforanderlighed,* by S. Kierkegaard, 1855.)

Kierkegaard's Attack upon "Christendom," 1854–1855, tr. Walter Lowrie. Princeton: Princeton University Press, 1944. (*Bladartikler* I–XXI, by S. Kierkegaard, *Fædrelandet,* 1854–55; *Dette skal siges; saa være det da sagt,* by S. Kierkegaard, 1855; *Øieblikket,* by S. Kierkegaard, 1–9, 1855; 10, 1905; *Hvad Christus dømmer om officiel Christendom,* by S. Kierkegaard, 1855.)

The Journals of Søren Kierkegaard, tr. Alexander Dru. London and New York: Oxford University Press, 1938. (From *Søren Kierkegaards Papirer,* I–XI[1] in 18 volumes, 1909–1936.)

The Last Years, tr. Ronald C. Smith. New York: Harper and Row, 1965. (From *Papirer* XI[1]–XI[3], 1936–48.)

Søren Kierkegaard's Journals and Papers, tr. Howard V. Hong and Edna H. Hong, assisted by Gregor Malantschuk. Bloomington and London: Indiana University Press, I, 1967; II, 1970; III–IV, 1975; V–VII, 1978. (From *Papirer* I–XI[3] and XII–XIII, 2 ed., and *Breve og Akstykker vedrørende Søren Kierkegaard,* ed. Niels Thulstrup, I–II, 1953–54.) Cited in notes as *J.P.*

At various times in recent years over twenty-five paperback editions of twenty Kierkegaard titles have appeared in English translation. For paperback editions currently available, see the latest issue of *Paperback Books in Print,* published by R. R. Bowker Co., 1180 Avenue of the Americas, New York, N.Y.

General works on Kierkegaard are listed in the bibliography, *Søren Kierkegaard's Journals and Papers,* I, pp. 482–88. Studies of a more limited and specific nature are listed in the appropriate section of topical notes in volumes 1–4 of *Søren Kierkegaard's Journals and Papers.*

Collation of Entries in this Volume With the Danish Edition of the *Papirer* and the *Breve*

Numbers in the left-hand column are the standard international references to the *Papirer*. Numbers in parentheses are the serially ordered references in the present edition.

Volume I A	Volume I A	Volume I A	Volume I B
11 (5061)	75 (5100)	194 (5153)	1 (5115)
12 (5062)	76 (5101)	202 (5154)	2 (5116)
13 (5072)	77 (5102)	204 (5155)	
14 (5073)	78 (5103)	220 (5156)	Volume I C
15 (5074)	79 (5104)	223 (5157)	
16 (5075)	80 (5105)	235 (5161)	1 (5050)
17 (5076)	103 (5113)	244 (5162)	2 (5051)
18 (5081)	109 (5114)	249 (5164)	3 (5052)
32 (5063)	118 (5117)	266 (5174)	7 (5053)
39 (5064)	120 (5118)	271 (5175)	9 (5054)
41 (5071)	123 (5119)	272 (5176)	11 (5055)
51 (5082)	143 (5132)	280 (5177)	12 (5056)
59 (5088)	144 (5133)	286 (5178)	16 (5058)
60 (5089)	147 (5136)	296 (5179)	17 (5059)
61 (5090)	156 (5140)	297 (5180)	18 (5060)
62 (5091)	161 (5141)	328 (5181)	19 (5057)
63 (5094)	162 (5142)	329 (5182)	25 (5065)
64 (5095)	166 (5143)	330 (5183)	27-33 (5066)
65 (5096)	169 (5144)	331 (5184)	34 (5067)
66 (5097)	173 (5145)	332 (5185)	35 (5068)
67 (5098)	179 (5146)	333 (5186)	36 (5069)
68 (5099)	182 (5147)	335 (5187)	37 (5070)
69 (5106)	184 (5148)	336 (5188)	46 (5077)
70 (5107)	186 (5149)	338 (5189)	47 (5078)
71 (5108)	187 (5150)	339 (5190)	48 (5079)
72 (5092)	188 (5151)	341 (5191)	49 (5080)
73 (5093)	189 (5152)		51 (5083)

Volume I C	Volume I C	Volume II A	Volume II A
52 (5084)	117 (5194)	164 (5261)	341 (5366)
53 (5085)	118 (5195)	166 (5262)	346 (5367)
54 (5086)	119 (5196)	167 (5263)	347 (5368)
60 (5109)	120 (5197)	171 (5267)	361 (5369)
61 (5110)	121 (5198)	182 (5268)	364 (5370)
62 (5111)	123 (5199)	185 (5269)	373 (5371)
64 (5112)	124 (5192)	189 (5270)	382 (5372)
65 (5087)	**Volume II A**	193 (5274)	386 (5373)
72 (5120)		200 (5279)	389 (5374)
74 (5121)	7 (5200)	202 (5280)	395 (5375)
75 (5122)	17 (5201)	203 (5281)	397 (5376)
76 (5123)	20 (5205)	204 (5282)	398 (5377)
77 (5124)	21 (5206)	205 (5284)	406 (5378)
78 (5125)	27 (5207)	206 (5285)	413 (5379)
79 (5126)	35 (5208)	207 (5287)	414 (5380)
81 (5127)	36 (5209)	208 (5289)	415 (5381)
82 (5128)	40 (5210)	209 (5302)	416 (5382)
83 (5129)	42 (5211)	210 (5303)	420 (5383)
84 (5130)	43 (5212)	212 (5304)	421 (5384)
85 (5131)	44 (5213)	216 (5305)	422 (5385)
87 (5134)	45 (5214)	222 (5306)	431 (5386)
88 (5135)	51 (5215)	228 (5324)	432 (5387)
89 (5137)	54 (5216)	229 (5326)	435 (5388)
95 (5138)	61 (5217)	231 (5328)	438 (5389)
96 (5139)	67 (5219)	232 (5329)	444 (5390)
100 (5158)	68 (5220)	233 (5330)	476 (5391)
101 (5159)	70 (5221)	238 (5331)	480 (5392)
102 (5160)	92 (5222)	240 (5332)	482 (5393)
103 (5163)	98 (5223)	241 (5333)	490 (5394)
104 (5165)	115 (5239)	243 (5335)	492 (5395)
105 (5166)	116 (5240)	255 (5337)	495 (5396)
106 (5167)	118 (5241)	259 (5338)	497 (5397)
107 (5168)	119 (5242)	270 (5351)	503 (5398)
108 (5169)	120 (5243)	275 (5352)	508 (5399)
109 (5170)	121 (5244)	300 (5356)	509 (5400)
110 (5171)	124 (5245)	312 (5361)	510 (5401)
111 (5172)	126 (5246)	319 (5362)	512 (5402)
112 (5173)	132 (5247)	328 (5364)	520 (5403)
116 (5193)	154 (5248)	340 (5365)	521 (5404)

Volume II A	Volume II A	Volume II A	Volume II C
533 (5405)	640 (5252)	749 (5322)	36 (5419)
534 (5406)	641 (5253)	753 (5323)	38 (5271)
540 (5407)	642 (5254)	757 (5325)	39 (5272)
542 (5408)	644 (5255)	760 (5336)	40 (5273)
546 (5409)	647 (5256)	768 (5339)	42–49 (5278)
548 (5410)	648 (5257)	769 (5340)	50 (5286)
549 (5411)	649 (5258)	770 (5341)	53 (5327)
557 (5412)	653 (5259)	771 (5342)	60 (5350)
560 (5420)	662 (5260)	772 (5343)	61 (5354)
561 (5421)	670 (5264)	777 (5344)	62 (5355)
565 (5422)	673 (5265)	778 (5345)	63 (5358)
567 (5423)	677 (5266)	779 (5346)	64 (5359)
572 (5424)	679 (5288)	780 (5347)	65 (5360)
574 (5425)	683 (5290)	781 (5348)	**Volume III A**
575 (5426)	684 (5291)	782 (5349)	
576 (5434)	685 (5292)	802 (5427)	15 (5437)
582 (5203)	686 (5293)	803 (5428)	16 (5438)
585 (5204)	688 (5294)	804 (5429)	17 (5439)
590 (5224)	690 (5295)	805 (5430)	18 (5440)
597 (5225)	691 (5296)	806 (5431)	19 (5441)
598 (5226)	693 (5297)	807 (5432)	20 (5442)
599 (5227)	696 (5298)	817 (5413)	21 (5443)
600 (5228)	700 (5300)	818 (5414)	22 (5444)
601 (5229)	702 (5301)	819 (5415)	31 (5445)
602 (5230)	712 (5307)	820 (5416)	35 (5446)
603 (5231)	714 (5308)	821 (5417)	40 (5447)
607 (5232)	717 (5309)	824 (5433)	42 (5448)
609 (5233)	720 (5310)	**Volume II C**	44 (5449)
611 (5234)	723 (5311)		50 (5450)
613 (5235)	728 (5312)	3 (5334)	51 (5451)
614 (5236)	730 (5313)	9 (5435)	52 (5452)
616 (5237)	732 (5314)	10 (5436)	53 (5453)
617 (5238)	733 (5315)	11 (5202)	54 (5454)
625 (5218)	736 (5316)	12–24 (5277)	55 (5455)
629 (5275)	737 (5317)	25 (5353)	56 (5456)
630 (5276)	739 (5318)	26–28 (5299)	57 (5457)
634 (5249)	740 (5319)	29–31 (5357)	58 (5458)
635 (5250)	742 (5320)	32 (5363)	59 (5459)
637 (5251)	745 (5321)	33 (5418)	60 (5460)

Volume III A	Volume III A	Volume III B	Volume IV A
64 (5461)	161 (5517)	130 (5549)	63 (5618)
65 (5462)	163 (5518)	132:3 (5550)	64 (5619)
66 (5463)	164 (5519)	168 (5553)	65 (5622)
67 (5464)	165 (5520)	172 (5566)	67 (5623)
69 (5465)	166 (5521)	173 (5567)	68 (5624)
71 (5466)	167 (5522)	189 (5568)	69 (5625)
72 (5467)	168 (5523)	**Volume III C**	70 (5626)
73 (5468)	169 (5524)		71 (5637)
74 (5469)	170 (5525)	4 (5485)	74 (5638)
75 (5470)	171 (5526)	5 (5486)	75 (5639)
77 (5471)	172 (5528)	8 (5487)	76 (5640)
79 (5472)	173 (5529)	12 (5488)	77 (5641)
80 (5473)	174 (5530)	24 (5489)	79 (5642)
81 (5474)	175 (5531)	26 (5514)	81 (5643)
83 (5475)	176 (5532)	27 (5536)	83 (5644)
84 (5476)	177 (5533)	28 (5537)	85 (5645)
90 (5490)	178 (5534)	34 (5545)	87 (5646)
91 (5491)	179 (5535)	37 (5546)	88 (5647)
93 (5492)	180 (5538)	40 (5547)	89 (5648)
97 (5493)	183 (5539)	**Volume IV A**	90 (5649)
103 (5494)	187 (5540)		91 (5650)
105 (5495)	190 (5541)	1 (5573)	93 (5651)
114 (5496)	198 (5559)	2 (5574)	96 (5652)
115 (5497)	203 (5560)	8 (5576)	97 (5653)
116 (5498)	207 (5569)	14 (5581)	101 (5654)
121 (5499)	208 (5570)	15 (5582)	105 (5656)
122 (5500)	209 (5571)	16 (5583)	107 (5664)
133 (5501)	220 (5554)	17 (5584)	110 (5666)
134 (5502)	221 (5555)	22 (5585)	111 (5667)
142 (5503)	223 (5556)	25 (5586)	113 (5668)
146 (5506)	224 (5557)	30 (5587)	114 (5669)
147 (5507)	225 (5558)	31 (5609)	118 (5670)
148 (5508)	227 (5561)	34 (5610)	119 (5671)
149 (5509)	228 (5562)	36 (5611)	122 (5672)
150 (5510)	229 (5563)	37 (5612)	123 (5673)
151 (5511)	245 (5564)	43 (5613)	126 (5674)
155 (5512)	246 (5565)	45 (5614)	127 (5675)
159 (5515)	**Volume III B**	53 (5615)	128 (5676)
160 (5516)	2 (5484)	56 (5616)	129 (5677)
		61 (5617)	

Volume IV A	Volume IV A	Volume IV C	Volume V A
132 (5678)	246 (5636)	124 (5606)	112 (5758)
133 (5680)	**Volume IV B**	126 (5607)	**Volume V B**
135 (5681)		127 (5608)	
136 (5682)	1 (5621)		47:13 (5726)
137 (5683)	10 (5620)	**Volume V A**	53:26 (5730)
138 (5684)	59 (5710)		72:22 (5731)
139 (5685)	60 (5658)	3 (5725)	147 (5721)
140 (5687)	78 (5659)	21 (5728)	148:5 (5722)
141 (5688)	79 (5660)	27 (5729)	148:25 (5723)
142 (5689)	97:1 (5657)	34 (5732)	148:29 (5724)
144 (5690)	125 (5707)	39 (5735)	232:1 (5734)
147 (5691)	126 (5708)	45 (5736)	**Volume VI A**
151 (5692)	140 (5661)	48 (5737)	
152 (5693)	141 (5662)	52 (5738)	4 (5768)
153 (5694)	142 (5663)	54 (5739)	8 (5769)
154 (5695)	159 (5686)	58 (5740)	10 (5770)
158 (5696)	**Volume IV C**	62 (5741)	11 (5771)
162 (5697)	2 (5572)	71 (5743)	12 (5772)
167 (5698)	6 (5578)	82 (5745)	13 (5777)
170 (5699)	8 (5579)	84 (5746)	28 (5799)
174 (5700)	9 (5580)	87 (5747)	29 (2800)
175 (5701)	10 (5588)	88 (5748)	31 (5801)
176 (5702)	15 (5589)	91 (5749)	32 (5802)
177 (5703)	18 (5590)	92 (5750)	40 (5803)
178 (5704)	22 (5591)	93 (5751)	41 (5804)
181 (5705)	24 (5592)	94 (5752)	42 (5807)
182 (5706)	34 (5593)	95 (5753)	44 (5808)
193 (5709)	41 (5594)	99 (5754)	45 (5809)
197 (5575)	42 (5595)	100 (5712)	47 (5810)
201 (5577)	43 (5596)	101 (5713)	53 (5811)
214 (5627)	44 (5597)	102 (5714)	54 (5812)
215 (5628)	45 (5598)	103 (5715)	55 (5813)
216 (5629)	46 (5599)	104 (5716)	56 (5814)
217 (5630)	83 (5600)	105 (5717)	57 (5815)
221 (5631)	97 (5601)	106 (5718)	58 (5816)
223 (5632)	98 (5602)	107 (5719)	59 (5817)
231 (5633)	101 (5603)	108 (5720)	61 (5818)
234 (5634)	107 (5604)	109 (5744)	73 (5819)
236 (5635)	123 (5605)	110 (5755)	75 (5820)
		111 (5756)	

462COLLATION

Volume VI A	Volume VI B	Volume VII¹ A	Volume VII¹ A
76 (5821)	17 (5791)	3 (5872)	111 (5898)
77 (5822)	18 (5792)	4 (5873)	112 (5899)
78 (5823)	35:14 (5793)	5 (5874)	113 (5900)
79 (5824)	35:15 (5794)	6 (5875)	114 (5901)
82 (5825)	35:19 (5795)	7 (5876)	115 (5902)
83 (5826)	35:24 (5796)	9 (5877)	116 (5903)
84 (5827)	40:33 (5797)	11 (5878)	117 (5904)
85 (5828)	41:10 (5805)	18 (5879)	118 (5905)
86 (5829)	89 (5850)	21 (5882)	119 (5906)
87 (5830)	90 (5851)	23 (5883)	120 (5907)
88 (5833)	100 (5778)	26 (5884)	121 (5908)
94 (5834)	130 (5783)	27 (5885)	124 (5909)
95 (5835)	131 (5784)	40 (5916)	125 (5912)
97 (5836)	132 (5785)	41 (5917)	126 (5913)
98 (5837)	192 (5853)	42 (5918)	127 (5914)
99 (5838)	193 (5854)	43 (5920)	128 (5915)
100 (5839)	194 (5759)	44 (5921)	129 (5924)
103 (5840)	199-201 (5760)	50 (5922)	147 (5937)
104 (5841)	222 (5761)	53 (5923)	148 (5938)
119 (5842)	224 (5762)	55 (5926)	150 (5939)
125 (5843)	225 (5763)	66 (5927)	154 (5940)
128 (5844)	226 (5764)	78 (5928)	155 (5941)
129 (5845)	227 (5765)	85 (5929)	156 (5942)
130 (5846)	229 (5766)	90 (5930)	157 (5943)
131 (5847)	231 (5767)	92 (5931)	158 (5944)
134 (5848)	233 (2831)	95 (5932)	160 (5945)
135 (5849)	235 (5832)	96 (5933)	164 (5946)
141 (5855)		97 (5886)	169 (5947)
142 (5774)	**Volume VI C**	98 (5887)	176 (5948)
143 (5775)		99 (5888)	184 (5949)
144 (5776)	1 (5798)	101 (5889)	202 (5951)
146 (5786)	2 (5779)	103 (5890)	214 (5957)
	3 (5780)	104 (5891)	218 (5958)
Volume VI B	4 (5781)	105 (5892)	219 (5959)
	5 (5782)	106 (5893)	220 (5960)
8:1-2 (5773)		107 (5894)	221 (5961)
13 (5787)	**Volume VII¹ A**	108 (5895)	222 (5962)
14 (5788)		109 (5896)	223 (5963)
15 (5789)	1 (5870)	110 (5897)	224 (5964)
16 (5790)	2 (5871)		

Volume VII¹ A	Volume VIII¹ A	Volume VIII¹ A	Volume VIII¹ A
227 (5965)	1 (5970)	156 (6011)	309 (6055)
229 (5966)	2 (5971)	158 (6012)	326 (6056)
231 (5856)	4 (5972)	163 (6013)	332 (6058)
233 (5857)	5 (5973)	164 (6014)	337 (6059)
241 (5858)	13 (5974)	170 (6015)	339 (6060)
246 (5967)	15 (5975)	171 (6016)	347 (6061)
Volume VII¹ B	16 (5976)	172 (6017)	352 (6062)
	18 (5978)	174 (6018)	366 (6064)
1 (5860)	23 (5979)	177 (6019)	383 (6065)
5 (5861)	27 (5980)	179 (6020)	384 (6066)
6 (5862)	33 (5981)	185 (6021)	385 (6067)
69 (5863)	34 (5982)	197 (6022)	388 (6070)
75 (5864)	35 (5983)	200 (6023)	390 (6071)
83 (5865)	36 (5984)	204 (6024)	394 (6072)
84 (5866)	37 (5985)	205 (6025)	397 (6073)
95 (5867)	38 (5986)	207 (6026)	407 (6074)
131 (5880)	42 (5987)	212 (6027)	414 (6075)
132 (5868)	44 (5988)	217 (6029)	415 (6076)
135:5 (5869)	45 (5989)	218 (6031)	417 (6077)
136 (5919)	46 (5990)	219 (6032)	424 (6078)
150 (5925)	49 (5991)	220 (6033)	440 (6079)
192:1–2 (5934)	61 (5992)	224 (6034)	444 (6080)
211 (5881)	68 (5993)	227 (6035)	445 (6081)
212 (2952)	71 (5994)	228 (6036)	446 (6082)
213 (5953)	81 (5995)	229 (6037)	447 (6083)
214 (5954)	82 (5996)	232 (6038)	450 (6084)
217 (5955)	84 (5997)	233 (6039)	452 (6085)
218 (5956)	99 (5998)	237 (6040)	453 (6086)
	100 (5999)	246 (6041)	455 (6087)
Volume VII¹ C	107 (6000)	249 (6042)	458 (6088)
	116 (6001)	250 (6043)	472 (6092)
5 (5950)	119 (6002)	252 (6044)	481 (6093)
Volume VII² B	120 (6004)	254 (6045)	486 (6096)
	121 (6005)	264 (6049)	487 (6097)
235 (5968)	124 (6006)	271 (6050)	496 (6098)
236–70 (5935)	133 (6007)	276 (6051)	502 (6100)
242 (5936)	135 (6008)	277 (6052)	504 (6101)
270 (5969)	139 (6009)	298 (6053)	507 (6102)
274:1–22 (5859)	153 (6010)	308 (6054)	508 (6103)

Volume VIII¹ A	Volume VIII¹ A	Volume VIII² C	Letters
533 (6104)	637 (6130)	1 (5977)	80 (5655)
544 (6105)	640 (6131)	2:1–61 (6028)	82 (5665)
545 (6106)	641 (6132)	3 (6117)	83 (5679)
548 (6107)	645 (6133)		101 (5711)
549 (6108)	648 (6134)	*Letters*	107 (5727)
557 (6109)	650 (6135)	2 (5051)	113 (5757)
558 (6110)	651 (6136)	4 (note 109)	119 (5806)
559 (6111)	652 (6137)	15 (5477)	120a (5852)
560 (6112)	653 (6138)	17 (5478)	134 (5910)
561 (6113)	654 (6089)	18 (5479)	136 (5911)
562 (6114)	655 (6099)	21 (5480)	149 (6003)
563 (6115)	666 (6127)	23 (5481)	150 (6063)
570 (6116)	669 (6128)	27 (5482)	152 (6030)
576 (6118)	679 (6140)	29 (5483)	153 (note 1650)
577 (6119)		42 (5505)	154 (6046)
589 (6120)	**Volume VIII² B**	49 (5513)	155 (note 1652)
590 (6121)		54 (5542)	156 (6047)
591 (6122)	116 (6068)	55 (5543)	157 (6048)
595 (6123)	118 (6069)	56 (5544)	161 (6057)
596 (6124)	166 (6139)	62 (5548)	166 (6090)
602 (6125)	186 (6094)	68 (5551)	167 (6091)
603 (6126)	188 (6095)	69 (5552)	
634 (6129)	274:1–22 (5859)	71 (5527)	

Notes

The following abbreviations have been used throughout the notes:

S.V.   *Samlede Værker* by Søren Kierkegaard, I–XIV, edited by A. B. Drachman, J. L. Heiberg, and H. O. Lange (Copenhagen: Gyldendal, 1901–1906).

Pap.   *Papirer* by Søren Kierkegaard, I–XI³ (20 vols.), edited by P. A. Heiberg, V. Kuhr, and E. Torsting (Copenhagen: Gyldendal, 1909–1948); 2 ed., I–XI³ and suppl. vols. XII–XIII, edited by Niels Thulstrup (Copenhagen: Gyldendal, 1968–1970). References to entries in the *Papirer* that are not included in *Søren Kierkegaard's Journals and Papers* are prefaced by *Pap.*, e.g., *Pap.*, I A 1. Cross-references within *J.P.* are by *Papirer* serial number (I A 9) or by footnote number.

ASKB   *Auktionsprotokol over Søren Kierkegaards Bogsamling* (Auction-catalog of Søren Kierkegaard's Book-collection), edited by H. P. Rohde (Copenhagen: Det Kongelige Bibliotek, 1967). This enlarged edition of the auction-catalog contains the basic serially numbered list of books indicated by number (*ASKB* 200), two appendices designated by I and II (*ASKB* II 200), and a section on books otherwise unlisted but in various ways known to have belonged to Kierkegaard, designated by U (*ASKB* U 100).

Letters   *Breve og Aktstykker vedrørende Søren Kierkegaard*, I–II (Letters and Documents pertaining to Søren Kierkegaard), edited by Niels Thulstrup, (Copenhagen: Munksgaard, 1953).

Notes 1–1805 appear in Volume 5; notes 1806–3403 appear in Volume 6.

1. Peter Christian Kierkegaard (July 6, 1805–Feb. 24, 1888), Søren Kierkegaard's brother, graduate student in Berlin and later in Göttingen and Paris, May 1828–Sept. 1830. Later he became a pastor and prominent Grundtvigian.

2. N. P. Asp (1799–1880) published in 1829 *Frimodige Yttringer om Studerendes Stilling i Staten.*

3. The word (*Forstrængelse* used here is not found in Molbech's dictionary of the time or in the present 27-volume *Ordbog over det danske Sprog* and is not colloquial speech. Already at the age of sixteen Kierkegaard had begun his practice of constructing new Danish words and expressions or borrowing from other languages, especially Greek and Latin.

4. The issue here has to do with averaging examinations in subjects, so that if a pupil fails in one, the average may bring him up to a passing grade. Asp's idea is that a pupil should be reexamined in the failing subject irrespective of a passing average.

5. Kierkegaard never learned English, but he was an avid reader of some English writers in German translations (Shakespeare, *ASKB* 1874–97, and Danish translations, *ASKB* U103; Shelley, *ASKB* 1898; Young, *ASKB* 1911; Byron, *ASKB* 1868–70).

6. Kierkegaard finished school at Borgerdydskolen in October 1830, and enrolled at the University of Copenhagen October 30, 1830.

7. S. C. W. Bindesbøll (1798–1871), teacher of religion at Borgerdydskolen, later Bishop of Lolland-Falster.

8. Ludwig Holberg Warncke (1787–1848), teacher of history and geography.

9. G. J. Marthensen (1800–1867).

10. G. F. Ursin (1797–1849), mathematician and astronomer, teacher of mathematics at Borgerdydskolen until named professor of mathematics at the Art Academy in 1827, author of the mathematics book mentioned in *Foranledigt ved en Yttring af Dr. Rudelbach mig betræffende* (*Armed Neutrality* and *An Open Letter*, p. 49).

11. Michael Nielsen. See letter 107, and dedication inscription in copy of *Tre opbyggelige Taler*, 1843.

12. Frederik O. Lange (1798–1862), classical philologist, teacher of Greek at Borgerdydskolen in the early 1820s.

13. Mrs. Rasmus F. Fenger, mother of Johannes F. Fenger (1805–61), with whom Peter C. Kierkegaard traveled to Berlin.

14. Peter T. Hald (1802–64), *De Summa animi perfectione specimen exegeticum*, 1828.

15. *Antistitum ecclesiae Danicae* (Copenhagen: 1817).

16. Petrea Severine Kierkegaard, a sister (Sept. 7, 1801–Dec. 29, 1834), married Oct. 11, 1828, to Henrik Ferdinand Lund (March 15, 1803–Aug. 24, 1875), later loan department manager of the National Bank and custodian of Kierkegaard's financial assets. Severine is the feminine form of the name Søren, itself a form of Severinus. Later letters frequently mention their children: Anna Henriette (1829–1909), Wilhelm N. (1831–1902), Peter Christian (1833–1904), and Peter Severin (1834–1864).

17. Nicoline Christine Kierkegaard, a sister (Oct. 25, 1799–Sept. 10, 1832), married Sept. 24, 1824, to Johan Christian Lund (Feb. 5, 1799–July 10, 1875), grocer and clothier in Copenhagen. Later letters frequently mention their children: Henrik S. (1825–1889), Michael F. C. (1826–1907), Sophie (1827–1875), and Carl F. (1830–1912).

18. Michael Pedersen Kierkegaard (Dec. 12, 1756–Aug. 9, 1838), formerly clothier, wholesale grocer, and importer in Copenhagen, married to

Kirstine Nielsdatter Røyen (ca. 1758–March 23, 1796) on May 2, 1794, and to Ane Sørensdatter Lund (June 18, 1768–July 31, 1834) on April 26, 1797.

19. See note 18.

20. Henrik Ferdinand Lund. See note 16 on Petrea Severine Kierkegaard above.

21. Niels Andreas Kierkegaard (April 30, 1809–Sept. 21, 1833), Kierkegaard's older brother, who emigrated to the United States and died unmarried in Paterson, New Jersey.

22. Presumably Marina Magdalene Lund, mother of Johan Christian Lund and Henrik Ferdinand Lund.

23. Anne Cathrine Lund (1800–1859) and Anna Lund (1807–79), daughters of Ole Troelson Lund and Karen Mouritsdatter Lund. See note 225.

24. See note 20.

25. Theology student J. A. Lorentzen (1805–30).

26. Kierkegaard himself copied the following in his father's letter copy book: "I do not know what it is with Søren; I cannot get him to write to you. Is it poverty of mind so that he cannot find anything to write about or childish vanity so that he will write nothing except that for which he could expect praise, and since he is not sure of his case in that respect he will write nothing at all?"

27. The texts of I C 1–3 are available in *Pap.*, XII, pp. 3–16. The three entries are from Kierkegaard's early period as a university student. See note 6.

28. Ibid., pp. 23–26 and I C 7. In dealing with problems of language, Kierkegaard made considerable use of C. G. Bretschneider, *Lexicon manuale Graeco-Latinum in libris Novi Testamenti*, I–II (2 ed., Leipzig: 1829). *ASKB* 73–74.

29. Most likely N. F. S. Grundtvig's sermon, "The Appeal of the Ten Lepers to the Lord," on Dec. 23, 1832, in Frederikskirken, Christianshavn, printed later in 1853 during the cholera epidemic which took about 5,000 of Copenhagen's 130,000 inhabitants within four months.

30. For text see *Pap.*, I C 11 and XII, pp. 28–36. See note 28. Kierkegaard came to know Latin very well and taught Latin at his old school, Borgerdydskolen, in 1837–38.

31. Ibid., XII, pp. 36–43.

32. The dating of this entry is placed by Niels Thulstrup (editor of the second edition of *Papirer;* see XII, pp. 49–51) in relation to H. N. Clausen's resumption of dogmatics lectures in 1833–34 and to Kierkegaard's plan (unfulfilled) to prepare for his examinations later in 1834. The notes, although incomplete, are in a reworked fair copy with additions and follow the structure of the lectures: On the Relation of Holy Scriptures to Reason; On Christian Dogmatics; Appendix to Part One; Part Two: Christian Anthropology; Part Three: The Person of Christ. The text is in *Pap.*, I C 19 and XII, pp. 52–125.

During the same summer of 1834 Kierkegaard read, with H. L. Martensen as tutor, F. Schleiermacher's *Der christliche Glaube* (2 ed., Berlin: 1830; *ASKB* 258 is 3 ed., 1835), from which excerpts are given in *Pap.*, I C 20–24, together with comments.

33. Presumably done in connection with C. E. Scharling's course on I and II Corinthians, spring semester 1834. For text see *Pap.*, XII, p. 46.

34. See note 33.

35. A. Lafontaine, *Skjebnens Vei;* a novel tr. H. P. Møller (i.e., P. S. Martin) (Copenhagen: 1826).

36. This piece on the master-thief is Kierkegaard's first literary attempt, and for some time he considered making a more extensive study of this theme, as well as of Faust and of the Wandering Jew.

37. See *Archiv for danske og norske Criminalhistorier,* ed. T. P. Hansen (Copenhagen: 1834), pp. 55 ff. (Peder Mikkelsen); the Robin Hood type referred to later in the entry is not found in this work.

38. See *Criminalhistorier uddragne af Danske Justitsacter,* ed. P. L. Benzon (Copenhagen: 1827), pp. 46 ff.; *Prefaces, S.V.,* V, p. 22.

39. Johan Paul Forster. See Anselm von Feuerbach, *Aktenmässige Darstellung merkwürdiger Verbrechen,* I–II (Giessen: 1828–29), II, pp. 123 ff., esp. 142 ff.

40. Søren Andersen Kagerup, executed for murder. See C. H. Visby, "*Psychologiske Bemærkninger over den, med Øxen henrettede, Morder* Søren Andersen Kagerup," in *Borgervennen,* 20–25, 1832; *Archiv* (see note 37), pp. 220 ff.

41. The text is given in *Pap.*, I C 26 and XII, pp. 131–32.

42. The text is given in *Pap.*, I C 31 and XII, pp. 132–39.

43. The entry is on a separate sheet and the antecedent is not traceable.

44. Exhaustion.

45. Presumably done in connection with C. E. Scharling's course in exegesis, conducted in Latin, the first term in 1834–35. The text is given in *Pap.*, I C 35 and XII, pp. 140–48.

46. See note 45. The text is given in *Pap.*, I C 36 and XII, pp. 149–65. See notes 28 and 30.

47. See note 45.

48. "The magnetized" are those under some form of hypnosis. See, for example, Franz Baader, *Philosophische Schriften und Aufsätze,* I–II (Münster: 1831–32; *ASKB* 400–401), II, pp. 1–37, 238–54.

This puzzling reference touches in part upon the legend that Mohammed's tomb hovers suspended at the center of a magnetic field. See II A 86.

49. Pückler-Muskua, Herman Ludwig Heinrich, Fürst von (1785–1871), *Tutti Frutti, aus den Papieren des Verstorbenen,* I–V (Stuttgart: 1834), V (not III), p. 202. The striking title of this travel book, known to Kierkegaard and known in Denmark, is important in interpreting the title of Kierkegaard's first book, *From the Papers of One Still Living* (1838), in which he wrote that H. C. Andersen "is better equipped to drive off in a coach and inspect Europe than to look into

the history of hearts" (*S.V.*, XIII, p. 91). Andersen had sought to carry out the second task in various works, including *Only a Fiddler* (1837), the object of Kierkegaard's critique; he had accomplished the first task with spectacular success in his European and English travels of 1831, 1833–34, and 1837.

50. See note 37.

51. Louis Dominique Cartouche (1693–1721), notorious French criminal and underworld leader.

52. Until the mid-twentieth century this symbol for the police was commonly used in Denmark (police department notices, automobile license plates, etc.).

53. The basis of the texts for entries I A 16 and 17 is *Søren Kierkegaards Efterladte Papirer*, I–III, ed. H. P. Barfod, IV–VIII, ed. H. Gottsched (Copenhagen: 1869–1881), I, p. 32, where the dates of the missing entry slips are given as February 9, 1835, and December 16, 1834. Presumably while writing entry I A 16 Kierkegaard remembered an earlier jotting and put the two slips together.

54. F. M. von Klinger.

55. H. C. Andersen, *Fodreise fra Holmens Canal til Østpynten af Amager i Aarene 1828 og 1829* (Copenhagen: 1829), p. 4.

56. "I would like to have a devil but not of my own kind."

57. "Besides, like a dry sponge, he absorbed the folly and the charlatanry that others spawned, a condition by which visionaries differ completely from philosophers, for the latter hate and despise someone else's hypotheses, while the former accept all the rubbish of the human mind and make it their own."

58. "Namely, that man is not made to associate with higher beings and that he may not venture to step out of the circle without punishment." *Historisches Taschenbuch*, ed. Friedrich v. Raumer (Leipzig: 1834), V.

59. The text of the omitted portions is given in *Pap.*, XII, pp. 206–7.

60. The author is F. M. Klinger (see I C 46).

61. The text is given in *Pap.*, I C 49, and XII, pp. 208–9.

62. A famous peasant clown in northern Germany in the fourteenth or fifteenth century.

The interest in Till Eulenspiegel in Scandinavia is partially indicated by two volumes in Kierkegaard's possession: *Ein gandske ny og lystig Historie om Ulspile Overmand Eller Robertus vom Agerkaal* (Copenhagen: 1724) and *Underlig og selsom Historie, Om Tüle Ugelspegel* (Copenhagen: 1781). *ASKB* 1467, 1469.

63. C. L. Stieglitz, *"Die Sage vom Doctor Faust."*

64. See note 36.

65. The omitted portion is given in *Pap.*, XII, pp. 210–11.

66. *ASKB* 1670.

67. "Doctor Faust," in *Zur schönen Literatur* (*aus Lessing's Nachlass*), *Gotthold Ephraim Lessing's sämmtliche Schriften*, I–XXXII (Berlin: 1825–28), XXIII, p. 177. *ASKB* 1747–62.

68. See note 58.

69. Lessing's *Litteraturbriefen* (the edition cited, Berlin: 1759, has not been available to the editors) is the same as his *Analekten für die Litteratur,* I–II (Bern, Leipzig: 1785). See *"Fünfzehnter Brief,"* I, pp. 210–14. Volume XXX, pp. 52–55, of Kierkegaard's set of Lessing (see note 67) contains letter 15 as no. 17 and in omitting the scene of the seven devils refers to the text in the *Theatralischem Nachlasse.*

70. See note 58.

71. See note 36.

72. See a later development of this theme in *Postscript,* pp. 24–47, especially 35–45.

73. See note 72. Nicolai Frederik Severin Grundtvig (1783–1872), pastor, poet, historian, and politician, has been perhaps the most influential single person in Danish religious and cultural life in the nineteenth and twentieth centuries. From his early years, Kierkegaard was rather critical of Grundtvig; his older brother, Peter Christian, became a leading Grundtvigian.

74. See N. F. S. Grundtvig, *Kierkens Gjenmæle* (Copenhagen: 1825), pp. 9–10; *Theologisk Maanedsskrift,* ed. N. F. S. Grundtvig and A. G. Rudelbach, XII, 1828, pp. 32–33 (*ASKB* 346–51); *Om Daabs-Pagten* (Copenhagen: 1832), p. 7.

75. In 1825 H. N. Clausen published a scholarly work entitled *Katolicismens og Protestantismens Kirkeforfatning, Lære og Ritus* (The Church Constitution, Doctrine, and Ritual of Catholicism and of Protestantism), in which he opposed ritualism and the concept that traditions are authoritative. He stressed the Bible as the sole and sufficient basis of Protestantism, but at the same time made the interpretation of the Bible dependent upon critical-historical research.

In *Kirkens Gjenmæle* (Copenhagen: 1825), Grundtvig attacked Clausen. Although their views of the Bible agreed, Grundtvig emphasized that in the sacraments there is a firm foundation, a tradition that can be traced back to the apostles and that our "matchless confession of faith" (p. 26) is the original confession of the Church and is the basis of Biblical interpretation. Since the Apostles' Creed is declared at baptism, Grundtvig placed special emphasis on baptism.

Kierkegaard's point here is that if Grundtvig wanted Christ's words as the solid basis for faith, he should rather have stressed the words of institution in the Lord's Supper as something already instituted during Christ's life, instead of the Apostles' Creed, which was formulated later.

76. H. N. Clausen and his adherents insisted that everything in the Bible and the Church be subjected to the endless approximation of historical-critical analysis. See I A 59.

77. Jacob Christian Lindberg (1797–1857), linguist, pastor, theologian, and adherent of Grundtvig. See *Postscript,* pp. 36, 38–41, 45.

78. See VII, 1826, p. 239.

79. The two possibilities posed here are the promulgation of the Creed

by the Apostles by virtue of their divine authority ("over") or its derivation from Christ's teaching ("under"). In the second case it would have been done for clarification in dealing with heretics and as such would belong to the work of the Church as it developed.

80. See J. C. Lindberg, *Historiske Oplysninger om den danske Kirkes symbolske Bøger* (Copenhagen: 1830), pp. 48 ff.; *Nordisk Kirke-Tidende*, 1834, col. 171–72.

81. See *Postscript*, pp. 39–43. Grundtvig called the Living Word his "matchless discovery." By Living Word he meant the pedagogical method of the spoken word versus the dead letter (books), and the ecclesiastical-theological principle of the spoken confession in the sacraments, the Lord's Prayer, and Apostles' Creed, particularly in the sacrament of Baptism. The historical issue involved here was dealt with also by Peter C. Kierkegaard, a Grundtvigian, who stressed the formative significance of the 40 days between Easter and the Ascension (*Jesu Christi Kirke i Folke-Kirkerne, Nordisk Tidskrift for christelig Theologi*, III–IV, 1841–42).

82. For example, Bishop R. Møller in the preface to C. C. Boisen, *Om Kirken og Præstens Forhold til samme* (Copenhagen: 1834), pp. vi–viii.

83. *Nordisk Kirke-Tidende*, 1834, col. 175–76.

84. I Corinthians 11:23.

85. See *Postscript*, p. 41.

86. See Clausen's review of Grundtvig, *Om Daabspagten, Maanedsskrift for Litteratur*, VIII, 1832, pp. 600–618; *"Tillægsbetragtninger,"* ibid., XI, 1834, pp. 26–61.

87. *Nordisk Kirke-Tidende*, 1834, col. 820 ff.

88. W. F. Engelbreth, *Sendebrev til Hr. Dr. theol. Prof. Clausen* (Copenhagen: 1834).

89. The reference is to Grundtvig and his adherents. See note 72.

90. See I A 59.

91. See note 73.

92. Presumably Peter Wilhelm Lund (1801–80), brother of Johan Christian Lund and Henrik Ferdinand Lund (married to Kierkegaard's sisters Nicoline Christine and Petrea Severine) paleontologist, natural scientist; he returned to Brazil in January 1833. However, Hirsch considers the letter fictive and as part of the "Faustian letters." See note 245.

93. Prosper Mérimée, *Les Ames du purgatoire* (Paris: 1834).

94. See Luke 12:16–21.

95. Hans Christian Ørsted (1777–1851), *"Forsøg over Klangfigurerne,"* Det kongelige Danske Videnskabernes Selskabs Skrifter, II (Copenhagen: 1807–8), pp. 31 ff.

96. Joakim Frederik Schouw (1789–1852) in his *Grundtræk til en almindelige Plantegeographie* (Copenhagen: 1822) gives names to the phytogeographical regions.

97. Jens Wilken Hornemann (1770–1841) in his *Forsøg til en dansk Oc-conomiske Plantelære* (Copenhagen: 1796) describes all the plants in Denmark, Holstein, Norway, Iceland, and Greenland, and also discusses their prevalence and spread in those countries.

98. See *Fragments*, p. 135; G. H. von Schubert, *Die Symbolik des Traumes* (2 ed., Bamberg: 1821), p. 38. *ASKB* 776.

99. See *Letters*, no. 262, in note 2648.

100. Kierkegaard by this time had been a university student for four years, ostensibly in theology. Five years later he completed doctoral work in theology (although in that faculty called Magister Theologiae at the time).

101. *Kjøbenhavns flyvende Post*, 143, 1830, in *Prosaiske Skrifter*, I–XI (Copenhagen: 1861–62), X, p. 478.

102. Polyæn, *Strategemata*, VII, 9, tells the anecdote that Cambyses' army, during the siege of Pelusium, drove ahead of them animals sacred in Egypt, to deter shooting by the besieged. See *The Concept of Anxiety* [*Dread*], p. 37.

103. Claudius Pulcher before the sea-battle near Drepana. See Cicero, *De natura deorum*, II, 3, 7; Valerius Maximus, *Facta et dicta memorabilia*, I, 4, 3.

104. The basis for the text is *Efterladte Papirer*, ed. H. P. Barfod, I, p. 43, in which the Latin phrase (something lacking) appears as a section title and not in editorial brackets. Thulstrup (*Breve*, I, no. 3, p. 36) brackets the Danish translation of the phrase as Barfod's editorial notation.

105. See Deuteronomy 34:1–4, with reference to Mt. Nebo rather than to Tabor, and Numbers 14:20–25.

106. The coastal road running north from Copenhagen, which was and is the main route to the carnival at Bakken, situated in Dyrehaug or Dyrehaven, a large woods with many deer (therefore Deer Park).

107. The goddess Thetis sought in vain to prevent fulfillment of the prophecy of Achilles' death in the Trojan war by dressing him as a woman. See P. F. A. Nitsch, *Neues mythologischer Wörterbuch*, I–II (Leipzig, Soran: 1821), pp. 18–19. *ASKB* 1944–45.

108. See note 106.

109. Entry I A 63 and those following through I A 80 are in the first regular journal (marked AA) that Kierkegaard kept. Here in translation they are ordered according to dates given in the text. They are a record of a vacation period that Eduard Geismar has called his "summer vacation of self-knowledge" (*Søren Kierkegaard*, I–VI, Copenhagen: 1927–28, I, p. 29) and go together with the letter (I A 72) written presumably to P. W. Lund on June 1, 1835. The Kierkegaard family had been shaken by the deaths of three children within the previous 30 months, and on July 31, 1834, Kierkegaard's mother died. No loose-sheet journal entries about these deaths or letters by Kierkegaard are extant, but H. L. Martensen states (*Af mit Levnet*, I–III, Copenhagen: 1882–83, I, p. 79) that the young student took his mother's death very hard. Martensen's mother said she had never seen a person so grieved over

a death. Michael P. Kierkegaard, perhaps sensing something of his son's intellectual and inner turmoil, gave him money for a summer vacation in North
Sjælland, and it did turn out to be a period of significant reflection and deep-
ened awareness for Kierkegaard.

During this time Kierkegaard apparently did write to his family, but none
of these letters is known to exist now. There is one letter from his father during
this period (*Letters*, no. 4):

My dear Son,

I send you these few lines in my own hand in order to lessen your worry
about my letting Peter answer your letters instead of writing myself. Thank
God, there is no other reason, internal or external, than that which you know
about and suppose: my ever increasing difficulty in writing, with which you are
quite familiar. Besides, in the past few days, I have been plagued more than
usually by my colic.

Your letter says nothing about how you are, and from this I conclude that
you are well, which makes me very happy. Your brother is also in good health,
and so are your brothers-in-law and their children.—

Please give affectionate and friendly greetings to Mr. Mentz and his wife
from us, and especially from me.

Your most loving and wholly devoted Father,
M. P. Kierkegaard

Copenhagen, July 4, 1835
[Address:]
To S. A. Kierkegaard, Student in Theology
at the Inn at Gilleleie

110. Helene-Kilde.
111. J. M. Thiele, *Danske Folkesagn*, I–IV (Copenhagen: 1818–23). *ASKB*
1591–92.
112. See ibid., I, p. 31.
113. Somewhat differently related in ibid., *Samling* 1, I, p. 29.
114. See note 111.
115. A feud involving various dukes and counts, also the mayor of Lü-
beck, following the death of Frederik I of Denmark, April 10, 1533. Duke
Christian became King Christian III in July, 1536.
116. Heinrich Ernst Schimmelman (1747–1831). He was instrumental in
the promulgation of the order of March 16, 1792, forbidding slave trade from
the Danish West Indies after 1803, making Denmark an early opponent of the
slave trade. As Danish Minister of Finance he was generally held politically
responsible for the bankruptcy of the Danish government in 1813. He was
named Foreign Minister in 1824 and was known as a patron of Danish and
German poets, including Baggesen, Oehlenschläger, Rahbek, Klopstock, and
Schiller.

117. Ole J. Kold, innkeeper of Rogaardshus. See II A 442. See letter of September 30, 1845 (not in *Breve*), *J.P.*, V, 5852.

118. A forest north of Copenhagen, one of Kierkegaard's favorite outing areas and the site of his most favorite place, Otteveien or Ottevejskrogen, the nook or crossing of eight paths. See notes 951, 952; *Stages*, pp. 33–36.

119. This view of nature and religion is absent in Kierkegaard's later writing and by implication is repudiated in *The Concept of Anxiety* [*Dread*], pp. 135–36. See also, for example, I A 333.

120. Hans Christian Lyngbye (1782–1837), pastor at Søborg and Gilleleie since 1827, also a botanist.

121. Nils Kristoffer Gyldenstjerne (1789–1865), ichthyologist and holder of the entailed estates Krapperup and Bjärsgård.

122. The source of these lines has not been located.

123. Gilleleie Kro [Inn].

124. Black Bridge.

125. Gilbjerg Hoved (Gilbjerg Headland), the northernmost part of Sjælland, 33 meters high, about 110 feet.

126. See note 109.

127. Matthew 10:29.

128. Kierkegaard makes fine double use of this term. On the one hand it points to the quiet marriage (Greek *Kryptos*, hidden, and *Gamos*, marriage), and on the other it is a botanical metaphor of quiet fruitfulness (Linnaeus's plant class 24, containing plants with hidden or indiscernible organs of fertilization and, without flowers and seeds, reproducing by means of spores, such as ferns, mosses, and fungi).

129. See *Repetition*, p. 94; *Stages*, p. 245; *Works of Love*, p. 138.

130. See Luke 2:19.

131. See John 6:15, 12:37.

132. Presumably Anton Günther (see II A 630 and 356, where the name is spelled correctly), author of *Peregrins Gastmahl, Eine Idylle in eilf Octaven aus dem deutschen wissenschaftlichen Volksleben* (Vienna: 1830). *ASKB* 1672.

133. J. G. Fichte, *Die Bestimmung des Menschen, Sämmtliche Werke*, I–VIII (Berlin: 1845–46), II, pp. 178–79. *ASKB* 492–99.

134. See I A 72, note 92.

135. See *Either/Or*, II, p. 356.

136. See Matthew 13:45–46.

137. See note 129.

138. Kierkegaard's first reference to Socrates. *The Concept of Irony with Constant Reference to Socrates*, Kierkegaard's dissertation, was published in 1841.

139. The name of a game in which one player sits on a stool in the middle of a circle, while a questioner quietly asks each of the remaining players what he wants to know about the stool-sitter. The questioner then puts these questions to the player on the stool, who tries to guess the author of each question.

The expression is also used in "An Open Letter to Orla Lehmann," *S.V.*, XIII, p. 28.

140. See *From the Papers of One Still Living, S.V.*, XIII, pp. 45–49.

141. See, for example, *Either/Or*, I, pp. 24, 25, 27; *Repetition*, pp. 75–76; *The Concept of Anxiety [Dread]*, p. 89.

142. Pythagoras.

143. See Matthew 5:45.

144. See Genesis 19:26.

145. If I may use this expression.

146. See note 133.

147. "It is, as with pleasant morning dreams, from whose drowsy confusion one can extricate oneself only by force, if one does not wish to go about in increasingly oppressive weariness and later drag through the day in sickly exhaustion." Novalis, *Schriften*, herausgegeben von Ludw. Tieck und Fr. Schlegel, I–II. *ASKB* 1776.

148. See note 120.

149. See *Stages*, pp. 181–83.

150. J. G. Burman-Becker, *Efterretninger om de gamle Borge i Danmark og Hertugdømmerne*, I Samling (Copenhagen: 1830), pp. 125 ff.

151. E. T. A. Hoffman, *Meister Floh*, "*Siebentes Abentheuer,*" *Ausgewählte Schriften*, I–X (Berlin: 1827–28). *ASKB* 1712–16.

152. "How did a man who searched out the most secret thoughts of his brethren speak to himself? Does not this fatal gift bring over him that frightful condition which came over the eternal Jew, who wandered through the bright tumult of the world without hope, without pain, in apathetic indifference which is the *caput mortuum* of despair, as if through an uncomfortable, comfortless wasteland?" See Gregor Malantschuk, *Kierkegaard's Thought* (Princeton: 1972), p. 28, for an interpretation of the significance of this passage as an expression of Kierkegaard's relation to his father.

153. Kierkegaard bought an amazing number of books for his use, as can be seen in *Auktionsprotokol over Søren Kierkegaards Bogsamling* (Auction-catalog of Søren Kierkegaard's Book-collection: *ASKB*), ed. H. P. Rohde (Copenhagen: 1967). In addition he made considerable use of the University Library, the Athenæum Library, the Student Association Library, and the library of Regensen.

154. In Nyerup (pp. 180–83) there is a section on *Jerusalems Skomager* (shoemaker of Jerusalem), Ahasverus, who, in another report (p. 182), is said to have been Pilate's doorkeeper, Cartophilus. See note 306.

155. Carl Frederik Lemming (1782–1846), Danish violinist and guitarist, an appointee of the Royal Theater, Stockholm, 1833–35. The Student Association records indicate that "chamber-musician Lemming from Stockholm" was granted admission for a fortnight (from October 17, 1835) as a "traveling member."

156. See Kierkegaard's letter to Regine, *Letters*, no. 16.

157. Most likely the entry is a draft of an introduction to a talk (see I B 2) given to the Student Association, November 28, 1835.

158. Do not touch me (John 20:17).

159. Far, O far away, are the uninitiated.

160. The Student Association *Rapportbog for Inspectionshavende*, October 1833–April 1837, states that philology student J. A. Ostermann gave a talk on Saturday, November 14, 1835. Ostermann's talk was printed in *Fædrelandet*, 71, January 1836, under the title "Our Most Recent Journal Literature." Kierkegaard appeared as a character called "the translator" in Henrik Hertz's novel, *Stemninger og Tilstande* (Copenhagen: 1839). For bibliographical details concerning the various publications mentioned later in this entry, see *Pap.* I B 2. See note 530.

161. See note 105.

162. See note 160.

163. On July 25, 1830, Charles X of France, who had assumed a kind of provisional dictatorship, promulgated the five ordinances of St. Cloud, suspending liberty of the press, dissolving the chamber of deputies, changing the election system, calling a new chamber, and appointing some ultra-royalists to the Council of State. Under the leadership of M. Thiers, the "fourth estate" made a collective revolt against what was generally regarded as illegal power. Insurrection broke out July 27. On July 29, Charles X, after Paris was out of hand, accepted the insurgents' condition that the five ordinances be withdrawn, but it was too late. The Duke of Orleans declared his acceptance of the office of Lieutenant-General of the Realm, and on August 2, 1830, Charles X abdicated. On August 9, 1830, Louis Philippe, Duke of Orleans, became "Citizen King," a constitutional monarch. The "three days of July" had effects elsewhere in Europe, particularly in Belgium, which declared freedom from the Dutch.

164. Polish revolution. Influenced by the July revolution in France, Polish students tried to capture the Russian regent, Grand Duke Constantine on November 29, 1830. They failed, but the insurrection spread. After months of struggle and the intervention of Russia, Poland was declared a Russian province on February 26, 1832.

165. This sentence from a Copenhagen newspaper is illuminating simply because of its length and complexity; most likely it would be impossible to find a similar sentence today in six pounds of the Sunday *New York Times*. Stylistically, it is quite like the writing of the exuberant twenty-two-year-old student who quotes it, suggesting that his style here was not at all exceptional.

166. The cane Nille uses upon her husband, Jeppe, in Holberg's *Jeppe paa Bjerget*. Erik (*Gamle Erik*, Old Erik) was common in Jutland dialects and was also employed elsewhere in Scandinavia as a name for the devil.

167. Christian Georg Nathan David (1793–1874), advocate of moderate

constitutional reform, founder of the weekly *Fædrelandet* in September 1834. Three months later he was charged, as editor, for the publication of three anonymous constitutional articles in *Fædrelandet*. He was acquitted by lower and higher courts but had to pay court costs.

168. The reference is to the King's message to the Chancellery, February 26, 1835, regarding a petition of February 20 urging no change in the ordinance on freedom of the press.

169. Daniel F. E. Auber (1782–1871), French composer. During the decade prior to the writing of this entry, numerous operas by Auber had been presented in Copenhagen.

170. See B. [Søren Kierkegaard], "Morning Observations in *Kjøbenhavnsposten*" (see note 530).

171. During the autumn and winter of 1835–36 Kierkegaard's reading included E. T. A. Hoffmann (*Meister Floh, ASKB* 1712–16), Schleiermacher (*Vertraute Briefe über die Lucinde*), *Ein Volksbuchlein* (on the Wandering Jew), Herder (*Zerstreute Blätter, ASKB* 1676–1705). See I C 55–69. See also entry on Goethe, I C 72; on Schleiermacher, I C 69; on Poul Martin Møller, I C 70; on Jens Baggesen, I C 78.

172. Friedrich Heinrich von der Hagen, *Erzählungen und Märchen,* I–II (Prenzlau: 2 ed., 1838). Not listed in *ASKB.*

173. See *Either/Or,* I, p. 19.

174. On February 10, 1836, Kierkegaard purchased *Goethe's Werke,* I–LV (Stuttgart, Tübingen: 1828–33). *ASKB* 1641–68. Volume XVIII is *Wilhelm Meisters Lehrjahre.*

175. *Jens Baggesens danske Værker,* I–XII (Copenhagen: 1827–32), purchased January 14, 1836. *ASKB* 1509–20.

176. See *Fragments,* p. 7.

177. Master Death, this I cannot understand. I am supposed to dance and I cannot even walk.

178. Martin Hammerich, *Om Ragnaroksmythen og dens Betydning i oldnordiske Religion* (Copenhagen: 1836). *ASKB* 1950.

179. On Kierkegaard's interest in mythology and legends, see Malantschuk, pp. 21–25 and index (see note 152).

180. Carl C. Rafn, *Nordiske Kæmpehistorier efter islandske Haandskrifter,* I–III (Copenhagen: 1823). *ASKB* 1993–95.

181. Ibid.

182. On the importance to the young Kierkegaard of Molbech's printed lectures on recent Danish poetry, see Malantschuk, pp. 48–49 (see note 152).

183. Kierkegaard had J. G. Herder's *Sämmtliche Werke,* I–LX (Stuttgart, Tübingen: 1827–30). *ASKB* 1676–1705. Molbech cites the 45-volume edition of 1805–20. The theme of ancient hymns was not pursued.

184. Pseudonym of J. P. F. Richter, author of *Vorschule der Aesthetik,* I–II (Vienna: 1815). *ASKB* 1381–83.

185. Pierre Jean de Beranger (1780–1857), French poet, writer of ballads, drinking songs, and political satires.

186. The text of the reading notes is given in *Pap.*, I C 89 and XII, pp. 224–28. This is one of many instances of extended reading in books not included in the *ASKB* listing.

187. *Ludwig Tiecks Schriften*, I–XV (Berlin: 1828–29). Not in *ASKB*, which does include 1848–49, *Sämmtliche Werke*, I–II (Paris: 1837).

"There is perhaps no invention of the imagination which, even if unconsciously, does not have the allegory as the very ground of its character. The double phenomenon of good and evil is that which the child understands most readily in all imaginative literature, which moves us anew in every portrayal, which speaks to us in manifold forms out of every enigma and arduously seeks to resolve itself into understanding. There is a way in which the most ordinary life is regarded as a fairy tale; likewise, one can become conversant with the most marvelous as if it were the most commonplace. It is possible to say that all of the most ordinary as well as the most marvelous, the lightest, and the jolliest have veracity and captivate us, only because this allegory in the last analysis serves as the mainstay of the whole, and that is precisely why Dante's allegories are so convincing; they have been painstakingly developed into the most graphic actuality. Novalis says: only the story that can also be a fable is truly a story. But there is also much sick and feeble literature of this type which only drags us about in concepts without engaging our imagination, and that is the most irksome kind of entertainment."

188. Heinrich Heine, *Die Romantische Schule* (Hamburg: 1836). Purchased February 16, 1836. *ASKB* U63.

189. Entries I C 96–99 comprise fifteen pages of reading notes from the Schubarth volume.

190. Hirsch considers the entry not as autobiographical but as part of the projected "Faustian letters." See notes 92, 245.

191. See note 190.

192. Chief clerk in the Copenhagen criminal-and-police-court.

193. The reference is to the use of the familiar second-person singular pronoun (*Du*) employed in a family and between close friends.

194. See *Either/Or*, I, pp. 40–41.

195. The edition (see note 151) of Hoffmann's works in Kierkegaard's library does not contain *Don Juan*.

196. See note 109.

197. Presumably P. W. Lund. See note 92. A letter from P. W. Lund is mentioned in a letter from P. C. Kierkegaard to Marie Boisen, June 28, 1836.

198. Hans Kristian Rask, who went to the same school (Borgerdydskolen) Kierkegaard attended and was a theology student during the first three years (1830–33) Kierkegaard was at the university.

199. Ditler Gothard Monrad, who began his theological studies the same

year (1830) Kierkegaard did and completed them in 1836, four years before Kierkegaard.

200. Peter Engel Lind, who finished Borgerdydskolen in 1831, one year after Kierkegaard.

201. See note 75.

202. In one of his earliest writings (*Papirer* II B 1–21, 1838) and his only attempt to use a dramatic form, Kierkegaard makes satiric use of the title *The Battle between the Old and the New Soap-Cellars* in discussing Hegelian philosophy. The reference is to the competition between three soap-stores located in the half-flight basements of buildings on Graabrødretorvet near the University of Copenhagen. One had a sign, The Old Soap-Cellar, another, The Original Old Soap-Cellar, the third, Here Is the Original Old Soap-Cellar where the Old Soap-Cellar People Live. See J. Davidsen, *Fra det gamle Kongens København* (rev. ed., Copenhagen: 1910), p. 19. See note 1175.

203. Pp. 127–29, 131–34. See note 188.

204. Kierkegaard customarily used another edition of Lessing. See note 67.

205. Subtitle ("A Flysheet from Cologne") of poem "Doktor Faust" in L. Achim von Arnim and Clemens Brentano, *Des Knaben Wunderhorn*, I–III (Heidelberg: 1806–8), I, p. 214. *ASKB* 1494–96, purchased March 14, 1836.

206. *Kjøbenhavns flyvende Post*, 11, 1828, col. 5.

207. See I C 100.

208. See I C 46, 49.

209. See I C 101.

210. *Faust*, XII (for edition, see note 174).

> What will you, poor devil give etc. (I,4).
> This was the poodle's real core, a traveling scholar?
> The *casus* is diverting (I,3).
> The Earth-Spirit (I,1). The modest truth
> I speak to you (I,3).

211. "Not even like you."

212. "My students by the nose."

213. L. Kruse, *Don Juan* (Copenhagen: 1807), pp. 125–26.

214. P. 217. See note 205.

215. Adelbert von Chamisso, Peter Schlemihl's *Wundersame Geschichte* (3 ed., Nürnberg: 1835). *ASKB* 1630.

216. I am condemned by the just judgment of God.

217. *ASKB* (1868–70) lists *Lord Byron's sämmtliche Werke . . . neu übersetzt*, I–X (Stuttgart: 1839). Kierkegaard may have used an earlier edition of Byron or he may have read about Goethe's discussion of Manfred and Faust in Schubarth's volume (see I C 96), pp. 45–46, 81–82.

218. See I C 107.

219. See *The Moment*, no. 10, in *Attack*, p. 278.

220. Figured bass was an old system of harmony in which a composition was written by giving the bass notes only; numbers were placed below them to indicate the complete chords.

221. *"Noveller,"* gamle og nye, af Forfatteren til *"En Hverdags-Historie"* [Thomasine Christine Gyllembourg Ehrensvärd], ed. J. L. Heiberg, I–III (Copenhagen: 1833–34), III, pp. 20–98, pt. 2 of *Familien Polonius*.

222. Ibid., pp. 122–23.

223. *Meister Floh, Sechstes Abentheuer, "Geschichte des Schneiderleins von Sachsenhausen,"* X, pp. 241–42. See note 151.

224. Ludwig Tieck, *Phantasus*, pt. II, *Schriften*, V. See note 187.

225. Two of Kierkegaard's three sisters were married to Lund brothers, Johan Christian and Henrik Ferdinand, and S. K. was frequently with their families. Among Kierkegaard's relatives there are two persons named A. Lund who would fit the date 1836: Anne Cathrine Lund (a second cousin of the Lund brothers) whom Henrik Ferdinand Lund married on April 2, 1836, after Petrea Severine Kierkegaard Lund's death (Dec. 29, 1834), and her sister Anna Lund. These two are Ole Lund's daughters, mentioned in entry 5049 (*Letters*, no. 2).

226. *Phantasus*, pt. I. See note 224.

227. See *Either/Or*, I, p. 88.

228. See note 174 for edition.

229. See *Either/Or*, I, pp. 43–134, especially pp. 55, 70, 84, 88–89, 91; II, p. 43.

230. Nicolaus Lenau, *Faust* (Stuttgart, Tübingen: 1836), pp. 49–51.

231. *Irische Elfenmärchen, übersetzt von den Brüdern Grimm* (Leipzig: 1826). *ASKB* 1423. A translation of T. C. Croker, *Fairy Legends and Traditions of the South of Ireland*, I–III (London: 1825–28).

232. For the listing in this rather extensive bibliography (63 titles) on Faust and *Faust*, see *Pap.*, XII, pp. 229–41.

233. Copenhagen: 1812 and 1823. *ASKB* U35. The text of this book with Kierkegaard's comments and underlining is given in *Pap.*, I C 107 and XII, pp. 242–60; see *Either/Or*, I, pp. 89–90.

234. This refers to p. 10 of the Faust book cited in I C 107.

235. Reference is to a footnote in Raumer, *Historiches Taschenbuch* (see note 58), p. 134: *"Die Sage von Dr. Faust:* (1) Moehsen, *Verzeichnisz einer sammlung von Bildnissen, grössentheils berühmter Aertze*, p. 16; (2) Trithem, *Epist. familiar.*, in *Operibus*, vol. II, p. 559. . . ."

236. This entry appears in S.K.'s handwriting at the end of the Faust book referred to in I C 107.

237. The reference is to pp. 13–14 of the Faust volume in I C 107.

238. See *Either/Or*, I, p. 26 (present text reads Virgil).

239. Heidelberg: 1807. *ASKB* 1440.

240. See note 58.

241. The text of this entry is missing. H. P. Barfod, secretary to Kierkegaard's brother Peter Christian Kierkegaard, lists the entry in his catalog of the journals and papers under a title composed of the initial words.

242. See note 241.

243. See note 151.

244. Jean-Nicolas Bouilly, *De to Dage eller Flygtningerne*, tr. N. T. Bruun (Copenhagen: 1802).

245. In his *Kierkegaard Studien*, I$^{1-2}$–II^3 (Gutersloh: 1933), II, pp. 490–92, serial pagination, Emanuel Hirsch makes a good case for the idea that Kierkegaard's first writing plan was a series of letters by a pseudonymous Faustian doubter. The present entry and the remaining I A entries given here represent Kierkegaard's initial work on this projected series, which was never completed. There is, however, an obvious relation in substance, tone, and form to the "Diapsalmata" written by the sardonic young Mr. A in *Either/Or*, I, pp. 19 ff. The back part of a notebook, marked CC by Kierkegaard and with pagination beginning from the back (the front and major portion was used for translations into Latin; see I C 11–12), contains entries I A 328–341. These are the core of the "Faustian letters." I A 329 touches on Gørres, *Die christliche Mystik*, and indicates that "the passage should be quoted"; this suggests that more than a journal type of writing was under way. II A 46 is entitled "A Preface" and indicates that the book "should be called 'letters.'" Working from content and within the 1834–37 time-span, Hirsch adds the following entries to the "Faustian letters": I A 34, 72, 104, 158, 161, 292, 328–39, 341; II A 22, 23, 24, 25, 26, 29, 30, 46, 48, 49, 50, 53, 54, 55, 56, 57, 59. See Sören Kierkegaard, *Erstlingsschriften*, ed., tr. E. Hirsch, *Gesammelte Werke*, I–XXXVI Abt. (Düsseldorf, Köln: Eugen Diederichs Verlag, 1956–69), Abt. XXX, pp. 114–137. See also II A 127, 599, 601, 603, 607, 609, 613, and 634.

That Kierkegaard had in mind a volume of pseudonymous letters by a fictive character not only has historical-literary importance but constitutes an early instance of the continuing riskiness of attributing personally and directly the contents of his pseudonymous works and his writing "as a poet." See especially "First and Last Declaration," *Postscript*, end, and *The Point of View*, pp. 39–41, 85–86.

246. See *Postscript*, pp. 324–25.

247. The medieval attempt to achieve one culture, one Church, and one language (Latin) is regarded here as akin to the effort to build the Tower of Babel.

248. Self-seeking.

249. See note 106.

250. See *Fragments*, p. 5.

251. See I A 223.

252. See H. L. Martensen, *Maanedsskrift for Litteratur*, XVI, 1836, p. 517.

253. A presumed practice of beginning any historical discussion with creation.

254. Anthology.

255. The reference is to an epistemological view that explained the correspondence of object and perception by way of the interaction of body and soul.

256. The preceding lines touch lightly on Hegel's concept of movement and becoming in logic and time. In 1714 King Carl XII of Sweden made his famous ride from Turkey to the fortress Stralsund in Poland in sixteen days, averaging about seventy-five miles a day. When he arrived, his boots had to be cut off. (See K. F. Becker, *Verdenshistorie*, I–XII [Copenhagen: 1822–29], IX, pp. 78–79; *ASKB* 1972–83). To the shoemaker, the immediate is an abstraction: "feet without boots," "boots without feet." The dialectical movement of boots and feet fitting each other is expressed by the squeaking. Unity is achieved when the boots have quit squeaking and fit the feet so perfectly that boots and feet can be separated only as they were in the case of Carl XII.

257. *Selskabet for Trykkefrihedens rette Brug* (founded 1835). See *Kjøbenhavnsposten*, 105, May 2, 1835, *Dansk Folkeblad*, 1, 1835, p. 1.

258. See *Fear and Trembling*, p. 79.

259. See *Kjøbenhavnsposten*, 69, March 9, 1836; 88, March 25, 92; March 28; 94, March 29; 316, November 9; and, especially, 340, December 3.

260. A fictional object of address in a fictional epistolary exchange. See note 245.

261. N. F. S. Grundtvig, *Christelige Prædikener eller Søndags Bog*, I–III (Copenhagen: 1827–30), III, no. 26, especially pp. 584 and 592 ff. *ASKB* 222–24. See note 81.

262. October 30, 1826. See *Kjendelse og Dom i Sagen Dr. Professor H. Clausen contra forhenværende residerende Capellan N. F. S. Grundtvig*, ed. J. Roed (Copenhagen: 1826), pp. 21–22. Instead of replying to criticism in *Kirkens Gjenmæle* (1825) by N. F. S. Grundtvig, H. N. Clausen had instituted an injury case in court. Grundtvig lost and was given a small fine and lifetime censorship (lifted in 1837). See note 75.

263. Shadow play on the wall.

264. J. Görres, *Die christliche Mystik*, I–IV$^{1-2}$ (Regensburg, Landshut: 1836–42). *ASKB* 528–32. "Since he [Napoleon] disappeared and the restoration spun out its boring allegories and the *juste milieu* discharged its high-flown metaphors, everything has again become a romantic wilderness; and young Germany sits in the swamp, and young Switzerland and young Italy and young France and young Spain and Britannia, carving whistles from the reed and whistling and crowing and cooing and wooing in all keys: apparently it is nothing but the stymphalic birds waiting for their Heracles to chase them away with his rattle. Thus all present time becomes myth; in the end even criticism

will no longer be able to resist the mythologizing principle; it becomes a fly on the nose of the world giant and cleanses its wings with its legs and does spotwork backwards for further cleansing."

265. See note 245.

266. A further characterization of the pseudonymous Faustian writer as a doubter, even to the point of radical doubt (suicide). See notes 92 and 245.

267. The fictive recipient of the Faustian letters. See note 245.

268. Niels Andreas (April 30, 1809) died September 21, 1833, in Paterson, New Jersey, U.S.A., where he had emigrated in 1831.

269. Søren Michael (March 23, 1807) died September 14, 1819, from an accident while playing at school.

270. See *Works of Love*, pp. 317–29.

271. Well, what is man?

272. See Matthew 10:30; Luke 12:7.

273. See *Either/Or*, I, p. 19.

274. Ibid., pp. 31–32.

275. G. J. Wenzel, *Manden af Verden eller Grundsætninger og Regler for Afstand, Tække, fiin Levensmaade og sand Hoflighed*, tr. N. T. Bruun (Copenhagen: 1818), p. 98.

276. The long delayed letter from Brazil arrived on the day of the widow's remarriage. See note 245 on the Faustian letters.

277. There is a shift in the relation of the visible polestar to the true pole. Here the brother says that the movement of life from happiness to the sorrow of separation is an expression of a single, unchangeable love, just as the shifting position of the visible polestar is an expression of its relation to the true pole. The metaphor is epitomized in the arithmetic symbol above.

278. The manuscript of this entry is missing. H. P. Barfod, *E.P.*, I, pp. 18–20, gives the date as December 2, with no year, and places it together with entries from 1833. The editors of the *Papirer* place it in the period 1836–37. In his catalog of the journals and papers, Barfod calls this entry a draft of a letter. In tone and in some details it is much like the "Diapsalmata" in *Either/Or*, I, pp. 17–42, and belongs together with I A 328 as a substantial element in Kierkegaard's projected pseudonymous work by a Faustian doubter. See note 245.

279. See *Either/Or*, I, p. 19.

280. See ibid., pp. 25–26, 27.

281. See Rafn, *Nordiske Kæmpehistorier*, I, pp. 96 ff. (Full reference given in note 180.)

282. A mysterious German youth who in 1828 appeared in Nürnberg without any knowledge of his past or awareness of his identity. See *Kjøbenhavns flyvende Post*, 65, 66, 70, 71, 73, 1828; *Dansk Ugeskrift*, II, 1833, pp. 309 ff.

283. See note 267.

284. See *The Concept of Anxiety*, p. 46; *Postscript*, p. 149.

285. See *Either/Or*, I, p. 33.

286. Ibid., p. 391 (where a saying of Caligula is used); II, pp. 101, 192.

287. The suffix *gal(e)* in the Danish *nattergal* (nightingale) means "to sing" (hence night-singer), but *gal* also means "mad, insane" (hence English "gale," a furious or "mad" wind). The word-play here has been shifted to the relation between "moon" and "lunatic" as the best possible approximation in translation.

288. See *For Self-Examination*, p. 43.

289. See *Either/Or*, I, p. 21.

290. Ibid., pp. 25, 39.

291. Play by L. Holberg.

292. See NUMBERS, CROWD, MASS, PUBLIC.

293. See *Either/Or*, I, pp. 19–20.

294. See note 141.

295. This entry is part of the projected "Faustian letters." See note 245.

296. See note 295.

297. See note 295.

298. See note 295.

299. L. Holberg, *Den honnette Ambition*, III, sc. 1.

300. See note 295.

301. *Kjøbenhavns flyvende Post*, 13, 1828, p. 3. In 99–101, 1827, the editor, J. L. Heiberg, gives a criticism of the production of Adam Oehlenschlager's tragedy, *Væringerne i Miklagaard*. In response to Oehlenschlager's comments on his review, Heiberg writes at greater length and more analytically about the play and about drama in general (*Svar paa Prof. Oehlenschlägers Skrift: "Om Kritiken i Kjøbenhavns flyvende Post over 'Væringerne i Miklagaard,' " Kjøbenhavns flyvende Post*, 7–8, 10–16, 1828). In no. 13, p. 3, Heiberg gives a discursive presentation of relations among kinds of comedy. Kierkegaard reproduces the essence of this discussion in outline form and significantly adds an observation on the absence of irony and/or humor in Heiberg's formulation.

302. Ibid., p. 4.

303. See note 36.

304. The University of Copenhagen dormitory for scholarship students and possessor of a rather extensive library, another one of the libraries Kierkegaard used to supplement his growing collection of books. See note 153.

305. J. Görres, *Die teutschen Volksbücher* (Heidelberg: 1807). *ASKB* 1440.

306. B. S. Ingemann, *Blade af Jerusalems Skomagers Lommebog* (Copenhagen: 1833). *ASKB* 1571, purchased February 9, 1836.

307. *Goethe's Werke*, I–LV (Stuttgart, Tübingen: 1828–33), XXVI, pp. 309 ff. *ASKB* 1641–68.

308. J. C. Lavater, *Physiognomische Fragmenter, zur Beförderung der Menschenerkentniss und Menschenliebe*, I–IV (Leipzig, Winterthur: 1775–78). *ASKB* 613–16.

309. The Danish is *den evig Jøde,* as in line 1 of the entry. This name and title are usually translated "the wandering Jew," but here the literal meaning, the eternal Jew, is required. See note 36.

310. See note 309.

311. See entry I C 117.

312. I am not young, I am not old,
My life is no life.

313. So I travel day and night,
The heart so full, the world so empty,
I have seen everything already
And still can have no rest.

314. I–IV (Braunschweig: 1833–36). *ASKB* 1907–10. A translation of Dr. Samuel Warren [pseud. Harrisson], *Passages from the Diary of a Late Physician.*

315. Hans Lassen Martensen (1808–84), professor of theology, University of Copenhagen, and P. J. Mynster's successor as Bishop of Sjælland (April 15, 1854). See notes 3258, 3275.

316. Review of J. L. Heiberg, *"Indledningsforedrag til det i November 1834 begyndte logiske kursus paa den kongelige militaire Høiskole," Maanedsskrift for Litteratur,* XVI, 1836, pp. 515 ff.

317. See *Fragments,* p. 5.

318. See Matthew 22:20–21; Mark 12:16–17; Luke 20:24–25.

319. Franz Baader, whom Martensen visited in Munich. See H. L. Martensen, *Af mit Levnet,* I–III (Copenhagen 1882–83), I, pp. 137–59.

320. See note 205. The expression "a flysheet from Munich" comes from *"ein fliegendes Blatt aus Cöln"* (referring to Dr. Faust) in L. Achim von Arnim and Clemens Brentano, *Des Knaben Wunderhorn* (see note 205), I, p. 214.

321. Poul Møller, *"Tanker over Muligheden af Beviser for Menneskets Udødelighed," Maanedsskrift for Litteratur,* XVII, January 1837, pp. 1–72, 422–53, in Poul Møller, *Efterladte Skrifter,* I–III (Copenhagen: 1839–43), II, pp. 158–272. *ASKB* 1574–76. "Episode" refers to ibid, pp. 177–180 (*Maanedsskrift,* pp. 18 ff.), where the author tells in dialogue form of a discussion about books, popularization of scholarship, and proofs.

322. *Allgemeines Reportorium für die theologische Literatur und kirchliche Statistik,* ed. G. F. H. Rheinwald (Berlin: 1837). *ASKB* 36–66 (I–XIX).

323. Even if he had dishonored the virgin mother.

324. Friedrich Schlegel, *Sämmtliche Werke,* I–X (Vienna: 1822–25). *ASKB* 1816–25.

325. Justinus Kerner, *Erscheinung aus dem Nachtgebiete der Natur* (Stuttgart, Tübingen: 1836), pp. 215 ff., esp. pp. 217–18. The quoted portion is a translation of Kierkegaard's Danish translation of I Corinthians 2:11 based on Kerner's German version, p. 219.

326. *Kiøbenhavns Aften-post,* XI, 1782.

327. *Kjøbenhavns flyvende Post.*

328. See notes 73, 75.

329. *"Kallundborgs Krønike eller Censurens Oprindelse,"* in Jens Baggesen, *Danske Værker,* I–XII (Copenhagen: 1827–32), I, p. 235. *ASKB* 1509–20.

330. Ibid. See *Postscript,* p. 270.

331. *Hervørs og Kong Hejdreks Saga,* in *Nordiske Kæmpehistorier* (see note 180), III, C.

332. Ibid., B, pp. 57 ff. The quotation is not quite exact.

333. See *Either/Or,* I, p. 33.

334. *"Vorrede i die klegliche Zukunft,"* ed. J. Görres (Frankfurt/M: 1817), p. 159. *ASKB* 1486.

> O mighty God! O just judge
> Have mercy upon me a poor poet.

335. H. C. Andersen, *Improvisatoren* (Copenhagen: 1835).

336. Wake, awake. See Görres (note 334), p. 117 (*"Hornruf"*), also pp. 113 (*"Nothgedrungener Abschied"*), 115 (*"Zweifache Mahnung"*), and 120 (*"Harter Entschlusz"*).

337. See *Kong Olger Danskes Krønike* in *Dansk og Norsk Nationalværk,* I–III, ed. K. L. Rahbek (Copenhagen: 1828–30), I, 2, pp. 28, 38, also pp. 26, 27, 29, 30, 117. *ASKB* 1457–59.

338. Ibid., p. 101 (*"otte Valske Mile"*; eight Italian miles).

339. Ibid., p. 44 (King Carvel).

340. Ibid., I, pt. 2, p. 289.

341. Ibid., pp. 157–59.

342. Ibid., p. 45 (Gloriant, betrothed to King Carvel).

343. Ibid.

344. Emanuel Schikander, *Tryllefløten,* music by Mozart (2 ed. Copenhagen: 1826), IV, 3. See *Either/Or,* I, p. 82. Kierkegaard heard *The Magic Flute* for the first time Jan. 26, 1837. See I C 125.

345. *Krønike om Keiser Carl Magnus,* in Rahbek (see note 337), I, 1.

346. See, for example, ibid., p. 179.

347. See L. Holberg, *Jacob von Tyboe,* II, 1.

348. Rahbek (see note 337), I, 2, pp. ii–iii.

349. Ibid., I, 2.

350. *"Die schwarzbraune Hexe-Fliegendes Blat,"* in *Des Knaben Wunderhorn* (see note 205), I, p. 34. See *From the Papers of One Still Living, S.V.,* XIII, p. 47.

> A hunter blew ably his horn,
> ably his horn,
> And all that he blew was
> lost.

351. See I C 107. Kierkegaard had read and annotated his copy of this

book. The entry itself is part of the projected Faustian letters. See notes 92, 245.

352. See note 241.

353. See Mark 8:36.

354. Peter Rørdam (1806–83), at whose home Kierkegaard first met Regine Olsen sometime between May 8–16, 1837 (see x⁵ A 149). Bolette (1815–87) was Peter's youngest sister. In the manuscript copy of this entry the words "Rørdam and by talking with Bolette" are crossed out. The dating of the entry is based on the internal coherence between II A 67 and II A 68 and upon Peter Rørdam, *Blade af hans Levnedsbog og Brevvexling fra 1806 til 1844*, ed. H. F. Rørdam (Copenhagen: 1891), p. 82.

355. See note 354. In the manuscript the entire entry is crossed out.

356. *Eine wahre Geschichte zur lehrreichen Unterhaltung armer Fräulein aufgeschrieben* (Berlin: 1810).

357. See *Either/Or*, I, p. 98.

358. 1837.

359. Translations of the German passages follow in serial order:

(1) Man is God, (2) God is God, (3) God is man.

[P. 10] "He does not have a definite direction to give his will like the Chinese emperor; he does not live in monastic quietism like the Lama; he is not a hero like Rostem; he is not an artist who, like Phidias, creates ideal images of the gods for Scopas and thereby experiences himself as the power of religion; through the title, through the name he knows himself as the unconditional power. This apotheosis is the caricature of the Hellenic apotheosis, which always appears as a conclusion."

[Pp. 21 f.] "Cognizant of itself as the quintessence of all actual powers, this master of the world is that awesome self-consciousness which knows itself to be the actual God; but inasmuch as he is only the formal Self that is able to tame them [the powers], his incitement and self-gratification are equally a monstrous dissoluteness."

[Pp. 23 f.] "Since the God in himself is man, he also becomes man."

[Pp. 30 f.] "The tragic element for the religion of art was the grief of incomprehensible death, which to be sure did not negate the enjoyment of beautiful serenity as in Egypt but did disturb in an uncomfortable way. The element of sadness in monotheism was the burden of the law which man certainly recognized as that of the holy God but not as his own. Even the autonomy of theoretical reason and the autocracy of practical reason in Deism are only secondary."

360. The creation eagerly waits.

361. See a parallel in *Fear and Trembling*, pp. 103–9.

362. See I A 175.

363. See I A 333.

364. *Ueber Lenaus Faust.* [See note 230.] *Von Johannes M.....n* (Stuttgart: 1836). See entry II A 50. Extended Danish version: H. L. Martensen, *"Betragt-*

ninger over Ideen af Faust. Med Hensyn til Lenaus Faust, Perseus," ed. J. L. Heiberg, no. 1 (Copenhagen: June 1837), pp. 81–164. *ASKB* 569. Nikolaus Lenau (pseud. of N. Niembsch), *Faust* (Vienna: 1836).

365. See *Either/Or,* I, pp. 55–56.

366. See note 364.

367. Ibid.

368. See *The Concept of Anxiety [Dread],* p. 93; see K. Hase, *Kirkehistorie,* tr. C. Winther and T. Schorn (Copenhagen: 1837), p. 88. *ASKB* 160–66. The Carpocratians of the second century believed that to become perfect one had to commit all acts, even the most base. Until perfection is attained, one is repeatedly born anew. This entry may have been intended as an item in the projected "Faustian letters" (see note 245).

369. Conveniently arranged for use by everyman.

370. Presumably intended for inclusion in the projected letters by a Faustian doubter. See note 245.

371. See note 370.

372. The "I" here is presumably the pseudonymous author of the "Faustian letters." See note 370.

373. See note 372.

374. Agreeable.

375. See note 370.

376. See I A 334.

377. See note 370.

378. See notes 241, 370.

379. See note 370; *Either/Or,* I, p. 19.

380. See note 354.

381. Justinus Kerner, *Die Dichtungen von Justinus Kerner* (Stuttgart, Tübingen: 1834), pp. 386–87. *ASKB* 1734.

382. See I A 333.

383. See *Either/Or,* "Diapsalmata," I, pp. 17–42, as the prime instance of aphorisms in Kierkegaard's writings.

384. See note 381.

385. See note 325.

386. For a brief discussion of Kierkegaard's journal writing, see *Journals and Papers,* I, pp. xiii–xv; Howard V. Hong, "Kierkegaard's Journals," Northwestern University *Tri-Quarterly,* XVI, Fall 1969, pp. 100–23.

387. G. C. Lichtenberg, *Ideen, Maximen und Einfälle,* ed. G. Jördens, I–II (2 ed., Leipzig: 1830–31), pp. 119–20. *ASKB* 1773–74.

388. J. G. Hamann, *Hamanns Schriften,* ed. F. Roth, I–VIII[1–2] (Berlin: 1821–43), III, p. 392. *ASKB* 536–44.

389. Hayo Gerdes, translator and editor of the German edition of the *Papirer* (S. Kierkegaard, *Die Tagebucher,* I–[V] [Dusseldorf, Köln: Eugen Diederichs Verlag, 1962–], I, p. 381, note 390), considers this entry and entry II A

127 to be the last of the "Faustian letters," an enterprise envisioned but not carried out. See note 245. E. Hirsch does not include II A 118 and 127 in the letters of a Faustian doubter.

390. The loose construction of this sentence is in the Danish text.

391. Condensed, abridged, as in a compendium.

392. Lichtenberg (see note 387), I, p. 122. See *From the Papers of One Still Living, S.V.,* XIII, p. 59.

393. By analogy to the duodecimo book (a size made by folding the printed sheet into twelve sheets), the duodecimo letters are 1/12 the size of the uncial letters.

394. See II A 662.

395. Wilhelm Lund (see note 92), anon. review, *Maanedsskrift for Litteratur,* VI, 1831, pp. 309–56. Johannes Carsten Hauch, *Kort Oversigt over en Deel rudimentarishe Organer,* in *Blandinger fra Soroe,* I, 1831, pp. 16 ff.

396. This entry may have been an item for the Faustian letters. See notes 245, 389.

397. See *Either/Or,* I, pp. 19–20.

398. See John 6:63.

399. See letter to Regine Olsen, *Letters,* no. 19; Christian Winther, *"Violinspilleren ved Kilden,"* *Sang og Sagn* (Copenhagen: 1840).

400. See letter to Regine Olsen, *Letters,* no. 19.

401. See *Either/Or,* I, p. 39.

402. See II A 132.

403. In the form of concealment. See II A 146.

404. The final selection of a subject was "concerning the concept of irony, with constant reference to Socrates," published in 1841.

405. Reflexive pronoun.

406. See *"Rom og Jerusalem, en historisk Parallel,"* *Theologisk Maanedsskrift,* ed. N. F. S. Grundtvig and A. G. Rudelbach, I, 1825, pp. 204, 214. I–XIII, *ASKB* 346–51. Also Grundtvig, *Haandbog i Verdens-Historien,* I–III (Copenhagen: 1833–42), II, p. 18.

407. See VII^1 B 205–10, in praise of autumn, Kierkegaard's last purely literary effort (apart from reviews), written late in 1846.

408. Johan Eduard Erdmann, *Vorlesungen über Glauben und Wissen als Einleitung in die Dogmatik und Religionsphilosophie gehalten* (Berlin: 1837). *ASKB* 479. For entire text of the excerpts and reading notes, see *Pap.,* II C 38–43, and XII, pp. 140–58.

409. See note 408.

410. Contradiction in adjectives.

411. Anton Günther, *Vorschule zur speculativen theologie des positiven Christenthums,* I–II (Vienna: 1828–29). See note 132.

412. See notes 315, 3258, 3275. The lectures were listed as "Prolegomena to Speculative Dogmatics," Mondays and Fridays, 5:00–6:00.

413. See note 408.

414. See I A 282; II A 197, 730.

415. See *Berlingske Tidende*, 296, December 13, 1837: "*Hydro-Oxygen-Gas-Mikroskop.*"

416. See *Either/Or*, I, p. 24.

417. J. H. Fichte, "*Speculation og Aabenbaring,*" Danish translation in *Tidsskrift for udenlandsk theologisk Litteratur*, ed. H. N. Clausen and M. H. Hohlenberg, V, 1837, pp. 747–77.

418. Philippians 2:12.

419. See note 408.

420. See note 417. The present entry consists of excerpts from Fichte's essay.

421. See Job 42:17.

422. See Titus 3:5.

423. See *Either/Or*, I, p. 212 ("Florine in the fairy story").

424. "I am not alone, good mother; I have with me a great following of troubles, cares, and suffering."

425. "Huldreich, where are you?"

426. "*Første Pentade,*" in *Danske Folkeviser og Melodier*, ed. F. Sneedorff-Birch (Copenhagen: 1837), p. 4.

427. Kierkegaard's father, M. P. Kierkegaard, grew up on "the Jutland heath" near Sædding, Jutland. Olaf Kierkegaard and P. F. Parup, in *Fæstebonden in Sædding Kristen Jespersen Kierkegaard's Efterslægt* (Copenhagen: 1941), a tabular genealogy of the Kierkegaard family, trace the family back three generations from Kierkegaard's time to Christen Jespersen Kierkegaard (1673–1749).

428. "Not a day without a stroke [line]." Attributed to Alexander the Great's painter Apelles (Pliny, *Historia naturalis*, 35, 36). See *J.P.*, I, p. xiv.

429. L. Kruse, *Don Juan* (Copenhagen: 1807), p. 23. The last production before January 2, 1838, was on April 1, 1837.

430. See A. Seidelin, *Visebog inholdende udvalgte danske Selskabssange* (Copenhagen: 1814), pp. 203–4. *ASKB* 1483.

431. Abbreviation.

432. The high, thick-soled shoes worn by actors in ancient Greek and Roman tragedy.

433. *Chenopodium bonus Henricus*, of the goosefoot family (in Danish also "Proud Henrik's goosefoot"), here used in colloquial form to exploit the adjective. See *Stages*, p. 362.

434. According to the Danish editors, the word is not found in Lucian, who does, however, use ὁμόνεκρος (companion in death) in *Dialogi mortuorum*, 2.1. Kierkegaard had two sets of Lucian: *Luciani Opera*, I–IV (Leipzig: 1829), *ASKB* 1131–34, and *Lucians Schriften aus dem Griechischen übersetzt*, I–IV (Zürich: 1769–73). *ASKB* 1135–38.

435. See the three presentations at meetings of the *Symparakromenoi* in *Either/Or*, I, pp. 135 ff., 163 ff., and pp. 215 ff.

436. *Dialogi mortuorum*, 22.1. See note 434.

437. From Professor H. L. Martensen's lectures at the University of Copenhagen, given the second semester of 1837–38 and the first semester of 1838–39. Entry II C 26 is in Kierkegaard's handwriting; entries II C 27–28 presumably were done by another student. For the texts see *Pap.*, XIII, pp. 4–116.

438. Poul Martin Møller (1794–March 13, 1838), writer and philosopher, professor of philosophy at the University of Christiania, 1826–30, University of Copenhagen, 1830–38. He was Kierkegaard's favorite teacher, a good friend, and a very significant personal and intellectual influence. See *Either/Or*, I, p. 238; *Repetition*, pp. 11, 29; *The Concept of Anxiety* [*Dread*], pp. 3 (dedication to P. M. M.), 136; *Postscript*, pp. 34n., 153, 277n. (read "eternal" for "external"), 314, 351; *Letters*, no. 17. *ASKB* (426, 1574–76) lists Møller's *Grundtrækkene af en philosophisk Propædeutik eller Erkjendelseslære* ... (Copenhagen: 1839); *Efterladte Skrifter*, I–III (Copenhagen: 1839–43).

439. Nicolai Peter Nielsen (1795–1860), actor and director. In connection with a concert Sunday evening, April 1, 1838, by C. F. Lemming, he read "*Glæde over Danmark*" (Joy over Denmark) by Poul M. Møller (*Efterladte Skrifter*, I, pp. 47–49). The line quoted is on p. 47 and together with the title phrase appears in the dedication of *The Concept of Anxiety* [*Dread*] to Møller.

440. See *Letters*, no. 17; note 438.

441. See I A 262, I C 101 and note 205, II A 7.

442. In Danish, *Evighedsblomster*, literally "flowers of eternity," flowers of the *compositae* family, especially the *immortelle* (immortal), which when partially dried keep their form and color.

443. *Fastelavnsris*, a decorated birch branch used by Danish children to wake up their parents on Shrove Monday.

444. See Mark 15:24.

445. J. F. Gjøwad (1811–91) L.L.B. (*juridisk Licentiat*), editor of *Kjøbenhavnsposten* from April 1, 1837. Three charges of infringement of the press laws were pending against Gjøwad and a fourth was made April 23, 1838. He was acquitted of the several charges on April 24, April 28, May 8, and November 6, 1838, but had to pay the court costs involved in two of them.

446. C. C. Rosenhoff (1804–69), editor, 1835–46, of the newspaper *Den Frisindede*.

447. See John 20:19.

448. The week beginning April 22, 1838.

449. C. D. Grabbe, *Don Juan und Faust* (Frankfurt/M: 1829). *ASKB* 1670. See *Either/Or*, I, 142; *From the Papers of One Still Living*, *S.V.*, XIII, p. 70.

450. Johannes Ewald, *Fiskerne*, II, 9, in *Samtlige Skrifter*, I–IV (Copenhagen: 1780–91), III, p. 213. *ASKB* 1533–36.

451. Görres, *Athanasius* (4 ed., Regensburg: 1838). *ASKB* 1673.

452. The reference can hardly be to *The Concept of Irony*, publication of which was still about three years in the future. It may be to *From the Papers of One Still Living*, a long review in book form (September 7, 1838) of *Only a Fiddler* by Hans Christian Andersen. The whole entry may very well be fictive or "poetic" (*digterisk*), as many of the seemingly autobiographical entries are.

453. From the one o'clock call of the night watchman. See *Instruction for Natte-Vægterne i Kiøbenhavn* (Copenhagen: 1784), p. 21. See I A 39; *From the Papers of One Still Living, S.V.* XIII, 45; *Christian Discourses*, p. 172.

454. See Philippians 4:4.

455. From the midnight call of the watchman. See note 453. See *Kingos Psalmer og aandelige Sange*, ed. P. A. Fenger (Copenhagen: 1827), no. 231, based on psalm 51, p. 521. *ASKB* 203.

456. This entry suggests a religious experience something like Pascal's and represents the opposite pole to another profound experience, "the great earthquake," which preceded it by at least a few months, perhaps two years. See II A 805. Walter Lowrie, *Kierkegaard*, pp. 168 ff., especially pp. 179–80.

457. See Daniel 2:1 ff.

458. See note 241.

459. *Zeitschrift für spekulative Theologie*, ed. Bruno Bauer. *ASKB* 354–57 (I–III, 1836–38).

460. See note 18. There had been a period of estrangement between father and son and the son lived away from home. The present entry is usually interpreted as an indication of a wholehearted reconciliation. See II A 232, 233, 243.

461. Possibly a reference to Gunnar in *Njals Saga*, ch. 75. Kierkegaard had *Nordiske Kæmpehistorier* (see note 180) and *Oldnordiske Sagaer*, tr. C. C. Rafn, I–XII (Copenhagen: 1826–37). *ASKB* 1993–95 and 1996–2007. See *Repetition*, pp. 71–72, where the episode is attributed to Justinus Kerner.

462. Mads Nielsen Røyen, a brother of M. P. Kierkegaard's first wife and owner until his death in 1827 of property (now called Petersborg) in Hillerød, north of Copenhagen.

463. J. H. Fichte.

464. Ferdinand C. Baur, *Die christliche Gnosis* (Tübingen: 1835). *ASKB* 421. Reviewed in Bruno Bauer's *Zeitschrift für spekulative Theologie*, 1836, I, pt. 2, pp. 209 ff.

465. Wilhelm Münscher, *Lærebog i den christelige Kirkehistorie*, tr. Frederik Münter and Jens Møller (Copenhagen: 1831). *ASKB* 168.

466. See C. W. F. Walch, *Entwurf einer vollständigen Historie der Kezerien Spaltungern und Religionsstreitigkeiten*, I–XI (Leipzig: 1762–86) I, pp. 816, 820, 822.

467. See notes 18, 460.

468. Emil Ferdinand Boesen (1812–1881), a close friend of Kierkegaard's from childhood and throughout his life.

469. See I Samuel 16:14 ff.

470. Apostolic, Gnostic, Novatian, Arian.

471. Hamann (see note 388), II, p. 105.

472. Steen Steensen Blicher, *Trækfuglene Naturconcert* (Randers: 1838). *ASKB* 1525.

473. *"Der Flug der Liebe,"* stanza 7, in *Des Knaben Wunderhorn* (see note 205) I, p. 231. Also in J. G. Herder (see note 183), *Zur schönen Literatur und Kunst,* VIII, p. 176.

> If I were a little bird
> And had two small wings,
> I would fly to you;
> But since that cannot be,
> I remain here.

474. Presumably most of entries II A 768–85 were jottings for possible use in any eventual exchange following the publication of *From the Papers of One Still Living* (September 7, 1838), a critical review of H. C. Andersen's novel *Only a Fiddler.*

475. This is the first use of the expression "armed neutrality." See note 474; *Armed Neutrality* and *An Open Letter,* pp. 28–29, 33–46.

476. See J. L. Heiberg, *Kong Salomon og Jørgen Hattemager,* sc. 3, *Skuespil,* I–VII (Copenhagen: 1833–41), II (Copenhagen: 1833), p. 317. *ASKB* 1553–59.

477. See Exodus 3:5.

478. *Kjøbenhavnsposten,* liberal Copenhagen daily newspaper edited 1837–39 by Jens F. Gjødwad (1811–91), with whom Kierkegaard had associations throughout his life.

479. See Jens Baggesen, *Nils Klims Underjordiske Reise,* based on the Latin work by Ludwig Holberg, in *Danske Værker* (see note 329), XII, p. 180. In Niels Klim's fall to the center of the earth the caraway kringle he threw away in sudden revulsion to earth food went into orbit around him. The orbit-figure, with Kierkegaard at the center, was used a few years later in a famous cartoon in the *Corsair* (285, March 6, 1846).

480. See note 478. The stated aim of *Kjøbenhavnsposten* was to meet the demands of the times and to concentrate on current local news of Copenhagen.

481. Adam Oehlenschlaeger, *Digte* (Copenhagen: 1803), p. 29.

482. See note 474.

483. Mental reservation . . . in mind.

484. See note 474; II A 533.

485. *ASKB* 756.

486. Julius Schaller, *Der historische Christus und die philosophie Kritik der Grundidee des Werks: das Leben Jesu von Dr. D. F. Strauss* (Leipzig: 1838). See II c 54. The omitted portions of the text are in *Pap.*, XIII, pp. 178–83. The allusions in "this book" (note book KK) are in entries II C 55, 57.

487. See I A 234, II A 7.

488. The manuscript is not in Kierkegaard's handwriting. For text see *Pap.*, XII, pp. 281–331.

489. For text see *Pap.*, II c 61 and XIII, pp. 184–95.

490. For text see *Pap.*, II c 62.

491. *Zeitschrift für spekulative Theologie*, ed. Bruno Bauer, 1838, III, pp. 125 ff. *ASKB* 357.

492. Presumably the reference is to N. F. S. Grundtvig's emphasis after 1824 on "the living word," which his adherents called the "matchless discovery" (see note 75). See, for example, *Postscript*, pp. 36, 39–40; also Kierkegaard's letter to innkeeper Kold, September 30, 1845, *J.P.*, V, 5852.

493. For text see *Pap.*, II c 29–30 and XIII, pp. 117–23.

494. An article in Friedrich Raumer, *Historisches Taschenbuch* (see note 58), IX, 1838, pp. 323 ff. For text of reading notes and excerpts see *Pap.*, II c 63.

495. See I Corinthians 15:42.

496. *ASKB* 423. For text see *Pap.*, II c 32.

497. To oneself. This entry is the beginning of Journal EE. See II A 189, *Either/Or*, I, p. 17.

498. See note 241. Perhaps the entry was the quotation used in *Either/Or*, II, p.1, from *Atala, Nouvelles* (Paris: 1838), p. 39.

499. Regine Olsen. See note 637. The Latin form *"Regina"* stresses the meaning "queen."

500. See Mark 9:5.

501. A prefiguring of Kierkegaard's later understanding of his vocation and his work (see I A 75; II A 520) and also of his Dante-Beatrice relation to Regine. The entry was written a year and a half before the engagement (September 8, 1840) and two-and-a-half years before the engagement was broken (November 11, 1841).

502. Fatherless, motherless, of unknown descent, having neither beginning of days nor end of life.

503. This line has not been located in Philo's works: The godless is fatherless, and the one who claims many gods is the son of a prostitute.

504. See *Either/Or*, I, p. 21.

505. Carl F. Flögel, *Geschichte der komischen Literatur*, I–IV (Liegnitz, Leipzig: 1784–87). *ASKB* 1396–99. "That whenever laughter first makes its appearance in the child, it is a nascent cry which is excited by pain or a suddenly arrested and repeated feeling of pain at very short intervals."

506. See *Either/Or,* I, p. 286.

507. *Goethe's Werke* (for edition see note 174), I, pp. 291–92 (no. 20, *Elegien* I, *Römische*).

508. Judge of the reflections and contents of the soul. Hebrews 4:12 has ἐνθυμήσεων rather than διαλογισμῶν, but no violence is done to the meaning.

509. Master of learning.

510. He learned from his sufferings.

511. The allusion is to certain Hebrew consonants which can serve also to indicate certain vowel sounds. Kierkegaard, following J. C. Lindberg, *Hovedreglerne af den Hebraisk Grammatik* (2 ed., Copenhagen: 1835), pp. 8, 17–18, and the interpretation given in L. Meyer, *Fremmed Ordbog* (Copenhagen: 1837), uses metaphorically the Danish version of *matres lectionis* or *literae quiescibiles: Hvile-Bogstaver.* According to Lindberg and Meyer, such a consonant may be sounded as a consonant, or, quiescent, it may "rest" [*hvile*] in the vowel which it indicates, while it remains unsounded as a consonant. The optimum toward which Kierkegaard points metaphorically is the full sound of vowel and consonant. See *Fear and Trembling,* p. 87. See also marginal note in II A 404; *Either/Or,* I, p. 22.

512. For an amplification of "rest," see Kierkegaard's Gilleleie letter, I A 75; index, Archimedean point.

513. Assertions.

514. Document paper with the tax stamp printed or affixed, thereby indicating that the required payment has been made or, metaphorically, that for Kierkegaard writing entailed demands upon the writer, that it was not the transcription of verbal assertions.

515. See *Either/Or,* I, p. 21.

516. See *Either/Or,* I, pp. 25–26, 27.

517. Ecclesiastes 12:1.

518. See *Either/Or,* I, p. 21. In the manuscript the italicized phrase is in English; "mey" is corrected to "my."

519. Kierkegaard had entered the university October 30, 1830. On July 3, 1840, at the age of 27, he took the final comprehensive examination for the *Candidatus Theologiae* degree. He defended his doctoral dissertation September 29, 1841. (The degree was called *Magister* in his faculty at that time but it was changed to *Doctor* a few years later.) See notes 570, 1173.

520. See note 36.

521. I Samuel 15:22.

522. See III B 2.

523. Low whisper. See Horace, *Odes,* I, 9, 19; *Q. Horatii Flacci Opera* (Leipzig: 1828); *Q. Horatii Opera,* I–II (Leipzig: 1816). *ASKB* 1248, A I 162–63. See *Prefaces, S.V.,* V, p. 7.

524. See Genesis 3:8.

525. *Either/Or,* I, p. 21.

526. See note 388. Ibid., VI, pp. 143–44. The text reads:
"Dieses Viereck [i.e., Judaism, Christianity, the Papacy, Lutheranism] ist mein ältestes und jüngstes thema und, so Gott will, das Ey zu meinem Schiblemini [*sic*]. Das Motto der erste Vers aus einem Liede von Luther:

Sie ist mir lieb die werthe Magd.

Meine Schürzen von Feigenblättern sind cassirt. Häfeli ist der Verfasser der Auflösung im Merkur, und mit Wieland bin ich ausgesöhnt. Starken traue ich nimmermehr ein Buch wie die freymüthigen Betrachtungen zu. Es scheint mir zu stark für ihn, oder wenigstens ist es seine Eigenliebe, hinter dem Schrein zu arbeiten."

("This foursome [i.e. Judaism, Christianity, Papacy, and Lutheranism] is my oldest and youngest theme and, God willing, the clue to my *Scheblimini*. The motto of the first verse from a hymn by Luther:

I hold her dear, the worthy maiden.

My aprons of fig leaves have been discarded. Häfeli is the author of the solution in *Merkur,* and I am reconciled with Wieland. Less and less I credit a book such as *die freymüthigen Betrachtungen [Candid Reflections]* to strong voices. I think it is too forceful to be coming from him, or at least he has a predilection for working behind closed doors.")

Scheblimini refers to one of Hamann's works, *Golgotha und Scheblimini. Von einem Prediger in der Wüsten* [Golgotha and Scheblimini. By a Voice Crying in the Wilderness] (1784), which was a polemic against Moses Mendelssohn's idea of a plurality of truths in religion. Hegel considered it Hamann's most important work.

See *Hamann's Socratic Memorabilia: A Translation and Commentary,* by James C. O'Flaherty (Baltimore: Johns Hopkins Press, 1967), p. 40.

527. See note 404.

528. See Hebrews 11:11–12. $\nu\epsilon\nu\epsilon\kappa\rho\omega\mu\acute{\epsilon}\nu o\varsigma$, "as good as dead," because of age, is used of Abraham.

529. "Past the appropriate age." See note 519.

530. See "Morning Observations in *Kjøbenhavnsposten,* no. 43," *Kjøbenhavns flyvende Post,* 76, February 1836, col. 1–6; *S.V.,* XIII, pp. 9–15.

531. Kierkegaard, somewhat grudgingly, was obliged to use most of his time preparing for the culminating examination at the university rather than in pursuing his own studies and writing. See note 519.

532. Going underground means concentration on preparation for his examination. See notes 519, 542, 573.

533. This entry quite accurately depicts the later history of Kierkegaard's influence. Kierkegaard was "discovered" about a century later.

534. Henrik Hertz, *Stemninger og Tilstande* (Copenhagen: 1839). Frithiof

Brandt in *Den unge Søren Kierkegaard* (Copenhagen: 1917), p. 4, identifies the characters in Hertz's book as Judge P. V. Jacobsen, Henrik Hertz, Hans Christian Andersen, P. L. Møller, and Søren Kierkegaard as the Translator ("the Satirist" in Hertz's first draft). On p. 243 Hertz states that he had left out the Translator's "satirical sallies." Kierkegaard was aware that Hertz had given an inadequate representation in a volume for which the author claimed historical accuracy (see Brandt, p. 8)—hence the expression "handiwork" with regard to Hertz's novel.

535. See *Either/Or*, I, p. 37.

536. See N. T. Bruun, *Figaros Giftermaal* (Copenhagen: 1817).

537. Pastor Peter Diderik Ibsen, from whom Kierkegaard took instruction in church music in 1839.

538. The court of Prince Christian, who became King Christian VIII on December 3, 1839.

539. See note 501.

540. See *Either/Or*, II, p. 85; *Letters*, no. 54.

541. See II A 782.

542. One who does what he wants to do. See notes 519, 532, 573.

543. In Hebrew a faint vowel sound, like *e* in *quiet.*

544. In Hebrew a marking of a consonant to denote pronunciation as a stop rather than as a spirant.

545. *Either/Or*, I, p. 22.

546. See note 73.

547. Jacob Peter Mynster (1775–1854), from 1811 a pastor of Frue Kirke in Copenhagen and from September 9, 1834, Bishop of Sjælland. Mynster was a friend of the Michael P. Kierkegaard family, so that young Søren came to know him at home and throughout his life associated Mynster appreciatively with his father. Kierkegaard read Mynster's writings regularly, just as he had heard Mynster's sermons read aloud at home. In later years he visited Mynster periodically, although he became critical, and increasingly so, of Mynster, but withheld open critique until after Mynster's death.

548. In the August 21, 1839, issue of *Kjøbenhavnsposten*, 229, there appeared an announcement by Rasmus Nielsen (later Professor of Philosophy, University of Copenhagen) of the subscription publication of *Grundtræk til en christelig Moral*, which he planned to publish "in the course of the winter." See *Postscript*, p. 165; "Public Confession," *S.V.*, XIII, pp. 399–400.

549. See Henrik Lund, *En udvalgt munter Samling af . . . Anecdoter* (Copenhagen: 1834), pp. 50 ff.

550. *Faust* (Stuttgart, Tübingen: 1834), p. 199. *ASKB* 1669. See note 174 for another edition. See II A 802. "Half child's play, half God at heart."

551. There is no clear clue to the reading mentioned. The text of the entry is from *E.P.*, I, p. 457, and there it is designated as being "on a loose slip."

552. This and the three subsequent entries seem to be part of some trial writing that was never completed.

553. "Not only limps . . . but conforms entirely to Jewish custom."

554. See, for example, *Either/Or,* I, p. 175; *Repetition,* p. 75; *Stages,* pp. 83, 208.

555. Presumably connected with Professor H. L. Martensen's lectures on Christian Symbolics during the academic year 1839–40. For text see *Pap.,* XIII, pp. 124–27.

556. Presumably related to H. N. Clausen's lectures during the academic year 1839–40. For text see *Pap.,* XIII, pp. 139–40.

557. "Admire nothing," attributed by Plutarch to Pythagoras, also a tenet of the Cynics.

558. From an Arabian root meaning "to admire."

559. See "Faith's Expectation," *Upbuilding [Edifying] Discourses,* I, p. 32.

560. See Genesis 31:2.

561. Pedagogue or teacher, literally, one who leads a boy.

562. See Exodus 3:10, 14.

563. "That the works of God might be made manifest in him."

564. See *Either/Or,* I, p. 22.

565. "Half child's play, Half God at heart."

A large portion of the manuscript texts of II A 802–807 (802, 803, 804, and the first lines of 805) came to light after the publication of *Søren Kierkegaards Papirer,* in which all six entries were given on the basis of H. P. Barfod's *Efterladte Papirer.* Entries 802, 803, and 804 are on separate sheets of the same kind of paper; the back of each is blank. The first two lines of 805 appear below 804, but the bottom of the page is cut off. There is some reason, therefore, to accept Barfod's inclusion of 805–807 together with 802–804 just as he has them printed in a separate section of *E.P.,* I, pp. 1–6.

There has been considerable dispute about dating these entries, for which no dates were given. The heading of 804, "Twenty-five Years Old," does not necessarily indicate that it was written on May 13, 1838, but it is not unreasonable to place it close to that date. Another use of the Goethe quotation (II A 557) is dated September 9, 1839. The quotation from Christian Winther first appeared in *Nytaarsgave for danske Digter* (Copenhagen: December 21, 1836). The contents point to dating the entries between Kierkegaard's birthday, May 13, 1838 (on the twenty-fifth year, see *The Point of View,* p. 80), and the death of his father, August 8, 1838, inasmuch as his death is not clearly mentioned in the prose entries. The one hindrance to that dating is the publication of the Ortlepp translation of *King Lear* (II A 804) on May 10, 1839. Less compelling but yet of some weight is September 9, 1839, the date of II A 557. All these entries may therefore be regarded as retrospective comments on his own life, his father, and his family, written approximately one year after his twenty-fifth birthday and his father's death.

The significance of these entries has also been controversial, except insofar as they all represent a retrospective look at the profound self-reflection beginning early in 1835 (I A 72, 75), the experience of indescribable joy (II A 228), the return of the prodigal son to Christianity (II A 730, 232), and Kierkegaard's reconciliation with his father (II A 231, 233).

The great earthquake (II A 805), despite the many interpretations given, can be understood very coherently as Kierkegaard's breakthrough, described above. The entry is in the past tense: "Then it was. . . ." The abandonment of possibility (which is the theme of the retrospective, interpretive entries II A 805–807) has been one interpretation, but Kierkegaard's new outlook did not entail the devastation of possibility; it broke with the past and was based on hope.

566. See note 565.

567. See note 565. The German quotation is from *King Lear*, V, 3, *W. Shakespeare's dramatische Werke*, tr. Ernst Ortlepp, I–XVI (Stuttgart: 1838–39; *ASKB* 1874–81, I–VII), VII, p. 108.

> So we'll live,
> And pray, and sing, and tell old tales, and laugh
> At gilded butterflies, and hear poor rogues
> Talk of court news; and we'll talk with them too—
> Who loses and who wins; who's in, who's out—
> And take upon's the mystery of things,
> As if we were God's spies; and we'll wear out,
> In a wall'd prison, packs and sects of great ones
> That ebb and flow by th' moon.

568. See note 565.

569. See note 565. The quoted clause is based on the second half of Deuteronomy 5:16, the Fourth Commandment.

570. Like the other entries in this group (II A 802–807), this entry is in the past tense. Kierkegaard's dilatory approach to his formal university studies, begun in 1830, came to an end later with his resolution, following his father's death, to concentrate on preparation for the final examination. See notes 519, 1173.

571. See note 565.

572. The text is missing. What is given here is from *E.P.*, I, p. xxii, H. P. Barfod's "Corrections and Additions." The "piece" refers to some writing on a visiting card dated December 20, 1839.

573. Bright intervals. See notes 519, 532, 542.

574. See II A 422, 497, 534, which together with the present entry indicate that Kierkegaard, studying assiduously in preparation for the degree examination in the summer of 1840, had to consciously discipline an ever-present urge to reflect and write also upon other themes. The numerous

unused trial writings and the entries from the period that found their way into *Either/Or*, I, reveal that Pegasus, although severely bridled, was quite active.

575. A title playfully attributed here, but later seriously and fatefully attributed to him by his brother P. C. Kierkegaard in the Roskilde speech, October 30, 1849, comparing H. L. Martensen and Søren Kierkegaard. See x^2 A 256, 273.

576. Professor C. E. Scharling, University of Copenhagen, held lectures on Romans the first semester, 1839–40. For text of exegesis, see II C 9 and *Pap.*, XII, pp. 264–76.

577. Presumably connected with Professor M. H. Hohlenberg's lectures on Christology the second semester, 1839–40.

578. Entries III A 15–84 are contained in two bound notebooks Kierkegaard used on what can only be called a pilgrimage to Jutland. He had completed his examination at the University of Copenhagen on July 3, 1840. This itself was an act of filial piety toward his father (see note 570), who had died August 9, 1838. The Jutland journey, begun presumably July 18 or earlier and ending August 7, 1840, was also an act of filial piety, a kind of pilgrimage to Sæding, on the meager west Jutland heath (see note 427), where his father had grown up before coming to Copenhagen at the age of twelve, and where his one remaining aunt, Else, still lived. For an echo of the coach horn figure, see *Repetition*, p. 78.

579. A bridge across the harbor channel between Copenhagen proper and Christianshavn. Larger ships quite frequently required, and still require, the drawbridge to be raised. See *Either/Or*, I, p. 24; *Letters*, no. 17.

580. See Matthew 20:1–6–16.

581. On July 3, 1840, shortly before the Sæding pilgrimage, Kierkegaard finished the degree examination after many months of preparation for it. See notes 519, 570.

582. See *Either/Or*, I, pp. 215–28.

583. Troels Lund (1802–67), painter of portraits and theatrical scenery.

584. In the census of February 1840 the following lived at Nyhavn 282: the Wilhelm Sass family, the Peter Andreas Børgesen family, including two sons, Viggo Christian Elias (b. 1814) and Johan Peter Guillaume (b. 1812).

585. Kierkegaard's name is on the Kallundborg–Aarhus passenger list of July 19, 1840.

586. A new steamship, *Christian VIII*, had been scheduled for the Kallundborg–Aarhus crossing (Sjælland to Jutland), but an old ship, presumably the *Dania*, was in service instead.

587. In 1833 N. F. S. Grundtvig, in a pamphlet, *Om Daabs-Pagten*, urged the dissolution of parish boundaries so that one could have all the rites of the Church in any parish he might choose. Discussion of this issue was current until 1855 (the year of Kierkegaard's death), when the parish limitations were lifted.

588. "Exclusive rights."

589. Carl Ulrik Boesen, brother of Kierkegaard's lifelong friend Emil Boesen and pastor (1835–49) of Knebel-Roelse, Mols District, northeast of Aarhus. Kierkegaard visited him later during his journey. See III A 53, 57.

590. Later spelled "Aarhus" and after 1948 "Århus." See III A 71, 79.

591. On the basis of the date of the ship's passenger list (see note 585), the date of this entry would be July 20, 1840.

592. "Insipid."

593. The census report of February 1840 lists Anders Kierkegaard, Ny Torv 2, servant of Peter C. Kierkegaard, Søren Kierkegaard's brother. Anders accompanied Søren Kierkegaard on the Jutland pilgrimage.

594. King Christian VIII and Queen Caroline Amalie visited Aarhus on July 20, 1840, and reviewed the local militia. They also visited other cities in Jutland, including Viborg.

595. The popular name of Stig Andersen Hvide (d. 1293), the Lord High Constable, Marshal of the Army, who was outlawed in 1287 in connection with the assassination of King Erik Klipping in 1286, and who had lived at Møllerup, near Kalløe.

596. See note 589.

597. See Romans 8:38–39.

598. See note 589.

599. A district on Djursland Peninsula, northeastern Jutland. See note 241.

600. General or common shipwreck.

601. By his own power.

602. See note 241.

603. A foreshadowing of Kierkegaard's later apprehensions about his relationship with Regine Olsen. See note 501.

604. A river eighty-five miles long, the longest in Denmark, emptying into Randers Fjord in northeastern Jutland.

605. An old manor house, situated on the Randers Fjord, converted into a home for unmarried women of rank.

606. August 2, 1840.

607. Hald Manor and the site of the medieval Hald Castle, near Hald Lake southwest of Viborg.

608. See note 594.

609. *Rigsbanksdaler* (rix-dollar, rdl.), the Danish currency until 1873, containing six marks of sixteen shillings each. In 1970 U.S. currency, a rix-dollar would be worth, as a very rough approximation, about $5.00. See note 1651.

610. See Psalm 127:2.

611. Use of property belonging to another.

612. In 1355 Niels Bugge was unsuccessfully besieged in Hald Castle by Waldeman Atterdag.

613. F. E. Hundrup, teacher of mathematics in the school at Randers.

614. J. A. Andresen, teacher of mathematics and French in the school at Slagelse.

615. See note 593.

616. At the time Holstebro was the most important wool and woolen cloth center in west Jutland.

617. Michael Petersen Kierkegaard, after leaving Jutland for Copenhagen, worked in a drygoods store and eventually had his own store. See note 18.

618. Pouel Pedersen Feld.

619. Troels Troelsen Lund, drygoods merchant in Helsingør, cousin of the father of Henrik F. Lund married to Kierkegaard's sister Petrea Severine.

620. A village between Holstebro and Ringkøbing.

621. Probably C. O. Gede, who was pastor 1835–42 in Harte-Bramdrup parish, near Vejle.

622. J. J. Gjeding, pastor in Idum parish since 1810.

623. In Danish "churchyard" or "cemetery" is *Kirkegaard*, which was also used to designate the two farms (*Gaard*) belonging to the Sæding parish. The family name with the "e" added is based on "church farm," *not* "churchyard" or "cemetery."

624. The wish that the student Kierkegaard would settle down and finish his university work, which he did after his father's death. This is also the "task" referred to toward the end of the paragraph. See notes 519, 570.

625. See note 241.

626. See *Either/Or*, I, pp. 28–29.

627. See note 428.

628. "Not a day without a tear."

629. Else Pedersdatter Kierkegaard (1768–1844), who had the paternal farm (*Gaard*). In 1802 she had married Thomas Nielsen, who took the farm name and was called Thomas Nielsen Kierkegaard (1771–1846).

630. A village south of Silkeborg on the road from Aarhus to Sæding.

631. Elias C. F. Ahlefeldt-Laurigen, son of the owner of Vestergaard on the island Langeland.

632. Presumably M. H. Rosenørn (1814–1902), born in Randers; B.L. degree, 1836; appointed Groom-in-Waiting, 1838.

633. Jens Jensen Kirkebye.

634. Niels Seding Memorial, December 5, 1821, an endowment "for the benefit of the school in Sæding parish."

635. See Ephesians 5:14.

636. No street address is given, presumably because the letter was delivered by messenger, not sent by mail.

637. Regine Olsen (January 23, 1822–March 18, 1904), daughter of Terkel Olsen (1784–1849) and Regine Frederikke Olsen (1778–1856). Kierke-

gaard met Regine Olsen at T. S. Rørdam's house in Frederiksberg just outside Copenhagen sometime between May 8 and May 16, 1837 (see note 354). On September 8, 1840, Kierkegaard proposed to her, and on September 10 she gave her acceptance. The chronological placement of this letter and other undated letters to Regine follows the sequence in Niels Thulstrup's Danish edition, which follows E. Hirsch's schema based on the contents (*Teologisk Tidsskrift*, 5 Række, II, 1931, pp. 198–212). On dating, see also Henning Fenger, *"Kierkegaards Onsdagskorrespondance"* [Wednesday correspondence; see *Letters*, no. 29] *Kierkegaard Studiet*, International Edition (Osaka, Japan), 6, June 1969, pp. 8–31.

    638. See note 579.

    639. A device which enabled the viewer to look back from the bridge to Børsgade 66, where Regine Olsen's family lived, while he appeared to be observing Trekroner, an island fortress in the Copenhagen harbor.

    640. See note 438.

    641. Grief ceases
        As does jesting
        As does the night
        Before one expected it to do so.

    642. Poul Martin Møller, *"Den gamle Elsker,"* *Efterladte Skrifter* (see note 438), I, p. 12. See *Letters*, no. 19; III A 95, *Repetition*, p. 38.

    643. Plato, *Symposium*.

    644. The setting of Plato's *Symposium* is a banquet.

    645. Two musicians journeyed thither
        From the woods so far away.
        One of them is deeply in love,
        The other would like to be so.

J. von Eichendorff, *"Musikantengruss,"* in *Dichter und ihre Gesellen* (Berlin: 1834), p. 2. *ASKB* 1633. See *Either/Or*, I, p. 352.

    646. See Matthew 13:44 and 13:45–46.

    647. See Romans 8:38–39.

    648. They stand there in the chilly wind
        And sing beautifully and sweetly:
        Oh, that a child who has had sweet dreams
        Might appear at the window.

See note 645.

    649. See Johannes Ewald, *"Rungsteds Lyksaligheder,"* stanza 1, l. 1, *Samtlige Skrifter* (see note 450), II, p. 348.

    650. See note 579.

    651. November 9.

    652. See Psalm 85:10.

    653. See note 642; *Repetition*, p. 11; III A 95.

    654. The letter was accompanied by a colored picture of an unveiled

woman holding a rose and a young man in Turkish dress. On the back were lines written by Regine Olsen and by Kierkegaard.

655. Not one hour passes in the night
When my heart is not awake
Thinking of you
And that you have given me your heart
A thousand times.

From *"Wenn Ich ein Vögelein wär,"* Des Knaben Wunderhorn (see note 205), I, p. 232.

656. From J. Ewald, *"Fiskerne,"* Samtlige Skrifter (see note 450) I, p. 234. See Letters, no. 26, for reference to "merman"; see also Fear and Trembling, pp. 103–108.

657. See note 637.

658. The document referred to is not extant.

659. See reference to "Wednesday correspondence," note 637.

660. Pastor P. D. Ibsen was pastor in Lyngby from 1833.

661. Conradine Christine Alberg (1786–1860) and her two sons.

662. A play on Caesar's expression in Suetonius (see note 697 for edition), ch. 27.

663. *The Concept of Irony.* See note 404.

664. See Genesis 22; Fear and Trembling, pp. 27–37.

665. See Job 1:21.

666. On November 17, 1840, following his pilgrimage to Jutland (departure from Kalundborg July 19, 1840, from Aarhus on the return journey August 6) and his engagement to Regine Olsen (proposal September 8, 1840, acceptance September 10), Kierkegaard entered the Kongelige Pastoralseminarium for two semesters (1840–41) of work in homiletics and catechetics. Entries III C 1–25 come from that period. At the same time he was working on his dissertation, which was completed by early summer 1841.

667. See *Either/Or,* II, pp. 342–56.

668. See note 647.

669. Thomas Kingo, *Psalmer og aandelige Sange* (see note 455), pp. 491–92. See Upbuilding [Edifying] Discourses, I, p. 68.

670. See note 647.

671. See *Upbuilding [Edifying] Discourses,* I, pp. 116–19.

672. See Ephesians 3:15.

673. See note 647.

674. See Matthew 22:2 ff.

675. See note 647.

676. Entries III A 85–145 are contained in a notebook without date and title. The Danish editors reckoned them as belonging to the year 1841. E. Hirsch (*Kierkegaard Studien,* I, pp. 61 ff.) dates them 1840, after the Jutland pilgrimage and including the time of Kierkegaard's engagement to Regine on

September 8–10 (see note 637) and the remainder of 1840. However, there is nothing in this notebook that limits them to the time surrounding the engagement. It is more likely that the entries belong to the period September 1840–October 1841. Their paucity is accounted for by Kierkegaard's intense and extensive work on his dissertation, *The Concept of Irony*, which was accepted on July 16, 1841, for public defense on September 29, 1841, and was published September 16, 1841.

677. J. Görres, *Der heilige Franciscus von Assisi ein Troubadour* (Strassburg: 1826).

678. Estranged, alienated.

679. See *Either/Or*, p. 20.

680. Reasoning.

681. See *Either/Or*, I, p. 20.

682. See *Either/Or*, p. 202.

683. Literally, hangs on someone's lips, i. e., listens intently. See *Either/ Or*, I, p. 413.

684. The text has the Danish forms of *Arabia Felix* (southeastern Arabia) and *Arabia Deserta* (northern Arabia).

685. *Letters*, Document XV. See note 676. The petition also specified that the oral defense (which lasted seven and one-half hours on September 29, 1841) would be conducted in Latin. Therefore it was not lack of competence in Latin that led to the dissertation being one of the first dissertations in Denmark written in Danish. *ASKB* lists forty-nine copies of the dissertation in Kierkegaard's possession at the time of his death.

686. See *Letters*, no. 18.

687. About life. From life. Kierkegaard's declaration of intention to draw upon life and to characterize the stages on life's way.

688. On October 25, 1841, Kierkegaard left on the *Königin Elisabeth* for Berlin and returned on the steamship *Christian VIII* from Kiel on March 6, 1842. The main occasion for the journey was to hear Schelling's lectures (see notes 700, 727, and 730). The timing was opportune for Kierkegaard. He had defended his dissertation on September 29, 1841 (10:00 A.M.–2:00 P.M.; 4:00–7:30 P.M.), and on October 11 the engagement to Regine Olsen was definitely terminated following return of the engagement ring, August 8, 1841.

Entries III A 146–96 are in a large notebook and contribute most of the journal entries definitely datable from the first Berlin period. Their paucity is accounted for by the numerous lectures he attended, the careful and extended rewriting of lecture notes (particularly on the Schelling lectures; see *Letters*, no. 68), the prodigious amount of writing on *Either/Or*, plus many long letters to his brother Peter, relatives, Emil Boesen, Professor Sibbern, and others.

689. See portion of note 688 on the engagement.

690. See *Either/Or*, I, p. 381; *Fear and Trembling*, pp. 46–49, 52–64, 79.

691. Adam Oehlenschläger, *Aladdin eller den forunderlige Lampe, Poetiske Skrifter,* I–II (Copenhagen: 1805), II, pp. 273–74; see also pp. 133, 139. *ASKB* 1597–98. See *Letters,* no. 20.

692. See *Letters,* no. 20; III A 174.

693. See Luke 22:62; Matthew 26:75.

694. Kierkegaard did not have much to do with the Danes in Berlin. See *Letters,* no. 49.

695. See note 468.

696. The letter to brother Peter is not extant. Peter's diary indicates that he received letters from Søren on November 4, 10, and 30, 1841.

697. Vespasian. See Suetonius, *Tolv første Romerske Keiseres Levnetsbeskrivelse,* VIII, 20, tr. J. Baden, I–II (Copenhagen: 1802–1803), II, p. 211. *ASKB* 1281.

698. Freely rendered from Suetonius: "his countenance was that of one making an effort."

699. Philipp K. Marheineke (1780–1846), professor of theology, University of Berlin. See III C 26. *ASKB* lists *Die Grundlehren der christlichen Dogmatik als Wissenschaft* (2 ed., Berlin: 1827) and *Institutiones symbolicae* (3 ed., Berlin: 1830). *ASKB* 644–45.

700. F. W. J. Schelling (1775–1854), in 1841 called from Munich to be professor of philosophy, University of Berlin. The lectures on *Philosophie der Offenbarung* were Kierkegaard's main reason for going to Berlin (see note 688; III C 27 and *Pap.,* XIII, pp. 253–329). They were eagerly awaited in Germany and elsewhere. Among those in attendance were Jakob Burkhardt and Friedrich Engels. Eventually Kierkegaard was disappointed in the lectures (see, for example, *Either/Or,* I, p. 31) and after attending them from November 22, 1841, to February 4, 1842, he left six weeks before their completion on March 18, 1842. See notes 688, 727, and 730.

701. Frederik Christian Sibbern (1785–1872), professor of philosophy, University of Copenhagen, 1813–70. Kierkegaard attended many of his lectures and owned a number of his works. *ASKB* 777–82, 1097, U105.

702. Refrain from the song *"Manden og Konen satte dem ned";* see *Folke-Visebog,* I–II (Copenhagen: 1847–48), II, pp. 18–19.

703. See note 694.

704. During October 1841–March 1842, Kierkegaard wrote in close to finished form: "The Reflection of Ancient Tragedy in the Modern," half of "The Diary of a Seducer," "The First Love," and "Shadowgraphs" for *Either/Or,* I, and "Equilibrium . . ." for volume II. See *Letters,* no. 54.

705. See note 17.

706. See note 16.

707. For text see *Pap.,* XIII, pp. 199–252. Kierkegaard had Marheineke's *Die Grundlehren der christlichen Dogmatik als Wissenschaft* (2 ed., Berlin: 1827). *ASKB* 644. The account of the lectures follows Marheineke's posthumously

published *System der christlichen Dogmatik* (Berlin: 1847) and Carl Daub's *Philoso-phische und theologische Vorlesungen*, ed. Marheineke and Dittbrenner, I–VII (Berlin: 1839). *ASKB* 472–472g.

708. Presumably the asterisk refers to a marginal addition, but the entire margin is missing. Kierkegaard had tried in various ways to get Regine to break the engagement herself. See *Letters*, no. 54; x⁵ A 149:11.

709. This was the case; Regine remained, Beatrice-like, the object of Kierkegaard's affection throughout his life.

710. After the engagement was broken, Regine's father entreated Kierkegaard to return. See x⁵ A 149:12.

711. See letter to Emil Boesen, *Letters*, no. 62.

712. For volume II of *Either/Or*, Kierkegaard intended a concluding portion, "Unhappy Love," as a parallel to "The Seducer's Diary," a piece that would give a truer version of the engagement. The piece was not written, and the present entry tells why. See III A 176, IV A 215.

713. See *Upbuilding [Edifying] Discourses*, II, pp. 20–21, for a universalized expansion of essentially the same theme.

714. See *S.V.*, XIII, pp. 478–79, also p. 396.

715. The Olsen family lived on the second floor of Nye-Børs 66, not far from Holmens Kirke.

716. Possibly what is meant here is that upon hearing a certain time rung out by the bells of Holmens Kirke, others in the family went about some regular duties and left the young couple to their "nocturnal whispers."

717. See *Either/Or*, I, pp. 435–36.

718. See *Letters*, no. 40, Kierkegaard to Regine, with reference to the sending and the return of a rose plant.

719. See *Works of Love*, p. 206, on loving forth love by presupposing it in another.

720. Henriette (Jette) Lund (November 12, 1829–May 16, 1909), daughter of Kierkegaard's sister Petrea Severine (1801–34) and Henrik Ferdinand Lund (1803–75) and author of *Erindringer fra Hjemmet* (Copenhagen: 1909), one of the significant books on Kierkegaard and his family and relatives. Kierkegaard had close relations with his younger nieces and nephews, and he was a great favorite with them. See *Letters*, no. 56.

721. In her *Erindringer fra Hjemmet* (Copenhagen: 1909, p. 118), Henriette Lund writes about her twelfth birthday (November 12, 1841), saying that Kierkegaard's houseman, Anders, had brought a letter from Uncle Søren (who was in Berlin in 1841, and it may be that the letter was from November, 1842). Earlier she had given Kierkegaard a school drawing and most likely had described it with the same expressions that Kierkegaard used about his drawing of a flower. Her initial disappointment was soon dispelled when Anders came with a package containing Poul Martin Møller's *Efterladte Skrifter*.

722. See III A 149.

723. Apparently an item for "The Seducer's Diary." See note 704.

724. See note 708.

725. See note 712.

726. That Kierkegaard, in the midst of all the lectures and his writing during the first Berlin period, thought continually of Regine is apparent in the journal entries and in his letters to Emil Boesen. See *Letters* no. 49, 50, 54, 60, 62, and 68.

727. See notes 688, 700, and 730. Schelling's eagerly awaited lectures on *"Philosophie der Offenbarung"* (Philosophy of Revelation), which drew auditors from throughout Europe, were given during the first semester of 1841–42. The second lecture was on November 11, 1841. On these lectures, see *Letters*, no. 49, 51, 54–56, 61, 62, 67, 68, and 70.

728. See Luke 1:41.

729. See *Either/Or*, I, p. 31.

730. For text see *Pap.*, XIII, pp. 254–329 (up to lecture no. 42, February 4, 1842, when Kierkegaard, presumably so engrossed in the writing of *Either/Or* and also disappointed in the lectures, concentrated on the writing). See notes 688, 700, and 727.

731. For texts of notes on "Logic and Metaphysics," see *Pap.*, III C 28 and XIII, pp. 330–33.

732. See Proverbs 24:26.

733. A draft item for *Either/Or*. See I, p. 412.

734. A draft item for the last part of *Either/Or*, I.

735. See *Letters*, no. 54. At this time Kierkegaard was working on "The Immediate Stages of the Erotic" and "Silhouettes," including the part on Donna Elvira. See *Either/Or*, I, pp. 45–134, 188–202. Mozart's *Don Juan* is treated in the masterly essay on pp. 43–134.

736. See note 468.

737. See Philippians 4:12.

738. Emilius D. Bærentzen (1799–1868), painter of the frequently reproduced portrait of Regine Olsen, lived on the same street as the Olsen family at no. 67. See note 715.

739. See note 708.

740. The Danish *snadder* is used for the feeding habits of aquatic birds.

741. See note 540.

742. See *Repetition*, p. 145.

743. See note 704.

744. God willing.

745. From L. Holberg, *Ulysses von Ithaca*, II, 3. See III A 225.

746. See notes 700, 727, and 730.

747. Doctor of both canon and civil law.

748. Master of two philosophies, a reference to Schelling's positive philosophy and negative philosophy.

749. Johannes Boesen (1768–1859), Sophie Hammerich Boesen (1779–1850).

750. See notes 16 and 17.

751. A work Kierkegaard needed in writing part of *Either/Or.* See I, pp. 229–77.

752. A bookseller in the stock exchange building in Copenhagen.

753. Crossed out in the manuscript. An Italian singer (1705–82) in the Spanish court. With his singing he was able to drive away King Philip's melancholy. J. L. Heiberg's *Farinelli* by Philippe de Forges, Juleo Saint-Georges, and Adolph Leuven was produced in Copenhagen in 1837 and 1838. See *Repetition,* pp. 7–8.

754. See III A 190.

755. See note 701.

756. See note 16.

757. Horace, *Ode* I, 32. We are asked for a song.

758. See II A 209.

759. See note 699.

760. Karl W. Werder (1806–93), Hegelian professor of philosophy, University of Berlin. Kierkegaard attended his lectures on "Logic and Metaphysics." See III C 28–29. He owned a copy of Werder's *Logik,* I (Berlin: 1841). *ASKB* 867.

761. See notes 688, 700, 727, 730.

762. Henrich S. Steffens (1773–1845), philosopher of romanticism, professor, University of Berlin. Kierkegaard possessed Steffens's *Caricaturen des Heiligsten,* I–II (Leipzig: 1819–21); *Anthropologie,* I–II (Breslau: 1822); *Christliche Religionsphilosophie,* I–II (Breslau: 1839); *Nachgelassene Schriften von H. Steffens* (Berlin: 1846); *De fire Nordmænd,* tr. J. R. Reiersen I–III (Copenhagen: 1835); *Was Ich Erlebte,* I–X (Breslau: 1840–44). *ASKB* 793–99, 1586–88, 1834–43.

763. The main work (1266–73) by Thomas Aquinas is entitled *Summa Theologica* (Theological Compendium or Summation). In ascending order Kierkegaard lists the summation, the summation of the summation, and the summation of the summations.

764. Berlin: 1812–13. *ASKB* 552–54.

765. An audience blown together from all sides.

766. See *Letters,* no. 54.

767. See notes 747 and 748.

768. See notes 404 and 685.

769. Henriette Lund. See notes 16 and 720.

770. Elise D. Dencker (1801–?), housekeeper in the family of Kierkegaard's sister Nicoline and brother-in-law Johan Christian Lund. See note 17.

771. See note 16.

772. See note 17. The letter is not extant.

773. See notes 688, 700, 727, 730.

774. See notes 16 and 17.

775. For text see *Pap.*, III C 34. *Pap.*, III C 31 and 33 also contain reading notes on the same volume. III C 31 is dated December 6. G. W. F. Hegel, *Sämmtliche Werke*, I–XVIII (Berlin: 1832–40), X, 3. *ASKB* 549–65 (IX missing).

776. See *Either/Or*, I, pp. 151–52.

777. See note 468.

778. However, in *Either/Or*, II, pp. 58–63, for example, Judge William affirms that only in marriage can erotic love be maintained and fulfilled.

779. See *Letters*, no. 49; III A 177.

780. "The Seducer's Diary," *Either/Or*, I, pp. 297–440.

781. The possibility that by reading *Either/Or* Regine will hate Kierkegaard, or the possibility that she sees through Kierkegaard's contrived deception and seeks a reconciliation.

782. Allusion.

783. See notes 700, 730.

784. See note 704.

785. Romans 1:11.

786. Luke 4:23.

787. Eugene Scribe, *Den hvide Dame*, tr. T. Overskou (Copenhagen. 1826), p. 12. See *Letters*, no. 239; in which Kierkegaard refers to the production of the opera on either October 12 or 18, 1841, and states that he was to meet someone (Emil Boesen) at the theater.

788. See note 749.

789. A. P. Adler's dissertation, defended June 25, 1840, was on this subject. See III A 1.

790. *Either/Or*, I, pp. 135–62. See note 704.

791. See note 468.

792. From the outside.

793. The microfilm text indicates that Niels Thulstrup's reading as *Storm* and Raphael Meyer's reading as *Strøm* are both defensible. The context, however, suggests the second reading.

794. See note 700; *Letters*, no. 62, 69.

795. See note 17.

796. See note 770.

797. See notes 16, 17.

798. See *Letters*, no. 52, 53, 56–59, 63–65, 67, of which one, no. 56, is included in this volume.

799. See note 704. *Either/Or*, I–II, was published February 20, 1843.

800. From L. Holberg, *Den politiske Kandestøber*, I, 1.

801. See note 700.

802. See note 468.

803. See notes 688, 700, 727, 730; *Letters*, no. 62, 68, 70. Toward the end of the series, Schelling lectured double periods.

804. See notes 704, 799.

805. May 5, 1813, was a Wednesday.

806. Presumably a name given by Kierkegaard to a driver who customarily took him on drives out of Copenhagen.

807. See note 702.

808. *Either/Or*, I, pp. 297–440.

809. Each of entries III A 220–26 is on a slip of paper and undated. Barfod dates them uncertainly as 1842(?) and Heiberg as 1840–42(?). Their contents seem to mark them as items for possible use in *Either/Or*.

810. See note 809.

811. See note 809.

812. See note 809.

813. See notes 745, 809.

814. Workhouse for indigents.

815. Entries III A 197–209, the first one dated May 1842, are from a green notebook marked JJ. Entries III A 227–29, the first dated May 1842, are also from notebook JJ but begin at the back of the notebook. Therefore this second group is interpolated prior to entries III A 207–209, since III A 207 is dated November 1842.

816. " 'Write,' said that voice, and the prophet answered, 'For whom.' The voice spoke, 'For the dead, for those you love in past generations.' 'Will they read it.' 'Yes, for they return as posterity.' " See note 183 for edition. The quotation is accurate except for the omission of some punctuation marks and of *schreibe* after *Die Stimme sprach*.

817. Rejected portions. The Latin expression here is usually used in the form *disjecti membra poetae*, literally, the limbs of a dismembered poet. See Horace, *Satires*, I, 4, 62, *Opera* (Leipzig: 1828). *ASKB* 1248. See note 815. Presumably this entry is the title for the following entries III A 228–41, all of which belong together with III A 242 and 243, which are on a sheet inside a folder marked "the earliest rudiments of *Either/Or*. The green book, some items which were not used." This folder most likely contained III A 244–46 also.

818. See note 817 and *Either/Or*, II, p. 291.

819. See note 817.

820. The title of a police inspector with the job of seeing to it that the streets were kept clean. See *Stages*, p. 424 ("public watchman").

821. See note 817.

822. See note 817.

823. A part of *Either/Or*, I, pp. 43–134.

824. A part of *Either/Or*, I, pp. 163–213.

825. A part of *Either/Or*, I, pp. 3–15.

826. See *Either/Or*, I, pp. 151–162.

827. *Die Ethik des Aristoteles* ..., I–II, tr. C. Garve (Breslau: 1798–1801). *ASKB* 1082–83.

828. W. G. Tennemann, *Geschichte der Philosophie*, I–VIII$^{1-2}$–XI (Leipzig:

1798–1819). *ASKB* 815–26. Kierkegaard read this rich work extensively and thoroughly. Volume IV, which treats of the Stoics, contains no outline such as follows in this entry. The entry is written in the notebook used for notes on Marheineke's lectures in Berlin the winter of 1842–43 (III C 26) but the entry itself states "Copenhagen." The four categories: the assumptions, what kind, how comprehended, for what purpose sought.

829. There are degrees only between accidents and not between the forms or natures of the individuals of a given species. Descartes, *Discourse on Method,* tr. F. E. Sutcliffe (Penguin: 1968), pp. 27–28. Kierkegaard had *Opera philosophica, Editio ultima* (Amsterdam: 1678). *ASKB* 473.

830. See *Prefaces, S.V.,* V, p. 68, where mention is made of this writing and publishing project which was not launched.

831. 1303 b 40–1304 a 4; *Die Politik Aristoteles,* tr. C. Garve (Breslau: 1799), pp. 407–408. *ASKB* 1088.

832. H. Ritter and L. Preller, *Historia Philosophiae Graeco-Romanae et fontium locis contexta* . . . (Hamburg: 1838), pp. 139 ff. *ASKB* 726.

833. Erasmus Darwin, *Zoonomie, od. Gesetze des organischen Lebens aus dem Englischen mit Anm. von Brandis,* I–III (Hannover: 1795–99).

834. J. E. Erdmann, *Versuch einer wissenschaftlichen Darstellung der Geschichte der neuern Philosophie,* I–III (Leipzig: I¹, 1834; I², 1836; II¹, 1840; II², 1842; III, 1852).

835. G. W. Leibniz, *Theodicee,* tr. J. C. Gottscheden 5 ed., (Hannover, Leipzig: 1763), p. 72. *ASKB* 619. Kierkegaard also had *God. Guil. Leibnitii Opera philosophica qua exstant Latina Gallica Germanica omnia,* ed. J. E. Erdmann, I–II, with continuous pagination (Berlin: 1839–40). *ASKB* 620.

836. In the preface.

837. "Reasonable thoughts on nature, what is it? That it is powerless without God and his all-knowing restraint; and how the one indivisible divine power works everything here in this world in and through its mediate causes according to its conferred effectiveness or ability."

838. See note 836.

839. Para. 97, *Theodicee,* p. 216; *Opera philosophica,* p. 529.

840. *Theodicee,* pp. 215–16; *Opera philosophica,* p. 529.

841. Para. 95, *Theodicee,* p. 215; *Opera philosophica,* p. 529.

842. Para. 260, *Theodicee,* p. 458; *Opera philosophica,* p. 582.

843. Para. 25, *Theodicee,* p. 783; *Opera philosophica,* p. 650.

844. *Theodicee,* pp. 731 ff.; *Opera philosophica,* pp. 635 ff.

845. *Theodicee,* p. 783n.

846. See *Fear and Trembling,* p. 119.

847. *Theodicee,* p. 210; *Opera philosophica,* p. 528.

848. *Theodicee,* p. 220; *Opera philosophica,* p. 530.

849. Followers of Gomarus, a Dutch Calvinist of the seventeenth and eighteenth centuries.

850. *Theodicee,* p. 330; *Opera philosophica,* pp. 553–54.

851. *Theodicee,* p. 334; *Opera philosophica,* p. 557.

852. E. T. A. Hoffmann, "*Das Fräulein von Scuderi,*" in (see note 151), III, pp. 177 ff. *Die Serapions-Bruder, Ausgewählte Schriften.*

853. This is sung, that is praised,
    Is said, is heard,
    This is written, that is read
    And what has been read is forgotten.

Leibniz, *Nouveaux Essais, Opera . . . omnia* (see note 835), p. 216. See *Stages,* p. 391.

854. *Theodicee,* p. 785; *Opera philosophica,* p. 651.

855. *Longi Pastoralia Graece & Latine,* ed. Ernst Seiler (Leipzig: 1843). *ASKB* 1128. See *Fear and Trembling,* p. 112. "For no one has ever escaped from love or ever will so long as there be beauty and eyes to see with." Longus, *Daphnis and Chloe,* Preface, para. 4.

856. See note 829; Part II, Article III.

857. Wonder, passionate longing, aversion.

858. See note 815.

859. *Nicomachean Ethics,* 1106 b 29–30, 35.

"[Again, it is possible to fail in many ways] (for evil belongs to the class of the unlimited, as the Pythagoreans conjectured, and good to that of the limited). . . .

For men are good in but one way, but bad in many."

860. Ibid., 1105 b 20–21. Passions, faculties, states of character.

861. *Die Ethik des Aristoteles* (see note 827), I, p. 587.

The Danish term attributed to Garve in IV C 18 is *Færdigheder;* the Ross edition (Oxford: Oxford University Press, 1910–52) of Aristotle's *Nicomachean Ethics* gives "states of character."

862. "Therefore, while he will fear even the things that are not beyond human strength, he will face them as he ought and as the rule directs, for honor's sake; for this is the end of virtue." *Nichomachean Ethics,* III, 10, 1115 b 11–14. See *The Concept of Anxiety* [*Dread*], p. 15.

863. To make; to do.

864. *Nicomachean Ethics,* VI, 4, 1140 a 1–23.

865. See note 835; *Theodicee,* p. 333–35; *Opera philosophica,* pp. 554–55.

866. See Fragments, pp. 92, 95.

867. See note 835; *Theodicee,* pp. 336–38; *Opera philosophica,* pp. 555–56.

868. See note 844.

869. See note 835; *Theodicee,* p. 737; *Opera philosophica,* p. 636.

870. Watching over or preservation and joint knowledge or conscience.

871. See note 828.

872. See note 828.

873. See note 835; *Opera philosophica,* pp. 418–26. The letter to Gabriel Wagner is in German; otherwise the entire volume is in Latin or French. Kierkegaard knew Latin well (see note 685) and had studied French.

874. See note 828.

875. The first philosophy. See Aristotle, *Metaphysics,* V, 1; *The Concept of Anxiety [Dread],* p. 19.

876. Final cause.

877. See note 875.

878. Reports on Schelling's lectures, III C 27. Lecture 3: "Thus we do have a priori knowledge, a pure rational knowledge—whether this is the first philosophy, I do not know—yet it certainly does belong to—*philosophia prima, Ontologia.*" Lecture 8: "This knowledge [the first, the a priori rational knowledge, i.e., identity philosophy] is purely logical *durchaus* [throughout]."

879. See note 828.

880. The lectures were not written, but the theme of motion (change, becoming, coming into existence) is central to *Philosophical Fragments,* especially the "Interlude," pp. 89–110. See also *Postscript,* p. 306. This entry comes from a period when Kierkegaard was reading Tennemann (see note 828), but Tennemann does not use the expression "lectures" for the divisions or sections of his work.

881. *Sophistical Fallacies* or *De Sophisticis Elenchis.*

882.

A.

Essence as Ground of Existence

(a) The Primary Characteristics or Categories of Existence

(α) Identity   (β) Indifference   (γ) The Ground

(b) Existence

(c) The Thing

B.

Appearance

(a) The World of Appearance or Phenomenal World

(b) Content and Form

(c) Ratio (Relation)

C.

Actuality

G. W. F. Hegel, *Encyclopädie der philosophischen Wissenschaften,* 1 *Theil,* 2 *Abt., Werke,* VI (Berlin: 1840), p. 416. *ASKB* 554. *The Logic of Hegel,* tr. W. Wallace (Oxford: Clarendon, 1874), p. xii.

883. "Beauty is a matter of size and order, and therefore impossible either (1) in a very minute creature, since our perception becomes indistinct as it approaches instantaneity; or (2) in a creature of vast size—one, say, 1000 miles long—as in that case, instead of the object being seen all at once, the unity and wholeness of it are lost to the beholder." *Poetics,* 1450 b 36–1451 a 1.

884. *Aristoteles Dichtkunst,* tr. M. C. Curtius (Hannover: 1753), p. 135. *ASKB* 1094.

885. "Magnificence [and observes in passing]: for pride implies greatness, as beauty implies a good-sized body, and little people may be neat and well-proportioned but cannot be beautiful." *Nicomachean Ethics,* 1123 b 6–8.

886. See note 835; *Theodicee,* pp. 469–70; *Opera philosophica,* p. 585.

887. These lectures were neither written nor given, but the themes appear in various works, particularly *Either/Or, Stages,* and *Postscript.* See G. Malantschuk (see note 152), pp. 38–48.

888. The cult of the genius.

889. See note 835; *Theodicee,* pp. 341–42; *Opera philosophica,* p. 556.

890. J. B. Bossuet, *Einleitung in die allgemeine Geschichte der Welt . . . ,* I–VII (Leipzig: 1758–86). *ASKB* 1984–90.

891. The entry is part of early work eventuating in *Stages on Life's Way,* April 30, 1845. See *Stages,* p. 209.

892. See Aristotle, *Natural History,* V, 4, 7.

893. "Aristotle says, of course, that if a male (partridge) flies over, whether only his chirp has been heard, or, if you please, only his breath has been sensed, the [female partridge] distinguishes his presence."

894. *Hieronymi Cardini Mediolarensis medici de Rerum Varietate libri* XVIII (Basel: 1581). *ASKB* 137.

895. "Among the miracles on earth, the earthquake has been variously described. It has been given four different names according to the results produced, viz.: volcanic, cyclonic, hurricanic, tornadic."

896. See note 894.

897. The printer, Bianco Luno (see note 1345), had *Either/Or,* I–II, ready on February 15, 1843, and on February 15 the distributor, C. A. Reitzel (see note 1170), had copies in his bookstore. Kierkegaard himself was actually the publisher and paid outright for all the production costs of the edition of 525 copies, which were sold out within two years, a very good record compared to the sale of his other books. See notes 905, 1276.

898. In *From the Papers of One Still Living,* Kierkegaard criticized H. C. Andersen's view that " 'genius is an egg that needs warmth, the fertilization of success; otherwise it will become a wind-egg.' " *S.V.,* XIII, p. 72n, quoted from H. C. Andersen, *Kun en Spillemand* (Copenhagen: 1846), p. 161. *ASKB* 1503.

899. Kierkegaard, as a cover for his pseudonymous writing and to eliminate authority (see note 958), promoted this impression not only by being an assiduous walker of the streets, concert-and-theater-goer, but also by contriving to be seen during the intermission of events he did not attend. See *The Point of View,* pp. 46–50.

900. The attitude expressed here is explained in *The Point of View,* pp. 93–97.

901. See *Either/Or,* II, pp. 343–56.

902. Tennemann, *Geschichte der Philosophie* (see note 828) I, pp. 105–106; *Fear and Trembling*, pp. 73, 79.

903. Tennemann, *Geschichte der Philosophie* (see note 828).

904. Ibid.

905. See notes 897, 1276. If Kierkegaard's unpaid full time as a writer is added to the full payment of the production costs of his first twelve books (1838–47), it is readily understood that he could scarcely regard his work as a financially rewarding occupation. See *Fragments*, p. 4.

906. See note 828.

907. "These are the pangs of labor, my dear Theaetetus; you have something within you that you are bringing to birth." Plato, *Theaetetus*, 148 e.

908. F. Astius, ed., *Platonis quae exstant Opera* ... I–IX (Leipzig 1819–32). *ASKB* 1144–54.

909. Johannes Climacus, the author of "Johannes Climacus eller *De omnibus dubitandum est*." The entire entry is from a draft of the above work. See *Johannes Climacus*, tr. T. H. Croxall, pp. 147–54.

910. See extended discussion in notes on REALITY, ACTUALITY. Johannes Climacus in this initial work (followed by *Fragments* and *Postscript*) frequently used *Realiteten* rather than *Virkelighed*, which is used primarily in the two later works. T. H. Croxall (*Johannes Climacus*), p. 148, fn. 1, and p. 149, fn. 1, rightly notes Climacus's shift in usage and that both terms mean "actuality."

911. T. H. Croxall (ibid., p. 17), interpreting another entry (v A 98) with some latitude, dates the work to mid 1842. A more probable time was the period after the publication of *Either/Or*, February 15, 1843, when Kierkegaard also found time for some newspaper articles (*S.V.*, XIII, pp. 407–17 and primarily pp. 460–85). "Johannes Climacus" was not published in Danish until it appeared in the *Papirer* in 1912.

912. See *Stages* (published April 30, 1845), pp. 264–65.

913. Ibid., p. 83.

914. Ibid., pp. 265–68.

915. "One fool always finds a bigger fool who admires him." Boileau, *L'art poétique*, I, 232. See *Fear and Trembling*, p. 66.

916. One bound by a vow.

917. See note 519.

918. See notes 404, 685.

919. See note 704.

920. See *Postscript*, pp. 225–33.

921. *Either/Or*, I, pp. 13–14.

922. Entries IV A 213–56 (here selected entries 5627–36) are written in Kierkegaard's copy of *Either/Or*.

923. See III A 164, 176.

924. See note 922.

925. *Either/Or*, I, p. 19. As used by Kierkegaard (who constructed the

plural form from the singular as used in the Greek translation of the Psalms, where it indicates a musical interlude), an aphoristic, lyrical reflection.

926. Ibid., II, p. 356.

927. Ibid., I, pp. 41–42.

928. The pseudonymous author of volume I of *Either/Or,* excluding "The Seducer's Diary."

929. See note 922.

930. Italicized portions are the underlined passages in Kierkegaard's own copy of *Either/Or,* I, p. 35 (English edition).

931. Substantially but not categorically correct, as is apparent from the use of some journal entries of 1842–43. See collation of manuscripts for *Either/Or, Papirer,* III, pp. 321–27. See *The Point of View,* p. 18.

932. See note 922.

933. See note 922; the entry is written in *Either/Or,* I, p. 43 (English edition).

934. Anonymous review in the Sunday edition of *Kjøbenhavnsposten,* 13, March 26, 1843.

935. See note 922. The passage referred to is in *Either/Or,* I, p. 29 (English edition).

936. Ibid., II, p. 325.

937. On the following two paragraphs, see ibid., pp. 343–56; IV C 60.

938. Masculine and feminine forms of the Latin for "grown-up" and of the Greek for "end" or "purpose."

939. See note 922; page references to the Danish first edition are to vol. II, p. 327 and p. 324 (English edition), respectively.

940. See note 922; entry is on the fly leaf of volume II.

941. See note 922; entry is on the division page of "Equilibrium," vol. II, p. 159 (English edition).

942. See note 828.

943. Jakob Peter Mynster, Bishop of Sjælland, a longtime friend of Kierkegaard's father and the object of Kierkegaard's great respect and affection. This entry is the first expression of negative criticism in Kierkegaard's journals and papers. See notes 547, 1295.

944. See *Stages,* p. 282.

945. Kierkegaard considered the pseudonymous *Either/Or* as given with his left hand (of lower rank or of lesser value) and received by readers with their right, and the opposite with respect to the signed *Two Upbuilding Discourses* (May 6, 1843). See *The Point of View,* p. 20.

946. See note 828.

947. See *Fear and Trembling,* especially pp. 27–29.

948. See IV A 85.

949. See *Fear and Trembling,* pp. 105–6, 108.

950. Entry crossed out in the journal.

951. Denmark's largest forest, primarily beech and evergreen trees, in north Sjælland above Copenhagen. See note 118; *Either/Or,* I, p. 400; *Stages,* pp. 33, 35–36.

952. One of Kierkegaard's favorite places when out for a ride. In 1903 a stone memorializing Kierkegaard was raised at Otteveiskrogen. See note 118; *Stages,* pp. 33–35.

953. See *Upbuilding [Edifying] Discourses,* I, p. 5.

954. *Two ... Discourses* was published May 5, 1843. Surprisingly, Kierkegaard uses here the term "sermons," although he usually makes a sharp distinction. See *Works of Love,* Introduction, pp. 9–11.

955. See IV A 76, 79.

956. See V A 24.

957. Quite likely Kierkegaard's awareness that he was bound to a particular task and life-direction ("From the very beginning I have been as it were under arrest. ..." *The Point of View,* p. 68), the occupation of a lifetime to which he was bound also by his melancholy and physical frailty. See also note 955.

958. Kierkegaard's authority. His frequently reiterated motto was "without authority" and his method indirect. See *On My Work as an Author* (together with *The Point of View*), p. 151; see note 899.

959. See note 388; ibid., I, p. 497.

960. An old, established Copenhagen paper devoted to announcements and advertising. See *Fear and Trembling,* p. 24.

961. See opera by A. E. Scribe, *Fra Diavolo eller Værtshuset i Terracina,* tr. T. Overskou (Copenhagen: 1843), I, 3, p. 3.

962. J. L. Heiberg, *De Danske i Paris, Skuespil,* I–VII (Copenhagen: 1833–41), V. *ASKB* 1553–59. Heiberg was the leading Danish writer and Hegelian philosopher of the time.

963. See note 609.

964. April 16, 1843.

965. See *Stages,* pp. 279–80.

966. Ibid., pp. 292–93.

967. Ibid., pp. 230–31.

968. Ibid., pp. 217, 222.

969. On May 8, 1843, fourteen months after returning from his first visit, Kierkegaard left for Berlin on the postal steamer *Königin Elisabeth.*

970. Karl Maria von Weber (1786–1826), German composer.

971. See *Repetition,* p. 71.

972. Ibid., pp. 36–40.

973. See note 468.

974. See *Repetition,* p. 145.

975. A word to the wise is sufficient.

976. See note 974.

977. Ibid., p. 39; see IV A 101.

978. Jacob M. Mini's cafe at Kongens Nytorv 3.

979. The title page of the printer's copy of *Repetition* (dated May 1843, on the basis of "Berlin in May 1843" in IV B 97:3; otherwise July 1843, on the basis of the date of the letter to the reader; see IV B 97:30). The following deletions were made: lines 2–5, "Philosophy" in line 6 (replaced by "Psychology"), line 8, and "Walter" in the last line. It was published simultaneously with *Fear and Trembling* on October 7, 1843.

980. A term used (IV C 4, December 2, 1842) by Kierkegaard in referring to a series of questions and observations in the back of a notebook (IV C 62–86). Many of these entries found their way into various works, particularly *Philosophical Fragments* and *The Concept of Anxiety*. Here the term is used as the heading of a sketch of *Fear and Trembling*, in which the expression is kept as the heading (p. 38) of Problems I–III (pp. 38–128).

981. Another provisional title (see note 980) of what eventually was entitled *Fear and Trembling*, published October 16, 1843. The Danish expression *Mellemhverandre*, literally "between each other," was coined by Kierkegaard from *mellemværende* (something between two persons, a "between-being") and is found in "From the Papers of One Still Living," *S.V.*, XIII, pp. 68, 69n., and *The Concept of Irony* (see index and Lee Capel's notes on pp. 361 and 373). Capel uses various translations responsive to the various contexts. Kierkegaard's own amplification, "movements and positions," points to the method of indirect communication. See, for example IV A 87.

982. Danish: *Piedestal*, a pedestal-like cupboard. Kierkegaard had such a cupboard, custom made, in which he kept letters etc. related to Regine. See X⁵ A 149 ("palisander").

983. See *Stages*, pp. 246–47.

984. Ibid., p. 247.

985. Ibid., p. 213.

986. See note 637. *Mutatis mutandis*, this is the theme of *Fear and Trembling*, especially pp. 49–64 and more particularly p. 57: "... with God all things are possible."

987. See "Guilty?/Not Guilty?" in *Stages*, pp. 179–444.

988. The entire entry is crossed out in ink.

989. See note 468.

990. See John 16:17.

991. Presumably *Repetition*, which was published October 16, 1843. Kierkegaard had finished it without knowledge of Regine's engagement to Johan Frederik Schlegel. Upon his return he rewrote the final portion.

992. *Fear and Trembling*, published same day as *Repetition*.

993. Phillip G. Grobecker (1815–83), comedian in the Königstädter Theater in Berlin. See *Repetition*, pp. 58–60.

994. "I fall over and am dead." "I fall dead and am over." "God knows."

995. This intended piece became part of *Stages,* pp. 220–22.

996. H. C. Andersen's version of Agnes and the Merman, *Agnete og Hav-manden,* was produced in the Royal Theater on April 20 and May 2, 1843.

997. The etymological observation is based on the meanings and the sounds of the Danish expressions *det Religieuse* (usually spelled *religiøs*) and *løser* (to loosen, to solve, to resolve, to release, to redeem). The observation is consonant with the meanings of the words, although the standard etymological reference is to the Latin *religare* (to bind) or to *religere* (to read over).

998. See *Fear and Trembling,* pp. 103–9 for the elaboration of this sketch.

999. See note 826.

1000. See *Stages,* pp. 236–37.

1001. Schack Staffeldt, "Elskovsbaalet," *Samlede Digte,* I–II (Copenhagen: 1843), II, p. 327. *ASKB* 1579–80. See *Repetition,* p. 107.

1002. See *Stages,* pp. 330–33. Nicolaus Notabene does not appear in *Stages* but is the attributed author of *Prefaces,* published in 1844, *S.V.,* V, pp. 3–70.

1003. "What Tarquinius Superbus said with the poppies in his garden the son understood but not the messenger." See *Fear and Trembling,* p. 21 (title page); *Repetition,* p. 149 (". . . write like Clement Alexandrinus in such a way that the heretics cannot understand what he writes"), the companion motto in the present entry, which is the motto in *Fear and Trembling.*

1004. J. G. Hamann (see note 388 for edition), III, p. 190, where the item is attributed to Valerius Maximus, VIII, 4, 2.

1005. "I would have perished had I not perished." J. G. Hamann (see note 388 for edition), III, pp. 151, 224. Possibly a reference to Kierkegaard's having learned late in June of Regine's engagement to Johan Frederik Schlegel. See note 991; x^5 A 149:20. See *Stages,* division page motto, p. 187; IX A 48.

1006. On the title page of the printer's copy of the manuscript of *Fear and Trembling* there were four quotations, the last three (IV B 96:1 a–c) of which were crossed out finally. The text of the present entry was originally the second of the deleted mottoes. See III A 203.

1007. *All's Well that Ends Well.* See note 241. The German title is from A. W. Schlegel and L. Tieck's translation, *Shakespeares dramatische Werke,* I–XII (Berlin: 1839–40), VII. *ASKB* 1883–88. See *Fragments,* p. 66.

1008. See III A 245, IV A 140. This projected writing was not completed. Kierkegaard, however, without appointment as "Street Commissioner," was Copenhagen's foremost peripatetic and street observer and conversationalist. See, for example, Andrew Hamilton, *Sixteen Months in the Danish Isles,* I–II (London: 1852), II, p. 269: "The fact is *he walks about town all day,* and generally in some person's company. . . . When walking he is very communicative."

1009. See *Stages,* p. 262.

1010. See note 1.

1011. May 30, 1843.

1012. A version of the Mohammed and the mountain proverb.

1013. Henriette Kierkegaard, Peter's second wife. See *Letters*, no. 150, 161, 167.

1014. Henriette Kierkegaard's parents.

1015. Willy-nilly.

1016. A version of the proverb from Aesop's fable about a boaster telling of his feats on Rhodes: *Hic Rhodus, hic salta.* "This is Rhodes; jump here."

1017. Particularly.

1018. A. P. Adler (1812–69), a pastor in Hasle and Rutsker, Bornholm, who in 1843 published *Nogle Prædikener* in the preface of which he claimed direct revelation. Later in the journals Kierkegaard refers frequently to Adler and in 1846–47 wrote *Bogen om Adler*, which remained unpublished. See translator's preface to the present English version, *On Authority and Revelation*, pp. v–x, and Kierkegaard's prefaces, pp. xv–xxvii.

1019. Events, disasters.

1020. Presumably H. L. Martensen's *Den christelige Daab* (Copenhagen: 1843). *ASKB* 652.

1021. Two pages of the journal are missing and the remainder of the entry given here is crossed out. See *Stages*, pp. 325–26, 329, 348.

1022. Ibid., pp. 76–80.

1023. An unused portion from a sketch that later became part of *Stages on Life's Way*.

1024. See *Stages*, p. 79.

1025. See note 1023.

1026. See *Stages*, p. 77.

1027. Ready at the printer on October 13, 1843. *Fear and Trembling* and *Repetition* had been printed by October 7 but were withheld until October 16 so as to be available on the same day as the *Discourses*, giving two pseudonymous works and the signed work on that day. On December 6, 1843, the third volume of *Discourses* was published, making three volumes (*Two, Three*, and *Four*) of discourses for the year 1843. This sequence was repeated in 1844, making eighteen discourses in six volumes during the two years.

1028. The entry here is an addition to the preface of *Three Upbuilding Discourses;* it had been used in the prior and first volume of such discourses, and eventually was used in all six volumes (*Two, Three, Four* in 1843 and again in 1844). The main point here is that he is without authority either as preacher or teacher: therefore discourses rather than sermons and "upbuilding" discourses rather than discourses "for upbuilding." To many Danes and in English to most readers the second distinction Kierkegaard makes is one without a difference. But Kierkegaard invests the phrases with his own meaning, although this meaning as a distinction is not apparent here but only in connection with an ascending scale of personal impingement and Christian uniqueness, culminating in *The Sickness unto Death,* which is "For Upbuilding and Awakening" (part of subtitle), *For Self-Examination,* and *Practice in Christianity.* See VI A 82, VIII¹ A 559, X¹ A 510. On Kierkegaard's distinctions between sermons, discourses, reflections, etc., see note 954; *J.P.,* III, note 1059; *Postscript,* pp. 242–43; *The Gospel of Suffering,* p. 3; *Christian Discourses,* pp. 257, 277; *Works of Love,* Introduction, pp. 9–13.

1029. See III A 245, IV A 132.

1030. Peter Vilhelm Christensen (1819–63).

1031. *"Litterært Qvægsølver eller Forsøg i det høiere Vanvid samt Lucida Intervalla"* [Literary Quicksilver or an Attempt at the Higher Madness together with *Lucida Intervalla*] appeared anonymously in *Ny Portefeuille,* February 12, 1843. It is included in *S.V.,* XIII, in an appendix (pp. 457–85) with three anonymous newspaper letters, on the basis of H. P. Barfod's and H. P. Holst's testimony (ibid., p. 396). E. Hirsch includes all four in an appendix to Abteilung 32 of the *Gesammelte Werke.* In late 1839 Kierkegaard writes of *"lucida intervalla"* (II A 576).

1032. See *Stages,* pp. 214, 286.

1033. Ibid., p. 211; IV A 79; note 547.

1034. See II A 805, IV A 107, 114.

1035. See *Stages,* p. 262.

1036. An unused entry for vol. I of *Either/Or,* published February 20, 1843.

1037. The entry is a mock-derisive expression of Kierkegaard's despair over Regine's engagement to Johan Frederik Schlegel. See note 991.

1038. See note 1027.

1039. Henrich Steffens, *Was Ich Erlebte,* I–X (Breslau: 1843). *ASKB* 1834–43.

1040. J. L. Heiberg, *"Litterær Vintersæd,"* *Intelligensblade,* 24, March 1, 1843, p. 289.

1041. See *Prefaces, S.V.,* V, p. 25.

1042. See *Stages,* p. 25.

1043. See notes 951, 952.

1044. See *Stages,* pp. 32–33.

1045. All the speeches at the banquet are about love. The first one, by the "Young Man," is particularly about Eros. *Stages,* pp. 46–60.

1046. Ibid., p. 37.

1047. See note 1045.

1048. See *Stages,* pp. 56–57.

1049. A short piece on the superiority of women by Heinrich Cornelius Agrippa ab Nettesheim, bound together unpaginated with *De Sacramento Matrimonii libellus* and *De incertitudine et vanitate omnium Scientarum et artium liber* (Frankfurt, Leipzig: 1622). *ASKB* 113. See *Stages,* pp. 128–29.

1050. See *Stages,* p. 45.

1051. Ibid., pp. 42–43.

1052. See note 430.

1053. See Tennemann (see note 828), VIII[1], pp. 323–24 fn. See note 241.

1054. See note 241. See Tennemann (see note 828), p. 314 fn.

1055. I. Kant, *"Traüme eines Geistersehers," Vermischte Schriften,* I–III (Halle: 1799), II. *ASKB* 1731–33.

"For those things which one knows so much in childhood, one is sure later on as an old man to remember nothing, and even a thoroughly-educated person can in the end at best become the victim of the sophistry of his youthful illusions."

"Is there a philosopher who has not at one time or another cut the sorriest figure when placed between the assertions of a reasonable but fully convinced eyewitness and his own inner opposition due to an insurmountable doubt."

Immanuel Kant, *Dreams of a Spirit Seer,* tr. John Manolesco (New York: Vantage, 1969), pp. 33, 30.

1056. *Repetition,* pp. 36–73. The section on the farce (*Posse*) is on pp. 50–68.

1057. This projected writing was not developed.

1058. Editor of *Either/Or,* I–II.

1059. The central feminine character in "The Seducer's Diary," *Either/Or,* I, pp. 297–440.

1060. In December each year an amazing number of New Year's gift books appeared in Copenhagen. Kierkegaard had in mind something of a parody particularly on J. L. Heiberg's *Urania,* designed for "the esthetically cultivated public" (*Intelligensblade,* IV, February 1844, p. 231). On June 17, 1844, the work appeared as "Prefaces," by Nicolaus Notabene. See *The Concept of Anxiety* [*Dread*], pp. 17–18 fn.; *Prefaces, S.V.,* V, p. 25.

1061. No doubt a reference to J. L. Heiberg's superficial treatment of *Repetition* in *Urania, Aarbog for 1844,* pp. 97–100. See IV B 126.

1062. Later used as a pseudonym. See *Crisis in the Life of an Actress,* pp. 65, 91; see also *The Point of View,* p. 14; *On My Work as an Author,* ibid., p. 150.

1063. By J. F. Hagen, in *Theologisk Tidsskrift,* VIII, 1844, pp. 191 ff. The response was not printed.

1064. The pseudonymous author of *Fear and Trembling.*

1065. The finished postscript of sixteen pages was not published, but the basic pattern was reproduced in *Philosophical Fragments* and *Concluding Unscientific Postscript to Philosophical Fragments.*

1066. See note 468.

1067. The journal was never launched. See *Prefaces, S.V.,* V, pp. 51–70, for a discussion of the proposed journal.

1068. See *The Concept of Anxiety* [*Dread*], p. 28.

1069. See *Johannes Climacus or De omnibus dubitandum est.*

1070. See *Upbuilding* [*Edifying*] *Discourses*, I, p. 7; III, p. 95.

1071. The Latin headings: Preface, Examination, Contemplation, Construction [or, literally, Building Up], Miscellany.

1072. H. L. Martensen's *Grundrids til Moralphilosophiens System* had been published in 1841. From 1842 Kierkegaard did considerable reading of Aristotle and about Aristotle in Tennemann (see note 828).

1073. See *Fragments*, pp. 50–52 and fn.

1074. Whether this is Kierkegaard's favorite professor P. M. Møller or the literary critic P. L. Møller is hard to tell—more likely the latter.

1075. See *Upbuilding* [*Edifying*] *Discourses*, I, pp. 47–48; *Postscript*, pp. 158–60.

1076. See IV C 97.

1077. See note 962.

1078. C. H. Weisse, *System der Aesthetik* (Leipzig: 1830). *ASKB* 1379.

1079. The addition of vowel markings, as in Hebrew.

1080. The work was published later in the year (June 17, 1844), simultaneously with *Prefaces*, by Nicolaus Notabene.

1081. Speak that I may see you. See *Stages*, p. 363.

1082. See *The Concept of Anxiety* [*Dread*], p. 56.

1083. See II A 584; *Either/Or*, I, p. 153.

1084. G. Schwab, *Buch der Schönsten Geschichten und Sagen*, I–II (Stuttgart: 1836), I, pp. 273–306 (3 ed., 1847). *ASKB* 1429–30.

1085. See note 324; *The Concept of Anxiety*, p. 62.

1086. For Kierkegaard's primary edition of Shakespeare, see note 1007.

1087. Kierkegaard had *Cenci* in *Percy Bysshe Shelley's Poetische Werke*, tr. Julius Seybt (Leipzig: 1844), pp. 93–137. *ASKB* 1898.

1088. See *Pap.* V B 53:29.

1089. Although in a notebook of preliminary work on *The Concept of Anxiety*, this and the following entry became parts of a draft of "In Vino Veritas" in *Stages*.

1090. A fictional and externalized formulation of Kierkegaard's experience with his father.

1091. An unused portion from a draft of " 'Guilty?'/'Not Guilty?' " in *Stages*, published April 30, 1845, about a year later.

1092. From draft of an intended postscript to *Stages*.

1093. Frater Taciturnus, the pseudonymous writer in this part of *Stages*, states here that his interest is not poetic narration but an effective delineation of the religious. Kierkegaard himself sought to do just that but repeatedly insisted that he was only a poet.

1094. See *Stages*, pp. 437–38.

1095. From draft of *Stages;* see p. 387.

1096. May 5 was Kierkegaard's birthday. Quidam's diary in *Stages* has entries dated January 5, February 5, March 5 (2), April 5 (2), May 5, June 5 (2), but none dated July 5. See *Stages*, p. 389 (reference to April 5 entry).

1097. From draft of " 'Guilty?'/'Not Guilty?' " See *Stages*, pp. 388–89.

1098. To meet the costs of the British devastation of Copenhagen in 1807 and other exigencies arising out of the Napoleonic Wars, the Danish government printed an enormous amount of unbacked currency. The currency reform of January 5, 1813, dropped the value 1:10 and the new rix-dollar was introduced. Subsequently the new currency dropped 1:100, and only after the establishment in 1818 of the National Bank, independent of the government, was financial stability achieved.

1099. This entry from the draft of *Prefaces* is a little token of Kierkegaard's practice of multiple writing; various works were frequently in progress at different desks at the same time. (See notes 1027 and 1110 on the clustering of multiple publications.) The accent on original sin places these lines in the sphere of *The Concept of Anxiety*, and and therefore this part was dropped from the final satirical formulations in *Prefaces:* "They ["our systematicians and philosophic optimists"] will easily perceive that there is no time to waste on a late-comer who has seen nothing of the world and has taken only an inland journey within his own consciousness . . . ." (*S.V.,* V, p. 48). The last words constitute a most fitting characterization of Kierkegaard's approach and authorship in the depths of the universal singular. See also I A 72, pt. 1.

1100. Michael Nielsen (1776–1846), who was principal of Borgerdyd-skolen, Copenhagen, when Kierkegaard was a pupil there and who retired in 1844. In 1843 Kierkegaard had sent him an inscribed copy of *Tre opbyggelige Taler*.

1101. Nielsen's letter is not extant.

1102. In October 1844 Kierkegaard moved from Nørregade 230 A (now 38) to the old home, Nytorv 2, which he and his brother Peter had inherited in 1838.

1103. Cicero, *Epistles*, V, XVI. "I am least of all qualified to offer you consolation, in that I have experienced so much distress at learning of your personal annoyances, that I am personally in need of consolation."

1104. ". . . that contrary to the observants he may combine eloquence with philosophy."

1105. Friedrich Heinrich Jacobi, *Werke*, I–VI (Leipzig: 1812–15), p. li. *ASKB* 1722–28.

1106. Although this idea was not carried out, something of the sort became part of *Three Discourses on Imagined Occasions* [*Thoughts on Crucial Situations in Human Life*], pp. 43–74. There is also a fulfillment of this idea in *Stages*, pp. 95–178. See V A 62.

1107. From draft of *The Concept of Anxiety* [*Dread*]; see p. 60.

1108. See note 1008.

1109. An unused portion of a draft of *The Concept of Anxiety* [*Dread*].

1110. Pp. 49–50. *The Concept of Anxiety*, by Vigilius Haufniensis (watchman of the habor, i.e., Copenhagen), was published June 17, 1844. *Prefaces* was published the same day, four days later came *Fragments*, and nine days later *Three Upbuilding Discourses*.

1111. See note 1105.

1112. From the printer's copy of *Four Upbuilding Discourses*, published August 31, 1844, thus completing the repetition of the sequence of *Two* . . . , *Three* . . . , and *Four* . . . in 1843.

1113. See V A 27, 62.

1114. See *Stages*, p. 299.

1115. *ASKB* 486. See *Stages*, pp. 301–2, on Melissa, the subject of the portion cited in Fenelon.

1116. See *The Moment*, no. 10, in *Attack*, p. 291.

1117. See note 73.

1118. See *Kjøbenhavnsposten*, 114, May 18, 1844.

1119. A pun on the Danish: *ølnordisk*, Old Norse, which refers to Grundtvig's important and well-known interest in Norse mythology.

1120. See V A 27, 39. This idea was carried out in *Three Discourses on Imagined Occasions* [*Thoughts on Crucial Situations in Human Life*], published April 29, 1845.

1121. *ASKB* 844. Kierkegaard also had Trendelenburg's *Platonis de ideis . . . ex Aristotele illustrata* (Leipzig: 1826), *Logische Untersuchungen* (Berlin: 1840), *Erläuterungen zu den Elementen der aristotelischen Logik* (Berlin: 1842), *Die logische Frage in Hegel's System* (Leipzig: 1843), *Niobe* (Berlin: 1846), *Geschichte der Kategorienlehre* (Berlin: 1846), and *Aristotelis De anima libri tres* . . . (Jena: 1833). *ASKB* 842–48, 1079.

1122. Daniel 2:1–7. See *Stages*, p. 330.

1123. Part of *Stages* (published April 30, 1845), pp. 25–93.

1124. Perhaps Kierkegaard meant a long journey, such as to Berlin, but that he did not do. However, he did make a considerable number of excursions to areas outside Copenhagen. See note 1127.

1125. See p. 62.

1126. *Stages*, pp. 25–93.

1127. A lake north of Copenhagen. During 1844 Kierkegaard took an unusually large number of carriage rides to his favorite woods and inns: January 1, Lyngby; February 15, Hørsholm; March 29, Bellevue; April 19, 21, Nyholte (Røjels Kro); 27, Lyngby, Dyrehaven; 29, Nyholte (Røjels Kro); May 2, Roskilde; 8, 11, 19, 22, Nyholte (Røjels Kro); June 1, Nyholte; 5, 8, Nyholte (Røjels Kro); 9, Nyholte (Røjels Kro); 11, Fredensborg, Frederiksborg; 17, Lundehuset; 21, 25, Nyholte (Røjels Kro); 27, Lyngby; August 2, 11, Lyngby; 23, Nyholte; 24, Dragør; 27, Lyngby; September 3, 12, Bellevue, Eremitagen;

20, Fredensborg; 23, Nyholte (Røjels Kro); October 3, Fredensborg; 8, Lyngby; 17, 26 Lyngby; November 8, 20, Fredensborg. The present entry is most likely about the Fredensborg trip on September 20, 1844.

During 1844 Kierkegaard published six books (3 volumes of *Discourses, Fragments, The Concept of Anxiety,* and *Prefaces*), finished a "Postscript" to *Either/Or,* and worked on *Stages.* The outings were both needed relaxation in the midst of strenuous work and a continuation of the diversionary tactic of the pseudonymous writer. See note 899.

1128. See note 951.

1129. See *Repetition,* p. 145.

1130. See *Stages,* pp. 37–38, 81–88.

1131. H. T. Rötscher, *Die Kunst der dramatischen Darstellung,* I–II (Berlin: 1841–44), I, pp. 394–97. *ASKB* 1391. See *Stages,* p. 410.

1132. Regine had said that she could not live without him. See note 1712.

1133. See *Stages,* p. 360.

1134. See *Kjøbenhavnsposten,* 254, October 28, 1844; 262, November 7; 264, November 9; *Corsaren,* 219, November 29, 1844. Christian George Nathan David, the founder of *Fædrelandet,* had, as editor, been involved in censorship trials in 1834–36. Later, as his political views moderated in the 1840s, he was at odds with some of his former political allies such as Orla Lehman.

1135. Jens Baggesen, *Jeppe* (see note 329), I, pp. 200–201.

1136. A personage in Baggesen's *Jeppe.* See *Either/Or,* I, pp. 26–27.

1137. The draft under this title contains material used in "In Vino Veritas" and in "Observations about Marriage" in *Stages.* The title was not used for a section heading, but it fits Parts I and II. See V A 110.

1138. See N. F. S. Grundtvig, *Brage-Snak om Græske og Nordiske Myther og Oldsagn for Damer og Herrer* (Copenhagen: 1844). *ASKB* 1548.

1139. A well-known convivial host in Copenhagen restaurants.

1140. See *Stages,* p. 40.

1141. A carnival on the northern outskirts of Copenhagen.

1142. Hans F. Helweg, who preached occasionally in Grundtvig's church in Vartov, Copenhagen.

1143. Part of *Stages,* pp. 25–93.

1144. Caricatures of the Holy. The phrase is the title of a work (I–II, Leipzig: 1819–21, *ASKB* 793–94) by Henrik Steffens.

1145. William Afham, pseudonymous reporter of "In Vino Veritas," *Stages;* see p. 77.

1146. Josty Cafe, still in operation in Frederiksberg Gardens.

1147. A name in this case is a property and a property a name.

1148. See *Stages,* p. 55.

1149. The amusement park Tivoli.

1150. The entire entry, considerably altered, appears in *Postscript*, pp. 164–67.

1151. Hans Peter Kierkegaard (1815–62), a half-cousin, son of Michael Andersen Kierkegaard, who lived at Købmagergade 45. Hans Peter, although severely crippled, was spirited and alert. His cousin Søren visited him from time to time. He was most likely the prototype for chapter VII, *Works of Love*, pt. 2: "Mercifulness, a Work of Love, Even if It Can Give Nothing and Is Capable of Doing Nothing."

1152. *Repetition* was published October 16, 1843.

1153. Ibid., pp. 72–73, 81.

1154. Records show that in February 1844 the occupants of 83 Lavendelstræde were a widow, Inger Marie Hansen, and her son Julius August. Their relationship to Kierkegaard is unknown.

1155. Preliminary work on this uncompleted and unpublished parody of contemporary writing constitutes a section of the *Papirer* (VI B 194–235), of which samples are given here in the following entries. This intended work, which does have some engaging portions, is unusual among the uncompleted writings in that very little of it found its way into Kierkegaard's other writings. Rosenblad (see VI A 146) and Rosenpind do not appear among the published pseudonyms. Willibald had already appeared as the main character in the philosophical drama "The Battle between the Old and the New Soap-Cellars," (*Pap.*, II B 1–21).

1156. Although Kierkegaard did not publish this piece or develop it further, he did pursue the theme. A letter from Henrik Lund (*Letters*, no. 262, April 12, 1850; see note 2648) is a lengthy reply to the "prolix task you gave me in your last letter" concerning the arrival times of migrating birds. "Tables" and the later reference to astronomy presumably point to J. L. Heiberg's *Urania, Astronomiske Aarbog* for 1844 (Copenhagen: 1843). *ASKB* 2157.

1157. The themes of this paragraph have their echo and amplification in part III, section C, of *Two Ages*, "The Present Age."

1158. Friedrich Faber, *Ueber das Leben der hochnordischen Vögel. Mit vier tabellen* (Leipzig: 1826).

1159. Kierkegaard frequently uses ironically this very common contemporary phrase.

1160. Ironically, the most widely known and now the most interesting of the cartoons of Kierkegaard in *The Corsair* (285, March 6, 1846, col 8–11) has a text akin to this phrase. Gyldendal Forlag, on a poster using the cartoon in connection with the publication of the third edition of *Samlede Værker* (Copenhagen: 1962), stated: "What was then malicious caricature is today literally true."

1161. See note 1155.

1162. See note 579.

1163. See note 1008.

1164. See note 1155.

1165. Ibid.

1166. Ibid.

1167. Ibid.

1168. Ibid.

1169. See note 73.

1170. C. A. Reitzel (1789–1853), the leading bookseller, publisher, and printer in Copenhagen at the time.

1171. See II A 243.

1172. See note 701.

1173. Brøchner reports, in his *Erindringer over Søren Kierkegaard* (Copenhagen: 1953), pp. 21–22, a conversation with Kierkegaard in which he said that he had had a vigorous discussion with his father about the examination, but that now after his father's death he was obliged to take his father's part in the debate and had decided to complete his university studies. See notes 519, 570.

1174. See note 1.

1175. The only piece Kierkegaard wrote in dramatic form was "The Battle between the Old and the New Soap-Cellars" (*Papirer*, II B 1–21). See note 202. In other works the police agent theme appears in references to himself as a secret agent, a spy, a police agent (see index), but no work, dramatic or otherwise, was written.

1176. Cornelia Olsen (January 10, 1818–March 26, 1901), older sister of Regine Olsen (January 23, 1823–March 18, 1904) and married to Frederik E. Winning, November 6, 1849. This is one of the few Kierkegaard clues not exploited in conjectural historical-psychological works: for example, the use of the name Cordelia in *Either/Or*, I, "The Seducer's Diary."

1177. Instructions accompanying the printer's copy of *Stages on Life's Way*, published April 30, 1845, one day after the publication of *Three Discourses on Imagined Occasions*. The first was a signed work, the second pseudonymous.

1178. Thomas H. Erslew, *Almindeligt Forfatter-Lexicon for Kongeriget Danmark med tilhørende Bilande*, I–III, 1814–40 (Copenhagen: 1841–53), *Supplement*, I–III, 1840–53 (Copenhagen: 1854–68). *ASKB* 954–69 (I–III and two sections of *Supplement*, I).

1179. The project was not carried out.

1180. Pseudonymous editor of *Stages*.

1181. See *Postscript*, p. 253.

1182. Luke 8:5–15, the text on January 26, 1845.

1183. For a time during 1844–45 Kierkegaard considered a volume of six discourses under the title stated in this entry; it was to include the three that appeared April 29, 1845, the day before *Stages*, under the title *Three Discourses on Imagined Occasions*, and a selection from other possible discourses suggested and briefly sketched in VI B 149–181.

1184. Besides Greek and Latin editions of Aristotle's works, Kierkegaard had K. L. Roth's German translation of Aristotle's *Rhetoric, Aristoteles Rhetorik* (Stuttgart: 1833), and Zell, Roth, Walz, and Spengel's translation, I–II of *Aristoteles Werke,* I–X (Stuttgart: 1833–41). *ASKB* 1069–73, 1074–75, 1092. See ARISTOTLE.

1185. Aristotle, *Rhetoric,* I, 1, 1355 a, 6–17.

1186. Ibid., I, 2, 1355 b, 26–27.

1187. Ibid., I, 2, 1355 b, 28–31.

1188. For instruction—for persuasion.

1189. Trust, faith.

1190. Ibid., I, 2, 1356 a 1–24.

1191. Disposition, character.

1192. Ibid., I, 2, 1356 a 25–30.

1193. Cause—cause of what.

1194. See note 1184.

1195. Aristotle, *Rhetoric,* I, 3, 1358 a 36–1359 a 29.

1196. The epideictic oratory for ceremonial occasions.

1197. See note 1191.

1198. See note 1184 and VI C 2–3.

1199. Aristotle, *Rhetoric,* presumably III, 1, 1404 a 7–12.

1200. See note 1184.

1201. At the time, Kierkegaard was considering writing something on "religious address" (see VI A 17, 27; B 129, 132; A 146). See note 1205.

1202. See note 1201.

1203. Ibid.

1204. The entire entry is a listing of titles or possible titles of works on which Kierkegaard was engaged during 1844–45. "Logical Problems" refers to *Postscript.* See VI B 89, 90.

1205. See note 1201. The theme of the Christian art of speaking or religious address was of live concern to Kierkegaard throughout his life; this involved the use of Aristotle's *Rhetoric* and the making of crucial distinctions between it and his projected work. "The Dialectic of Ethical and Ethical-Religious Communication" (VIII² 79–89) was begun but was not finished and never published. The substance, however, appears throughout the authorship.

1206. Pseudonymous author of *Fear and Trembling.*

1207. Aristotle, *Rhetoric,* II, 23, para. 14; 1399 a 20–25.

1208. *Aristoteles Rhetorik,* tr. K. L. Roth (Stuttgart: 1833). *ASKB* 1092.

1209. See VI A 31, 55.

1210. See VI B 194.

1211. See VI A 146. This entry and the following five entries are an outline of Kierkegaard's thinking and provisional writing, which eventuated in *Concluding Unscientific Postscript,* published February 28, 1846.

1212. See *Postscript,* p. 7.

1213. Ibid., pp. 25–47.

1214. Ibid., pp. 25–35.

1215. Ibid., pp. 35–45.

1216. Rubric 3 is crossed out in the manuscript.

1217. See *Postscript*, pp. 49–55.

1218. Ibid., pp. 57–544.

1219. Ibid., pp. 59–66.

1220. See note 1218.

1221. See note 1219.

1222. J. N. Madvig (1804–86), Danish philologist and politician, at one time Minister of Church and Education.

1223. See *Postscript*, pp. 64–65.

1224. Ibid., pp. 15, 201.

1225. Ibid., pp. 45–47.

1226. See *Fragments*, pp. 28–88, 111–32.

1227. See *Postscript*, p. 145.

1228. See note 3296.

1229. Ibid.

1230. Ibid.

1231. See *Postscript*, pp. 182, 208–9, for example.

1232. Ibid., p. 184, for example.

1233. One of Kierkegaard's favorite metaphors of the venture of faith. See *Stages*, pp. 402, 425, 430; *Postscript*, pp. 126, 182, 208, 256; *Works of Love*, p. 334; *Attack upon Christendom*, p. 43 (see also p. 111).

1234. See note 1227.

1235. From a draft of *Postscript;* see p. 74 of present English edition.

1236. Ibid.; see p. 75.

1237. Ibid.; see p. 78.

1238. See VI B 15.

1239. See note 1235; *Postscript*, p. 85.

1240. Ibid., see p. 211, ll. 6–8.

1241. To be, being. See Poul M. Møller (see note 438), III, p. 350.

1242. Rasmus Nielsen, *Den propædeutiske Logik* (Copenhagen: 1845), pp. 115–16. *ASKB* 699. See note 1939.

1243. See VI A 55, 146.

1244. Kierkegaard writes in the same vein about himself and Regine (see IV A 107).

1245. See Genesis 4:16.

1246. The moment is presumably the publication of *Stages on Life's Way* (April 30, 1845), and the entry indicates that Kierkegaard considered that the series of pseudonymous writings would be completed with the *Postscript* on which he was working at the time. The "guide" appeared in the *Postscript*, also pseudonymous, but with a last minute "First and Last Declaration" at the end (on unnumbered pages), which acknowledged his "poetic" authorship of the pseudonymous works. See VI A 41, 85; "A Glance at a Contemporary Effort in Danish Literature," *Postscript,* pp. 225–66.

1247. Published April 30, 1845.

1248. See *Postscript,* p. 261.

1249. Ibid., pp. 261–65.

1250. Ibid., p. 265.

1251. Ibid., p. 263.

1252. A certain one. See *Stages,* pp. 404–9.

1253. Ibid., p. 258.

1254. " 'Guilty?'/'Not Guilty?' " in *Stages,* pp. 179–444, a counterpart to "The Seducer's Diary" in *Either/Or,* I, pp. 297–440. The entry here is from a draft of *Postscript;* see pp. 255–57.

1255. This sale of remainders is the first step toward the eventual composite publication of *Eighteen Upbuilding Discourses,* which appeared May 29, 1845. The volume comprised the *Two, Three,* and *Four* discourses published in each of the years 1843 and 1844.

1256. See note 1177. On May 13 Kierkegaard left on his third visit to Berlin and returned May 24. This journey and sojourn were less significant and productive than the earlier ones.

1257. Lauritz Terpager Hagen (1791–1873), retired pharmacist, who was also on the *Geiser.*

1258. See *Either/Or,* I, pp. 175–88.

1259. Intimate. Literally, "you and you," the familiar form of the second person singular pronoun in German and in Danish, which has been lost in English except for, paradoxically, the distancing form of the ecclesiastical "thou." This small entry as a disclaimer and *Works of Love* as a positive development are perpetual barriers to those who insist nevertheless that Kierkegaard's basic position is solely a *Du und Du* God-relationship without what in *Fear and Trembling* (pp. 44–60) is called "the double movement of infinity."

1260. P. 186 fn. *ASKB* 865.

1261. See VI A 53; Weil, pp. 176–78, 209; *Postscript,* p. 389 fn.

1262. Concerning hidden things the Church does not judge.

1263. See *Kjøbenhavnsposten,* 113, May 19, 1845; *Fædrelandet,* 1894–95, May 23, 24, 1845.

1264. See note 1119.

1265. Michael Petersen Kierkegaard had died August 9, 1838, and was buried in the family plot in Assistents Kirkegaard (note difference in spelling) in Copenhagen. See note 623.

1266. J. J. Engel, *Ideen zu einer Mimik,* I–II (Berlin: 1785), I, p. 269. *ASKB* 1403–4.

1267. See *Stages,* p. 44.

1268. Ibid., p. 122; *Postscript,* p. 253 fn.

1269. See *Stages*, p. 363; also *Postscript*, p. 252.

1270. The indirect method of the pseudonymous works. See, for example, *Postscript*, pp. 246–47.

1271. *Neues Reportorium für die theologische Literatur und Kirchliche Statistik*, ed. H. T. Bruns, II, 1, April 1845, pp. 44 ff. See *Postscript*, pp. 245–46 fn.

1272. See VI A 40.

1273. Pseudonymous author of *Prefaces*. See *S.V.*, V, p. 3.

1274. See V A 111; *Postscript*, pp. 164–67.

1275. See Shakespeare quotation, *The Point of View*, p. 4.

1276. At this time (1845) Kierkegaard was still his own publisher, defraying the entire cost of production of the sixteen books already published, none of which had been sold out (1838–45), in editions of 525 copies (*The Concept of Anxiety*, 250 copies). In 1845 the stock of *Discourses* was remaindered (see *Letters*, no. 119), and when all other remainders were sold to Reitzel, August, 1847 (see *Letters*, no. 152), only *Either/Or* was sold out. Through honoraria in the later years, Kierkegaard eventually more than recovered expenditures on book publishing, but he received almost nothing for his undiverted time and work as a writer. Fortunately his inheritance (see note 1796) made the phenomenal enterprise possible. See notes 897, 905, 1796; x^3 A 99.

1277. See *Kjøbenhavnsposten*, 135, 142, June 14, 23, 1845; *Fædrelandet*, 1914, 1915, 1924, 1926, 1927, June 16, 17, 28, July 1, 2, 1845, on a projected loan fund for artisans and on Danish hospitality shown to the Scandinavian Student Congress.

1278. See *Either/Or*, I, pp. 282–84.

1279. The entry is an item in the proposed "Writing Sampler." See note 1155.

1280. *Prussia* is deleted in the manuscript. However, the King of Prussia did visit Denmark; he arrived in Copenhagen the morning of June 18, 1845, and left at 1:30 A.M., June 22. See *Berlingske Tidende*, 143–47.

1281. See J. L. Heiberg, *De Uadskillelige* (Copenhagen: 1827), sc. 3.

1282. See note 3269.

1283. Denmark's oldest regularly published newspaper, founded in 1749 by Ernst H. Berling. Although Berling was an immigrant from Mecklenburg, the paper and its name had no special connections with Berlin or with Germany, and obviously should not be translated as the *Berlin Times*.

1284. See note 1155.

1285. See VI B 233.

1286. M. W. Brun's *De skandinaviske Brødre* [*The Scandinavian Brothers*] had a disastrous premiere performance June 13, 1844.

1287. The Scandinavian Student Congress met in Denmark June 23–28, 1845, and was warmly welcomed.

1288. Presumably where Per Madsens Gang (Alley) entered Strøget, the main "Walking Street" in Copenhagen.

1289. Mr. Povelsen did give his speech on the evening of June 24, 1844, in Christiansborg.

1290. Joel 3:1.

1291. See note 1119.

1292. On June 25, 1845, the Scandinavian Society had a festival day in Dyrehaven with a program including an improvised talk by N. F. S. Grundtvig.

1293. Povl Frederik Barfod (1811–96), politician, poet, and historian, not to be confused with H. P. Barfod, editor of the first edition of Kierkegaard's journals and papers (*Efterladte Papirer*).

1294. See note 547.

1295. The last two paragraphs, including most likely the item about an empty church, are largely fictive and ironical; even though the piece was not published, it stands as one of the earliest (see note 943) intimations of a critique of Kierkegaard's and his father's cherished pastor and friend, J. P. Mynster.

1296. *Stages*, pp. 179–444. The entry was written after *Stages* was published on April 30, 1845.

1297. Ibid., see p. 404.

1298. Kierkegaard himself saw the possibility of his becoming a rural pastor (see note 1359). In the reading of the banns there is an echo of his engagement to Regine and her subsequent engagement to Johan Frederik Schlegel.

1299. See *Postscript*, pp. 413–14, 450–51.

1300. See *Postscript*, pp. 402–3.

1301. See *Postscript*, p. 398.

1302. See note 1155.

1303. See Christian F. Wadskiær, *Poëtiske Reflexioner* ... (Copenhagen: 1747), p. 3.

1304. Danish: *Regnspaaer* (curlews).

1305. The west gate of the old walled city of Copenhagen, now the name of an underground train stop.

1306. One of the marsh-lakes just outside the walls of old Copenhagen.

1307. A dissertation on Lord Byron, defended in Copenhagen on April 29, 1845, and reviewed on the same day in the *Berlingske Tidende*.

1308. See note 354.

1309. In I C 80 Kierkegaard says he does not know the source of this story. The editors have not been able to track it down.

1310. See *Either/Or*, II, p. 141.

1311. Title page (together with VI B 90) of *Postscript*. See VI A 146.

1312. See VI B 89. The word "Simple" is an addition to the title in the draft manuscript. Later it was replaced by "Unscientific" in the printer's copy. See VI A 140. *Concluding Unscientific Postscript* was published February 28, 1846.

1313. Ole J. Kold, innkeeper at Fredensborg. See note 117. On September 20, 1845, Kierkegaard had made an excursion to Fredensborg. See note 1127.

1314. This may be a play on an expression associated with Grundtvig. See note 81.

1315. See note 1327. In *E.P.*, III, p. 219, H. P. Barfod writes: "At least as early as November 1845 S.K. was on the point of publicly opposing *The Corsair;* evidence for this seems to exist in the following draft written on a loose quarto sheet." See *S.V.*, XIII, pp. 421–31 for the challenge written by Frater Taciturnus and published in *Fædrelandet,* 2078, December 27, 1845.

1316. Editor of *Either/Or.*

1317. *Postscript,* p. 328.

1318. Martin Luther, *Werke,* ed. Otto von Gerlach, I–X (Berlin: 1840–41), p. 195. *ASKB* 312–16.

1319. See *Prefaces, S.V.,* V, pp. 31–34.

1320. See Luke 16:19.

1321. See *Works of Love,* p. 297; Suetonius, *Vespasian,* 23.

1322. See note 505.

1323. See note 1155. During 1845–47 Kierkegaard kept working sporadically on this parody of New Year's gift books (with J. L. Heiberg's *Urania* particularly in mind). Amid other numerous and more important writings underway at the time, this book was never completed and published.

1324. J. L. Heiberg's *Urania, Aarbog for 1844* (*ASKB* 2157) had a gold border and gold design on white covers front and back, a double border on every page, large print throughout, and extra large initial letters of each section. See *Prefaces, S.V.,* V, p. 27.

1325. See Adam Oehlenschläger, *Digte* (Copenhagen: 1803), p. 238.

1326. See *Prefaces, S.V.,* V, p. 25.

1327. "If one goes a step further and places an author like Victor Eremita [pseudonymous editor of *Either/Or*] above Attorney Lehman (which certainly is proper, since Lehman will die and be forgotten, but Victor Eremita will never die. . . .)" *Corsaren,* 269, November 14, 1845, p. 14.

1328. The entry is from the end of a draft of "The Activities of a Traveling Esthetician and How He Still Happened to Pay for His Dinner" (*S.V.* XIII, pp. 422–31), published in *Fædrelandet,* 2078, December 27, 1845.

On December 22, 1845, P. L. Møller's *Gæa, æsthetisk Aarbog* for 1846, was published. It contained a long piece by Møller entitled "A Visit to Sørø," a large portion of which was a rather supercilious review of the pseudonymous works. "The Activities of a Traveling Esthetician . . ." was Frater Taciturnus's reply to P. L. Møller's piece.

1329. Where the spirit is, there is the Church.
Where P. L. M. [Møller] is, there is *The Corsair.*

See note 1328. The closing paragraph of the article in *Fædrelandet* (*S.V.*, XIII, pp. 422–31) constituted the opening of Kierkegaard's public attack on *The Corsair,* which carried on its political satire and destruction of personal reputations anonymously. The single Latin line stated publicly what was known in literary circles and had already been published in Erslew's *Forfatter-Lexicon,* "Peder Ludwig Møller," II, p. 406 (Copenhagen; 1847, but published in sections from 1843)–that P. L. Møller was a writer for *The Corsair.* Møller left Denmark later in 1846 and never returned (see note 1708). The owner and editor, M. Goldschmidt, gave up *The Corsair* October 2, 1846, and travelled abroad for a year. In the meantime, *The Corsair* launched a continuing campaign of ridicule and personal attack upon Kierkegaard, resulting in his being unable to remain the foremost peripatetic conversationalist of the Copenhagen streets (see note 1008). Although Kierkegaard felt this keenly (see VII[1] A 98), he had known the risks involved in taking on *The Corsair* single-handed. The entire *Corsair* affair was a prolonged event consciously initiated by him, through writing as an ethical act, in order to precipitate the murkiness of anonymity and to diminish the power of journalistic intimidation.

1330. "... for example, whether it is not a greater pleasure to eat dry bread and drink water with Hilarius Bookbinder than to drink champagne with Boethius." *Corsaren,* 251, July 4, 1845, p. 3.

1331. See note 1328.

1332. See notes 1328, 1329.

1333. *The Corsair* repeatedly caricatured Kierkegaard's physique and his clothes. See 277, January 9, 1846, col. 2–5; 278, January 16, col. 13; 279, January 23, col. 11; 284, February 27, col. 13; 285, March 6, col. 14; 289, April 3, col. 13. See note 1590.

1334. See note 1328.

1335. *S.V.*, XIII, p. 430.

1336. *Fædrelandet,* 2079, December 29, 1845.

1337. See note 1329.

1338. See notes 1327, 1330.

1339. VI B 192, 193.

1340. Insertion or contribution.

1341. A review of *Three Discourses on Imagined Occasions* and *Stages, Berlingske Tidende,* 108, May 6, 1845, col. 3; see *S.V.*, XIII, pp. 418–21.

1342. A draft of Kierkegaard's acknowledgment of his relation to the pseudonymous writers, written in February 1845 for last-minute inclusion (see VII[1] A 2) on unnumbered pages at the end of *Postscript,* published February 27, 1846. See note 1357.

1343. Jakob Peter Mynster's pseudonym formed by the middle consonant of each of the names.

1344. Page number in the first edition. See *Postscript,* p. 255, last line.

1345. Bianco Luno (1795–1852), who did Kierkegaard's printing.

1346. *Stages*, pp. 179–444.

1347. Page number in first edition. See *Either/Or*, I, p. 440.

1348. Ibid., p. 419.

1349. Page number in first edition. See *Stages*, p. 288.

1350. See note 922.

1351. See, for example, IV A 107, B 140, 141.

1352. *From the Papers of One Still Living, S.V.*, XIII, pp. 58–60; See *Two Ages, S.V.*, VIII, p. 22.

1353. Novels by Thomasine Gyllembourg.

1354. From a draft of Kierkegaard's long review, published in book form March 30, 1846, of Thomasine Gyllembourg's *Two Ages*.

1355. Ibid.

1356. From the printer's copy. See note 1354.

1357. The Declaration was on a separate sheet, not bound together with the manuscript. See note 1342.

1358. See VII¹ B 83.

1359. On this theme, see introductory essay, *Armed Neutrality* and *An Open Letter*, pp. 3–24. Kierkegaard very seriously and over a considerable period of time considered halting all writing after the *Postscript* and taking a rural parish or a post at the pastoral seminary.

1360. Proofs of *Concluding Unscientific Postscript*, published February 27, 1846.

1361. Published March 30, 1846.

1362. See VII¹ A 9, 114, 116, 128, 169, B 211.

1363. H. P. Barfod, in *Til Minde om Biskop Peter Christian Kierkegaard* (Copenhagen: 1888), pp. 13–15, tells of this occasion during the boyhood of Kierkegaard's father, Michael Petersen Kierkegaard, as related by Kierkegaard's brother Peter.

1364. See notes 1243, 1262.

1365. God judges when no one speaks.

1366. *ASKB* 1439.

1367. See VII¹ A 4. With the *Postscript* as the terminal work, Kierkegaard had set a period to what he considered his esthetic writing. See note 1359. He did not consider *Two Ages* (published March 30, 1846) as writing in the usual sense, inasmuch as it was at least in part a review of someone else's work. For a time he also considered making "The Book on Adler" a review and titling it as such. See VII² B 242.

1368. Michael Nielsen (1776) died February 11, 1846. Kierkegaard cherished him as a secondary school teacher and the principal of Borgerdydskolen. See note 1100.

1369. Hans Carl Sager (1808–1885), baker and director of Copenhagen's welfare department.

1370. This unusual Danish expletive, a habit with M. Nielsen, is untranslatable. Various meanings are still current. In some parts of Jutland it is used as a reassuring and encouraging utterance to horses, something like "steady, now," or "take your time." Others report occasional usage of the expletive in Copenhagen Danish, without any precise meaning or at best a fill-in like "Well, now." Holger Lund, in *Borgerdydskole* (Copenhagen: 1887), p. 145, states: "Nielsen's speech, particularly when he was speaking with urgency or making an explanation, was always interwoven with the sound: 'sene, sene.' Others designate the sound with 'sīn, sīn.' "

1371. J. P. Mynster. See note 547.

1372. From final draft of *Two Ages* (published March 30, 1846), but omitted from the printed work.

1373. See note 1276.

1374. See notes 1359, 1367.

1375. See notes 1262, 1243.

1376. "A wise man has no particular need, and yet he has need in many instances. Accordingly, although a wise man may be content with self, yet he needs friends, not that he may have someone to sit by his side when he is in distress but that he may have someone by whose side he may sit when he is in dire need, one for whom he can give his life willingly."

1377. *Zeitschrift für Philosophie und spekulative Theologie*, ed. J. H. Fichte.

1378. See *Corsaren*, 285, March 6, 1846, col. 8–9.

1379. See note 547.

1380. See 108, May 6, 1845; "An Explanation and a Little More," *S.V.* XIII, pp. 418–21.

1381. See pp. 3–6.

1382. Ibid., pp. 551–52. See note 1342.

1383. "Let him die!" the opposite of "*Vivat!*"

1384. Parallel with the use of the latter part of journal JJ and of assorted loose sheets, Kierkegaard also wrote (beginning March 9, 1846) entries in a notebook which he marked NB[1] and titled "Report" on the *Corsair* affair (VII[1] A 97–128, 147; VIII[1] A 1–106). He continued using notebooks and marking them NB[2], NB[3], etc., until the end of his life. The last one, NB[35], was begun December 3, 1854.

1385. See note 1360.

1386. See note 1342.

1387. See note 1361.

1388. See *The Point of View*, pp. 44–45.

1389. See notes 1328, 1329.

1390. See notes 1359, 1367.

1391. See *The Point of View*, pp. 53–63.

1392. Ibid., pp. 64–73.

1393. See note 1328.

1394. See "The Dialectical Result of a Literary Police-operation," *S.V.*, XIII, pp. 432–35.

1395. See P. L. Møller's letter, in response to "The Activity of a Traveling Esthetician," published in the next number of *Fædrelandet*, 2079, December 29, 1845.

1396. See *The Concept of Irony*, pp. 266–67.

1397. See *Corsaren*, 270, November 21, 1845; M. Goldschmidt, *Livs Erindringer og Resultater*, I–II (Copenhagen: 1877), I, p. 264.

1398. See pp. 3–4.

1399. See notes 1359, 1367.

1400. Among the unpublished papers there are various drafts and some completed versions of *Corsair* pieces which were not published (VII¹ B 1–73).

1401. Meïr Goldschmidt was twenty-one when the first issue of *Corsaren* appeared on October 18, 1840.

1402. Kierkegaard criticized the same lack of a life-outlook in Hans Christian Andersen. See *From the Papers of One Still Living*, *S.V.*, XIII, pp. 68–76.

1403. Meïr Goldschmidt has written of his meetings with Kierkegaard on the street in *Livs Erindringer og Resultater*, I–II (Copenhagen: 1877). See note 1529.

1404. See note 1327, also 1330.

1405. See VII¹ B 1, 5, 6.

1406. The manuscript of *Concluding Unscientific Postscript*, by Johannes Climacus, was delivered to the printer in mid December 1845 and was published February 27, 1846.

1407. A reference to Goldschmidt's admiration for Kierkegaard, *The Corsair's* praise of Hilarius Bookbinder and Victor Eremita, and Kierkegaard's subsequent challenge to *The Corsair*. See notes 1327, 1329, 1330, 1529.

1408. See note 1406.

1409. See note 1405.

1410. A review of *Two Ages* by the author (Thomasine Gyllembourg) of *En Hverdags-Historie*.

1411. See notes 1327, 1330.

1412. See note 962.

1413. See note 547.

1414. *Henry IV*, I, III, 2. See [*The*] *Crisis* [*and a Crisis*] *in the Life of an Actress*, p. 81.

1415. Glaucon's speech in II, 360 c–361 d.

1416. Peter Johannes Spang (1796–1846), chaplain and later pastor of Helliggeistes Kirke in Copenhagen 1840–46.

1417. *Platons Werke*, tr. F. Schleiermacher, I¹⁻², II¹⁻³, III¹ (Berlin: 1807–28), III¹, pp. 127–28. *ASKB* 1158–63.

1418. See *The Point of View*, pp. 10–14. This entry and those following are the beginnings of *The Point of View,* which was published posthumously in 1859 by Kierkegaard's brother Peter Christian Kierkegaard.

1419. Ibid., pp. 66–68.

1420. Ibid., p. 67; see note 521.

1421. See *The Point of View,* p. 49; notes 899, 1008, 1329.

1422. Søren C. Barth (1803–95).

1423. See N. J. Thue, *Læsebog i Modersmaalet for Norske og Danske* (Kristiania: 1846), pp. 486 ff.

1424. See notes 1359, 1367.

1425. Regine Olsen. See note 637.

1426. See note 1329.

1427. See note 1327, also 1330.

1428. See note 1529.

1429. See note 174; ibid., XXVI, book 13, pp. 219, 227, 229–31, 236–37.

1430. Christian Molbech (1783–1857), historian, linguist, literary critic; named Councillor of State June 28, 1845.

1431. See *The Point of View,* pp. 39–41.

1432. See notes 1359, 1367.

1433. During *The Corsairs*'s campaign this happened with the name "Søren."

1434. Rasmus V. Christian Winther (1796–1876), one of Kierkegaard's favorite Danish poets.

1435. Hans Peter Holst (1811–93), best known for his epic poem *Den Lille Hornblæser* (1849).

1436. Presumably Poul Frederik Barfod. See note 1293.

1437. See *Gæa,* 1846, p. 174.

1438. See *Prefaces, S.V.,* V, pp. 29, 37.

1439. Edited by Claudius Rosenhoff; no. 58, May 19, 1846, contained an article "S. Kjerkegaard and His Reviewers."

1440. H. C. Ørsted (1777–1885), renowned Danish physicist, also author of *Aanden i Naturen.*

1441. By the immortal gods!

1442. A reference to the small village to which Erasmus Montanus returned from Copenhagen in Holberg's play of the same name.

1443. See note 962. The name of J. L. Heiberg, son of the anonymous author of *En Hverdags-Historie,* Thomasine Gyllembourg, appears on the title page as the editor of the work, also as the editor of her *Two Ages,* the subject of Kierkegaard's review, published March 30, 1846.

1444. See note 1443.

1445. See note 1.

1446. See note 1443.

1447. See *S.V.,* VIII, p. 16.

1448. Kierkegaard's main relaxation, especially now that his customary walking and talking on Copenhagen streets had been spoiled by the pervasively spread ridicule of *The Corsair*, was to take carriage rides to the woods and towns north of Copenhagen (see note 1127). During 1846 the following journeys are recorded: Hørsholm, March 25; Sorø and Pedersborg, April 2–3; Lyngby, 11; Fredensborg, 20; Fredensborg, June 8; Charlottenlund, Nyholte (Røjels Kro), 19; Nyholte (Røjels Kro), 21–22, July 11; Hørsholm, 18; Fredensborg, Hillerød, 28–29; Nyholte (Røjels Kro), August 2; Charlottenlund, Ordrup, 6; Charlottenlund, Nyholte (Røjels Kro), 15; Kongenlunde, Amager, 17; Hørsholm, 22; Nyholte (Røjels Kro), 31; Fredensborg, Frederiksborg, September 3; Charlottenlund, Nyholte (Røjels Kro), 16, 26, October 3; Sorø 28; Fredensborg, November 24; Nyholte (Røjels Kro), December 7; Lyngby, 17.

1449. See *The Point of View*, pp. 76–83.

1450. See note 18.

1451. See note 637.

1452. See *The Point of View*, p. 68.

1453. See II Corinthians 12:7.

1454. See note 1359.

1455. The *Corsair* affair.

1456. Danish: *Bedemand.* Here an "undertaker-man" is regarded as a kind of actor, a professional mourner, and therefore twice removed from the hero type.

1457. See note 1619. "The envious is a martyr, but the devil's."

1458. A provisional title for what became *Upbuilding Discourses in Various Spirits* (published March 13, 1847), of which the first, "Purity of Heart," best fits the title before the alteration in this entry.

1459. Johan Arndt, *Fire Bøger om den sande Christendom* (Christiana: 1829). *ASKB* 277. Quotation not located.

1460. See *Upbuilding Discourses in Various Spirits*, Part One (*Purity of Heart*, p. 151). See notes 1500, 1502.

1461. Quoted (as from I, 13) from Cicero, I, 12, by H. Ritter, *Geschichte der Philosophie alter Zeit*, I–IV (2 ed., Hamburg: 1836–39), I, p. 327. *ASKB* 735–38.

1462. On May 2–3, 1846, Kierkegaard left for Berlin and returned May 16. Translations of the entries (VII¹ A 130–46) from this fortnight, mostly on religious themes, are in *J.P.*, I–III. See Collations.

1463. From draft of *Upbuilding Discourses in Various Spirits*, published ten months later, March 13, 1847.

1464. See note 1222.

1465. Torkel Baden (1765–1849), Latin scholar.

1466. See notes 1328, 1329.

1467. Henrik Hertz (1798–1870), Danish dramatist and poet. See *Two Ages, S.V.*, VIII, p. 87 (*The Present Age*, p. 42).

1468. *Prædikener paa alle Søn-og Hellig-Dage i Aaret,* I–II (3 ed., Copenhagen: 1837) I, pp. 166, 257. *ASKB* 229–30.

1469. The Danish editors of the *Papirer* have unearthed an advertisement in *Flyveposten,* 224, September 26, 1846: The panorama at Vesterbro no. 9 (now 49) is "provided with the following new equipment . . . the mechanical peepshow or lucky star, where everyone gets a temperament chart."

1470. A group of hills near Kolding in Jutland. The second of a series of *Sprogfester* (Language Festivals) was held there on July 4, 1844, in support of the Danish cause in the Schleswig controversy with Germany. N. F. S. Grundtvig was one of the speakers.

1471. From the printer's copy. A later change was the omission of "Styles."

1472. In June 1846 Kierkegaard bought some additional books by A. P. Adler. See note 1486. Entry VII² B 235, the unpublished manuscript of *The Book on Adler* (current English translation entitled *Authority and Revelation*), is dated 1846. The preface is dated January 1847. See note 1018.

1473. Provisional title of *Bogen om Adler.* See note 1472. See VII¹ A 9 on writing reviews, and VII¹ B 135:5 (from draft of *Two Ages,* in which "Literary Review" is omitted).

1474. See note 1384.

1475. See note 1328.

1476. The world wants to be deceived [therefore let it be deceived]. Attributed to Pope Paul IV but found earlier in S. Brandt, *Narrenschiffen.* See *Irony,* p. 271; *Stages,* p. 313; *Judge for Yourselves!,* pp. 153–54; *The Point of View,* p. 45; X¹ A 320.

1477. See notes 899, 1008, 1329.

1478. Carl Mettus Weis (1809–72), lawyer, amateur musician, and governmental careerist primarily in the Ministry of Culture, and author of pieces on philosophy of law, such as *Staten og dens Individer. Indledning i Retsvidenskaben* (Copenhagen: 1845). *ASKB* 922.

1479. See note 1476.

1480. See notes 1018, 1472.

1481. Pseudonymous author of part three of *Stages,* an experiment entitled "Guilty?/Not Guilty?"

1482. Author of a diary found and used by Frater Taciturnus, *Stages,* pp. 188 ff. See note 1481.

1483. F. Helweg, "Mag. Adlers senere Skrifter," *Kirketidende,* 45, 46, July 19, 26, 1846.

1484. The pseudonymous authors of the works beginning with *Either/Or* and ending (at that time) with the *Postscript.*

1485. *Nogle Prædikener* (Copenhagen: 1843). *ASKB* 49.

1486. *Nogle Digte, Studier og Exempler, Forsøg til en kort systematisk Fremstilling af Christendommen i dens Logik, Theologiske Studier,* all published in Copenhagen, 1846. *ASKB* 1502, U11, U12, U13. See note 1492.

1487. *Nogle Prædikener*, preface.

1488. See notes 1018, 1472.

1489. Jens Hostrup, *Gjenboerne*, first presented in the Hofteater by the *Studenterforening* on February 20 and again on March 9, 1844, has among the characters a theologian named Søren Kirk.

1490. The play was presented in Odense December 19, 26, 1845; January 1, 11, 18, 28, February 23, and March 9, 1846.

1491. June 27, 30, July 2, 1846. Søren Kirk was then called Søren Torp.

1492. Within the family.

1493. See note 315.

1494. See notes 962, 1443.

1495. See note 1342.

1496. The *Corsair* affair.

1497. See notes 899, 1008, 1329.

1498. A review of *Fragments* by J. F. Hagen (signed "80"), written in October 1845, which appeared in *Theologisk Tidsskrift, Ny Række*, 1846, IV, 1 (vol. x), p. 175.

1499. See note 1476.

1500. See *Upbuilding Discourses in Various Spirits*, Part Three [*The Gospel of Suffering*, pp. 5–168]. See note 1460.

1501. See Acts 5:40–41, Philippians 1:7–13, Acts 26:29, II Corinthians 6:10, Philippians 4:4, James 1:2, Matthew 6:25–34.

1502. *Upbuilding Discourses in Various Spirits*, Part Two [*What We Learn from the Lilies of the Field and the Birds of the Air*, with *The Gospel of Suffering*, p. 220]; Part Three [*The Gospel of Suffering*, pp. 146–47, 150]. See note 1460.

1503. Ibid., Part Two, p. 220; Part Three, pp. 150, 156.

1504. See *Christian Discourses*, p. 127.

1505. Philippians 4:4.

1506. James 1:2.

1507. Part Two of *Upbuilding Discourses in Various Spirits*. See notes 1460, 1500, 1502.

1508. VII^1 A 248.

1509. See notes 1246, 1359, 1367.

1510. The *Corsair* affair.

1511. Abstractly.

1512. See notes 1246, 1359, 1367.

1513. See note 1359.

1514. See *Upbuilding Discourses in Various Spirits*, Part One [*Purity of Heart*, p. 5].

1515. Regine Olsen. See IV A 215; *Stages*, pp. 288–89, 364 fn., 387.

1516. Pforzheim: 1846. *ASKB* 459. The book was purchased November 20, 1846.

1517. See *Upbuilding Discourses in Various Spirits*, Part One [*Purity of Heart*, p. 27].

1518. The publishing project sketched here and in the following entry was not carried out, although portions appeared in other forms. See notes to VII^1 B 213.

    1519. See VII^1 A 160.

    1520. See VI A 147.

    1521. See VII^1 A 69.

    1522. See V A 51, VI A 28.

    1523. See II A 12.

    1524. See VII^1 A 15.

    1525. See VII^1 B 218.

    1526. The volume "Minor Works" was not published. Instead, no. I became "An Occasional Discourse" [*Purity of Heart*], Part One of *Upbuilding Discourses in Various Spirits,* published March 13, 1847; no. II, *Bogen om Adler,* remained unpublished; no. III became Part Two following "An Occasional Discourse"; no. IV became Part Three of the same work. See notes 1460, 1500, 1502.

    1527. *The Corsair.*

    1528. See note 1329.

    1529. See note 1329. In his *Livs Erindringer og Resultater* I–II (Copenhagen: 1877), I, pp. 427–29, Goldschmidt writes of the *Corsair* affair and his decision to leave *The Corsair:* "After the replies, which I wrote myself, some accompanied with cartoons, my colleagues carried on, and thus the affair was constantly raked up, with side-cuts at him. How distasteful this was to me, I cannot say. My impression of the whole business first emerged clearly at a crucial moment.

    "As long as the name Kierkegaard was never mentioned, there was still a tinge of impersonality about the controversy. He himself wrote pseudonymously, and he was attacked under one of the many names he himself had invented; consequently he could not personally step out of the fiction in which he had surrounded our conversations, and when he met me—which happened rarely now—it was with the same courtesy as before, although neither he nor I showed a desire for conversation.

    "But then he publicly named himself Victor Eremita, Frater Taciturnus, etc., etc., and immediately thereafter he met me on Myntergade and passed me by with an intense, very bitter glance, without wanting to give a greeting or to be greeted.

    "In the bitterness of that glance, just as in Kierkegaard's entire personal appearance and manner, there was something that verged on the comic. But this vanished and gave place to loftiness, the ideality, which were also present in his personality. There was something about that intense, wild glance that drew the curtain, as it were, from the higher right that Kierkegaard had asserted earlier and that I had not been able, rather was unwilling, to see, although I did indeed suspect it. It accused and depressed me: *The Corsair* had won the battle, but I myself had acquired a false No. 1. But a protest also arose in my mind during that moment packed with meaning: I was not one to be looked down upon, and I could prove it. On my way home I decided that I would give up *The Corsair,* and when I told them at home that I was going to do it, they said, Praise God! so happy but so little surprised, as if they had known about it before I did."

1530. See note 1329.

1531. To Kierkegaard, his confronting *The Corsair* was an ethical, social act of general benefit. Loner though he was, he nevertheless felt abandoned by the commoners on the streets, who after the incessant ridicule by *The Corsair,* avoided or taunted him, and also by the literary-political elite, who although now relieved as objects of the *Corsair*'s treatment, in turn gave Kierkegaard the silent treatment or criticized the action as rash or called the whole thing a trifle not worth thinking about.

1532. See note 1359.

1533. Nature.

1534. J. P. Mynster, Bishop of Sjælland. This entry on cultural-political accommodation of the religious is an expression of Kierkegaard's central criticism of Mynster. This critical view developed slowly and its open expression came late, because of personal reasons (his own lifelong affection for Mynster, his father's friend), in hope of an "admission" from Mynster, and out of apprehension lest political use be made of open criticism of Mynster and the empirical Church. See note 943.

1535. See note 1233.

1536. See Matthew 19:26, Mark 10:27, Luke 8:27.

1537. See I Corinthians 9:26.

1538. See note 438; xi^1 A 275.

1539. A rural pastorate. See note 1359.

1540. See vii^1 A 123; also viii^1 A 663, 673.

1541. See note 1500.

1542. See II Corinthians 5:11; *Works of Love,* p. 337; *For Self-Examination,* p. i.

1543. See vii^1 A 222.

1544. See *Upbuilding Discourses in Various Spirits,* Part Three [*The Gospel of Suffering,* p. 167].

1545. See note 1472.

1546. See note 1472.

1547. Part Two of *Upbuilding Discourses in Various Spirits,* "What We Learn from the Lilies of the Field and the Birds of the Air," is composed of three discourses: I. "Contentment with Our Common Humanity"; II. "The Glory of our Common Humanity"; and III. "The Happiness of Our Common Humanity Consists in First Seeking the Kingdom of God." See *The Gospel of Suffering* and *The Lilies of the Field,* pp. 165–236. viii^1 A 15 ("Part Two").

1548. See *Danske Ordsprog og Mundheld,* ed. N. F. S. Grundtvig (Copenhagen: 1845). *ASKB* 1549.

1549. See *Apocrypha,* Jesus Sirach 4:26, 28.

1550. The publication of *Upbuilding Discourses in Various Spirits* (see notes 1460, 1500, 1502) was announced in *Adresseavisen,* 61, March 13, 1847.

1551. Subsequently published on September 29, 1847.

1552. "An Occasional Discourse" [*Purity of Heart*]; see notes 1460, 1500, 1502.

1553. Ibid., see p. 133.

1554. Ibid., p. 134.

1555. See *What We Learn from the Lilies of the Field and the Birds of the Air,* together with *The Gospel of Suffering,* pp. 204–13.

1556. See note 1547.

1557. See VIII^1 A 13.

1558. See Acts 3:6; *Works of Love,* p. 304.

1559. *What We Learn from the Lilies of the Field and the Birds of the Air,* together with *The Gospel of Suffering,* p. 188. See note 1547.

1560. Also translated as "change." See *Fragments,* pp. 90–93.

1561. Generation-destruction; growth-wasting away; another kind; generation.

1562. Adolf Trendelenburg, *Geschichte der Kategorienlehre. Zwei Abhandlungen* (Berlin: 1846). *ASKB* 848.

1563. See VIII^2 B 81:34, VIII^2 B 85:5.

1564. Affection; be changed.

1565. Trendelenburg, pp. 381 ff.

1566. See note 1562.

1567. See note 193.

1568. C. Molbech, *Dansk Ordbog* (Copenhagen: 1833). *ASKB* 1032.

1569. *Schillers und Fichtes Briefwechsel,* ed. J. H. Fichte (Berlin: 1847), p. 41.

1570. Danish has two words, *Tankestreg* (literally "thought-line," an invitation to pause and think in order to add what may have been omitted purposely or to become attentive to the special significance of the portion following the thought-line), and *Skillestreg* (separation-line or division-mark), for the dash. Here Kierkegaard assumes the distinction.

1571. See note 1570. Here *Tankestreg* is meant.

1572. Simultaneity.

1573. Frithjof Brandt, in *Den unge Søren Kierkegaard* (Copenhagen: 1929), pp. 125–59, interprets the parrot ("Let us be men. Let us be men.") in Hans Christian Andersen's story as a parody on Kierkegaard, who either did not take it that way· or ignored it here.

1574. See VIII^1 A 27.

1575. Peter Engel Lind (1814–1903), a schoolmate at Borgerdydskolen and at the University of Copenhagen.

1576. See notes 1460, 1500, 1502. Part Three has the subtitle "Christian Discourses."

1577. See I Peter 3:4.

1578. See *Det Gamle Testaments Poetiske og Prophetiske Skrifter*, tr. J. Møller and R. Møller, I–II¹⁻² (Copenhagen: 1828–30), I, p. 38. *ASKB* 86–88 (duplicate, 89–91).

1579. Moriz Carriere, *Die philosophische Weltanschauung der Reformationszeit in ihren Beziehungen zur Gegenwart* (Stuttgart, Tübingen: 1847). *ASKB* 458.

1580. "Man is on a higher level when he meets misfortune."

1581. "Better act and regret than not act and regret."

1582. The writing was begun (VIII² B 79–89) but the lectures were never finished or delivered. See notes 1201, 1205.

1583. The second plan was carried out in the form of a book which was published September 29, 1847, under the title *Works of Love*.

1584. See note 1430.

1585. See p. 254.

1586. See note 1170; *Letters*, no. 157.

1587. *The Book on Adler*. See notes 1018, 1473.

1588. Jens F. Giøwad (1811–91), journalist, editor of *Fædrelandet*, middle-man between Kierkegaard and the printer and bookseller of the pseudonymous works.

1589. See note 1328.

1590. *The Corsair* had a series of ridiculing cartoons concentrating also on various personal aspects of its caricatured object, including legs and trousers. The parodies were picked up quite generally, and Kierkegaard was subjected to considerable annoyance when he went out in public. See note 1333.

1591. Regine Olsen. See notes 637, 2017.

1592. See letter to his brother Peter, *Letters*, no. 149.

1593. Birthday.

1594. See note 1384.

1595. See note 1.

1596. See VIII¹ A 100.

1597. July 6, 1839.

1598. NB[1]. See note 1384.

1599. See VIII¹ A 82, 121.

1600. See notes 1333, 1590.

1601. See note 1599.

1602. See VIII¹ A 82.

1603. Yes, good luck!

1604. See note 1441.

1605. See *Upbuilding* [*Edifying*] *Discourses*, IV, pp. 49–74; note 1453.

1606. See notes 118, 951, 952, 1448. During 1847 Kierkegaard made the following carriage excursions from Copenhagen: Lyngby, February 5, March 1; Fredensborg, 6; Lyngby, 16, 18; Nyholte (Røjels Kro), 27, April 6; Fredensborg, 8; Nyholte (Røjels Kro), 16; Roskilde, 22; Sorø (Pedersborg, Peter Christian Kierkegaard), 29–May 1; Nyholte (Røjels Kro), 7; Lyngby, 17; Nyholte (Røjels Kro), 25, 29; Fredensborg, June 4; Sorø (Pedersborg, P. C. K.), 14–16; Fredensborg, 29, July 10; Nyholte (Dyrehaven, Røjels Kro), 14; Lyngby, 18, 20; Fredensborg, 27; Fredensborg, August 5–6; Nyholte (Dyrehaven, Røjels Kro), 13; Nyholte (Røjels Kro), Frederiksborg, 29; Fredensborg, Frederiksborg, September 1–2; Nyholte (Røjels Kro), Dyrehaven, 10; Fredensborg, Frederiksborg, 20–21; Nyholte (Røjels Kro), 28; Frederikssund, October 1; Lyngby, 3; Sorø (Pedersborg, P. C. K.), 11–13; Nyholte (Røjels Kro), 20; Rudersdals Kro, 31; Lyngby, November 3; Nyholte (Røjels Kro), 9; Frederiksborg, 15; Lyngby, December 2; Nyholte (Røjels Kro), 4, 10. No excursions are recorded for the remainder of December 1847. The only excursion recorded for the year 1848 is the one to Fredensborg, August 26 (IX A 262).

1607. See notes 899, 1008, 1329.

1608. At the time Kierkegaard was considering a journey to Stettin and a longer journey in the fall. See VIII^1 A 227.

1609. *The Gospel of Suffering.* See note 1500.

1610. See notes 1796, 1783, 2692; VII^1 B 211.

1611. Earlier in 1847 there were numerous reports of disturbances in Berlin and various other German cities, Paris, Ghent, and also in the Danish cities of Odense and Flensborg.

1612. Death-leap.

1613. See VIII^1 A 178.

1614. Inconsequential.

1615. See Romans 1:1: set apart.

1616. See Plutarch, *De virtute morali* 12, 452d, vol. 4, p. 240, in *Plutarchs moralische Abhandlungen*, tr. J. F. S. Kaltwasser, I–V (Frankfurt/M: 1783–93). *ASKB* 1192–96.

1617. See note 1619.

1618. A popular lithograph of P. N. Sølling, who had introduced a new type of pilot-boat for use along the Norwegian coast. See *Works of Love,* pp. 300, 302.

1619. See VIII^2 C 2:1–61.

1620. C. A. Reitzel. See note 1170.

1621. See note 1345.

1622. Kierkegaard's books were generally printed in editions of 525 copies. Only 250 copies of *The Concept of Anxiety* were printed. See note 1276. On *Postscript,* see X^1 A 584.

1623. See note 609 on Danish money, also note 1651.

1624. Let him die.

1625. See notes 1329, 1529.

1626. See notes 1328, 1329.

1627. *Works of Love,* VIII of Part Two, pp. 306–16.

1628. Presumably Ditlev Andersen V. Nutzhorn (1800–1865), a physician.

1629. The date of his father's death (August 8/9, 2 A.M., 1838).

1630. See *Letters,* no. 152.

1631. Nytorv 2, the family house Kierkegaard and his brother Peter had purchased at the auction where their father's estate was liquidated.

1632. See note 688.

1633. *Aristipp und seiner Zeitgenossen, C. M. Wielands sämmtliche Werke,* I–XXXVIII, Supplement, I–VI (Leipzig: 1794–1805, 1797–98), XXXIII–XXXVI.

1634. *Euthanasia. Drei Gespräche über Das Leben nach dem Tote,* ibid., XXXVII. The editors were unable to locate the quoted line: "how man must go about dying cheerfully and painlessly." The book consists of three dialogues about life after death.

1635. See notes 1243, 1262.

1636. See note 1384.

1637. See notes 1201, 1205, 1582.

1638. See note 962.

1639. The *Corsair* affair.

1640. A play by Henrik Hertz (Copenhagen: 1836).

1641. See note 315.

1642. See notes 547, 943.

1643. See note 1631.

1644. See note 1583.

1645. *Works of Love* is in two parts.

1646. This entry (together with VIII A 158, 229) is an early indication in the journals and papers of Kierkegaard's breakthrough to a new self-understanding and conception of his task.

1647. See notes 1018, 1472, 1473, and Walter Lowrie's Preface to *On Authority and Revelation,* pp. lx–xi.

1648. Kierkegaard's *The Book on Adler.* See note 1647.

1649. See notes 1328, 1329, 1529.

1650. P. G. Philipsen (1812–77), a Copenhagen publisher and bookseller who had purchased the remainders of the eighteen discourses of 1843 and 1844. See *Letters,* no. 119. The letter is in reply to Philipsen's letter:

Copenhagen, August 23, 1847

Mr. S. Kierkegaard, Magister!

In accordance with our verbal agreement the following is respectfully submitted in reply to your written request:

Bianco Luno has stated that the cost of a printing of 1,000 copies, including the printing and the paper, will amount to 948 rdl., 3 mk., 12 sk.

I intend to reduce the price to make it at least 1 rdl. cheaper than the first printing. The discount to my colleagues must be reckoned as 25 percent, since I give a free copy with every tenth copy, and in addition I still have the bookbinder and the advertisements.

Having permitted myself a summary of all expenditures, I find myself in a position to offer you 500 rdl. for the second printing of *Either/Or*, payable as follows: 400 rdl. next New Year, and 100 rdl. when the printing has been sold out. For these sums you will receive my note.

I admit that this is not much, but in relation to my own expenses it is not so little.

Awaiting the favor of your reply, I remain

Respectfully yours,
P. G. Philipsen
Letters, no. 153 August 23, 1847

1651. On Danish money, see note 609. On the basis of the production prices stated in Philipsen's letter and the retail prices on the paperback books (*Letters*, no. 152), the estimate of $5.00 for one rix-dollar may be too high.

1652. See note 1650. Letter no. 156 is in reply to Philipsen's letter reaffirming his earlier offer:

Dear Magister:

You have good reason to smile at my vacillation. When I am with you, I forget all my calculations, I see and hear only the author of *Either/Or*, and I say yes to everything that flows from your lips.

Not until I am here in my room am I able to make my estimate. I have once more very closely calculated my expenses and all the risks, and as a result I can only refer you to my letter of the 23rd of this month and can undertake the publication of *Either/Or* only on the conditions contained in it.

As the discrepancy between what was stated in my letter and in our conversation is not very considerable, I earnestly request you to forgive my vacillation.

As soon as you have read these lines without anger and notified me in writing of your consent, I shall immediately make all the necessary arrangements.

August 28, 1847.

Yours truly,
P. G. Philipsen
Letters, no. 155 August 28, 1847

1653. See notes 1170, 1630. *Either/Or*, 2 ed., appeared May 14, 1849.

1654. See note 1651.

1655. See notes 1018, 1472, 1473.

1656. See *On Authority and Revelation* (English translation of *The Book on Adler*), pp. 5–11.

1657. Ibid., pp. 11–56.

1658. Ibid., pp. 57–68.

1659. This portion became part of *Two Minor Ethical-Religious Essays* ("On the Difference between a Genius and an Apostle" and "Has a Man the Right to Let Himself Be Put to Death for the Truth?"), by H. H., published May 19, 1849. See notes 1969, 2116.

1660. See VIII^1 A 264.

1661. See note 315. Martensen had been named Royal Chaplain in 1845.

1662. *Works of Love*, p. 288.

1663. See VIII^1 A 298.

1664. See *The Gospel of Suffering*, title page and pp. 118–19. See VIII^1 A 224.

1665. See *Works of Love*, p. 342.

1666. Sophie Henriette Glahn Kierkegaard (1809–81), second wife of Peter Christian Kierkegaard. In 1847 Peter and Jette lived at Pedersborg, near Sorø.

1667. See note 1.

1668. Source of the quotation has not been located.

1669. Thomas Kingo, *"6te Morgen-Sang," "Nu rinder Solen op,"* stanza 10, ll.3–4, 6 (see note 455), p. 399.

1670. Son of Henriette and Peter C. Kierkegaard.

1671. See notes 547, 943, 1534.

1672. Henrik Steffens, *Christliche Religionsphilosophie*, I, *Teleologie*, II, *Ethik* (Breslau: 1839). *ASKB* 797–98. The two quoted portions: "thus the frightful certainty that also internally, in history, evil = the crowd;" "the Savior has died for the whole world but is risen only for the true Christians."

1673. Although the book was never written and the pseudonym was never used, no. 1 appeared separately in *Fædrelandet*, June 24–27, 1848, under the title *The Crisis and a Crisis in the Life of an Actress;* at least parts of no. 2 were completed but remained unpublished (VII^1 B 205–10); no. 3 on a Danish actor in the part of Hummer in J. L. Heiberg's *De Uadskillelige* was begun (VIII^2 B 172–74); and considerable work was done on no. 4 (see VII^2 B 271–95), but this also remained unpublished.

1674. See *The Sickness unto Death*, p. 208. This development and reflections on it led to the published piece *On My Work as an Author* (August 7, 1851) and the longer piece, published posthumously, *The Point of View* (see especially pp. 74–75). See also *Armed Neutrality*, pp. 35–39, 44; *For Self-Examination*, pp. 12–13, 18.

1675. See, for example, II A 23.

1676. See *Fear and Trembling*, p. 129.

1677. See note 1666.

1678. Possibly *Works of Love*, published September 29, 1847.

1679. See note 1606.

1680. See notes 1008, 1329; *Letters*, no. 211.

1681. See *Repetition*, p. 3.

1682. See note 547.

1683. See "Was Bishop Mynster a 'Witness to the Truth'. . . ?" *Fædrelandet*, 295, December 18, 1854, in *Attack*, p. 9.

1684. Presumably Royal Archivist C. J. Hiorthøy (1770–1843).

1685. *Christian Discourses*, published April 26, 1848.

1686. See note 547. The dedication to Mynster was omitted in the published work. See VIII² B 118.

1687. Grand Cross of the Order of Denmark, Order of Denmark, and others.

1688. See notes 1685, 1686.

1689. See note 547.

1690. See notes 547, 943, 1534.

1691. See note 1583.

1692. See note 547.

1693. See notes 1008, 1329; *Letters*, no. 211.

1694. On this theme, crucial for Kierkegaard, see, for example, *On Authority and Revelation*, p. 112; *The Sickness unto Death*, pp. 230, 248, 256–58; *Two Ethical-Religious Essays* (together with *The Present Age*, pp. 151–154; *Practice [Training] in Christianity*, p. 139.

1695. See notes 547, 943, 1534.

1696. See note 1694.

1697. During the so-called Spjellerup period, after earlier years dominated by a mixture of romantic and rationalistic influences, Mynster came to a personal appropriation of historical Biblical Christianity. See X⁴ A 474.

1698. Kierkegaard saw this possibility and hoped for its realization, and in this connection he intended to dedicate *Christian Discourses* (1848) to Bishop Mynster (see VIII² B 116, 118; VIII¹ A 560).

1699. Presumably a reference to Holberg's drama *Jeppe paa Bjerget* [the mountain].

1700. Perhaps no other writing by Kierkegaard received as much rewriting as *The Book on Adler*, which nevertheless was not published. See notes 1018, 1472, 1473, 1647.

1701. A side-issue.

1702. See note 1656.

1703. See on *Authority and Revelation*, pp. 11–18.

1704. Ibid., pp. 19–56.

1705. Ibid.

1706. See note 1659.

1707. See *On Authority and Revelation,* pp. 143–89.

1708. P. L. Møller (see notes 1328, 1329) hoped to replace Adam Oehlenschläger as Professor of Esthetics at the University of Copenhagen. To that end he collected his critical writings in *Kritiske Skizze fra Aarene 1840–47,* I–II (Copenhagen: 1847), which Paul Rubow characterizes as not being a qualifying work for a university post but rather a memoir (*Dansk Biografisk Lexicon,* XVI, p. 434).

1709. The article on P. L. Møller in *Salmonsens Konversations Lexicon* (2 ed., Copenhagen: 1924), XVII, p. 577, states that Møller left Denmark in 1846 for permanent residence abroad. Rubow concurs. Kierkegaard in this paragraph employs the historical present tense for events of 1846.

1710. Secret understanding.

1711. Virgil, *Aeneid* II,3. "Beyond all words, O queen, is the grief thou bidst me revive." Kierkegaard's line adds *"me"* and places *"jubes"* before rather than after *"Regina."*

1712. Regine Olsen and Johan Frederik Schlegel were married in Vor Frelsers Church, Christianshavn, on November 3, 1847. See note 2375.

1713. *Ludovici Blosii Opera omnia* (Louvain: 1568). *ASKB* 429. Ibid. (Cologne: 1572), p. 412. "This is the supreme rule for the highest perfection. Wherever you shall have found yourself, leave yourself behind."

1714. See notes 899, 1008, 1329, 1448.

1715. See notes 547, 943.

1716. See note 1489.

1717. No. 283, December 6, 1847, in which *Rigstidenden* of Norway is quoted: "Mr. Smith was somewhat absent-minded yesterday and got all confused in the Søren Kierkegaardian syllogisms."

1718. See notes 1716, 1717.

1719. See note 1624.

1720. See note 1276.

1721. See note 1.

1722. See notes 1631, 1796.

1723. See notes 609, 1651.

1724. See note 1666.

1725. See notes 1, 1670.

1726. *Works of Love* had been published three months earlier (September 29, 1847). The title in the singular was not used later, as suggested here.

1727. The series was neither prepared, nor given, as lectures. On August 7, 1851, *On My Work as an Author* was published.

1728. This plan was not carried out.

1729. See note 1028.

1730. 4:17. See *Christian Discourses* (published April 26, 1848), pp. 171–83.

1731. See Matthew 19:27–28; *Christian Discourses*, pp. 184–96.

1732. *Christian Discourses*, pp. 197–209.

1733. Ibid., pp. 210–20.

1734. Ibid., pp. 210–11.

1735. Ibid., pp. 212–14.

1736. Ibid., pp. 228–38.

1737. See Matthew 5:11; Luke 6:22.

1738. See *Christian Discourses*, pp. 231–36.

1739. See Luke 6:26.

1740. See Romans 13:11; *Christian Discourses*, pp. 221–27.

1741. Ibid., pp. 239–50.

1742. [T. Kingo,] *Den Forordnede Kirke-Psalmebog* (Copenhagen: 1833).

1743. Grundtvig, an extremely productive writer, also of hymns, and others were pressing for a new hymnal. Mynster was not persuaded. The great influx of Grundtvig's hymns into the hymnbook came under Mynster's successor, H. L. Martensen. See his *Af mit Levnet*, I–III (Copenhagen: 1883), II, pp. 58–69, III, pp. 25–33.

1744. See notes 455, 1742.

1745. See note 1742; ibid., pp. 147–48. Title line: "Heartfelt I long for a blessed end."

1746. *Nyt Aftenblad*, 294, December 17, 1847. The review had appeared in installments on December 14, 15, and 17.

1747. Ibid., 295, December 18, 1847.

1748. See *Nord og Syd*, 1, 1848 (printed December 1847), pp. 1 ff. M. Goldschmidt returned to Denmark (see note 1329) in October 1847 and made preparations for a new journal, *Nord og Syd* (1848–56) (quite different from *Corsaren*).

1749. Ibid., pp. 33–34.

1750. Ibid., pp. 227–28.

1751. Ibid., pp. 121–22.

1752. Reference to Goldschmidt's practice of anonymity and use of stand-in publishers of *The Corsair*.

1753. Main character in Holberg's *Mester Gert Westphaler*. G. W. drank *Dus* (see note 193) with the executioner.

1754. See notes 547, 943.

1755. Part two of *Christian Discourses*, published April 26, 1848.

1756. Part Three of *Upbuilding Discourses on Imagined Occasions*.

1757. See notes 547, 943.

1758. See VIII¹ A 388.

1759. See VIII¹ A 100; *Letters*, no. 149. This entry indicates that Kierkegaard has come to take time and life as a gift.

1760. See notes 1127, 1448, 1606.

1761. See notes 118, 951, 952.

1762. By "family" only Peter C. Kierkegaard is meant. From numerous other references it is clear that the father and mother are not referred to, and the last of the other five brothers and sisters had died fourteen years before.

1763. Publication of *Fortsættelser fra Pedersborg*, a journal edited by Peter C. Kierkegaard, was begun in February 1848.

1764. In a conflict with Bishop Mynster, Peter C. Kierkegaard won out.

1765. The last section of *Christian Discourses*, "Thoughts that Wound from Behind," p. 167.

1766. See note 521.

1767. See note 1734.

1768. *Tausend und eine Nacht*, tr. G. Weil, I–IV (Stuttgart, Pforzheim: 1838–41), III, pp. 560 ff., especially pp. 579–83, 590–94. *ASKB* 1414–17.

1769. A title already used for Part III of *Christian Discourses*. See VIII¹ A 548.

1770. See note 1028.

1771. Part One of *Christian Discourses*, published April 26, 1848.

1772. This paragraph was later crossed out, leaving a two-part book which eventually became two separate works: *The Sickness unto Death* and *Practice in Christianity*.

1773. This title was not used even as a subtitle for *Practice in Christianity*, but the expressions are found there. See pp. 116–17, 139.

1774. Nevertheless these discourses were included as Part Three of *Christian Discourses* by S. Kierkegaard, published April 26, 1848. See VIII¹ A 560.

1775. "Discourses at the Communion on Fridays," Part Four of *Christian Discourses*.

1776. See VIII¹ B 116, 118, 415.

1777. Eventually published as *Two Minor Ethical-Religious Essays*, by H. H., May 19, 1849.

1778. See VIII¹ A 558.

1779. See Matthew 6:17, one of the passages marked in Kierkegaard's 1820 *Nye Testament*. See VIII² C 3.

1780. See X⁶ C 1. The dating is the conjecture of the Danish editors of the *Papirer* and may be much too restrictive. From the various kinds of markings (pencil, ink, etc.) and the appearance of marked passages in the works from *The Concept of Anxiety* (1844) to *The Moment* (1855), it may well be concluded that Kierkegaard read this New Testament carefully for over a decade. Since geographical necessity requires that it be placed in one spot, a mid-point between 1840 and 1855 is merely a compromise that points back and ahead. See Bradley Rau Dewey, "Kierkegaard and the Blue Testament," *Harvard Theological Review*, LX, 4, October 1967, pp. 391–409.

1781. See *Christian Discourses*, pp. 22–23.

1782. Freely quoted. See *Christian Discourses*, p. 238.

1783. In the context of the old Slesvig-Holstein issue, Prince Frederick of Augustenburg put himself at the head of a provisional government proclaimed at Kiel in March 1848. A Danish army subdued the rebels as far as the Eider River. A new national assembly of Germany decided to incorporate Slesvig, and a Prussian army under Wrangel drove the Danes back and entered Jutland. On August 26, 1848, an armistice was signed in Malmø and the government of the two duchies was entrusted to a commission composed of two Prussians, two Danes, and a fifth member by common consent of the four. War was renewed between March and July, 1849, and a second armistice was signed between Prussia and Denmark. Germans in the duchies increased their army under General Willesen. The Danes trapped Willesen's army at Idsted on July 23, 1849. In July 1850 Prussia concluded a treaty with Denmark and gave up claim to the duchies. In London, May 8, 1852, the leading European powers signed a treaty concerning the succession after Frederik VII, and there was no further outbreak until his death in 1863. From 1848 on, the financial situation of the country was precarious and inflation rampant.

1784. Delivered by Kierkegaard to Bianco Luno, March 6, 1848 (*E.P.*, V, p. 41).

1785. See note 547; VIII^1 A 366.

1786. See John 3:1–21; *Prædikener paa alle Søn-og Hellig-Dage i Aaret* (see note 1468), II, pp. 51–64.

1787. See note 1783.

1788. H. A. Brorson, *Psalmer og aandelige Sange*, ed. J. A. L. Holm (Copenhagen: 1838). *ASKB* 200.

1789. Eventually written in four chapters as Part One of *Practice in Christianity*, published September 27, 1850.

1790. Matthew 11:28.

1791. See *Practice [Training] in Christianity*, p. 21.

1792. Ibid., p. 22.

1793. "Self-encapsulation," although exuding the odor of jargon, is also close to the meaning of *Indesluttethed*, an inclosing of oneself. This may be like Abraham's (*Fear and Trembling*, pp. 121–25), but it may also be self-inflicted, even though for some good reasons.

1794. See note 1793. In this entry with seven instances of *Indesluttethed*, both of the better translational candidates have been used.

1795. See note 1796.

1796. Kierkegaard and his brother each inherited a substantial sum (with part of which they bought the family house at the liquidation auction) from their father at the time of his death, August 9, 1838. During the next ten years Kierkegaard lived, fairly well, on this money and paid full publication costs of his first nineteen books (see notes 905, 1276), only one of which sold out. F.

Brandt and E. Rammel, in *Kierkegaard og Pengene*, p. 54 (Copenhagen: 1935), pointing out that Kierkegaard received a writer's honorarium from Reitzel after August 1847, reckon that Kierkegaard's total net from sales and honoraria was an average of 300 rix-dollars per year over seventeen years. This they calculate as equalling 1,500 Danish crowns in 1935, or approximately $300 annually, which in 1973 would be roughly $1,500. In 1846 Kierkegaard entertained the idea of seeking a state grant (VII¹ B 211), which was not uncommon as patronage of the arts and letters. He did not pursue this notion. In December 1847 the brothers sold the house (Nytorv 2), and Kierkegaard kept part of his share of the proceeds in government bonds, which deteriorated badly in the war period (see note 1783), put some into shares which were held through the bad times of 1848–49, and kept some in cash, which also deteriorated because of rampant inflation. See note 2692.

1797. Anders W. Christensen, Kierkegaard's house-man, had been conscripted by the military. See note 1783.

1798. See note 1783.

1799. The Danish term is *sympathetisk*, although C. Molbech, *Dansk Ordbog*, I–II (Copenhagen: 1859) does not list it. Kierkegaard frequently uses a loan word and in its elemental meaning. *Sympathetically* (*syn*, with, plus *pathos*, suffering or passion) here means with suffering and passion on his own account and also on Regine's behalf.

1800. Published over a year later: July 30, 1849.

1801. James 1:13–14.

1802. Ephesians 6:12.

1803. John 8:34.

1804. See *The Sickness Unto Death*, pp. 225–26, 227.

1805. See VIII¹ A 680.